State, Peasant, and Merchant in Qing Manchuria, 1644–1862

CHRISTOPHER MILLS ISETT

State, Peasant, and Merchant in Qing Manchuria, 1644-1862

STANFORD UNIVERSITY PRESS 2007
Stanford, California

Stanford University Press
Stanford, California

Library of Congress Cataloging-in-Publication Data

Isett , Christopher Mills
State, peasant, and merchant in Qing Manchuria, 1644–1862 /
Christopher Mills Isett.
p. cm.
Includes bibliographical references and index.
ISBN 0-8047-5271-0 (cloth : alk. paper)
1. Peasantry—China—Manchuria—History. 2. Peasantry—China—Manchuria—Social conditions. 3. Political leadership—China—Manchuria—History. 4. Social structure—China—Manchuria—History. 5. Manchuria (China)—Politics and government. 6. China—History—Qing dynasty, 1644-1912.
I. Title.
HD1537.C5I72 2006
330.951'803—dc22

2006011775

Printed in the United States of America

Typeset at Stanford University Press in 10/12.5 Minion

FOR MY TEACHERS

Contents

Tables

Preface

Along the way to completing this study, I have incurred debts to many individuals and institutions. Without their assistance this work would not have been possible, and I am grateful for the opportunity to thank them now.

The generosity of several foundations and granting institutions made the research possible. A year in Japan in 1992–93 was funded by the Chiang Ching-kuo Foundation through the American Council of Learned Societies. Research fellowships from the Committee for Scholarly Communication with China and Fulbright-Hays funded a year in China in 1993–94. I wish also to thank the Department of History and Center for Chinese Studies of the University of California, Los Angeles, for graduate funding over the years. Finally, the Graduate School of the University of Minnesota provided generous grants that funded two return visits to China and Japan in 1998 and 2001.

As a young and naïve graduate student doing research for the first time in Japan and China, I benefited from the generosity of many senior scholars, who gave freely of their time and guided me through the archives with kindness and patience. In Tokyo, Professor Linda Grove arranged a graduate research position at Sophia University and introduced me to the scholars working on northeast China. She graciously shared both her time and her expertise. Professor Enatsu Yoshiki of Hitotsubashi University gave most generously of his time and expertise, walking me through the stacks on more than one occasion. Professor Hamashita Takeshi, formerly of Tokyo University, introduced me to the library staff at the *Tōyō bunka*. He kindly made a point to seek me out for lunches and to solicit queries. The staff at both *Tōyō bunka* and the Asia Economic Research Institute provided patient and unending assistance in finding the Japanese materials. I wish to thank them all.

In China, Professor Kong Jingwei, formerly of Jilin University's Department of Economics, and the senior historian of China's northeast, provided unflagging advice and help. In the winter of 1994, he personally accompanied me to the provincial archives in Changchun, provided introductions to the provincial archives in Shenyang and the city archives in Jilin city, and arranged my two tours in the countryside. Professor Cao Xingsui, now of the Beijing Agricultural Museum, provided a wonderful environment for research at Nanjing Agricultural University's Center of China's Agricultural Heritage, where he was working in fall 1993. Professor Cao and his wife Jin Ping have continued to open their home to me over the years, providing a family oasis in busy Beijing and fabulous home-cooked meals. Professor Jing Junjian, formerly of the Chinese Academy of Social Sciences, has been a generous host on more than one occasion. A model scholar, he has guided me through legal sources and helped in my earliest readings of the legal records. Many individuals assisted me in the countryside, and I wish to thank the villagers of Liujiatun, Jilin province, and Mengjiatun, Heilongjiang province, who put up with my absurd questions about farming. In particular, I wish to thank Mr. Jiang Shizhong of Hulan county, who took care of me during my visit to Mengjiatun. In addition to these individuals, I wish to thank the knowledgeable staffs of the Jilin Provincial Archives, the Jilin City Archives, and the Liaoning Provincial Archives for their assistance in tracking down archival materials. In Beijing, the staff at the First National Archives was extremely helpful, and I especially wish to thank the unflappable Zhu Shuyuan, who handled my requests for help with goodwill and humor.

I owe more than I can ever repay to my teachers and colleagues in the West. My graduate student colleagues were always willing to criticize and compliment, and I particularly wish to thank Clayton Dube and Yasuhiko Karasawa. David Wakefield, who passed away prematurely, was a wonderful and inspiring friend. I still miss him very much. Since I left UCLA, several colleagues have given generously of their time and read and commented on parts or all of the book manuscript. In no particular order, I wish to thank Pamela Crossley, Peter Perdue, Michael Chang, William Rowe, Furichi Daisuke, and John Shepherd. I also thank Lynda Bell and the second anonymous reader for Stanford University Press. Special thanks are due to my former classmates Matthew Sommer and Bradley Reed, whom I burdened with parts of the dissertation and all of the book. They saved me from mistakes, and their questions and suggestions made this a far better book. Of course, all errors and infelicities remain my own. Finally, I wish to thank John Feneron and Muriel Bell at Stanford University Press for putting up with my procrastinations and shepherding the book. I also wish to thank William Rowe and the journal *Late Imperial China* for allowing me to republish large parts of Chapter 5.

At the University of Minnesota, fellow probationary faculty provided invaluable and timely feedback. I especially thank Thomas Wolfe, J. B. Shank,

David Chang, Hiromi Mizuno, Kevin Murphy, and Liping Wang. Ann Waltner and M. J. Maynes read the book in detail and provided unflagging encouragement and assistance. David Good provided help in clarifying the argument. My debt to them all is profound. Lastly, I thank my graduate student RAs, Ma Yuxin, He Qiliang, and Fang Qing, who tirelessly entered data, catalogued legal cases, and hunted down gazetteers and passages from the *Qing Veritable Records*.

Ultimately, a book is an intellectual endeavor, and so my greatest debts are to my teachers, past and deeper past: it is to them that I dedicate this book. Neil Kemp's sardonic style yet passionate teaching on Tudor and Stuart history instilled in me a great love for history at a very early age. Shortly afterwards, Colin Evans introduced me to the pleasure of social theory. I remember my time spent in their classrooms fondly. At the University of Michigan, where I received both my B.A. and an M.A., professors Ernest Young, Harriet Mills, Kenneth Lieberthal, and Michel Oksenberg were model teachers and scholars. Each encouraged me to pursue my interests in China and taught me the skills needed. Though a scholar of colonial America, Professor John Shy was instrumental in my decision to go to Taiwan to study Chinese in 1985 and to attend graduate school soon after. He was an unparalleled teacher, and his two courses, which book-ended my undergraduate life, convinced me to pursue history. At UCLA, professors Fred Notehelfer, Herman Ooms, Josh Muldavin, Scott Waugh, and especially Kathryn Bernhardt were inspiring teachers and mentors. Kathryn's comments and interventions in the dissertation workshop were a model in graduate student training. Finally, James Lee—who was at Cal Tech at the time—was most generous with his time as I was writing the dissertation.

My greatest intellectual debts go to my two closest mentors, Philip Huang and Robert Brenner. Bob's influence is evident enough. His theoretical insights into economic development in general, and his invaluable contribution to the debate on the transition to capitalism in particular, were major reasons for my going to UCLA. I can not hope to repay his generosity and support over the years. Philip provided an indescribably rich learning and research environment. His reading and writing seminars were models in open discussion and critical debate. I can only hope to emulate his style. His book *The Peasant Economy and Social Change North China*, which I first read in 1986, while living in Taiwan, got me interested in Chinese social history. I have tried to follow his attention to both trees and forests.

Lastly, I wish to thank my family. My parents, Robin Wallace and Robert Isett, provided love and support. I only now understand and appreciate what it requires to be a parent. My children, Isabella and Sebastian, are always happy to bring me back to the present. I thank them for that and for their unquestioning patience. I owe a karmic debt to Huang Wenmei who has been a constant source of encouragement and joy. In 1994, she sat in archives with me in Beijing, Shenyang, and Jilin and helped hand-copy many of the legal documents used here and also accompanied me to the countryside to do interviews. Sadly, I do not possess the poetic touch needed to express my affection and admiration for her.

Measurements and Conventions

Readers should note that in the Qing, one *shang* equaled 6 *mu* in Fengtian (Liaodong) and 10 *mu* in Jilin and Heilongjiang. In the twentieth century, the *shang* was standardized at ten *mu* throughout Manchuria. One *mu* is the equivalent of one-fifteenth of a hectare or one-sixth of an acre. One standard *shi* equals 100 liters or approximately 160 catties. The weight of a *shi* varies by crop. One *shi* of soybeans or sorghum is roughly 130 kg; one *shi* of millet is 117 kg and one *shi* of *beizi* is 85 kgs (Yi 1990, 450). Ages are expressed in *sui*. A person is one *sui* at birth and one *sui* older with the arrival of every new year. Thus, a person's age expressed in *sui* would be approximately 1 to 2 more than an age expressed as "years old." Units of currency included the *wen* or copper cash, *diao* or string of one thousand copper cash, and *liang* or silver tael.

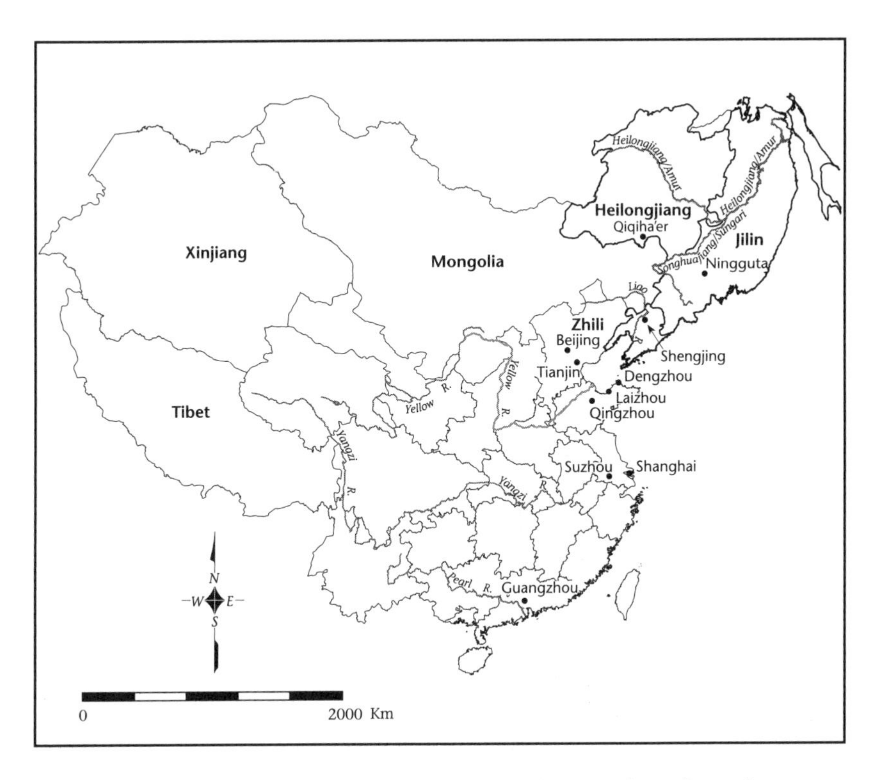

The Qing Empire, circa 1820. (Source: China Historical Geographic Information System, CHGIS)

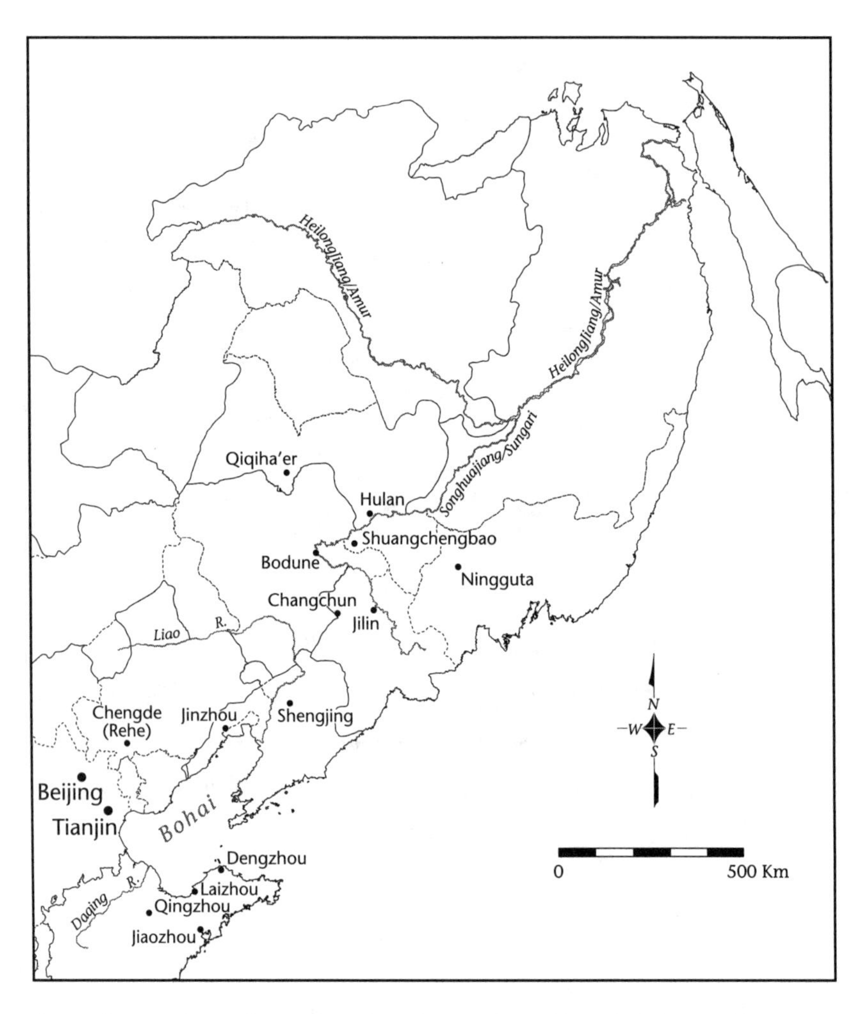

North China and Manchuria, circa 1820. (Source: China Historical Geographic Information System, CHGIS)

Manchuria, circa 1820. (Source: China Historical Geographic Information System, CHGIS)

State, Peasant, and Merchant in Qing Manchuria, 1644-1862

Introduction

THIS STUDY seeks to lay bare the relationship of the sociopolitical structures that shaped peasant lives in Manchuria (northeast China) during the Qing dynasty and the development of that region's economy. The study is in three parts: it begins with an analysis of the ideological, political, and economic interests of the Qing ruling house in defending its homeland in the northeast against occupation by non-Manchus and examines how these interests informed state policy and the reconfiguration of the region's social landscape in the first decades of the dynasty; it turns to an examination of how this agrarian configuration unraveled under challenge from settler peasant communities and gives an account of the resulting property and labor regimes; the study ends with an account of how that social formation configured peasant economic behavior and in so doing established the limits of economic change and trade growth.

The Setting: Temporal, Geographic, and Political Boundaries of the Study

Historical studies require a temporal beginning and end, even though the forces at play carry over from one era to the next. The temporal parameters of this study are set by the establishment of Qing rule in 1644 and the opening of the Manchurian port at Niuzhuang to foreign trade in 1862. Both moments marked disjunctures in the history of the northeast and serve, therefore, as fitting bookends.

That said, at first glance the year 1644 may not appear to be the most appropriate beginning. The ethnically Manchu imperial house that ruled over China from 1644 to 1912 as the Qing dynasty had consolidated its authority over the northeast by 1616. By the time of its invasion of north China in 1644, the Manchu ruling house ran a well-developed state and had established an agrarian system that relied upon the farm labor of free peasants, slaves, and soldiers (the major social elements of post-1644 agricultural production). But, what makes 1644 a useful starting point is the fact that this preexisting agrarian regime was dismantled in the immediate wake of the Manchu invasion, as the ruling house transferred the bulk of its subjects to China Proper. That resettlement effectively wiped Manchuria's social terrain clean. With the social landscape thus pruned to the ground, in the 1650s the ruling house set about restructuring the Manchurian countryside to serve a new imperial agenda. That reconfiguration of the agrarian order is this study's point of departure.

The second disjuncture, which fixes the temporal end of this study, is the opening in 1862 of the Manchurian entrepôt of Niuzhuang to foreign trade as a Treaty Port. The opening of Niuzhuang to foreign traders initiated a period of unprecedented growth in international demand for Manchuria's agricultural goods. The Qing's decision in 1860 to counter imperialist expansion in the northeast by ending its ban on immigration and encouraging colonization allowed for a rapid expansion in agricultural production and agricultural exports. By the 1890s, trade began to draw significant capital investments in railways and modern manufacturing plants that served as the spearheads of Russian and Japanese imperial adventures in the region. New forces were in play after 1862 that bore the potential of restructuring social arrangements and reshaping Manchuria's economy, distinguishing that period from what came before.[1]

The geographic focus of this study is roughly commensurate with the contemporary provinces of Liaoning, Jilin, and Heilongjiang. The focus of the study lies in Liaoning and southern Jilin, however, as that was where agricultural settlement was most concentrated by 1862. For much of pre-Qing history this region lay outside of or was only partially incorporated within the Chinese imperium. Ming power did not extend beyond the lower Liao river plain. Under the Qing, Manchuria was for the first time brought fully into the imperium. However, because of Manchuria's particular standing as the ruling house's homeland, the dynasty chose to govern Manchuria in ways that set it apart administratively and even socially from China Proper, but was akin to its rule in central Asia. Of particular note, the ruling house appointed members of the Conquest Elite to govern the region and established a secondary capital with its own government in the Manchurian city of Shengjing (a.k.a. Mukden, the contemporary city of Shenyang). The demarcation of the region as separate from China Proper was affirmed in the ruling house's use of the Chinese term *Manzhou* (Manchu continent) to designate the region. It is from this term that our English "Manchuria" derives. Administratively, the region was often simply known as Shengjing or Fengtian, terms that strictly speaking defined clearly demarcated administrative districts in southern Manchuria. This sense of Manchuria's separateness from China Proper remained until the very end of the Qing dynasty. Not until 1907 was the region politically and socially incorporated into China Proper. In that year, Manchuria (*Manzhou*) became simply the Three Eastern Provinces (*Dongsansheng*), a designation that defined its administrative and political parity with the other provinces of the empire. It is this region—its transformation—that is the subject of this study.

An Approach to Understanding the Economy in History

The analytical approach taken in this study asserts that long-term, macroeconomic patterns are the outcome of particular social and political arrangements. These arrangements, or social property relations, configure how individuals attain access to the basic elements of production: in the early modern world these would have been labor, tools, and—above all else—land. By determining how individuals attain access to the means necessary for economic activity, social property relations establish the parameters of rational economic choices, or the rules of reproduction (what individuals must do to survive economically). In so doing, social property relations determine the long-term pattern of economic change.

This argument draws directly on the insights of Robert Brenner's work in social theory and comparative history.[2] Brenner holds that it is the given property relationship (the relationship between producers and nonproducers, among producers, and among nonproducers) that establishes the best economic strategies for individuals and social classes to pursue as they seek to maintain their social positions. By determining the opportunities and constraints acting upon individuals and social groups, property relations establish rules of reproduction which, when articulated, configure long-term patterns of economic development *while* reproducing the social relations in which people and classes are embedded. Because social property relations are politically determined (determined by the political balance between the major social classes), individual economic actors cannot alter them but instead must take them as they are. They must, therefore, pursue to the best of their abilities those ends that secure their individual reproduction *within* the prevailing property system.

One implication of this model is that economic growth—defined as sustained increases in the growth of output per unit of labor input—is not the result of the workings of the market, the growth of trade, or the elaboration of the division of labor; nor is it the result of onetime shifts in technologies such as the finding of coal or the development of factory production; nor is it the result of gains in accumulation via colonization, or other forms of forced expropriations; and, finally, nor is it the outcome of cultural proclivities such as a commercial or entrepreneurial spirit.

In making this argument, I draw explicit comparisons between Manchuria's (and China's) pattern of growth and that of contemporaneous Europe, particularly England. I do so because I see England in this period undergoing what can only be described as the quintessential pattern of Smithian growth (i.e., modern or capitalist economic growth), understood to be the incessant reallocation of labor from one specialization to another specialization that yields a higher rate of return made possible by the growth of market demand or lower relative costs, ipso facto raising the productivity of labor. I see that pattern as distinctly different from the Malthusian or Ricardian-Malthusian pattern of growth, which is characterized by the allocation and reallocation of labor in ways that yield a steady decline in the productivity of labor and ipso facto stagnating or falling daily or hourly wages. The comparison between England and China is drawn to highlight those differences which I believe are telling of both the underlying causes of development (Smithian growth) and nondevelopment (Malthusian growth) and their divergent patterns once they are established. This view is clearly contrary to R. Bin Wong's (1997) typology of preindustrial economic patterns that collapses Smithian and Malthusian growth and subordinates the dynamics of the former to the constraints of the latter, a disagreement to which I return in the conclusion of this study.

In early modern England, in contrast to China (and much of continental Europe) the main economic agents had lost the capacity to secure their economic reproduction either through the extra-economic coercion of the direct producers or through the possession of the full means of subsistence. In Brenner's original thesis the restructuring of English property relations was itself the upshot of the demographic crisis of the fourteenth century. Briefly stated, a prolonged period of class struggle between lords and peasants in the fourteenth and fifteenth centuries brought on by dwindling agricultural surpluses and labor shortages ended in the sixteenth century with lords holding on to their lands (and indeed the bulk of land in England) and peasants freed of their serf status but without direct access to the land they needed to reproduce themselves (Brenner [1982] 1985b).[3] The major economic actors were thus rendered dependent upon the market by this outcome, a condition that required each to match the efficiency of the other or face "going out of business." Lords and peasants alike were compelled by the forces of competition to allocate their resources in a manner that would maximize their rate of return (the gains from trade). They could only achieve this by furthering specialization, deepening the division of labor, reorganizing production toward greater efficiency, and accumulating and investing capital in the latest labor-saving methods. England experienced, as a result, a Smithian pattern of economic evolution, or self-sustaining growth, that commenced in the sixteenth century and brought it, in the eighteenth and nineteenth centuries, to the edge of the Industrial Revolution.

The key to England's economic evolution in the early modern period and beyond was thus the consolidation of a system of social-property relations in the countryside that broke decisively from that which had prevailed during most of its medieval epoch. In the medieval period, agriculture had been largely in the hands of economic agents who, like their counterparts in late imperial China, by and large held direct, nonmarket access to the land, tools, and labor power that they required for their reproduction. Peasants possessed their plots, defending their rights (especially to inherit) by manorial custom and their peasant communities. Lords, for their part, generally took a rent by extra-economic coercion (Postan 1966). Thereby freed from the competitive constraint, medieval English peasants, like those in late imperial China, tended to subdivide holdings, as well as to marry early and to have many children. This was in the service of ensuring the survival of sons who would support them in case of illness or old age. The outcome was high fertility, which made for an initial period of rapid population growth and ever tinier plots that peasants could only counter by sacrificing labor productivity. They worked ever harder for ever slimmer returns.

England transcended the limits of its medieval epoch when, in the aftermath of socioeconomic collapse associated with the Black Death, there emerged a novel set of social property relations that rendered both lords and peasants dependent upon the market for their livelihood. Following the severe population decline of the late fourteenth century, peasants succeeded, by way of resistance and flight, in destroying the prevailing system of lordly exaction by extra-economic compulsion. Nevertheless, from the fifteenth century onwards, having failed to reinstate serfdom, lords did succeed in asserting their absolute property rights to the greater part of the land. They consolidated their hold on what were, in terms of western European norms of the time, unusually large demesnes. They expanded, moreover, those already large demesnes by appropriating peasant customary land left vacant in the demographic downturn. They acceded, finally, to land held by customary tenants who lacked both the right to pass on their holdings by inheritance and the right to invariable fines on the transfer of their holdings. The emergent class of commercial landlords, unable, as the feudal lords had been, to take their rents by extra-economic coercion, were obliged to depend on rents determined by supply and demand (i.e., what the market would bear). The emergent class of direct producers, now largely separated from their means of subsistence (the land), though still possessing the means of production (tools and the like), were correspondingly obliged to maintain themselves through taking up commercial leases on a competitive land market. Compelled therefore to produce competitively to survive economically, these tenant farmers had to adopt an approach to their economic production that diverged sharply from that of England's medieval peasantry, as well as from their counterparts in China and most of continental Europe.[4]

I argue in this book that in Manchuria peasants' communities succeeded in securing for themselves direct and nonmarket access to the land that they required for their livelihood. By virtue of their possession of the land (as well as their labor, tools, and the like), peasants in Manchuria were shielded from the requirement to allocate their resources in order to maximize their returns via exchange and were, instead, free to allocate their resources in ways that, while individually sensible, nonetheless ran counter to the aggregate requirements of economic development. The upshot, I argue, was a Malthusian-Ricardian pattern of development in which the total output of the economy grew by a combination of labor intensification and the extension of arable land, but which was unable to realize any improvements in labor productivity.

Historiographical Questions

Though this is ultimately a study of economic outcomes, my adopted mode of analysis requires that the study move from the realm of the political and social to the economic, for it is in the realm of high and low politics and social transformation that social property relations are given. In the words of Perry Anderson, "it is the construction and destruction of States which seal the basic shifts in the relations of production, so long as classes subsist" (1974, 11). This study therefore begins at the level of Qing objectives in Manchuria and their repercussions for the countryside in the late seventeenth and early eighteenth centuries. It then turns to the contestation between state goals and the interests, objectives, and practices of frontier communities. It examines the outcomes of a peasant victory in the eighteenth century that afforded peasants control over their labor, tools, and most importantly their land. Only after addressing the unfolding of the sociopolitical terrain does this study turn to examine economic behavior and the long-term pattern of economic change. The three parts of this study correspond roughly to the state, society, and economy.

Manchuria's Place in the Qing Empire

More than any other factor shaping the political and social history of Manchuria during the Qing dynasty was the fact that the so-called Conquest Elite (the ruling house, its coterie of noble followers, and its elite military units—the Banner Armies) originated there. This fact imbued the northeast with special meaning and value for the Qing dynasty, and beginning in 1680 it led successive emperors to adopt policies to prevent the colonization of Manchuria by Han peasants.

As alien rulers in China, the ethnically Jurchen Qing—the designation "Manchu" was not adopted until 1635—faced challenges that were common to previous alien dynasties and that are known by scholars as problems of "minority rule." The first challenge was governing the far more populous Han—with whom the Qing Conquest Elite shared few if any cultural bonds—and securing the allegiance of the literati or scholar-officials who clung tightly to traditional notions of government and governance. The second challenge—and the one with greater implications for Manchuria—was preserving the ethnic and cultural distinctiveness of the Conquest Elite, something that the ruling house believed underwrote its hegemony in East Asia while living among the Han Chinese.

An earlier generation of scholarship underscored the Qing adoption of Neo-Confucianism to argue in essence that the ruling house largely abandoned its pre-Conquest Manchu ways to become part of the larger Chinese civilization. The "universalist" assumptions that lay at the heart of Confucian teachings not only explained what was necessary if Manchus wished to join Chinese civilization, but in fact made it possible for them to do so. Reacting against this analysis, recent English-language studies have placed Manchu ethnicity at the center of their analyses of Qing rule and have recast our understanding of how the empire was held together both institutionally and ideologically.[5] Stated very briefly, it is argued that the Qing Conquest Elite never abandoned its Manchu identity and it never ruled fully in the Chinese style. At most, the Qing opted for a hybrid constitution that departed from both traditions.

Here is not the place to delve into this literature, but suffice it to say that it has signaled three points that require highlighting in this study. First, the imperial dynasty considered the maintenance of the martial prowess of the Conquest Elite—and particularly its foot soldiers in the banner armies—to be essential to its hegemony in Asia. Second, martial prowess and nomadic resilience were both understood to be the product of the Manchurian ecology and an associated way of life that existed before the Conquest. Third, it was believed that the acculturation of the Conquest Elite to Han ways would dissipate those characteristics that underwrote Qing power and, *pari passu*, to the loss of Qing hegemony in East Asia. The Kangxi emperor's decision in 1680 to tightly control Han settlement in the northeast was the logical extension of those concerns.

The State, Qing Lands, and the Policy of Han Exclusion

To the Qing emperors, the northeast was part of the imperial patrimony. The region's resources were therefore to be used exclusively for imperial benefit. The Qing understood the productive possibilities of agriculture in the northeast, having exploited the labor of captive Chinese peasants on the Liao river plain in the 1620s and 1630s. With the establishment of the new dynasty in 1644, the Qing sought to assert a monopoly over Manchuria's potential farmland, creating in the process what I will call the Qing lands. The early Qing sovereigns carved out vast "territories" of cultivable land in Manchuria for the settlement of demustered banner warriors. These men were given land grants within these territories and then sent down to the countryside to farm (or rusticated) along with their families. The land grants they received were known as "bannerland" and those rusticated were known as "banner households of the farming colonies." In addition, the Qing established "manors" (*zhuang*) which provided the elite of the Conquest Elite with rental incomes garnered from serf labor. The manors were attached to the agencies of the imperial household as a source of privy revenue, conferred upon the Qing nobility as imperial largesse and distributed to parts of regional government bureaucracy as sources of operational revenue. No sooner had the imperial house made these arrangements, however, than commoners started to settle in Manchuria. Many settled alongside and on the Qing lands, which they occupied through illegal purchase or by squatting. It was, therefore, also with an eye to preserving the integrity of Qing land (and holding on to the revenue sources they provided) that the Qing ruling house tried to prevent Han settlement.

Yet, the sovereign's desire to exclude Han Chinese from the northeast pit the patrimonial and ideological interests of the ruling house against the ideological views and administrative interests of parts of the civil bureaucracy.[6] Many Qing field administrators saw colonization of the frontier as a means to alleviate rural poverty and add revenue to the coffers, and the emperor concurred in principle (Rowe 2001, 56–57). By the second half of the eighteenth century, the population of the north China provinces Shandong and Zhili, which lay closest to Manchuria, outstripped local food supplies. Poor harvests were having devastating effects. And yet the Qing continued to enforce the prohibition against colonization of Manchuria and Mongolia. In 1750, after a series of particularly devastating famines in Zhili and Shandong, the Qianlong emperor formalized what was already unofficial policy by closing the borders to Manchuria. Tension between imperial and bureaucratic interests on this matter is evident in the sovereign's continued need to inform his bureaucrats of the necessity to keep the Manchurian borders closed and to return all illegal colonists to China Proper.

Whereas the emperor's interest lay with securing a Manchuria untrammeled by Han settlers, the civil bureaucracy's natural inclinations lay with opening the northeast to immigration. For reasons of both ideology and political control, the civil bureaucracy was committed to what its officials termed "the people's livelihood" (*minsheng*) which, in the final analysis, meant pursuing policies that ensure peasants had adequate supplies of grain (Rowe 2001, 187–189, 202–204). In that endeavor, administrators encouraged peasants in the most densely populated regions of the empire to migrate to the frontiers, sometimes provided startup seed and draft oxen, and even granted a tax hiatus, enlisting landed magnates in the process. The latter were offered degrees and office on the basis of how many recruits and how much land they opened (Guo 1991, 239–247). However, when it came to the question of Han colonization in Manchuria, the patrimonial concerns of the ruling house took precedent over any bureaucratic commitment to *minsheng*. Consequently, despite clear evidence emanating from its own field administrators of problems associated with mounting population pressures and accompanying ecological degradation on the neighboring north China plain, and despite the clear evidence that landless peasants were risking the illegal crossing into Manchuria in order to secure a homestead, the ruling house remained opposed to opening the borders to the northeast. It was only because Russian incursions threatened Qing control of the region that the sovereign finally opened the borders to settlers in 1860. At this point in time, sinicization of Manchuria was preferable to Russian colonization, and establishing the facts of Qing territorial claims on the land became the imperial court's overriding concern.

In this regard, Qing behavior does not accord with the prevailing historiographical view of the Qing state. Not without justification, some have argued that Qing officialdom was committed to fostering social stability through the promotion of agricultural expansion as an expression of its adherence to Confucian notions of what constituted proper rule (Wong 1997).[7] One might be tempted to argue, therefore, that the prohibition against Han migration to Manchuria was the exception that proved this rule. But in this case, I believe the exception speaks to and complicates our understanding of the Qing state. And, indeed, it was not the only exception.[8] Recent scholarship emphasizing the Manchu origins of the Qing has highlighted the need to understand Qing rule in China Proper as part and parcel of a much larger imperial project. That project had a set of ideological and political imperatives that did not always line up with the concerns and interests of the civil bureaucracy and Han officialdom. The sovereign's ultimate objective was maintaining his own hegemony and different and conflicting strategies and agendas were followed in pursuit of that goal. A commitment to such classically Chinese notions as *minsheng* was not so much foundational to Qing notions of how to govern, as it was perhaps conditional to the dynasty's broader strategic goals. Whereas there was no paradox inherent in such tensions, ideological discord did lead to practical inconsistencies as local officials navigated the rocky straits between the requirements of imperial policy on the one side and the requirements of rural social and political order on the other.

State and Village

Efforts by the Qing to limit the number and impact of Han peasants in the northeast notwithstanding, hundreds of thousands of them risked the illegal crossing into Manchuria. Once in the northeast, they hoped to establish a homestead and avoid detection by the authorities. Settling under these conditions, peasants faced considerable challenges, not the least of which was securing claims to their farms. Because the state proscribed the customary proprietary claims of settlers, peasants and their communities had no choice but to develop for themselves the means to acquire and hold land. That migrant-settlers were successful in this regard speaks to two points of interest.

The first is that peasants secured these claims while avoiding detection by the authorities, a fact that raises questions about both the state's ability to implement key policies in the countryside and the peasants' ability to assert their interests over and against the state. The second is that peasant communities were able to establish and maintain institutional arrangements that underwrote property systems to protect their claims *on their own*; suggesting that the normative functions of the state were unessential to the establishment of property claims.

On the first point, this study suggests that even when the stakes were high from the sovereign's perspective, the capacity of the emperor to mobilize the bureaucracy to influence local affairs remained significantly circumscribed. Since Peter Perdue's (1987) influential study of the opening of the central China province of Hunan during the Ming (1368–1644) and Qing eras, it has become commonplace in the English language historiography to hold that the late imperial state was interventionist in ways that ameliorated worsening peasant welfare and fostered economic expansion.[9] The more recent historiography has moved beyond Perdue's cautious thesis of an activist state that was nonetheless limited in its effect to argue that the Qing state was not only especially solicitous of peasant interests (Wong 1997), but that it was "liberal" and even "modern" in its guardianship of the economy and its ability to effect social and economic change (e.g., Dunstan 1996; Marks 1998).

This recasting of the Qing state as an agent capable of intervening in the lives of its subjects has focused principally on its efforts to affect grain movement and supply and to provide famine relief, and promote interregional trade integration (e.g., Marks 1998; Rowe 2001). By all accounts, the state registered successes that were impressive. However, because these interventions often occurred at nodes in urban and transportation networks where the state was best positioned logistically and institutionally to intercede in local affairs and to elicit the support and assistance of local notables in its efforts, it is not surprising that it had some effect. The famine relief efforts that are the focus of much of the new historiography were, moreover, exceptional instances of state-society relations. Not only were they atypical of the day-to-day interactions between bureaucrats and rural society, they were also instances when an emperor, frustrated by his lack of control over the bureaucracy, could energize and focus its attention and, hopefully, tighten his grip on it in the process.[10]

For the most part, the Qing state had limited ability to affect the daily lives of its subjects. The late imperial state's limited presence in the village can be traced to the earlier resolution of the destabilizing contradiction lying at the heart of the pre-Song (960–1279) state. The pre-Song state was an uneasy alliance between the sovereign and a strong and for the most part independent aristocracy that not only circumscribed the sovereign's ability to act but on occasion rose up in arms against him. The configuration of the late imperial state had resolved this contradiction by trimming the aristocracy back to members of the imperial family and by staffing the apparatus of state with dependent bureaucrats. In contrast to the pre-Song state, the late imperial state offered less in the way of institutional and social challenges to imperial authority.[11] The late imperial sovereign guarded his autocratic powers over the bureaucracy by requiring ideological conformity but also by ensuring officials remained sufficiently detached from local society. While that arrangement prevented officials from building political power bases from which to challenge imperial authority, it also hampered their ability to affect the village.[12] If these innovations precluded the emergence of private powers capable of challenging imperial authority, they also unintentionally attenuated imperial reach into the village by ensuring field administrators at the county level could put down only the shallowest of social roots.[13] Thus, augmentation of monarchical power and control within the late imperial state was accompanied by a weak state presence in and control over the village. As we shall see, the Qing's use of the banner chain of command to administer Manchuria did not do much to enhance imperial presence or control there because it suffered from the same weaknesses.

This brings me to the second point. For their part, villagers in the northeast were well provided with strategies and means for circumventing detection by the state to secure claims to land.[14] Recent scholarly work in legal history has focused on the overlapping realm between the formal legal system and customary practices to show how the former underwrote the latter (e.g., Allee 1994a, 1994b; Huang 1996; Macauley 1998). In this view, the formal system of the code and courts backed customary claims in the legal realm of *hu hun tiantu xishi* as much directly through formal litigation and adjudication as indirectly by virtue of the peasants' knowledge and fear of formal litigation. To the extent that scholarship has examined how peasants enforced claims outside the courts, the emphasis has therefore been on the interaction between the law and custom in and around the court, to show that the courts were part and parcel of the smooth functioning of the property system (e.g., Huang 1996, 122–130).

The evidence of a functioning set of customary norms for regulating property in Manchuria, by contrast, directs our attention not to the effects of the courts, direct or otherwise, but to the way that custom operated independently of and in tension with the Qing formal legal system; it requires an examination of the ways peasants and their communities were able to enforce property claims and police their property system *on their own*. But, if peasants and their communities in the northeast had to find ways of handling their affairs outside the courts, they also had to conceal their efforts from officials who were tasked with enforcing a property regime that was incongruent with the one taking shape on the ground. The manner in which commoners came to settle and occupy much of the land in the northeast speaks also to customary practices as a potential means for resisting the state and providing an alternative vision for social organization.

Property Relations and Agricultural Development

To the extent that the English language literature has drawn connections between Qing property systems and economic change, it has argued that peasants' strong legal and custom control of land allowed them to allocate their most valuable resource—their land—in ways that elicited modern economic growth via productivity gains (e.g., Rawski 1972, 24; Chen and Myers 1976; Buoye 2000, 25–32).[15] These conclusions are disputed by Chinese scholars such as Li Wenzhi (1993) and Fang Xing and others (1992, 2000). They contend by contrast that the appearance of strong peasant claims to the land in the early Qing constituted an impediment to modern economic growth, even if such claims allowed peasants to keep more of their surpluses and granted them greater freedom in the deployment of their labor. These scholars have argued that the advent of modern economic growth is associated not with peasants' secure property rights per se but with competitive property arrangements of the sort associated with English farming from the sixteenth century on. If the new property regime translated into greater security in land, cultivators may just as well have reasoned that household integrity was best served by avoiding the rigors of the marketplace with both its rewards and significant risks. Indeed, judging from comparative historical work, secure property rights are associated historically with instances of economic growth and nongrowth alike. Maurice Dobb (1947) and Robert Brenner (1976 [1985a], 1982 [1985b], 2001) have shown that despite the securing of property rights by the broad mass of rural producers in large areas of continental Europe in the early modern era, real economic growth in this period was confined to a narrow range of countries.

The approach taken in this study is distinguished from the neo-classical model of U.S. scholarship by its emphasis not on the clarity or strength of property rights per se (i.e., whether different social actors, be they peasants, landlords, or merchants, are able to get the most income out of their land as a result of their legal/customary relationship to it), but on how property arrangements configure the individual's relationship to the market. In short, I argue that shielded from the competitive pressures of the market by the virtue of their possession of land, peasants in Manchuria were under no compulsion to buy necessary inputs on the market. They were therefore relieved of the necessity to enter into competitive production to survive and instead able to allocate their resources to pursue social goals that were in their rational self-interest but had nonetheless uneconomic outcomes. First and foremost, peasants eschewed specialization and dependence upon the market to the fullest extent possible, preferring to diversify their production in order to secure as many of their needs without turning to the market. Needless to say, the ability of peasants to pursue these non-Smithian strategies rested upon possession of their means of reproduction, especially land, without which they would have been compelled to buy from the market and thus have no choice but to specialize to successfully compete.

Consequently, agriculture in Manchuria underwent what can only be described as a Malthusian-Ricardian–type expansion. On the one hand, as peasants filled up vacant land, thereby bringing more and more land into production, total agricultural output rose. The settlement of Manchuria in turn spurred the development of a Ricardian division of labor, one that was rooted in ecological differentiation across large distances. Peasants in Manchuria found themselves dependent upon other regions of the Qing empire for cotton cloth, which they had no choice but to acquire by exchanging grain and soybeans surpluses in their possession. While this dependency upon cotton imports accounts for the development of long-distance trade between Manchuria and north China and Jiangnan, securing cotton did not require peasants to specialize. Given the obvious risks to specialization, moreover, peasants had good reason not to do so by choice and every reason to obtain the bulk of their needs directly instead.

On the other hand, it is not clear that had peasants wished to innovate in ways that made labor more efficient that they would have had the wherewithal to do so. As others have noted, the onset of declining farm size made it increasingly uneconomical to try to save labor (Elvin 1973; Chao 1986). Consequently, peasants had to turn to agricultural techniques that—all else being equal—would feed the same number of people as before. But they had to do so on smaller holdings and so under increasingly disadvantageous circumstances. The upshot was a gradual trend toward labor intensification (as peasants expended greater amounts of labor) and diminishing labor productivity (as marginal returns to labor fell with each addition of work time expended). In short, peasants shifted from low-yielding, labor-extensive farming methods to higher-yielding, labor-intensive ones.

State, Merchant, and Commerce

It is my contention that the Malthusian-Ricardian pattern was replicated in China's other macroregions, though with different limitations and different timelines, and it was those variations that configured Manchuria's commercial fit and economic function with the rest of the empire. Peasants on the empire's "peripheries," such as Manchuria, the middle Yangzi, and Taiwan, by virtue of the fact of their later settlement and greater availability of land, produced (up to a point) more grain than they could consume (Zhang Guoxiong 1993a; Jiang 1992). By means of long-distance trading networks and merchants, that grain surplus was made available to the longer-settled "cores" such as Jiangnan and Lingnan, where the population was far more dense by contrast and where food deficits had appeared by the early 1700s (Jiang 1992).

Historical examinations of trade in the Qing, broadly conceived, have focused much of their attention on two issues. First, what was the state's role in the distribution and circulation of grain and how did this change over time? Second, were merchants agents of economic development?

On the first issue, the low levels of labor productivity in agriculture (sufficient for only the slimmest surpluses) and the high and rising density of the rural population in China Proper presented the state with significant policy challenges. One could say that the Qing state was *structurally* committed to monitoring harvests, grain prices, and the circulation of grain by the fact that only ten to fifteen percent of grain harvested was surplus (Guo 1994; Fang et al. 2000). There were chronic grain shortages on the north China plain, in the Yangzi delta, and in Lingnan in the eighteenth century, forcing the Qing state to expend significant bureaucratic resources to redistribute grain surpluses (Will 1990; Will and Wong 1991; Wong and Perdue 1983). What did it mean, therefore, that the state ceded the circulation of grain to merchants toward the end of the eighteenth century?

Helen Dunstan views this ceding of ground to merchants as "liberalization" (Dunstan 1996, 8–9, 260, 262–263).[16] However, I think there is good reason to believe that Qing grain commerce after the late eighteenth century should not be characterized as liberal in either practice or ideology. If the Qing sovereign donned the ideological mantle of guarantor of his subjects welfare, as represented in the terms "people's livelihood" (*minsheng*) and "nourishing the people" (*yangmin*), and fostered by his ritual plowing of the sacred plot outside Beijing, then he could not fully cede the commercial terrain to merchants without revealing the "emperor had no clothes." Nor would it have been politically prudent to do so, given the constant potential for social unrest.[17]

The fact that the Qing state depended increasingly on merchants to move grain, whether in times of dearth or feast, does not by itself suggest that merchants were agents of economic transformation. For good reason, merchants and commerce are central to the neo-classical or Smithian paradigm, which takes the emergence of division of labor as its point of analytical departure. This is not the place to discuss the merits of this position, though the historical record would certainly seem to speak against it; whereas merchants and trade have historically been quite ubiquitous, sustained economic growth is rare.[18] Far more important, I believe, is the question of whether merchant capital made its way into production and, in so doing, took on a new function. For centuries, merchants in China and elsewhere pursued a strategy of arbitrage profit-making, which they accomplished by buying cheap and selling dear. Yet, rarely were they a dynamic force for real economic growth. *At the very least*, that would have required that merchants invest capital in the production processes. In this regard, the social theorist and historian of Europe Charles Tilly (1990) posits that whenever and wherever merchant capital remained historically confined to the circulation of commodities, and therefore did not enter into the production process, sustained economic expansion characterized by ongoing increases in labor productivity did not occur.

Merchants in Manchuria could rely upon peasants' need to exchange some of their output for cotton cloth to acquire the grain and soybeans they needed to secure their profits. But, given the fact that peasants were not subject to the full disciplining effects of the market (by virtue of their possession of land), merchants could not be guaranteed a return on any investments they made to improve agriculture production. Thus, rather than invest in improving agriculture, merchants in Manchuria did what was fairly typical of merchants in the early modern era. They used their political clout to establish merchant organizations to protect their market positions. To the extent that they forwarded capital to peasants, because merchant loans bore high levels of interest, these functioned to allow peasants to reproduce themselves from year to year, but not to expand labor productivity. In the long run, these types of activities gave merchants some protection from the erratic market swings associated with early modern agriculture, but on their own these behaviors were incapable of propelling improvements in either agriculture or manufacturing.

Sources and Methods

In his study of the rural economy of north China, Philip Huang noted that Chinese agrarian history of the late imperial period is hampered by a lack of sources (1985, 33). This is particularly so for China's northeast where to date the major studies of Manchuria in Chinese and Japanese have relied heavily on standard Qing sources such as gazetteers, the Veritable Records of the (*shilu*) Qing dynasty, and the Qing's Collected Statutes (*huidian*). Sudō Yoshiyuki's (1944) classic examination of Qing land policy in Manchuria exhausted all such sources on the subject. Chinese scholars of the northeast such as Kong Jingwei, Yi Baozhong, and Diao Shuren have made use of the same sources. As a result, their work on the Manchurian land system has been very derivative of the earlier Japanese scholarship. I draw upon both scholarships in this study, making use of their references to pertinent regulations, changes in policy, and imperial concerns especially. But these sources, and the scholarship that has come from them, are decidedly state-centered. To understand what went on in the Manchurian village requires a look at new sources. The Japanese scholar Enatsu Yoshiki (1980, 1989), for instance, has made innovative use of Japanese ethnographic surveys from the 1930s to re-create the history of an imperial estate in southernmost Liaoning. James Lee and Cameron Campbell (e.g., 1997), on the other hand, have used Qing household registries of rusticated Han bannermen to examine changes in household formation and other demographic behavior. I have made up for the paucity of standard Qing sources on the northeast by using legal records from the eighteenth and nineteenth centuries.

The late imperial legal system had two classifications of legal cases. The most common type of case was what the legal system referred to as *hu hun tiantu xishi* or "household, marriage, land, and other trivial matters." These were nonviolent disputes over such matters as debts, property, and betrothal agreements and were handled almost exclusively at the local level by county magistrates. Because these cases rarely made it out of the local county court, and the records of most courts have been destroyed or lost, such cases have survived in only a few county-level archives. The most widely used collection of "marriage and property" cases come from Ba county in Sichuan, the Danshui subprefecture in Taiwan; and Shuntian prefecture on the north China plain.

In the northeast, only a handful of such *xishi* records survive, all from the Boduna (Jilin) military yamen. Absent a bountiful prefectural-level archive, this study makes significant use of the more abundant records that have survived from the joint court sessions of the Shengjing Board of Revenue and Imperial Household Department in Shengjing and of the Office of Scrutiny (*xingke*) and Fengtian Office (*Fengtian si*) of the Board of Punishment in Beijing. The sessions of the Shengjing Board of Revenue and Imperial Household Department handled nonviolent criminal activity on the imperial estates in Fengtian. In content, they resemble "marriage and property" cases, though the court that handled them was part of the imperial household bureaucracy. Of these, I use the trial records of illegal sales of Qing manorial land as well as criminal investigations of estate malfeasance. The benefit of these court records is that the investigations focus on how land was bought and sold, the ways settlers obtained access to manor land, and the way in which others colluded to conceal these illegal goings on from higher officials.

The second category was death penalty or capital cases, the records of which survive in Beijing. All death penalty cases other than those slated for "immediate execution" (*li jue*) were presented to the emperor for review during the Autumn Assizes. The court records themselves are summations of the case and lower court findings and recommended sentencing. Most of Manchuria's capital cases were reviewed by the Board of Punishment's Office of Scrutiny, which reviewed most of the Autumn Assizes cases. But some of Manchuria's death penalty cases were reviewed by the Board of Punishment's Fengtian Office (*Fengtian si*), one of the seventeen provincial offices within the Board of Punishment.

There are many methodological problems associated with using trial records as windows on plebian society and social change. First, court records are not equivalent to surveys. Without independent verification, we have no way of knowing if the incidences these records relate are representative of general conditions, practices, or trends. Second, court records are by definition accounts of social conflict and irreconcilable differences. Alone, they leave the impression that late imperial society had no extra-legal means for resolving disputes. There are ways, however, by which we can read past the implicit biases of the court records to find social history. James Scott, for instance, argues that we often have little choice but to recapture plebian life and customary practices in the very documents that those seeking to stamp out such practices create (1990, 1–16). In making the arguments that I do about social change and practices I try to take from Qing court records the snapshots they provide of rural life and the customary practices employed by peasants and their communities to manage their affairs, without letting the implicit biases of the source influence how I understand the representativeness and efficacy of such practices.

In making those kinds of judgments, I rely heavily on other sources including other types of official communications, missionary observations, gazetteers, but especially Japanese ethnographic surveys of rural conditions in the twentieth century. While reading the Qing legal cases, I make much use of the latter precisely for the sorts of insights they provide into plebian life that Qing court records often only hint at. The practice of using twentieth-century ethnographic work in this fashion was pioneered by Japanese legal historians such as Niida Noboru (1962) and Shiga Shūzō (1967), who used rural surveys of Taiwan and north China in their studies of Qing law and legal custom, and continues to be used by Japanese historians today such as Kishimoto Mio (1997, 1998). In the United States, scholars have followed suit: Arthur Wolf and Huang Chieh-shan (1980) in their study of Taiwan, Philip Huang (1985, 1996) in his studies of the rural economy and Qing legal system, and David Wakefield (1998) in his examination of household property division (*fenjia*).

Whereas there are few sources from the Qing that shed light on rural Manchuria, twentieth-century sources make for an embarrassment of riches. Japanese colonial interests in Manchuria mean that it is one of world's most thoroughly documented peasant societies in the twentieth century. Japanese ethnographic investigations and surveys of economic conditions of China were the product of Japan's attempt in the first half of the twentieth century to carve out an empire in Asia.[19] In Manchuria, most surveys were conducted in the 1930s and 1940s by the research arms of either the Ministry of Commerce and Industry of the Japanese-run Manchukuo government (1931–1945) or the Southern Manchurian Railway, a quasi-official arm of the Japanese state. This study makes much use of the investigations of the former, especially a multi-volume report on rural customs and agricultural practices and a household-by-household investigation of the economic conditions.[20] What these sources show—something the Qing court records were never intended to show—is how peasants went about regulating their affairs. Drawing from first-hand interviews, the reports describe such things as how peasants bought, sold, and rented land, how they divided property among sons and handled disputes between neighbors over adjoining fields, how they planted their fields and how much labor was required, and how they married their sons and daughters. In addition, I conducted my own field interviews with elderly peasants in Liujiatun, Jilin and Mengjiatun and Zhangjiatun, Heilongjiang, three villages also surveyed by the Japanese in the 1930s. I read all of these surveys alongside the Qing sources to obtain a much fuller sense of rural life and customary practices and to fill in information that is absent in the Qing sources.

Recapitulation of the Study

As I have already explained, the approach taken in this book requires that I move from the political to the economic. The work begins, therefore, by examining the ruling Qing dynasty's interests in its homeland in the mid- to late-seventeenth century and how these shaped the agrarian social structure and affected social change in the eighteenth century. Thus, I examine how these interests resulted in a particular set of policies and strategies for the region that shaped the ways in which the countryside was ruled. I also look at the peculiar historical conditions that granted the state unprecedented freedom to establish an agrarian order that suited its interests and needs in the region. I show how the state established a land system and corresponding agrarian order that suited its imperial needs and then excluded Han peasants from settling in the region in order to preserve that order.

I then turn to the challenges this order posed for the large number of peasants who settled in the northeast illegally in the eighteenth and nineteenth centuries. This includes how peasant communities organized and maneuvered politically in response to these challenges, and, in the process, how peasants restructured agrarian property relations. I show that at the level of the village Han peasants successfully secured control of land, even though they had settled illegally and the state refused to recognize their legal rights of ownership.

On the basis of this sociopolitical account of the unfolding agrarian social formation of the eighteenth century, I offer an interpretation of long-term economic change and the dynamics of agricultural change and export trade. I begin by arguing that the village-level consolidation of a set of social property relations that secured for the bulk of economic actors direct and nonmarket access to land, tools, and labor provided a shield from market competition that in turn allowed peasants to pursue goals that—while perfectly rational—were nonetheless incompatible with economic growth. I conclude with an account of the pattern of economic change and its implications for the long-term dynamics of Manchuria's trade, merchant activities, and state interventions in the economy.

PART ONE

Asserting Hegemony in the Homeland

Dynastic Objectives and the Creation of an Agrarian Order, 1644-1700

PART ONE establishes the study's point of departure. By laying out the sociopolitical and institutional arrangements configuring the Manchurian landscape circa 1700, Part One provides both a blueprint of those structures that informed subsequent developments and a backdrop against which those developments become observable. Part One maps how the ideological, geopolitical, and economic interests of the early Qing ruling house framed state policy and actions in its Manchurian homeland and, in the process, how it established an agrarian order in Manchuria that in 1700 diverged in fundamental ways from the one evolving contemporaneously in China Proper. The chapters in Part One show how the ruling Qing house established in the northeast an agrarian regime that simultaneously underwrote first the region's ideological function (the preservation of a dynastic Manchu/Qing identity distinct from that of the Ming); second its geopolitical function (provisioning a base for military operations in central Asia and a preserve for the nurturing of Manchu martial qualities); and third its economic function (providing revenue to the Conquest Elite). The chapters in this part then go on to examine both the social and administrative ramifications of these goals by mapping the juridical and social categories associated with the new agrarian regime and describing the administrative hierarchies that kept them in place.

CHAPTER ONE

Manchuria's Place in the Early Imperial Project

As the homeland of the Qing Conquest Elite, Manchuria occupied a unique and vital place in the political configuration of the empire. Manchuria was variously called by Qing emperors and officials alike "the land from whence the dragon [ruling house] arose" (*long xing zhi di*), the "cradle" of the Manchu people (*faxiang zhi di*), and the place of "Manchu genesis" (*manzhou genben*).[1] These phrases point to the association in ideology of Manchuria, as a geographic and cultural site, with the origins of the Qing dynasty and even the source of its power. That historical association with the founders of the Qing dynasty shaped the ways in which the ruling house thought of the region and, in turn, conceived of the region's function in supporting its quest for hegemony in East and Central Asia.

The historiography has highlighted two broad themes in tracking Qing policy toward Manchuria. One set of concerns was ideologically driven: the need to maintain a geographical site where Manchu culture could be preserved in an unadulterated form. In this view, successive Qing sovereigns considered Manchuria to be the repository of such Manchu traits as martial prowess and nomadic resilience that served simultaneously to secure Qing political power in Asia while marking the Manchus as ethnically apart from others.[2] The other set of concerns was geopolitical: the need to stabilize Manchuria's northern border with Tsarist Russia, to pacify the Mongols on the adjoining eastern steppes, and to keep open a line of retreat in case the imperial project failed and the Conquest Elite had to return home.[3]

Less emphasized has been the economic dimension. To the extent that economic interests have featured in historical analyses of Qing action in Manchuria, especially in the West, the historiography emphasizes lucrative imperial monopolies in ginseng, gold, fur, and other exotic goods. In the Western literature, far less attention has been paid to the reordering of land and labor systems in the second half of the seventeenth century and how those served Qing objectives. Yet, Manchuria was conceived by the emperors as part of their personal patrimony. And, though they were obliged to use these resources in ways that benefited the broader Conquest Elite—a heterogeneous group that included the imperial household, the Qing aristocracy, and rank-and-file banner soldiers and their households—the lands of the northeast provided the ruling house with important sources of direct and indirect privy revenue. In short, the ruling Qing house had ideological, geopolitical, and economic/fiscal interests in the northeast that were each linked in some way to Manchuria's unique standing as the ruling house's homeland. No other part of the empire could claim that standing nor, consequently, would any other part of the empire quite resemble Manchuria's political, social, and economic architecture.

Manchuria in the Imperial Imagination

For the emperors—and for the banner warriors who "followed the (Qing) dragon" into China Proper in 1644—Manchuria served as an aide-mémoire of their origins: it was the constant geographic referent of the ruling body's cultural attributes and social form. With the passage of time, the need for that referent became more pressing (Crossley 1990, 20). As the Conquest Elite living within China Proper became accustomed to Han ways, anxiety over Manchu and banner acculturation began to afflict the ruling house and the highest levels of the court (Crossley 1987; 1990, 21–26; Rhoads 2000, 53–58, 89–90; Elliott 2001, 277). Concern for the loss of banner military skills dates to the 1680s, forty years into Qing rule, at the exact moment when the Kangxi emperor set out to restructure the northeast's agrarian order as part of an overt effort to prevent the region's colonization by north China settlers (Crossley 1989, 85; Sudō 1944, 179–188; Elliott 2001, 258, 262). These anxieties overlaid older ones, particularly concerns over inter-ethnic conflict that dated to the brutal struggles between Liaodong-dwelling Han and their Manchu rulers in the 1620s (Roth-Li 1975, 65–78; Roth 1979, 16–31; 2002, 46–49). To preserve Manchu control of the northeast and minimize inter-ethnic conflict, in 1680 the Kangxi emperor commanded stations along the southern Manchurian border to turn commoners away, required all migrants to apply for a pass before entering the northeast, and ordered his officials in the northeast to segregate rusticated bannermen from Han commoners to prevent conflict between them (Yi 1993, 210; Xu 1990, 94). After 1680, the policy of protecting the Manchu homeland from Han settlement was a central pillar in the Qing imperial edifice.

The Kangxi emperor was concerned primarily with the practical implications for Qing power of the loss of banner military skills. Since the days when

Nurgaci first forged a federation of Jurchen tribes and clans in the 1590s, the constitution of the Manchu polity bore a deeply martial imprint associated not only with warfare but also hunting (Kessler 1976, 105–107). The militarization of that early polity went deeper still, extending from the realm of mundane to the ideal. Warfare not only configured the social and political organization of the pre-Conquest Manchus through the banner armies but also informed the ways by which Nurgaci and his son Hung Taiji acquired and projected charismatic rulership and imperial authority in the decades before the Conquest (Lee 1970, 24–40; Crossley 1987, 772).

Predictably, therefore, immediately after the Conquest and in the eighteenth century, as the Conquest Elite settled into garrison life in China Proper, reports of the loss of Manchu martial preparedness and skills vexed the sovereign, who saw in this development a threat to Qing political hegemony in East Asia. With the Qing empire extending well beyond China Proper, covering geographically diverse terrains and incorporating peoples of widely divergent social formation, the Qing emperors' political authority over these spaces and populations was dependent—or so it was believed—upon the Manchus retaining the same political and military capabilities, traits, and advantages that had won them the empire in the first place (Lee 1970, 20–23, 51–57; Fletcher 1978a, 39–40). To be sure, by the middle of the eighteenth century, Qing hegemony no longer rested solely on the military abilities of the Banner Armies. In numbers, Chinese regulars in the Green Standard Army surpassed active banner warriors in the 1680s (Kessler 1976, 105, 108).[4] However, the relative decline in the number of Manchu bannermen in the armed forces does not gainsay their continued importance to Qing hegemony. While the new dynasty had pacified China Proper by 1685, with the suppression of the Rebellion of the Three Feudatories and the conquest of the last holdout of Ming loyalism on the island of Taiwan, the Qing imperial project was still far from complete. The vast territory of Xinjiang was not brought under Qing dominion until 1759, after a long campaign that featured large numbers of banner troops (Millward 1998, 29–32; Hostetler 2001, 33). Moreover, the importance of the banner forces to the maintenance of Qing authority over China Proper continued, where they secured strategic cities and the capital (Crossley 1990; Rhoads 2000; Elliott 2001). Given their continued importance to the Qing imperium, any indication that the banner forces were losing their martial abilities through acculturation to Han ways necessarily worried the ruling house (Crossley 1994, 361).[5]

But, monarchical anxiety over acculturation was not limited to deteriorating fighting skills. Over the course of the eighteenth century, the Qianlong emperor, who had come to think of these and other attributes as defining the Manchus as people, was increasingly concerned with the ideological and political consequences of disappearing Manchu ways. Qianlong, who was anxious that Manchus might lose their identity and become culturally indistinguishable from Han Chinese, saw horseback riding and archery not only as military skills but as the "habits" or "customs" that in part defined the Manchu as a people. Thus, when he spoke of "Manchu customs," he spoke of traits that simultaneously secured Qing military hegemony in East Asia and differentiated Manchus from others. In this new context, Manchuria was seen as the geographical site of pristine Manchu culture, the preservation of which the imperial house increasingly tied to the survival of the dynasty itself (Crossley 1990, 24, 26–27). Thus, the Qianlong emperor celebrated the natural qualities of the Manchurian landscape and the unadulterated northern Tungusic tribes who inhabited Jilin and Heilongjiang and who continued to live as pure Manchus. For the ruling house, the attributes and ways of life that marked Manchus as distinct and that nurtured the martial character of the Conquest Elite came to be closely associated with the northeast and its geography (Crossley 1990, 31–46; Elliott 2000, 616–617).[6]

In a series of studies, Pamela Crossley has argued that in the eighteenth century there was heightened anxiety over the loss of Manchu martial skills, along with other so-called Manchu traits, that resulted from the purposeful reconfiguration of the ideological framing of imperial rule. Under the Qianlong emperor, notions of imperial sovereignty and dominion abandoned the then archaic Manchu binary of conqueror and subject, master and slave. In the new conception of imperial dominion, the empire was understood to be constituted by a taxonomy of racial genealogies. Over the realm perched the lone emperor whose transcendent person now held the diverse peoples of the empire together (Crossley 1987, 779–780; 1989, 99). As the representation of the emperor shifted from that of conqueror of disparate parts and peoples to that of a singular transcendent figure giving unity to a multiracial empire, there was a parallel taxonomic need to assign the empire's peoples—including the Manchus—to established genealogies.

Moreover, as Crossley points out, the Qianlong emperor often conflated cultural traits and genealogies with geographic locations and cultural habits in his quest to create order out of multiplicity (Crossley 1990, 31–46). Qianlong associated the Manchu character with the landscape of the northeast—its forests, hills, streams, sacred sites, and ancestral burial grounds—and he demonstrated real anxiety over the prospect of Han peasants turning hunting grounds, gravesites, and pasture into homesteads (e.g., GZSL 1964, 15208 [1035]). With these concerns in mind, the Qianlong emperor described his tour of southern Manchuria:

> Shengjing is Our dynasty's bountiful homeland. The people's hearts and customs are simple and sincere and it is their nature to be loyal. . . . This year, We toured the ances-

tral tombs and met with the officials and soldiers of the region, attending to all public matters gladly and assiduously. . . . Today, very many commoners live there without a permanent home and merchants converge to the point that the people of this place and their customs are changing. They too have become extravagant and wasteful [like the commoners]. If we do not make every effort to correct this expeditiously, We fear customs will be transformed, [the Manchus] will abandon their ways, and their descendants will become profligate. (GZSL 1964, 3023 [206]).[7]

More than two decades later, in 1777, Qianlong commented: "The Three Eastern Provinces are the Manchus' birthplace. We must preserve the upright and ancient customs of the Manchu and so make every effort to avoid being saturated by Han customs" (GZSL 1964, 15208 [1035]). Lamenting the reported disappearance of Manchu traditions and practices in Fengtian and fearing similar developments in northern Manchuria, the Qianlong emperor added, "[t]oday, We see that the customary practices of Jilin are like those of Shengjing: they too are gradually wasting away. As the number of commoner settlers increases daily, so the ancient Manchu customs are lost (*liumin ri jian jiaceng, zhi shi manzhou jiu su*)."

Qianlong appears to have equated the Manchus with a specific set of cultural practices, which included military skills as well as language and shamanism, to geographic locations. In this reconfiguration of the empire and emperor, Manchus were ideally speaking seminomadic hunters and warriors. Thus, Manchus who abandoned hunting and lost their martial skills as they picked up the language and effete styles of the Han literati were ideologically problematic.[8] Any cross-racial acculturation threatened to tear apart Qianlong's carefully crafted ideological canvas. By the reign of Qianlong, anxieties over lost Manchu habits and ways on the one hand and the new ideological imperative for pure types on the other combined to generate intense concern over the status of the Manchurian homeland. Increasingly, the northeast was conceived as the locus of pure Manchu cultural traits; its terrain functioned both to nurture hunting/martial skills and to signify ethnic differences between Manchus and others. As Crossley (1999) argues, "Manchus were the descendents of culturally distinguished, genealogically coherent successions of peoples in the Northeast" (299). The result was the establishment in Qing ideology of a proto-racialized ecology that perpetuated the Qing policy of Han exclusion from Manchuria (cf. Elliott 2000, 608–614, 617–619).

Manchuria and the Geopolitics of Empire

Bordering on the kingdom of Korea, China Proper, the Mongolian steppe, and Tsarist Russia, Manchuria occupied a position of geostrategic importance to the Qing. It could function both as a springboard for Qing forays into central and northeastern Asia and as a bulwark against potential challengers from those same regions. Finally, it was the place to which the Qing could strategically retreat if necessary. For each of these reasons, preserving control over Manchuria was thus considered key to securing Qing hegemony in East Asia and, in turn, the imperial house believed the ban on Han migration to be necessary to its dominion over Manchuria.

The principal strategic threat to Qing hegemony in northeast Asia came from Tsarist Russia which, as early as the 1660s, had already made forays along the Amur river into territory the Qing considered to be part of its domain. By the 1670s, successive adventurers in the employment of the Romanovs had constructed fortified outposts, established trade relations with local tribes, and opened farming colonies along the Amur (Ravenstein 1861, 9–44). By the early 1680s, Russian soldiers and settlers had occupied the northern bank of the Amur, opened nearly three thousand acres of farm land, and established a major presence at Blagoveshchensk near the Qing town of Aigun (Ravenstein 1861, 45). The Qing court responded by fortifying the town of Aigun, strengthening its garrison, and establishing the first regular banner garrison in Heilongjiang in 1684. But, it was not until 1685 that the Qing turned its full attention to these developments. With the south of China pacified that year, substantial Qing forces were redeployed to the far northeast to drive out the Russians. After a series of clashes, Qing armies reached the Shilka river, destroying all Russian settlements between there and Aigun in the process (Ravenstein 1861, 45–53). The Qing campaign concluded with the treaty signed between the Romanov and Qing empires in June 1689 at Nerchinsk. That treaty fixed the boundaries between the two empires and prohibited Russians from navigating any part of the Amur.

Despite the treaty, Qing concerns remained, particularly over Russian influence on the allegiance of the frontier Jurchens—as Robert Lee (1970) calls the largely Tungus-speaking peoples of the far northeast—over whom the Qing claimed suzerainty. Keen to enforce sovereignty in the Amur basin, the Kangxi emperor ordered the boundaries between the Muscovite and Qing empires marked with stones and expanded frontier garrison forces. However, policing the new border with Russia (and deterring the increasingly belligerent Olöt in Mongolia) proved too much for the thinly spread banner garrisons of Heilongjiang, while the attenuated supply lines trailing from the Amur southward, through Ningguta and Shengjing to Beijing, posed great logistical problems that inhibited augmenting Heilongjiang's banner garrisons (Lee 1970, 50). It was far more practical and cheaper to enlist the services of the local Tungus tribes in the effort to secure Qing sovereignty on the Amur (Lee 1970, 50–51; Fletcher 1978a, 42–43).

However, the frontier Jurchens were problematic deputies in the Qing plan to secure control of the lower Amur basin. Despite a tributary status with the imperial house, the Qing was unable to ensure their allegiance and compliance. The threat of a frontier Jurchen rebellion worried the ruling house, whose own experience against the Ming was a lesson in the need to keep tributary tribesmen under control. In response, Lee has argued, the Qing pursued strategies that would ensure the Jurchen tribesmen remained in a "primitive" political state that would not threaten Qing dominion in Manchuria (Lee 1970, 21–22). Lee argues that the initial material deprivation and archaic political forms that characterized the northeast's frontier and its peoples proved an asset to the Qing in its efforts to dominate. The Qing strove to maintain these conditions by keeping the frontier Jurchens isolated from the benefits of Han civilization. Qing emperors spoke of the need to maintain the "simple and sincere ways" of the frontier tribesmen, a clear nod of imperial approval for preserving the archaic political and social formations (GZSL 1964, 3023 [1753, 206]). Thus, Lee concludes that to prevent the frontier Jurchens from acquiring the political and material wherewithal to challenge Qing territorial claims in the northeast, and to ensure their continued subordination to Qing interests in the dynasty's relationship with the Muscovite empire, the ruling house sought to keep the Han at some distance from the far northeast (Lee 1970, 22; cf. Fletcher 1978a, 39).

Manchuria as Imperial Patrimony

The early Qing emperors knew of the productiveness of agriculture in southern Manchuria from the dynasty's experiences there in the 1620s and 1630s. The pre-Conquest ruling house and aristocracy began relying upon estates and serfdom for income in earnest after seizing the fertile Liao river plain in the 1620s and Hung Taiji greatly expanded the pre-Conquest state's dependency upon taxes levied on free peasants in the 1630s. After 1644, the Qing emperors asserted their patrimonial claims over all the northeast's resources, including its farmland.

One of the early acts of the Qing state upon establishing power in China Proper was to reorganize Manchuria's property regime to best serve the welfare and revenue needs of the Conquest Elite. Beginning under the Shunzhi emperor, and accelerating under Kangxi, the Qing state dedicated increasing amounts of the northeast's fertile and cultivable plains for uses that benefited the ruling house, the aristocracy, and the rank and file bannermen. By 1700, of the nearly thirty-three million *mu* of land set aside by the state for cultivation, twenty-eight million *mu* were slated to be farmed for or by members of the Conquest Elite and only five million *mu* were provided for Han Chinese (Zhao

2001, 203). The Qing policy of Han exclusion, which came to include both restrictions on migration and the forced separation of Han commoners from noncommoners in the Manchurian countryside, functioned to protect Qing claims to this vast amount of land and to keep the Han population in the region small.

The state dedicated the greater part of that land for cultivation by rusticated bannermen. These were rank-and-file banner warriors whom the imperial house discharged and dispatched to the Manchurian countryside where they were expected to farm for a living. A lesser amount was set aside for pasture, on which to raise military horses, or formed into large agricultural manors (*zhuang*) to provide the highest echelons of the Conquest Elite—including the imperial family—with rental incomes. Remaining land was set aside for Han commoners already settled in Manchuria whom the state did not return to China Proper. However, to prevent conflicts over land, Kangxi decreed both in 1680 and 1689 that rusticated bannermen and commoners live apart, that each tend to his own fields, and that neither purchase or occupy the land of the other. To protect the newly created bannerlands, as well as the estates, the Kangxi emperor restricted migration to the region after 1680, though a full ban was not promulgated until the middle of the eighteenth century. In 1740, the Qianlong emperor ordered a significant restriction on entry and the opening of land by commoners (GZSL 1964, 1743–1745 [115]; 5385 [356]; QHS 1991, 1000 [158]). He required all commoners living in the northeast to register in the *baojia* or return to their native place within ten years' time; he ordered that all merchants and temporary laborers who traveled to the northeast be given a provisional entry permit that had to be returned on departure; and he prohibited merchants and laborers from bringing family members. In 1750, he prohibited immigration more forcefully, commanding "migrants from the interior are not permitted to covertly cross the pass" (*buxu neidi liumin zai xing tou yue chukou*) (QHS 1992, 1001 [158]; Zhao 1998, 198; Xu 1990, 91).

In sum, in the eighteenth and nineteenth centuries Han exclusion was justified on the grounds that it was necessary first to preserve Manchu military ability and preserve a distinct Manchu way of life; second to guard against the territorial ambitions of Tsarist Russia and the unincorporated frontier tribes of the Amur river basin; and third to secure the Qing patrimony in land and other resources from Han depredations.

Managing Frontiers in the Qing

John Shepherd's (1993) analysis of the Qing's concerns and agendas in governing the frontiers highlights how strategic and revenue concerns informed the state's attitudes toward frontier colonization. Shepherd's study of Qing Taiwan points to the tensions within the bureaucracy between competing concerns over maintaining borderland security, establishing administrative control, and extracting revenue on the frontier (408).[9] Shepherd argues persuasively that when considering whether to extend state presence on the frontier or to facilitate peasant colonization of new territories, the state weighed the relative gains and costs in terms of revenue, security, and control. One common concern that Shepherd highlights was the fact that whereas further colonization offered the possibility of new land taxes and improving the lot of the peasantry, in the short (and even medium) run the costs of administration and pacification of the frontier often exceeded revenues. Colonization, whether legal or otherwise, often committed the state to maintaining social stability in a social context where communal struggles among settlers, as well as between settlers and aborigines, were often endemic. Not infrequently, the Qing response to such dilemmas was simply to prohibit colonization altogether, as it did on the island of Taiwan in the eighteenth century (Shepherd 1993, 398–403).

In regards to Manchuria, however, beginning in the seventeenth century the ruling house expanded the regional administration well beyond what the region's economy could support in taxes. The state forewent increases in tax revenue by limiting and then by prohibiting colonization and by purposely keeping the tax rate on bannerland well below normal levels (see Chapter 2). The bulk of the funds needed to pay for the administration of the northeast came from China Proper (Lee 1970, 70, 75–76). In essence, the peasants of China Proper subsidized the dynasty's strategic and patrimonial interests in its homeland. To be sure, the early administration and pacification of frontiers more generally was always financed by peasants from long-settled regions, but as Shepherd shows the Qing state looked forward to the time when an incorporated frontier might pay its own way. Manchuria was unlike Taiwan, in this regard. Insofar as the region and its people were unequivocally part of the Qing empire after 1644, they had to be administered even if that meant a continual transfer of revenue. The fact that the region was administered differently reflected the dynasty's specific interests in the region and its desire to protect those interests (Fletcher 1978a, 42). Given these interests, making Manchuria fund its own administration was not a consideration until the last decade of the dynasty, when reforms brought administration in Manchuria in line with that of China Proper.

The Qing ruling house did not think of Manchuria as a frontier, and it did not refer to it as such in its own writings. It certainly did not equate Manchuria with frontiers such as Taiwan. For one thing, the aborigines of the far northeast were understood very differently in a taxonomic/genealogical sense than those of Taiwan, or other parts of China for that matter. The native peoples of Jilin and Heilongjiang were judged to be Manchus, and the emperors often considered them to be more purely so than the acculturated Manchus who lived in China Proper. Though the rusticated bannermen who farmed Manchuria's bannerlands were not all ethnically Manchu, the ruling house nonetheless considered them part of the Conquest Elite. In the Qing administrative taxonomy, they were simply bannermen who farmed. There was therefore no court debate over the expense and benefit to governing the northeast in the way that there were such debates over colonization and administration of Taiwan and other regions (Shepherd 1993, 182–191).

In sum, the convergence of multiple policy agendas around the issue of Han exclusion lent that policy its staying power and distinguished Qing actions in the northeast from its actions in other frontier regions, especially those in the south. Ironically, the commitment of Qing emperors to that agenda cost the dynasty sovereignty over parts of the region in the second half of the nineteenth century. Had the Qing permitted and encouraged Han colonization early on, Russian claims to these territories may not have been successfully pressed in 1860 (Fletcher 1978b, 332, 348). Ultimately, as Fletcher suggested, the exclusion of Han commoners was not simply impractical, given the demographic pressures pushing peasants to the northeast, but self-defeating. Thus, changes in geopolitics of Russian expansionism meant that the commonly cited rationales for Han exclusion no longer held water after 1850 or so, and the region was subsequently opened for settlement (1978a, 39–40).[10]

Asserting Qing Hegemony in Manchuria in the Reign of Kangxi

The Qing ruling house did not set out in 1644 with a systematic program to close off the northeast to Han settlement, nor did it begin with a fully developed understanding of how its homeland would come to fit into the empire. It was not until 1680, after a period of open and encouraged Chinese colonization, that the Kangxi emperor made the exclusion of Han commoner settlers a primary objective of Qing rule in the northeast. Coming late, the policy had somehow to incorporate those Chinese colonists already settled in the northeast and who had done so with the ruling house's encouragement.

Re-settlement had been encouraged in the northeast because of the need to restore agricultural production that, following the Manchu invasion, was in disarray in large parts of the north.[11] In 1649 the Shunzhi emperor's regent Dorgon decreed that permanent property rights be granted to any "drifter" or "landless person" (*liumin*) who brought abandoned farm land anywhere in the empire into production or who opened waste land (Guo 1991, 240). Two years later, Dorgon singled out southern Manchuria for special attention, specifying that "commoners willing to go to the northeast to open land are to be registered at the Shanhai pass, recorded at the Board, and then given land on which to dwell" (cited in Yi 1993, 196).[12] The early results of the latter policy were lackluster. Thus, in 1653, Shunzhi offered official rank and office to any local dignitaries who recruited a substantial number of colonists to settle in south Manchuria, under a policy known variously as "Regulations on bestowing office on those who recruit settlers to Liaodong" (*Liaodong zhaomin shouguan li*) or the "Regulations on drifters opening land in Liaodong" (*Liaodong liumin kaiken li*) (Yi 1993, 198–199).[13]

Yet, even as the Qing encouraged resettlement in this period, it was opposed in principle to unregulated settlement. Within southern Manchuria, the Qing court required that settlers settle east of the River Liao (i.e., in Liaodong), while the entire region of Heilongjiang and the greater part of Jilin were entirely off limits to any settlers. To make this perfectly clear, beginning in 1661 this vast region was demarcated by the rebuilt and then extended Willow Palisades. This was a willow-branch constructed barrier that stretched from the south Manchurian town of Fengcheng southeast to the sea, northeast to Xingjing, northwest to Kaiyuan, and southwest to Shanhaiguan. A second branch extended the line northward to the contemporary city of Jilin (Diao 1993, 61; Xu 1990, 91–92; Yi 1993, 196–197, 199–200; Zhang 1999, 80; Edmonds 1985).[14]

In 1668, however, Kangxi terminated the policy of offering rank to landlords who brought recruits to resettle in Liaodong. The rationale for ending the policy was never clearly articulated, though it seems likely that the recovery of agricultural production on the north China plain undermined the original reason for expanding agricultural production in southern Manchuria. Though Qing land registration figures are problematic, it appears that by 1660 cultivated area in north China had recovered to late sixteenth-century levels. Population too was recovering, though at a slower pace (Huang 1985, 327, table C.1). These trends suggest a recovery and stabilization of agriculture. While economic recovery on the north China plain would certainly have made the resettlement of northeast a less pressing economic need, the Qing house was also beginning to look with some alarm at a growing Han presence in the northeast at a time when the Kangxi emperor wished to shore up Manchu privileges in the region. The Kangxi emperor, who took over the reins of power from Oboi in 1669, wanted to reinforce the banner garrison forces in the northeast, return bannermen to farming, and increase the number of manors. Coinciding with the abrogation of the recruitment scheme, the Kangxi emperor reiterated in 1668 and again in 1670 the Qing prohibition against commoners and bannermen in the northeast comingling and working each other's land (Xu 1990, 94).

Kangxi also began to expand and strengthen Manchuria's banner and civil bureaucracies to better restrict the movement of the legally resident Han commoner population and to restrict new migrants from entering. The Kangxi emperor ordered all resident Han commoners in Manchuria into the *baojia*, a subcounty system that assisted civil magistrates in the monitoring and policing of the civil rural population (see Chapter 2). He also expanded the local civil bureaucracy, adding several new counties and prefectures to southern Manchuria, and appointed new magistrates to run these districts. With better control over the commoner population, the Kangxi emperor then moved to set aside for imperial use most of the land in Fengtian and Jilin and all land in Heilongjiang. The area of total Qing land registered as cultivated in Fengtian and Jinzhou grew from 2.65 million *mu* in the Shunzhi era to seven million by the end of the seventeenth century. It reached 14.2 million by the Yongzheng era (Sudō 1944, 161–162; Zhao 2001, 199–200, 202–203; SJTZ 1965, 1234 [24]).[15] The actual area reserved for Qing uses by the Kangxi emperor was greater still, approaching thirty million *mu* in Fengtian alone. With the expansion of Qing lands came the need to control the movement of Han both into and within the northeast. Bringing an end to the policy of recruiting settlers was part and parcel of that goal.

Despite Kangxi's best efforts to prevent large numbers of Han from entering the northeast—he posted guards at all the passes and required any Han who wished to enter the northeast to apply for and display a permit from the Board of War (Yi 1993, 198–199)—they continued to cross the border illegally. Moreover, those whom Kangxi permitted to reside in Manchuria after 1668 were habitually invading the Qing lands, despite repeated demands that this end (Xu 1990, 94). Much to his dismay, this had led to conflict between rusticated bannermen and Han settlers. After several years of watching these developments unfold, in 1680 and again in 1689 the Kangxi emperor acted decisively to end them. The resulting edict established the basic administrative and juridical framework that would structure rural life in Manchuria with varying degrees of influence until the last decade of the dynasty.

In the 1680 edict, the Kangxi emperor commanded regional and local officials to segregate Manchuria's rural populations (QHS 1991, 375 [289]). Henceforth, Han commoner peasants (*minren*) were to live in designated commoner villages (*mintun*) where they cultivated commoner land (*mindi*). These communities and their formal lands were to be administered by civil officials. By contrast, rusticated bannermen were to live in banner colonies/encampments (*qitun*) where they cultivated bannerland (*qidi*) and were supervised by officials of the banner administration. The physical borders between the communities, which were overlaid with juridical status or caste boundaries (to be discussed in the next chapter), were to be clearly demarcated, and both populations were forbidden to cross over them. Long-standing prohibitions dating from the

Ming era that forbade commoners from occupying manorial land, whether by sale or squatting, remained on the law books, as did laws forbidding serfs from fleeing the manor. Bannermen, serfs, and commoners were, thereby, prohibited from living as neighbors, from intermarrying, from hiring each other's labor, and from farming each other's land.

The 1680 decree had little effect and was therefore reiterated in the edict of 1689. This second edict began by noting that "the established boundaries of the banner and commoner fields and land in Fengtian and associated places are not clear." Because of this "bannermen and commoners cultivate land side by side, which leads to endless conflicts and lawsuits." To bring an end to these conflicts and the casual ways in which commoners and bannermen farmed each other's land, the Kangxi emperor declared: "henceforth, commoners are not permitted to cultivate land within the banner territories, while bannermen may not cultivate within the commoner territories" (QHS 1991, 376 [289]; BQ 1985, 328 [18]). For reasons already noted, there was no need for Kangxi to make reference in either edict to serfs and manorial lands; when the Qing Code was adopted in 1646 it legally fixed serfs to their lords' manor and had forbidden them from selling manorial land to commoners. Thus, not only could bannermen, commoners, and serfs not work each other's land, each population was forbidden to live, marry, or labor with the other (BQ 1985, 328 [18]; SZSL 1964, 3494 [262], 3542 [266]). The desired effect was to immobilize Manchuria's rural population, to shore up institutional distinctions between serfs, rusticated bannermen, and commoners, and to assign each of those castes to its respective and bordered territory. The goal was to minimize social conflict *and* to prevent the devolution of all Qing lands into Han Chinese hands.

To enforce the edict of 1689, the geographic borders and status boundaries that distinguished bannermen, serfs, and commoners were overlaid with a corollary set of administrative organs to form a complex tripartite system of bureaucratic jurisdictions for each population and land type. This arrangement set the northeast administratively apart from China Proper until reforms in 1907, when a civil governor-generalship was established to oversee the entire northeast and civil governors replaced military governors in Fengtian (Shengjing), Jilin, and Heilongjiang (Lee 1970, 152; Zhao 1998, 235–237). Before then, civil administrators were limited to those places where Han Chinese had formally and legally settled, whereas ultimate regional authority lay with military rather than civil governors (Sudō 1944, 181). The imperial house's preference for military governors—especially those from the Manchu banners—reflected in part its belief that these men were more trustworthy than Han civil officials, even if they too needed to be watched very closely (Lee 1970, 63, 75). The deployment of military governors as the highest-ranking regional administrators was not limited to the northeast, to be sure. It was also the practice in the Qing Central Asian territories of Xinjiang, Mongolia, and Qinghai, where banner generals oversaw civil officials who administered only in those places of legal Han settlement. Each of these territories similarly lay on the very edge or beyond the traditional range of Han Chinese settlement, where the Qing court feared that excessive Han settlement would heighten conflict between local ethnic groups and Han Chinese and threaten frontier stability (Millward 1998, 202). The emperor assigned military generals to govern in these regions in recognition of these facts; yet while the same fears applied in Manchuria, there were more specific reasons to insist on the military governorship in the northeast. One of these was the need to insist on the priority and protection of Qing patrimonial interests in the region, not least of which included the integrity of what I call the Qing lands.

The effects of the 1680 and 1689 edicts thus reverberated across eighteenth- and nineteenth-century Manchuria; thereafter, the major policy concern of regional officials in the northeast—one which occupied much if not most of their time—was how to deal with the growing number of illegal Han settlers who the Qing believed threatened to compete for resources with the Conquest Elite, transform Manchus into Han culturally, and undermine Qing efforts to hold on to the northern frontier.

Divergent Outcomes in Agrarian Social Formations and the Social Basis for Qing Hegemony in Manchuria

The Qing ruling house's restructuring of Manchuria's countryside to serve its objectives instantiated after 1680 an agrarian order that differed fundamentally from that emerging concurrently within the core economic and political zones of China Proper. That the Qing was able to pursue a line of action that by 1700 had produced in Manchuria an agrarian order very different from that taking form elsewhere in the empire was due to the very different demographic and sociopolitical conditions that prevailed there. The most important of these differences was the absence in the northeast of well-positioned and oppositional agrarian social classes or groups with which the Qing might otherwise have had to negotiate for control over land and the agricultural surplus. By the 1650s, there was no regional or local elite to speak of in the northeast and the few remaining peasant communities were so shell-shocked by the military struggles of the period of transition that they could muster only minimal resistance against a Qing state invigorated by recent victories and bent on restructuring rural production relations to serve its interests. By contrast, in China Proper local elites and peasant communities were on the whole far better positioned to defend their interests, not only vis-à-vis one another, but also vis-à-vis their new masters.[16]

Developments in the seventeenth century, preceding and attending the Qing Conquest, left a significantly altered social landscape by 1700.[17] Taking advantage of the turbulent social conditions created by mid-seventeenth century wars and rebellions and the attending demographic losses that improved the bargaining position of agricultural producers, formerly servile agricultural laborers, tenants, and peasants secured changes to their social and customary standings. Many of these gains were then consolidated in law in the eighteenth century. Broadly speaking, throughout most of China agricultural laborers shed the servile status that had been forced upon them in the mid- and late Ming (Jing 1983a, 1983b). The so-called master-servant distinctions that in the Ming had differentiated employers and hired hands were mostly gone from practice by the mid-eighteenth century (Jing 1983b, 281–292).[18] Similarly, servile tenants who had been bonded either for life or for short periods to large and powerful Ming gentry families succeeded in expunging their lowly legal and customary status by taking flight, burning the records of their contractual obligations, and through sustained rebellion (Li 1993, 22–37).

In north China, formerly servile tenants and laborers emerged from the Ming-Qing transition largely as legally independent small holders, having taken advantage of the depopulation caused first by peasant rebellion and then the Qing invasion to accede to vacated land, often with the support of the new Qing state. In China's south, agricultural producers who did not gain direct ownership of land nonetheless consolidated strong claims to the land they worked, usually by buying top-soil ownership rights, purchasing permanent tenure, or by opening land for a landlord in exchange for permanent tenure. A variety of customary forms of such rights took shape, with names that expressed their permanency: titles such as *yongyuan gengzuo*, *yong geng*, and *yongyuan gengzhong* (to cultivate permanently), *chang geng* (extended cultivation), *shi geng* (cultivation for life), *chang zu* (extended rent), and *yong dian* (permanent tenancy). Thus, by the mid- to late-eighteenth century the sorts of control enjoyed by the late Ming ruling class over land, labor, and persons had more or less come to an end. Many of these gains were then written into law.[19]

The upshot of these developments was the emergence in the early eighteenth century of a set of social property relations in the countryside of China Proper that secured for peasants control over their own labor and what amounted to the effective possession of their land. The Qing state, in turn, largely accepted the new agrarian status quo. On the one hand, it was not in the Qing's interest to assist landlords in regaining their prior political authority over plebian society insofar as landlord abuses in the late Ming had sparked rural unrest. On the other hand, the Qing was probably incapable of refashioning rural production relations in China Proper to enserf peasants as it had following the occupation of the Liao river plain in the 1620s. Instead, the Qing's best possible strategy was to extract revenue by extending its reach over, and strengthen its grasp on, the agricultural surplus *within* the emerging relations of production (Beattie 1979, 56–87; Mazumdar 1998, 211–217; Walker 1999, 71–73).

By contrast to China Proper, a very different demographic and political environment prevailed from Zhili to southern Manchuria in the mid- to late seventeenth century. In short, this region had been cleared of its traditional gentry elite. In the northeast, Ming notables and large landholders either fled in advance of the Manchu armies or offered their services to their new masters, and thereby joined the ranks of the Manchu elite. In much of Zhili, the Ming grandees who held large estates had fled the peasant army of Li Zicheng, abandoning their estates. The peasant population throughout the region was badly mauled by the combined effects of rebellion and pacification. At the end of 1644, the areas around Beijing as well as much of Jinzhou and Fengtian prefectures were significantly depopulated (Wang 1990, 72; Xu 1990, 91; Wu et al. 1990, 96). The further depopulation of the northeast followed in the second half of the 1640s when the Shunzhi emperor transferred all banner households and their retinues south, through the Great Wall and into northern China (Zhao 2001, 196).

The full effects of these developments are difficult to determine, but early Qing accounts suggest the countryside in southern Manchuria and north China was significantly emptied of people. Wang Yipeng noted of Manchuria ten years after the invasion in 1654 that "it is often said Guandong's [Liaodong peninsula] soil is fertile. What a pity the farmland has turned to waste and there is no one to farm it!" (He 1992, 862–863 [35]). The Qing Veritable Records recount that throughout south Manchuria "there are only empty cities and extinguished villages; shattered roof tiles and crumbling walls. . . . For one thousand *li*, this place is vacant. Though there are farm fields, there are no people" (SSL 1964, [12]; also 142–143 [12]). A 1661 account in the Veritable Records states:

> [E]ast of the [Liao] river, though there are many fortified towns they are all desolate. Only Fengtian, Liaoyang and Haicheng districts barely meet the standards of prefectures and counties. Moreover, the two districts of Liao [yang] and Hai [cheng] are without fortifications such as Gaizhou and Fenghuang cities, while the people amount to no more than a few hundred. In Tieling and Fushun there are only exiles and they do not know how to cultivate and moreover they do not multiply. Most of the exiles who came alone run off while those with families die in this place without ever having made any improvements to the region. . . . To the west of the (Liao) river there are even more fortified towns though the people are sparse. Only in Liaoyuan, Jinzhou, and Guangning do people manage to gather. (cited in Zhu 1990, 79).

Twenty years later, the Jesuit Ferdinand Verbiest (1686, 227) traveled with the Kangxi emperor to southern Manchuria in 1682 and recorded:

> All the Towns and Villages which I saw in Leaotum (Liaodong), and which are pretty numerous, are entirely ruined. There is nothing to be seen every-where but old demolished houses, with heaps of bricks and stone: some houses have been lately built within the Precinct of the Towns, but without any order: some are of Earth, and others of rubbish of the ancient buildings, most covered with straw, and but very few with tile. Of a great many Towns and Villages that were in being before the War, there is not now the least sign remaining.

Conditions where not apparently much improved on the north China plain where "there is more than 94,500 *qing* of waste land, but because of the cataclysms of war there is no one to farm it" (SZSL 1964, 180 [11]; cf. 142 [12]). Whereas the Qing was required to deal with entrenched and established social classes throughout most of China Proper, from Beijing to Shengjing the new dynasty was in a position to restructure the land and labor regimes more or less as it saw fit because the rural landscape had been wiped clean.

Just as this environment posed very different problems from that of other parts of the early empire, it also offered alternative possibilities. Given the favorable conditions occasioned by rural depopulation, the Shunzhi and Kangxi emperors moved to reinvigorated and expand serfdom. In southern Manchuria, serfdom was already a major part of the pre-Conquest agricultural system of the 1620s and 1630s. After 1644, the emperors added more manors and serfs. They also reserved vast tracts of land for the permanent resettlement of bannermen beginning in the late 1640s, re-creating a system of military farms that was in use before the Conquest and that would ostensibly bind rusticated bannermen to the land. On the north China plain, in the immediate aftermath of the invasion, the estates of former Ming grandees and aristocrats were redistributed as largesse among the Qing aristocracy along with peasant lands that were either abandoned or expropriated during the invasion. Again, demobilized bannermen were rusticated to work banner farms. By the late 1670s, the basic structures of the renovated agrarian system were in place around Beijing and in southern Manchuria (Yang 1963, 177; Wang 1990, 72–74; Huang 1985, 87–88; Sudō 1944, 136–146).

In the early years of Qing rule, especially to the 1690s, there appears to have been no clear preference on the part of the court for what would be the eighteenth-century policy of supporting the spread of an independent peasantry. The historian Li Wenzhi has shown, for instance, that under the Shunzhi and Kangxi emperors the Qing in fact reversed a trend in Zhili toward the equalization of land holdings and the strengthening of the smallholder that had begun with Li Zicheng's peasant rebellion. The Qing put an end to such developments when it expropriated peasant land and Ming estates to redistribute to the new aristocracy and to banner soldiers (Li 1963, 78; also Huang 1985, 87). A similar reversal occurred in southern Manchuria beginning in the late 1660s when the Kangxi emperor expropriated vast tracts of land from peasants that his father's policies had encouraged to settle in the northeast. Kangxi formed manors from their lands and bound the settler peasants to these as serfs (Enatsu 1989, 5–7). In both places, the fact that the invasion and subsequent reassertion of social order had cleansed these regions of their former residents greatly facilitated—if not made possible—these reversals. Subsequent developments in property arrangements were themselves the simple continuation and extension of the property systems that had characterized rural production under the Manchus in the pre-Conquest era. Beginning with their occupation of the Liao river plain in the early 1620s, the pre-Conquest ruling elite enserfed and enslaved captured Chinese whom they put to work on the aristocratic manors as well as the military farming colonies attached to the banner armies (Sudō 1944, 42–60, 97–106). Yang Xuechen (1963) has reasonably argued on these grounds that the early Qing court preferred to strengthen and spread manorialism when it could, even as it insisted on a more formal and regularized means for doing so (177, 184).[20]

Examined over the longer run stretching from 1621 to the 1690s, it does indeed appear that Yang is correct in his assessment. When and where political conditions were made favorable by a combination of demographic decline and military assault on rural society, the Shunzhi and Kangxi emperors both expanded manorialism and distributed land grants to the rank and file banner soldiers as rewards for their loyal service. But conditions within late seventeenth-century China were not universally favorable to the establishment of such land and labor regimes, even if the Qing had desired to expand these regimes beyond north China. In large areas of China, from Anhui to Jiangsu, Zhejiang and Fujian, peasants revolted against their former masters. In many cases, they succeeded in capturing and then defending their control over their master's former lands through these struggles (Li 1993, 22–37). The political pacification by Qing forces that followed in these regions, though often brutal, concentrated in urban areas such as Yangzhou and thus did not empty the land of its residents. Even if it had wished, the Qing state could not in all likelihood have enserfed peasants under such conditions. The new state was willing to strengthen the small-holding free peasantry—consolidating in law many of its gains—in order to create a counter-weight to the landed Ming elite. However, when and where the Qing could not consolidate the small-holding peasantry and therefore acquiesced to landlordism, it nevertheless protected tenants from the private powers of landlords in law while insisting on its right to collect the land tax out of rents (Mazumdar 1998, 214–216; Walker 1999, 71).

While some scholars have supposed a Qing predisposition to support the small-holding peasant economy and have read this to be the outgrowth of an historical commitment to elements of Confucian ideology on the part of the imperial state that stretched from classical times (e.g., Wong 1997, 138–139), there was nothing predetermined in the Qing adoption of this long-standing discourse. The contrast between the agrarian regimes of late seventeenth-century Manchuria and Zhili on the one hand, and the cores of China Proper on the other (and pre-Conquest Manchuria and post-Conquest China Proper), suggests the Qing had *at most* no predilection to any particular agrarian system. What the contrast suggests is that the early Qing rulers pursued a much more contingent and opportunistic strategy, in which outcomes were determined not by adherence to foundational discourses but the class/political forces at play on the ground. Once a path was paved, I would argue, the relevant imperial discourse followed.

The Edict of 1689 and the Remapping of Manchuria's Social Landscape

If the Qing had a coherent and early vision for the Manchurian countryside, it was autarchy. The blueprint for the agrarian regime, as mapped out in the regulations, code, and imperial edicts of the Shunzhi and Kangxi eras, called for the segregation of the peasantry by caste; the closing of internal borders to migration between banner zones, commoner zones, and manors; and the closing of the external border that separated Manchuria from China Proper to migrants and traders alike. The majority of the initial agricultural producers—both serfs and rusticated bannermen as well as early commoner settlers—were juridically bound to the land they worked. They were prohibited from leaving their villages, restricted to selling their land to—and hiring the labor of—members of their own communities, and even restricted to marrying persons of the same caste.

Thus, after 1680 commoner peasants were permitted to live only in state-designated communities of commoner peasants (the *mintun*) that lay within commoner zones (*minjie*). By virtue of segregationist policies, these people were effectively bound to their villages too. They were restricted in their economic lives to working commoner land and hiring their fellow commoners, and in their social lives to marrying fellow commoners. In the often-stated words of Qing officials, commoners and noncommoners were forbidden from "intermingling" (*za chu*). The respective territories and villages occupied by estate serfs, rusticated bannermen, and commoners were, moreover, overseen by discrete administrative bodies and rural agents within the northeast's regional government. The complex division of administrative oversight that grew out of segregation in the northeast reflected the state's determination to keep interaction between different communities to a minimum, in the hope that this would better secure the sovereign's hegemony over the region.

The agrarian order thus formed made possible a pattern of surplus expropriation and distribution that favored the ruling Qing body. In theory, there was little to no lateral exchange of surplus, whether among Manchurian peasants or between them and the peasants of China Proper. The state's intent, judging from the juridical prerogatives and institutional arrangements in place by around 1700, was to establish a static and self-sufficient agrarian order that was capable of meeting, through rents, land taxes, and forced procurements, the needs of the regional banner garrisons and the regional government, as well as the ceremonial and consumption demands of the Qing ruling body. When land filled up and peasants—particularly rusticated bannermen and serfs—found themselves with insufficient holdings to support themselves, the state provided by moving the landless to uncultivated areas to open new land and there reproduce and extend the agrarian regime. Ideally, within the Manchurian agrarian order the principal mode of "exchange" took the form of tribute, or direct state and elite expropriations in rent and taxes, that was made possible by fixing the rural population to the land and their communities in one way or another.

As we shall see, the social basis of the agrarian order was maintained by the coercive power of the state. Power was required to fix peasants to their communities. Power was required to expropriate the peasants' land and the agricultural surplus. Finally, power was required to close the northeast off from China Proper and to enforce the bans on migration and export trade. However, as Part Two of this book demonstrates, the state in the end was unable to enforce this agrarian regime, which unraveled as all caste communities challenged the limitations imposed upon their mobility, defied state prohibitions against the exchange of land and labor between segregated communities, and in the process established a new set of norms by which they would organize their economic and social lives.

CHAPTER TWO

The Agrarian Order in Late Seventeenth-Century Manchuria

BY THE END of the Qing dynasty in 1912 Han migration and settlement had thoroughly transformed Manchuria's social landscape.[1] Though formally abrogated in 1905, much if not most bannerland existed in name only by this time. Manors continued into the Republican era, but many of these had long since been farmed by a combination of serfs and commoner peasants. Though most of the demographic transformation of the region occurred after 1860, when the prohibition against migration was lifted to counter Russian expansion in the northeast, Han Chinese were immigrating across the eighteenth century and had already established strong customary claims to banner and manorial lands by the mid-nineteenth century. According to Ho Ping-t'i perhaps two-thirds of Qing lands were occupied by commoners by the 1770s (Ho 1959, 159–160). Though his source for that figure is unclear, this seems as reasonable an estimate as any.

To gauge the nature and pace of the transformation of Manchuria, and to account for the form it took, it is necessary first to map out the lay of the land at the beginning of the Qing. This, however, presents a significant problem. Sources that shed light on the constitution of rural seventeenth-century Manchuria are in the form of normative prescriptions and therefore tell us how the state intended things to be and not how they were. Still, imperial edicts, bureaucratic regulations, and the law framed the backdrop against which subsequent historical developments unfolded and, though the state never came close to securing the agrarian regime as it intended, the rural institutions it did create, as well as the decrees and proclamations these institutions were charged with enforcing, necessarily configured subsequent actions of the rural population. This and the following chapter describe the formal substance of these institutions. This chapter focuses on the prescriptive categories of the three main peasant communities in the countryside—rusticated bannermen (*xia tun qiren*), serfs (*zhuangding*), and commoners (*minren*)—and the laws and regulations pertaining to them. The next chapter examines the overlay of administrative offices that were charged with holding these categories in place.

The Manchurian land system, as envisioned by the Qing, was part and parcel of a broader set of juridical prescriptions that assigned every person of the rural population to a specific caste that in turn served to define and delineate the boundaries of the legally permissible community. Chapter 1 pointed to the Qing's creation of new administrative or juridical categories of peasants, and it indicated how, on the basis of these categories, the ruling house would segregate agricultural producers into territorially bound enclave communities in which commoners lived in commoner villages, rusticated bannermen lived in banner villages, and serfs lived on manors. The constituents of these communities were not combined on the basis of a priori or shared "ethnicity," so much as on the grounds of juridical categories that served state power interests. The community and its members were administratively and juridically defined primarily in terms of their normative relationship to the crown (for instance, whether or not they were members of the Conquest Elite or its bondsmen, or whether they were part of the conquered, subject Han population). To be sure, the formation of ethnic distinctions between state-established communities might follow upon these prescriptive categories (though that remains an open question), but that was not the state's intent when establishing the communities in the first instance. They were in this sense castes. This chapter unpacks the prescriptive taxonomies of the three peasant communities circa 1700.

Rusticated Bannermen

In the decades that followed the Manchu conquest of China, the Qing monarchs de-mustered a large number of banner warriors and sent them to farm in the countryside around Beijing and throughout the northeast. In the early years of Qing rule about thirty million *mu* of land was engrossed as so-called bannerland, though initially only a fraction was put to farming (SZSL 1964, [71]). Most of the land was left as waste, to be opened later when growth of the banner population necessitated an expansion of arable land. By the 1690s, there was approximately seven million *mu* of registered bannerland under cultivation in Fengtian; by the time of the Yongzheng cadastral survey of 1724–25, there was fourteen million *mu* in Fengtian and another nine million in Jilin and Heilongjiang combined (SJTZ 1965, 1227–1236 [24]; Zhao 2001, 202–203, 207–208, 215–216, 220–221; Diao 1993, 46–47, 117–118; Yi et al. 1992, 37–38).[2] As for the number of bannermen sent to farm, standard Qing sources provide no figures. These sources do however put the total size of the garrison force in the northeast at fifty thousand in 1700, where the number stayed until the middle of the nineteenth century (Diao 1993, 116; Rhoads 2000, 33). By 1700, the rusticated banner population was certainly greater than the garrison force, which it was expected to support in grain and other items. There may have been as many as one million rusticated bannermen by the middle of the nineteenth century, though any estimate remains speculative.[3]

Putting soldiers to farm work in this fashion was not novel to the Qing. The Ming dynasty had established soldier-farmer colonies as part of its frontier strategy, as had earlier dynasties.[4] The pre-Conquest Manchus had adopted a similar strategy. Beginning in 1613, the early Manchu ruler Nurgaci rusticated bannermen, along with their Han Chinese bondservants. These households were made to farm to provision Nurgaci's growing army with food supplies and the like. At the height of the system, two-thirds of all male bannermen engaged in agriculture (Diao 1993, 19). It appears, however, that most military colonies were abandoned in 1644 when bannermen and their dependents were ordered into China Proper as part of the Manchu invasion. In 1648, when the regent Dorgon ordered the restoration of banner garrison towns in Manchuria, he also resuscitated the military colonies. They were now simply called "banner encampments" (*qitun*) and the land around them was thereafter called "bannerland" (*qidi*). The newly rusticated banner population would provision the northeast's isolated garrisons with grain and other items needed to feed the active duty soldiers and their horses.

Vast tracts of land surrounding each garrison town were subsequently divided into "banner zones" (*qijie*), one for each of the banner armies in the resident garrison. In Fengtian prefecture, for instance, where units from eight different banners were garrisoned, the surrounding countryside was divided into eight radiating sections, one for each banner. The local commander then assigned households under his command to live and farm in the zone designated for that banner household's affiliation. Every head of household sent to the countryside then received the standard thirty-six *mu* land grant, along with tools, start-up seed, a year's grain provisions, and a share of a draft animal (Sudō 1944, 189; Diao 1993, 46). As the size and number of banner garrisons in the northeast grew over the next decades (the total garrison population tripled between 1650 and 1720), the ruling house correspondingly increased the number of colonies and rusticated households to ease the cost of provisioning these forces (Diao 1993, 45–46).[5]

It was the sovereign's clear expectation that rusticated banner households work the land to which they were assigned. They were regarded first and foremost as cultivators and were expected to secure their subsistence by farming and consuming the fruits of their own labor (Wang 1990, 79). The Kangxi emperor's edict of 1689 was unambiguous on this matter for it had not only criminalized the sale of bannerland to commoners but it also prohibited bannermen and commoners from cultivating each others' fields (QHS 1991, 376 [289]).[6] Thus, the act of turning bannermen into cultivators—or rustication—was expressed in the officially used phrase, "sending down to the countryside to farm" (*xia tun zhongdi*), and rusticated banner households were described in official sources variously as "banner households of the farming colonies" (*tun qihu*), "households of the Eight Banner Armies sent down to the villages to farm" (*Baqi xia tun zhongdi renhu*), and "banner households sent down to the villages to cultivate" (*qihu xia tun gengzhong*). Implied in the bureaucratic language was the expectation that rusticated bannermen become peasants, farming the land both to secure their sustenance and as part of their official duty to the emperor.

In this regard, rusticated bannermen were functionally distinct from garrisoned bannermen, who were in fact forbidden to labor for a living. The latter, as Pamela Crossley (1990) tells us, were the "occupiers." They were posted throughout the empire to maintain Qing military hegemony (49).[7] By contrast, rusticated bannermen, whom Crossley calls "producers," were a type of state peasant insofar as they were required by law to farm land held by the ruling house (49). In a turn of phrase that expressed the official understanding that the social function of rusticated bannermen (as well as the manner in which they secured their livelihood) was distinct from that of garrisoned bannermen, bureaucrats spoke of the former as "bannermen who cultivate land for a living" (*qiren zhongdi du ri*). This rhetorical formulation was even internalized by rusticated bannermen who similarly described themselves when testifying in local courts. Thus, for instance, during the 1794 homicide trial of commoner peasant Zhai Hai, witness Zhao Jincheng said of himself, "I am a bannerman who makes his living by tilling the land" (*xiaode shi qiren zhongdi du ri*) (XT 1794, 3.28); in another homicide case, rusticated bannerman Lin described himself as "living in *Xiajiawopeng tun* where I make a living by tilling the land" (*zai Xiejiawopeng tun juzhu, zhongdi du ri*) (XB 1850.8.18).[8]

The normative expectation of the rusticated bannerman was articulated succinctly by the Qianlong emperor in 1740: "With respect to the bannermen's fields," he proclaimed, "bannermen are not to rely upon the hired labor of commoners nor are [the fields] to be used entirely to garner rent [*zu*]. Rather, [rusticated bannermen] must exert themselves throughout the three seasons (Spring, Summer, and Autumn). Leading and working alongside others, they are to fulfill their duties as farmers." If Qianlong's intent were not clear enough, he concluded the pronouncement: "when some refuse to farm, the officials, who establish the rule of law by nurturing and punishing the people, are to summon those charged with oversight and reprimand them in accordance with the regulations" (GZSL 1964, 1924 [127]; cf. 1743–1745 [115]).

Later, when it became evident that bannermen were often inadequate farmers, or simply lacked a predisposition for the bucolic life, Qianlong would modify the ruling house's position, but still insisted that rusticated bannermen remain on the land. Thus, seven years later, in explaining the original objectives of rustication, Qianlong wrote to the governor of Zhili province, where many bannermen were rusticated in the environs of the capital, saying "rusticated banner households [*qihu xia tun gengzhong*] were originally commanded to learn to farm and become self-sufficient." He added that only after it was evident that many rusticated bannermen were poor farmers had he modified his policy to permit rusticated bannermen "to hire laborers and avail themselves of this assistance as they oversee farm work." Nevertheless, affirming Kangxi's edict of 1689, Qianlong maintained: "it has never been permitted to rent out or summon tenants to cultivate their land" (QDTD 1988, 1338).

To ensure that rusticated bannermen remained in the countryside, the ruling house prohibited them from leaving their villages. It did so by applying banner regulations against "desertion" (*sizi chujing*) (QHS 1991, 1285 [856]).[9] All bannermen in the northeast, whether garrisoned or rusticated, were forbidden to travel further than one hundred *li* (thirty-three miles) from their assigned post without permission from their commanding officer. Punishment for those who did was harsh. An absconding bannerman received for the first offense one hundred lashes of the whip, one month of the *cangue*, and tattoos on the left side of the face.[10] The punishment increased with every subsequent violation. For the third and final offense, a bannerman was stripped of his banner status and made the slave of a soldier stationed at a frontier post (QHS 1991, 1295 [857], 1321 [861]).[11] The immediate effect of these regulations against desertion was to tie rusticated bannermen to their villages, or at the very least to the narrow "banner territories" in which their villages were located.

While initially rustication was considered a means to provision hard-to-reach garrison towns in the northeast with locally grown food, increasingly the ruling house used rustication to the Northeast to solve the problem of indigent and idle bannermen that plagued the garrisons of China Proper. By 1700 the deterioration of banner welfare within China Proper was evident to all at court. It was especially bad in Beijing which had the largest concentration of banner households (Li 1985, 92; Crossley 1990, 49; Rhoads 2000, 49–51). Impoverishment resulted from the selling off of lands that had been appropriated within China Proper to support the banner garrisons, the failure of cash dispensations to keep up with inflation, and the growing size of the banner population. The problem was compounded by the rising number of bannermen without an active duty role. Whereas banner status was hereditary, military positions were not guaranteed. It had always been Qing practice to select from among the banner population only some of its adult males for military service. The Qing

Board of War eventually fixed the number of active banner troops at 200,000 in an attempt to control rising costs associated with a large active duty force. Supplementary positions were added in the eighteenth century, but these were not sufficient in number to keep up with rising demand for posts (Li 1985, 92, 95–96; Rhoads 2000, 36, 48). Subsequently, the proportion of bannermen serving fell from one in three in the 1630s to one in ten in the late Qing (Crossley 1990, 17; Rhoads 2000, 34–35). As the total banner population grew, and as an ever smaller percentage were assigned to military duty, more and more men were left "idle," an official designation known as *xiansan*.

Compounding the problem further was the fact that the rising cost of the banner system was leaving the state financially strapped. In addition to the annual salary received by active banner soldiers, which went to supporting both the soldier and his dependents, the state provided periodic cash and grain hand-outs to those in need, repaid private debts, and bought back banner property that had been improperly sold off (Crossley 1990, 49–52). By one estimate, by the middle of the eighteenth century the banner system ate up as much as one-quarter of state revenues and was understood by all at court to be contributing to the state's dire fiscal problems (Elliott 2001, 307, 310; Crossley 1990. 49–50).[12] A substantial part of the cost borne by the state went simply to supporting household dependents of active duty warriors (Crossley 1990, 52–53; Elliott 2001, 310). Yet, as the fiscal burden of the banner system grew, tax revenues from standard sources failed to keep pace with overall government expenditures. For institutional, economic, and ideological reasons, the Qing state's rate of take of agricultural output, by far the largest taxable source of production in the economy, was fixed by the Kangxi emperor in 1713. Subsequent emperors adhered to that principle and did not raise the quotas. While the effects of the freeze were ameliorated by the increase in cultivated acreage and by supplementary levies and surcharges, there were limits to how much new revenue could be added so long as Kangxi's edict remained the ruling principle (Wang 1973, 53, 81–82; Zelin 1984, 74–78, 105–115, 307–308). In short, the combination of the rising size of the banner population, restrictions on the movement and employment of the banner population, and the state's limited revenue streams resulted in a growing body of impoverished bannermen.

Not surprisingly, given the implications of the problem, the matter of the "Eight Banners' welfare" (*Baqi shengji*) attracted the attention of Qing officials associated with the so-called Statecraft School of thought (the *jingshi* tradition). These bureaucrats advocated a series of programs to improve the economic livelihood of the idle bannermen, including rustication either to the bannerlands of southern Manchuria or to government estates (*zhuangyuan*) in Jilin and Heilongjiang (see He 1992, 861–883 [35]; Crossley 1990, 55–56).[13] The secretary of the Board of Revenue, Chen Zhilin, whose 1655 essay on the subject was included in the canonical Qing statecraft compendium, cited Zhou dynasty (1122 BC–255 BC) precedents to support his proposal to alleviate impoverished bannermen by providing them with farm land (in He 1992, 864 [35]).[14] In 1741 the leading authority on banner issues of the moment, Liang Shizheng, who was a close confidante of the young Qianlong emperor, and whose views on the subject of the banners most certainly corresponded with the emperor's, explained rustication thus: "His imperial majesty, the Yongzheng emperor, planning for the benefit of subsequent generations, seeing the population of bannermen growing numerous by the day, and finding the treasury wanting, desired that bannermen be sent to Heilongjiang, Ningguta, and other such places to dwell and till the land so that they could secure a living on their own" (in He 1992, 867 [35]).[15] Rustication was seen as one means to deal with the "Eight Banner welfare" crisis: the provision of land grants in Manchuria simultaneously repaid the ruling house's historical debt to the descendents of the banner warriors who had won the Qing empire and reduced banner dependency upon the dole.

Given the intense interest of the ruling house to diminish banner poverty and to relieve itself of some of its fiscal responsibilities, it is no wonder that the Qing ruling house applied the draconian measures described above in its effort to bind rusticated bannermen in the northeast to the land. Examining these measures, some scholars have argued that because the bannerland system was framed by a politico-legal formula which tied bannermen to land that was held by the imperial household, rusticated bannermen were serfs and the bannerland system akin to European manorialism of the high middle ages (Diao 1993, 51–52; Wang 1990, 72, 75). While it is true that certain aspects of the social relationship between sovereign and rusticated bannerman resemble elements of serfdom, to make the argument on the basis of these similarities alone is to overlook serfdom's social function, both in the European and Qing contexts. That function is, in the words of Classical historian G.E.M. de Ste. Croix (1981), to facilitate the increased exploitation of the peasantry (250).[16]

By that definition rusticated bannermen were not serfs. They paid no rent and the state levied no tax on Manchuria's bannerland until forty-five years after the first wave of rustication. Even then, the take of tax was miniscule, less than that levied on commoner land in north China (see Chapter 3). Furthermore, the act of rustication entailed demobilization, but not the loss of banner status. To be sure, that status could be ended, but only after petitioning for its removal or if the ruling house chose to take it away as punishment for certain offences. Consequently, rusticated bannermen who stayed in the banner system (and this would appear to have been the majority) remained "regular bannermen," or *zhengshen qiren*. As such they were ostensibly entitled to a share, however small, of the privileges and the spoils of conquest. Undoubtedly, rusticated bannermen stood socially and normatively on the periphery of the Conquest Elite, and with the passage of time their standing within that group fell further (Crossley 2002, 312).[17] But juridically speaking they remained its members and *ipso facto* not the normative or social equivalent of serfs or *zhuangding*. In fact, rusticated bannermen could legally possess the latter in the form of bonded servants, whereas *zhuangding* could not "own" other bonded servants (Wang 1990, 76–77; Jing 1993, 101–102).[18] Sociologically speaking, rusticated bannermen were peasants who were required to farm state-held lands for fiscal and other reasons but whose social function did not directly facilitate ruling class reproduction via rent payments.

Serfs and Serfdom in Manchuria

Whereas a significant proportion of agricultural work in late sixteenth-century China was performed by servile or bonded laborers and tenants, by the end of the seventeenth century a series of peasant uprisings, coupled with the social and political chaos attending the Manchu conquest, meant that thereafter a declining proportion of agricultural laborers remained legally bound to a master. The majority of these were manors owned by the Qing Conquest Elite.

Chinese and Japanese scholars have accounted for the disappearance of bonded labor from most of the Chinese countryside between the late sixteenth and seventeenth centuries in terms of a broader structural transition from "gentry landlordism" to "commoner landlordism." In this interpretation, gentry landowners during the Ming had succeeded in using political power derived from their holding high office in the state to subsume peasants within their households as dependent agriculturalists. With the collapse of the Ming and the attending peasant rebellions, however, the gentry lost what had been their juridical and customary hold on agricultural producers so that by the eighteenth century most peasants in China were formally free. Serfdom persisted thereafter only on the manorial lands of the Conquest Elite in Manchuria and north China's Zhili province. There the ruling Manchu dynasty held sway over the rural population and so could tie peasants to their masters' land and household.

Given that the pre-Conquest elite had relied upon manorialism and serfdom for much of its income in the two decades before 1644, it was natural that the Qing would try to reinvigorate and export the practice thereafter (Roth-Li 1975, 58, 86–89; Roth 1979, 20; Diao 1993, 9–12, 26). While it seems that, like the soldier-farmer colonies, the manors had also fallen into disarray when Manchu forces invaded China Proper in 1644, the imperial house reinstituted manorialism in south Manchuria and around Beijing soon thereafter.[19] In the process, land in north and northeast China that was abandoned as peasants fled the invading Manchus and the manors of the former Ming aristocracy were expropriated en masse. In other instances, lands still farmed by peasants were expropriated. These lands were formed into manors and when possible the peasants who had worked it were enserfed. By the 1720s, the imperial household held just under two million *mu* of manorial land (*zhuangdi*) in the northeast, while another 660,000 *mu* had been assigned to the regional government to help cover administrative costs. The land in Manchuria held by the nobility is not known, but most scholars agree it exceeded that held by the emperor (Diao 1993, 63, 80–81; Wu et al. 1990, 50, 74; Yi 1993, 233–234, 236).[20] In north China, 17.6 million *mu* of land was appropriated and distributed among bannermen and nobles, or about twenty-nine percent of registered arable land (Huang 1985, 87).

Those who worked manors (*zhuang*) were designated *zhuangding*, peasants who were serfs by virtue of the fact that they were legally bound to the land on which they labored.[21] *Zhuangding* were acquired in several ways. Some were taken from among the prisoners of war seized during and after the conquest. Others were taken after they submitted (*touchong*) freely to vassalage in return for the political protection of their new masters. (Though it is clear that many serfs registered by their masters as having submitted of their own free will had in fact been pressed into servitude.) Others were convicts sent to the northeast to labor. Still others were free peasants who were enserfed as their fields were expropriated to create new manors that were in turn divided among the Manchu nobility (Diao 1993, 71–73, 79–84, 92–93; Yang and Zhou 1986, 218–219, 222, 284; Yi 1993, 238–239; Entasu 1989, 7; Yi et al. 1992, 101–104; Chang 1972, 251–254).

Beginning in the early 1620s, the pre-Conquest Manchu elite had come to depend on manors and serf labor for part of its revenue. It appears that these manors fell into disrepair immediately after 1644 as Manchu nobles and their lieutenants departed the northeast and left their serfs and lands unattended. The subsequent resuscitation and expansion of manorialism in the 1650s and 1660s under imperial auspices coincided with the general rise in mortality and demographic decline and the widespread flight of bonded agricultural labor that attended the Ming-Qing transition in China Proper (Yi 1992, 196–197; Zhu 1990, 79; Kessler 1976, 16–17). These conditions would have lent weight to the decision to restore and even expand serfdom. Though sources are hard to come by, severe and persistent labor shortages throughout north China and the northeast would have pushed labor costs up and rents down, disadvantageous conditions for landholders. By using serf labor, the Qing elite could squeeze rents that were above what could be taken if they had to recruit tenants, in which case they would be compelled by the general labor shortage to offer terms that reduced their rental incomes. (Of course, the ruling class's ability to enforce serfdom depended on whether it could, in the first instance, tie peasants to the land and then enforce rent payments.) By all estimates, manorial rents were very high, at least initially. In the late seventeenth century, half of all grain output on a manor went to the lord in rent alone. In addition, serfs provided labor services, were charged fees and fines, and made an annual tribute payment of meat, fowl, eggs, and other such products (Diao 1993, 77–78; also see Zhao 2001, 292). Consequently, serfdom afforded the Qing ruling class rates of expropriation that far exceeded the rentier landlord's typical take, and far exceeded the state's land tax rate levied on commoner landholders (cf. Diao 1993, 77–78; Wang 1973, 127–128; Chang 1972, 253–254).[22]

What made such a high take possible was the legal power that the master wielded over the serf's person. Qing law defined the *zhuangding* as household dependents (*huji neiren*), a status that marked them as a type of "bondservant" (*nupu*). Bondservants as a social group in the Qing took many forms, though most were domestics who performed household chores or clerical work. The serf's status as bondservant not only made it a crime to leave the master's household, it also made it a crime for the serf to sell his master's property, a legal power wielded by the nobility that protected the integrity of its property (Statute 93).[23] What distinguished *zhuangding* from other bondservants, however, was the fact that they were attached to and compelled to farm their masters' manorial lands. Describing the legal responsibilities of *zhuangding*, Wu Zhenchen (b. 1664), who served as a bailiff on a government manor in Jilin during the reign of the Kangxi emperor, wrote: "When not engaged in cultivation, [the *zhuangding*] are to busy themselves. . . . Every person is responsible [each year] for remitting 12 *shi* of grain, 300 sheaves of fodder, one *jin* of pork, 100 *jin* of charcoal, 300 *jin* of coal, and 100 sheaves of hay. All of their worldly possessions are the state's (*fan jiazhong suoyou xi wei guanwu*)" (Wu 1985, 85). Wu expressed the facts that the master owned both the serf's labor and the land to which the serf was fixed, a formal arrangement that secured for him the right to extract revenue from the manor.

The legal and customary formula that in turn underwrote this social relationship by lending the master political power over his serfs was inscribed in the legal prescription *jian*. In the Qing, the term *jian* denoted a person of "debased" or "mean" status. It applied to all "bondservants" or *nupu*, including *zhuangding* and other social categories. Persons of *jian* status ran the gamut from theatrical performers to servants and even included a number of ethnic and regional subgroups such as Shaoxing's "indolent persons" (Ch'ü 1961, 129–133; Bodde and Morris 1967, 172: Zhang Jinfan et al. 1998, 268–269). At root, *jian* denoted a person whose labor was owned by another and who was, therefore, a dependent (Jing 1993, 100–109; Niida 1943, 959, 963–964). As a social category *jian* always stood in opposition to *liang*, the legal and customary signifier of nondebased status (Ch'ü 1961, 131). Thus, the social and legal meaning of *jian* not only rested upon the dichotomy between *jian* (debased) and *liang* (nondebased) but also between servant (*nupu*) and master (*zhu*). Recognizing the categorical distinction between servant and master, the Qing legal system singled out *jian* persons for special handling, as did other dynasties before it. Entire classes of crime applied specifically to those marked as *jian*, while crimes that crossed the status divide between the debased and nondebased were singled out for extraordinary treatment because they violated foundational social power distinctions (Ch'ü 1961, 128, 230–231; Meijer 1980, 335).[24]

The manor lord's political authority over the serf was thus rooted in the latter's dependent status as *nupu* and the attending normative prescriptions entailed both in the legal formula *jian* and the social category *zhuangding*. In this fashion, *jian* denoted a juridical relationship that secured for manor lords extra-economic power over their serfs while the social category *zhuangding* provided additional politico-legal powers that were necessary to ensure the continuity of the manorial system and the expropriation of rents and dues. These extra-economic powers were necessary because those attached to manors were given permanent tenure rights to land as condition of their enserfment. Moreover, the *zhuangding* were permitted to pass their land on to sons under the generally practiced custom of *fenjia*, or household property division, and they were permitted to exchange land with other serfs of the same manor. Given these rights and claims to land, and given the nobility's reluctance and inability to remove non-paying serfs from the land (they were reluctant because serf labor was essential to realizing their manorial incomes), the only means by which the nobility might secure manorial revenue was via compulsion and policing.

Commoner Peasants in Manchuria

The prescriptive and bureaucratic category "commoner" or *minren*, as it was deployed in Manchuria, was made necessary by the region's particular agrarian regime. In the Qing administrative language for China Proper, *min* (civil) was commonly used in opposition to *bing* (military) to differentiate between civilly and militarily administered populations. The distinction was most commonly found in the garrison towns, such as Hangzhou, where the city and population were divided between areas under civilian and military or banner control. In

Manchuria, the term *minren* (civil person, or commoner) was consistently used in memorials, edicts, and records of court proceedings as both a prefix and common noun. It denoted a person or body of people that was not associated with the banner system, whether as "full bannermen" (*zhengshen qiren*), which included both garrisoned and rusticated bannermen, or as *zhuangding*, who were registered under their masters' banner.

This usage of *minren* was necessitated by the ruling house's strategic agenda in the northeast. To construct an order that preserved Manchuria for members of the Conquest Elite, the state needed a classificatory term to denote those persons to be curtailed or excluded. Prior to 1644, Han commoners living in the conquered territories primarily in southern Manchuria were subsumed under the Manchu-language classification *nikan. Nikan* referred to all persons living in the Chinese style, whose primary habitat was within the territories of the Ming dynasty (Crossley 1999, 91–92).[25] With the Qing conquest of the Ming empire, those peasants dwelling in southern Manchuria who were not part of the banner system—that is, neither rusticated bannermen nor manor serfs—came to be designated as commoners (*minren*) in the Chinese vernacular used in administrative communications. *Minren* differentiated these people from the many *nikan* subsumed and continuing to live within the banner system and the large number of Han serfs.

From the Qing's vantage, after 1644 in the northeast "commoner" was a designation for those Han who had settled in Manchuria, both legally and illegally, and were not incorporated into the banner system. The classification as commoner was required for the regional administration to draw two distinctions. Authorities needed to differentiate Han Chinese living in civilly administered rural areas as free peasants from both rusticated Han bannermen who remained within the banner hierarchy and were subject to banner regulations and Han serfs who worked aristocratic holdings (Enatsu 1989, 5–7). In the bureaucratic lexicon of northeast administration, therefore, *minren* stood in contrast to *xiatun qiren* (rusticated bannermen) and *zhuangding*.

Despite the necessity of the administrative differentiation between these categories, the distinction between Han and "commoner" remained an unstable one in imperial discourse. Whereas the Kangxi emperor cited conflicts and disputes between bannermen and commoners in Manchuria as the rationale for his 1689 edict that segregated these communities, the Qianlong and Jiaqing emperors justified continued segregation and the prohibition against commoner migration in more "ethnicized" language. In essence, the fear that Manchu ways and livelihood were deteriorating had replaced banner-commoner conflict as the chief rationale for these policies (e.g., RZSL 1964, 1544 [111]; 1609–10 [116]). Paralleling that shift, the Qianlong and Jiaqing emperors now conflated "Han" and "commoner" in ways that suggested that all Han in Manchuria were "commoners." Deploring the effects of the spread of "Han habits and customs" in the northeast, for instance, the Qianlong emperor blamed the migration of what he called "commoners" from north China. By drawing a genealogical line between migrant commoners and Han habits, the Qianlong emperor seemed blind to the thorny presence of those north Chinese already incorporated into the Eight Han Banners as well as those pressed into serfdom on noble manors (GZSL 1964, 15208 [1035]). While virtually all "commoners" in the northeast were from China Proper and therefore Han Chinese, it is clear that not all Han Chinese in the northeast were "commoners," even by Qianlong's own standards. The genealogical pairing of commoner and Han customs was an awkward one and an indication of the often strategic and unstable ways in which Qianlong constructed ethnic or racial types (Crossley 1987, 1989).

Though the sovereign at times conflated commoner and Han, field administrators generally did not. In everyday bureaucratic communications, officials working in Manchuria used the term *minren* exclusively to refer to those who were neither *qiren* nor *zhuangding* (e.g., HZ 1771, 4.21; HZ 1774, 12.13; HZ 1781, 10.20; HZ 1806.8.21; HZ 1806. n.n). This was also the case in Qing Xinjiang, where James Millward (1998) notes that the term *minren* was used far more commonly than Han, and where it was used in contrast to terms such as *Huimin* or Muslims (153). In the administrative idiom of the Qing empire, *minren* were those persons living outside the eight provinces of China Proper who were nonetheless administered by the civil bureaucracy. The introduction, persistence, and tremendous frequency of the term's use in Manchuria—as in Xinjiang—was made necessary by the need to distinguish administratively between different communities and castes.[26]

With the hardening of distinctions between types of land and categories of people that followed the decrees of 1680 and 1689, and the accompanying segregation of Manchuria's population into enclave communities of bannermen, serfs, and commoners, the category "commoner" thus entered the northeast's administrative vernacular. In the Manchurian context, the category "commoner" was the marker for both people and "habits" the state sought to confine to civilly administered districts and whose influence the Qing intended to keep to a minimum by limiting "commoner" movement. Thus, after 1689 all commoner peasants permitted to live in the northeast were required to remain within the commoner territories (*minjie*) and live in commoner villages (*mintun*). They were also restricted to cultivating commoner land (*mindi*) and were administered by civil bureaucrats (*min guan*) (BQ 1985, 328 [18]; QHS 1991, 376 [289]).[27]

Manchuria's field administration was, therefore, designed to control the movement of the rural population and particularly to bind commoners to their villages and the territories designated for their habitation.[28] To prevent commoners from departing the so-called commoner territories for the banner and manorial lands, the regional government expended substantial energy and resources in policing the countryside and enforcing the territorial and juridical boundaries that segregated and demarcated the *minren* population (see Chapter 3). All things being equal, these restrictions would have had little effect on commoner peasants, who could still move freely between the civilly administered villages and zones within the northeast. However, because the Qing state had set aside the greater part of cultivatable land in southern Manchuria for banner and manor use (more than four-fifths of the thirty million *mu* of land designated by the Kangxi emperor for cultivation in 1680 was bannerland) and had banned commoner settlement altogether from central and northern Manchuria, commoner mobility was in fact significantly restricted. As a result, the commoner peasants of the northeast faced significantly greater limitations on their mobility than the peasantry of China Proper.[29] Yet the state's active intervention in the countryside to control commoner peasant mobility—which proved largely unsuccessful in the course of the eighteenth century—contrasted with its limited objectives at the level of the commoner village. There, the state intervened only minimally to structure the ways in which commoners organized their lives so that, within this narrow zone, Manchuria's agrarian regime did not depart from China Proper's.

The state's primary interventions in the daily lives of commoners were for the purposes of securing the land tax and maintaining a modicum of social order: the state had no designs on restructuring the property rights among commoners or compelling commoner peasants to perform agricultural work in ways it visited upon rusticated bannermen and serfs. As a result, commoner peasants were able to import customary practices wholesale from their native places for regulating village economic affairs. Local officials in Manchuria were commanded to "let [commoners] do as they will" (*ting qi zi bian*) with their land insofar as their practices did not spread outside the borders of the commoner villages and territories (Yi 1993, 251). However, the Qing was adamant that commoner customary land practices not leave the commoner territories and, more to the point, commoners not be permitted to deploy their customary notions of property and ownership to acquire banner and manorial lands. In the administrative language of the northeast, *minren* stood in juxtaposition to both *qiren* and *zhuangding*, a set of relational normative categories that in principle underpinned the agrarian regime.

The Formal Land System and Social Categories

When Japan acquired the Liaodong peninsula following the Russo-Japanese war (1904–1905), the colonial government ordered an investigation of Manchuria's property system. The result was a nine-volume compendium of formal land arrangements. The work was overseen by Amagai Kenzaburō, who subsequently did more to advance our historical understanding of the peculiarities of the Manchurian property systems than any other scholar (MT 1914; 1969). His catalogue of the types of land is widely adopted in the Japanese historiography and has been accepted in the Chinese scholarship, though its provenance is not always recognized or acknowledged in the latter.

Amagai used the Japanese term *ippan kichi*, literally "regular bannerland" (Ch. *yiban qidi*), to refer both to the bannerland (Jp. *kichi*; Ch. *qidi*) worked and held by rusticated bannermen *and* the manor land (Jp. *kanchi*; Ch. *guandi*) worked by serfs and owned variously by the imperial house, aristocracy, or the state. Though Amagai recognized that these two forms of land were distinguished by different production and social relations, he also recognized that together "bannerland" and "manor land" stood in juxtaposition to "commoner land" (*mindi*). Under Qing practice, both "manor land" and "bannerland" were attached to the grantee's banner. Thus, Amagai's collapsing of "manor land" and "bannerland" under a single category reflected the assumption that the banners, and all that was affiliated and attached to them, including land and people, were part of the Conquest Elite and the imperial patrimony.

This conflation is evident in the Qing sources. Qing authorities conducting rural surveys to uncover land that had been illegally sold to commoners registered bannerland and manor land alike as "bannerland conditionally purchased by commoners" (*min dian qidi*). For example, a 1793 land survey uncovered that a serf household had sold land to several Han commoners and, though the land was part of an imperial estate, the official described it as "bannerland conditionally sold to commoners" (LPA 1793, 8820, 8857).

By collapsing banner and manor land into a single category in this fashion the Qing was drawing a distinction between what I will call "Qing land" (what Amagai calls "*ippan kichi*") and commoner land, as well as between rusticated manor serfs and bannermen and commoners. Commoner land constituted a separate category because commoners stood outside the banner system. By contrast, manor and banner land, as well as the serfs and rusticated bannermen who farmed it, were part of it. In this construction, the Qing state was not drawing lines between Manchu and Han ethnic groups per se, but rather between those peasants who were part of the banner system and those who were not. The distinction was not *ethnic* but *institutional*.

The segregation of commoners, rusticated bannermen, and serfs into separate village communities was part of the imperial court's broader goal to define and configure the land system associated with bannerland, manorial land, and commoner land. The physical and juridical boundaries that mapped these lands also mapped the social boundaries between rusticated bannermen, serfs, and commoners. Some Chinese scholars have taken this as evidence that the Qing practiced a form of *ethnic* privileging and segregation in Manchuria that ultimately heightened and hardened "ethnic contradictions" (*minzu maodun*). It is not clear how either the land system or its related pattern of residency corresponded to a priori ethnic distinctions, however.

Rural communities and their inhabitants, as they were defined by the state, were not strictly differentiated by language, place of origin, appearance, lineage, or any other standard notion of an a prior ethnic difference. To be sure, *minren* were overwhelmingly if not entirely from China Proper. But, as noted, so were the serfs and bailiffs working and living on the manors (Enatsu 1989, 6; Fletcher 1978a, 43). Similarly, a fairly large number of rusticated bannermen were ethnically Han, having submitted to Manchu rule before 1644 (Enatsu 1989, 6–7; 1991, 9–13; Lee 1970, 33–36; Diao 1993, 60–62, 79–81, 91–94, 98–99; Wu et al. 1990, 60–65, 73–74).[30] What distinguished rusticated bannermen, serfs, and commoners in the first instance was not communal differences per se but institutional alignments vis-à-vis the state. Whereas rusticated bannermen were attached to specific banners, commoners were not, and, whereas serfs were bondservants incorporated within the banner system, commoners were free peasants.

This is not to say that these castes could not form the basis of future ethnic identities in a fashion argued by Mark Elliot (2001) for the banner garrisons in China Proper. But what is striking is the extent to which social identities among the rural population of the northeast remained oriented toward, and configured by, forces other than ethnicity, The evidence for this comes from the large number of legal court records used in Chapters 5 and 6. Serfs and rusticated bannermen who appeared before the courts, whether for homicide trials, prosecution for illegal land sale, or as a result of a dispute, identified themselves by name and provided information about their age, village, commanding officer, and banner affiliation. They never spoke of themselves as Manchu or Han—neither did they specify in most cases whether they belonged to a Manchu or Han banner. Similarly, those who were clearly free Han peasants from north China identified themselves exclusively as "commoners" or *minren*, never as Han Chinese. Commoners provided the only hint of their "ethnicity" when they referred to a home town in China Proper.

There is little evidence in Manchuria of the excessively antagonistic relations between bannermen and commoners of the sort noted by Mark Elliott (2001), who sees the record of conflict between these populations as evidence that legal and institutional distinctions were shaping ethnic identities among average subjects (230–232). By contrast, the documentary evidence from over three hundred legal cases, including homicides, criminal prosecutions, and non-violent disputes, shows that the Manchurian village was no more divisive than that of China Proper, and there is no indication that disputes and crimes were overlaid by ethnic rivalries or prejudices. Indeed, neither those involved or those who witnessed these murders and disputes, nor the officials who judged them, made any reference to ethnic differences, even though by the late eighteenth century, if not earlier, the Manchurian village was a socially hybrid place. It is clear from the legal records that commoners lived side-by-side with rusticated bannermen and serfs and that these different populations thought of each other as fellow-villagers (*tongtun*) and as friends who got along well (*suo hao wu chou*). They visited (*chuanmen'er*), they were lovers and inter-married, they were drinking partners who chatted and gambled (*gaoxing shangliang wanxi*), they worked together in the fields as fellow hired hands, and they recruited each other as farm hands and tenants (Isett 2004, 169–170). Insofar as the court records of homicides and land disputes from Manchuria present a close approximation of the spoken language used by common folk in reference to each other and themselves, that language shows no signs of ethnic identities.

In conclusion, the Qing dynasty explicitly curtailed the expansion in Manchuria of a free and small-holding peasantry. Toward that end, it infused the countryside with legal prescriptions against mobility and carved up the rural population into distinct status groups—serfs, rusticated bannermen, and commoners—whom it then segregated into enclave communities. The state then enforced a sort of agrarian autarky in which the primary mode of exchange/expropriation ran vertically, from cultivator to sovereign. As a result, agrarian production relations in Manchuria were marked *in law* by sharp vertical and horizontal status cleavages, significant immobility of cultivators, and heightened extra-economic coercion with regards to serfs. Whether the state could put law into practice depended of course on enforcement and relative balance of power between it and rural society.

CHAPTER THREE

The State in the Village

THE QING DYNASTY'S PROJECT in Manchuria required a proactive administrative presence. The consolidation there of the particular agrarian regime was predicated upon the Qing ruling house's ability to create and protect land systems through both coercion and enforcement: coercion to fix populations to their communities and enforcement to ensure populations did not cross physical and status boundaries and to prevent Han migrants from settling. This project necessitated an early and significant bureaucratic presence that contrasted with the Qing state's generally thinner presence in other frontier regions.[1] To be sure, coercion and local policing were characteristic of Qing rule generally, but the Qing project in Manchuria required an aggressive and interventionist regional administration to reconfigure land and social arrangements from the ground up. However much, for instance, the Qing state intervened *coercively* in eighteenth-century Taiwan to prevent settlement and colonization, it had no intention of overhauling and restructuring agrarian social and productive relations there (Shepherd 1993, 137–154, 182–208). But, because securing Manchuria's novel land and social arrangements depended in large part upon the state's ability to police and shape the countryside, the disaggregation of those arrangements in the eighteenth century suggests a certain weaknesses in the form of agrarian administration. In this chapter, I examine how the Qing sought to plug the state into Manchuria's villages in its efforts to secure hegemony over the region.

Manchuria's Regional Bureaucracy Circa 1700

The highest-ranking authorities of Fengtian, Jilin, and Heilongjiang were the military governors (*jiangjun*) who held banner rather than civil rank and appointment (Zhao 1998, 193). In the early years of Qing rule, a single military governor resided in Shengjing to administer the entire northeast. A second military governor was appointed in 1653 to govern the border regions north of Shengjing. Finally, in 1683 a third was added to the far north to address more effectively the Russian incursions along the Amur that led to the Treaty of Nerchinsk in 1689. Thus, by 1700 administration of the far northeast was divided between the jurisdictions of the Jilin and Heilongjiang military governors, who were administratively subordinate to the Shengjing military governor on some but not all matters (Zhao 1998, 193).[2] Though the Qing employed the same military administrative system in its Inner Asian dominions, its reliance upon military appointees from the banner armies to administer Manchuria served the sovereign's specific interest in maintaining direct authority over the homeland (Lee 1970, 24).

The presence of the Qing secondary capital in Shengjing complicated questions of administrative jurisdiction in the region, however, and ensured that the military governors were not all powerful. Mirroring arrangements in Beijing, the Qing maintained an Imperial Household Department in Shengjing along with five ministries, each headed by a vice secretary (*shi lang*) and each with its own administrative prerogatives and responsibilities.[3] Their presence in Shengjing tended to diminish the authority of the military governors, who had to share some jurisdictional oversight with the ministerial vice secretaries in matters such as justice and tax collection. The authority of the Shengjing military governor was diluted further by the presence of the Fengtian Prefect. The Prefect was the highest ranking civil appointee in the northeast and thus the de facto governor of the commoner population (Lee 1970, 62). Until 1765, the post of Fengtian Prefect was of little consequence since the Shengjing military governor held the office concurrently. Thereafter, however, the office of Fengtian Prefect was held concurrently by the Shengjing Board of Revenue vice secretary, a reform that enhanced the latter's powers and broadened his administrative oversight (Lee 1970, 63). In his study of the Qing administration in the northeast, Robert Lee (1970) maintains that fragmented and shared jurisdictions and authority precluded any single official in the region from achieving autonomy and thus served to undergird the sovereign's control over his officials and the region (62). The division of authority and jurisdiction so evident at the regional level extended to the countryside as well. There, jurisdiction over the banner and commoner villages as well as the manors was split up. The banner populations were overseen by the banner bureaucracy, at the top of which sat the military governors. Commoners were overseen by civil officials who reported to the Fengtian Prefect, but also to the vice secretaries and the military governors on some matters. Oversight of the manors depended upon whether the manor was owned by the emperor, a member of the aristocracy, or was attached to one of the five boards in Shengjing as a source of revenue.

Banner Zones

The banner zones (*qijie*) were the territories around each garrison town dedicated to the settlement of rusticated bannermen and in which the banner villages (*qitun*) were situated. Every rusticated banner household lived in a banner village within the zone designated for its particular banner. Somewhat misleadingly, in 1745 the Qing official He Tai drew an analogy between the administration of the civil and banner populations. (Misleading because the administration of the former was conterminous to a geographic area, whereas that of the latter was conterminous to an organization.) The banner army, he stated, was analogous to the province; the regimental commander or colonel (*canling*) to the prefecture; and the company commander (*zuoling*) to the county. Below the company commander, households were organized in units of no less than ten households, which He Tai compared to the civil *lijia* and *baojia* systems, which organized and registered households for tax collection and policing (in He 1992, 868 [35]).

Each garrison town and its surrounding bannerland was overseen by the garrison commandant (*chengshou wei*), an office in the banner bureaucracy usually held by a deputy lieutenant-general of the banner army (*fu dutong*), though occasionally by a colonel (*canling*) (Sudō 1944, 191–193; Lee 1970, 72).[4] The responsibility of the garrison commandant included overseeing all bannermen and their dependents within his jurisdictions, including those who lived in the banner villages. Ideally, therefore, through the chain of command that flowed from sovereign to military governor to garrison commandant, the emperor secured direct authority over his banner subjects in the villages.

Prior to 1644, the lowest command unit within the banner army was the company (Man. *niru*, Ch. *niulu*), a unit of between 150 to 200 mounted men (Lee 1970, 28–29). But because the company did not correspond precisely to the banner village, two subgarrison functionaries were created after 1644 to facilitate the garrison commander in his oversight of the rusticated banner population. One of these functionaries operated above the banner village and the other within it.[5] The former held the banner rank of *zuoling* (major). He reported directly to the garrison commandant and was charged with reporting crimes and dunning taxes in the banner zones. Assisting him were assigned *lingcui* (clerks) who possessed the skills needed to keep administrative records and mounted troops (*xiaoji xiao*) who accompanied the tax collectors on their rounds (Sudō 1944, 149, 193; 1972b, 400–401; Lee 1970, 28; Li 1988, 306–312).

Accounts of tax collection in the banner zones give some sense of how the layer of administration lying between the garrison town and the banner village functioned. Beginning in 1693, a tax was levied on all bannerland in Manchuria. The levy was small, however, at a mere one Guandong *sheng* in beans and one sheave of hay levied on every *shang* of land (BQ 1985, 329 [18]; QHS 1991, 376 [289]), an amount that was less than 1.25 percent of output.[6] The lightness of the bannerland tax reflected the Qing ruling house's paternalist attitude toward the banner population. It also reflected the fact that rustication was understood not as a source of revenue but rather as a means of saving revenue by making bannermen support themselves. The entire garrison bureaucracy was mobilized every year to collect the tax. Providing further details of administrative responsibilities, the 1727 edition of the Eight Banner *Gazetteer* explains: "The *xieling* and *chengshou wei* of each zone are charged with oversight and tax collection; the *zuoling* . . . and the *xiaoji jiao* are charged with administration and tax dunning. If anyone refuses to remit the tax then the supervising and tax-collecting officials are immediately to arrest and punish him" (BQ 1985, 329 [18]; cf. Yamamoto 1941, 15).

Until the mid-1720s, the *zuoling* and *lingcui* were the full extent of banner bureaucratic presence in the banner villages. But around 1725 a new post was created within the banner village itself to assist the garrison commandant and those *zuoling* charged with rural oversight. According to Japanese scholar Yamamoto Yoshimitsu, the office was the *shoubao* and its establishment coincided with the first comprehensive cadastre (*qingcha*) of the northeast, conducted over two years in 1724 and 1725.[7] The *shoubao*, who was always a rusticated bannerman who lived in the banner village he oversaw, was expected to coordinate oversight with the *lingcui*, and in this function was similar to the headmen and such who oversaw commoner villages throughout China Proper and Manchuria (Yamamoto 1941, 13).[8] Given the timing, the post of *shoubao* was probably created to assist in the land survey. The appointee's familiarity with his village was undoubtedly considered by provincial authorities to be of some help. Upon the completion of the 1724–25 survey, the post of *shoubao* was evidently retained to help maintain the household registers and tax records. But, over time the range of the *shoubao*'s responsibilities grew to include reporting criminal activity within the village—including illegal sales of bannerland to commoners—and detaining suspected criminals. It is evident from the legal court records that by the High Qing, the *shoubao* was a local constabulary in the banner village.

These records always include the statement of the nearest *shoubao*, whether he witnessed the crime or not. The *shoubao*'s statement appears at the very beginning of the case record and provides details of the crime scene and corroborates both the crime's time and its place. Clearly, the *shoubao* was by the middle of the eighteenth century the equivalent of the village policeman and, in this function, he was analogous to the *xiangyue* or *dibao* who policed civil populations both in Manchuria and China Proper and whose testimonies similarly appear at the beginning of court records (for instance, see XT 1762, 2.5; XT

1794.3.26; XB 1823.6.3). Like the office of the *xiangyue* and *dibao*, the *shoubao* was unsalaried. He was a villager and like his fellow rusticated bannermen he was expected to farm, pay taxes, and provide military service if called upon (GZSL 1964, 1745 [115]; Yamamoto 1941, 13–14). The *shoubao*'s character and responsibilities were concisely summarized: "he is upright and honest and his responsibilities include assisting in the prompting of taxes, investigating illegal activities, and seeing if any households have moved or land gone unregistered. He is to report such things in the registers. Order in all matters ultimately depends upon the enquiries of the local *shoubao*" (cited by Yamamoto 1941, 13–14; also see Sudō 1972b, 394–395, 400–402).

As was true in the administration of other communities in the northeast, the Qing state was clearly seeking to place as much of the fiscal burden of policing as possible on the village, while simultaneously precluding the emergence of local strongmen by seeking out lowly villagers to perform many of these tasks. In this sense, Qing policy in the banner zones resembled its standard practice elsewhere in the empire.

Manor Oversight

Manors existed to provide the banner aristocracy and imperial household with a rent income. This income was expropriated from the serfs who were attached to a manor and considered their masters' dependents. Because of the juridical arrangement that characterized production relations on the manor, oversight and compulsion were key to the successful garnering of rent and the securing of the labor force. First, because serfs were not subject to eviction—not only did serfs hold permanent tenure as a condition of their enserfment, but it made no sense for a manor lord to sell, manumit, or evict his serfs since they provided a major source of his income—they were under no compulsion other than that brought to bear by the manor lord to pay rent. Second, because serfs always had reason and opportunity to flee their manors—there was plenty of vacant land in the northeast where an absconded serf might set up home—and because they fled with some frequency, the viability of the manor system rested upon the manor lord's ability to tie his serfs down. Close oversight of the manors and the threat of harsh punishment for both rent defaulters and absconders were therefore integral to the manorial system.

Manor oversight was the responsibility of the bailiff or estate steward (*zhuangtou*), a hereditary title given to prized bondsmen, many of whom were *baoyi* slaves of Manchu princes or the monarch.[9] Manor-holding members of the Qing aristocracy had no interest in managing their own estates. Their time was occupied in high politics and courtly life in the capital or in holding salaried bureaucratic office. Thus, the aristocracy left enforcing day-to-day order on the manor to their bondservants whom they appointed as bailiffs and over whom they had little direct oversight. By contrast, the bailiffs of the imperial estates (*huang zhuang*) and official estates (*guan zhuang*) were overseen by a middle layer of bureaucratic officers stationed in the northeast. After 1733, bailiffs on the official estates were overseen by the *Nongtian si* (Farmland department), an office within the Shengjing Board of Revenue (Li 1988, 268) and those on imperial estates by the *Kuaiji si* (Accounts department) of the Shengjing and Jinzhou Imperial Household departments.[10]

Most bailiffs were of Han Chinese origin. Many had been incorporated into one of the eight Han banners before 1644 and by definition they were therefore *zhengshen qiren*, or "full bannermen" (Diao 1993, 70–71; Jing 1993, 93–100). They then received their posting as reward for meritorious behavior in their masters' services. The bailiffs of the imperial grain estate at Junjiatun in Jinzhou, for instance, were all from one family in the Han Yellow Banner Army (Enatsu 1989). According to historian Enastu Yoshiki, the first bailiff of the Junjiatun manor was a Han Chinese from Dengzhou prefecture in north China named Jun Suncai. Jun had been incorporated into the Han Yellow Banner Army after submitting voluntarily to the imperial household, and in 1669 he was granted a bailiffship as reward for his military service.[11] Bailiffs such as Jun were provided with generous land grants within the estates as emolument. They could use this land as they saw fit, renting it to serfs and, by the mid-eighteenth century, to commoners as well. In return, they assisted their lords by collecting rent, tribute, and the head tax from the manor serfs. They also registered and kept track of the serf population and cultivated area, reported serf flight, and assisted in the apprehension of absconding serfs and uncovering and reporting illegal land sales. Finally, they reported shortages of serf labor, tools, and draft animals, as well as any natural disaster that reduced the manor's productivity (Zhao 2001, 291–294).

There was, however, a major problem associated with the employment of bailiffs. Physically far from their lords, with hereditary authority to oversee estates, bailiffs were well positioned to take control of manorial land from their masters. This was even the case with those who oversaw government or imperial estates and were thus subject to closer oversight. Many bailiffs did just this over the course of the Qing, accruing substantial properties through abuse of office (Enatsu 1989, 7–16; Yang and Zhou 1986, 312). It was with an eye to preventing such developments that manor lords tried to control their bailiffs through bonds of vassalage and dependence. Like serfs, bailiffs were bondservants and by definition their masters' personal dependents or housemen. The bonds of vassalage entailed in the bailiff's dependency provided his lord with both normative and legal powers over him. On the one hand, it was the bailiff's hereditary duty as his master's bondservant to serve his master by loyally fulfilling all responsibilities. This was the normative requirement of vassalage entailed in houseman status. On the other hand, as dependents and bondservants, bailiffs were also subject to laws and regulations that stipulated punishment for transgressions of the master-servant relationship. This was the juridical force brought to bear on those who broke the rules of personal dependency.

A 1779 legal case of a bailiff who brought suit against his superior demonstrates the asymmetrical sets of obligations, claims, and legal authority that strengthened the hand of the master in disciplining his bailiffs. The case stemmed from a suit brought by a bailiff against his superior in the banner hierarchy. The superior was found guilty of the accused crime, yet the bailiff was also charged with the offense of "a bondservant (*pu*) bringing suit against his master (*zhuren*)" (Jing 1993, 96–97; GZSL 1964, 15848 [1076]).[12] The normative value at the heart of this bailiff's crime was that suing one's lord or his representative was a transgression of the status differences between lord and servant and, as such, required punishment.

Bailiffs who committed crimes against their masters were sentenced simultaneously for the transgression of both a general legal principle—such as stealing property, striking or killing another person, and adultery—and for the transgression of a status boundary—the boundary between master and servant, a legal principle that applied to all dependent persons. Under Qing law, this double breach was cause for harsher punishment. The punishment for a bailiff who sold his lord's property was thus set two degrees above the level specified for the crime of "selling another's property."[13] The status distinction between master and servant in the case of lords and their bailiffs extended to the former's right to punish the latter for failing to remit manorial rent. The punishment was, moreover, harsh. For failing to remit one-tenth or less of the rent quota, the bailiff received fifty lashes of the whip, with the number of lashes increasing for every ten percent increment in the amount of unpaid rent (QHZ 1983, 363–364 [624]; DC 1970, 93.7, 95.11; QD 1989, 387–388; Zhao 2001, 292).

Though bailiffs were their masters' vassals or housemen and, like serfs, attached to their masters' household as bondservants, they were not legally or functionally analogous to serfs.[14] That fact was captured in the following statement of the Farmland Office of the Imperial Household Department—an office charged with overseeing the bailiffs of the manors held by the imperial household—following a series of investigations into the management of an imperial grain estate. In defining the conditions and responsibilities of the bailiff, the Farmland Office pointed out that "though a bailiff of this office (*si*) and serf of a different surname [to that of the bailiff] are not master and bondservant, the serfs do fall under the bailiff's authority. . . . Furthermore, the management of the estate is the responsibility of the bailiff himself, while the responsibility of meeting the rent (*zu*) quota is that of the serf" (LPA 1815, 25944). The point made was that though a bailiff could legally possess his own bondservants and use them to farm his land, he could not treat his master's serfs as his own bonded servants. Thus, while the bailiff was tasked with overseeing his master's serfs, he held no private authority over them (Jing 1993, 100–111). The bailiff's powers were limited to oversight; it was the lord's prerogative to punish his serfs.

The bailiff was therefore simultaneously a hereditary overseer, a hereditary bannerman, and a hereditary bondservant, as defined by his duties, his banner affiliation, and his dependent status respectively. It is because of the bailiff's multiple social and legal roles that Jing Junjian (1993) has suggested there is a certain ambiguity to the legal standing of the bailiff. Along one axis, the bailiff was a vassal. The office of bailiff was bestowed upon bondservants who had demonstrated service to their master, and it was in this sense a reward for loyalty and meritorious behavior, or upon persons with demonstrated and useful skills taken as captives and forced into servitude. As hereditary vassals, bailiffs were subject to extraordinary punishment for any crimes committed against their masters. The master-servant relationship thus gave manor lords juridical powers to discipline those charged with overseeing their patrimony, a necessary power given the difficulty in asserting control across the great physical distances that separated estate holders from their estates. Along another axis, the bailiff was an overseer and on these grounds he stood socially and legally both separately from and above the serf. The bailiff was charged not only with collecting rents but also with monitoring and disciplining serfs on his lord's behalf. Just as a bailiff committing a crime against his master was tried and punished as a bondservant breaking the normative boundaries between them, so a bailiff who abused his master's serfs was punished for failing to perform his duties to his master (e.g., LPA 1815, 24127).

The perpetuation of bailiff vassalage was useful in the struggle between lord and bondservant over the control of manorial land and the collection of rent, enabling very high rates of expropriation. Yang Xuechen and Zhou Yuankang (1986) estimate that on princely manors (manors held by members of the imperial aristocracy) rent in kind took about one-third of grain output, while tribute in such items as ducks, geese, pigs, and so forth took twice as much in cash value (306–307). Over and above that, each adult male serf paid in cash an annual fee of 1.5 *tael*. Yang and Zhou's estimates suggest that all in all total dues came to about eighty percent of the grain yield of a standard serf holding.[15]

The rate of take on crown (imperial) and government manors was less extreme, but nonetheless considerably higher than that paid by free tenants to their rentier landlords. In the late seventeenth century, a Shengjing imperial or government grain estate of 720 *mu* remitted 120 *shi*, or about one-third of its total grain output, assuming a yield of 0.5 *shi* per *mu* (QDTD 1988, 390, 415; Diao 1993, 74; Wu et al. 1990, 77; Yi 1993, 240).[16] In addition, every estate remitted four thousand sheaves of hay, as well as tribute in eggs, poultry, charcoal, and other items, plus the head tax. On the government manors of Ningguta, a serf with sixty *mu* was expected to remit twelve *shi* in grain rent, from a total harvest of perhaps thirty *shi*, plus three hundred sheaves of hay, one hundred catties of pork meat, one hundred catties of charcoal, and three hundred catties of coal (Wu 1985, 234). In the 1720s, tribute was eliminated on the Ningguta manors, and a single serf working sixty *mu* was subsequently charged a flat rent of thirty *shi*. That was still the equivalent of half his output (Yi 1993, 240). In addition to rent and tribute, after 1693 all serfs on government-owned manors were required to remit as a poll tax 2.6 *sheng* of grain per annum per *mu*, or about one-third of a *shi* of grain annually, which supplied the regional granaries (QDTD 1988, 388; Diao 1993, 86).

All in all, before 1750 rent and fees taken on the imperial and government manors took in excess of half the grain yield. At a time when free tenants in China Proper paid in rent about forty to fifty percent of their grain output to their commoner rentier landlords, the higher rate of expropriation achieved on manorial lands—particularly those of the nobles—was possible because of the heightened levels of coercion possible under Qing manorialism. Given the distances between the manors and the nearest state officers, and the rights and claims of permanent tenancy of serfs and bailiffs alike, perpetuation of bondservant status among bailiffs and serfs was key to the workings of the system. That said, given that rents on manors were fixed, it is clear that as yields rose overtime the relative rate of lordly take would have fallen.

Rural Control in the Commoner Territories

The removal in 1680 and again in 1689 of all commoners to commoner villages (*mintun*) (and the concomitant hardening of physical and juridical boundaries separating commoners from rusticated bannermen and manorial serfs) was accompanied by the extension, deepening, and clarification of the field administration for overseeing the so-called commoner zones (*minjie*). It is no coincidence that the earliest expansion of civil administration and control, lasting roughly from 1650 to 1700, coincided with the initial expansion of Qing lands (both bannerland and manors). Those projects required the application of political force and compulsion against the rural population both to create and to secure the new land systems.

Not surprisingly, regional civil government was confined to southern Manchuria until the mid-eighteenth century, especially Liaodong and Liaoxi, where most commoners were settled. The earliest civil administration offices were established in Liaoyang and Haicheng counties, both formed in 1653 and subordinated to Fengtian prefecture after 1657. In 1662 and 1665, six counties (Jin, Guangning, Gaiping, Kaiyuan, Tieling, and Chengde) and three departments (Liaoyang, Jin, and Ningyuan) were added. That was where civil administration stood in 1700.[17]

The geographic spread of the civil field administration was accompanied by the institutional penetration of state presence into the commoner villages. Thus, in 1668, all commoners in the northeast were ordered to register in *baojia* and *lijia*, subvillage organs that assisted county magistrates in overseeing the rural populations (Diao 1993, 198–199). In principle, as Hsiao Kung-chuan (1960) showed in his classic study of rural control, each of these "parapolitical" organs was tasked with particular duties. The *baojia* assisted local government in the task of registering and policing the rural population. Under the *baojia* system, every rural household was in principle assigned to a unit (the *pai*) of ten households headed by a *paitou* or *paizhang* (literally, the *pai* head or leader). A unit of ten *pai* formed a *jia*, headed by a *jiazhang*, and ten *jia* formed a *bao*, headed by a *baozhang*. Those selected as *paitou* and *baozhang* were expected to assist the local magistrate in maintaining population registries, tracking local residents, and noting the appearance of newcomers, as well as policing and reporting crimes. The parallel but functionally distinct *lijia* system assisted magistrates in the registration of the rural population for the head (poll) and land taxes. In principle, every 110 village households were combined to form a single *li*. The heads (*lizhang*) of the ten largest tax-paying households in the *li* were responsible for keeping tax records for the ten households under them, a unit known as a *jia* (Hsiao 1960, 25–143). The *paitou*, *baozhang*, and *lizhang* were all villagers selected from among the peasantry, theoretically in consultation with the local magistrate.

Distinct both organizationally and functionally from the *baojia* and *lijia*, in the rural areas the Qing state also established *she*, a unit of several households or villages intended to facilitate cooperation and assistance among villagers. The *she* was headed by a *xiangyue*, originally conceived as a Confucian lector whose responsibilities included the moral edification of villagers. In the eighteenth century, however, the *xiangyue* had become the local constabulary and the *she* a policing jurisdiction, while the office's pedagogical responsibilities had all but gone (Hsiao 1960, 184–254; Huang 1985, 224n). In Manchuria, for instance, it was noted at the end of the Qing that "since the time when the [post of] *xiangyue* was established, in addition to dunning taxes, they have investigated instances of theft and gambling, and reported cases of murder and assault. While the local official is far off in the town, he can rely upon the *xiangyue* as his ears and eyes" (MC 1906, 193–196; cf. Li 1978, 80 [7]).

Hsiao Kung-chuan demonstrated how in the eighteenth century the organization and function of the *baojia*, *lijia*, and *she* merged. In particular, he traced the way in which the *baojia* morphed into a unit for both policing and tax dunning and the *lijia* either attenuated or disappeared altogether (Hsiao 1960, 89). He believed this to be the result of the merging of the poll tax into the land tax under the Kangxi emperor, a change in the tax system that eliminated the need to maintain the poll tax rolls, a task formerly assigned to the *lijia*. Because the *baojia* already registered the population, the task of registering land for the land tax soon fell to the *baojia* as well, rendering the *lijia* fully obsolete. As they did in China Proper, so the parapolitical organs overseeing commoner peasants in Manchuria, the *baojia*, *lijia*, and *she* merged in various ways to form hybrid units that performed multiple tasks. From the sources at hand, it is not entirely clear when this metamorphosis occurred. However, it is clear that it was well under way by the mid-eighteenth century.

Different orientations took shape. In Gaiping county, for instance, the *baojia* and *she* were combined to form a single chain of command for assisting the magistrate in policing commoner villages. According to the Kangxi era Gaiping county gazetteer: "At the beginning of the Qing, the entire area [of Gaiping county] was divided into twelve *she*, with ten *jia* to every *she*. Each *she* appoints a *xiangyue* (constable) and *baozhang* (ward headman)." The Gaiping orientation suggests that the *baozhang*, as head of the *baojia* system, were subordinated to the *xiangyue*, and the *baojia* thereby were subsumed under the *she*, creating a single hierarchy for registering and policing the peasantry (Yamamoto 1941, 20).

By contrast, in Jinzhou prefecture to the south, the *baojia* system was absent altogether and the *lijia* appears to have taken over the former's policing functions. Thus, as the *baojia* was subordinated to the *she* in Gaiping, so in Jinzhou the *lijia* was subordinated to the *she*: "every year each *she* must record the name of one *zongli*. Every *she* consists of ten *jia* and each household must record the name of one *shenli*. The *shenli* is to dun taxes (*cui liang*) and establish order" (JZFZ 1985, 826). In the Jinzhou orientation, the *zongli* (an agent of the *lijia*) appears to have become the equivalent of the *xiangyue* while the *shenli* functioned as a *lizhang*. While the lowest rung of the *lijia* retained its tax-dunning functions, it had also taken on the policing functions of the *baojia*. Similar arrangements were to be found in Tieling, Ningyuan, Kaiyuan, and Liaoyang counties in the late seventeenth and early eighteenth centuries, where villagers were grouped in *lijia* subordinated to *she* (TLZ 1985, 774; LYZ 1985, 740; KYZ 1985, 2470; NYZ 1985, 2414–2415, 2418). In each of these cases, a single hierarchy was created for both registering and policing villagers.

What appears to have occurred by the early eighteenth century is that within the village the lowest rungs of the *baojia* and *lijia* hierarchies—the *pai* and the *jia* respectively—became congruent with the entire village community while the *paitou* and *lizhang* lost their distinct titles and functions and merged into a single agent overseeing the entire village. The head of the amalgamated *pai* and *jia* was often called simply the "head of ten households," or *shijia zhang*, a generic term not part of the original nomenclature but clearly identifying the person's duty as overseer of multiple households (NSS 1937, 147–149; Yamamoto 1941, 22–32). Above the village, the *baojia* and *lijia* hierarchies disappeared altogether, superseded by the *she*, leaving *xiangyue* in charge of overseeing both registration and policing for the local magistrate. The Manchurian *she* thereby consisted not of a specified number of households, as Hsiao describes it, but of a number of villages, covering as much as thirty square *li* (Yamamoto 1941, 22–23). Evidence compiled by Yamamoto (1941) from late nineteenth-century Fuzhou suggest that a *xiangyue* oversaw between three and fourteen villages (22).

The particular forms taken by Manchuria's parapolitical agencies by the eighteenth century are perhaps best explained by the frontier conditions and concomitantly sparse population. With commoner villages thinly populated and widely dispersed across the countryside, it was logistically easier for rural functionaries to perform multiple rather than specialized tasks. Since many of those who performed these tasks regarded their responsibilities as burdensome, it seems logical that when adapting subcounty agencies to local circumstances in Manchuria, magistrates would streamline the tripartite system of *baojia*, *lijia*, and *she* into a single, hierarchical organization combining all tasks.

Rural Agents and the Limits of Rural Control in Qing Manchuria

It was standard practice elsewhere in the empire for the Qing state to rely upon unsalaried informal and semiformal agents and brokers to assist in the tasks of administration (Hsiao 1960; Huang 1985; Mann 1987). The practice constituted a form of indirect taxation of local society which was thereby made to bear the costs of its administration. The need to place administrative costs onto rural society in this way had much to do with the Kangxi emperor's pledge in 1713 to "never raise the land tax assessment" (*yongbu jiafu*) fixed for the empire. Efforts by the Yongzheng emperor to get around that pledge by allowing local administrators to raise revenues by regularizing the collection of surtaxes, and tying these to budgetary lines, were short lived, as Madeleine Zelin (1984) shows. Yongzheng's son and successor the Qianlong emperor returned to Kangxi's low tax policy while steadfastly opposing local attempts to increase administrative budgets (Zelin 1984, 304). Propagandized to good effect as an indication of benevolent Qing rule, the fixing of tax rates simply gave impetus to the adoption of various modes of indirect taxation, some of which future monarchs, including Qianlong, regarded as corruption but nonetheless tolerated as a necessary evil. As a result, much of the tax burden on the peasantry by the High Qing came not from the *direct* taxation of land by the central government, but from the *indirect* and semilegal taxes levied by local authorities on peasant households (Wang 1973, 82; Ch'ü 1962, 132, 135, 140–142; Hsiao 1960, 113–124; Reed 2000, 175–177). Rather than pay for local administration through the redistributive channels of the Qing bureaucracy, much of the cost of local administration was levied directly (Ch'ü 1962, 22–32, 44–49, 64–67, 87–88, 112–113). The local government's continued reliance upon rural agents selected from the peasantry to help oversee the countryside was analogous insofar as the practice burdened the locality with the cost of its own administration.

The decision to recruit from among villagers, rather than other social classes, especially local elites, cannot be explained by pecuniary needs alone, however. The choice was also guided by the sovereign's desire to circumvent local elites. Big landlords and merchants already held considerable sway over local populations by virtue of their economic power and their control over lineages and other social organizations. The Qing state, not wishing to augment its influence by delegating oversight powers to them, elected instead to recruit from the lower rungs of Qing society (Esherick and Rankin 1990, 6). Since the Song dynasty (960–1279), which marked the ascendancy of the autocratic emperor and the end of aristocratic authority, the Chinese sovereign had aggressively guarded against the emergence of local strongmen capable of challenging imperial authority.[18] This meant not delegating policing or taxing powers to these men. Thus, unwilling to turn to local elites to assist in tax collection and policing, Qing authorities instead turned to those who resided in the villages. These men posed no serious challenge to imperial authority, while their intimate knowledge of local conditions lent the state some traction in the countryside. Even so, the Qing state limited these rural agents to auxiliary tasks in an effort to preclude their emergence as local strongment. In principle, rural agents were prohibited from administering punishment and collecting taxes, powers that were reserved for the *yamen* (Hsiao 1960; Ch'ü 1962).

While these institutional arrangements helped keep local elites in check, they did so at the expense of the state's ability to project its power into the countryside. The problem for authorities in Manchuria and elsewhere in the empire was that parapolitical agents inhabited two worlds. They were simultaneously agents of the state and members of a community and their allegiance was split accordingly (see Chapter 5). Consequently, eliciting full cooperation from rural agents was a constant challenge for the local official. As it turns out, these agents could be expected to cooperate when the interests of villagers and the state coincided. They regularly reported violent crimes, for instance, and helped in the apprehension of those who committed them. But, they just as often protected the village by concealing developments that while harmful to the state were beneficial to villagers. Thus, as we shall see, rural agents refused to report the illegal sale of Qing land, sales that local communities accepted and sanctioned but that the state considered criminal. One can speculate that things may have turned out differently had rural agents been more fully incorporated into the state as tax-farmers, such that they received salaries tied to the amount of tax revenue they gathered. (This was how the Ming and Qing states taxed commercial transactions in market towns [Mann 1987].) Had the late imperial state made it in the financial interest of rural agents to protect its interests, the state might have had less trouble preventing the devolution of Qing lands into the hands of commoners. As it was, however, the crown was unwilling to yield the kind of authority that tax farming would have required.

In the end, the paradox of the Manchurian agrarian regime was the coexistence of a rural order commonly associated with sub-enfeuded polities on the one hand and a centralized tax-office state associated with an attenuated local presence on the other. Qing officials such as Shuhede serving in the northeast were themselves aware of the weak state presence. Discussing the problem of uncovering illegal migrants, he memorialized in 1740 that:

> on examining the situation, we see that though there are *zuoling*, *xiangyue*, and *paitou* in the localities of Fengtian, they can not be everywhere at once. In 1729, on the basis of a memorial from the then Military Governor, Ge'erbi, *baojia* were ordered established. Though this command was carried out, commoners from outside (China Proper) have continued to settle here over the years. Among them, there are those who have registered in the county records and rolls and those who have not. (GZSL 1964, 1744–1745 [115])

Shuhede was clearly aware that the weak link in rural oversight in Manchuria was the subcounty agent. Unless these agents fulfilled their duties, *yamen* officials had no means to secure the agrarian regime; they could not keep immigrants out, nor, probably, could they keep rural communities segregated. Yet the regional government in Manchuria not only relied upon subcounty functionaries to perform standard tasks such as the registration of the local population and reporting crimes, but also to assist in the state's program to prevent commoners from occupying banner and manorial land.

The management of a peasant economy rooted in forms of servile and immobile labor is generally associated with states constituted by agents who are positioned to enforce that immobility by virtue of their proximity to the site of production.[19] Yet the physical and social distance between the centralized bureaucratic offices of the regional banner and civil administration and the countryside was substantial enough that regional officials in the employment of the emperor had little knowledge of what was going on in the villages. This situation was not particular to Qing rule in Manchuria, however, or to Qing rule more generally. Indeed, the famed late Ming scholar and official Gu Yanwu (1613–1682) had written critically of these same aspects of post-Song bureaucratic rule (the so-called *jun-xian* or "prefecture-county" system of administration). He went so far as to advocate a partial return to "feudal" (*fengjian*) administration, even suggesting that the Qing state abandon the rule of avoidance, whereby local officials could not oversee their home counties, and return to patrimonial governance. He argue that local magistrates be selected from local elites who would serve hereditarily in their home districts. This, Gu argued, would not only result in less autocratic rule (by which he meant the emperor would have less power over the community) and better local government but would also give administrative power to those who best knew local conditions and ways. Gu maintained that such a reform would thus enhance political control even as it weakened imperial autocracy (Min 1989, 92–95).

In the end, however, given the social distance between administrators and the local population that characterized Qing administrative practices, bureaucratic officers in Manchuria were ultimately unable to maintain the close supervision necessary to preserve an agrarian order rooted in an immobile peasantry. As the peasantry acted in its own interest, and as these actions went unnoticed and unchallenged, state authority retreated.

PART TWO

Peasant and State in the Eighteenth and Nineteenth Centuries

PART TWO SHOWS that the ruling house's early success in securing hegemony over the northeast was contingent upon particular historical conditions—specifically, a politically and demographically weakened peasantry. It shows that once these conditions no longer prevailed, the Qing land system became increasingly untenable.

Through a close analysis of court records from the eighteenth and nineteenth centuries, Part Two examines the social and political forces that undermined Kangxi's agrarian regime in Manchuria and that by the end of the eighteenth century had given rise to a set of property relations that secured "peasant possession" in land. Part Two reveals, in the first instance, how rural communities succeeded in concealing from the state the transfer of Qing land to commoners. It shows, in the second instance, how communities successfully found ways to regulate property claims on their own. Part Two also shows how Qing officials adapted to developments on the ground, in their efforts both to prevent the further devolution of Qing land and to ensure that, in so doing, they minimized the possibility for social unrest. Torn between their mission to maintain the Qing land system and their need to ensure social peace, officials adopted strategies for coping with both sets of demands.

Part Two then examines how, once secured, peasant property claims functioned in practice. First, it shows that peasants, whether customary proprietors or tenants, attained a tenacious hold on the land despite the absence of "legal protections": it shows that this hold was underwritten by customary principles and secured in the institutional practices of the village. Second, Part Two traces the spread in Manchuria of novel wage relations alongside the new property regime and explores what this meant for the peasantry and economy. On the one hand, it is clear that the legal and customary bonds of servitude that had applied to field hands in the Ming disappeared in the eighteenth century, a development that conforms to trends that have been long noted by legal and social historians of China Proper. On the other hand, it is also clear that the appearance of wage laborer did not signal a structural transition in the economy toward agrarian capitalism, as some have maintained.

I end by suggesting that peasants in Manchuria, as in China Proper, by virtue of the reigning property relations of the eighteenth and nineteenth centuries, were protected from being fully separated from the land—a condition that is the hallmark of capitalist development. Part Three will then show that agrarian property relations in the northeast shielded peasants from the full effects of market forces, a condition that allowed them to pursue goals that were incommensurate with the requirements of economic development.

CHAPTER FOUR

The State and Agrarian Property Relations

IT HAS BEEN ARGUED that the maturation of the land market in the early Qing ushered in a modern property system by the end of the eighteenth century. It is claimed that by taking advantage of new market opportunities, individuals were able to maneuver to dissolve pre-existing patrimonial constraints on their claims to land and upon the exchange of property. As a result, individuals were able to realize the productive value of property better than at any time previously (Buoye 2000; Pomeranz 2000). Yet, many studies have shown that the commodification of land was accompanied by the multiplication of rights and claims rather than their narrowing. Thus, despite the long-term commercial patterns that marked the Ming and Qing dynasties, as well as the mounting conflict and competition over land that attended the eighteenth-century population boom, the thick undergrowth of custom and convention that sanctioned multiple claims was never fully cleared and a generalized pattern of absolute rights to property did not take root.[1] In short, peasants developed ways to use their property to secure the funds they needed for survival without having to relinquish fully their claims to it. As peasants layered the land with claims to it and its product, predictably social tensions mounted. Nevertheless, these practices persisted into the twentieth century when the Republican government faced the daunting challenge of developing new property law to regulate many of those practices (Huang 2001, 65–68, Bourgon 2004).

Disputing the claim of Ramon Myers and Chen Fumei (1976) that the Chinese peasantry had established absolute rights in land by the Qing, Peter Perdue concludes that despite the rising price of land and attempts by landowners and others to profit by circumventing customary notions of ownership and claims, "absolute property rights of ownership and alienation never came to predominate" (1987, 150). Sucheta Mazumdar comes to similar conclusions in her analysis of custom and property systems in Guangdong; she finds that the ability to alienate land was greatly circumscribed by custom and lineage power (1998, 220–240). Similarly, Melissa Macauley, Kishimoto Mio, Yang Guozhen, and Li Wenzhi show that customary practices persisted that secured peasants' claims to land even after they had "sold" it (Macauley 1998, 229–237; Kishimoto 1997; Yang 1988, 274–275; Li 1993, 16–18).[2] It has been noted, moreover, that magistrates continued to observe custom when adjudicating legal matters, even when local practices went against codified principles intended to clarify property rights (Yang 1988, 115; Allee 1994b). Moreover, despite an interest in knowing from whom to collect the land tax, the local administrators continued to tolerate multiplex and multi-layered property claims and even illegal arrangements so long as basic tax obligations were met (Macauley 1998; Ocko 2004, 190; Osborne 2004). Finally, Thomas Buoye, who has made the strongest claim to date for the ascendancy in the Qing of what might best be described as the market logic in land rights—a system of modern and fully commercial property rights—records the rising tension and conflict that characterized and accompanied attempts by some to capture full control and alienability in land (2000, 92–107, 166–192).

Despite the Qing efforts to the contrary, peasant communities in Manchuria succeeded in establishing many of the same claims to property as their counterparts in China Proper. This chapter is primarily concerned with the types of claims peasants in Manchuria held over the land and how they were asserted. However, given the peculiarities of the banner and manorial land systems, where much of the peasantry's buying, selling, and renting land took place, attention must also be paid to how the state's intervention shaped the content of these claims.

Qing Law and Property Claims in Land

The state's principal concern—written into law—regarding property was that landowners pay the land and transfer taxes (Jing 1994, 66; Huang 1996, 148). Thus, Statute 95 of the Qing Code, which addresses the buying and selling of land, opens not with a declaration of rights to alienate or own property but with the admonition that the transfer tax be paid and then proceeds to prescribe punishment for those who fail to do so.[3] The statute was a reflection of the state's general ambivalence on the question of private property. Thus, Qing law did not speak to the question of absolute property rights in land; conventionally understood as the right of individuals or corporate bodies to own property free of unreasonable restraint by the state or other social groups. The closest the code came to any such statement was to codify the punishment of those who occupied land that by custom belonged to others (Statute 93; Jing 1994, 43). Under Qing law, therefore, the rights of property owners appeared as a "negative principle"—the right not to have one's property stolen—rather than as a positive one—a declaration of the general inviolability of private property. Moreover, the only "positive" statement pertaining to land rights contained in the code constituted a forceful circumscription of the property holder's privileges. The law guaranteed all sons the right to an equal distribution of their father's or grandfather's property, thereby denying patriarchs the right to dispose of their property as they saw fit among their heirs (Statute 78.1; Wakefield 1998, 14–21).

Simply stated, absolute rights to property (and of person) were inconceivable on a political terrain in which the self-described function of the state/sovereign was not to act as disinterested mediator between private citizens, individuals, or corporate groups but as moral edifier of the emperor's subjects (Ch'ü 1961, 249–252; Huang 1996, 7; Sommer 2000, 67). Thus when it came to property, the state was concerned with clarifying property ownership to avoid social conflict and disputes over land that otherwise burdened the local courts with litigation and generated social disharmony (Perdue 1987, 163; Huang 1996, 105–106; Macauley 1998, 61–65, 97). Accordingly, the Qing state intervened to prohibit those practices that disrupted the "natural" social hierarchies that underwrote social harmony, understanding practices to have either beneficial or malevolent effects that had to be appropriately encouraged or repressed (Ch'ü 1961, Bourgon 2004, 89). The state's priorities are evident in the fact that it was not until 1768 that the Qing legally recognized the use of land sale contracts as evidence of ownership, and only then as a practical application in the adjudication of land disputes (Zhang 1998, 104–105). Absent any intent to create a systematic and consistent body of property law, field administrators were in turn left to propose ad hoc regulatory interventions under the rubric "correction of mores and practices" (*zheng fengsu*) to criminalize practices that were socially disruptive.[4] To be sure, as others have shown the late imperial state handled local disputes over contracts, land, and debts through mediation and adjudication under the so-called category of *hu hun tiantu xishi* (literally, small matters pertaining to the family, marriage, fields, and land) (Huang 1996, 78–100). Yet the practice of law in such cases did not create corresponding legal principles.[5] The state handled these matters because not to do so was to invite social instability, and to do so was one of the few means by which the state could in fact interject itself into local society for the purpose of social control.

Customary Practices in Land

Given the Qing legal framework, it is not surprising to find that peasant claims to property were secured at the level of the village, first and foremost.[6] The law courts facilitated the smooth functioning of custom by enforcing both directly and indirectly much of what was customarily acceptable (Allee 1994b, 134–135, 138; Huang 1996, 2–3, 110–120). Indeed, there was much resonance between Qing legal practice and customary practices in land. What is of interest about the Manchurian case, however, is that customary practices in land functioned in the complete absence of sympathetic or facilitating courts. As we shall see, in many instances peasants' claims to land were sustained by communities even as the state was trying its best to do away with those claims.

What made peasants' assertion of their claims to land possible in the Qing (and perhaps earlier) was the fact that communities had effective institutional means for recording exchanges of land, regulating claims, and managing disputes. Recent research in Qing legal history has shown that lawsuits were often resolved at the village level after they were filed but *before* they went to formal trial (Huang 1994, 143; 1996, 13, 61–68, 123–124; Allee 1994a, 229–231; Macauley 1998, 63, 363–364, n 80). Ethnographic evidence from the twentieth century points to the existence of a vital realm of village-level mediation that was institutionally apart from the courts and provided peasants with an effective instrument for handling disputes and intervillager affairs (Duara 1988, 94, 181–191; Huang 1996, 21–75, 118–119). In Manchuria too, there is clear evidence that villages were effective sites for the regulation of peasant claims over land; the next chapter describes how this was possible. In both Manchuria and China Proper village self-regulation worked in a context in which the state had resisted endowing individual villagers with political authority over others for fear of devolving power to the locality (see Chapter 5). Those powers were guarded by the state. Absent a formally empowered state representative in the village, informal mechanisms that relied on villagers of good standing and *gravitas*—sometimes backed by the village powerful—sufficed to manage matters of great importance to peasants and their communities (Chen and Myers 1976, 6–10, 24–25).

Transferring Claims to Land

Chapter 5 will examine village strategies and institutions that in Manchuria secured de facto property claims of villagers despite the illegality of those same claims in law. Here I examine how these same institutions facilitated the buying and selling of land and, in so doing, established the grounds upon which claims could be made. Though the evidence is often taken from Manchuria, much of what I discuss here was true for China generally. I will do this by examining the land "contract" or "deed," not as a legal but as a social document.

The Chinese land sale contract or deed carries a boiler-plate quality when confronted as a formal document. The semiliterate scribes who wrote them often worked from models, a practice that tended to standardize contracts within and across regions and that standardized language has most often elicited formalist analyses that focus on the rights and claims expressed in the contract (see Chen and Myers 1976; Hamashita 1983). In this view, the language of the contract represents formally the normative rules of property in operation. However, by concealing the social acts and obligations that stood behind the contract (as well as those that were anticipated within it) this approach fails to account for how the norms formally expressed in the contract were socially reproduced—in essence, the formalist approach misses the day-to-day social play that stood behind the norms. It is only when land contracts are viewed alongside ethnographic accounts of the performance of the land sale—and are therefore seen as social as well as legal documents—that their full character and function are revealed.[7]

Ethnographic surveys from the northeast (and elsewhere in China) show that each article in a land contract corresponded to a specific social action, meaning the contract was not only a delineation of claims but also an historical account of the transaction. Each aspect of the sales contract gave force to the other. A proprietor who wished to sell land began by locating a broker or middleman (*zhong ren* or *zhongjian ren*) to assist in finding a suitable buyer. The middleman, as we shall see, was there to ensure customs were followed, to act as a broker in mediating an agreement, and to be the chief witness to the proceedings should disputes arise after the sale. His first task, according to the Japanese ethnographic surveys, was to verify the owner's claim to the property. This action was mirrored in the deeds' opening statements that explained the basis of the owner's right to sell the land, usually explained as "his own" (*ziji*) or an "ancestral inheritance" (*zuyi*). A statement that explained the owner's reasons for selling his property usually preceded that statement. This generally was a declaration that he needed money "because I am empty-handed" (*yin shouzhong kongfa*) or "because I have insufficient funds" (*yin zhengyong bu zu*). Such statements undoubtedly lent the contract an air of authenticity, but they also reflected the reality of many land sales. The sense that the seller had lost out was captured in the customary requirement, standard to large parts of China including the northeast, that the buyer host a meal celebrating the purchase—sellers of land did not host celebratory meals (Huang 2001).

Having authenticated the seller's claim to the land, the middleman then approached potential buyers. Custom required that the land be offered first to those who held what twentieth-century ethnographers called "the right of first purchase" (*xianmai quan*), which was in fact the right of first refusal. The people who held this right varied from place to place, but always included the seller's relatives and any person who held a lien or had purchased the property conditionally. It usually extended to those whose land lay adjacent to the plot being sold and sometimes to any person considered a villager. It was the middleman's responsibility to offer these people the opportunity to decline the purchase at the asking price. Only after these individuals had declined the offer could the middleman take the property to other parties. But the fact that these persons had been approached and turned down the invitation to buy the land was *always* noted in the land contract, usually immediately following the contract's opening statements (MTDG 1935, 155–156; TKK 1937, 186–187, 197).

Once a buyer was found, the middleman accompanied both parties to the property. Together, they estimated the land's productivity, measured the area, and noted its precise location, boundaries, any easements, and any building or structure on the property. These particulars were all noted on the contract. The buyer and seller then negotiated a price and the terms of the sale with the middleman acting as mediator. Once the price was set, a contract was written up. If the sale was outright, this was noted. If it was conditional, then this was noted and the time period within which the seller could redeem the property might be noted. The contract finished with a general statement declaring the sale was made without duress, such as "the seller willingly sells" (*qingyuan mai*) and "both parties agree willingly to this sale" (*ci xi liang jia qingyuan*), and that the middleman was responsible for mediating any disputes arising from the contract. The contract ended with the signatures—usually the ideogram for "ten" (十) under his name—of the seller, middleman, witnesses, and scribe (Shimizu 1945, 11–15).

The language of the land contract, which presents the agreement as fait accompli and therefore irrevocable in principle, replicated in exact sequence the tasks of the middleman who, according to Japanese ethnographers, began by verifying ownership, then cleared away preemptive purchase rights, measured and evaluated the land, and finally witnessed the exchange of the cash price. There were additional aspects to the middleman's task that were not typically mentioned in the contract, but were nonetheless essential. Most important of these was the timing of the sale and whether it required further clarifications of rights and claims. To avoid such problems, most land sales occurred after the harvest and before field preparation work began for the following year's planting (TKK 1937, 184; MTDG 1936, 153, 187).[8] However, there were ways to accommodate peasants who were in dire need of cash and had already prepared their land for the next year. The practice of selling land that had been planted, for instance, was known as "selling young (green) sprouts" (*mai qingmiao*) or "selling a young (green) field" (*mai qingtian*). In such cases, the broker was required to confirm that indeed the labor had been expended and then assist in evaluating its cost to the buyer (TKK 1937, 185).

This account of the land sale lends further support to the notion to be discussed in Chapter 5 that middlemen and facilitators stood in for the community to police and regulate property claims. In the absence of village courts, or a legal system that proactively secured such claims, the account also points to the primacy of village institutions in underwriting many property claims. Furthermore, it suggests how it was possible that multiple claims to land were not only sanctioned but put into practice, even in the face of the state's attempts to regulate these. Villages were after all small units in which individuals and families functioned in close cooperation and social proximity to others, in which significant social pressures were brought to bear against those who broke rules that jeopardized others and the community.

The "Right of First Purchase"

By the Qing dynasty, if not earlier, the content and form of land contracts were fairly standardized, as a result of using boilerplates to write contracts.[9] For this reason, contracts in Manchuria resembled those of other regions. This standardized phrasing did not however mean that contract language was pro forma, although some have suggested this for certain aspects of the contract. Thus, Thomas Buoye has argued, following Yang Guozhen, that the statement contained in all land contracts recognizing what in the twentieth century has been called "right of first purchase" (*xianmai quan*), especially as it related to relatives and kin, was a dead letter (Buoye 2000, 68; cf. Yang 1988, 18). However, Yang Guozhen provides little in the way of evidence to support the claim, whereas the homicide cases upon which Buoye rests his argument do not demonstrate the unenforceability of such claims. In many of the cases Buoye cites the event of the homicide, which left one party to the dispute dead, prevented any possibility of a formal or informal resolution of a dispute over the "right of first purchase," leaving the status of the land still open to question. In other instances, the cases cited suggest in fact that the right remained active enough that relatives received payments to relinquish it (Buoye 2000, 101). Rather, these sources often indicate that the failure to recognize the right of first purchase was reason for complaint, social acrimony, and violence (Buoye 2000, 101, 185–186; 2004, 114–115).

The fact remains that renunciation of future claims by relatives remained part of the standard contract language *and* social practice of the land sale, while the practice of selling land to relatives who held the right of first purchase was common. On the basis of more than seven hundred examples of land sale contracts from the Qing, Xu Tan shows that the practice of selling land to relatives was alive and well. Her sources suggest that on average about one-third of all land sales went to relatives who held the right of first purchase and, moreover, that there was little change across the eighteenth and early nineteenth centuries, when commercial forces were having their fullest effect (in Fang et al. 2000, 1609–1616). When these numbers are broken down by province there does not appear to be any correlation between the persistence of this right and heightened commercial trends. In other words, commercialization did not lead to a decline of kin purchases. Guangdong and Fujian were arguably among the most commercialized zones in Qing China, yet Xu's sources show that kin were far more likely to buy land from each other there than in other provinces (cf. Mazumdar 1998, 224–228). To be sure, Xu's sources do not speak directly to the enforcement of the "right of first purchase," but they are an indication that kinship relations had an important role in the land market.[10]

Other sources, principally ethnographic surveys and foreigner observations of the Chinese countryside from the late nineteenth and twentieth centuries, amplify the findings of Xu's data. These show that the "right of first purchase" was not a distant memory but was still recognized and enforceable in large parts of rural China (Johnston 1986, 143–144; Jamieson 1888, 72; Jamieson 1921, 103; Jernigan 1905, 139; Gray 2002, vol. 2, 108–109).[11] The earliest ethnographic observation I have found of the practice in Manchuria dates to 1877. In that year the U.S. Consulate to Niuzhuang wrote in his analysis of property customs: "It is advisable in case of a mortgage [conditional sale] (and necessary in case of a sale) to consult the neighbours before completing the transaction" (U.S. CR Dispatch 338, May 19, 1887). Fifty years later, peasants were still required to offer land they hoped to sell first to relatives, among other village members. In the most comprehensive study of Manchurian property rights, Shimizu Kinjirō points out that the right of first purchase was vigorously enforced in Manchuria for the most part, with seller and middleman required to offer the land to relatives, neighbors, fellow villagers, and, of course, anyone with a lien on the land. Shimizu also noted that peasants did on occasion assert their right to preempt a purchase (Shimizu 1945, 16–17, 35–39; also see TKK 1937, 197; MTDG 1935, 155–156; MTK 1939, 72, 107, 128).[12]

The persistence of language in land sale contracts recognizing the right of first purchase—as well as attempts to assert this right—was one of an array of claims and rights that secured for peasants a very tenacious hold on the land. R. Bin Wong has singled out the strength of peasant attachment to the land in late imperial China as a defining *distinction* between its agrarian social formation and that of early modern western Europe. Whereas peasants in early modern western Europe, Wong argues, were easily dispossessed of their land, and thereby more easily rendered fully dependent upon the market for their employment, peasants in contemporaneous China remained more firmly attached to their land. Chinese peasants by contrast either remained in full possession of their land, securing their reproduction primarily through farming, or were rendered only partially dependent upon the wage labor market ("semiproletarianized") (Wong 1997, 47).[13] The tenacious hold the Chinese peasant had on the land was a definitive feature of the late imperial agrarian social formation, of which the "right of first purchase" was just one form. Other means by which peasants staved off full dispossession include the practices of "conditional sale" and "supplemental payments," to which we now turn.

The Conditional Sale

In Qing customary practice, land could be sold in two ways. It could be sold "outright" in a practice known as *juemai*, in which case the right of the seller to redeem the land was said to "die" with the sale (*simai*, literally "dead sale"). Or, it could be sold "conditionally" (*dianmai*), in which case the right of the seller to redeem the property was said to "live on" (*huomai*, literally "live sale"). Clear evidence of the peasantry's persistent and tenacious grip on the land was the fact that most land alienated in Qing China was sold conditionally. Only after peasants failed to redeem land they had sold in this fashion was it sold outright.[14]

Under the conditional sale, the seller (*ye zhu*) or *dian*-maker retained both customary and legal rights to redeem the property at the original transaction price. That was anywhere from one-third to seventy percent of the land's full sale price (Jamieson 1888, 81; McAleavy 1958, 406–407; U.S. CR Dispatch 331, May 19, 1887).[15] The conditional buyer (*dian zhu*) or *dian*-holder took possession of the land, which he could use as he wished with only a few restrictions (Hoang 1888, 121, 123–127; Schurmann 1956, 514–515; McAleavy 1958, 406–407; Huang 2001, 72–78). What the *dian*-holder did with the land had no bearing on the *dian*-maker's right to "redeem" (*huishu*) it, however. The *dian*-holder was required by both the Qing Code (Statute 95) and customary practice to return the land to the *dian*-maker upon return of the conditional sale price (Zhou and Xie 1986, 45; Jing 1994, 67). If the *dian*-maker were either unable or unwilling to redeem the land, however, then the *dian*-holder could purchase the land outright by paying what was called the *zhaotie*. By law and customary practice, the *zhaotie* was the difference between the original sale price and the full market value of the land at the time of the final sale (Huang 2001, 75).

Qing records of homicide trials and criminal investigations into illegal sales of banner and manorial land suggest that in Manchuria most if not all sales started as conditional exchanges. Indeed, so ubiquitous was the exchange of banner and manorial land by the conditional sale that the Qing authorities spoke *only* of "bannerland *conditionally* bought by commoners" (*min dian qidi*) in their communications. They never referred to land that had been illegally "sold outright." When the Qing state finally formalized the prohibition against the sale of bannerland to commoners in the Code during the Jiaqing era (until then, the prohibition existed only in the Board of Revenue regulations), Qing jurists worded the new substatute to criminalize only the "conditional" sale of bannerland to commoners. Rusticated bannermen and serfs had good reason to sell their land to commoners conditionally. Knowing these exchanges were illegal, but in need of cash, they could raise money and still hope to redeem their property before the authorities found them out.

The preference for the conditional over the outright sale is also explained by the fact that most households in the late imperial period derived most of their sustenance from farming. Peasants simply had few economic options outside of agriculture. On the one hand, they lacked the skills or capital needed to enter into town-based manufacturing. On the other hand, rural-based manufacturing had developed in conjunction with farming as a way to round out consumption needs rather than in towns as an alternative to agriculture, so that in most cases land remained essential to household survival (Huang 1985, 193–195; 1990, 80–86; Xu and Wu 2000, 375–380; Brenner and Isett 2002, 629–631).[16] Given these constraints, maintaining access to land was essential to the continuation of the peasant household and the conditional sale helped in this effort. It allowed the poor and misfortunate to raise money needed in a crunch while retaining some control over their land (Perdue 1987, 138; Huang 2001, 73; 1990, 106; Macauley 1998, 230).[17]

This does not entail that peasants had a sentimental attachment to land, a notion effectively critiqued by Myron Cohen (2004, 48).[18] There were clearly social reasons that were "unsentimental" and pushed peasants to keep control of their land. First, land was the ground on which male social standing and patriarchal control stood (Huang 2001, 81). Second, land ownership was in many communities the principal criterion for defining membership, which came with important claims to common land, foraging, and other unclaimed resources that helped fill out basic needs. Third, land ownership also gave fathers control over sons, especially their labor.[19] Thus, male heads of household throughout China purposely delayed the partition of family property until the last possible moment, often holding out to their deaths, because their control over property was what kept sons around as they waited for their inheritance (Gates 1996, 93). The late imperial state, as a matter of principle, supported the patriarch's control over his land and his sons in this regard (Ch'ü 1961, 29; Wakefield 1998, 21, 116; Zhang 1998, 300–302). Finally, possession of land improved the likelihood that peasant sons could marry. While not having land was no disqualification, young girls were sometimes in short supply (this was especially so on the Manchurian frontier in the eighteenth and early nineteenth centuries) and even under better circumstances males without land were often unable to find brides (Wolf and Huang 1980, 140–141, 222). On the opposite side of the coin, married peasants who had lost their land not uncommonly lost their wives shortly thereafter. With the loss of land and wife, a male lost his social standing in the community (Sommer forthcoming). Thus, access to land not only underwrote peasant subsistence in what was still a substantially agricultural and insecure environment but made possible an array of highly desired social goals as well as access to social goods such as wives. The conditional sale, which gave peasants the chance to buy back their land once better times came, if they wished to do so, thus reflected a fundamentally rational desire on the part of the male peasant to remain both on the land and at the head of his family.

Qing Regulation of the Conditional Sale

In law, the Qing state sanctioned the conditional sale, just as it also sanctioned the outright sale. Its primary concern was simply that the *dian*-holder pay the transfer tax (Statute 95; see Jing 1994, 66; Huang 1994, 148–149). The state prohibited the conditional sale under only two conditions. First, land could not be sub-*dian*-ed without the *dian*-makers authorization. Second, banner and manorial land could not be conditionally sold to commoners. In the eighteenth century, the Qing state did however have occasion to regulate the conditional sale; but its goal was not to end the practice but to reduce court litigation by clarifying and placing limits on it.

The decision to regulate the conditional sale in the early eighteenth century was precipitated by rapid price inflation that worked to the advantage of *dian*-makers who could redeem their property at the preinflation price. *Dian*-holders as a result were forced to accept cash payments that had significant lost purchasing power. The courts were consequently flooded in the early 1700s by suits as peasants fought to prevent or compel land redemptions. The state's first response, in 1730, was to end attempts to redeem fraudulently land that had been sold outright. New regulations mandated that all land sale contracts include language that specified whether the sale was redeemable or not (Statute 95-3). The 1730 edict, however, did not prevent peasants who had sold their land conditionally from redeeming it many years and even decades after the fact. Sons whose fathers had conditionally sold land several decades before continued to seek to redeem their property and buyers responded by bringing suits to prevent them.

In an effort to minimize conflict and litigation, in 1753 the state added an amendment to the code specifying that conditional sale contracts signed within the previous thirty years continued to be redeemable, unless the contracts specified otherwise; however, any land sale older than thirty years was declared irredeemable, regardless of the contract terms (Jamieson 1921, 100; Zhang et al. 1998, 289–290; Huang 2001, 73–74; Jing 1994, 69–70). That same year, the Board of Revenue stipulated in its regulations that all contracts were thereafter required to specify a maximum ten-year time limit on the redemption (Zhang 1998, 290). A grandfather clause was written to allow those who had legitimately conditionally sold their land between 1723 and 1753 to redeem it at the original price. After 1753, the right to redeem land was limited to ten years from the date of the contract. In both cases, however, the state supported the *dian*-maker's right to pay only the original sale price.

It is far from clear what effect if any these regulations had. In China Proper, Philip Huang finds that despite the commercial developments of the Qing, and despite new regulations, "conditional sales persisted in to the twentieth century when the expectation continued to be that conditionally sold land was redeemable for indefinite or very long periods" (Huang 2001, 85, 92–94; cf. McAleavy 1958, 411).[20] In Manchuria, commoners were already buying land against state mandate, so it is unlikely peasants would have heeded these new regulations simply because they were the law of the realm. An examination of a series of thirty-eight legal land sale contracts included among numerous in court records, dating from the 1820s to the 1840s, suggests that payment of the transfer fee was the important factor in determining whether or not the ten-year time limit was specified in the contract. Of the twenty contracts that bore official seals denoting that the transfer fee had been paid, all stated or implied a finite time limit on the land's redeemability, ranging from three to ten years. By contrast, of the eighteen contracts that bore no official seal, only one made mention of a time limit to the seller's claims. Under Qing law, deeds that bore no official seal were technically illegal, since they were instruments for avoiding the payment of taxes on the transaction and as such were used among peasants only (Perdue 1987, 137). Evidently peasants who concealed their conditional sales from the state to avoid detection, whether to avoid the transfer tax or because the sale was illegal, felt no need to heed the new regulations.

Qing legal records from Manchuria show beyond a doubt that the right to redeem land could extend indefinitely. For example, between 1760 and 1763 the Kongs conditionally sold 1,332 *mu* of manor land to eight commoners. Twenty five years late, the Kongs had neither redeemed the land nor received a *zhaotie* payment. The land was still held conditionally by the buyers (LPA 1786, 8499, 8509, 8512; also see XB 1880, 2001; LPA 1779, 2322). Twentieth-century ethnographic investigations demonstrate this remained the case as late as the 1940s. In his examination of twentieth-century property systems, Shimizu notes that some conditional sales could be redeemed at any time in the future. Those agreements were appropriately called "thousand-year living sales" (*dian huo qian nian*) (Shimizu 1945, 93). Others noted that some contracts explicitly stated "there is no limit in years" (*buju nian xian*) to the redemption (TKK 1937, 243–244; MTDG 1935, 161). Even the fixing of a time limit did not preclude peasants from redeeming land after the fact. Thus, Republican government surveys show that villagers upheld the right of a *dian*-maker to refuse a *zhaotie* when offered, if he was too poor to make the redemption payment. This practice gave the unfortunate extra time to come up with the money needed to redeem his land (MS 2000, 40).

Ignoring imperial edicts that prohibited customary practices was not in itself unusual. Matthew Sommer (2000) and Kishimoto Mio (1998) have documented the widespread practice among poor male peasants of wife selling, an act criminalized by the state yet so accepted by peasants that they exchanged wife-sale deeds to verify such transactions. Sommer and Kishimoto even show that practices commonly associated with the sale of land applied equally to the sale of women; males who sold their wives often demanded *zhaojia* payments against them.[21] Examples of peasant disregard for state regulation of local land practices also abound. Yang Guozhen describes the failure of the state to put an end to the system of split ownership, known as "two masters to a field" (*yitian liangzhu*) in Jiangnan and Fujian (Yang 1988, 115). Under that practice the land was split between "subsoil" and "surface" rights. The owner of the former held the right to collect rent on the land, but the owner of the latter was protected from rent increases and was free to do what he wished with the land (Yang 1988, 100–113, 117). The 1730 Fujian provincial regulation that prohibited the separation of land into top-soil and bottom-soil rights was not only flouted in Fujian, the practice also spread to Taiwan (Yang 1988, 113, 284–290, 329–359; Shepherd 1993, 227–230). Peter Perdue (1987, 139) notes that despite provincial regulations in Hunan that prohibited landlords from seeking rent deposits and criminalizing the *zhaojia*, both practices persisted.

Given the limited resources available to the local magistrate, policing customary practice was difficult if not impossible. It also appears that in many of the documented cases, state mandates were trumped by continued support within the peasantry for adhering to old ways, even in the face of the mounting social tension and competition for resources that characterized the eighteenth century. In the northeast, attempts to regulate the conditional sale had little or no effect. Communities continued to recognize the right of *dian*-makers to redeem their property long after the sale, both in principle and practice, into the twentieth century.

Multiple "Supplementary Payments" in Custom and Law

Under Qing customary practice, sellers of land could return to buyers years later to demand supplementary cash payments on the grounds that the value of the land in question had risen since the time of the sale (Jing 1994, 68; Kishimoto 1997). The demand for supplementary payments, along with the prevailing preference for the conditional sale, is an example of what Franz Schurmann (1956) described as the Chinese practice of alienating property by degrees. In his study of property, Schurmann suggested that the dominant mode of land exchange lay between full alienation and full inalienability. Land was exchanged, he noted, in part, thereby creating a "multiplicity of social relations" (514–516).

Under one practice of "supplementary payments," a seller could return to the buyer and demand a second or third *zhaotie* payment on a single piece of land (Huang 2001, 75, 90–91). While the receipt of the *zhaotie* in theory ended the seller's right to redeem property, it did not sever entirely his claims to the land's value or productiveness. The origin of the multiple *zhaotie* is not clear, but it was very similar in spirit to another practice, that of the *zhaojia*. Under that practice, the seller could return to the buyer and request additional or supplementary payments of cash over and above the original land sale price. The receipt by the *dian*-maker of the *zhaojia* had no bearing whatsoever on his right to redeem the property at a later date.

Before examining the differences between multiple *zhaotie* and the *zhaojia* and how each worked, we should first realize they appeared under similar conditions and, it seems, were driven by the same logic. Both spread in tandem with rising land prices and both, in effect, were recognitions of the fact that sellers of land were able to make claims against the increase in its value (Kishimoto 1997). The acceptance of the multiple *zhaotie* and *zhaojia* seems to imply that sellers of land held rights to share in the increased value of land on the grounds that it had formerly been theirs to work. Thus, Hill Gates (1996, 100) argues that the Chinese understood their property as "concretized labor," developed "by the sweat and toil of real work by real people in the past." Anne Osborne (2004) finds that on frontiers, where settlers often abandoned land they had brought into production, peasants could return to reassert their claim to a field after they had abandoned it and others had occupied it. The claim was commonly asserted on the grounds that they had expended labor on the land in the past (127–129). Family members who toiled in these fields were often themselves buried near them and their gravesites, in turn, established family claims to the land, thereby closing the circle binding labor and property (Gates 1996, 108 n 1; cf. Huang 2001, 79–80; Osborne 2004, 143–145). Because of the strength of such customary claims, officials in the northeast criminalized the commoners' practice of burying their dead on banner or manorial land (see cases LPA 1798, 31499; 1815, 24127). The extension of labor in the past appears, therefore, to have been grounds for asserting claims to the productiveness of land even after its alienation. So entrenched and accepted were these associations that despite efforts by the state to regulate and even criminalize practices such as the multiple supplementary payment, they persisted throughout Manchuria and China Proper into the twentieth century (FTTZ 2003, 2602).

The state believed the multiple *zhaotie* fomented conflict and a litigious society. In 1730, as part of the state's effort to regulate the conditional sale, it limited the number of legally permissible *zhaotie* payments to one (Huang 2001, 75). The new statute had nothing to say regarding the *zhaojia*, however. Nevertheless, Li Wenzhi and Philip Huang both believe that after the 1730 edict not only the multiple *zhaotie* but the *zhaojia* as well became increasingly rare (Li 1993, 513; Huang 2001, 90). While Li more or less assumes this to have been the case without providing evidence, Huang bases his conclusion on the land records of the Shen household of Suzhou, a substantial series of contracts that covers the period from 1659 to 1823 (see Hong 1988, 91–144).[22] While the multiple *zhaotie* may have become less common, this was certainly not so for the *zhaojia*. Demands for and payments of the *zhaojia* remained fairly commonplace in the eighteenth, nineteenth, and twentieth centuries in all of China's macroregions. Yang Guozhen and Peter Perdue emphasize that demands for the *zhaojia* persisted respectively in Fujian, where it was commonplace for three or more *zhaojia* to be demanded and received, and in Hunan, where the *zhaojia* continued despite its criminalization under provincial regulations in 1680 (Yang 1988, 274–275; Perdue 1987, 139; cf. Osborne 2004, 150; Feng 2004). Mark Allee cites a case from Taiwan in which the sellers, having repudiated the right to any supplemental payment or right to redeem in the sale contract, nonetheless requested and received at least one such payment within six years of the original sale (Allee 1994b 161). Clearly, the law had at best limited effect in narrowing these sorts of claims.[23]

Kishimoto Mio (1997) sees the spread of the *zhaojia* as a response to the rise in land prices in the eighteenth and nineteenth centuries that buttressed the bargaining position of the *dian*-maker. In order to redeem his property, the *dian*-maker was required by custom and law to repay the preinflated and original price. Obviously, many *dian*-holders were loath to accept the *huishu* redemption price because it meant a pecuniary loss. By openly or implicitly threatening to redeem the land at the original sale price, the *dian*-maker could thus push a *dian*-holder to pay the *zhaojia* time and again (Huang 2001, 75). But, the spread of the *zhaojia* may *also* have been a response to the criminalization of the multiple *zhaotie*, which it resembles in practice. It seems that both were closely associated with the conditional sale and like the *zhaotie* the *zhaojia* implied the alienation of land by degrees. The criminalization of the multiple *zhaotie* in 1730 would have simply encouraged greater use of the *zhaojia*. In either case, the continuation of the right to the *zhaojia* had to be guaranteed by the community and it is yet another explanation for why peasants continued to prefer to sell their land conditionally.[24]

The persistence into the early twentieth century of the *zhaojia* in Manchuria,[25] as well as the indefinitely redeemable sale and right of first purchase, reflected the continued capacity of peasants to maintain a tenacious hold on the land—as the best possible strategy for survival—and to mediate the implied multiple and conflicting claims. This was, of course, not unique to the northeast. The fact that the *zhaojia* was practiced in south and central China, despite state attempts to prohibit it, is evidence that there too peasants not only effectively defended their interests in land but also developed norms and means to regulate and enforce at the village level a variety of multiple claims.

The Sub-dian

The sub-*dian* is further evidence that in the Ming and Qing eras the development of a market for land did not peel away secondary and tertiary customary claims to leave hard and clear individual rights in property. Under the customary practice of sub-*dian* the *dian*-holder conditionally sold the land to a third party. The only customary stipulations were that the sub-*dian* could not extend in time beyond the original *dian* and the original *dian*-holder was obliged to buy the land back from the sub-*dian*-holder if the original *dian*-maker wished to redeem it (MTDG 1935, 162–163; McAleavy 1958, 407). The only legal stipulation (Statute 95) was that the sub-*dian*-holder not conceal the transaction from the *dian*-maker (Jing 1994, 66).[26] In Manchuria, however, the prohibition against commoners acquiring banner or manorial land extended to the sub-*dian* as well.

The only other customary stipulation was that in cases when the original owner wished to sell the land, he had to notify the *dian*-holder who then attended the transaction and recouped his money. According to the U.S. Consular in Niuzhuang:

> When an owner sells his mortgaged land, to other than the mortgagee, he simply notifies the mortgagee to be present during the transaction and especially during the transfer of the money. Said mortgagee would then be recouped by the mortgager in the presence of the purchaser and the mortgage deeds duly handed back and destroyed. No preference need be given to the mortgagee in the case of contemplated purchase; but if he is a powerful man he may intimidate the owner and intending purchaser, and thus secure the land below its actual value. (U.S.CR Dispatch 312, May 19, 1887)

The records from two murder trials give a further sense of the complex ways in which peasants exchanged claims to land as they sought to keep their households together. In the first case, commoner Dong Yulin testified that in 1798 he conditionally purchased six *mu* of land from fellow villager and commoner Ning Huai for fifty-four strings.[27] After farming the land for three years, Dong found himself "without money" (*mei qian shiyong*) and sub-*dian*-ed (*zhuan dian*) the land to Li Hongyou, a rusticated bannermen from a neighboring village, for forty strings. Dong's situation continued to worsen, however. A year later, he went to Li's home to ask for the *zhaojia*. Bannerman Li Hongyou agreed but on the condition that the original *dian* contract signed between commoners Dong and Ning be turned over to him; in a sense, by accepting the *zhaojia* Dong was agreeing to take himself out of the loop. In this instance, it seems that the *zhaojia* functioned as a *zhaotie* payment and by taking it Dong Yulin was conferring on Li Hongyou the standing of *dian*-holder (XT 1804.11.4).[28]

In the second case, Zhang Yongfu testified at trial that sometime in the 1860s he had conditionally purchased a section (*duan*) of land from bannerman Guan Chengxin for 3,500 cash (*wen*). Zhang subsequently fell on hard times and in 1872 conditionally sold the same piece of land back to Guan at the same price. Testimony at trial made it quite clear that this was not a redemption. The magistrate noted: "because Zhang Yongfu's family was poor (*jiazhong pinhan*), he conditionally sold the land back (*zhuandian gei*) to Guan Chenglin for the same price." Zhang's situation grew worse still. In late 1872 and early 1873, Zhang sent his son to Guan's house twice to ask for the *zhaojia*, but was refused both times. This case went to trial after Zhang murdered Guan in a dispute over the land and *zhaojia* (XT 1879.4.5). Rather than reflecting a rejection of the legitimacy of the *zhaojia*, it is clear that Guan's refusal to make the *zhaojia* payment reflected the extraordinary nature of the land arrangements between himself and Zhang. Guan was after all in the peculiar position of being both the *dian*-maker and *dian*-holder and, presumably, under such circumstances Zhang's request for the *zhaojia* was considered beyond the pale. (Guan, after all, could presumably have just as easily demanded the *zhaojia* from Zhang under the terms of the initial conditional sale!)

Schurmann's "multiplicity of social relations" produced by the conditional sale (*dian*)—the dominant form of land sale not only in the northeast but in the empire as a whole—the sub-*dian*, and the *zhaojia* were expressions of the peasantry's hold on the land and its ability to defend against full separation from its means of subsistence. It was undeniably an expression too of what Purdue sees as the peasantry's ability to raise cash in a market that recognized the alienability of land by degrees (Perdue 1987, 137–138). But, the fact that land was alienable and that there was a market for land was not sufficient for the emergence of absolute rights in land, either de facto or de jure. Instead of narrowing rights, the market in land facilitated peasants' ability to raise cash in ways that continued to recognize customary practices that sustained multiple claims to land. There was no linear trend in the northeast (or China Proper) running from the market to absolute property rights.

In sum, what was striking about developments in Manchuria's property system in the Qing was that the establishment of the market in banner and manorial land not only multiplied the ways in which peasants could transfer land but also the layers of land claims that could be simultaneously asserted. Under the principles of 1680, rusticated bannermen and serfs received a single land grant that they held in perpetuity. These peasants could petition the state to engross more land as their households grew, and they could transfer property through household division to their sons. However, no lateral exchange of property between unrelated households was permitted. Property rights, it could be said, were highly circumscribed under the agrarian regime of 1680; patriarchs controlled the patrimony and sons held a claim to this land that they could fully exercise at the moment of household division. But when the state sanctioned the sale of land between bannermen and serfs, rendering it a commodity by decree, possession of land became divisible. Then, as peasants turned to selling land across communities on their own initiative, the divisibility of claims widened to include persons outside the caste.

The market was not effecting a narrowing and hardening of property rights; rather, peasants used the land market in ways that created multiple and simultaneously held claims. The conditional sale, the sub-*dian*, the *zhaojia*, and the "right of first purchase" appeared and spread along with the expansion of Manchuria's population, the development of agricultural production, and the growth of trade in the eighteenth and nineteenth centuries. Communities continued to accept and enforce these practices into the twentieth century *despite* the significant growth of interregional trade and the mounting competition for land that characterized the period from 1890 to 1940, at which time these practices remained sufficiently vigorous to be recorded by ethnographic surveyors and investigated and analyzed by legal reformers.

I believe the argument, expressed by Thomas Buoye, that a "modern" or commercial property system (commonly understood to be one and the same) was emerging in the Qing is misplaced. In his view, land in the pre-Qing era was held as patrimony, with corporate rather than individual rights predominant. The advance of market forces and pressures (witnessed in the increase in total trade and mounting demand for land) in the eighteenth century provided opportunities and incentives for individuals to challenge patrimonial claims and to assert individual property rights. The suggestion is that patrimonial rights were incompatible with market forces, and one or the other had to give way. It is conceivable, however, that commercial interests—the desire to make money—were not incompatible with a property rights regime in which, as we have seen, multiple and patrimonial claims to property were simultaneously expressed, sanctioned, and even asserted (see Cohen 2004, 45–46).

Peasants who requested multiple *zhaojia* or sold their land conditionally and held on to rights of redemption for thirty years or more were pursuing interests that were perfectly congruent with any impulse they may have had to "gain" from the market. Their possession of property continued to be the necessary condition for production and market engagement, even if peasants and rural communities had to exert such claims in opposition to the state. The persistent undergrowth of customary property rights alongside commercial expansion and activity is perfectly congruent with the complex and competing claims to property characteristic of early modern peasant societies over broad areas of the world.[29] The widespread evidence of such practices in the twentieth century, moreover, suggests that in late imperial China, despite commercial expansion and rising competition for land, complex customary arrangements persisted that secured for peasants a strong grip on land (see Gray 2002; Jamieson 1888, 1921; Johnston 1986; Jernigan 1905; MS 2000).

Rent Relations

Not all peasants in Manchuria held land as property and, therefore, not all had the security in land that this entailed. Some rented land. The questions are: how pervasive was tenancy, how did the state regulate rent relations, and what sort of security in land did tenants hold?

The first question is much harder to answer with the sources at hand. It is evident from those sources available that for migrants, tenancy and wage work were often the first steps toward permanent settlement in the northeast (e.g., XT 1762.2.25; MQ 1747, A148–101). Not all illegal migrants wished to settle in sparsely inhabited areas or expend tremendous effort to bring wasteland into production. Still others did not have the capital, tools, and draft animals needed to do so. These migrants settled instead where others had already established a presence, and often this was on bannerland or manors. Returning from his 1743 eastern tour of Fengtian, the Qianlong emperor noted that whereas in the past bannermen and serfs in the area "had done all of the cultivation themselves, today only a few work the land on their own while most recruit commoners to rent and to cultivate it" (GZSL 1964, 3023 [206]).

The earliest attempt to gauge in some fashion the relative number of tenants to owners came in 1888 when the Reverend John Ross, commenting in his report on Manchurian property rights for the Royal Asiatic Society, stated that "the great majority of the farms in Manchuria are owned by the cultivators" (in Jamieson 1888, 80).[30] It is not until the twentieth century, however, that substantive evidence first became available. A 1930s Japanese survey of 1,651 households in thirty-seven Manchurian villages shows that fifty-four percent of households rented some land, but that only twenty percent rented all their land (MKK 1938, 3, table 1; 56, table 23). Given the nature of Qing documentation, the best we can say is that a minority of peasants were tenants. The proportion perhaps did not surpass the twenty percent found in the 1930s.

State Regulation of Tenancy in Manchuria

Given that commoners were renting Qing land, and the sovereign's recognition that rusticated bannermen were inadequate farmers in need of assistance, the state had perforce to intervene between rentier bannermen and tenant commoners to protect its interests in land. The sovereign's principal concern was that commoner tenants in Manchuria would acquire permanent rights to the land they rented. That fear was well-placed, given the preponderance of fixed rents and permanent tenancy in China Proper (Yang 1988, 91–133).

The Qing code's general pronouncements on the landlord-tenant relationship were limited to supporting the right of landowners to garner rent on the one hand, and prohibiting them from exercising private "justice" against their tenants on the other (Huang 1994, 147–148; Zhang et al. 1998, 284). The relevant substatute (312–3) was added to the code in 1727 and had two goals. First, the Qing wished to put an end to Ming-era practices whereby landlords exercised private power against their tenants. While the law was written to forbid powerful families from privately punishing those who rented their fields, edicts in 1679 and 1681 were more specific, forbidding powerful households from enslaving their tenants and the poor in general (Mazumdar 1998, 215). The Qing state thereby supported peasants in their struggle to free themselves of the servile and bonded status that had entangled them in the late Ming. At the same time, however, the Qing also wanted to make sure landlords could remit the land tax, which they paid out of their rent revenue. The state therefore protected the right of landlords to collect rent. The Qing dynasty was thus eager to support tenant gains, as an instrument in its efforts to diminish the power of elites over local society and, correspondingly, to strengthen its own, but not at the expense of lost revenue.[31] While the Qing had established the general legal framework for managing landlord-tenant relations with the addition of the 1727 substatute, thereafter its interventions were much more ad hoc. They were limited to encouraging greater "harmony" between landlord and tenant when social tensions between the classes threatened rural social stability (Perdue 1987, 152).

In Qing Manchuria, as always, the presence of banner and manorial lands complicated matters. In the dynasty's early years, immediately following the decree of 1680, the principle held that: "bannermen and commoners can not cultivate each other's land." Not only were commoners forbidden to buy banner and manorial land, they could neither rent it nor work it as wage laborers. By the middle of the eighteenth century, however, the Qing state had softened its position, making it legal to recruit commoners. Still, permission was granted in very guarded language. In 1740, the Qianlong emperor declared: "With respect to the bannermen's fields, bannermen are not to use hired commoners exclusively, nor are [the fields] to be used entirely to garner rent (*zu*). Rather, [bannermen] must exert themselves throughout the three seasons (spring, summer, and autumn). Leading and working alongside others, they are to farm" (GZSL 1964, 1924 [127]).

The use of the negative voice clearly reflected some ambivalence with the state of affairs. The shift in policy echoed a widely held belief at court that rusticated bannermen were poor farmers. The Jiaqing emperor remarked once that: "Because bannermen are ignorant of farming they often rent their land to commoners and collect a rent and commoners thus benefit" (cited in Yi 1993, 204). Given this state of affairs, it was considered better that they make a living by recruiting commoners than for the state to be burdened with the cost of supporting them. However, it remained the sovereign's wish, expressed by Qianlong, that commoners be permitted to work banner and manorial lands *only insofar as* this did not lead to bannermen and serfs abandoning their land fully to others. This ambiguity played out in the ways in which the state tried to regulate rent relations in Manchuria.

When, in 1740, the Qing state moved to protect tenants throughout the empire from arbitrary evictions and rent-jacking, under the new Board of Revenue regulation "forbidding the raising of rents and arbitrary dismissal of tenants," it included the following clause in reference to both banner and manorial land:

> when commoners rent bannerland, though the land belongs to the owner, and the tenant remains [in possession] for a long period, the landowner may not arbitrarily raise rents or dismiss the tenant. If the tenant fails to pay rent, then the landowner may remove him; if the tenant creates trouble, then the officials can remove him; or if the landowner wishes to take up the cultivation of the land himself, then the land must be returned to him. But, if none of these conditions apply, bailiffs and local bullies who collude to dismiss tenants and raise rents are to be punished according to the law. (Cited in Zhang et al. 1998, 286)

For good measure, the regulation added that landowners could not scheme to remove tenants by falsely claiming they wished to cultivate the land themselves. If a landowner evicted a tenant by asserting his desire to farm it, but within three years rented it out again to a new tenant, then the original tenant could sue under the regulation for reinstatement (Zhang et al. 1998, 286; Zhou and Xie 1986, 292). The Qing state intended to extend protections against evictions and rent-jacking to commoner tenants in the northeast as both Qianlong's pronouncement and the Board's new regulations recognized permanent or "long-term" tenancy (*changzu*) of banner and manorial land by commoners.

In 1769, however, the Qianlong emperor moved to prohibit any commoner from renting banner and manorial land in Manchuria for a period longer than three years, thereby ending the right of commoners to "long-term leaseholds" (*changzu*) on banner and manorial land (QHS 1983, 1031 [160])). (A limit of one year was established for bannerland outside Manchuria [Huang 2001, 77].[32]) The prohibition came in reaction to the spread to the northeast of customary practices already common in China Proper whereby tenants acquired permanent rights to land they farmed, often by purchase. Known variously as *yonggeng* (indefinite cultivation), *shigeng* (generational cultivation), *changgeng* (long-term cultivation), *yongdian* (indefinite tenancy), and *changzu* (long-term rental), these rights protected tenants against eviction and increases in rent (Yang 1988, 94, 96–97, 100–101; Li Wenzhi 1993, 96–113).

By the mid-eighteenth century, commoners in Zhili had secured *changzu* or "long-term rent" on bannerland, and this practice was already evident in the northeast (Yang 1988, 96). The effect was to devolve still more land into the hands of commoners. The Qianlong emperor's 1769 edict was an attempt to prevent the spread of permanent tenure, while still allowing rusticated bannermen the ability to earn income from renting land to commoners. The three-year rental limit was also intended to simplify the search for illegally sold land that was being misrepresented as leaseholds. Local authorities were now required to investigate all incidences in which commoners had been in possession of banner or manorial land for longer than three years, under the assumption that this land was not rented but purchased.

Aspects of the 1740 and 1769 regulations were at odds. Whereas the 1740 regulation protected commoner tenants against eviction and rent squeezing, the 1769 edict required landowners to evict commoner tenants at the end of the third year of tenancy. The state had an opportunity to clarify matters, but it did not. In 1791, the Board of Revenue commanded that bannermen be allowed to remove commoner tenants and raise rents at will, apparently abrogating the edict of 1740. However, only nine years later the original regulation protecting commoners from eviction was restated (Zhang et al. 1998, 286). This confusion in law mirrored the conflicting impulses of Qing officials and the monarch. As a general principle, the monarchy and the bureaucracy intervened in rent relations to mollify tensions between landlords and tenants and to encourage reciprocity and landlord paternalism (Perdue 1987, 150–154). Yet, the dynasty also remained bent on pursuing Kangxi's project of preserving Manchuria for the Manchus. The upshot of these conflicting tendencies meant that so long as commoners were "guest" laborers and tenants—that is, they were assisting rusticated bannermen and providing rent income to the aristocracy—their presence on Qing land was often tolerated. But they were not to gain a permanent foothold on this land and so it remained the policy of the state to insist that commoner tenants could be removed after three years. As Chapter 5 shows, whether or not such provisions were enforced depended much on local conditions.

One might expect bannermen and serfs to take advantage of the law to evict tenants and raise rents—or threaten tenants with eviction to compel higher rents—but there is no evidence of this in the court records. Part of the reason for this may have been knowledge that officials were not always willing to enforce the three-year limit when it was transgressed. For example, in the midst of an investigation into acts of corruption committed by Bailiff Xie, it was found that he had threatened to evict Zhao and other commoners tenants if they did not forgive debts he had accrued. In the course of the investigation it was found that the commoners had rented land from the bailiff for nineteen years. Rather than remove the tenants, the magistrate punished the bailiff for extortion and ordered him to desist in his attempts to evict the commoners. The magistrate openly worried that eviction of the commoners would set a bad precedent and deter efforts to attract other commoners to farm manorial land and that this would lead to a loss of imperial revenue. He suggested the tenants be permitted to continue cultivating the land as long as they paid the rent (LPA 1761, 13964). As was so often the case in rural Manchuria, in the final analysis, the state's policing of the countryside fell well short of what was needed to secure stated dynastic goals.

Rent Relations in Practice

Bannermen and serfs held permanent rights to the land they worked as a condition of their original attachment to it. By 1800, if not earlier, commoner tenants had also secured strong customary rights to banner and manorial land, despite the three-year limitation demanded by the 1769 edict (Yi 1993, 243). Of twenty-six trial records that reveal the length of tenure, in thirteen examples the leases had lasted more than ten years. For example, Zhao Haoli and Ma Shixiu rented manorial land from 1742 to 1761 (LPA 1761, 13964); the Yangs rented manorial land from 1753 to 1800 (LPA 1800, 25220); Zheng Fen rented manorial land from 1771 to 1793 (QDTD 1988, 037); Geng He rented bannerland from a *cuiling* from 1773 to 1796 (LPA 1796, 21760); Li Minghua and four other commoners rented manorial land from a bailiff for more than twenty years, from before 1778 to 1798 (LPA 1798, 31499); and the Qiao brothers rented manorial land from 1790 to 1798 (LPA 1798, 25171). In only one legal case was it testified that the tenants had agreed when they were recruited to give up the land in three years (LPA 1758, 13959). In the remaining cases, there was no indication of the length of the rental agreement.

Commoner tenants in Manchuria secured long-term leaseholds by a variety of means. Some did so by paying a deposit (MMZ 1922–23, 3.86; FTTZ 2003, 2606 [113]). Commoner Kang Zibao paid thirty strings of cash in 1848 and farmed until 1858, when he voluntarily ended the arrangement with his landlord (XB 1858.4.28); commoner Zhao Fu rented manorial land in 1793 for ten years and also paid a deposit for the right to do so (JCA 1805, 27674). In 1792, commoner Ai Guorong rented nine *mu* from commoner Zhang Rong, who in turn had rented the land from bannerman Dong Jiu. Ai paid a deposit of six thousand strings of cash and Zhang Rong agreed to rent him the land indefinitely (XT 1796.9.27).

Others acquired permanent tenancy by agreeing to bring wasteland into production. When the practice involved a bannerman and bannerland, it was called "asking a bannerman to be one's landlord" (*tou qiren wei dong*) (Yang 1988, 96). A commoner would approach a bannerman or serf and ask whether there was land to be opened in their vicinity (FTTZ 2003, [113]). In return for permanent rights, the commoner agreed to open this land and pay rent. Sometimes, the landlord made the arrangement more legitimate by petitioning local officials for permission to open the land himself. Afterwards, he paid the appropriate taxes or rents but kept hidden the fact that he had rented the land out to a commoner. A complicated example of the practice of *tou qiren* is evidenced in the case of the Yangs. The convoluted arrangements began when Serf Zheng Yiyan recruited fellow serf Liu Zehui to open some wasteland he had received from the bailiff. Liu did not open the land, however, but recruited commoner Yang Yulin to do so. Under the original arrangement, Yang paid a rent to Liu, as well as the appropriate taxes to the state. No deposit was paid, however, but by opening the land Yang had acquired permanent rights to it. After Liu Zihui passed away, his household fell on hard times and moved to Jinzhou. For many years thereafter, no one came to collect rent or the tax from the Yang household, which nonetheless continued to farm the land. Upon Yang Yulin's death, his son, Yang Rong, inherited the land and continued to work it. In 1800, the actual landowner, the son of Zheng Yiyan, came to claim the land from the Yangs. But by this time the Yangs had such a well-established claim to it that the two households simply agreed the Yangs would continue to work the land and pay rent to the Zhengs. Liu Zihui's son, who was summoned to participate in the mediation, agreed to abandon any claims he might have had to the land (LPA 1800, 25220).

In a similar fashion, commoners Yu Erya and Gao Ju obtained permanent rights to manorial land in Fengtian. According to testimony, in 1798 commoners came to an estate in Chengde county and settled there legally as tenants. In the same year, one of these commoners, Lan Bin, received permission to open nearly a thousand *mu* of wasteland. The land was subsequently opened and, for the next five years, rent on the land was paid to the state. In 1803, however, there was a poor harvest and the rent payment was not met. A prompter (*lingcui*) was then sent to investigate. It was found that the land had never been worked by Lan Bin. Indeed, Lan Bin had not even opened the land, having, from the very outset, sublet it to commoners Yu Erya and Gao Ju. Each year, Yu and Gao paid leasehold rent to Lan Bin at 1.2 strings of cash per *mu*. From this, Lan Bin paid one string of cash per *mu* in rent to the state, pocketing the remainder. When this was uncovered, the estate's bailiff ordered Yu and Gao to pay rent directly to the state, and cease paying the leasehold rent to Lan Bin. When Lan Bin found out that Yu and Gao were no longer paying him the leasehold rent, he brought suit at the local *yamen* claiming that Yu and Gao had plotted to occupy his land. The prefect adjudicating the lawsuit found in favor of the tenants, however. Bringing the lawsuit to an end, the prefect advised the Shengjing Imperial Household Department *yamen* to grant Yu and Gao Ju permanent rights (*yongyuan quan*) to the land because of "the great effort with which they had opened the land and brought it into production" (LPA 1809, 22381).

While some peasants purchased permanent tenure and others acquired it by opening land, still others held what amounted to permanent tenancy by renewing their contracts year after year without incurring an increase in rent. These practices were in line with contemporaneous developments in other parts of the empire (Yang 1988, 91–133; Zhou and Xie 1986, 288–331; Fang et al. 2000, 1771–1852). The abundance of wasteland and the low ratio of land to labor would partially explain how this was possible in the northeast. Though this would fail to explain how permanent tenancy and fixed rents were secured under contrary conditions in China Proper. Moreover, Manchuria's slow but steadily rising yields (see Chapter 6), along with rising population in longer-settled areas, should have led to greater competition for land between tenants, resulting in greater insecurity of tenure and a strengthening of landlord bargaining positions. The terms of lease should therefore have become less advantageous to tenants.

Yet, the legal records point to the ability of tenants to renew their leaseholds with some ease, even into the second half of the nineteenth century. For example, in 1826 commoner Wang Yongxiang rented ninety *mu* of manor land from *cuiling* Tasiha's father for sixty *diao* a year. During his trial for murder, Tasiha testified that Wang and his father had a verbal agreement as to the rent and terms of tenure. In 1850, Wang Yongxiang died. His son, Wang Hai, remained on the land and he continued to pay the same rent (XB 1855.7.?). In another example, the Li and four other commoner families had rented manor land from the bailiff of the imperial estate in Laoheshangbao for many years. The case came before the local *yamen* when it was reported that these commoners had buried deceased relatives on manor land. Since it was illegal for commoners to bury their dead on manor land, commoners Li Minghua, Chen Gong, Yang Guofa, Wang Wenren, and Wang Jing were all summoned to the Fengtian prefectural yamen in 1798 for interrogation. According to testimony, each family had been in the village for "many years" and had always rented land. Over the years, each household had come to the bailiff to request permission to bury family dead on the land. Each time, permission was given. Li Minghua testified he had grown up with his brother in the village. His grandfather had been buried on the land and he had buried his own son in 1778, his father in 1783, and his wife in 1792 there. Chen Gong testified that his "ancestors" had rented land in the village. He had heard his father say his grandfather was buried in it in 1750. During the investigation, the prefectural *yamen* was very concerned that manor land had been sold rather than rented. Obviously, his suspicion was raised by the length of leaseholds, which exceeded the limited nonrenewable three-year lease mandated for all manor land. Nevertheless, the court found that in each case the leaseholds were not covers for illegal land sales. The prefect ended the case by issuing certificates to each of the commoner tenants that stated this to be the case and granted them permission to continue working the land (LPA 1798, 31499).

It seems that even when landlords held the contractual right to expel tenants, and despite the tendency over time for the productivity of land to rise, landowners were not well enough positioned politically to turn tenants off the land. Tenants in longer-settled regions moreover continued to benefit from the persistence of frontier conditions to the north. John Ross noted in the 1880s that "when any district, or even farm, in Southern Manchuria becomes congested, some of the young people, or possibly the whole family, after selling out, hive off to the ownerless but rich plains in Northern Kirin [Jilin] or beyond the northern bank of the Sungari" (in Jamieson 1888, 80).

If tenants in the northeast had fairly secure tenure under various long-term arrangements, could landlords raise rents? The court records suggest that at the end of the nineteenth century, tenants in Manchuria held significant security in land *and* protection from regular increases in rent (FTTZ 2003, 2606). Rent in the Qing was most commonly fixed and was collected in either kind or cash (Yi 1993, 324). According to John Ross, in the 1880s most tenants in Manchuria were sharecroppers who paid a fixed rent of between one-third and four-tenths of output (in Jamieson 1888, 80). In the 1930s, fixed rents took one of two forms, as it probably did in the Qing. "Living rent" (*huozu*) or sharecropping was a proportion of the harvest, usually between forty and fifty percent and usually collected in kind. "Dead rent" (*sizu*) was an absolute amount collected in cash or kind that ranged anywhere from thirty to sixty percent of output, depending on the quality of the land and the harvest (MKK 1938, 18, 20; MTDG 1935, 174, 202). The court records support Ross's observation. Whatever the terms, these records suggest that once a tenant acquired land, the rent rarely increased. In the just discussed case of the Laoheshangbao imperial estate, for example, each family had rented land from the same bailiff family, which renewed their agreement annually but never once raised their rent across several generations (LPA 1798, 31499). From another legal record we learn that Wang Yongxiang's rent on ninety *mu* of land was not raised in the nearly thirty years he rented it from Tasiha's family (XB 1855.7.?). Zhao Haoli rented twenty *shang* for "many years," paying an annual rent of 2.2 strings per *shang* without any increase. Ma Shixiu, who rented two hundred *mu* from a bailiff, never once had his rent raised in nineteen years (LPA 1761, 13964). Xu Tianyu and twenty-one other commoners rented a combined one thousand *mu* for "many years" without the rent changing (LPA 1755, 6494). Zhang Feng rented land for twenty-two years before his landlord asked to raise the rent (see below). Geng He worked the same land for thirty-three years without a rent increase (LPA 1796, 21760). Yang Rong rented land for forty-eight years without an increase in rent (LPA 1800, 25220). In each of these cases, the landowner lived nearby and had plenty of opportunity to discuss raising the rent.

This is not to say that landlords never tried to raise rents, just that it was very difficult for them to do so. While there are a handful of court cases that began as a direct result of a landowner seeking to increase rents, none provides evidence that landlords were customarily or legally guaranteed the right to raise the rent. In 1771, Zhang Fen rented 28.3 *mu* that he thought belonged to Yang Tianwei. In 1791, twenty years after the original rental agreement, Yang wanted to double the rent from forty to eighty strings of cash, but Zhang procrastinated even after the middleman to the original agreement came to "settle" the matter. In the fall of 1792, Yang again demanded an increase in rent and this time Zhang flatly refused, claiming falsely the land's true ownership was in question (QDTD 1988, 123–129). Before the dispute was resolved, Yang Tianwei killed Li Guangsheng.

In a second example, Zhao Fu rented three hundred *mu* from Ma Shiren in 1793. They signed a ten-year contract and Zhao paid a 150 string deposit. The rent was fixed at eight *dou* (0.8 *shi*) of grain per *shang*. In the early months of 1803, when the contract was set to expire, Ma died without any sons. The land passed to his nephew, Ma Qi. After taking control of the land, Ma Qi tried to raise the rent by two *dou* and demanded another four hundred *diao* in deposit—presumably to extend the leasehold. Zhao refused. The rent remained as it was and no new deposit was paid. Two years later, Zhao and Ma fell into a dispute over some land that Zhao claimed he had rented from a third party but which Ma insisted was his. Ma demanded that Zhao pay rent on this land. Relations between the tenant and landlord deteriorated and Zhao decided to abandon the original leasehold. He sought to return the original three hundred *mu* and demanded his deposit back. This time, Ma refused to pay, claiming Zhao owed him back rent on the disputed land. The case was resolved in court when the magistrate agreed with tenant Zhao's request to end the leasehold and found that the disputed land was not Ma's (JCA 1805, 27674). In this case Zhao eventually quit the lease not because Ma demanded a higher rent—that matter was settled and the rent remained unchanged—but because the two fell out after Ma falsely claimed ownership of other fields that Zhao worked.

In neither example did the landlord in fact succeed in garnering an increase in rent. This is not to say, however, there were no upward pressures on rents in Manchuria over the long haul. As land filled with new settlers, demand for land correspondingly rose, and as land yields increased, with greater and greater labor inputs, landlords might succeed in edging rents upward. Nevertheless, the conditions under which landlords could secure a higher rent remained *circumscribed*. It appears that social barriers, buttressed by a relative shortage of labor, protected tenants against regular increases in rent to match productivity gains and demand for land.

In sum, tenants in Qing Manchuria managed to secure a fairly strong grip on the land they rented. They did this by either bringing the land into production, paying a deposit, or simply renewing the contract yearly with little or no fuss. Furthermore, they secured a degree of protection against rising rents. While this protection was provided in law, peasant communities could of course have undercut such rights had they so desired. (After all, Qing law was frequently flouted by peasants in the northeast; so that the mere fact of a law was insufficient to deny or secure any rights in land.) Consequently, while rents may have risen over time, along with the productivity of land, landlords could not raise them automatically, even when leaseholds were up for renegotiation. Along with the various means peasants used to protect themselves from full dispossession of their property (the conditional sale and *zhaojia*), "long-term rent" (*changzu*), whether by purchase or default, protected peasants from separation from the land and full market dependency.

The foregoing discussion has shown how the agrarian regime mandated in 1680, which was characterized by property systems that bound cultivators to their land and villages—though with different degrees of intensity—gave way to an alternative set of property relations. These new relations operated alongside the old. The vertically oriented social relations that facilitated the expropriation of agrarian surplus by the Manchu ruling body and the Qing state were maintained even as new horizontal property relations and modes of surplus extraction spread among petty landowners, cultivators, and laborers. On the manorial and banner lands, the state, monarchy, and aristocracy continued to collect a rent and tax directly from cultivators—the serfs and rusticated bannermen respectively—who were still legally tied to their villages. Even as cultivators sold or let their land to commoners, these levies continued to be met. Those petty landowners who let their land out to commoners met these levies out of the rent they received in return. Those who had sold their land either paid the levies on behalf of the commoners or had the commoners pay them directly, with the acquiescence of tax collecting agents.

Concurrently, the property relations that horizontally linked the different juridical communities of the rural population spread across the countryside in the trail of peasant settlers. These new property relations gave peasants greater latitude in the allocation of their land and labor than had the mandated property regime of 1680. Undoubtedly, this in turn underwrote peasant colonization and settlement and the absolute growth of the agricultural economy. Nonetheless, the "new" property regime was structurally no different from that found on the north China plain and much of the empire; producers in the northeast had secured for themselves direct and nonmarket access to their land.

Commerce and Colonization Compared: Colonial North America and Qing Manchuria

At this point, a brief but constructive comparison can be made that highlights the ways divergent property regimes take root under different colonial contexts and how these regimes configure social relationships to the market in very different ways. The social theorist Ellen Meiksins Wood (2003) argues forcibly that in contrast to other forms of European expansion in the early modern era, which focused on the capture of trade lanes and commercial wealth, English imperial expansion especially in the Atlantic world, beginning with Ireland in the late seventeenth century, was geared toward settlement and the development of commercial agriculture (Wood 2003, 79; Canny 1998, 15). This was particularly evident in the colonies of Virginia and Maryland which the Virginia Company had hoped to settle for the development of commercially viable industries and the exploitation of land through the cultivation of marketable crops. Settlers were recruited in ways that would require they provide the goods the company needed to expand its trading empire. When these plans failed and the large merchant houses behind the company pulled out, a new breed of investors from among London's more humble merchant ranks redirected the modus operandi of the colonies, while maintaining its commercial trajectory. Making speculative land purchases, and investing capital and time to develop these lands, these merchants ushered in the plantation economy. Initially specializing in tobacco, and only later cotton, the plantations were commercial enterprises, worked initially by contracted laborers who provided the goods merchants would then trade back to the metropol (Brenner 1993, 92–95; McCusker and Menard 1985, 122–127; Bushman 1998, 356).

By contrast, the peasant-led colonization of Manchuria was small scale and ad hoc. There were no financial backers with commercial interests to secure. The settler's primary objective was the acquisition of a small homestead on which to secure subsistence *directly*. Commercial interests followed on the heels of migrants, as merchants saw opportunities to profit by arbitrage buying and selling across regions of the empire. But, at this point merchants had to fit themselves into the already existing social formation. Thus, whereas settlers to the early colonies in Virginia and Maryland were tied into the market before they even embarked on their voyage, by virtue of their contract obligations, the settlers of Manchuria were in some respects escaping dispossession and market dependency in north China by taking to land and the promise of securing direct subsistence in Manchuria. Having acquired land they were shielded from the market and were therefore able to pursue desirable strategies (such as diversified agricultural production) that, while perfectly rational, were, as we shall see in Part Three, nonetheless incommensurate with the requirements of the sustained and systematic improvements in labor productivity that drive economic growth. The land market that developed suited those goals insofar as it offered peasants a means to "alienate" land that did not precipitate their immediate separation from it.

CHAPTER FIVE

The Social Basis of the Transformation of Agrarian Manchuria

Over the course of the eighteenth century, as commoners settled in the northeast, and as rural communities developed mechanisms and norms for enforcing and sanctioning commoners' claims to Qing land, a new property system took form. But because the state refused to recognize the new property regime, it had to be secured at the level of the village. This necessitated the appearance in rural Manchuria of customary practices that mediated property claims as well as institutions that policed them. The result was a heightened disjuncture—sustained over a prolonged period of time—between social and juridical practices. That tension played out in the ways in which peasants and their political communities regulated property on the one hand and how state authorities closest in proximity to the village responded to those efforts on the other.

Migration and Settlement

A successful challenge to Kangxi's agrarian regime could not have developed without the significant presence of commoners in the northeast. Migration was therefore the necessary precondition for its demise. Most migrants settling in Manchuria were from the north China provinces of Zhili and Shandong, where in the eighteenth and nineteenth centuries life for many was increasingly harsh. The combined effects of rising population density and a fragile ecosystem forced many to leave.

By the Yongzheng era, registered arable land per capita on the north China plain had fallen below ten *mu*. It fell further to four *mu* by the 1760s and three *mu* by the mid-nineteenth century (Lu 1987, 24; Xu 1998a, 77, table 2–16).[1] As population pressure grew in the core agricultural districts of the north China plain, in an effort to maintain their standard of living, peasants intensified labor inputs, migrated internally to less densely populated parts of north China, such as hillsides and the Shandong peninsula, or left the region altogether to go to Inner Mongolia and Manchuria (Xu 1998a, 60–68).[2]

The pressure to migrate was made greater still by the frequent disasters that struck the north China plain and Shandong Peninsula (Will 1990, 66).[3] In almost every year of Qing rule, one or more districts in Shandong province suffered from natural disaster and famine. During the 268 years of the Qing dynasty, drought struck in 233 different years and floods in 145; the Yellow River burst its banks on 127 separate occasions and tidal inundations occurred on 45 (Lu 1987, 27–29). In one out of every three years a district or county in Shandong suffered from disasters that afflicted at least twenty percent of its farmland and only two years passed during the entire Qing when Shandong was disaster free (Xu 1998a, 10). In Zhili and Shandong, large- and medium-scale famines were frequently reported by officials.[4] At those times, tens of thousands flooded into Manchuria. In the two years after the 1743–1744 famine that devastated Zhili, for instance, the Fengtian prefect uncovered forty-seven thousand newly arrived commoners who had made their way north and were still living in Fengtian.[5] Wondering what to do with them, he received instructions from the Qianlong emperor to allow them to reside in the northeast so long as they registered in the *baojia* (for the meaning of the *baojia* see Chapter 3) (GZSL 1964, 5381 [356]). When land surveys were conducted ten years later, local officials found and registered 2.76 million *mu* of newly opened commoner land, some of which had been opened by refugees (Sudō 1944, 204–205).

Even under noncrisis conditions, the simple facts of household division and declining farm size were sufficient to propel migration to Manchuria and Mongolia. Many males went for seasonal employment as farms hands every spring and summer, returning in the fall. Others migrated to the northeast permanently, an act described as "rushing the pass" (*chuangguan*). The northeast's appeal was clear enough to the Qing court: land was available for the taking. Describing the situation in 1803, the Jiaqing emperor commented that "the poor and those without employment from Shandong and Zhili all come to Fengtian where they husband the land and become proprietors (*zhongdi wei zhu*). They gradually construct grass huts for shelter and in this manner they cluster together more and more" (RZSL 1964, 1544 [111]; also see RZSL 1964, 3773 [256]). The reasons for leaving north China were vividly articulated by the compiler of Shandong province's Rongcheng county gazetteer. Looking back upon a century of population growth and change, he wrote: "The land [here] is so unfruitful and the people so poor that no matter how diligently they work they cannot survive by farming. Finding it difficult to sustain themselves, when crops fail people leave their villages and flee to the Capital, Liaodong, and Mongolia. Many have taken up their households and fled. That is why this place withers and grows poor" (RX 1976, 141–142 [3]). Migrants typically explained their decisions to migrate as responses to poverty. According to testimony provided in his trial for attempted rape, commoner Chen Tianzhang stated: "I am from Leting county, Yongping prefecture in Zhili province. Today I am thirty-one *sui*. I had no parents at home and because I was unable to make ends meet [there] I came to Fengtian where I have made a living by hiring out as a wage laborer wherever possible" (XT 1762, 290).

There were of course significant regional and temporal variations to the pattern of Manchuria's colonization and settlement. Up through the end of the dynasty, most of the increase in population and cultivated land area occurred in present-day Liaoning and southern Jilin provinces, areas that were located closer to the source of north China migrants. This is apparent when late Qing acreage figures are compared with those of the 1950s. By the end of the dynasty two-thirds of Liaoning's 1957 arable area had been opened and just under sixty percent of Jilin's. By contrast, just under thirty percent of Heilongjiang's arable land in 1957 had been opened by 1912. The relative extent of south Manchuria's settlement is evident also in the fact that, although Liaoning in 1912 accounted for two-fifths of total acreage in the northeast, it was home to three-fifths of the region's population. Cultivated land per person in Liaoning in the early twentieth century, at about four *mu* per person, was substantially lower than in Jilin and Heilongjiang, at about eight *mu* per person. In 1912, Liaoning more closely resembled north China, where there were about three *mu* of cultivated area per person, than it did Jilin and Heilongjiang.[6]

In the seventeenth and eighteenth centuries, settlement tended to cluster around old Ming towns, many of which were used by the Qing to garrison troops. Settlement also tended to concentrate first on the friable alluvial soils of accessible river plains and drainage basins such as the Liao and the upper reaches of the Songhua. These places were excellent for newly arriving farmers, many of whom came with the most rudimentary of tools and lacked the tools needed to work heavy soils. Using population figures in the Qing gazetteers, Ding Yizhuang (1991a) has reconstructed migration and settlement patterns for the first century and a half of Qing rule (336–337). She discerns three distinct periods. During the reigns of the Kangxi and Yongzheng emperors (between 1662 and 1736), new settlement concentrated to the west of the Liao river, principally along the Dajun river in Jinzhou prefecture. This pattern is discernible during this period in the records of women in Manchuria who were honored by the state for conforming to Confucian feminine morality. The 1736 *Shengjing General Gazetteer* (SJTZ) categorizes these women by their status as "commoners" and "bannermen" and also includes their place of residence in the northeast. All commoner women so celebrated lived in present-day Liaoning, and most of these in southernmost Jinzhou prefecture. Not a single commoner woman appears among those honored for the Jilin and Heilongjiang regions, even though numerous bannerwomen are listed (SJTZ 1965, 2119–2184 [37]).

In the Qianlong period (1736–1795), Ding observes, the center of Han settlement shifted to areas northeast of present-day Shenyang, between the cities of Kaiyuan and Tieling. Settlement there was facilitated by the main imperial thoroughfare that passed through Kaiyuan and Tieling from Beijing to the northeastern frontier. In the first half of the nineteenth century, the center of migration shifted once again, this time to southern Jilin. The settlement of the Yitong river plain around Changchun city, for instance, began in the last decades of the eighteenth century, when the Mongol prince Gorlos was granted permission to open land there to commoners. By 1828, twenty to thirty thousand recently arrived settler households were estimated to be in Jilin (Ding 1991a [339]). Ding Yizhuang ends her study in the middle of the nineteenth century. But a fourth period of migration is worth examining, dating from the 1860s when parts of Jilin were opened to settlement, and extending past 1880 when all of the northeast was opened. This period witnessed unprecedented growth in the population of central and northern Manchuria, the continued settlement of Jilin, and the opening of much of Heilongjiang province as far north as the Amur river.

Settlement and the Expansion of Field Administration

In Chapter 2 it was shown how the Qing ruling house's overriding interest that Han Chinese not colonize Manchuria gave rise to the early establishment of a large administrative presence there. The pattern differed from that outlined by G. William Skinner (1978) who suggested that frontier field administration followed one of two patterns. In some cases, civil administration was established alongside or shortly after colonization, in an effort to bring Han settlers under the control of the state. In other cases, where strategic or military concerns existed alongside or predated the standard concerns of civil administration, military jurisdictions were established ahead of significant Han settlement. Civil administration followed later as colonization proceeded (Skinner 1978, 45–50; also see Shepherd 1993, 198–208). In Manchuria, the Qing established a large military administration early on, as Skinner's typology suggests. But, the Qing sovereign was unwilling to expand civil administration beyond a certain point, no matter how far Han settlement proceeded in Manchuria. In 1733, the Qing monarchy with few exceptions stopped expanding the civil administration in an effort to delineate the geographic extent of legitimate commoner presence. At that time, there were twelve civilly administered counties and departments in Fengtian and only one in Jilin, though Changchun subprefecture was added in 1800.

Explaining the Qing position on the subject of civil administration, in 1776 Qianlong contrasted his position on Shengjing, where some increase in civil administrative units had been permitted, with that on Jilin, where it was not allowed:

> because Shengjing is in close proximity to Zhili and Shandong [provinces], vagrants have been gradually accumulating [in number] there. If they were to be expelled all at once, then it would necessarily cause all to lose their livelihood. Thus, departments and counties are to be established to administer [those people]. As for Jilin, it does not border on the Han lands (*yuan bu yu handi xianglian*), thus commoners are not to be allowed to settle there. (GZSL 1964, 15038–15039 [1023])

Despite suggestions to the contrary contained within this proclamation, the Qianlong emperor was unwilling to legitimize further commoner settlement even in Shengjing. Consequently, with the exception of Changchun, no new civil districts were created between 1734 and 1876, by which time the policy of Han exclusion had ended. Throughout the eighteenth and for most of the nineteenth centuries, in Manchuria civil administration remained underdeveloped relative to commoner settlement, while military oversight and military prerogatives remained dominant (SJTZ 1965, 1160–1165 [23]). Ultimately, the ruling house's particular objectives in Manchuria dictated that the field administration evolve in ways distinct from those suggested by Skinner.

Mixed Communities in the Eighteenth Century

Despite attempts to limit and prohibit Han migration, Han settled in large numbers (Sudō 1944, 181–183, 194–197). To be sure, measuring the levels of migration is difficult with the sources at hand. However, revisions of official Qing numbers presented in Appendix A suggest that the northeast's population surpassed one million by 1750 and two million by 1800. It surpassed five million by the mid-nineteenth century and topped fourteen million by century's end.[7] Given what the works of James Lee and Cameron Campbell have said on the subject of natural rates of population increase among banner populations, it is clear that most of Manchuria's population growth came from migration (Isett 1998, 34–37).

Once in Manchuria, Han migrants did not much care for the boundaries drawn to delineate legitimate sites for commoner residency so that by the mid-eighteenth century, if not earlier, commoners were living with alarming frequency in banner villages and on manorial lands. As early as 1678 Fengtian Prefect Jinnai complained that commoners had settled illegally in Chengde, Tieling, and Kaiyuan, and added that they "indiscriminately mingled" (*za chu*) with bannermen. In 1715, thirty-five years after Kangxi's decree of 1680, Fengtian Prefect Haolin reported that bannermen and commoners encroached on each other's land with impunity. To his subordinates, Prefect Haolin reiterated that any transgression of the physical boundaries separating communities was forbidden and added for good measure that the prohibition applied to the exchange of cultivated land as well as the opening of and squatting on land in waste (SZSL 1964, 3494 [262]).

Across the eighteenth and nineteenth centuries, the sovereign and his field administrators in Manchuria expressed alarm at the "indiscriminate mingling" (*za chu*) of communities. "Indiscriminate mingling" became a catch-all expression of angst over the failure to keep Han out of Manchuria and to maintain appropriate juridical and physical boundaries between commoners, serfs, and bannermen. As discussed earlier, the Qianlong emperor took a particular interest in what he saw as the rising tide of illegal Han settlers and squatters that threatened the Manchu way of life, as did some of the highest officials in the land (GZSL 1964, 3023 [1753]; 15208 [1035]; He 1992, 861–883 [35]). Before Fujun's 1806 observations on the problems associated with "indiscriminate mingling," Qianlong had already noted that "first commoners are hired as wage laborers (*gugong*), then they steadily rent land from the bannermen, until a point is reached when the number of tenants is especially high. The bannermen all seek leisure and do not know how to work [the land]" (GZSL 1964 [102]).

Eighteenth- and nineteenth-century court records of homicides, "civil" disputes, and prosecutions of illegally settled commoners support and amplify the notion that the legal and physical boundaries established by the state had failed to segregate commoners from rusticated bannermen and serfs. Perhaps more disturbing, from the state's perspective, court records show that commoners had set deep roots in banner villages and manors. They had become established and working members of these communities. To be sure, these records are by their nature accounts of social conflict (often, they are the result of a murder). Yet, when read closely they are also evidence of significant levels of social cooperation, neighborliness, and more between commoner and noncommoners.

The records of a 1796 homicide recounts commoner Cui Xin's illicit sexual affair with the Mongolian wife of a Chengde bailiff. Cui Xin and the bailiff had known each other for some time and, it was reported, they were on good terms. Living nearby in the county of Yu, Cui Xin worked as a carpenter and often went to Bailiff Wang Yaoshun's village to perform jobs. Bailiff Wang testified that he had even borrowed over three thousand *qian* from Cui. It was about that time that Cui Xin had begun an illicit sexual affair with Wang's Mongolian wife, Wulata'na. The affair continued for "some time," perhaps ending just prior to Wulata'na's murder at the hands of Cui Xin in the winter of 1796 after the two lovers quarreled (XT 1796.11.2).

An attempted rape case from 1762 shows again how closely commoners and bannermen lived, as well as the opportunities for predatory sexual acts such proximity occasioned. The case reveals that commoner Chen had for several years been hired by rusticated Han banner households in one village to assist in the cultivation of their fields. At the time he tried to rape the wife of his banner employer, he had been hired as a year laborer and worked, lived, and ate with the household (XT 1762.2.25). (This case is discussed in some detail in Chapter 6.)

The records from the 1796 homicide trial of rusticated bannerman Li Bao and his cousin Li Wushi, who were eventually convicted of the double murder of commoners Liang Taian and Liang Hong'an, show that rusticated bannermen and commoners were hiring each other's labor, living in the same villages, and even intermarrying (XT 1796.8.25). Ironically, the case occurred in Xiuyan county, near Fenghuang town, in precisely the region where scholar Zhang Qizhou asserts that the banner population observed the "great taboos" concerning marriage, one of which was the taboo against marriage to commoners (cited in Rhoads 2000, 41–42).

A remarkable case from 1753 describes how commoner Cui Yuyuan from Zhili came to live with and then formed an illegal household with a married bannerwoman and local prostitute, Du Hou, in Haicheng. Du's husband had disappeared and Du and Cui subsequently became lovers. They soon began living together. After a while, Du Hou decided that for propriety's sake Cui should take a wife—Du was still married and so she and Cui could not. According to Du's plan, the three would live together and Du and Cui would continue their relationship. Du arranged for and lent Cui Yuyuan money to marry a sixteen *sui* bannerwoman named Su. Six months after the marriage, Cui Yuyuan beat his young bride Su to death after she refused Cui's command that she work as a prostitute to recoup the bride price he had borrowed from Du (XT 1753.9.25). Examples of "indiscriminate mingling" such as these abound in the court records (many of which will be examined in detail below) and demonstrate without a doubt that state-imposed boundaries between populations had failed to work.

The Problem of Rural Control in Qing Manchuria

The growth of mixed communities was a clear sign of the state's inability to secure one of the central pillars of its agrarian regime. As long as populations remained segregated, there were few opportunities for commoners to occupy banner and manorial lands. But once communities became integrated, and peasants found ways to regulate the exchange of land among themselves, Qing land easily devolved into commoners' hands. The challenge posed to the agrarian order by the breakdown of communal segregation was recognized at all levels of the state. The precise nature and source of this challenge was evaluated and stated most fully in an 1806 memorial written by Shengjing Military Governor Fujun (1748–1834), a Mongol official with many years of administrative experience in the northeast. At the time of this communication he was serving as the highest authority in the region:

After investigating the bannerland (*qidi*) of Shengjing [south Manchuria], I have found that not even five in ten [bannermen] cultivate their own land. The majority have leased (*zu*) land to commoners (*minren*) who do the actual cultivation themselves. It is the natural course of things that those with excess and those with deficiencies lend to and borrow from each other. Such is inevitable. As time passes, however, those who have leased out land turn to selling it conditionally (*dian*), and in this fashion the [present] unscrupulousness has been accumulating. Today the property of the banners (*qi chan*) no longer belongs to them. On reading the old [official] records, we find that in the past, and on more than one occasion, cadastral surveys (*qing cha*) were conducted. [However] within ten or more years of any resolution, the problem reappears. The dilemma is such that all sides go before [the court] and bring suits. Both sides try to hide the fact that they have engaged in illegal sales, and those who purchased the land conditionally (*shou dian*) dress up their statements. . . .

I conclude that this is all because bannermen and commoners co-mingle (*qi min za chu*), which permits the discussion of leasehold (*zu*), which soon leads to conditional sales (*dian*). From local officials to the yamen runners, everyone believes that the land is being leased when in fact it is being sold. These activities are discovered only when the bannermen (*qiren*) are unable to remit their taxes, when they force increased payments,[8] or when they compel the recovery of the land. Because the local constable (*xiangbao*) has no authority, even though he is aware that commoners are conditionally purchasing land, it is difficult for him to report these matters. This is because inspections are not conducted jointly [by the magistrate and sub-county functionaries agents]. (HZ 1806, n.n.)

In Fujun's view, the difficulties confronting the Qing state were twofold as it tried to maintain, and in some instances restore, the agrarian regime constructed by Kangxi.[9] First, peasants cooperated in the development of ways to conceal illegal sales from the authorities, a matter to which I will return shortly. Second, local officials were unable to root out illegal sales because they could not elicit the full cooperation of the parapolitical agents who were responsible for uncovering and reporting such goings on. Thus, Fujun lamented, oversight was so poor that local officials uncovered illegal land sales only when they were brought to their attention, such as when taxes or rents were not remitted to the state, unrelated crimes were investigated, or property disputes got out of hand.

The ultimate cause of the breakdown of rural order, in Fujun's eyes, was therefore "indiscriminate mingling." Comingling of commoners and rusticated bannermen gave rise to opportunities to buy and sell bannerland in the first instance, so he argued. But, Fujun understood, preventing populations from interacting required that regional and local authorities leverage inordinate levels of discipline.

On the one hand, given the physical distances that separated authorities from the villages, there was the problem of how to monitor and discipline the rural agents upon whom the state relied for day-to-day policing of rural affairs. The rural agents—*xiangyue* and *baozhang* who oversaw the commoner villages, the *zuoling* and *shoubao* who oversaw the banner zones, and the bailiff who oversaw the manor—all resided at some distance from the authorities who, in turn, were too few and overburdened to monitor them effectively. Regional and local authorities were thus poorly positioned to exact from the rural agents the level of cooperation required to monitor the countryside.

On the other hand, the late imperial state's preference for unsalaried rural agents over salaried civil servants, or tax farmers, cost the Qing the level of cooperation needed to maintain the agrarian regime of 1680. These rural agents had a foot in both the *yamen* and the village and their allegiance was correspondingly divided. So long as the needs of the state and those of the village were in accord, there was no reason to expect rural and village-level agents to work against state interests. However, when state and village interests were in opposition, then rural agents could prove problematic assistants, obfuscating at best and deceiving at worst.

Hampered in this way by institutional confusion and noncooperation between rural agents and authorities, and facing active peasant opposition in the forms of misrepresentations and village sanctioning of criminal acts, regional and local officials were handicapped in their enforcement of the law.

An Example of the Problem of Rural Control: The Case of Nuomizhuang Manor

A series of records stemming from allegations of abuse by the bailiff of the imperial manor at Nuomizhuang provides exceptional insights into the difficulties field administrators (in this case the Shengjing Imperial Household Department and Shengjing military governor) faced in their efforts to govern the countryside and secure control over Qing lands. Though this case is concerned only with crown lands, Fujun's memorial of 1806 shows clearly that analogous conditions existed on the bannerlands. The case of Nuomizhuang, therefore, speaks to the larger issues at stake. It began in 1815 when Mrs. Ma, née Wu, brought a countersuit before the Fengtian prefectural *yamen* citing abuses committed by their bailiff, Zhou Lin (LPA 1815, 24127, 25944; 1816, 24129, 24130, 26006, 26008; 1817, 26053).

The conclusion of the investigation resulting from Ma's suit showed that not only had a series of bailiffs abused their office for personal gain, but also that bailiffs and the manor's serfs had illegally sold substantial amounts of manor land to commoners. The case was particularly disturbing for both the Fengtian prefectural *yamen* and the Shengjing Imperial Household Department, which held dual jurisdiction over the case, because these abuses had been committed over a number of decades without detection. Echoing Prefect Fujun's analysis of the problem of local control, the crimes committed on the Nuomizhuang manor only came to the attention of local officials because of Mrs. Ma's lawsuit. That suit, moreover, was not brought out of concern for criminal activities occurring on the manor, but to settle old scores held by Ma against the Zhou household. The case of Mrs. Ma illustrates the institutional distance separating rural communities from the state. It illustrates how little knowledge local officials had of matters within their own jurisdictions and how easy it was, therefore, to conceal criminal actions from local officials.

While Mrs. Ma's original suit against Bailiff Zhou Lin alleged that he had illegally sold Qing land to commoners, official investigation soon revealed that the Zhou family had illegally acquired the office of bailiff. In 1775, Zhou Lin's grandfather, Zhou Bi, had used influence to have himself assigned after the dismissal of Mrs Ma's father-in-law, Ma Huan. Furthermore, the investigation revealed that the Zhou family had abused the office to extort money from the manor's serfs. Finally, and most distressing from the state's perspective, the investigation uncovered that a substantial amount of estate land had been sold illegally to local commoners by the Zhous, as well as by the manor's serfs, over several generations—all this without field administrators finding out.

On receiving Ma's suit, the Shengjing Imperial Household Department was eager to uncover whether the bailiffs from the Zhou family had indeed mismanaged the estate and abused their office. The Office of Farmland of the Shengjing Imperial Household Department was ordered to look into the circumstances of the Zhou family's assumption of the bailiffship of Nuomizhuang and to see whether rent payments had been evaded and estate land sold illegally.

It was soon discovered that the Ma household had been the manor's original bailiffs. According to testimony presented at the Fengtian prefectural *yamen* in 1815, former Bailiff Ma Huan of Nuomizhuang, the father-in-law of Mrs. Ma, had failed to collect the requisite rent from the serfs under his supervision in 1775. For this, Ma Huan was dismissed. Zhou Bi was given the office of bailiff that same year (LPA 1815, 24127).[10] When Ma Huan was bailiff, the estate had

had more than 5,400 *mu* of land in the villages of Nuomizhuang, Gengjiatun, Qingduizi, and Xiongyue. Of this, approximately 1,800 *mu* was distributed among the serfs of the estate and the remaining 3,600 *mu* was managed by the bailiff directly (LPA 1815, 25944). After assuming office in 1775, Zhou Bi found that a total of 300 *mu* of land from the estate had been illicitly sold to commoners by the former bailiff, Ma Huan, and several serfs. After asking the prefectural *yamen* how best to handle the illicitly sold land, Zhou Bi was instructed to redeem (*shu*) the land at the cost of 4,900 strings of cash[11] and to "cultivate the land himself, paying the necessary rent (*zu*) [to the state]" (LPA 1815, 24127, 25944).

Sometime later, perhaps in 1814, long after Zhou Bi had passed away, serf Ma Jin, son of the former Bailiff Ma Huan and husband of Mrs. Ma, brought a suit against Zhou Bi's son and the new Bailiff Zhou Shixun. In that suit, Ma Jin claimed that his father, Ma Huan, had not illegally sold all of the three hundred *mu* of land redeemed by Zhou Bi under court order. Ma Jin argued that the land not illegally sold should be returned to him. At this point a runner was sent down from the prefectural *yamen* to investigate and mediate the case. A resolution was reached; Bailiff Zhou Shixun agreed to return to Ma Jin 180 *mu* of the 300 *mu* in exchange for Ma's return of 2,400 strings of cash. The prefect agreed to the mediated settlement.

The matter did not end here, however. In 1815, soon after the settlement had been reached, the wife of the now deceased Zhou Shixun and mother of the new bailiff, Zhou Lin, claimed that Ma Jin had taken the 180 *mu* of land without paying the 2,400 strings of cash.[12] Moreover, she claimed that Ma Jin had turned around and sold the 180 *mu* to "people from outside the estate," a not-so-oblique reference to commoners living on and around the manor (LPA 1815, 24127; 1816, 24129). While investigating this accusation, the presiding prefect discovered Zhou Lin had used influence in 1775 to acquire the post of bailiff illegally after Ma Huan's dismissal. Because the office had been assumed fraudulently, Zhou Lin was dismissed and the baliffship was returned to the Ma family and assumed by Ma Jin (LPA 1815, 25944).

In retaliation, Mrs. Zhou subsequently accused newly appointed Bailiff Ma Jin of illicitly selling estate land to commoners, plotting with serfs and commoners to illegally occupy estate land worked by the Zhous, expropriating money from serfs to buy a wife,[13] and failing to pay rent on the three thousand *mu* of estate land his household now managed (LPA 1815, 24127). It was at this point in time that Bailiff Ma Jin's wife, Mrs. Ma, brought the countersuit that caused the full investigation of the manor. In the suit, she accused the Zhou family and several of the estate's serfs of illegally occupying, cultivating, and selling manor land (LPA 1815, 25944; 1816, 24130).

In response to the allegations of Mrs. Zhou, in the winter of 1816 the prefect opened an investigation into Bailiff Ma Jin's management of the estate. The prefect interrogated Mrs. Ma and her son, Ma Fuxi, along with eight commoners and serf Guo Ruisheng. Ma Fuxi denied Mrs. Zhou's accusation that his father illegally sold land to the commoners, and his testimony was corroborated by serf Guo and the eight commoners.[14] In response, Zhou Lin retracted his mother's suit, claiming that in her dotage she had "unwittingly and foolishly" brought a false suit against the bailiff. He even went so far as to say that all the land cultivated by commoners had been rented legally and that the Mas had not sold any land illicitly.

Nevertheless, the court was not satisfied and ordered further investigations into the allegations of illegal land deals. In the summer of 1817, serf Guo Ruisheng was again interrogated regarding the land he cultivated. This time he confessed to having conditionally sold (*dianmai*) some manor land to commoners. According to Guo's account, his father had conditionally purchased 120 *mu* from Ma Jin in 1804. In 1810, Guo's father was short of cash and decided to conditionally sell sixty-six *mu* of the land for 1,200 strings of cash to Wu Pei, another serf. In 1814, Guo Ruisheng redeemed twenty-four *mu* of this land, leaving Wu Pei with forty-two *mu*. A short time later, however, Guo Ruisheng conditionally sold the twenty-four *mu* back to Wu Pei.

If the land arrangements were not complicated enough, Wu Pei had turned around and conditionally sold his remaining forty-two *mu* to commoner Fu Guo. When interrogated, Fu Guo claimed he did not know at the time of the land sale that this was manor land registered to Bailiff Ma, and he did not know that Wu Pei had himself purchased the land from Guo Ruisheng (LPA 1817, 26053). After hearing testimony, the presiding judge handed down a guilty verdict against Ma Jin, Guo Ruisheng, Wu Pei, and Fu Guo.

In passing sentence, the judge stated that irregularities in the rental agreement between Ma Jin and Guo Ming had cast suspicion on their testimony, suggesting that the land had in fact been sold rather than rented. He expressed his thinking on the case as follows: "Though it was stated [in the contract] that rent was to be paid, the amount [of rent] was not specified. Moreover, rental contracts are to be limited to three years [by law]. Yet this contract was for ten years. Evidently, Ma Jin et al. are guilty of having [feigned] the rental of land with intent to sell it conditionally (*dianmai*)." Apparently, state officials in the Shengjing bureaucracy were sufficiently acquainted with local practices in land sales to know fraudulent rental contracts when they encountered them. Here, the judge explicitly refers to regulations that limited commoner leaseholds of Qing land to nonrenewable three-year contracts. The fact that in this case, the practice of renting Qing land to commoners for prolonged periods was identified as an illegal sale suggests that some officials were aware of peasant subterfuge.

The court found Guo Ming guilty of knowingly and fraudulently reselling sixty-six *mu* of conditionally sold manor land to Wu Pei. Ma Jin and Guo Ming were sentenced in accordance with the code to one hundred blows with the heavy bamboo and three years of penal servitude, and the magistrate ordered the land and sale price forfeited to the court. Guo Ming, accused of the crimes of illegally selling manor land and reselling conditionally purchased land without the original owners' knowledge, was punished for the former, which was the more severe of the two.[15] Guo Ruisheng was handed the same sentence for having illegally sold twenty-four *mu* of manor land to Wu Pei. As for Wu Pei and Fu Guo, the court stated that even though they had unknowingly sold crown land they had nevertheless broken the law. They were each similarly sentenced in accordance with the code to one hundred blows with the heavy bamboo and three years of penal servitude. The land and sale price were ordered forfeited to the court (LPA 1817, 26053). With these convictions, the case was finally brought to a close.

Rural Agents and the Illegal Occupation of Banner and Manor Land

On the manor of Nuomizhuang, the institutional and normative mechanisms for disciplining and watching over village-level agents had clearly failed the regional government. From the state's perspective, the most alarming revelation in the case was that for forty years or more, from as early as 1775 until 1815, commoners had purchased manor land, entirely unbeknownst to the regional government and the Shengjing Imperial Household Department. Also alarming to officials was the fact that bailiffs—the very individuals charged with policing manors—were intimately involved in these sales. Examples of rural agents concealing and engaging in the illegal sale of Qing land abound. In the separate but analogous case of rural agent malfeasance, a *xiangyue* was implicated in the sale 13,000 *mu* (2,167 acres) of bannerland (HZ 1806.8.21). In another example, a *yamen* secretary, Zhang Jianlong, was found to have illegally sold eighty-seven *shang* (870 *mu*) of bannerland. In the same case, two officers in the Jilin military *yamen*, De Lu and Tai Shanbao, were found to have sold several "districts" of bannerland (LPA 1843, 02503).

As noted earlier, the paradox of the Manchurian agrarian order, as it was envisioned by the earliest Qing emperors, was the coexistence of property systems and labor regimes that have historically been associated with sub-enfeuded polities that are adapted to close supervision of village society, on the one hand, and a tax-office state that was ill-designed for localized applications of power, on the other hand. In the classical cases of the feudalisms of medieval Europe and Warring States Japan (1467–1600), for instance, peasants were kept bound to the land by local "overseers," who were either vassal warriors of more powerful nobles or petty nobles themselves. Whatever the circumstances, these "overseers" were part of the expropriating class and it was, therefore, in their interest to keep the peasants under them bound to the land. They were strategically positioned to do so, moreover, because they commonly lived *in situ*, nearby or alongside the peasantry, and because they were armed—on some occasions they had under their command small bands of their own vassal warriors with which to enforce serfdom.

The post-1644 agrarian regime in Manchuria, by contrast, was policed by bureaucratic officers with no foothold in the village aside from the rural agents. Whether civil magistrates in the civil bureaucracy or garrison commanders in the banner bureaucracy, field administrators were officed in the towns and, more importantly, they had limited staff with which to oversee the countryside under their authority (Liu 1988, 267–268).[16] Ultimately, the physical and social distance between the centralized bureaucratic offices of the regional government and the villages was so great that regional officials had little knowledge of what was going on in the villages, despite frequent alarms sounding the imminent collapse of the agrarian regime.

Asserting Han Customary Practice in Property

While the limited reach of the state disadvantaged its efforts to enforce the Qing land system, without the concomitant emergence within the village of the means to regulate property in land, peasants could not have taken possession of it as they did. In his 1806 memorial, Fujun reported on villagers' strategy of concealing the sale of Qing land by "dressing up statements," a deception found also among the peasants of Zhili, who similarly hid illegal sales of bannerland to commoners (Yang 1988, 96). Villagers in essence maintained two accounts of the sale of Qing lands—one fictitious and one actual.[17] As we shall see shortly, while villagers understood such exchanges to be sales, they represented them as leaseholds (*zu*) to local and regional officials. Because the renting of banner and manor land to commoners had been made legal by 1740, so long as the duration of the leasehold did not surpass three years, by misrepresenting the illegal sale in this fashion peasant communities facilitated the exchange of land among themselves without attracting the attention of the authorities.[18]

The records of the just-discussed case of Mrs. Ma tell precisely how the disguised land sale was expected to work. Commoner Xing Dexiang, the middleman to a series of sales of Nuomizhuang manor land to commoners, testified that the buyers and sellers of the land "feared being found out and so they purposely substituted [the character] '*zu*' (rent) for '*dian*' (conditional sale) in the contract." It was their intention, he confessed, to use the subterfuge of the fake leasehold to dupe local officials into thinking the land had not been sold at all (LPA 1815, 24129, 25944). In this case, the presiding judge remarked that "though the land sale contract stated that rent was to be paid, the amount of rent was not specified; rental contracts are limited to three years [by regulation], yet this contract was for ten years. Evidently, Ma Jin et al. are guilty of using a leasehold with the intent to sell the land conditionally."

Yet, no matter how effective, the practice of misrepresentation was only a means for concealing land sales from local officials and rural agents. It provided no guarantee that commoners who bought Qing land could assert their claims to it. After all, the Qing courts, which in China Proper acted as final arbiter of land disputes, did not recognize the legitimacy of these exchanges. Qing law mandated the forfeiture of illegally sold Qing land, as well as punishment of all those involved in the sale, including the buyer and seller, and middlemen, witnesses, and guarantors. Thus, a commoner who purchased Qing land knew full well that in the event of a dispute over the land's status neither he nor his descendants could take their claim of proprietorship to court, because the purchase was considered a criminal act. Given the situation, we must assume that, when commoners bought land, the serfs and rusticated bannermen who sold it to them, fellow villagers who came forward to act as witnesses and guarantors to the sales, and the buyers themselves must have been confident that the village would sanction these exchanges; they must have further assumed, with some certainty, that village institutions would suffice to mediate disputes satisfactorily. Though guarantors in such instances were occasionally liable for losses incurred when an arrangement fell apart, more often then not they were the principal witness to the agreement and principal mediator when things went bad. In most instances, their responsibility was less pecuniary and more enforcement. In the final analysis, therefore, what made the sale of Qing lands to commoners possible was the development of customary mechanisms within villages for regulating property claims and asserting property norms (cf. Cohen 2004, 88; Osborne 2004, 156–157; Brockman 1980, 129).

Customary Practice and Subterfuge at Work in Sanctioning and Securing Claims to Land

A late eighteenth-century case of the sale of manor land to two commoners illustrates both how peasants evaded state detection and how they deployed customary practices to regulate property claims. The saga began in 1772 when just over two hundred *mu* of land belonging to an imperial grain estate (*liangzhuang*) in Gai prefecture, on the Liaodong peninsula, was confiscated by regional officials as "bannerland sold to commoners" (*min dian qidi*) (LPA 1794, 8820, 8857). In 1783, Su Yi, the son of the deceased serf who had earlier illegally sold the land, successfully petitioned the regional government to get it back.[19] Upon retrieving it, Su Yi was approached by the estate's bailiff. The bailiff had been asked by a commoner from a neighboring village, a man named Chen Jun, to broker an arrangement that would give Chen the right to cultivate the land rent-free for two years. The court records explain that it was Chen Jun's father who had illegally bought this same land from Su Yi's father. When the state confiscated it, however, the Chens were not compensated and thus lost all of their investment. When Chen Jun heard that Su Yi had recovered the land in question, he asked the estate's bailiff to mediate an arrangement whereby he would be compensated for the financial loss suffered by his family a decade earlier. With the bailiff as mediator, Su Yi agreed to turn the land over to Chen Jun for two years. To compensate the Chens for their loss, the agreement with Su Yi stipulated Chen would not pay rent.

When the arrangement came to an end in 1785, Su Yi was in need of money so he decided to sell conditionally just over half of the two hundred *mu* to Chen Jun. Two years later, in 1787, he sold conditionally a further twenty-four *mu* to Chen Jun's brother, Chen Rong. To evade detection by the state, the Chens later admitted in court that they had counterfeited contracts that represented the conditional sales as leaseholds. As just described in the unrelated case of Mrs. Ma, the terms of this sale were hidden within the lexicon of a leasehold—the conditional sale price was represented as a "rent deposit," while the length of time during which Su Yi could redeem his land was recorded as the "duration of the leasehold."[20] The judge stated in his finding that "[i]n reality, no interest was charged on the loan and no rent was collected on the land," meaning that the "leasehold contract" was fraudulent and designed to hide an illegal sale. Middlemen and witnesses were summoned to broker and validate each exchange, ensuring that it was carried out according to customary norms, and to formalize the exchange of property publicly by signing the contract.

Over the next decade, Su Yi rapidly sank deeper into poverty. In 1787, several years after he had conditionally sold most of his land, he approached the Chen brothers separately and asked each for *zhaojia* payments, which he received. As noted in Chapter 4, the *zhaojia* payment was made on the understanding that increases in the value of land since the time of its sale should be shared, though not necessarily in equal proportions, by the new and former possessors of the land (TKK 1937, 248–249; Kishimoto 1997, 264–270). After he received the first *zhaojia* payment, Su Yi's situation continued to deteriorate. In 1788, he asked for and received a second *zhaojia* payment. To maintain the subterfuge, the *zhaojia* payments were represented in the contract as "increases in rent." In 1794, Su Yi again approached the Chens, this time through a middleman, and asked for a third *zhaojia* payment from each brother. Chen Jun agreed, though no mention was made of whether Chen Rong did so as well. Again, the *zhaojia* was noted and again it was represented as an increase in rent. Despite these payments, Su's situation grew ever more desperate. Later that year, penniless and destitute, Su

Yi left the village. He abandoned his wife, who died shortly afterward, and his two children.

The example of the Sus and the Chens, with their complex relationship of debt and obligation, reveals just how powerful a force customary practice and convention were in the daily lives of peasants. In this case, village custom—not the formal apparatus of the Qing legal system—sufficed first to convince Su Yi to compensate the Chens for their father's financial loss and then to persuade the Chens to make multiple *zhaojia* payments to Su Yi when the latter faced economic hardship. Nothing in law required Su Yi to compensate Chen Jun for the losses his father had incurred in the original land purchases. Indeed, in the eyes of the Qing courts the original sale was criminal and so the Chen family had no legal claim on the land. Yet, through his actions, Su Yi recognized that, until the original purchase price was returned, the Chen family retained a claim to the land their father had purchased from his. The normative issue at stake—whether or not the Sus owed the Chens for their father's losses—arose from a complex sense of outstanding debt between families, spanning two generations, upon which the Chens successfully played to get remuneration.

Equally, there was nothing in law compelling either Chen Jun or Chen Rong to make *zhaojia* payments to Su Yi. The Qing Code had nothing to say regarding the legality of the *zhaojia*—and there is not a single legal case from Manchuria in which the state addressed its legality. Rather, both the payment and receipt of *zhaojia* were entirely matters for negotiation between buyer and seller (TKK 1937, 249; Huang 2001, 74–75; Kishimoto 1997). Often, as noted in Chapter 4, the *zhaojia* was given because it was preferable to having the land redeemed by the *dian*-maker. Nevertheless, it was the customary acceptance of the conditional sale that ultimately made the *zhaojia* possible and recognized as a legitimate practice.

The records of this case also point to the important role played by other villagers in the brokering and sanctioning of such arrangements. First, Chen was assisted in his request for compensation by the estate's bailiff, who acted as a go-between. The bailiff acted to legitimate Chen Jun's request by interjecting his stature and power in the community, in recognizing and securing such claims. Second, when Su Yi conditionally sold land to the Chen brothers in 1785, a number of villagers acted as witnesses and guarantors to these sales. Later, when Su Yi needed more money, three of these witnesses approached Chen Jun on Su's behalf and asked for the *zhaojia*.

Japanese ethnographic surveys conducted in the twentieth century show that the negotiation of weighty matters required the participation of fellow villagers who, representing the common interest of the community, ensured that "transactions" were concluded in accord with accepted principles. Acting as middlemen, go-betweens, witnesses, guarantors, and mediators, those who facilitated everything from buying and selling land to dividing up the family property were central figures in village social life in the Qing, as they still were in the early twentieth century.

Customary Practice and Mediation in the Village

Philip Huang (1996) argues that in Qing China the *threat* of a lawsuit—actual or otherwise—was often key to the smooth and efficacious arbitration of disputes in the village. He suggests that the threat of fines, as well as the possibility of punishment, even for minor infractions of the code, were together often enough to push disputants to speedy resolutions before a case went to court (51–57). But, when disputes arose from criminal acts to which both sides were party—such as the illegal sale of Qing lands—then the threat of a lawsuit was ineffectual. To be sure, the understanding that disputes could not be taken to court, or the fear that unsettled quarrels might bring an illegal sale to the state's attention, may have pushed disputants to village mediation. But the fact remains that in the case of illegal sales to commoners of Qing land it was precisely because the state would not find in favor of *either* party that commoner peasants' securing of claims to this land depended upon villagers' self-enforcement of customary property norms.

To secure possession of land in this way was no easy matter, however, even with the institutional means for self-regulation in place in the village. The amount of land sold illegally in a Manchurian community of several clustered villages could run into the thousands of *mu*, and the time span over which it was sold might cover several decades and cross generations (LPA 1786, 8499, 8509, 8512; JCA 1795, 65418; HZ 1806.8.21; Isett 2004, 146). We are therefore talking not only about the misrepresentation of illegal land exchanges that had occurred in living memory, but also, more strikingly, about the need to recollect the actual circumstances of misrepresented exchanges that had been made when the present disputants were young children or, in many instances, before they were even born. Further complicating villagers' self-regulation of property claims was the fact that written contracts for land exchanges were falsified.[21]

To have kept track of these transactions in a manner that enabled commoners to buy, misrepresent, and yet secure their claims to land—without arousing the state's attention—suggests the participation of many villagers in the charade. At the very least, it suggests the recognition by the village's own leadership that these sales, though criminal from the state's perspective, were considered legitimate among peasants. To carry this all out undoubtedly required long memories and the institutional means for transmitting accounts of sales from one generation to another. This raises an obvious question. Once the land was sold, and the deal concealed behind a sham rental contract, how did Manchuria's rural communities handle disputes over claims to land without turning to the courts? More generally, what were the institutional means for anchoring and maintaining the customary practices pertinent to the assertion of property claims?

Throughout much of rural China lineage heads and the local gentry had roles in mediating disputes, though whether they had a monopoly over mediation depended upon conditions *in situ* (Huang 1996, 58–61; Beattie 1979, 127–132; Mazumdar 1998, 86, 124, 217–230; Gates 1996, 103–120). But in much of Qing Manchuria these groups were either absent or few and far between. Mirroring northern Chinese villages, lineages and therefore lineage heads were uncommon in Manchuria and remained so into the twentieth century. The most extensive Japanese investigation of village life in the 1930s found that of the 681 households surveyed in nineteen villages only seventy-eight claimed to belong to a lineage, while the highest proportion of households claiming common descent in any one village was eighteen percent (NSS 1937, 69, table 11). It also appears that Qing policies in the region—in particular its restrictions on migration—and general frontier conditions precluded the formation of a vibrant local gentry, at least until the second half of nineteenth century (Lee 1970, 83; Enatsu 1991, 24–25, 53–57). In China Proper, the gentry dominated local politics and society (Hsiao 1960, 284–287, 316–318). They were able to do so by virtue of a combination of landholding wealth, lineage position, and because they held civil degrees. With the degree came privileges, including access to the *yamen* where the state's representatives sat as local administrators. Whereas gentry were ubiquitous in China Proper, albeit unevenly distributed, Manchuria's gentry was by comparison highly attenuated. According to Chang Chung-li's (1955) well-known study of the Qing gentry, there were a mere 2,091 "regular" or degree-holding gentry in early nineteenth-century Fengtian. That number rose to 4,832 in the second half of the century, but only after an increase in Fengtian's degree quota (100, table 6; 164, table 32). Consequently, as a percentage of population, Fengtian's gentry (including their family members) was considerably smaller than that of any other region of the empire.[22] The thinness of Manchuria's gentry population is confirmed by Yoshiki Enatsu's (1991) study of Fengtian politics in the transition from the Qing to the Republic. Enatsu finds that Fengtian's Republican local elite were more or less entirely the creation of late Qing administrative reforms begun in 1907 after the province's civil governor Xu Shicheng took office (24–25, 53–57).

Whereas in other regional contexts the gentry were active in rural control (Hsiao 1960, 264), the absence of an entrenched gentry in Manchuria—coupled with the impracticality of turning to the courts to handle disputes over illegally sold land—meant that villagers in the northeast had to find ways to regulate land arrangements on their own. Consequently, it seems that the task of securing commoner property claims in Manchuria fell to those within the village who occupied formal and informal leadership positions and/or were held in esteem for their brokering and mediation skills. These were not necessarily powerful people, however, in the sense that they dominated or controlled village politics, but they were more established villagers with standing and reputations for fairness and common sense—people with "personal prestige," as Hsiao Kung-chuan (1960, 269) remarked.

Facilitators and the Regulation of Property Claims

The participation of other villagers in negotiating, guaranteeing, and witnessing arrangements made what were otherwise private transactions between two parties into matters of communal record. The public nature of the process was, therefore, a means not only for self-policing—ensuring customary norms were being followed—but also a means for ritualizing these norms, thereby establishing a basis for shared normative behavior. The smooth functioning of village custom and life in China depended to some degree upon mediation and arbitration (Hsiao 1960, 290–292).

The central role of the facilitator in regulating village affairs is captured in the language of the land contract which typically ended with the following admonition:

> Both parties are willing in this matter [of the exchange of land]. There are no misgivings or disputations whatsoever (*ci xi liang jia qingyuan, bing bu fanhui zhengjing*). Any dispute is to be submitted to the middleman and handled by him (*cha zhengjing zhi shi kao quan zai zhongjian ren, yimian chengshou*). For fear of there being no verification [of this agreement], we have written up this contract (*kongkou wuping lizi wei zheng*). (LPA 1761, 165; 1791, 33312; 1855, 32993; JCA 1787, 21312)

Statements found in land contracts about the facilitator's responsibilities were not *pro forma*. Indeed, it would be difficult to imagine how they could have been, given that the facilitator was both broker *and* witness. A witness, by definition, is a person whose social function is not fulfilled until they have related what they have observed as evidence. Twentieth-century investigations of customary practices conducted by Japanese show that facilitators (middlemen and brokers) were bound both by convention and village expectation to carry the memory of the arrangement and to mediate disputes.

That function is evident enough in Qing court records as facilitators are called upon to mediate disputes. In our first example, the middleman to a rent agreement/debt repayment was called upon to mediate a dispute after one party failed to keep up its side of the arrangement. Bannerman Zhang Yongbiao owed 280 *diao* to fellow bannerman Liu Shikuan. Unable to pay the debt, Zhang agreed to let Liu cultivate ten *shang* (sixty *mu*) of his land for six years free of rent. The agreement specified that neither interest on the loan nor rent on the land were to be charged, indicating that Liu obtained full rights to the land for the six years. Rather than work the land himself, however, Liu Shikuan rented it back to Zhang Yongbiao's nephew, a man surnamed Yang, for forty strings of cash per year.[23] (This was a fairly common arrangement after land was conditionally purchased or used to secure a loan, though more often the land was rented directly back to its seller.) To facilitate the arrangement, Zhang Yongbiao, who was obviously known to both Liu and Yang, acted as middleman. It was agreed at the time that tenant Yang would pay part of the rent upfront and the remainder after the fall harvest. However, in the third month of 1821, well before harvest time, Liu, accompanied by a hired laborer, approached Yang and asked for the full amount. Perhaps Liu was hoping that, with his hired hand along for support, he would be able to intimidate Yang into agreeing. But Yang told Liu to take the matter up with their middleman, Zhang Yongbiao. Liu then went to Zhang's house to discuss the matter; during that discussion a brawl broke out between Zhang's son and Liu, and Liu was killed (XB 1821, 01477).

In a second example taken from court accounts, village mediators were called in to facilitate an inheritance dispute four decades after the household property had been divided. In this case, the original guarantors and witnesses had already passed away by the time of the dispute, but others in the village stepped forward to help mediate. In 1821, serf Du Jin sued his paternal cousin once removed over his inheritance. Du Jin's grandfather had died many years before and the family property had been divided between two sons, Du Qingzhang and Du Mingzhang, who each received 27.5 *shang* or 165 *mu*. Soon after the division, however, Du Jin's father, Du Qingzhang, died. At that time, Du Jin was still an infant, so he went to live with his uncle Mingzhang. Mingzhang also took control of his nephew's inheritance. Years later, when he reached maturity, Du Jin asked his uncle for his inheritance so that he might set up a separate household. At the time the harvest was poor and the family circumstances were quite dire. Mingzhang told his nephew that he was too young to handle the land on his own and, given the difficult times, they were better off sticking together and working side-by-side. Du Jin was convinced, apparently, because he testified that he had willingly dropped the matter. After Mingzhang died, however, his grandson (Du Jin's cousin once removed) took charge of the household and began to sell conditionally some of the family's land. Du Jin brought suit against his cousin, fearing he would soon lose his inheritance. The problem was that the middleman and witnesses to the original property division were no longer around, so at this point two villagers, serf Zhang Wanli and commoner Li Youtai, who were friends of Du Jin, stepped in to mediate a resolution. It was agreed that Du Jin would receive his father's share of the inheritance and Du Jin dropped the suit (LPA 1821, 23917).

Our final example comes from the records of a dispute between two cousins, Liu Chaotai and Liu Chaorui, over the division of their grandfather's property ten years earlier. At that time, Liu Chaotai could not afford to pay the *panfei* of forty *diao* for his share of the family property, so his cousin, Liu Chaorui, paid the amount for him. In return, Liu Chaotai agreed to rent his share of the divided land to Liu Chaorui for ten years, or until the debt was paid off. (It is not clear from the court records precisely how they intended this arrangement to work. Presumably, the rent charged to Liu Chaorui was below customary levels or perhaps, as in the just discussed case of the unrelated Liu Shikuan, Liu Chaorui got to cultivate the land rent-free. Forty *diao* was less than the going rent for one *shang* for a ten year period, but then Liu Chaorui had to expend his own labor working the land to get his money back.) The head of the extended Liu family, Liu Duan, brokered both the household division and the agreement to repay the debt. When the time came for Liu Chaorui to return the land, he refused to do so, denying that he and his cousin had ever agreed to the arrangement in the first place. He even claimed that the land in question had been his all along. At this point it appears that the local *yamen* got involved and found Liu Chaorui to be in the wrong. He was ordered to return the land to his cousin. Two years later, however, Liu Chaorui had still not complied with the court's order. Liu Duan then stepped in to mediate and judged that Liu Chaorui should return the land to Liu Chaotai's family. Liu Chaorui finally relinquished it and told his cousin's son—Liu Chaotai having died in the intervening two years—"to spread manure" on the fields and "plant them" (LPA 1809, 20440).

Given the seriousness of such matters—due to the fact that they bore long-term consequences for family and village livelihood alike—only certain people in any village were considered up to the task of facilitating property exchanges. First, facilitators were village members—usually though not exclusively defined as someone who had land within village boundaries. These people were conversant with the dos and don'ts of local practices and, moreover, they could be expected to remain in the village where they were available to recall an agreement's details (NSS 1937, 5–8; TKK 1937, 77; NSS 1937, 153–156). The unwritten convention that facilitators were village members made good sense in an illiterate society and in a legal system which required deeds and the like as proof of claims. Under these conditions, practice is knowledge and a working knowledge of how things are done, as well as a memory of how they were done in the past, carries tremendous force in human affairs (Liang 1996, 120–125, 149–152, 165–

166). This combination of knowledge and continuity was essential for a good middleman, mediator, or facilitator (Isett 2004, 150–151).

Second, given the critically important role of memory in regulating village affairs, as well as memory's associated problems, a facilitator had to be more than just a villager. That is to say, being well versed in village practices or a long-time resident was an insufficient qualification. To be an effective middleman, witness, or guarantor also required a reputation as someone whose word carried weight in the community. Describing land sales in 1887, the U.S. Consul to Niuzhuang wrote: "two respectable witnesses known to both parties must sign the paper; and there must be a surety who can replace the whole sum in question, if it be found that there was a flaw in the title deeds or some other irregularity in the transaction" (U.S. CR Customs Report Dispatch No. 338, dated May 19). Facilitators had to be in good standing or "respectable." But, for a person's words to carry weight it was also important that he be considered by fellow villagers to be fair and impartial (MTK 1939, 31–32, 35–36, 106; Shimizu 1945, 5–6, 35–46; Hsiao 1960, 291).

It is easy to see why these qualities were so highly valued. First, only persons with sufficient *gravitas* were able to convince one or both disputants to compromise and move toward a settlement. Second, a facilitator had to be able to smooth over tensions and mollify anger, all the while mediating a resolution. Because villages were often small—in Manchuria they were often composed of twenty or so households—and because peasants lived in close proximity to one another, it was necessary to minimize social friction in all affairs. Unresolved anger and frustration of a few could disrupt village life and even threaten the general consensus necessary for the proper functioning of property systems and other socioeconomic relations (Liang 1996, 120–125, 149–152, 165–166; Huang 1996, 61–63). It is telling that villagers considered a good mediator to be someone who ensured that all parties saved face, even if the final decision significantly favored one party over another (Hsiao 1960, 291–292). If a facilitator was held in high regard by fellow villagers, and considered fair and incorruptible, his task would be all the easier.

To preserve the appearance of disinterest and impartiality, villages developed rules of propriety that frowned upon paying middlemen or guarantors any cash for their services. Paying a middleman suggested that he could gain financially from the land sales he brokered or the leaseholds or the hiring of wage laborers he arranged. Such motives would conflict with his duty as an honest broker of transactions and fair mediator of disputes. Similar expressions of distaste are reserved today for those who use money to develop social relationships. In his study of the northeast village of contemporary Shuangchengbao—a village of former rusticated bannermen—the anthropologist Yan Yunxiang (1996) explains that the use of cash in social networking is considered by villagers to be in "poor taste"; it is a sign of vulgarity and a failure to understand the rules of proper etiquette and decorum expressed in the unwritten code that "a respectable man should avoid the appearance of gift exchange as payoffs" (125–126). Analogously, in the 1930s rules required that after major transactions, such as land sales, the buyer invite the middleman to feast at the next festival or celebratory occasion such as the New Year or the wedding of a son (Shimizu 1945, 6). Of course, we can see how middlemen accumulated a form of what Pierre Bourdieu called "social capital" and prestige. This could be used to try to secure loans or obtain some position of village leadership (LPA 1794, 8857).[24] In this regard, the invitation to a public celebratory feast (rather than a private meal at a home) served to recognize and reinforce publicly the middleman's important social role in the village, giving him social capital, which he could "cash in" at a later date, while still maintaining his all-important aura of detachment and fairness.

The Manchurian village did not have its own "courts" for handling contractual arrangements and there was certainly nothing comparable to "common law" in the Anglo-Saxon tradition.[25] But it did have other means for regulating its own affairs. In effect, brokers and middlemen policed customary practice. The participation of a broker (required in all land sales), whose principal task was to ensure each party to an arrangement followed protocol in relation to the other, effectively guaranteed that agreements did not violate accepted village practices, while assisting in mediating disputes (NSS 1937, 190–194; MTDG 1935, 154–155; Shimizu 1945, 20–21). Through the participation of facilitators, the exchange of land became more than a simple arrangement between two individuals or households. The middleman effectively stood in for the broader community and its general interests. In so doing, facilitators and brokers constituted an institutional framework for securing and reproducing customary practices in land that in Manchuria made possible the devolution of Qing land into the hands of commoners (MTDG 1935, 153–164; Shimizu 1945, 14, 20–22; TKK 1937, 187–192, 196–198, 253–259; NSS 1937, 117–120, 190–194).[26]

The Imperial Response to the Devolution of Qing Land

By the Qianlong era (and probably earlier), in the northeast customary practices in land did not conform with Qing law. With opposing norms established for regulating the exchange of property and for enforcing property claims, and with means to conceal exchanges from local officials, substantial amounts of both banner and manor land had been transferred into the hands of commoners. Though it is not possible to determine exactly the total proportion of Qing land commoners had illegally purchased or occupied, Ping-t'i Ho believed (without explanation) that it may have been as high as two-thirds by the 1770s (Ho 1959, 159–160). Whatever the relative levels, it was certainly high enough to push the state into action (Sudō 1944). Across the eighteenth and nineteenth centuries the Qing court implemented a series of plans each designed to recover illegally sold land and to restore the status quo of 1680.

The Qianlong emperor responded to the unfolding developments of eighteenth-century rural Manchuria with open expressions of anxiety. Gazing across the Manchurian landscape on his 1753 tour of Shengjing, he saw Manchu customs dissolving as commoners settled in the northeast. He observed that:

> This year, We toured the ancestral tombs and met with the officials and soldiers of the region and attended to all public matters gladly and assiduously. . . . Today, very many commoners live there without a permanent home and merchants converge to the point that the people of this place and their customs are changing. They too have become extravagant and wasteful. If we do not make every effort to correct this expeditiously, We fear customs will be transformed, [the Manchu people] will abandon their ways, and their descendants will be profligate too. (GZSL 1964, 3023 [206])

Nearly twenty-five years later Qianlong lamented the outcome of many of the developments he had earlier anticipated:

> Today, We see that the customary practices of Jilin are like those of Shengjing. They too are gradually wasting away (*ri qu yu xia*). As the commoner settlers increase daily, so the ancient Manchu ways are lost (*liumin ri jian jiazeng, zhi shi manzhou jiu su*). . . . The three eastern provinces [Fengtian, Jilin, and Heilongjiang] constitute the Manchus' place of origin (*gen ben zhi di*). We must preserve the upright and ancient customs of the Manchus and lament tainting by Han customs (*bing liwan jianran hanren xiqi*). (GZSL 1964, 15208 [1035])

Fear of losing customs was accompanied by anxiety over the deteriorating welfare of bannermen (*baqi shengji*) (Li 1985, passim). The court tied these circumstances to commoner invasions of bannerland in Manchuria. In 1740, Qianlong thus explained that the increase in commoners, and their occupation of bannerland, were undermining the bannerland system and thereby threatening the livelihood of banner households:

> Shengjing is the land from which the Manchus came and is thus of tremendous importance. Today, the commoners who have congregated in this region are many and they have occupied the land. . . . Would it not be best if bannermen cultivated this land? But the bannermen are unable to cultivate the land and so it is left vacant.

Having asked the rhetorical question, Qianlong provided the answer by commanding that "all the benefits of this place are to revert to the bannermen" (GZSL 1964, 1743 [115]). In an effort to stem the devolution of Qing land, beginning in the second half of the eighteenth century, the court experimented with various policies to rectify the situation.

Qing Policies to Identify and Recover Illicitly Occupied Land

One solution to the problem was to buy back land illegally sold to commoners. Under the Qianlong emperor's predecessor, the Yongzheng emperor, the state offered a one-time amnesty for those who came forward and admitted to having illegally sold or bought Qing land. Commoners were even compensated after the land was returned to the seller. The Yongzheng program led to problems, however. Because the land was returned to the original banner or serf household without recouping the cost from them, serfs and rusticated bannermen found they could sell their land to commoners, report the sales themselves, and thereby keep both the sale price and recover their land (Yi 1993, 216)! The policy was swiftly brought to an end when field administrators realized what was happening. For some time thereafter no major efforts were made to recover Qing lands.

Then, in 1769, the Qianlong emperor ordered regional officials to conduct a general survey of the northeast to uncover illegally sold Qing land. To encourage cooperation with the survey, he offered amnesty to those who stepped forward and admitted to having illegally bought or sold Qing land. As in the Yongzheng amnesty, state funds were used to buy back the land that had been sold to commoners.[27] But to halt the abuses that had plagued Yongzheng's arrangement, under the Qianlong plan those who had conditionally sold land had to buy it back from the state if they wished to cultivate it again. They were given ten years in which to do so. At the expiration of the grace period, land not bought back by the original sellers was to be distributed to needy rusticated banner households other than the original holder (Yi 1993, 216–217). By the following year, at a cost of 147,661 *taels*, the state had redeemed a total of 524,721 *mu* of "bannerland conditionally purchased by commoners" (*min dian qidi*), which included manorial land. By 1774, 775,620 *mu* had been redeemed at a cost of 228,940 *taels* (HZ 1771, 4.21; HZ 1774, 12.13).[28]

Despite the cadastral survey and efforts to encourage voluntary self-reporting, regional officials were aware that only a fraction of illegally occupied land was in fact redeemed in this fashion. They were also aware that the illegal occupations of banner and manor land by commoners continued apace, despite their efforts. Acknowledging this fact, Fengtian Prefect Henglu and the Shengjing Board of Revenue Secretary Tanggutai concluded their report on the outcome of the 1770 cadastre with a warning for local officials to be vigilant for further illegal sales. All rusticated bannermen and commoners subsequently caught illegally buying and selling bannerland, they commanded, were to be punished to the full extent of the law, and the land and sale price were to be forfeited to the state without recompense. Interestingly, Henglu and Tanggutai went on to order harsh punishment for any *lingcui* or *shoubao* who sought to impede official investigations in order to conceal illegalities in their villages, thereby acknowledging that rural agents were undermining official efforts to maintain the integrity of the bannerland system (HZ 1771, 4.21). On this point, their admonition proved to be prescient. As we saw in the case of Su Yi, whose family land had been redeemed by the Qing state in 1772 as part of the Qianlong program, when Su retrieved his father's land he immediately resold it to the commoners Chen Jun and Chen Rong with the aid of the manor bailiff.

The 1769–1770 amnesty and buy-back did not signal a *volte-face* in the state's position on the sale of Qing land to commoners. Once the buy-back ended, regional and local authorities were instructed to handle illegal sales of Qing land just as they had done prior to 1769 (HZ 1781, 10.20). Central government authorities were, moreover, well aware that many peasants had not come forward to report illegal sales during the buy-back program and ordered local officials to continue efforts to ferret out these people and to punish them. To impress upon bureaucrats the need to put an end to these sales, the emperor ordered the reprimand of all officials who failed to uncover illegal sales.

> During the 1770 cadastral survey there was hiding and non-reporting. After [the program ends], land that was uncovered is to be confiscated, and the owner and buyer are to be punished under the statutes against concealing matters from officials. If they are found guilty of having sold land either conditionally (*dian*) or outright (*mai*) then they are to be punished according to the statutes. The land and cash price are to be confiscated together by the state and those officials who failed to investigate are to be severely reprimanded. (LPA 1788.3.6 [8599])

Rather than softening the state's position, the 1769–1770 buy-back program and similar policies that followed were attempts to clear the ground of illegal settlement and clean up the land registry records so the state could start afresh. In many instances, including the above cited case of Mrs. Ma, local officials continued to mete out the full measure of punishment required by law for the illegal sale of Qing land to commoners (also see LPA 1785, 10660).

To discourage further illegal migration, the state also adjusted its tax policies to discriminate against newly opened lands worked by commoners. Under the original tax code, the state distinguished between red-registry commoner land (*hongce mindi*), which referred to all commoner land registered in 1683 at the time when commoners were segregated into commoner zones, and surfeit commoner land (*min yudi*), which had been opened subsequently but was nonetheless legal because it lay within the commoner zones (FCZS 1914, 27–29; Yi 1993, 218, 248–250). Initially, fields opened in this way were termed "land raised to the rank" of tax-paying land (*shengke di*).[29] The rate of taxation was comparable to commoner red-registry land. But, under the Qianlong emperor, in 1765, the tax was raised on surfeit land (Yi 1993, 250). Then, in 1780 it was recommended that regional officials raise the tax on surfeit commoner land opened thereafter so that the tax burden exceeded that typically levied in Zhili and Shandong. The new penalty tax rate was approved and beginning in 1781 all new commoner surfeit land was taxed at the optimum rate of eight *fen* per *mu*. In addition, an extra tax of 0.4 *sheng* of grain per *mu* was levied to supply the military granary (HZ 1781, 10.20). Surfeit commoner land subject to the penalty tax was appropriately called "augmented tax land," or *jiafu di* (Yi 1993, 250–251; FCZS 1914, 25–26).[30]

The goal of the penalty tax was to convince commoners to return to north China. Given the comparatively lower levels of agricultural technique in Fengtian and Jilin, the new tax most certainly exceeded in relative terms that of Shandong and Zhili. In a memorial reporting progress in the implementation of the new tax, Shengjing Military Governor Suonuomucejun wrote:[31]

> Because the land in and around Shengjing and Jilin is fertile and expansive, many migrants come to illegally open land here. On all of the previously and illicitly settled land in the Shengjing area, the taxes in monies and grain are to be set according to the amounts levied in the interior [China Proper] in order to reduce gradually the bad practice of commoners coming to settle. During the period of two years in which they carried out the investigations, the amount of unregistered land uncovered because of law suits between bannermen and commoners amounted to 1,200 *shang* (7,200 *mu*). Upon handling these matters, the illegal migrants in the area [of Shengjing and Jilin] will return to their native homes to make their living because the taxes are set similarly to those in the interior and so there is no benefit to be had. Thus, the amount of land forfeited will rise and the Manchus can cultivate it. They can thereby obtain the surfeit land, becoming its proprietors, which is good for their livelihood. If after giving this land to the Manchus they do not personally cultivate the land and instead give it to commoners to cultivate in secret, while illicitly collecting rent, upon discovery by the Military Governor the bannermen and commoners are to be punished. The land is to be forfeited to the state for the purpose of redistribution among other bannermen. Thereafter, the Military Governors are to periodically conduct investigations. After three or five years, this Board is to request the commission of an official to come forth and conduct a thorough survey of the land. If in these districts land is still illegally occupied by commoners, then the Military Governors and other officials are to be disciplined. (HZ 1781, 10.10; also see HZ 1781, 11.16)

Suonuomucejun's account of the new policy shows that the state had not adjusted its position on commoner settlement nor had it softened its attitudes toward rusticated bannermen. Suonuomucejun intended the new policy to deter further colonization *and* to put rusticated bannermen back to farming the land.

The records of a 1788 case involving the illegal occupation of nine thousand *mu* of manor land by commoners speak directly to Suonuomucejun's second aim—that of putting rusticated bannermen back to work on the land. In making his judgment, the presiding magistrate in this case noted:

on examining the law it is found that in regulations of the Board of Revenue regarding the "forfeiture of land illicitly opened by commoners to Manchu bannermen to cultivate and pay taxes" that in all cases when commoners illicitly open land, the local official is to select from among those bannermen without land within his district, and who have the ability to farm, to give them the forfeited land in units of one hundred mu. *These bannermen are to be ordered to cultivate the land using their own labor.* Any bannerman who does not use his own labor but instead rents the land out to commoners and collects taxes is to have his land confiscated and it is to be given to another bannerman. (LPA 1788, 11823, emphasis added)

By the end of his reign in 1796, with an eye to protecting the interests of the Qing dynasty and the banner population, the Qianlong emperor had attempted on several occasions to arrest the unraveling of the banner and manor systems. The 1750 ban on migration, the state buy-backs of sold land, the implementation of various penalty taxes, and even the continued threat of punishment had, however, minimal effect, such that in 1805 the Fengtian Prefect Fujun could conclude that "though matters in regard to bannerland purchased by commoners have been reviewed for many years, there is much evidence that there are still cases of conditional buying and selling." He estimated only half of all bannerland was cultivated by bannermen (HZ 1806, n.n.). A year before, following the recommendation of Fujun, the Jiaqing emperor had commanded a novel solution to this old problem that encouraged bannermen and commoners to report illegal sales voluntarily. Recounting the policy in 1805, Duo Qing of the Board of Revenue in Beijing noted that:[32]

In the memorial of the Shengjing Military Governor, Fujun, proposing a solution to the matter of commoners conditionally buying bannerland, declared that henceforth when bannermen come forward and register [illegal sales of land], the land is to be forfeited to the state and rented back to the original banner proprietor. The rusticated bannerman is to pay the rent according to the regulations, but the state is not to press him for the conditional sale price nor are punishments to be administered [against him]. But, in these cases, outstanding taxes and interest are to be pressed from the commoners [who conditionally bought the land] and they are to be punished. In cases of commoners who come forward and register [illegal occupations of land], then the land is to be forfeited to the state but they are not to be punished. Furthermore, the [commoners] are not to be pressed for past taxes and interest. In addition, it was decided that [these commoners] are to be exempted from taxes for a period of one year in compensation for the lost conditional sale price. (HZ 1805, 2.20)

The expressed goal of the proposed policy was to avert the shortcomings of previous programs, which, in the authorities' own reckoning, had failed to elicit self-reporting of illicitly occupied land.[33] The following year, in 1806, this policy was significantly adjusted to compensate commoners for the loss of the conditional sale price that came with the land's confiscation. When rusticated bannermen registered the land, then commoners were given two more years to cultivate it tax free in order to earn back part of the conditional sale price. Commoners who reported having illegally purchased bannerland were given four more years to cultivate the land tax free. If bannermen and commoners reported the land together, the commoners were allowed three more years on the land tax free. In each case, at the end of the period, the land was returned to the bannerman, who was then liable for the land tax. In changing the policy, Fujun noted:

> these bannermen and commoners are all poor and unfortunate people. If today they were to report their land then in accordance with one regulation they will be pressed for the conditional price and according to another they will be pressed for taxes and interest. They will not be able to avoid the turmoil of being dunned. Moreover, having been fined their circumstances are pitiful. So we should make an exception. The punishments due to all bannermen and commoners who have already registered their land, along with the policy of pressing for the conditional price, taxes, and interest, are to be fully abrogated. (HZ 1806 7.28)

In this fashion, the state redeemed the land without having to mobilize funds. It simply waived several years of taxes, which it would not have earned anyway had the land's cultivation continued to be concealed. Despite the novelty of the policy, officials reported that it had failed to elicit much cooperation. For the most part, villagers evidently felt secure in their own institutional means for managing property claims and concealing their purchases from local officials. They saw no need to report on themselves and, in so doing, lose their land.

Despite consistent failure to uncover illegally occupied Qing land or to elicit the cooperation of peasants to report this land themselves, the court continued to insist that local and regional authorities implement the letter of the law. Thus, as late as the 1850s, the court insisted that those involved in the illegal sale or occupation of Qing lands in Manchuria be punished. In 1852, when the imperial court issued the "regulations for the buying and selling of bannerland" (*qidi maimai zhangcheng*) to legalize the sale of bannerland to commoners within China proper, the edict began with a declaration that it did not apply to the northeast:

> Aside from the illicit sale and illicit conditional sale of bannerland in Fengtian, which are still regulated under the old statutes and that are still to be strictly enforced, henceforth bannerland in such places as Shuntian and Zhili, regardless of whether it was engrossed land or homesteaded, or whether it belongs to the Capital's bannermen, those living in the countryside, or commoners, this [land] may all be mutually bought and sold, and will be subject to the regulated tax. (cited in Zhang et al. 1998, 243)

Seen in light of the sovereign's continued antagonism toward both commoner settlement in Manchuria and their occupation of Qing lands, policies enacted to recover Qing lands were not signals of reform. Each action was an effort to reassert order and clarify the land records so that local officials could remove recent migrants and better police against their incursions in the future.

Field Administrators, Peasant Defiance, and the Politics of Local Compromise

In the face of continuing migration, regional and local officials were increasingly in the difficult position of having to maintain, and in some instances restore, the mandated agrarian regime, even as efforts to do so often threatened to disrupt local social order. At times the state appears to have been aware of the dilemma posed, as when the Qianlong emperor reflected in 1776 that removing commoners from Fengtian would deprive them of their livelihood, with all the negative repercussions thus entailed (GZSL 1964 [1023]; cf. SZSL 1964, 1678 [71]), or when field administrators noted that dispossessing commoners of their land could provoke unrest. In a dramatic statement to this effect, the Board of Revenue official Duo Qing memorialized the court in 1805 stating: "if we continuously investigate [illegal land sales], I worry since many bannermen and commoners will not be able to afford [to pay the fines] and because there are so many involved. I fear that because the foolish people will dwell on their lost property some will go to the extreme of killing themselves *or worse*" (HZ 1805, 2.20). One can only imagine what was worse than suicide for a Qing official, but open rebellion is certainly a possibility! As migrants settled in larger and larger numbers, and acquired more and more Qing land, the task of restoring the mandated agrarian regime met peasant resistance. Across the eighteenth and nineteenth centuries, field administrators in Manchuria were thus having to juggle conflicting priorities. On the one hand, they were charged with enforcing the emperor's will by implementing his laws and policies and securing social stability. On the other hand, they were ideologically committed to nurturing the "people's livelihood" (*minsheng*), by virtue of their inculcation in neo-Confucian thought. As the following two cases from the eighteenth century demonstrate, while enforcing the law of the land might spark social unrest, appeasing peasants would maintain social order but contradict state policy. Stuck in the middle, local officials searched for means to navigate the rocky straits between law and order.

The Case of Commoner Hou Duo

The details of a legal case stemming from the criminal sale of manor land in Jilin illustrate the conflicted position of local officials. According to the case record, the extent of illegal land deals on the Dengerlezhi estate came to the attention of the Bodune military *yamen* in 1791, when the Bodune military governor, traveling through the estate on inspection, asked Bailiff Yu whether his estate's land was sufficient to meet the estate's immediate needs and rent payments. Yu admitted that one-third of the eighteen thousand *mu* of land allotted to the manor had been illicitly sold to commoners by the estate serfs (JCA 1795, 65418).

On returning to his office at the military *yamen*, the military governor sent two officials to investigate and decide how to handle the illegal land sales. Taking into consideration that commoners had spent large sums of money to acquire the manor land, and that to dispossess them of their land would leave them with no livelihood, a compromise was found that contained within it some aspects of Fujun's strategy of 1806 to recover Qing land. It was decided that any original allotments of land (i.e., the red-registry land given to the serfs) that had been purchased by commoners would be returned and all documents associated with their sale handed over to the *yamen*. However, land in excess of their original allotment (i.e., the surfeit land) that had been sold to commoners would remain in the commoners' possession for another five years and then be returned. In this way, compensation was afforded to some commoners, but not all. Those who had purchased red-registry land were clearly out of pocket, while those who had purchased surfeit land would have five years in which to make alternative plans before they were removed.

When Bailiff Yu moved to confiscate the red-registry land and gather the title deeds peasants had used to record their sales among themselves, he was sued in court by seventeen commoners who accused him of seeking to "take their land forcibly for personal benefit." Commoner Hou Duo, the principal plaintiff in the case, argued that the land in question had been his for some time. He testified that not only had he purchased it, but the bailiff had even sanctioned the purchase when he added Hou's name to the manor's rent rolls and started to collect from him the manor rent due on the property.

Hou related how he had come by the land in question. He stated that he had arrived in Xincheng in 1776 with his daughter and sons and purchased by conditional sale three sections (*duan*) of land from the serf Li Fang. The following year Bailiff Yu informed him the manor rent on the land was to be increased and he protested, arguing that since he had purchased the land conditionally it was not his and therefore he should not have to pay the rent. He related how Bailiff Yu had told him to take the matter up with serf Li Fang, who still held the right of redemption to the land. Hou did this, telling Li that he was reluctant to pay the increased rent since he did not own the land outright, and suggested that Li was responsible for paying the increase in rent. According to Hou, Li had responded that he had no intention of redeeming the land and that Hou "pay the increased rent and become the land's proprietor" (*zeng liang wei ye*). Hou Duo did so and, under the assumption that the land was now his, began to pay the rent at the increased rate.

Of course, this was all highly irregular. Hou Duo should never have been allowed to buy manorial land in the first place. Yet, the bailiff recognized the purchase and even started to collect a share of the manor rent from Hou. Here we have a clear example of the complicity of rural agents in the buying and selling of Qing land. For Bailiff Yu the decision to enter Hou Duo on the manor roll, along with other commoners, was based on his need to meet the manor's fixed quota of rent, which by his own admission he was hard-pressed to do. In his court testimony, Bailiff Yu recounted how over the years many of the estate's serfs had fled, leaving the estate undermanned. Yu was faced with the option of either being punished for not meeting the manor's annual rent quota or collecting rent from commoners who had purchased or occupied manor land. He did the latter.

Having paid the state rent on the land, with the bailiff's full knowledge and sanction, Hou Duo was understandably outraged when in 1791 that same bailiff came to confiscate the land on the orders of the military governor. In his plaint, and in court testimony, Hou Duo argued that since he had paid the rent on the land for many years, the land was rightfully his and could not be taken away by the bailiff, nor by implication by the state. Just as the land tax was collected on the basis of land ownership—and its payment was in other parts of the empire sometimes sufficient to assert land claims in the courts (Osborne 2004, 140–142, 154)—so the estate rent was collected on the basis of permanent tenure. This is clearly what serf Li Fang had in mind when he told Hou to pay the rent and become the land's owner, and this is clearly the argument Hou articulated in his case against the bailiff.

In 1791, Hou and the other sixteen commoners on Denglezhi manor brought their accusations against Bailiff Yu at the Xincheng prefectural *yamen*, but the prefect was less than sympathetic to their cause and had them beaten and then ejected from the court. To the prefect, the commoners' case was worse than frivolous or without merit, it was libelous and therefore criminal. As far as he was concerned, the land belonged to the state, the commoners were forbidden by law to possess it, and the bailiff was acting within his duties to confiscate it. Overturning the earlier ruling, the prefect now ordered that all the land (including surfeit land) be confiscated immediately, and that it be returned to waste.

Bailiff Yu, however, hesitated to implement this new command. He pointed out that if the land were returned to waste, then the manor would be left with insufficient arable land either to meet its rent dues to the state or to guarantee the livelihood of the resident serfs. Bailiff Yu now reported that many serfs had returned to the manor in 1791 in the hope of recovering their land after the military *yamen* had ordered it confiscated. Yu was now concerned that the returning serfs, who were still without land, might starve to death. Just as important, he reported that since the time of the suit's filing that year's crop had begun to "sprout." In other words, the commoners had already invested that year's initial labor to prepare and plant the fields and the crops were just beginning to push through the topsoil. Their labor, having been invested in the land, had secured for them certain customary rights to the crop if not the land and yamen staff were reluctant to ignore this.[34] Fearing a disturbance if the land were confiscated at this point in time, Bailiff Yu reported that he dare not make a move against it. This fear was well grounded, since Hou Duo and the other commoners had already demonstrated incredible nerve by filing their initial suit against him. Searching for a remedy, Bailiff Yu even suggested that the situation be resolved by granting the commoners permanent ownership of the land, and thereafter collect from them the commoner land tax. Bailiff Yu was becoming an advocate for the commoners' position.

The case picks up again in 1795, four years after the bailiff had been ordered to remove the commoners. At this time the commoners were still farming their illegally purchased fields, having successfully prevented Bailiff Yu from carrying out his orders. A newly arrived prefect now reopened the case. He reinstated the original decision: the commoners were to return the original allotted land without receiving cash compensation, but could hold on to the surfeit land for another five years without having to pay any rent. This last arrangement, the new prefect argued, would allow the commoners to recover the money they had spent when they purchased the land conditionally and so would properly compensate them for their labor and expenses.[35] The court record ends there.

The case of Hou Duo illustrates how customary practice served on the one hand to articulate and establish claims to land within the village, and thereby facilitate the day-to-day grind of agricultural production and securing of household subsistence, and on the other to challenge state power in the ongoing contestation over land and, by association, labor and the agricultural surplus. The case also shows how local and regional officials compromised to assuage peasants and, in so doing, maintained local social order. In this case, the courts decided that Hou and his fellow commoners deserved compensation for the capital they had expended in buying land, and this was finally provided by allowing them to keep the "surfeit land" for another five years.

The Case of Kong Xingdai

The case of plaintiff Kong Xingdai is another example of the dilemma facing regional officials who saw the need to compensate commoners for their investments in capital and labor, but still wished to prevent the devolution of Qing land. In 1785, serf Kong Xingdai, who was attached to an imperial grain estate of the Plain Yellow Banner of the Imperial Household Department, went before the Shengjing Board of Revenue to reclaim land that had been confiscated from his family as "bannerland conditionally purchased by a commoner" (*min dian qidi*).[36] Kong Xingdai explained that in the 1760s the family holding of estate land had been divided by his father between Kong Xingdai and his two brothers, Kong Xingji and Kong Xingzong, in three equal shares. Beginning in 1751, the Kong brothers gradually sold their inheritance to a number of commoners. During the cadastral survey of 1771 Kong Xingdai and his brothers came forward to register the land with the local officials as "bannerland conditionally purchased by commoners" in the hope of avoiding punishment. The land was confiscated and the Kongs were given ten years to repay the redemption price and thereby retrieve the land from the state. They had failed to do so, but in 1785 Kong Xingdai came forward and expressed his desire to reclaim the Kong family's land in its entirety, Xingdai's two brothers having died and their sons being outside the village working as wage laborers (LPA 1786, 8499, 8508, 8512).

An investigation was ordered to verify Kong's story, which was soon found to be false. It was reported that between the winter of 1751 and the winter of 1763, Kong Xingdai, his two brothers, and five other members of the Kong family had indeed conditionally sold 1,332 *mu* of red-registry and surfeit land to eight different commoners. In every land sale, the Kongs and the commoner buyers drew up false leasehold contracts to disguise the sales and in none of the cases did the Kongs redeem the land (LPA 1786, 8499). It was found, however, that the Kongs had in fact never reported the land to the state in 1771. Moreover, it was found that as early as 1766 the local *yamen* had uncovered these illegal sales. But, rather than confiscate the land, as would have been appropriate under the policy of the time, the magistrate at that time decided to allow the commoners to continue farming the Kongs' land. He even had them pay the manor rent due on it. He then falsified *yamen* records to cover up this fact, and those that followed continued to maintain the same arrangement (LPA 1786, 8508).

After uncovering these facts, the Shengjing Board of Revenue contemplated what to do. What complicated matters was the fact that the commoners, as in the case of Hou Duo, had been paying rent on the land to the state for nearly twenty years. It was, at first, suggested that the illicitly exchanged red-registry land be forfeited entirely and the commoners receive half of the original sale price as compensation. It was also recommended, however, that the commoners continue to cultivate the surfeit land and pay land taxes on it; by implication, the commoners would then become the permanent proprietors of the surfeit land. The fairness of both policies was questioned by the Shengjing Board of Revenue, however.

In the thirty-first year of the reign of the Qianlong emperor [1776] the fact that these commoners had purchased through conditional sale estate land from Kong Xingdai et al. was not uncovered. Today, it would be unfair to suggest that the *serfs* [could redeem the land] by paying only half [of the original sale price] to the commoners. . . . Nevertheless, although for the past ten years these commoners cultivated the land and paid the manor rent, that had amounted to less than leasehold rents they would have . . . paid [if the land had been leased to them by the serfs]. In this respect, the commoners have benefited. (LPA 1786, 8499)

The case was finally resolved by the forfeiture of all of the illicitly exchanged red-registry land without the payment of a redemption price. This land was then returned to the serfs. The commoners, however, were given permanent rights to the surfeit land, even though it lay within the estate, because, the judge explained, they had "cultivated it for many years." To facilitate the payment of taxes on the Qing-cum-commoner land in the future, the judge ordered the acreage and location of each piece of surfeit land registered under the name of its new proprietor and that this registry be stored at the prefectural *yamen* (LPA 1786, 8499, 8521).

Insofar as customary norms and practices diverged from or challenged the mandates of the state, these norms supported an alternative vision of how to organize day-to-day social, political, and even economic life.[37] Confronted with this alternative vision, the state had to react. On the one hand, retaining the sovereign's hegemony over the region remained the state's primary objective, underwriting the Qing government's drive to preserve Qing lands and prohibit commoner migration and settlement across the eighteenth and nineteenth centuries. There is, for example, the above cited 1815–1817 case of Nuomizhuang manor. In that instance, regional and local officials felt no need to recognize commoner claims: the land was confiscated, no compensation was offered, and both the serfs and commoners involved were sentenced in accordance with the code (LPA 1815, 25944; 1816, 24130; 1817, 26053).

On the other hand, regional and local officials also realized that securing state control locally might on occasion require striking a compromise with peasants in order to dissipate brewing troubles before they grew out of hand, or to preclude problems from arising altogether. In the final analysis, the loss of local control was potentially as much a threat to the Qing agenda as was the constant flow of illegal migrants into the northeast; so that at times political hegemony was best secured by granting concessions in order to prevent social unrest. Such was the case in the examples of Hou Duo and Kong Xingdai; local officials understood that if commoners were denied access to land and forced to return home, given the large numbers involved, they might protest. Deprived of land, they faced starvation. Either way, local order would be threatened and so concessions were granted. It appears that when and wherever possible regional officials fully applied the law and had commoners removed; but when expelling peasants from the land might provoke threats to political order and state power these same officials yielded ground to the peasantry by offering commoners continued access to some land in one form or another.[38]

The important point from the perspective of the Qing court was that officials always preserved the state's prerogative to evict the next batch of illegal commoners that came along, even as it yielded to the one in front of them. Consequently, the state reserved the right to decide how it was going to deal with these problems as they arose, while continuing to deny in principle the right of commoners to migrate to the northeast and settle on Qing lands. Ideologically speaking, either action was justifiable depending upon what underlying principle was being emphasized; loyalty to the Qing and bureaucratic professionalism required applying the full letter of the law, whereas neo-Confucian normative thought dedicated the bureaucrat to securing the "people's welfare" (*minsheng*). Here we see a clear indication of how the Qing state's commitment to *minsheng* was conditional. Whereas officials in the northeast recognized that policing actions against the devolution of Qing lands were harmful to commoner's welfare, the decision of whether to act upon this concern appears to have been a simple matter of calculating the political risks involved if they did not.

The Nature of Property in the Eighteenth and Nineteenth Centuries

Whereas it is evident that Manchuria's peasantry had found a means to exchange land across caste boundaries, to regulate claims to property that were not recognized by the state, and in the process to conceal illegal acquisitions of land from it, the fact that such developments remained wholly within the sphere of customary practice meant that the property claims were by definition de facto as opposed to de jure. By their nature, a certain precariousness and conditionality therefore pertained to all claims to property that was, from the state's perspective, illegally obtained. This disjuncture between customary practices and law created an opportunity for extortion, which I have analyzed elsewhere (Isett 2004, 155–158).[39] Despite the shared material interests of villagers in maintaining customary practices and observing norms as the basis of all property claims, the asymmetry between the law and custom on the matter of property rights and claims in Manchuria created space for abuse. Property under these conditions could never be absolutely held.

The singular difference between rural Manchurian customs and the formal law engendered a certain precariousness in the functioning of customary practices in property which was absent in China Proper. The conditionality of property claims under these conditions belies the notion proposed by some mainland Chinese scholars that Qing lands had become private property (*sichan*) in the eighteenth and nineteenth centuries (Yi 1993, 212–220, 241–242; Diao 1993, 133–138, 186–189). Instead, what we have is best understood as a form of what Robert Brenner terms peasant possession of land (1985b [1982], 1997). "Ownership" is conventionally understood as an absolute claim founded on legal principles. Commoners in Manchuria did not "own" the land they had purchased from bannermen and serfs because, of course, the legal system did not recognize the transferal of claims. What commoners held were customary claims that gave them possession without formal proprietorship. This formulation is expansive enough to incorporate the range of claims to land that pertained in the peasant communities of northeast China and also allow for the retention of some notion of property control as conditional and contended.

CHAPTER SIX

Wage Labor and Wage Relations in Qing Manchuria

Between the late Ming and early Qing a combination of commercial and political forces issued in the demise of servile agricultural labor and the concomitant spread of nonservile agricultural wage labor.[1] Examining these developments, several historians maintain that agricultural field hands—who in the Ming were subject to the extra-economic coercion of landowners—were by the early eighteenth century subject to the compulsion of the market. In their view, this transformation was a sign of the advance of commercial forces in people's lives and, therefore, evidence of proto-modern economic development.[2]

Yet, it is also evident that the early Qing period witnessed the growth of the relative size of the land-holding population, a pattern that, once established, held more or less for the duration of the dynasty. By all estimates the proportion of the rural population that was rendered fully dependent upon wage labor employment for its reproduction remained small in the Qing. While developments in agricultural production relations between the late Ming and mid-Qing point to the end of the viability of extra-economic coercion of landowner over field hand, the same developments also indicate how well protected peasants were from being fully separated from the land and becoming fully dependent upon wages for their reproduction (Mazumdar 1998, 237; Fang et al. 2000, 1863; Wong 1997, 47).

Given the nature of dynastic designs in Manchuria, there was no reason to expect that by 1800 both Manchurian rent and wage relations would mirror those that were taking shape in north China. It was true that social developments in north China, and in much of the rest of China proper, had resulted in the widespread disappearance of servile statuses among tenants and agricultural laborers alike. However, in Manchuria and parts of Zhili province nearest the capital, the Qing monarch and aristocracy, backed by the full power of the state they controlled, had succeeded in greatly restricting the mobility of cultivators. They had created new forms of bonded labor and infused the countryside with status hierarchies and distinctions.[3] Agricultural production in the northeast was characterized, therefore, by an array of political relations that not only facilitated but maintained extra-economic compulsion.

The *Gugongren* in Manchuria

Given the legal status distinctions that separated rusticated "full bannermen" (*zhengshen qiren*) from Han commoners, were some in the countryside positioned to press others into forced service? There were, to be sure, many types of bonded and servile labor dotting the Chinese and Manchurian landscape in the early Qing. Many were residual customary and legal statuses of the disintegrating Ming agrarian order. Among those were slaves (*nu*), hereditary servants (*shipu*), and indentured tenants (*dianpu*). New categories were also introduced by the Manchus including the "bondservant" (Ch. *baoyi*; Man. *booi*) (Elliott 2001, 82).

Among the Ming categories, the one with greatest staying power was the *gugongren*, a type of servile wage laborer that the Qing perpetuated *in law* when it adopted wholesale the Ming legal code in 1646 (Jing 1983a, 1983b). However, as Jing Junjian has demonstrated, despite Qing codification the *gugongren* status applied to few by the late eighteenth century (Jing 1983a, 1983b; Huang 1985; Chao 1986). The question is: was this also the case in Manchuria where a large part of the early rural population was affiliated with the ruling banner system, an institutional affiliation that came with privileges and power over the Han?

The Origins of the Gugongren in Ming and Qing Law

In 1588, under the Ming Wanli emperor, a distinction in law was made between contracted agricultural laborers who were servile, and therefore of a lower status than their employers, and those who were their employers' status equals. According to Jing Junjian, whose work remains the definitive source on the subject, the Wanli statute stemmed from a memorial written by then Censor-in-Chief Wu Shilai. The need for revisions in the Ming Code arose because wealthy and powerful commoners and degree-holding gentry were in violation of a law that limited the right to own and use slaves (*nubi*) to aristocratic households (the so-called households of the "Great Officials" [*gong chen zhi jia*]) (Jing 1983a, 267). The question before the censor-in-chief was what to do when field hands, who by custom were servile, committed crimes against their commoner employers. To punish them under statutes for crimes committed by slaves against the "Great Officials" would muddle important status distinctions in Ming law between the aristocracy and commoners. Yet, it was incomprehensible to the status-conscious Ming that laborers who were servile by custom could be tried and sentenced as their employers' status equals. Censor Wu's solution was to devise for these servile laborers a new legal category that satisfied the courts desire to enforce status distinctions between the Great Officials and commoners on the one hand and between commoner employers and their servile field hands on the other. That category was the *gugongren* which was codified in 1588 under the statute: "Slaves who beat the household head" (*nubi ou jiazhang*) (Jing 1983b, 265–267).

The substatute applied to a certain strata of agricultural laborers who performed labor for the employers for extended periods of time and who often lived with their employer. They were therefore not part of the casual day labor market, a type of farm hand about which neither the Ming nor the Qing Code had anything to say. Thus the legal definition held that: "Henceforth, in the families of the officials [*guan*] and commoners [*min*], all hired laborers who have signed contracts, agreeing to a finite period [of employment], shall be treated as *gugongren*. Only those employed for short periods, for small wages, shall be treated as commoners" (Jing 1983a, 268; also Chao 1986, 145). Thereafter, Ming jurists were at pains to distinguish between laborers who were customarily considered their boss's dependents, because they were employed for long periods of time, and casual day laborers and the like who remained customarily independent or "free" (Jing 1983b, 247–252, 256–257).

The Wanli *gugongren* substatute was copied wholly into the Qing Code. However, by that time the social and customary terrain was shifting in ways that rendered this legal category socially problematic. As Chinese and Japanese scholars have demonstrated, peasant rebellion and a demographic downturn in the seventeenth century had significantly diminished the social power of the gentry and big landlords over the peasants who labored in their fields. The mainland Chinese literature has understood this as the end of a sort of "manorialism" (also labeled "gentry landlordism," or *jinshen dizhu*), under which agricultural production was led by degree-holding and aristocratic landholders who held their laborers and tenants in bondage and servitude, and its replacement by "commoner landlordism" (*shumin dizhu*), under which larger nonaristocratic landholders recruited labor and tenants (e.g., Fang 1983, 88–90; Li 1993, 60–81).

The Qing state recognized this change in society in 1727 by abolishing several categories of servile persons and thereafter local authorities also began to apply a stricter interpretation of the Wanli statute. Rather than reading the statute as defining the *gugongren* by either his long-term employment or the use of a written contract, as had formerly been the case, Qing jurists now insisted that the *gugongren* status applied only when both conditions were fulfilled (Chao 1986, 146). Interpretation of the Wanli statute was narrowed further in 1759, when the legal category *gugongren* was said to apply only when, as part of the customary terms of their employment, agricultural laborers had signed written contracts, had been employed for at least one year, and the hired hand and his employer called each other master and servant (*zhu pu zhi fen*) (Jing 1983a, 286; also Chao 1986, 146).

The strengthening and expansion of the small-holding peasantry in the early Qing challenged a range of "status" distinctions in the law that no longer had the basis in customary practices they once did. One of these was how to define long-term laborers who hired out to fellow villagers under contractual terms that corresponded to those defining the *gugongren*, but who worked for their neighbors rather than big landholders or members of the degree-holding gentry. Philip Huang has called these new employers of long-term laborers "small-scale rich peasants" to emphasize their humble social and economic standing. These men were certainly better off than their laborers, but not so much so that they were able to assert customary prerogatives over their hired hand's persons (Huang 1985, 94, 96). Under such circumstances, hired hands were no longer considered customarily servile. By 1780 the state had come to the same realization. In that year it reformed the Wanli statute, rendering the *gugongren* status inapplicable under most circumstances (Jing 1983a, 291–293; 1983b, 246).[4] Magistrates were now required to inquire into the contractual terms enunciated at the time of hiring and to investigate the nature of the laborer's working relationship with his boss before passing judgment. It was formal practice in the eighteenth and nineteenth centuries for magistrates to ask about the length of employment, whether there was a written contract, and most importantly whether laborer and employer used the prefixes "master" (*zhu*) and "servant" (*pu*). A common way of describing status equality between an employer and his laborer was to say that "they ate at the same table" (see Huang 1985, 95).

Even with these revisions, problems of the substatute's application persisted. Jing cites Qianlong-era homicide cases from Zhili, Henan, Shaanxi, Guangdong, and Jiangsu to illustrate how jurists struggled over the application of the *gugongren* statute. In a 1745 homicide case, the bondservant of a banner noble family from Zhili killed a long-term laborer hired by a commoner. The presiding magistrate sentenced the bondservant for the crime of "a slave who kills a non-debased person" (*nupi ou liangren zhi si*), but upon reviewing the case, the Zhili governor general reversed the lower court's decision. He contended that "as for bondservants and hired laborers [*gugong*], one is servitude for life while the other is servitude for one year. Both are people who have submitted to service. How can we determine the slave to be 'debased' [*jian*] and the hired laborer to be 'non-debased' [*liang*]?" (cited in Jing 1983b, 277). In this instance, the governor general of Zhili, not a legal novice, clearly applied the narrowest possible reading of the Wanli statute by equating the simple fact of year-long wage employment with "debased" status.

Using another case from Zhili, Jing references the 1735 example of agricultural laborer Shi Maoer, who was beaten to death by his boss. The presiding magistrate decided that because there was no contract signed in this case, it would be inappropriate to consider Shi a *gugongren*. But the governor general disagreed. He responded: "in village custom it is necessary to write up written contracts when hiring someone from outside (i.e., a non-native) because of the anxiety [that occurs] when a person's background is unknown. In this instance, Shi Maoer was from the same village [as his employer]. He was, therefore, known and there was mutual trust." The governor general concluded that: "Shi was, however, hired for a definite period of time and wages were agreed verbally; and though there was no contract, Shi had been employed twice before. Thus, he is not the equivalent of a short-term laborer [*duangong*] who hires for a few days or months." The governor general recommended that Shi's employer be sentenced for killing his *gugongren*. Finally, the Board of Punishment in Beijing reversed the governor's decision, reinstating Shi's "non-debased" status on the grounds there was no written contract (Jing 1983b, 272–273; also Chao 1986, 146).

There was clearly much inconsistency in findings on the matter of *gugongren* in these early years of the eighteenth century. Why Shi was found to be a commoner but not Wang under the very same statute and legal definitions is difficult to fathom. Their social background and the conditions and terms of their employment were not dissimilar enough, it would appear, to warrant the very different decisions. More than any other factor, the different judicial outcomes appear to result from the divergent "senses" of the situation rather than concrete "sociological" findings. The eighteenth century was a period of transition in laboring statuses and evidently jurists were still struggling to apply the law against the shifting social ground that attended the Ming-Qing transition (Huang 1985, 98–99).

The Gugongren Status in Eighteenth Century Manchuria

The records of two capital crimes committed in Manchuria in the early Qianlong period illustrate similar problems centering on the applicability of the *gugongren*. In each case, the employer was a rusticated bannerman and the hired hand a Han commoner and in each case the question before the courts was whether, in their relationship to their employers, these laborers were *gugongren.*

The first example was a fairly cut-and-dried case involving a Han commoner wage laborer who murdered his bannerman boss and who was found not to be a *gugongren*. In the third month of 1738 commoner Lan Youxin was hired by rusticated bannerman Yi Lai to work for three months. At the time, the two men verbally agreed to wages of five *taels*, which was to be paid in full at the end of the contracted period. When Lan fulfilled his three months employment, he was unable to return home because of a pustule on his foot. Yi continued to put him up as he recovered and so delayed paying Lan the last of his wages. When Lan eventually returned home he was still owed the money. A while later, Lan and Yi bumped into each other in the village and began to chat; they soon got into a heated argument after Yi cast aspersions on a mutual acquaintance. Yi struck Lan. The next day, still incensed, Lan went around to Yi's home and demanded the remainder of his wages. Yi refused to give him the money and, for added effect, berated Lan. Later that evening, as he confessed in court, Lan snuck into Yi's house and hacked him to death with a hatchet as he slept (XT 1739.4.2).

The judge, who was in this instance the prefect of Fengtian, was particularly interested in uncovering the circumstances of Lan's employment in order to discern whether the *gugongren* statute applied in his case. He asked Lan whether they had used a "written contract and guarantor." Lan replied there was no written contract and that they had no need for a guarantor since he and Yi had known each other well (*bing mo xie li wenqi yi wu baoren*). The prefect was satisfied that Lan was not a *gugongren*. The Shengjing Board of Punishment's vice minister, who reviewed the prefect's decision, agreed, concluding, "according to the Code in cases where those who hire their labor do so by written contract and agree to one year of employment, the designation *gugongren* applies (*yi gugongren lun*). Only in cases where they hire out for short-term wage work, by month or by day, and are paid little does the designation commoner apply (*yi fan lun*)." The vice minister had in fact cited the Ming statute as it appeared in the Qing Code nearly word for word. He then sentenced Lan Youxin to decapitation after the autumnal assizes for the intentional murder of Yi Lai. Had Lan been a *gugongren* he would have been sentenced to immediate decapitation upon review.

By comparison, the second example shows clearly the sort of confusion still surrounding the *gugongren* status in the eighteenth century. The accused in the case, commoner Chen Tianzhang, testified that after working for bannerman Lu Zhao in 1760 he returned the following year to ask for work again. But Lu Zhao was not hiring that year, so Chen found work with Lu Zhao's nephew, Lu Chenxian. Lu Chenxian testified that since he and his father knew Chen from the time he had worked for Lu Zhao, they did not bother using a contract or finding a guarantor (XT 1762. 2.5). Shortly after being hired, Chen was arrested and confessed to the attempted rape of Lu Chenxian's wife. Chen testified that after a morning of work in the fields, he, Lu Chengxian, and Lu's father all returned to the house to eat. After their meal, father and son returned to the field, but Chen remained behind to fix his smoking pipe. Chen confessed that he then began to flirt with Lu's wife and, when she refused him, he tried to rape her.

The presiding judge found that the *gugongren* statute did not apply in Chen's case and sentenced him accordingly to death by strangulation after the autumnal assizes. Again, had Chen been a *gugongren* the sentence would have been immediate execution. The Three High Courts, however, on reviewing the case, objected to this finding; it argued that status distinctions between employer and laborer applied in this case. The jurists of the Three High Courts noted that: "[we now] know that Chen Tianzhang hired himself to Lu Yongtai's household as a month laborer. To be sure, he was employed for a short period and there was no written contract; and yet it is clearly the case that Chen is a servile person. How can we dare not to employ status distinctions in deciding his punishment? . . . Being a 'labor hired without a contract' hardly accords with the definition of a commoner." The Three High Courts concluded: "The Secretary [of the Shengjing Board of Punishment] used the statutes on attempted rape and stabbing to decide on death by strangulation, but this [sentence] is not grounded in the law. Thus it is necessary to have the Secretary continue the investigation of the case." The document ends at this point.

What is striking about this case is the element of confusion over Chen's status. By all appearances, the lower court had in fact found correctly. The 1759 revision had mandated that the *gugongren* status applied only when there was a written contract and the laborer's period of contracted employment was a year or longer. In addition, it specified that "master-servant distinctions" had to be observed. The written record of Chen's trial shows, however, that none of these criteria applied in his case. He was hired for just two months, no contract was signed, and there was strong evidence that the Lus regarded Chen as their status equal. Indicative of his status equivalence was the fact that he ate with his employer; more striking, while his employers went back to work in the field after lunch, Chen had stayed behind, relaxing and fixing his pipe! Even the concluding remarks of the Three High Courts belied its decision to reverse the lower court's original sentence. In summarizing the case, the Three High Courts stated that a *gugongren* was a person hired for one year who had signed a written contract at the beginning of his employment; yet it also declared that in Chen's case the fact that he had not signed a contract was insufficient grounds to sentence him as a nondebased person.

The circumstances of Chen's case resemble the earlier-cited example of Shi Maoer, though in that case the Three High Courts came to the opposite finding while citing the same rationale. It will be remembered that whereas the governor general judged Shi Maoer to be a *gugongren*, the Three High Courts reversed the decision on the grounds that not having a contract was an indication of his *liang* status.

In his analysis of the Chen Tianzhang case, Matthew Sommer (2000) has argued that the confusion surrounding Chen's status was a sign of the increasing disparity between legal prescriptions and social representations to be found in the Code on the one hand, and changing customary and social practices/realities unfolding on the ground on the other. The back-and-forth on Chen's status is evidence of the problems the Qing judiciary faced when matching an outdated statute in the Code—along with jurists' outmoded preconceptions of the long-term laborer as a social category—to the novel agrarian social conditions of the early and middle Qing. If this were the case, then this example also shows that Qing jurists who worked closer to the ground had a very different—and probably better—understanding than their superiors of the social content of the practices used by peasants in hiring agricultural labor.[5]

We see in the trials of Lan and Chen that local and central courts were not imposing legal categories upon local society arbitrarily, even if they imposed the categories incorrectly. Rather, they were trying to evaluate social and customary practices on a case-by-case basis in order to determine whether the formal standards of what were in effect legal understandings of status categories corresponded. Yet, even as the officials in these cases struggled to apply the *gugongren* substatute appropriately, those against whom the status could be applied were becoming fewer. Indeed, they were so few in the nineteenth century that magistrates no longer probed so doggedly into the details of contractual and social relations between employers and their laborers. Instead, judges were perfunctorily recording witness testimony that boss and hired hand "ate at the same table" or "did not distinguish themselves as master and servant" to indicate status equivalence.

The Social Basis of the Demise of the Gugongren in the Qing

The Qing state's revisions of the *gugongren* statute reflected the rise of the casual and short-term labor market that attended the transition to an economy dominated by the small-holding peasant. Specialized terms for the casual labor market (*yong shi, gongfu shi*) began to appear in China in the early Qing and, by the end of the eighteenth century, if not earlier, short-term laborers outnumbered long-term laborers (Fang et al. 2000, 1857–1858). As the opposite side of the coin, the revisions to the *gugongren* statute reflected a dramatic change in the class character of those who hired labor. Whereas in the Ming much peasant labor was used on the estates of the aristocratic households and degree-holding gentry, in the Qing more and more labor was hired by modest peasants and larger village landowners. With these changes in agrarian structure, as the case of Chen Tianzhang showed, the *gugongren* statute, in its pre-1780 form, created legal confusion. Not the least of which was how to categorize those longer-term laborers who were not much different socially or economically from their employers yet, under the 1588 statute, might be considered servile.

Under these circumstances, what, for instance, was a magistrate to make of the legal status of a small-holding peasant like Xie Yingyin? Was he the social and therefore legal superior of his laborer or his equal? Xie was sixty *sui* and lived with his son. His brother was an itinerant carpenter, which left Xie and his son to work the family holding. At sixty *sui*, Xie was what peasants in the northeast called a *banlazi* or "half-hauler," someone capable of half the workload of a healthy, adult male known as a *chenggong* (NJ-Taonan 1936, 153). The son's age was not given, but judging by his father's age he was probably a *chenggong*. With only one family member capable of a full load of work, Xie hired year laborers to assist. In 1825, he hired a man named Zhang, who used to come by the village begging to work by the month or the entire year. Xie testified that he knew Zhang before employing him and that Zhang lived with Xie during his employment. Zhang was somewhat of a spendthrift; within two weeks of beginning work, he had already borrowed and used up seven thousand cash against his future wages. When he asked to borrow another eight thousand, Xie's patience broke. The two men started arguing and a fight ensued, during which Xie struck and killed wage laborer Zhang (XB 1826.4.17).

Before 1780, laborer Zhang might have been considered a *gugongren*. He was hired for the year and—as we have seen—the fact that no contract was signed did not stopped jurists from applying the *gugongren* statute in the past. Indeed, it is difficult to find significant differences between Zhang's conditions of employment and those of Chen Tianzhang. However, it is also clear that employer Xie's social standing, as a simple small-land-holding peasant, would not have justified the use of the appellation "master" as it was customarily used in either the Ming or Qing dynasties. Though the court records tell us nothing of the size of Xie's holding, it could not have been too large to have required the work of just three adult males, one of whom was elderly. Hazarding a guess, Xie probably held no more than sixty to eighty *mu*, or ten to thirteen acres. Xie was a "small-scale rich peasant," at best. That would explain why he and Zhang regarded each other as social equals who "ate at the same table" and did not call each other by the status markers "master" (*zhu*) and "servant" (*pu*) (XB 1826.4.17).

The social conditions revealed by this case are fairly typical, judging from other nineteenth-century homicide records. Many of those who needed labor in nineteenth century Manchuria had small holdings that they could mostly work with household labor. They hired help only for periods ranging from a single day to three or four months to assist when the workload on the farm peaked. These hired hands were what villagers called "short-term laborers" (*duangong*) and, for the most part, were hired from among their neighbors or from nearby communities. By contrast, fewer employers hired what villagers called "long-term laborers" (*changgong*) who were recruited to work for a year or longer and usually lived with their employer. To be sure, the legal cases should not be treated as if they were surveys. It is the case however that short-term laborers appear twice as frequently as long-term laborers in the court records, even though long-term laborers had more frequent interactions with their employers and therefore more opportunity for conflict. This ratio matches exactly the findings of twentieth-century surveys conducted by Japanese investigators of the Manchurian countryside (Isett 1998, 368, table 8.10). It also corresponds with the general pattern surmised by Chinese scholar Xu Tan, who also argues that in the Qing short-term labor was far more commonly employed than long-term labor (in Fang et al. 2000, 1857).

Against this setting, it was certainly difficult for employers to force servile status upon their hired hands who increasingly resembled them in general socioeconomic standing. Nevertheless, the small and middling peasants' need for hired labor alone cannot explain the social disappearance of the *gugongren* and other types of servile or bonded field hand. First, in the Ming dynasty small landholders had hired labor too, yet the *gugongren* category existed in both law and custom (Chao 1986, 143–147). Second, the Qing sovereign most certainly could have revised the code in ways that would have retained the servile status of those laborers who worked for degree-holding gentry. This was the intent of the original Ming statute, and similar adjustments to the Qing Code would have preserved the all important social and legal distinctions between the peasantry and the literati and between the literati and Qing aristocracy. The Qing did not choose to do so, however.

Explanations for the demise of the *gugongren* status, along with the shedding of other forms of servile status in agricultural work, have emphasized a number of factors. But at the center of most accounts sits the market and market mechanisms. In this view the spread of trade and the monetization of economic transactions on the one hand made for efficiency gains that employers captured by replacing bonded labor by wage labor and on the other hand opened up new avenues for those peasants without land.

In his archetypically market-driven account, Chao Kang explains the demise of servile agricultural labor in terms of the relative movement of prices over time. In Chao's view, as the Ming and Qing population booms made land increasingly expensive relative to labor, the fall in wages that this implied encouraged landowners to substitute more flexible and therefore more efficient wage labor for bonded labor, until the latter more or less disappeared from agricultural production (Chao 1986, 139). The same market mechanisms feature prominently in many Marxist explanations, though are read through their effects on social property relations between landholders and laborers. For instance, in Liu Yongcheng's view the rise of trade and increasing circulation of commodities exasperated economic inequalities and social differentiation and thereby issued in the creation of a large, landless class of peasants eager to hire out as wage laborers. Simultaneously, and as a result of the same mechanisms, a class of commercial farmers successful in trade took form which then turned to hiring wage labor because of its intrinsically more efficient character (Liu 1981, 3–18). Consequently, more efficient wage labor supplanted bonded labor. Elements of this argument are echoed by Xu Tan (2000). In her view, commercial forces intensified class conflict that in turn struck down servile status. Consequently, the commercialization of production and the incentives this created for landlords and employers to improve production by adopting new methods and tools destabilized production relations and the ensuing class conflict ended with laborers and tenants shedding all servile status (in Fang et al. 2000, 1864–1871, 1903–1907).[6] In each of these cases, trade was the *deus ex machina* and changes in the legal framework recognizing the end of such servile laboring statuses as the *gugongren* was its super-structural resonance.

But in either form the commercialization model is hard to reconcile with Chinese and other historical records. First, commercial forces were clearly at work in the early and mid-Ming and the population certainly grew by a considerable amount (Brook 1998a; Heidjra 1998). Yet, during this time the use of servile labor in agriculture appears to have intensified. In some areas of the country, the free tenants and laborers of the early Ming had disappeared altogether by 1600, if not earlier. In other areas bonded labor came to account for a significant proportion of the peasant population and was often associated with the most intensively commercial agriculture (Walker 1999, 33; Wakeman 1985, 621–622; Shih 1992, 134; Mazumdar 1998, 199–200). The trade-based arguments of Chao, Liu, and Xu cannot account for why commerce and population growth encouraged the substitution of wage for servile and bonded labor in the Qing, yet led to contrary outcomes in the Ming.[7] Nor can their arguments explain the timing of the end of servile labor regimes. Chao for instance argues that it was the cheapening of wage labor that made bonded labor redundant, and yet common forms of bonded labor and servile tenancy disappeared between the mid-seventeenth and early eighteenth centuries, at precisely the moment when population was falling most rapidly (due to peasant rebellion, famine, and the Qing Conquest campaigns) and labor was therefore becoming increasingly hard to come by. If the cheapening of wage labor had encouraged landholders to substitute bonded labor, why did bonded labor in fact disappear when the population was declining and the cost of labor therefore rising?

Second, it does not follow that falling population and rising wages that accompanied the Ming-Qing transition allowed bonded labor to free itself on the basis of its improved bargaining position. For one thing, the extra-economic control that landlords and the powerful wielded over their servile laborers in the Ming was secured on the basis of their political power in the local community, backed by the state and its legal courts, not on the basis of market arrangements (Walker 1999, 33; Fu 1961, 68–153). The difficulty of obtaining labor was just as likely to drive individual landlords to try to ratchet up their extra-economic power over local communities in order to capture the labor they needed, rather than accept passively the substitution of expensive wage labor. This was what occurred in eastern Europe under fairly similar macroeconomic conditions. Following the Black Death of the fourteenth century, the so-called "second serfdom" took root in Eastern Europe in the sixteenth and seventeenth centuries before the population had recovered from the plague and at a time when peasants had a better bargaining position vis-à-vis their lords. That eastern European lords were able to tie their serfs back to the land was because of their effective political organization. Moreover, serfdom remained strong in eastern European alongside population growth as lords took advantage of the European-wide upswing in grain prices in the following centuries to ratchet up surplus extraction for the grain export trade. In that case, commerce and serfdom went hand in hand (Dobb 1947; Anderson 1974; Brenner 1985b [1982]; Kula 1976; Kochanowicz 1989).

To be sure, a market for wage labor was by definition a necessary condition for the emergence of an agricultural wage laboring class. Moreover, the bargaining hand of tenants and laborers was certainly strengthened in the immediate aftermath of the population collapse that accompanied the Ming-Qing transition. Nevertheless, neither the existence nor even the expansion of trade could have been sufficient for the demise of *gugongren* and other forms of servile agricultural labor. The substitution of free for servile labor in Qing China was the result of the loss of the gentry's and big landlords' power over their servile laborers at a time when labor was more difficult to come by then before. This came as a result of rising protest and resistance that caused worsening social conditions and the loss of political order that attended the Ming-

Qing transition (Tanaka 1984, 192–211; Shih 1992, 136–140; Wiens 1980, 28; Li 1993, 22–37).[8] It was only upon their failure to reassert political control over their field laborers in the aftermath of bondservant rebellions that landlords came to accept the new wage relations and adapted the management of their holdings accordingly (Li 1993, 124–145).

Thus, to uncover the source of the *gugongren*'s disappearance, I believe we must return to the peasant uprisings that shook rural society from the 1620s and 1630s and continued into the first decades of the eighteenth century. These disturbances, many quite violent, ended with tenants and laborers freeing themselves of their prior legal dependent statuses (Li 1993, 27, 36–37; Walker 1999, 47–50, 66–67). The new Qing state, having restored local order, was either unable or unwilling to assist local elites in restoring their former authority over the peasantry. Covetous of its authority over local society, the new dynasty was eager to reduce the gentry's and big landlords' hold over the countryside as it sought to establish its own basis of power and tap into the agricultural surplus. The Qing state actively moved to protect laborers and tenants from the private authority of the gentry and big landlords on the one hand, and promoted the strengthening and expansion of the land-owning, independent peasantry on the other, until the latter became the state's principal source of revenue.[9] By the early eighteenth century, still recovering from peasant rebellions and the Manchu invasion, local gentry and big landlords lacked both the political power to restore privately the *status quo ante* and the support of the new state for such an enterprise. Unable to tie peasants back onto the land or reabsorb them into their households, big landowners were compelled to turn to new modes of organizing production and expropriating surpluses (Beattie 1979; Huang 1990, 58–59; Walker 1999, 69). The disappearance of the *gugongren* from the late imperial countryside coincided with the expansion of the small landholding peasantry and the market for wage labor, but was ultimately the result of the weakening of gentry control over local society (Li 1993, 67–71, 78–81, 124–136).

Turning to Manchuria, there is no evidence to suggest that those affiliated with the banner system who resided in the countryside were able to press commoner peasants into servitude. Thus, while there is evidence that a small number of rusticated bannermen and bailiffs possessed Han slaves (see JCA 1806, 3684; also see Wang 1990, 76–77), there is no evidence that they used the labor of *gugongren* or similar servile field hands in agricultural production. That this would be the case was certainly not predictable given the persistence of the Conquest Elite's legal and social privileges. Recent work has revised the once-dominant understanding of the Qing state to show that the banner system was not ancillary to but definitive of its constitution.[10] The banner-commoner dichotomy helped secure dynastic power, as it buttressed the banner/Manchu-commoner/Han binary and sustained the prerogatives of the former over the latter. One might expect rusticated bannermen, rural banner agents, bailiffs, and even serfs to deploy their standing within the banner system to press commoners into some form of service. The Qing state did, for instance, require that rusticated bannermen and serfs register commoners whom they hired for longer periods as household members. Yet, despite the obvious ways in which this might have allowed bannermen to subsume these laborers as household dependents, this did not occur. More striking still is the clear evidence that when investigating crimes, Qing magistrates accepted the possibility that rusticated bannermen who labored for commoners were *gugongren*. If true, this would of course have constituted a complete reversal of social power relations.

The Status of Wage Laborers in Law and Custom in Manchuria

In the fifty-nine court cases involving agricultural laborers that I have located and examined,[11] there is only one instance of the court applying the *gugongren* statute, and as seen there is some question as to whether the Wanli statute was misapplied in that case. (There is similarly only one mention of a slave.) In all other instances, standard declarations of social and customary equality were expressed such that employers and laborers alike stated that they "sat together and ate together" (*tong zuo tong chi*), did not make "master-servant distinctions" (*wu zhu-pu mingfen*), and that they "knew each other and shared no animosity" (*renshi bing mei chou*).

Expressions of a laborer's customary independence of his employer's household are evident in an early Qianlong case in which the bondservant to a rusticated bannerman was murdered by a hired hand. The question before the magistrate in this case was whether the hired hand was also his employer's servant and thus commensurate in status with the man he murdered. As in such cases, the form of the answer had bearing on the punishment.

According to testimony, the accused, a commoner named Shao Lun, had immigrated from Laiyang in Shandong to Fengtian in search of his elder brother. Unable to find him, he turned to "making his living by selling his labor abroad" (*zai wai maigong duri*). In 1736 he arrived at the village of Chazigoutun, where he found employment as a day laborer working for bannerman Yang Yongkui. Because he had no home, Shao Lun was given a room to share with Yang's bondservant, a Han Chinese named Zhang Youku. Over the next few days Shao and Zhang worked together hoeing Yang's fields. One day it rained, however, and the two men remained indoors and drank. Intoxicated, Zhang made impolitic references to Shao's native place, suggesting that "no decent folk ever came from Shandong." Shao objected and added similarly disparaging remarks for good measure. This was evidently more than Zhang could bear and the two men came to blows. Shao Lun claimed that in the struggle he used a club to strike Zhang, who died the following day from his injuries (MQ 1737, A71–45).

With Shao Lun's confession to murder, this was an open-and-shut case. All that remained before sentencing was for the magistrate to uncover the precise nature of Shao Lun's relationship to his employer, bannerman Yang Yongkui, to determine the appropriate sentence. The question at hand was whether Shao had "killed another's bondservant during an affray" or "killed a fellow bondservant during an affray." The verdict depended upon Shao's customary status vis-à-vis Yang, since Zhang Youku's status as Yang's bondservant was not in dispute. After questioning Shao, the presiding magistrate concluded that Shao Lun and his employer's bannerman Yang Yongkui were status equals, even though one was a commoner and the other a bannerman. Consequently, Shao was found to have committed the crime of "killing another's bondservant." Passing judgment, the magistrate stated that "while working as a laborer for Yang Yongkui, Shao Lun beat to death Yang's bondservant [Zhang Youku]" (*dasi yin pu*).

Another case in point is the court record of an 1826 homicide trial. According to testimony, commoner Shi Dezhi murdered his employer, bannerman Wang Liangren. Shi Dezhi, a twenty-nine *sui* commoner who lived in a village three *li* (one mile) from the deceased's home, was hired to work two and a half months. Shi began work in the spring of 1826. During his employment, he both lived and ate with his employer. One day in the early summer, Shi Dezhi had returned from working in the fields in the rain when Wang Liangren demanded he fetch some water. Shi Dezhi complained that he had only just changed into dry clothes and refused to go out again. Wang Liangren berated Shi Dezhi for his idleness and the two men started fighting. Shi Dezhi struck Wang Liangren with a club, killing him instantly (XB 1826.9.23).

During questioning, the magistrate specifically asked Shi Dezhi, members of Wang's household, and neighbors in the banner village whether employer and hired hand had observed any customary master-servant distinctions. In his finding, the magistrate declared: "Shi Dezhi and Wang Liangren were acquaintances and there was no animosity between them. This year, on the seventeenth day of the fourth month, Shi Dezhi was hired by Wang Liangren's household to work as a month laborer. He sat with Wang Liangren and they ate together; moreover they did not differentiate themselves as master and servant." The magistrate was satisfied that Shi was of "nondebased" (*liang*) status and accordingly sentenced him under Statute 290 of the Qing Code for the crime of "killing another during an affray," which required his "execution by strangulation after the autumn assizes." Had the magistrate found reason to believe commoner Shi Dezhi was a servile laborer, and therefore "debased" (*jian*), he would have been required to sentence Shi to execution by decapitation without delay, under Statute 313. The Three High Courts agreed with the finding of the lower courts and ordered the sentence carried out.[12] These court cases are illustrative of the general recognition by officials and peasants alike that commoner laborers in the northeast were the status equals of their bannerman bosses in the early nineteenth century.

Despite continued discrimination between bannermen and commoners in a variety of realms, these ethnojuridical differences did not result in customary or legal status distinctions in the wage labor relationship. As testified in numerous court cases, rusticated bannermen, serfs, and commoners in the Manchurian countryside considered each other social equals, and magistrates judging these cases saw no reason to think otherwise. More surprising is the fact that, among Qing jurists, neither banner affiliation nor standing as a "regular bannermen" (*zhengshen qiren*) precluded servile status as a wage laborer. Adjudicators were not only trying to uncover the customary status of commoner wage laborers who worked for bannermen, but also that of bannermen and serfs who were hired to work for commoners. In the eyes of the state, it seems, banner affiliation did not preclude the applicability of *gugongren* status. Thus, as late as 1864, the magistrate handling the murder of the young boy and bannerman Zhao Yaodu at the hands of his employer, commoner Yu Tai, specifically asked about the social nature of their relationship to uncover whether Zhao was contractually servile to Yu (XB 1864.4.26). Upon questioning, Yu Tai testified that there were no "master-servant" distinctions between himself and Zhao Yaodu. Similarly, in 1843 bannerman Bai Fuliang who killed his commoner boss was found to be his employer's status equal after the court determined that both men "ate at the same table" and neither employed "master-servant distinctions" (XB 1844, 02495).

What is interesting about both cases was the possibility, implied by the magistrates' line of inquiry, that rusticated bannermen who hired out to commoners might be customarily and legally considered their employer's servile laborers. The possibility that a bannerman might be his commoner employer's servile laborer represented a reversal of the banner privileges that Edward Rhoads (2000) notes were institutionalized at all levels and in every area of the Qing state and its judicial system, from official appointments to the exam system to the law (42–45). In neither case were the bannermen found to be their commoner employers' servants, to be sure. But the facts of the magistrate's questioning and the recording of responses are telling in themselves for what they say about official presumptions of the status hierarchy that separated the banner and civil populations in rural Manchuria.

Customary equality between laborers and their employers took root in the northeast alongside the spread of those customary practices that underwrote peasant possession of land. On the one hand, the strengthening of *all* cultivators' customary hold over their land established the material basis for customary equality between commoners and those attached to the banner system. On the other hand, the rise of the small landholding peasant to numerical dominance, and his need to hire labor for both short and long periods, dissolved the social distinctions in wealth and power that had previously characterized relations between servile laborers and their big land-owning employers. On the basis of these developments, those peasants affiliated with the banner structures—whether rusticated bannermen or serfs—found that at the village level they could not reconstruct customary and social hierarchies of power that would enable them to enforce relational status distinctions between themselves and commoner peasants. Institutional distinctions imposed by the state between banner-affiliated households (whether rusticated bannermen or serfs) and commoner households were thus paralleled in rural Manchuria by the emergence of more equitable social relations.[13]

Agricultural Wage Labor and the Mode of Agricultural Production

Much ink has been expended in the Chinese historiography discussing the emergence and historical role of agricultural wage labor and in particular the large landowners who employed them. Chinese scholars have termed these "managerial landlords" (*jingying dizhu*) in order to distinguish them from rentier landlords. Whereas the latter garnered income from tenants who rented small plots, the former are considered large-scale, capital-intensive, commercial farmers whose distinguishing characteristic was their employment of efficient wage labor. They are considered in short the progressive expression of China's commercial revolution and the seed of what scholars refer to as China's "sprouts of capitalism." The immediate historical reference is the classical case of English agrarian capitalism that began to take shape in the mid- to late sixteenth century and was characterized by a tripartite relationship of landlord, commercial tenant, and wage labor (cf. Dobb 1947, 125; Brenner 1985b [1982], 301; Allen 1992).[14] The theoretical references are Marx's discussion of the transformation of class relations in the English countryside that appears at the end of volume one of *Capital* and Lenin's study of Russian agriculture prior to 1917 (Marx 1976, 877–913; Lenin 1956).

In the "capitalist sprouts" literature, the managerial farmer is the social manifestation of an indigenous structural transformation in the economy. The thesis' *locus classicus* lies in the scholarly work of Jing Su and Luo Lun (1959, 1978), though others continue to make it in one form or another.[15] Jing and Luo maintained, in their ground-breaking study of the north China plain, that in the late imperial period incipient capitalist property relations had taken form as a consequence of the mutually reinforcing effects of commercialization and social differentiation. Market forces, they argued, on the one hand issued in the agglomeration of ever larger holdings as commercially successful producers sought to take advantage of the economies of scale in crop farming, and on the other hand created a growing body of failed peasants who having lost their land joined the ranks of landless agricultural wage workers. The result, Jing and Luo argued, was an epoch-making transformation of agricultural production led by the "managerial farmer" that was only cut short by imperialism in the second half of the nineteenth century.

To make the argument, Jing and Luo accumulated a mass of historical evidence and deployed novel methodologies such as field interviews. Since Jing and Luo wrote, however, two criticisms have been leveled not at their methods and sources but at their interpretation. First, the largest of what Jing and Luo claimed were estates that were worked as unitary farms by wage labor were in most instances divided up into smaller holdings and then rented out to tenants who farmed mostly with household labor. The typical "large farm" was in fact quite small. Second, their claim for the emergence of a class of agricultural laborers was found to have been much exaggerated. The majority of laborers in agriculture were not landless laborers but members of smallholding peasant households. These households used the income derived from hiring out its members to round off family consumption needs that their small plots were unable to meet.[16]

Nevertheless, the errors of their interpretation do not gainsay Jing and Luo's emphasis on the transformative and progressive implications of the emergence of the large-scale farm employing wage labor. Historically, the path to agricultural development has been through increases in economies of scale. The only two European nations to experience sustained growth in labor productivity in agriculture in the early modern period (the Low Countries and England) were also the only two to witness steady increases in farm size and the squeezing off of the land and eventual disappearance of the small-holding peasantry (Allen 1992; Rösener 1994, 120–122; O'Brien and Keyder 1978, 132). As Jing and Luo note, larger farms benefit from the elimination of disguised underemployment of household labor, from the ability to adjust labor costs to labor needs more efficiently through the use of hired hands, from having more capital for better and heavier working tools and more and stronger draft animals, and from the greater use of fertilizer (Jing and Luo 1978, 112–113, 181–189). For essentially these reasons, in early modern England and the Low Countries the supersession of small farms and the emergence of large ones made a critical contribution to the growth of labor productivity, especially in basic food production (Brenner 19885b [1982], 299–317; 2001, 300–302, 314; Brenner and Isett 2001, 626–627).

Wage Labor and Scale of Production in Rural Manchuria

Historians of rural Manchuria have pointed to the similar presence of large holdings worked by wage labor as evidence of proto-capitalist development and/or the modernization of agricultural production (Yi 1993, 325, 471–473; Liu 1995, passim). These works have emphasized developments in the period following the opening of Niuzhuang to foreign trade in 1862, even though holdings previously were on average greater in size and commercial forces were already in motion by that time.[17] As with the large landowners studied by Jing and Luo, a close examination by scholars of Manchuria demonstrates that most rented the greater part of their land out to others in small holdings. This was certainly true at the end of the Qing, when surveys were first made of the rural social structure and landholding patterns (Yi 1993, 323). In the fourteen Fengtian counties in 1909, those with holdings of three thousand *mu* or more rented on average more than eighty percent of their land out. Thus, in the 1880s the reverend John Ross, who worked as a missionary in Fengtian, observed that "[t]here are many proprietors of 100 acres, and not a few of 200; but, though they are to be found, proprietors of more than 500 acres are rare. . . . When a family small in numbers owns a large farm, it is usual to let the farm in small lots of from five to thirty acres" (cited in Jamieson 1888, 80–81). Large landowners with large families—Ross writes of households with as many as two hundred people!—may have worked some or all of their land, with or without wage labor; but the majority of large landowners would clearly not have had sufficient family members and would therefore have rented their land out.[18]

There is no evidence in the Qing sources of the emergence of large-scale, commercial farming in Manchuria, nor is there any evidence of a large and fully market-dependent wage-laboring class that might work such holdings. Everything points instead to the accession to most arable land by small landholders whose needs for wage labor were far different. That development was itself the outcome of the pattern or mode of colonization that characterized Han settlement in the northeast. As we have seen, colonization was not characterized by large-scale engrossments, but by a combination of small land grants and the slow and gradual reclamation of wastelands by individual households. It is easy to see how Qing policies might foster this pattern. In the northeast, the only individuals permitted to engross land on a significant scale were the highest members of the Qing Conquest Elite—the monarchy and nobility—and their estates were farmed by serf households in small allotments. As for rusticated bannermen, regional authorities limited how much land they could open. Initial land grants were limited to thirty-six *mu* in south Manchuria and sixty in the Jilin and Heilongjiang. Thereafter, rusticated bannermen had to petition banner authorities to undertake the cultivation of new land. While legal petitions were often granted, bannermen were nonetheless not permitted to engross vast holdings. This was part of a broader strategy documented by Robert Lee (1970) by which the Qing emperors precluded the emergence in Manchuria of a regional, landed elite that might challenge dynastic claims over the territories.[19] As for Han settlers, they could not easily engross vast holdings privately—assuming they so desired and had the wherewithal—because the scale of such operations would have made them easier targets for field administrators who were supposedly on the lookout for them. Consequently, those who did engross large holdings were mostly privileged bondservants serving as bailiffs to the imperial and aristocratic households who, it appears, used their power and connections to accede to land within and around their estates (Enatsu 1989, 12–13). Though a few bailiffs had emerged as significant local power brokers by the end of the Qing, archival evidence suggests that most bailiffs were burdened by debts as they borrowed cash to meet their rent quotas. Most land engrossment thus proceeded on a relatively small scale under the radar of the local officials.

In Manchuria, Qing policies had the effect of fostering the establishment and reproduction of the small land-holding economy, some of it intentional and some not. Consequently, despite the important differences in land arrangements between Manchuria (and parts of Zhili where estates and bannerlands were also found) and China Proper, we see Qing policies supporting the consolidation of the peasant small farm as the basic unit of production in the countryside everywhere. The policies of keeping land taxes and surcharges relatively low, promoting peasant homesteading on the frontiers, and the abrogation of gentry rights to privately punish tenants and laborers were part and parcel of a strategy to support the small-holding peasantry, which in turn was easier to tax and posed much less of a political threat to state power than estate holders or substantial landlords (Huang 1985, 86).

To be sure, the nature of the sources permits only modest speculation on the scale of farms, the size of the holdings of those who hired out, and the proportion of fully landless laborers. Beginning with wage labor, we may reasonably assume that because land was relatively plentiful, and because there was little large-scale private engrossment, only a minority of agricultural laborers were fully landless. The only conclusive sources available are, unfortunately, from the twentieth century. A survey of the landholding patterns of 681 households shows that in the mid-1930s just under seventeen percent of farm workers (five percent of the total population) hired out for the entire year in north Manchuria, where the land-to-labor ratio was comparable to the most densely populated areas of the Qing.[20] These people were presumably either fully landless, or came from farms so small their labor was redundant to their families (TKK 1937, 17–18, table 7).[21] People who hired out for the day or by the month—people for whom wage work usually supplemented their income from farming their own holdings—outnumbered yearlong laborers two to one (Isett 1998, 368, table 8.10).[22] At a time when commercial forces were more strongly felt than at any time prior—when Manchuria was meeting eighty percent of world demand for soybeans—there is no evidence of a substantial class of rural dispossessed that acquired both its earnings and sustenance entirely from the market, just as there is no evidence for substantial commercial farming enterprises hiring labor.

As for the large holdings at the end of the Qing to which Yi Baozhong and others point as evidence of a modern, capitalist farming, most of these were farmed in small rented plots. Again, data are scarce for the Qing but in 1917 the average farm in southern Manchuria was just over forty *mu* (seven acres); in Jilin it was one hundred *mu* (seventeen acres); and in Heilongjiang it was 180 *mu* (thirty acres) (Adachi 1925, 142, 144). Rougher estimates suggest farms in southern Manchuria were larger in the Qing, as might be expected given the lower population levels and how household division practices diminished farm sizes over time. Using population data compiled in Appendix A, and assuming an average of six persons per household (Lee and Campbell 1997, 110, table 6.1), then in 1800 the average holding was a little over one hundred *mu* (18.6 acres), by 1850 it was just under seventy *mu* (11.6 acres). These farms were of course large by Chinese standards. But agricultural methods were also less labor intensive than those of agriculturally similar north China so that farms of this size did not require as much in the way of labor inputs.

Turning to the court records, we see that few large landholders ever appeared in court. Presumable, the truly wealthy and powerful had other ways to handle disputes, or the means to avoid appearing in court. However, there are also no examples of wage laborers in the court records who worked on large holdings as part of a gang of hired hands and who could not have bribed their way out of court. But there is evidence pointing to rich peasants who held and worked holdings somewhat in excess of one or two hundred *mu* using hired wage labor, as well as peasants with even small holdings of thirty to fifty *mu* who also employed field hands. Armed with some knowledge of the number and age of adult laborers in a household from the court records and a sense of the intensity of farm work from other sources, it is possible to make some suppositions about farm sizes.

Yu Bangcai was one example of a peasant who seems to have employed larger than average amounts of labor. He lived in a village near Changchun, Jilin in the middle of the nineteenth century at a time when that area was still sparsely populated by the standards of north China and south Manchuria. At forty-nine *sui*, Yu Bangcai was the head of his household and what peasants in the northeast still call a "big half-hauler" (*da banlazi*). By Manchurian count, a "big hauler" is between the ages of seventeen and nineteen or forty-five and fifty *sui* and had less endurance than a "full laborer" (*chenggong*), who was between the ages of twenty and forty-four *sui*. However, a "big hauler" is capable of heavier and more effort than a "hauler" (*banlazi*), who is between the ages of fourteen and sixteen or older than fifty *sui* (NJ-Panshi 1936, 276; KKK 1937, 34–36). At forty-nine, Yu was therefore past his working prime and on his way to being a "hauler" (*banlazi*). In addition to himself, he had two sons who were in their twenties and who were therefore "full laborers." One son was married and had an infant boy incapable of any work. The family had not yet divided its property, so the three men still farmed the holding together (XB 1851, 2514).

Yu employed a thirty-two *sui* "year laborer" (*niangong*) named Ren Tingfu. In addition, he recruited someone who in the northeast was called a *bangqing* named Li Desheng. The *bangqing* was a type of field hand peculiar to this region, somewhere in between a conventional wage laborer and a tenant. The *bangqing* lived with the landowner's household and assisted in fieldwork, though in some cases the *bangqing* worked a proportion of his employer's land on his own. In either case, a *bangqing*'s wages were a portion of the harvest paid in kind and were always more than the wages received by a standard long-term laborer. He was taken on almost as a shareholding employee. According to twentieth-century surveys, the *bangqing* was a fairly common type of field hand in Jilin and Heilongjiang, leading one to believe the arrangement had much to do with the difficulty of securing labor and cash currency in more sparsely settled areas (KKK 1937, 6–14). Employing a *bangqing* was perhaps a way for Yu Bangcai to guarantee a laborer at a place and time when labor was more difficult to come by than land.

The Yu family farm employed five adult male laborers, four of whom were capable of the heaviest work, judging by their ages. Undoubtedly Yu had a larger than average holding to have required this much labor, but the court record does not tell us how large. A source dating to thirty years prior to this case, and describing conditions in the same region, states that one adult male and a draft animal working *tirelessly* could cultivate one hundred *mu* (ten *shang*), and with a second draft animal and the help of a hired hand, could cultivate twice as much (Saying'e 1939, 178).[23] Taking the average area worked by an adult male to be one hundred *mu*, Yu possessed at most a holding as large as five hundred *mu*, or roughly eighty acres.[24]

This was indeed a large holding, but there appears to have been nothing typical about it. Rich peasants such as Yu Bangcai, who commanded larger pools of labor, appear rarely in the legal and other historical records. Far more common in the sources are middling and even small landholding peasants who hired wage labor by the day or month to assist when seasonal chores demanded greater labor inputs than the family could provide. At the end of the Qing, when hard numbers are first available, more than half of all surveyed households in Fengtian (south Manchuria) hired some labor during the year at a time when the average holding was about forty *mu* (FNDS 1909, 4.3:1–6).[25] A century earlier, holdings were certainly larger, but as noted the land was also worked far less intensively and for lower yields.

Turning again to the court records, we see evidence that middling and smallholding peasants employed small amounts of wage labor and that they did so for short periods of time. For example, in the spring of 1875 Zhang Chuanlu hired a laborer named Cai to assist in preparing and planting the fields (XT 1875.4.29).[26] According to the records of the case, Chuanlu was forty-three *sui* and lived with his younger brother, sister-in-law, and their daughter. His parents and wife were dead and he had no children of his own. There is good reason to believe, moreover, that Chuanlu's brother was away. He never testified in court, even though adult male relatives were usually questioned in homicide cases, especially when they lived in the house of the defendant or deceased, and he was not cited as working in the fields with Chuanlu and Cai. Even with a modest-sized holding, Chuanlu would have needed the assistance of a hired laborer at the busiest times of the agricultural season.

It was also common for households without adult males to hire field hands to assist. Such circumstances probably arose frequently when the adult male capable of work had gone off and not returned, or was dead or incapacitated by illness or injury, and other household males were either too old or too young to take up heavy farm work. An example was seventy *sui* Shi Keju who had fifty *mu* and lived alone with his eleven *sui* grandson. Shi was clearly too old to work the land himself, and his grandchild too young. So he depended upon hired laborers and in the summer of 1867 he hired a day laborer to help with the summer weeding (XB 1867.6.17).[27] In a similar example, Xie Yingyin was also elderly, at sixty *sui*, and lived with his only son, who was a mere fourteen *sui*, and his older brother. The brother, however, made a living as a carpenter and was not at home. Xie Yingyin's wife had passed away sometime before, leaving the elderly Yingyin and his son Shiliang to work the holding. Unable to work the farm on their own, Xie hired a forty *sui* laborer for the year to help (XB 1826.4.17).

Judging from other court records, Shi Keju and Xie Ying were fairly typical employers (e.g., XB 1822, n.n.; 1837, 01601; 1844, 02495; 1851, 2514; Isett 1998,

210–219, 230–236). As was the case in the twentieth century, when Japanese surveys document that day and month laborers outnumbered year laborers nearly two to one (NJ-Series 1934–1936), so it appears that in the Qing most of those who hired field hands recruited short-term laborers for the day or month. They hired these laborers, moreover, during periods of peak labor demand, to assist in field preparation and planting, weeding, or the fall harvest and threshing, chores that required an intensity of work that household labor could not meet. Finally, they hired only one or two at a time.

The labor market was differentiated in ways that reflected both the labor needs and structure of Manchuria's small landholding peasant economy. Twentieth-century ethnographic work shows that labor was hired by the day, month, or year. As in China proper, the designation given to the types of laborer was an indication of the length of their contract (Myers 1970, 50–51, 90–91; Huang 1985, 80–81). "Day labor" and "month labor" (*rigong* and *yuegong*) were known collectively as "short-term labor" (*duangong*) whereas "year labor" (*niangong*) was known as "long-term labor" (*changgong*). Day labor was hired by the day whereas "month labor" was usually hired for three to four months, covering the period from the early spring to the late summer (for field preparation, planting, and weeding), or from the early summer to the late fall (for weeding, harvesting, threshing, and hauling). Year labor was hired from the first or second lunar month of the year until the end of the lunar year and helped not only with field work but also other chores around the farm, including fixing tools, watching and herding livestock, preparing fertilizer, carrying goods to market, and helping with domestic work (Isett 1998, 208–214).

Because, agricultural production was dominated by smaller farms that could be worked by family labor with only moderate assistance from hired hands, most labor needs were met by hiring day and month laborers. There was far less demand for long-term laborers. As the opposite side of the coin, because the economy was dominated by smaller holders there were few fully landless laborers seeking full-time employment. Most wage workers came from households with holdings too small to absorb all family labor but who were not yet fully separated from the land.[28]

Farm Size, Wage Labor, and Their Significance for Economic Development

Following the establishment in the countryside of de facto peasant possession in land, confirmed at the village level through peasant self-governance, and following the replacement of some forms of servile labor by nonservile agricultural wage labor in farming, no further structural transformations were forthcoming. Developments as they stood were of course not without import. In theory, households were now able to adjust their labor inputs with greater sensitivity to labor needs because wage labor could be hired at times of peak workload to assist household labor already in the fields. Conversely, the development of mechanisms for handling land sales and rentals allowed households in theory to adjust the size of their holdings in line with family labor.

However, these developments were predicated upon and embedded within a social formation that established limits to economic growth. In this regard, *pace* the proponents of the "capitalist sprouts" thesis, we can point to the fact that in Manchuria there were no discernable trends toward increasing economies of scale and greater reliance upon wage labor in agriculture—either in the Qing or early twentieth century.[29] Moreover, any advantage that the Manchuria peasant may have had in farm size over other parts of China in the early Qing dissipated with time. Between 1750 and the early twentieth century, the average size of farms in the northeast shrank from perhaps 150 *mu* (twenty-five acres) to forty *mu* (eight acres), by which time, it should be noted, perhaps sixteen percent of those laboring in agriculture were full-time wage laborers. As Chapter 7 demonstrates, this decline in farm size alone constituted a partial barrier to the improvement in the productivity of labor.

As noted, Chinese scholars such as Jing and Luo and Xu Tan are correct to emphasize the significance of the appearance of large-scale commercial farming and market-dependent agricultural wage labor for economic growth, even if the actual extent of these developments in Qing China was limited. On the one hand, as Jing and Luo note, larger farms benefited from greater economies of scale and often had higher productivity due to the elimination of disguised underemployment, the use of more and better tools, the availability of more and better draft animals, and the increased use of fertilizer. On the other hand, the appearance of a substantial wage-laboring class that, in Xu Tan's (in Fang Xing et al. 2000) words, was fully separated from the land would have made for a substantial "home market" for cheap consumable goods and thus propelled the process of commercialization and industrialization. The problem for Jing and Luo and Xu Tan is that there is no evidence for increasing economies of scale in agriculture as a whole or for the appearance of a substantial wage-laboring class.

The importance of such developments is clear enough when we return to the classic case of capitalist development. As Ellen Meiksins Wood (2002) points out in her analysis of early modern England, a growing body of landless and market-dependent laborers constituted a huge market that needed to buy all of its basic necessities because it no longer produced them directly. Though their wages were initially low, the relative weight of wage laborers in the population made for a significant home or domestic market; as their number grew relative to the entire population, and as their wages rose with gains in productivity, they propelled the commercialization of production more generally (Wood 2002 , 99; cf. Coleman 1977, 102–103, tables 8 and 9; Clark 2004, 28–31; Wrigley 1985, tables 7.4, 7.5). The dramatic commercialization of food output was but one outcome of this process; by 1800 something in the order of ninety percent of food output in England was marketed, compared to ten percent or so in China as a whole (see Chapter 8). Simultaneously there ensued in early modern England a classical process of social differentiation resulting in the rise of a class of substantial commercial tenant farmers, the yeomen. The increase in the size of farms and the stepped-up accumulation of capital was part and parcel of this process and resulted in the secular rise in agricultural productivity (Brenner and Isett 2002, 626–628). Between 1500 and 1750, agricultural labor productivity grew by between fifty-two and sixty-seven percent (Allen 2000, 20, table 8; Wrigley 1985, 720, table 1).[30] Proponents of the Chinese "capitalist sprouts" argument are hard-pressed to point to comparable developments in Qing China, a fact that Xu Tan herself cedes at points in her analysis (in Fang et al. 2000, 1906).

To make explicit the structural differences in their respective agrarian regimes, for now we need only compare the size of farms and the size of the wage laboring class in early modern England and Qing Manchuria. Where by 1800 Manchurian farms averaged a little over one hundred *mu* (a little over sixteen acres), England's averaged nine hundred *mu* (150 acres). Even the more substantial cultivators in Manchuria (and north China) managed holdings that were smaller than the English average. Take the just-discussed example of Yu Bangcai, for instance. Judging from the amount of labor he commanded, Yu *may* have had a farm in the 1850s that, at eighty-three acres, was still only half the size of the *average* English farm in 1800. More to the point, the average farm size in the northeast was falling whereas farm size in England was rising.

As the obverse of those developments, by the time of England's "Glorious Revolution" in 1688, when the country was still overwhelmingly agrarian, perhaps as much as half of those in agriculture were separated completely from the land and worked as wage earners (Chambers 1972, 38–39, table 2; Lindert 1980, 702–704, table 3, 705). Though Qing era sources for Manchuria only allow for educated estimates, there is no evidence pointing to comparable developments there. Nor is there evidence for comparable developments anywhere in the empire. In the 1920s and 1930s, when the average north Manchurian farm was somewhere between fifteen and thirty acres, a mere sixteen percent of the rural population who worked in the fields were wage laborers. In China as a whole, agricultural wage laborers were between eight and ten percent of the population in the early twentieth century.[31]

Developments in holding size in Qing Manchuria (and north China)—far from signaling the emergence of large-scale, commercial farming employing efficient wage labor in the English fashion—point to the continuation of the peasant pattern of property holding and falling farm sizes. Across the Qing, though Manchuria's large peasant holdings were bigger than anything possible on the north China plain, they were no bigger than the typical peasant holdings of medieval England and early modern France (cf. Miller and Hatcher 1978, 143; LeRoy Ladurie 1987, 184, 192; Thoen 2001, 114);[32] and agricultural wage laborers in Manchuria were mostly from small landholding families rather than fully landless wage laborers. The typical wage labor came from a household whose holding was too small to make full use of his labor. He was what Philip Huang (1985), R. Bin Wong (1997), and others have called the "semi-proletarianized peasant." In this regard, the agricultural wage labor market in Manchuria is further evidence of the ways in which the agrarian social formation of the late eighteenth and nineteenth centuries shielded peasants from full market dependency.

Structurally speaking, therefore, rural Manchuria (and China Proper) looked nothing like rural England. If institutions do matter in history, as more and more historians of China's late imperial economy rightly emphasize, then the different growth potentials of each social formation needs to be taken into account. In its basic outlines, rather than looking like England or the Low Countries, the structure of farming in Qing China approached that of early modern France and other parts of continental Europe such as Flanders. In those parts of Europe, until very late, farming was also done by small-scale landholding peasants with limited capital who produced a small agricultural surplus (O'Brien and Keyder 1978, 138) and who relied upon wage labor (and proto-industry) to supplement farm incomes and thereby make survival possible (Thoen 2001, 114). Household labor in France remained trapped on the land for lack of off-farm alternatives, leading peasants in turn to favor labor-intensifying over labor-saving means of farming. Historian Roger Price (1975, 62–71) sums up the situation when he writes that the weight of France's rural population before the 1840s made for a "labour intensive rather than capital intensive system" in which peasants preferred to substitute the inefficient sickle for the labor-saving scythe (cf. Price 1996, 105–107; Moulin 1991, 50–54, 100–101, 114–115; O'Brien and Keyder 1978, 132, 137–138). Not surprisingly, agriculture in places such as rural France and Flanders lagged behind England into the second half of the nineteenth century (Allen 2000; Maddison 2001; O'Brien and Keyder 1978, 137–139).

Consequently, while older modes of political compulsion were increasingly absent from agricultural production in rural China, wage labor remained firmly embedded within a broader set of social property relations that, I would argue, continued to constitute a barrier to development. Rather than undermining the dominant property system in a way that might occasion a structural break capable of unleashing economic growth, the spread of new agricultural wage relations in the Qing served to perpetuate the dominant property relations by providing households with an outlet for redundant family labor that brought in income, buoyed up standards of living, and, as it did in other parts of China, ultimately strengthened the peasant's grip on land (Huang 1985, 195–199, 201).[33]

PART THREE

State, Trade, and Peasant Agriculture

Developments in the Manchurian Economy

PART THREE PROVIDES an account and explanation of developments in agriculture and trade in the eighteenth and nineteenth centuries. In it, I show that while the agricultural economy grew both extensively (via the colonization of more and more wasteland at the hands of more and more immigrants) and intensively (as peasants applied greater and greater amounts of labor to their plots), it did not grow in relative terms (with steady and incremental improvements in output per unit of labor input). That pattern of growth was, I argue, the upshot of the consolidation, discussed in Part Two, of a specific set of social property relations in the eighteenth century. I argue that, by virtue of the fact of peasant possession of land, peasants in Manchuria were not required to specialize for the market and were therefore free to pursue valued social objectives which, over time, made it ever more difficult to specialize, accumulate capital, and improve labor productivity in agriculture. I argue that the practice of partible property division among sons, made possible by peasant ownership of land, led to declining holding size and a population growth rate that exceeded the expansion of arable land. I show that peasants responded to diminishing plot size by raising output, in an effort to maintain the same levels of consumption as before. But in order for them to do so, given both the diminishing quantities of not only land but also and especially capital they could dispose of per worker, they could not avoid increasing labor inputs for any given output. A long-term trend to declining labor productivity was therefore unavoidable. That this pattern was sustainable for such a long period is explained by the fact that peasants could always open new land farther north.

Second, I show that by 1800 Manchuria was integrated within the Qing long-distance trading system (and by implication, the empire-wide division of labor) and served a vital function supplying China's densely populated cores (particularly Jiangnan) with much-needed grain and soybeans used in the manufacture of oil-cake fertilizers. Using revised acreage and population data and other sources I also provide rough estimates of Manchuria's export capacity in grain and soybeans. While exports were considerably lower than some previous estimates, it is clear that Manchuria supplied what, in another context, Kenneth Pomeranz (2000) has called "ghost acres," thereby making possible the labor-intensive route of agricultural development followed by the cores.

Part Three then argues that given the structural limitations on agricultural expansion in Manchuria, regional officials closely monitored grain and soybean exports to protect the region's peasants from poor harvests. On the one hand, authorities recognized merchants and grain circulation as an acceptable good in the abstract, but on the other remained skeptical of merchants as individuals and on guard for merchant profiteering. I also show that because peasants did not have to respond to the market, by virtue of the protection afforded them by their possession of land, they did not respond to rising food prices by producing more for the market. Individually merchants therefore could not be sure they would acquire the goods they needed to reproduce themselves. Moreover, since merchants had no means of guaranteeing returns on their investments in agriculture, because they had no political control over agricultural producers and because peasants were not themselves subject to the disciplining effects of the market, merchants were unwilling to invest their capital in improving agricultural production. Under these conditions, merchants found that the best means to ensure profits was to come together politically to form merchant organizations and commodity guilds to regulate themselves and to protect their market positions by precluding competitive price cutting.

CHAPTER SEVEN

Household Formation, Property Division, and Agricultural Change in the Peasant Economy

THE PHYSICAL TRANSFORMATION of the rural northeast under the Han hoe and plow was configured and made possible by the spread of a social property regime derivative of north China. That entailed more than the simple transferal (and replication) of the practices of one region to another. The appearance and spread of customary practices were framed by the expectations and practices specific to the north Chinese peasants who migrated to the northeast,[1] by the willingness of already established communities to take on these practices as their own, and by the state's and the regional government's desire to contain commoner settlement and prevent commoners from occupying Qing land. Precisely because the property system in Manchuria was secured through subterfuge, foot-dragging, and counterfeiting, rather than a once-and-for-all-time seizing of the land, the ability of rural communities to adapt to local political conditions, while regulating and articulating claims through shared customary norms and practices, was all the more important to the success of the peasant challenge to the early Qing dirigisme in the northeast.

To be sure, during the Qing peasant possession of land remained de facto rather than de jure in the northeast—secured in the villages rather than the courts. Nonetheless, that was sufficient to furnish peasants with the security in land that shielded them from the requirement to specialize for the market and, through the reproduction of these property arrangements, instantiated the long-term pattern of Ricardian-Malthusian expansion. Shielded from the economic requirements of specialization, on the one hand peasants could pursue social objectives that while individually rational were nonetheless incommensurate with the requirements of long-term economic growth. On the other hand, they did not have to match the productive abilities of others by investing in labor-saving methods or reorganizing production along more efficient lines in a systematic and ongoing manner. Absent pressures to innovate, there was no sustained improvement in labor productivity in agriculture, whereas the pursuit of valued social goals made it ever more difficult for peasants to specialize and accumulate had they so desired.

Property Relations and Peasant-Led Growth in Qing Manchuria

Manchuria poses a problem for the two dominant modes of interpretation in the fields of economic and Chinese history. The Smithian or neo-classical model that characterizes most of the recent scholarship on China's late imperial period argues that increases in population made for rising trade and an elaboration and deepening of the division of labor.[2] These works argue that as peasants were induced to divert more and more of their energies to producing for the market, the resulting specialization issued in ongoing improvements in labor productivity and rising wages. The implied assumption is that peasants with access to markets on the one hand specialized in the expectation that they would benefit from trading with others and on the other innovated in the expectation of higher daily "wages" or less work for the same "wages."

While studies drawing on the Smithian paradigm argue that the burgeoning division of labor and accompanying specialization occasioned improvements in labor productivity, the other dominant mode of analysis—the neo-Malthusian approach—argues that the relative movement of the price of land and labor was a disincentive to the application of labor-saving tools. The falling cost of labor and the rising cost of land that issued from population growth encouraged the substitution of labor for capital. Moreover, as land was ever more scarce, peasants searched out ways to raise yields and the land's population carrying capacity. But they did so by disproportionately intensifying labor inputs because labor was increasingly cheap relative to capital. Consequently, they could not avoid a steady decline in the productivity of their labor.[3]

By both accounts, Manchuria in the eighteenth and nineteenth centuries was ripe for economic expansion. Relative to China Proper, the northeast's population was low and the cost of labor high, while the unfavorable climate pushed peasants into the empire-wide division of labor where they marketed surplus grain and soybeans for cotton goods and other southern agricultural products and byproducts (Wu 1985, 271; Chao 1977, 14; Jing and Luo 1978, 47, 50–51). Despite migration and a natural population increase over the course of the eighteenth and first half of the nineteenth centuries, Manchuria's land-to-labor ratio remained far better than that of the cores, while trade links with China proper deepened and the appearance of new market towns in Manchuria linked peasants in the northeast to their counterparts in Shandong—and later in Jiangnan and Lingnan—through coastal trade. Yet these seemingly propitious conditions notwithstanding, economic development—defined as the sustained relative increase in output per hour work—was not forthcoming. Manchuria followed a "Ricardian-Malthusian" pattern of growth.

The explanation for this pattern does not lie, as the neo-Malthusians would have it, in the cheapness of labor per se. Indeed, it could not because by comparison to the north China, labor was scarce in eighteenth century Manchuria and wages were higher, suggesting that innovation would have been rational if it reduced labor inputs. Even in 1803, when James Lee and Cameron Campbell detect Malthusian pressures in the southern Manchurian community of Daoyi, wages in the northeast were still higher than those in China Proper (RZSL 1964, 1544 [111]). Labor and land were in demand in the northeast (though not equally so everywhere and at all times). In southern Jilin in the 1930s labor was still so scarce that women with bound feet worked in the fields (Zhang Guizhou, 1994i). The explanation for Manchuria's Ricardian-Malthusian growth pattern lies, I believe, in the social property system that had taken form by the middle of the eighteenth century. In short, because peasants had secured possession of their land they did not have to subjugate themselves to the rigors of market dependency in order to maintain household integrity and peasants continued to secure the bulk of their subsistence directly. They did so because whatever the possible rewards of the market, to expose themselves fully to its rigors and the requirement that they specialize production was too great a risk. They preferred moreover to pursue other social strategies that in the short run improved their chances of maintaining the integrity of their households, even if over the long run these same avenues made for "uneconomic" outcomes. In particular, patriarchs strove to have as many sons and grandsons *as possible* for reasons of old-age support and ancestral worship and then facilitated their household formation by dividing up the family estates equally among heirs. These social goals made specialization all the more difficult since expanding the scale of farming was the surest means to meeting the market's requirement that producers systematically improve labor productivity.

Diversified Production as the Most Rational Means to Household Reproduction

But, why did peasants—especially the earlier settlers who appear to have held larger than average holdings—not head off the Ricardian-Malthusian developments by subjugating their household strategies to market discipline in ways that would have initiated economic growth in order that they might pursue Smithian ends, specialize, and gain from the market? All things being equal, peasants would presumably have wanted to specialize in order to take advantage of the efficiency of others, as the Smithian paradigm suggests. But all was not equal and, as a consequence, peasants had good reasons for not subjecting the entirety of their household strategies and laboring activities to the rigors of the market. Thus, in the 1930s, when rural markets were better developed than at any time prior, and when railroads crisscrossed the region, only one-third of grain and other crop output was marketed (Isett 1998, 393; NJ Series 1934–1936). One major reason for not specializing was the risks associated with the market itself, especially the market in food. Harvest failures were frequent yet unpredictable and their effects could last for several years, downgrading peasant tools and farms as peasants sold off items and fields in a desperate attempt to stay alive. Lee and Campbell (1997) have shown, for instance, that prices for grain and soybeans in Manchuria were extremely volatile, moving "by as much as a factor of two or three within three years" (33). To avoid the effects of poor harvests on food supplies and prices, peasants were better off trying to diversify grain production rather than specialize in the hope that drought, floods, blight, and other calamities would not take the better part of the harvest.

In addition to medium-run fluctuations, prices also rose and fell over the course of a year in ways that significantly disadvantaged the peasant household. In times of good harvest and plenty, most peasants found that they had to sell their surpluses precisely when prices were falling most rapidly, as their fellow peasants also began to unload their surpluses. Again, data from the twentieth century show that almost two-thirds of all grain and beans marketed in south Manchuria were sold in the three months following the harvest; in north Manchuria eighty-five percent of grain and beans marketed was sold in that period (NHB 1937, 25). The sudden influx of grain in the market drove prices down by nearly thirty percent from the summer high, when rural stores from the prior year's harvest were at their lowest (NHB 1937, 35, 38; also see MTDG 1935, 318–320). The rapid decline in price was noted in 1880 by the British consular to Niuzhuang, who reported that the price of soybeans fell thirty percent between March and November (GB.CR 1971, vol. 13, 88). Of course, peasants would try their hardest to sell in the late summer before prices began to fall, but most were simply unable to do so because their reserves were too low (MTDG 1935, 318). Clearly, trade networks and trading infrastructure were such that merchants could not move surplus grain out of the region fast enough to buoy up prices.

For most households, a combination of small surpluses and household consumption needs compelled peasants to sell off whatever surpluses they had immediately following the harvest to meet other needs and costs. In the 1930s, fall and wintertime expenditures on clothing accounted for as much as forty percent of total annual expenditures on household essentials. It was at that time that peasants were also traditionally required to settle debts, pay off wage laborers, and make rent payments (NHB 1937, 38–40). To meet these obligations and needs, peasants were compelled to sell their surpluses at the same time, thereby pushing prices down. Predictably, those peasants with the smallest holdings and smallest harvests were compelled to sell off the greatest part of their surpluses when prices were falling fastest. Japanese investigators found that the less well-off small land-holding peasants sold more than seventy percent of their marketed output in the months immediately following the autumn harvest. By contrast, when prices were rising from late May to the end of the summer, these same households managed to unload only ten percent of their total marketed output (NHB 1937, 31). Consequently, the average price received by the most well-off households was six times that received by the poorest and more than twice that received by moderately well-off households (NHB 1937, 35).

Swings in food prices associated with poor harvests and market congestion could have devastating effects on all peasants but especially on those who specialized. Peasants were themselves obviously aware of these problems and, given both the lack of alternative economic outlets—particularly in non-agricultural work—and the negative implications of failure, they chose not to specialize. Again, data from the twentieth century show this. Whenever possible they strove to secure basic subsistence in grain production first.[4] They did this by diversifying production in agriculture, first and foremost. By planting crops with different natural strengths and resistances to diseases and pests, drought and water-logging, they improved their chances of avoiding a complete harvest failure. In the 1930s, for example, peasants planted a diversified array of crops.[5] Thirty percent of the land was planted in sorghum, fifteen percent in millet, eight percent in maize, sixteen percent in soybeans, and eight percent in wheat. Much of the remainder was planted in *beizi*—a hardy but low-yielding crop suited to poorly drained soils—as well as some buckwheat, barley, beans, and vegetables (NJ-Series, 1934–1936). Though the nature of Qing sources do not allow for precise measurements, they do show that peasants in the early and mid-nineteenth century practiced similar multi-course rotations, which generally had only one-third to one-fifth of the land in any one crop (Yang 1967, 368). The 1909 *Agricultural Investigation of all Fengtian Province* records thirty-four different multi-course rotations of three, four, and even five crops in use. The most complex of these was a five-course rotation of maize, millet, beans, sorghum, and wheat (FNDS 1909, 4.1, 36–42; Wilm 1927, 1047–1048).[6] By diversifying production in this manner, peasants were able to reduce overall risks from disease, insects, and poor weather, while securing a fuller range of their food needs directly.

But not all were able to plant their fields in rotations. In the 1930s, peasants with holdings of ten *mu* or less often planted their entire farm in sorghum or millet in a biennial rotation. But since they consumed most or all of their grain output this was in no sense a form of Smithian specialization. The smallholder's preference for sorghum and millet was due to these crops' superior caloric output per *mu* and hardiness (Buck 1937, 67; Liu and Yeh 1965, 29; Piper 1924, 309–312, 315–316; Isett 1998, 362–364). Larger farms tended to be more diversified, planting a greater variety of crops, and because of their size they generated more predictable surpluses that allowed for a more market oriented production (Wilm 1927, 1047; NJ-Series 1936). These large holders could and did market crops such as soybeans and wheat, but they also devoted significant amounts of land to lower value subsistence grains such as sorghum and millet whose value lay in their higher caloric output, hardiness, and the animal feed, fuel, and building materials that remained after the grain was threshed.[7] In all likelihood a similar phenomena existed on larger holdings in the Qing. Lower yields in the Qing would mean that all else equal more land had to be devoted to subsistence production, leaving less land for commercial farming. But, the point is that even these middling and larger producers would have been unwilling to devote the entirety of their production to the market by fully specializing because of the risks to subsistence and their other social goals.[8] Much of their labor and land would have remained outside the circuits of the market and its imperatives.

In short, by avoiding specialization, and by orienting production toward securing directly as many subsistence needs as possible—*which peasants could do by virtue of the reigning system of social-property relations*—peasants were under no compulsion to buy necessary inputs and could thereby avoid full *dependence* upon the market. Peasants in Manchuria were thus freed from the necessity to enter into competitive production to survive and could pursue valuable social goals such as property division that while rational nevertheless made it increasingly hazardous to specialize.

Property Division and Household Formation

Over time, as households in Manchuria divided their property among sons the average holding size fell, just as it did in China Proper. Declining holding size in turn made it increasingly difficult to specialize and accumulate in ways that would foster rising productivity of labor and economic growth. The Chinese term for property division is *fenjia*, or "dividing the house." By law and custom, in Qing and twentieth-century Manchuria (as in China Proper), property—from land to liquid capital to tools and movables—was divided equitably among all sons (Chikusa 1964–1967, 704–718). This was the case on commoner, banner, and estate lands alike.[9] Daughters received little or nothing in the way of cash or movables and certainly no tools or land, except under particularly unusual conditions (Chikusa 1964–1967, 697–699; Bernhardt 1999, 49–52, 196–197).[10]

Twentieth-century studies show that household division was carried out in the presence of any living parents, a paternal uncle as witness (or, if not available, another close senior male relative on the father's side), and the sons receiving the property. The value of all tools, furniture, and household items, down to the chopsticks, were calculated and then divided. Since individual tools and the like might not be divisible and many households had no more than one of a larger or more costly implement, liquid capital was divided in ways that would compensate sons who did not receive movables or received movables of a lesser value (NSS 1937, 117–118). To ensure that property in land was divided as equally as possible, each son received land of equal amounts and quality. Before dividing household property, land was therefore measured and the quality and productivity of each contiguous field gauged as good, middling, or poor. The fields were then divided in equal-sized and quality strips of land so that each son received not only the same amount of land, but also land of equal productivity (NSS 1937, 118). After the division of property, each son established a separate household (though they might continue to live under one roof), with charge over a separate purse and independent management over his share of the land (Chikusa 1964–1967, 687–696, 704–718).

While there is much twentieth-century ethnography detailing the practice of *fenjia*, there are few Qing sources that provide insights into the practice of household division in Manchuria. Accounts of it in the legal records are, for example, few and far between.[11] Nonetheless, the division of household property was sometimes mentioned in Qing-era trials when those in court were required to provide a standard statement of self-identification (who they were, where they lived, and their relationship to persons directly involved in the case under judgment) or in disputes over property. For instance, in the testimony provided in an 1818 case that involved outstanding taxes owed by two banner households, the defendant in the case, Sun Yinqing gave the following account of his land holdings. He declared that in 1801 he and his brother, Sun Yingfan, had converted imperial pasture land to arable land. For twelve years, the two brothers farmed jointly. In 1813, however, Sun Yingfan insisted on dividing the property and each took half. When Sun Yingfan died, his only son, Sun Zhiliang, inherited his property (LPA 1818, 21772).

In a second and unrelated case, commoner Yang Tianwei, who was sixty-five *sui*, testified that he had divided his land among his three sons, each of whom lived separately thereafter. Yang stated that he lived with his youngest son and grandson on a thirty-*mu* holding (QDTD 1988, 37).

In a third separate case, Mrs. Bai, née Shen, who ended up in court after she had an adulterous affair with her paternal cousin, testified at her 1856 trial that she and her husband, Bai Riyou, along with their two sons had previously lived in a large household with her parents-in-law and two brothers-in-law. In 1827, her husband's family's property was divided and thereafter each brother lived separately (XB 1854, 04410).

While it is generally acknowledged that households in China Proper and Manchuria divided property among sons in more or less equal portions, patriarchs did pursue strategies to delay the effects of partible inheritance on family wealth. In his study of *fenjia*, David Wakefield (1998, 156–161) has shown that at the time of household division it was not an uncommon practice for one son (usually the eldest) to receive a larger share of the family holding in return for his pledge to care for the parents. This larger allotment was called "land for nurturing the elderly" (*yanglao di*) and in Manchuria was usually not redivided upon the parents' death (NSS 1937, 118). The eldest son (or grandson) might also receive a larger allotment—what Wakefield called the "eldest son's" and "eldest grandson's portion"—which Arthur Wolf (1970) has suggested was sometimes provided to afford the price of a wife, thereby ensuring the eldest male heir would marry and continue the line.

Wakefield found, however, that the provision of the older brother's share was not universally practiced. It was common in south China, where it was used as part of a lineage-building strategy often associated with getting one son into official service (Wakefield 1998, 173–184), but rare or absent on the north China plain, where lineage building was far less pronounced (156, 161, 162–165). It also appears to have been more significant among the minority wealthy than the poor (Wolf 1970, 196). Given that peasants in Manchuria were migrants from north China, and given that Manchuria's lineages were few and weak, it is not surprising therefore that twentieth-century Japanese ethnographic studies of Manchuria do not mention the practice, even though the elder brother was expected to care for the ancestral sacrifices there as everywhere else in China (Chikusa 1964–1967, 580–582; 1978, 157; NSS 1937, 114–120).[12]

Significantly, Wakefield also demonstrated that whether peasants set aside *yanglao di* or gave the eldest son or grandson a larger portion of property, those practices did not facilitate accumulation of larger holdings on average. Wakefield showed that while in some instances the elder brother's share did make for significantly unequal distribution of land among sons, in most cases the extra allotment was nothing more than a symbolic gesture (Wakefield 1998, 156–161).[13] He also demonstrated that when the eldest son died and an extra allotment was provided to his son instead, the amount was always smaller than the main shares going to the uncles.

To be sure, peasants might also try to slow down the process of property division by delaying the breakup of the household, thereby extending the time when family property and sons' labor were under the control of a single patriarch. This practice might potentially allow households to build and maintain larger holdings, but only if certain branches of the family were cast off without land. Lee and Campbell (1997, 114), in their study of the Manchurian banner community of Daoyi, in Fengtian, found that the most common expression of this practice was the formation of complex household, usually consisting of two or more brothers living with one or both parents and in some cases extending to include cousins and uncles (cf. Chikusa 1964–1967, 582–583). They also find that in the nineteenth century most people in Daoyi lived in such "multiple-family households," half of which comprised married brothers living together and one-quarter of fathers living with their married sons (1997, 109–111).

The Qing homicide records do provide further evidence for the presence of such complex households, again in the statements of defendants and witnesses. One example is that of the family of Wang Liangren, whose family history was provided in the court by his relatives after he was murdered by his wage laborer in 1826. According to a surviving son's testimony, the family consisted of Wang Liangren, his wife, four sons, two daughters-in-law, and one grandchild (XB 1826, 01510). Li Bao, sentenced in 1835 for the murder of his neighbor over a land dispute, testified that he lived with his mother, father, wife, son, daughter-in-law, two grandsons, and one granddaughter (XB 1835, 01569). Yu Fenghan, the unmarried son of Yu Bangcai, testified in 1851 that before his father was killed he had lived with his father, brother, sister-in-law, nephew, and niece (XB 1851, 2514).

That people lived together did not mean they managed their purses or land jointly, however. The presence of such households can not therefore be seen as evidence that landholdings were held together in all cases. In China Proper, some if not many multiple-family households functioned as multiple economic units and, given the troubled history of record keeping and policing in rural Manchuria, we should not assume that banner household registers captured household divisions when they occurred. There is evidence in the court records, for example, that multiple families living under one roof maintained separate budgets and farmed separate plots in a common Chinese practice known as "dividing the stove" (Wolf and Huang 1980, 58). The records of a 1799 homicide is a case in point. According to testimony presented by a witness to what began as a debt dispute, two brothers had divided the family estate (*fenjia*) soon after the death of their father, as was common practice (Wakefield 1998, 44–52). They chose however to continue living under the same roof, dividing up the house between them. The elder brother, who was thirty-eight *sui* at the time of the trial, lived in the eastern side of the house with his mother, wife, and son. The younger brother, who was twenty-five *sui* and unmarried, lived on the western side of the house alone (XT 1799.7.20). According to the younger brother, each brother worked his own share of the family land and minded his own purse. The existence of large and complex households was not, therefore, evidence that in all cases the patrimony remained intact.

Yet even for those households that did keep the patrimony in one piece, there is no evidence that they held more land per laborer than the average small household. John Ross observed large families living under one roof on several occasions in Manchuria. However, he also remarked that the amount of land per household member among such families was not much more than what he found among small holders. Ross wrote:

> It will sometimes be found that the nominal owner of a very large property is not a man of wealth, as those dependent on the land are numerous, consisting of what we consider many families under one patriarchal head. I know of several such families possessing several hundred acres, but as the family numbers little under two hundred individuals, living in large blocks of houses, with a common gate and a single kitchen, it will be understood that the family is not necessarily a wealthy one. (as cited in Jamieson 1888, 80–81)

What Ross's observation suggests is that large households with substantial holdings were not an expression of a desire to form and maintain large farms with the goal of saving labor. It would seem instead that patriarchs in these cases desired to exploit the labor of familial dependents by keeping them bound within the household. As Lee and Campbell's findings suggest, patriarchs were able to use their power within the family to "squeeze" surpluses from male agnates who were kept within the house (Lee and Campbell 1997, 130). They did this by not providing dependents with costly brides and by suppressing their consumption, evidenced in both their lower rates of marriage and lower life expectancies. In this manner, the main line of the household was better off and better able to ensure marriage and survival for its sons (133–156; cf. Gates 1996, 112–115).

All in all, despite the availability of various practices for diluting the effects of property division on landholding size, there is little evidence to suggest such practices succeeded. In this regard, Qing Manchuria was not all that different from the rest of the empire where, as David Wakefield (1998, 187–191, 198–199) notes, peasants not only continued to divide holdings into very small units beyond what was economically efficient, but they also fragmented their holdings to a high degree, all in an effort to ensure as many sons survived as possible.[14]

Consequently, average peasant holdings in the northeast fell in size over the course of the Qing, just as they tended to do throughout the empire. Whereas early Qing sources tell of households in Manchuria working 80 and 120 *mu* farms, by the first decades of the twentieth century family farms averaged less than 60 *mu*, with the majority of farms smaller still (Adachi 1925, 142, 144). The effects of household property division are evident enough in the twentieth century, when the first systematic surveys of farm size were conducted. The peasantry of the early settled regions of south Manchuria (Fengtian), where household formation and property division had been going on longest, had on average the smallest holdings in Manchuria. The opposite was true in central and northern Manchuria, where household formation and division of property had been going on for a shorter period. Thus, in the late 1910s the average peasant holding in the Fengtian region was 42 *mu*, compared to 100 in Jilin and 180 in Heilongjiang (Adachi 1925, 142, 144, 147–148). Ramon Myers's (1976) work is instructive in this regard. In his examination of the Japanese *Survey's of Actual Village Conditions* (cited here as the NJ–Series 1934–1936), which covered thirty-seven villages, he found that the earlier the village was settled the smaller the average village holding. Thus, by the mid 1930s those peasants who lived in villages settled in the period between 1883 and 1908 farmed an average of 95.2 *mu*, whereas those living in villages settled between 1833 and 1882 farmed an average of 63.4 *mu*, and those in villages settled before 1833 worked a mere average of 31.3 *mu*. The average land owned per household for these same villages was 108, 51.6 and 26.7 *mu* respectively (Myers 1976, 599, table 1).

Not surprisingly, therefore, data collected in a 1930s Japanese investigation of ten thousand households from throughout the northeast indicate that very few households were successful in accumulating large holdings. Just one percent of land-owning households possessed more than one thousand *mu* (166 acres) and just under five percent more than five hundred *mu* (eighty-three acres) (NK 1937b, 47, 67; also see NSS 1937, 89, table 15, 97–102). However, more than two-thirds of households had holdings under the average size of sixty *mu*, or ten acres. And again, conditions were worse for those in longer settled areas. According to the *Fengtian Gazetteer*, by the 1930s the average holding in longer-settled Fengtian was ten mu, or just under two acres (FTTZ 2003, 2590). Clearly, the pressure to divide household property could not be put off forever so that peasant land holdings shrank. The reasons are simple enough. As Lee and Campbell (1997) show, whether it came early or late, the breakup of complex households and the division of household property was instigated by the death of the patriarch, who while alive maintained household discipline and integrity but whose death was occasion for dissolving the household.

Important to our understanding of the implication of household formation strategies is the fact demonstrated by Lee and Campbell (1997, 120) that Daoyi's population had not always lived in complex household units. Rather, they were more likely to live in such units as land in and around the community became scarcer, a development that manifested in Daoyi in the early 1800s. The turn to more complex households in Daoyi is best understood therefore as a *response* to mounting Malthusian pressures that commenced around 1800 or so, along with the diminishing availability of untapped land that these pressures entailed.[15] Coming in the wake of declining land-to-labor ratios, delaying household division through the formation of more complex holdings was a means to offset mounting Malthusian pressures felt in Daoyi. But precisely for this reason, the practice cannot be considered an "optimizing strategy" in support of economic specialization and expansion. That avenue would have had to have been pursued in advance of the appearance of Malthusian pressures and moreover, if effective it would have headed off these same pressures. But, neither was true.

Moreover, whatever one has to say about the constitution of Daoyi families, it is clear that many households over the period were in fact small, usually an indication of poverty in the Chinese context (Cohen 1976, 73–74).[16] Just over half of Daoyi households (just under fifty-three percent) had five or fewer members, with an average of a mere 2.7 persons per household. The remaining forty-seven percent of households were by comparison significantly larger, averaging 9.5 persons. Because of the very large number of small and fragmentary households, the average household size for the period 1792–1873 was a fraction under six persons, only slightly more than Ho Ping-ti's well-known average of 5.3 persons per family for the entire empire in 1820 (Ho 1959, 56). Thus, the Lee and Campbell data indicate that just under half of all households in the Daoyi population had managed to remain together in any meaningful sense, while just over half were reduced to living in a small family, with perhaps an unmarried uncle, brother, or cousin on the side (1997, 110, table 6.1). The mounting Malthusian pressure, which Lee and Campbell note was having an effect by the 1810s, would have driven cousins, uncles, and younger brothers to join relatives to form these small households and offer their labor in exchange for food and housing.

Patterns of Holding Engrossment and Fragmentation

Unfortunately, the banner rolls used by Lee and Campbell do not include landholding records, so the question of whether household formation strategies succeeded in building up larger and larger estates or whether holdings grew smaller over time can only be deduced from their sources indirectly. There are,

TABLE 7.1

The Distribution of Households by Holding Size on Four Manors, 1754–1860

Location	Year	0–9 *mu*	10–29 *mu*	30–99 *mu*	100–199 *mu*	200–499 *mu*	500 + *mu*	Total households
Gaizhou	1753	0	2	15	0	0	0	17
Gaizhou	1791	4	2	16	23	5	5	55
Gaiping	1818	3	14	21	5	7	5	55
Liaoning	1860	8	16	16	2	0	0	42

SOURCE: LPA: *Fengtian sheng gongshu.*

however, records of serf holdings on the imperial estates, though these are problematic because I have been unable to locate diachronic data for a single village or manor. Nonetheless, single registries for different estates in Fengtian can be used to reveal something of long-term trends in holding patterns. Knowing that all serf households in Fengtian received an initial allotment of thirty-six *mu*, it is possible to gauge what proportion of households in a particular estate experienced an increase or decrease in the size of their holdings (see Table 7.1).[17] Whereas there were significant restrictions on serf movement, the effect of movement on the ratio of land to labor and holdings size was obviated to some extent by the rights of serfs to open wasteland within the estate.

The earliest land registry from a manor shows that the majority of households in 1753 still possessed close to their original grant of thirty-six *mu*. The range of holding sizes on this estate remained narrow by the standards of the other three estates in our study—the smallest holding was twenty-four *mu* and the largest ninety *mu*. The majority of households (fifteen out of seventeen households) possessed holdings of between twenty-four and forty-eight *mu*. Only two households had engrossed much land, but with holdings of sixty and ninety *mu* apiece neither had managed to accumulate particularly large holdings. By comparison, land registries of other manors and for later periods show far greater differentiation. In particular, they show an increase in the proportion of households with holdings under thirty *mu* as well as those of one hundred *mu* or more. On the second of the Gaizhou estates, located at Panshanzhai, a general pattern of engrossment is discernible in the 1790s. Holdings ranged from 3 to 778 *mu*, with thirty-three out of fifty-five households in possession of more than 100 *mu* of land. Only two households possessed holdings near the original thirty-six *mu* allotment. It appears that the eighteenth century was still a period of expansion in Gaizhou.

The two-front assault from engrossment and property division on small landholders is most apparent in two cadastre surveys of the nineteenth century. The 1818 cadastre of fifty-five households on the East Route in Gaiping county shows holdings ranging from 6 to 856 *mu*, with twenty-one households in possession of holdings under 36 *mu* and seventeen households in possession of holdings in excess of 100 *mu*. The extent of engrossment was quite extraordinary in this village; five households possessed in excess of five hundred *mu*, and occupied forty-five percent of the village's total cultivated area. By contrast, the bottom twenty-one households (those possessing less than the original allotment of thirty-six *mu*) occupied a mere five percent of the manor's total cultivated area. The 1860 cadastre survey of the village of Miaoershan shows farms ranging from 6 to 120 *mu*, with more than half of all farms under the original allotment of 36 *mu*. There were fewer engrossers in this village, with only two households possessing in excess of one hundred *mu*. Instead, small and middling holders predominated, suggesting perhaps that even land engrossers were suffering from the long-term effects of household subdivision by the second half of the nineteenth century.

Together, these registries suggest that following a period of land engrossment, marked by low population and abundant wasteland, a period of subdivision set in, marked by rising population and diminishing wasteland. That shift from stable or expanding holdings to declining average holdings coincides with the observation of Lee and Campbell for Fengtian that the "1810s were a watershed that marked the beginning of a prolonged period of intensified Malthusian pressures," that they also show resulted in rising grain prices and declining migration into the area (Lee and Campbell 1997, 44–47). Squeezed between engrossment and subdivision, small and micro-landholding peasants were a greater and greater proportion of all households.

The History of the Cai Family's Landholdings

In 1931, Japanese ethnographers reconstructed the fortunes of the Cai family of Caiwobaotun, Heilongjiang, starting in 1850, the only such reconstruction I have ever located. This case study illustrates the processes that led, over time, to social differentiation in rural Manchuria and ultimately forced even large and complex households to divide their property. In short, the investigation shows that the Cai family history followed the Chinese truism that "wealth never survives more than three generations" (*fu buguo san dai*). Within the space of three generations the peak holding of four thousand *mu* was reduced to a pittance.

Originally, the Cai family were rusticated bannermen living in Fenghuangcheng, in Zhili (TKK 1937, 92–98). Probably in the 1820s or 1830s,[18] the founding patriarch of the Manchurian branch of the Zhili Cais moved to Shuangchengbao in Heilongjiang, where he began by renting land from another rusticated banner. It was his son who built the family fortune when, at the age of thirty *sui*, he and a common descent relative decided to move farther north to Suihua county and open land there. Over several years, he engrossed 3,850 *mu*.

For the next two generations, the Cais lived as an extended household under one roof, as the male line of the family grew prodigiously. The Cai patriarch who first settled in Suihua had three sons and eleven grandsons.[19] The entire family managed to remain under one roof until circa 1900 when the household divided the property after the second generation had passed away. It was the grandsons, the fourth generation to live in Manchuria and third in Suihua, who decided to divide the family's property and set up separate households. The reason given to the Japanese investigators was that managing the large household had become too difficult, as can be imagined. At the household division in 1900, each of the eleven grandsons in the three branches of the Cai family received between 350 and 400 *mu*.

When the three branches of the Cai family divided property again in the 1910s and 1920s, there were by this time nine great grandsons who each received between ninety and four hundred *mu*. Over the next two decades, a combination of illness, disasters, opium addiction, and household division reduced all but one to making their way as landless wage laborers and beggars. The long-term pressure to subdivide landholdings, well documented throughout north, central, and south China, was clearly also at work in Manchuria. No matter how hard peasants sought to put off the point of household division, the time came when it had to be undertaken.

Rising Population, Declining Farm Size, and Falling Grain Surplus

Across the eighteenth and nineteenth centuries, Manchuria's population grew at a faster pace than cultivated acreage, propelled both by migration from the north China plain and natural increase.

With the tendency toward early and near universal marriage among women, it was difficult to keep the number of births per woman low. In Daoyi, only five percent of women remained unmarried at twenty-five *sui*, and fully fifty-six percent were married at twenty *sui*, eighteen or nineteen years old by Western count (Lee and Campbell 1997, 86–87, table 5.2). Lee and Campbell estimate that the total marriage fertility rate (TMFR) among married cohorts from twenty to forty-four *sui* was 6.3 in the years 1774–1873 (90, 219). Given that more than half of all women were already married by twenty *sui*, a TMFR that took the low female marriage age into account would be higher still.[20]

Lee and Campbell's TMFR figure for Daoyi is by their own recognition an estimate based upon incomplete records. Poor official record keeping in Daoyi was entirely in keeping with what we know of bureaucratic oversight in Manchuria as a whole, where commoners lived illegally among serf and banner communities without soliciting much official attention. It is not surprising, therefore, that by their own estimates Lee and Campbell believe fully one-half of all persons (one-third of males and two-thirds of females) were never registered on the banner rolls, a proportion that is in turn predicated on their belief that all those who survived to sixteen *sui* (age fifteen) were registered (17 n 3, 66). There were good reasons to keep children, especially males, off the banner rolls after they reached sixteen *sui*, however. As Lee and Campbell note males in the banner system were liable for uncompensated service to the state, including military service, which heads of household would certainly wish to avoid (Lee and Campbell 1997, 44). Underreporting of males in the Daoyi population may have been higher still (Wolf 2001). Taking all of these things into account, there is every reason to believe that once converted to total fertility rate (TFR—the measurement of total fertility of the society and therefore the best means for gauging population growth rates),[21] total fertility among Manchuria's female population was probably not far from the human historical and pre-modern norm of 6.0 (Wood 1994, 48, figure 2.1).[22] Indeed, James Lee has acknowledged elsewhere that China's TFR was higher than contemporaneous Europe's which was in turn lower than 6.0 (Lee and Wang 1999, 84).

With a total fertility rate that was not too far from the premodern human norm, and with population growth compounded by migration, the number of people in Manchuria increased fairly rapidly in the eighteenth and nineteenth centuries. Knowing that most people held land and urbanization rates were low (see below), a simple examination of population and acreage data tells the story. Predictably the average cultivated area per person in the farming population steadily fell, and since it is likely that few peasants in the northeast were fully landless, it is clear that farms too declined in size (Myers 1976, 559, table 1). Whereas in 1800 there was perhaps twenty *mu* per capita, by the 1850s this had fallen to eleven *mu* and seven *mu* by 1900 (Appendix A). With about six persons per household, farms over the same period had fallen from 110 *mu* to 70 *mu* to below 50 *mu*.

The decline in per capita acreage predictably resulted in a Malthusian squeeze on resources that is evident in Fengtian by the turn of the nineteenth century in the rise in grain prices (Lee et al. 1992, 160–161, figures 5.3 and 5.4). To be sure, some of the rise in Manchurian grain prices had to do with similar though more deeply felt processes at work in other parts of the empire. In the eighteenth century, Qing officials in the empire's core regions were noting the correlation of rising population density, diminishing availability of uncultivated land, rising grain shortages, and rising grain prices. Those on the peripheries were also noting the obverse relationship between low population densities and low grain prices (Rowe 2001, 158–159). In eighteenth-century Manchuria, Qing officials similarly noticed and commented on the effects of migration and rising population on prices. In their view, mounting population pressure and, by implication, the failure of Manchuria's peasants to respond to rising demand by increasing output sufficiently were significant factors in driving up grain prices. In 1803, it was observed, commoner settlers "have been gathering and concentrating and rising prices are unavoidable because the number of people grows daily. However, prices are still lower than in the interior [China Proper].... Looking to the future, as the number of commoners in the northeast increases, prices will be higher than they are now. Though there will still be a grain surplus, the number of consumers will rise and so must prices" (RZSL 1964, 1544 [111]).[23]

The repercussions of this rising population pressure on relative levels of grain output per person were evidently felt by peasants, though only crude estimates of output per capita are possible (Table 7.2). As acreage per person shrank and yields rose only slowly, liberal estimates of grain output per person (after deducting production costs) show a decline from 4.6 *shi* in 1750 to 3.1 in 1850 to 2.3 in 1900, and more conservative estimates, taking into account fallow farming, suggest that grain available per person in the population declined from 2.8 *shi* to 2.4 to 2.3 over the same period. With per capita grain consumption at a minimal level of 2.1 *shi*, and with peasants having to acquire salt, cooking oil, cotton cloth, and other nongrain essentials out of agricultural output (given the absence of industrial jobs, wages had to come out of total agricultural output), it is clear that by 1800 peasants in longer-settled Fengtian had to find ways to raise output.[24]

Compelled to live on less and less land, peasants strove to raise output in order to maintain the same levels of consumption as before. Unlike in other parts

TABLE 7.2

Crude Estimate of Unhusked Grain Output per Person in the Population after Deducting Production Costs

Year	Grain per capita	Grain per capita with fallow
1725	3.5	2.3
1750	4.6	3.0
1775	4.2	2.8
1800	4.3	2.8
1825	3.2	2.4
1850	3.1	2.4
1875	2.5	2.5
1900	2.3	2.3

EXPLANATORY NOTE: For the first column, I assume for the sake of simplicity that all land is planted in grain, production costs are thirty percent of output (MNK 1942; SNS 1937) and the grain extraction rate is eighty-eight percent, after Liu and Yeh (1965, 29 table 2). For the second column, I have assumed that the area of land in fallow fell from one-third (1725–1800), to one-quarter (1801–1850), to zero (1851–1900). Grain yields are the same as those used in Table 8.3.

of China, where peasants typically took up by-employment to add to household income, this option appears to have been unavailable in Manchuria (see below and Chapter 8). Consequently, peasants in Manchuria had to find ways of raising grain output if they were to continue to feed themselves adequately. But because peasants could only have found it increasingly difficult to sustain the same tool inventories—especially in large tools—and support the same number of large draft animals as before, given the decline in the size of their holdings, they were perforce required to raise output by increasing labor inputs. What followed was a typical peasant pattern of growth via labor intensification exemplified in the work of Esther Boserup (1965). Posed as a critique of Thomas Malthus's conclusion that population growth necessarily outpaced the growth of food supply, Esther Boserup's study argued that population growth leading to falling output per person in the population, rather than issuing in extreme immiseration, may instead elicit productivity expansion via ever-more intense levels of work and the application of new—and especially labor-absorbing—methods to achieve higher yields. However, because the types of innovations in agriculture Boserup associated with peasant-driven development—such as the elimination of fallow farming, more careful tillage, and greater applications of fertilizer—were intermittent, gradual, and required disproportionately greater labor inputs, the Boserupian pattern of economic expansion must in theory be brought to a stationary state (Boserup 1965, 41).[25]

Peasant-Led Development in Manchuria

Thus shielded from the pressures of market-dependent competition, peasants were able to allocate their resources to pursue social goals that were in their own interest but that were nonetheless noneconomic in the strict sense of maximizing the gains from trade. Significant investments in capital were usually one-off—most commonly at the time when land was converted from waste into arable. Moreover, because peasants were not required by competition to match the technical level of other producers, and because of the risks associated with such investments, changes in agricultural technique were very slow in coming.

This is not to say that improvements or shifts in productive activity were not forthcoming. Indeed, such developments were essential given the need to raise output to support the growing population even as plots grew smaller. In this regard the peasants of the northeast had one ecological limitation not shared by their north China cousins. The northeast has a shorter growing season and lower average cumulative temperature that makes the region unsuited to thermophilic crops such as cotton and overwintering crops in the field. Unable to grow cotton, peasants in northeast China had to forgo spinning and weaving, a major source of supplementary earnings for peasants in late imperial China. Moreover, because winter wheat, which is planted in the fall and harvested in early summer, was unsuited to the long and arduous Manchurian winter, the north China rotation of three crops in two years was not possible (Xu 1991, 112; Huang 1985, 61). As a result, ecology dictated that labor intensification in Manchuria follow a slightly different route.

That said, there was much room for labor intensification in eighteenth- and nineteenth-century Manchuria because of the very extensive but low-yielding farm methods preferred by early settlers. Because the northeast had a low labor-to-land ratio for much of the Qing, the earliest settlers found that they could abandon intensive methods used in north China for extensive methods. In particular, they found that they could practice fallow farming as an effective means to sustain yields and support their households in food. Raising farm yields in Manchuria, therefore, began by peasants abandoning fallow farming for permanent cropping. But as they abandoned the fallow they also found they had to work harder to maintain soil fertility and structure: so they added fertilizer, they weeded more intensively, they thinned their crops to reduce unwanted nutrient absorption, they tilled better and plowed deeper, and those whose farms were large enough to permit it took up more complex rotations. But, as practiced in the eighteenth and nineteenth centuries, the changes in farming methods were labor intensifying, so that for every increase in output entailed by these technical advances there was an equivalent or greater expenditure of labor.[26]

Rising Population and the Abandonment of the Fallow

Over one and a half millennia prior to the colonization of Manchuria by Han peasants in the Qing, peasants on China's Central Plain (Guanzhong) had abandoned fallow farming—the practice of replenishing soil structure and fertility by taking land out of cultivation for a year or longer. They were obliged to do so by a growing population and the concomitant need to increase overall output of food, especially grain (Hsu 1980, 12, 150–152). Peasants in the more densely populated regions of early China took to planting their land continuously (Hsu 1980, 13). But because they were working their land more intensively than before, peasants had to counter the accelerated depletion of soil nutrients and the breakdown of soil structure that accompanied permanent cropping or face declining yields. They thus gathered human excrement, pig manure, and even silk worm droppings, composted waste, and ploughed weeds into the ground, all in an effort to replenish organic matter in the soil. Peasants also took to weeding and thinning crops to maximize the amount of soil nutrients going to the crops (Hsu 1980, 260–262; Bray 1984, 132, 589–590). As land became too scarce to allow anything but grain cultivation, peasants also gradually abandoned the raising of large livestock for anything but beasts of burden. The cost of the land required to support these animals was presumably too great. By the second century A.D. the classic grains-only agriculture that characterized most of agriculture in the late imperial period was already in place in some parts of China.

By the beginning of the late imperial period, fallow farming had long since disappeared from the densely settled lands of the core regions and had been replaced by labor-intensive and continuous farming (cf. Elvin 2004, 180–186, 211–214, 463–464). However, Han peasants who migrated to and colonized the frontiers and highlands, where they found land readily available, often abandoned labor-intensive high-yielding farming techniques of their parents and reverted to the labor-extensive and low-yielding farming methods of a much earlier mode of agricultural production. In the sparsely settled Hunan highlands, for instance, settlers took up slash-and-burn farming, whereby the land was cleared, cultivated for two to three years, and then abandoned (Perdue 1987, 27). Settlers of the Bashan region of Sichuan and Shaanxi often planted land they had cleared for three to five years and having exhausted it moved on (Vermeer 1998, 255). Late seventeenth-century settlers on Taiwan similarly abandoned the very labor-intensive farming practices of their Fujian home villages. On arriving on Taiwan, and for some time after, they turned away from paddy farming and took up labor-extensive swidden cultivation and dry-cropping millet (Cao 1991, 290–291; Shepherd 1993, 168–169). While such extensive practices would eventually give way once again to more intensive use of the land (Perdue 1987, 134–135; Zhang 1986, 15–16), for the early settlers the return to lower-yielding fallow farming and the like was an expression of the abundance of land and the corollary absence of population pressure. We see similar developments in the northeast. Whereas by the end of the Qing the fallow had all but disappeared in heavily settled Fengtian, it was still practiced in parts of sparsely populated Heilongjiang (FNDS 1909, 4.1. 36–42; HZG 1965, 1547). Indeed, the single instance of reported fallow from Fengtian notes that soil-enriching brassica were commonly cultivated in place of fallow.

The return to extensive farming is discernable from early accounts of farming in Manchuria, particularly its least settled regions (Yi 1993, 274). Fang Gongqian, a native of Anhui's Tongcheng, writing in retirement in Yangzhou of his years spent in exile in the northeast with his father—the reknowned and unfortunate literati Fang Bao—disparaged the farming techniques of late seventeenth-century Manchurian peasants. The contrast with the intensive rice paddy farming of his native Tongcheng, as well as his adopted home on the northern edge of the Yangzi delta, were most certainly on his mind. Describing farming near Ningguta, he noted that "the land is opened in the first year and by the following year it is ready [for cultivation]. In the third, fourth, and fifth years the land remains fertile; but in the sixth or seventh years it is abandoned and [the peasants] move on to open new land" (Fang 1993, 101–102).

Fang Gongqian had described instances of long-fallow farming whereby peasants farmed land consecutively for several years until it was exhausted. They then abandoned it to waste or rested the land in fallow for many years. New land was opened and similarly worked until it too was exhausted and the peasant moved on again, or returned to the now-replenished fields abandoned several years prior. Edward Parker (1920, 54–55), an American agronomist who worked in southern Manchuria in the 1910s, described the same farming methods. He found that yields were sufficient in the first years of cultivation as settlers took advantage of the accelerated breakdown of naturally present humus in the soil, a process that occurs when soil is first brought under cultivation. Once the naturally occurring nutrients in the soil were depleted by several years of consecutive planting, without rest or the replacement of lost organic matter, the soil became depleted and, as our Qing observer also noted, Parker found that yields fell off dramatically. As late as the early twentieth century, the agricultural methods were evidently so labor-extensive in some regions visited by Parker that when the land was returned to fallow, rather than purposively planting the fields in "green manures"—plants which could then be plowed back into the soils to restore and improve soil fertility quickly—peasants simply abandoned fields to waste, allowing naturally occurring deposits of organic matter to build up over several years before returning to farm it again (Parker 1920, 51–52, 271–272).

Though long-fallow farming made for very low yields, because so little labor was deployed per unit of land—no time was spent weeding or fertilizing the fields, while plowing ridges and furrows appears to have been an option—peasants could work farms sufficiently large to meet their basic subsistence needs. So long as uncultivated land was sufficiently available, they could hope to produce enough grain to support themselves and their families.[27] But, as the population grew and unclaimed land became scarcer, peasants found themselves having to support the same number of people on less land. Simultaneously, as communities became more established, unclaimed resources such as the wasteland surrounding villages, an integral part of the long-fallow system, were increasingly claimed by others within the community. Under these conditions, peasants no longer had access to enough land and resources to support themselves in grain, so long as they kept to labor-extensive and low-yielding long-fallow farming.

In more densely populated areas, peasants thus took up short-fallow farming. This implied higher yields but also more labor-intensive farming methods. Under short-fallow farming, peasants no longer replenished soils by returning their fields to waste for several years—or abandoning them altogether for new land—but instead rested between a half and a third of their land every year. In this way, every field rested for a full year once every other or third year (Adachi 1925, 152; HZG 1965, 1547; Yang 1967, 368).[28] Because short-fallow farming rested a portion of the land every year, giving it time to recover lost nutrients from the previous year or more of cultivation, yields could in theory be sustained for prolonged periods of time, and perhaps indefinitely if peasants also better managed their soils.

Despite the improvement in average yields over long-fallow farming, a household practicing short-fallow farming still required a fairly large holding to subsist because the short-fallow required that one-third or more of the land go uncultivated. According to a Republican-era survey, the short fallow was found to be practiced among peasant households with average holdings of 120 *mu* or more in northern Manchuria, where it was called the "resting method" (*xiuxian fa*). Peasants who practiced it put half of their land each year in fallow. Since the land in fallow was not used for cattle or sheep raising or put to some such productive use, peasants using the *xiuxian fa* survived on the grain output of the remaining sixty *mu* (HZG 1965, 1547). With yields of 0.4 to 0.5 *shi* per *mu* (as reported by the same survey), a household of four practicing the short fallow could produce just enough grain to survive, after deducting production costs and accounting for expenses on basic requirements such as cloth, cooking oil, salt, and other necessities.[29] As a result, short-fallow farming was only possible under relatively sparsely populated conditions. Beyond a certain point, therefore, it too could not sustain the rising population and had to be abandoned for permanent cropping, which raised the carrying capacity of the land but also required better soil management.

In the nineteenth century, some agricultural land in the most densely populated region of Fengtian was already being farmed continuously, without a fallow. Yang Tonggui described three different field management methods he observed while traveling through south Manchuria in the first half of the nineteenth century. The most commonly employed field rotation he noted was known locally as "greater field" (*datian*). This was a three-course rotation of soybeans in the first year, sorghum in the second year, and millet in the third year. Variations might include buckwheat, as well as hemp and beans, which were sometimes intercropped with grains. Yang also observed that peasants near Shengjing (Shenyang) practiced rotations that they called *zhengcha* and *yingcha*. The former was a three-course rotation of soybeans, setaria millet, and an unspecified grain. The latter was a two-course rotation of soybeans and millet. Finally, Yang also found that some peasants in the region practiced what was called locally the "recurrent rotation" (*chongcha*), which was in fact no rotation at all. Under the *chongcha* the land was planted every year in millet or sorghum (Yang 1967, 368). Yang made no mention of fallowing in the vicinity of Shengjing, suggesting that it had disappeared by this time. The elimination of the fallow in southern Manchuria, which most certainly occurred gradually, raised total output simply because land that was formerly rested was now planted. All things equal, this alone significantly raised the population-carrying capacity of the land, but it also required increases in the level of work, especially to maintain soil fertility. Thus, whereas peasants on the frontiers were certainly able to farm smaller plots more intensively without over-extending their labor, when land was plentiful they selected instead to cultivate extensively (cf. Bray 1984, 132).[30] Only when land became quite scarce did they switch to the most intensive methods.

But to work smaller holdings and feed their households, peasants would have had to work harder—or adopt labor saving tools and methods—to perform the tasks needed to raise yields. Yang Tonggui was struck in particular by the fact that peasants in the northeast expended little if any labor improving and maintaining soils, a habit he contrasted with tillage practices of China Proper. Some of their cropping methods, such as the "recurrent rotation," which put little in the way of nutrients back into the soil, were as a result detrimental to soil vitality (Yang 1967, 368; cf. Parker 1920, 271). But even under less detrimental rotations, Yang noted, farming methods in southern Manchuria remained crude. Peasants, he noted, expended little labor or time preparing the land or caring for the growing plants. They plowed shallowly; they "prepared" the fields for planting crudely (by which Yang probably meant they did not add any fertilizers, since that was a key function of field preparation); they did not harrow the land, which would have improved the soils' retention of moisture; they did not weed or irrigate their fields; they used the most simple of tools; and, because they left great distances between the ridges and furrows, they "unnecessarily" reduced the amount of seed they could plant and ipso facto the grain they might harvest (Yang 1967, 368).[31]

Judging from twentieth-century farming surveys, it seems that peasants in the early nineteenth century could have worked the land more intensively if they had so desired. Japanese surveys show that in the 1930s a single adult male along with a draft animal worked an average of twenty-five *mu*, but because he worked more intensively he could still produce enough to support himself and a few family members, with yields in grain approaching one *shi* in the best of cases (Myers 1976, 599, table 1; NJ Series 1934–1936). But that average worked did not represent the possible limits of one man's labor: in some instances, a single adult male was noted to have farmed twice the average amount of land.[32] To be sure, there were brief periods in the agricultural calendar when tasks such as field preparation and harvesting required some assistance—to guide draft animals when plowing, for instance—but there is no reason to believe that the labor was not available for such work, or for that matter some labor could not be eliminated through more use of draft animals. As one might suspect, peasants in the early nineteenth century worked far more land than the average twentieth-century peasant. According to one source, in the first decade of the eighteenth century one adult male (*yi fu*) could farm eighty *mu* and was capable of attaining yields in the range of 0.25 to 0.5 *shi* of grain per *mu* (Yang 1993, 46). Another source states, on the basis of experience in the banner settlement of Shuangchengbao, that in the 1820s one adult male employing a single draft animal and working tirelessly could cultivate one hundred *mu* (ten *shang*). With a second draft animal and the help of a hired hand, he could cultivate twice as much (Saying'e 1939, 178).[33] Finally, according to a 1908 source there were still districts in Liaoning where a single male adult could work more than 100 *mu* (ZWZ 1908, 1.3). But, in such instances crude and lower-yielding farming methods predominated. In a good year, it was noted, yields in early nineteenth century Shuangchengbao were between 0.4 and 0.5 *shi* of grain per *mu*, whereas the 1908 source gives yields of 0.2 *shi* per mu, far below twentieth-century yields (Saying'e 1939, 191; ZWZ 1908, 1.3).[34] Thus, whereas twentieth-century data show that peasants could achieve higher yields, peasants were doing so on much smaller plots.

It appears, therefore, that from the late seventeenth to the early twentieth centuries, so long as land was available for the taking, peasants in Manchuria *selected* to work extensively, farming larger holdings for low yields. The extra effort required to attain higher yields (but on smaller plots) was clearly not worth the peasant's while, so long as land was plentiful and yields sufficient to support the household with the expenditure of less labor. Thus, given the prevailing conditions in the northeast, peasants chose—as Francesca Bray suggests peasants in China and elsewhere were apt to do (Bray 1984, 132–133; also see Boserup 1965, 66)—to revert to more labor-extensive and lower-yielding farming methods when the opportunity arose on the sparsely populated northeast plains. This was a perfectly rational strategy. By working larger holdings, peasants were laying claim to as large a homestead as possible in anticipation of the day when they would divide their land among their sons. Returns to their labor were of less concern than the provision of future generations with land. By holding and working large farms, therefore, peasants were securing the land that upon division would provide their sons with what they needed to form their own households.

It was only with rising population pressure and declining acreage per capita that peasants in the northeast took to farming the land more intensively. As the average holding size fell, peasants had to raise agricultural output to sustain the same levels of consumption as before, or to simply prevent consumption levels from falling perilously close to bare subsistence levels. Like their counterparts in China Proper, only later in time, as the population grew peasants in Manchuria adopted cultivation methods that required greater and greater labor inputs. This gradual and intermittent shift in farming methods issued in a slow but not insignificant increase in total food crop output (which can only be crudely estimated) that in turn allowed for the support of more persons on a given unit of land. But, peasants found that with each of these shifts they were expending equal or disproportionately greater amounts of their own labor for every increment in output.

Rising Labor Intensity in Agriculture and Declining Returns to Labor

As peasants abandoned fallow farming and began to work their fields more intensively, they also found that they had to work harder to maintain soil structure and fertility or face declining yields. Labor inputs consequently rose quite dramatically as they began to gather, prepare, and spread manures, weed the land and thin the crops, plant crops more closely together, till more carefully, and perhaps cart water to the fields.

This pattern is observable from the Japanese survey of Ningcheng county, which provides an excellent account, based upon village records and interviews, of the shift in farming methods that accompanied rising population in this area of west Jilin (NJ-Ningcheng 1936, 180–181). From the time commoners first settled in Ningcheng in the 1720s until the 1830s, the population remained sparse and land plentiful. Under these conditions, peasants practiced long-fallow farming. They farmed the land for ten consecutive years and then rested it for eight to ten. But as population mounted, due to migration and natural increase of the already settled inhabitants, desirable land on the alluvial plain in Ningcheng filled up until peasants found they could no longer afford to rest land in fallow. Beginning in the early nineteenth century, peasants in Ningcheng began to abandon fallow farming and started to plant their fields continuously. With greater intensity of farming, land yields began to fall and peasants in Ningcheng were compelled to begin applying fertilizer sometime in the late 1880s (NJ-Ningcheng 1936, 181). But, the disappearance of grazing land was beginning to put pressures on livestock that provided manures.

First, peasants took to farming the low-lying fields that formerly went to pasturing their livestock and grazed their animals on the nearby hillsides (NJ-Ningcheng 1936, 180–181). However, by the late nineteenth century, as population continued to rise, peasants pushed farming onto these same hills. Eventually the village decided to keep by pact about one hundred *mu* of hilltop land uncultivated for villagers to pasture their livestock (196). Because of these developments, peasants who wished to apply manures found they had to expend considerable energy collecting it from the pastures and carting it to their fields. But, the quantity of manure was not sufficient even for the typical triennial spreading, and so peasants also gathered human feces and urine, which they composted with green and rotten vegetables, the husks and stalks that remained after threshing and winnowing, and humus rich soil. This mixture was then spread on the fields. At the same time, peasants in Ningcheng also took to weeding and thinning their crops and building up larger ridges to protect the young seedlings and improve the water retention of the soil, all in an effort to raise and sustain yields. When Japanese surveyors investigated Ningcheng in the 1930s, peasants were continuously cropping all their land, spreading manure triennially, weeding every field two or three times annually, and thinning crops. Some were even intercropping legumes with grains (NJ-Ningcheng 1936, 151–162, 186–187, 200–205). Depending on the quality of land and topography, in Ningcheng county grain yields in the 1930s ranged from 0.5 to 1.0 *shi* and bean yields from 0.3 to 0.8 *shi* (171).

The developments in Ningcheng were replicated throughout the northeast, though commencing at different points in time and proceeding at different rates. All things being equal, the elimination of fallow entailed no decline in labor productivity; the same amount of labor would be applied, but now over more of the land. However, all things were not equal. The fallow had been key to sustaining yields and its elimination increased the stress on soils and threatened to suppress the productivity of land and labor alike.[35] Peasants who reduced or abandoned the fallow had to find alternative ways to maintain soil health. In China, as in Manchuria, this has historically meant taking up and improving crop rotations, adding more fertilizer, and by means of improved tillage methods, weeding, and thinning of crops (Bray 1984, 133).

Multicourse rotations that alternate the crops planted in each field from year to year are beneficial for several reasons. Simple rotations of short- and long-rooted crops such as millet and sorghum break up hardpan layers that might otherwise form and reduce moisture available to the plant and generally improve soil structure. Such rotations also alternate between shallow and deep layers that part of the soil from which the plant is taking nutrients, thereby improving overall soil structure (Parker 1920, 60–62; NJ-Ningcheng county 1936, 186). Rotations also reduce the chances that disease and pests specific to one plant carry over from one year to the next (though the best results occur when grains are not planted in succession as was most often the case in Manchurian rotations) (Parker 1920).

For all their benefits, however, it seems that rotations did not by themselves raise plot yields. Their benefit lay primarily in the fact that peasants could plant all their land and thereby raise their total output (Parker 1920, 80). Whether peasants could sustain yields with the more intensive use of land that followed the abandonment of the fallow depended upon the rotation employed and whether or not they labored harder to maintain organic content of the soil. In fact, according to Edward Parker Manchuria's standard grain crops—millet and sorghum—added little in the way of humus back to soil, while taking quite a lot of nutrients out of it. Sorghum and millet are what agronomists call "humus destroying" crops because they tend to deplete soils very quickly unless cultivators take counter measures to reintroduce nutrients.[36] Most peasants in Manchuria compounded that problem by digging up sorghum roots for fuel and using the stalks for framing buildings, fences and the like, rather than plowing that matter back into the soil to add to the soil's organic content (Parker 1920, 54; Wilm 1927, 1050).

The greatest challenge posed by continuous cropping was therefore restoring or maintaining nitrogen levels in the soil. Nitrogen levels could be maintained or raised by several means: making more of the nitrogen in the soil available to the crops by weeding out competitors and thinning weak crop plants; introducing a nitrogen-fixing crop such as soybeans; releasing more of the organic nitrogen in the soil, usually by adding lime to reduce acidity, which then spurs nitrogen mineralization; and adding more nitrogen in the form of manures and compost. Of the available methods, adding more nitrogen is the only one that raises yields (Overton 1996, 106). Spreading fertilizer rich in nitrogen in sufficient quantities helps retain soil productivity and allows the elimination of the fallow without reducing yields. If enough fertilizer is added, yields can also be raised. But depending on how this is done, the application of fertilizer can depress labor productivity.

The methods used by peasants in Manchuria to collect and spread manures entailed significant increases in labor inputs and in all likelihood suppressed labor productivity. According to the 1909 survey of Fengtian, as well as Japanese surveys from the 1930s, those peasants who spread fertilizer did so an average of once every three years. Most prized was the *huangfen* or feces produced by draft animals, of which mules and horses produced 7,200 catties a year and donkeys about 5,400 (Huang 1985, 148). In Manchuria, this was collected from farm animals and gathered along the major cart routes where it was deposited by horses, donkeys, and mules hauling the soybean crop to the coast (Parker 1920, 389). Peasants also collected manure from hogs, chickens, goats, and other small animals and even gathered their own feces and urine from latrine ditches. In addition, peasants composted, which involved digging large ditches and filling them with mud gathered from nearby rivers as well as vegetable and other organic matter gathered from fields, hillside, and other wasteland. The compost was then mixed with whatever manure and human excrement was on hand (MT 1925, 60–68; NJ-Panshi county 1936, 240–243; Wilm 1927, 1048). Finally, peasants also dug up humus-rich subsoil to mix with manure and compost before spreading (Parker 1920, 389; Wilm 1927, 1048).

To be sure, much of this work was done during the agricultural off-season when there was little else to do, and expending labor in this way made sense. Nevertheless, the methods employed meant that the work added to the overall level of labor intensity in crop production (FNDS 1909, 4.3–5). The amount of fertilizer spread varied by the mix and its overall availability, ranging from as little as five hundred catties of manure per *mu* every three years to as much as four thousand catties of compost every three years.[37] The typical range was between five hundred and fifteen hundred catties per *mu* every two to three years (MMZ 1922–23, 194–198; also see FNDS 1909, 4.1, 21–27; NJ-Yaonan county 1936, 126; NJ-Panshi county 1936, 242; MT 1942, 119–120). In Panshi and Yaonan counties, applying five hundred catties of fertilizer required about 0.2 days of work per mu.[38] In longer-settled Gaiping county, where farming was very labor intensive, though yields comparable to those elsewhere in southern Manchuria, hauling and spreading the standard 1,200 catties of fertilizer required three-quarters of a day per *mu* (MNS 1937, 46–50). Those surveys do not say how much time was spent preparing fertilizers, but studies of four other south Manchurian counties (Liaozhong, Liaoyang, Xinmin, and Yushu) suggest that just under half a day was spent in gathering and preparing fertilizer for every *mu* of land fertilized (NKK 1939).[39] On a sixty-*mu* farm (approximately ten acres), peasants spreading twelve hundred catties of fertilizer once every two to three years would have expended twenty-four and thirty-six days respectively per year just preparing and spreading fertilizer. Clearly, the gathering, preparing, and spreading of fertilizer added tremendously to the intensity of work.

The additions of labor did not stop there, however. Peasants who fertilized their fields would have found that it stimulated weed growth that had to be countered with more intensive weeding lest plant competitors absorb so much of the nitrogen as to counteract the value of adding it. It was common in the 1930s for peasants to perform two rounds of weeding and one round of thinning per growing season, which on a sixty-*mu* holding in Panshi and Ningcheng counties added forty days of work—fifty days if a third round of weeding was needed. Peasants in these counties who took up harrowing to improve moisture retention added another four to eight days of work to their schedule, depending on the size of draft animals, and added another fifteen days of labor to rebuild the ridges and furrows afterwards.[40] Other figures suggest even higher rates of work: again, in Gaiping county weeding and hoeing

TABLE 7.3

Labor Inputs in Grain Farming per mu in the 1930s

Task	Days of labor per *mu* (one day = ten hours)
Land preparation	0.06–0.1
Forming ridges and furrows	0.06–0.1
Planting	0.375–0.6
Rolling	0.033–0.055
Fertilizing (prep and spreading)	0.65
Weeding (two rounds) and thinning	1.0–1.8
Horse-harrowing	0.06–0.14
Harvesting and hauling	0.24
Threshing	0.25

EXPLANATORY NOTE: All data aside from fertilizer preparation and spreading from NJ-Ningcheng county (1936, 199–208; 205–206) and NJ-Panshi county (1936, 242, 260–262); Fertilizer preparation and spreading figure combines time spent hauling fertilizer noted in the Ningcheng and Panshi county surveys with days preparing fertilizers from NKK (1939). The latter figure is not given for the Ningcheng and Panshi studies.

typically took 3.6 days per mu, or 216 days on our sixty-*mu* farm, and in the four counties of Liaozhong, Liaoyang, Xinmin, and Yushu this work took on average 1.6 days per *mu*, or 96 days on the sixty-*mu* farm (MNS 1937, 46–50; NKK 1939). Finally, plowing, planting, harvesting, hauling, and threshing in the 1930s required about 58 days of labor on a sixty-*mu* farm in Panshi and Ningcheng (NJ-Ningcheng county 1936, 199–208; 205–206; NJ-Panshi county 1936, 242, 260–262), though these same tasks required 1.5 days per *mu* or 90 days on a sixty-*mu* farm in Liaozhong, Liaoyang, Xinmin, and Yushu counties (NKK 1937).

From Yang Tonggui's account of farming it is evident that peasants in the nineteenth century expended far less effort in all of these areas than peasants in the twentieth century. Indeed, from Yang's account it appears that the peasants he observed were not fertilizing their fields, harrowing, or weeding. The average amount of labor invested in fertilizing the land, weeding and thinning, and better tillage in the 1930s was perhaps as much as double the level of all labor inputs described by Yang. It was certainly more than double the amount of time spent in all other field work combined in the 1930s (Table 7.3). Yet, since the early nineteenth century typical grain yields had risen at most seventy-five percent, from 0.4 or 0.5 *shi* to 0.7. In Ningcheng, where there was a significant pattern of labor intensification, millet and sorghum yields still ranged from 0.25 to 0.5 *shi* per *mu* in the 1930s (NJ-Ningcheng county 1936, 225). Even if yields had risen further its is unlikely that they would have compensated for the rise in labor intensity. In the surveyed villages of Liaozhong, Liaoyang, Xinmin, and Yushu counties, grain yields were about one *shi* per *mu*. Yet the work expended just gathering and spreading fertilizing and weeding (1.7 days per mu, assuming one round of fertilizer every three years) was more than all other field work combined (1.5 days per mu). But, as noted, even these figures do not capture the full levels of labor intensification since other field tasks would have intensified as well over time, as peasants took more care planting, building up ridges, and rolling their fields. Thus, even a doubling of yields would have been offset by a more than doubling of labor inputs.

Stagnating or declining labor productivity is confirmed in part by a twentieth-century experiment performed on sorghum (the most commonly grown grain in the region) by Japanese agricultural scientists in the 1920s. That study suggests that the *annual* spreading of fertilizer raised sorghum yields by fifteen percent over what was achievable without fertilizer (MT 1928a, 154, table). Of course, the increase in yield would have been less for the typical triennial spreading. Clearly the relative increase in labor expended to gather, prepare, haul, and spread the typical fertilizer application every year—plus the added time for weeding and rebuilding ridges that accompanied increased fertilizer use—outpaced that increase in yield (Table 7.3). This all suggests that the intensification of labor entailed in sustaining or raising yields was accompanied by stagnating or falling levels of labor productivity.

Despite these efforts to sustain or raise yields, there is evidence of significant limitations on what was achieved. Though it appears the three-course rotation combined with triennial applications of fertilizer helped to raise and sustain higher yields, there is also evidence that the failure to intensify labor inputs still further, especially with greater applications of fertilizer, may have caused some backsliding under some conditions. According to the agronomist Edward Parker (1920), in districts in Manchuria where fairly labor-intensive cultivation had gone on for seventy-five to hundred years, soil structure and fertility nonetheless deteriorated to the extent that yields were half of what they used to be. Despite rotations and triennial spreading of fertilizer, Parker noted there was a decline in soil fertility over the long run; peasants failed to counter sufficiently the constant drain on nutrients: "the tillage is very shallow, there is no use of green manure crops [crops like alfalfa that are plowed back into the soil], pasture crops or meadow crops, and all crops are inter-tilled. Humus is rapidly exhausted from these soils by these practices as well as the common practice of digging out crop stubble for fuel. The farmers of this region conserve such animal and human excrement as is available; but it is insufficient to counterbalance the plant food taken out by crops and exported from the country" (390). In short, Parker believed there was insufficient nitrogen making its way back into the soils of Manchuria, which he blamed in part on the structure of Manchuria's export economy: the export of soybeans had created a nitrogen deficit in the northeast.

Agricultural Improvement Without Rising Labor Productivity

That there was dynamic change to farming practices is indisputable. But so long as the expansion of output was propelled by assarting and by working harder for lower daily returns, "growth" in Manchuria remained involutionary and ultimately circumscribed. In this regard, a quick examination of European history is instructive. In the past decade, historians of medieval and early modern Europe have argued that the abandonment of the fallow and the taking up of increasingly complex crop rotations are expressions of agricultural dynamism in the premodern era. They point to rising yields and improved carrying capacity of the land as evidence, and to be sure, the reduction or elimination of the fallow has been key to raising total output (e.g., Campbell 1983, 1991, 1995). However, in these instances the reduction and eventual elimination of the fallow was clearly also accompanied by greater applications of labor, made necessary by the implied turn to continuous cultivation and the need to sustain the structure and fertility of soil under the increasingly intensive usage that followed. Peasants who gave up the fallow historically turned to intensive and multiple weeding, putting animals in stalls and spreading manures by cart and hand, more intensive tillage, thinning to remove weak plants, and even careful watering. Predictably, this pattern of intensification led to declines in labor productivity in the medieval era. Thus, for all his attention to the dynamism of the system, Bruce Campbell (1991) sums up his account of medieval English farming thus: "Under medieval technology and economic conditions . . . high output per unit of land was bought at the expense of low output per worker" (210).[41] While such developments must be considered "improvements" wherever they occurred, historically they have issued in declining or at best stagnating productivity of labor (also see Bray 1984, 589–591; Boserup 1965, 41).[42] Their benefit lies in the raising of the land's population carrying capacity.

Limits of Agricultural Productivity and Its Effects on Urban Development in Qing Manchuria

There is a clear historical correlation between levels of labor productivity in grain cultivation and levels of urbanization. Economies burdened with low levels of labor productivity in food production have historically simply been unable to release labor from agriculture. Moreover, because such economies are often associated with labor-intensive farming methods, it is evident that any reduction of labor in agriculture would initiate declines in grain output. By contrast, economies with higher relative levels of labor productivity in grain production can release labor to the towns and industry. England's agricultural revolution of the sixteenth and seventeenth centuries did just that: between 1600 and 1800 the percentage of the population living in towns of ten thousand or more rose from six to twenty-four percent, while the nonagricultural population rose from thirty to sixty-four percent (Wrigley 1985; Allen 2000). The low level of urbanization in late imperial China was conversely the result of low labor productivity in Chinese agriculture. The proportion of the total Qing population in urban towns of two thousand or more was seven percent at most, less still for towns larger than ten thousand (Chao 1986, 58–59; Huang 1990, 332–333; Cao 2001, 829; Skinner 1977b ,245, table 6B). The inability of Chinese agriculture to release labor was a major brake on urbanization (Brenner and Isett 2001, 633–636).

Circa 1910, the earliest year for which estimates of urban population are possible for Manchuria, perhaps eight percent of the people lived in towns of five thousand or more (Wang 1971, 161). While greater than China's national average at that time, it was nonetheless low by comparison to Europe a century and a half prior, in 1750, and lower still than Europe's most urbanized countries.[43] The low level of urbanization in Manchuria reflected a low level of productivity in agriculture. To be sure, the absolute number of towns in the northeast certainly grew over the Qing. By 1910, when the entire population of the northeast was perhaps eighteen million, the number of towns with a population in excess of five thousand numbered sixty-two (though several of the largest towns grew as a result of Russian railway construction and were therefore recent phenomena) (Wang 1977, 161). There is no reason to believe, however, that the urban population grew any faster than the overall population. The low level of urbanization in Manchuria was an upshot of the low level of labor productivity in agriculture.

Because Manchuria's peasants could muster little surplus above basic subsistence, rural demand for manufactured goods must have remained narrow. To be sure, part of what peasants earned in the market had to go to buying cotton cloth imported from other parts of the empire as well as other local manufactures (iron implements, food oil and the like) that peasants could not secure directly. But, as Chapter 8 shows, such purchases did not stimulate the development of local industry. What was left after deducting food and cloth expenditures was simply insufficient to foster much beyond very basic town-based manufacturing. Consequently, the range of functions served by northeast towns remained narrow. First and foremost, Manchurian towns served as administrative centers, housing the banner garrisons and staff of the regional government. They were also sites of merchant organization and activity; in particular they were the locations from which merchants orchestrated inland trade (Zhang 1990, 168–172). What urban-based manufacturing and processing there was served nobles who resided in the secondary capital at Shengjing, resident administrators throughout the region, town-based merchants, and those who serviced them. Thus, Zhang Yaomin's (1990) catalog of manufacturing in Qing Manchuria points to a narrow range of industries. Aside from distilleries, oil mills, and flour mills, there were state-run shipyards and arsenals; simple iron tool making; woodworking for tools and simple furniture; cloth production for the state; salt production, and some small-scale coal mining (172–184). With the exception of salt (the production and distribution of which was run by state and state-backed monopolies), some cooking oil, and a modicum of flour and alcohol, and iron for implements the towns basically offered peasants no other goods. In sum, without a large and growing domestic market, made possible by the rising productivity of labor in food production, urbanization and industrialization (whereby a growing proportion of the population works outside of agriculture) were not forthcoming in Qing Manchuria.

Technology and Innovation in Early Modern English and Late Imperial Chinese Agriculture

Broadly speaking, the literature on the late imperial Chinese economy has argued, in one form or another, that the absence of labor-saving innovation was the single greatest barrier to agricultural development in the Qing. Ramon Myers (1970), for instance, concludes in his study of the peasant economy of the north China plain that there was no growth because peasants did not offset the inefficiencies entailed by their smallholdings with the application of new technologies and knowledge (159–166; cf. Faure 1989, 36–40). Similarly, Mark Elvin argues that China's economy was trapped in underdevelopment because of a combination of technological stasis and lack of liquid capital (1973, 203–204, 303). More recently, R. Bin Wong (1997) and Kenneth Pomeranz (2000) have suggested that positive economic growth in the eighteenth century was brought to a standstill in the nineteenth century by resource constraints that could only be overcome by a shift to new and principally coal-fueled technologies, which then feed back to agriculture in the form of chemical fertilizers and machines powered by nonanimal energy. By way of comparison to northwest Europe, they argue that institutional arrangements and unfavorable geology in China precluded the exploitation of the sort of inorganic technologies that they hold were necessary for sustainable economic expansion (Wong 1997, 56, 58; Pomeranz 2000, 207).

In one way or another, these interpretations understand technology to be exogenous to the economy; the necessary technologies, in this view, were not sufficiently forthcoming, but if appropriately introduced or made available they would have transformed production given China's already propitious development of market dynamics. However, what is striking about the examples of early modern economies such as England and Holland, which exhibited sustained and significant levels of real economic growth, was the extent to which growth was achieved entirely on the basis of methods that, far from being exogenous, were long practiced though not widely disseminated before the seventeenth century (Thirsk 1984, 288–289, 204). Between 1600 and the commencement of the classical period of the Industrial Revolution in 1750, the productivity of labor in English agriculture doubled on the basis of traditional methods (Allen 2000, 20, table 8; 1992, 223–227, table 11-8). It continued to grow, moreover, well into the nineteenth century *before* new inorganic steam-powered machinery and chemical fertilizers were ever brought to bear.[44] The achievements of English agriculture were thus secured well into the first half of the nineteenth century on the basis of methods and tools that were for the most part known in the sixteenth century.[45]

There were, according to Mark Overton, four major innovations in English farming during the agricultural revolution.[46] First, farmers and landlords rationalized farms by removing barriers, aggregating holdings, and building up expansive and contiguous fields for better economies of scale and reduced wastage. Second, farmers introduced new crops such as nitrogen-fixing turnips, clover, lucerne, and sainfoin and improved field management methods through the adoption of convertible husbandry, the Norfolk four-course rotation, and the adoption of more labor-efficient tools such as better drills for planting (Overton 1996, 107–111, 117–121; also see Thirsk 1984, 184–189; Kerridge 1967, 181–325; Yelling 1977, 187–189). Third, farmers increased their number of animals, particularly large animals useful for their manure and ability to haul. Improved cattle were put to pasture in fields that were often planted in clover and later plowed up and planted in grains. Farmers replaced the slow and weaker oxen with the stronger and faster horses for pulling and carting, and they dramatically increased the total number of horses they employed per acre (Overton 1996, 125–128; also see Wrigley 1988, 36–44). Fourth, farmers improved tillage—in particular, hoeing, weeding, and greater use of fertilizers—while simultaneously continuing to sustain increases in the productivity of labor. They could do this because they modified, developed, and used specialized tools while also making far greater use of horses in tillage. Though there were important examples of capital-intensive innovations in the sixteenth century—such as the floating of meadows and draining of fenlands—the revolution in English agriculture was largely by the way of increased specialization and reorganization of holdings requiring significant but, in absolute terms, not very large capital investments (Brenner 1985b [1982], 49, 308–310). There was, in short, little that was exogenous or inorganic in the developments of this period or, for that matter, in much of the nineteenth century (Overton 1996, 88–132).[47]

The basic elements of the innovations behind the English agricultural revolution were present in Manchuria, but they were not combined in ways that advanced productivity of labor. Manchuria's peasantry was aware of the benefits of legumes to the soil; the improvement in soil structure and elimination of disease associated with rotations; the benefits from improved soil drainage and irrigation; and the increase in yields achieved with greater applications of fertilizers and improved tillage. They also knew of the greater pulling power of the horse over the ox and donkey and understood they could complete the most labor-intensive chores more quickly if they harnessed more horses to the task. Peasants also knew from experience of the boost in yields that came from putting land in leys for several years before planting in grains. Finally, peasants knew that dispersed and fragmented fields made for wasted time, the result of having to set up and stop work as they moved from field to field. In short, the basic ingredients of England's agricultural revolution—rotations, leys, legumes, better field organization, more draft animals—were known to peasants in Manchuria—just as they were to continental peasants and landlords in large areas of early modern Europe where they were similarly not adopted in the same combinations as they were in England and Holland (Grantham 1978, 1980; Berend 2003, 26–31, 159–167).[48]

It is commonplace in the literature to explain the tendency to adopt labor-intensive rather than labor-saving methods as the result of the cheapness of labor in China. The superabundance of labor reduced its cost relative to land, tools, and draft animals, making for the rational substitution by peasants of their labor for capital (Elvin 1973; Chao 1986). This explanation also implies that when the cost of labor rises (following demographic downturns or when production shifts to the frontiers) pari passu labor-saving tools and draft animals would be adopted in ways that reduced labor inputs (costs) while sustaining yields. But, there is little evidence that that occurred. First, there is no evidence that labor-saving innovations were taken up in a systematic fashion following significant demographic downturns such as that accompanying the Ming-Qing transition. Second, there is no evidence that peasant settlers on frontiers such as Manchuria (or on Taiwan and in Hunan) took up labor-saving tools that allowed them to sustain yields but with less labor. Rather, it appears that where there was abundant land peasants chose to lower labor inputs by simply working the land less intensively—by not fertilizing their fields, not weeding, not harrowing—and thereby settled for low yields.

The reason for the absence of innovations of the sort that would propel improvements in labor productivity, I believe, lies in the system of property relations that had taken shape in the eighteenth century and continued into the nineteenth. Because peasants in the northeast had secured de facto possession of their land through village organization, they had no need to commit themselves to production for the market except to purchase the few subsistence goods they could not produce or manufacture on their own. They had, moreover, every reason not to become fully market dependent. Harvest failures were frequent and full dependency on the market was a risk peasants forwent. Peasants selected, as the best strategy to maintaining the household, to secure as much as possible of their food needs on their own and to do so by diversifying production to the greatest extent possible. They grew different kinds of crops with different strengths, they grew all their vegetables, and usually raised a pig and some fowl for personal consumption. Only after their food needs were met did they sell their surpluses to purchase cloth, salt, and oil.

By orienting their production in this manner, peasants were not fully subject to the competitive constraints of the marketplace and, therefore, did not have to match the efficiency of others in what were their primary areas of production. There was, as a consequence, no systematic tendency to adopt labor-saving methods. Furthermore, it was difficult for them to improve the efficiency of labor given the propensity to divide their wealth among their sons. The lack of innovation, in sum, was not due to the absence of technology, or the relative cost of labor per se, but rather the absence of pressures that accompany market-dependency and that compel the adoption of what were often already known but not widely practiced methods in ways that raise the productivity of labor in agriculture.

CHAPTER EIGHT

The Content and Growth of the Manchurian Trade, 1700-1860

In the aftermath of the devastation wrought by the Ming-Qing transition, Manchuria's agrarian economy recovered only slowly. Not until the 1720s did the region show signs of being able to support itself, and then only provisionally. In 1700, Fengtian still required regular grain subsidies, receiving 160,000 *shi* of relief grain from north China in 1696. Aware of the region's low agricultural productiveness, after lifting the empire-wide ban on maritime and coastal trade in 1685, the imperial court and Manchuria's regional government continued to enforce a ban on the maritime export of Fengtian food grains and soybeans.[1] By 1750, however, agricultural production had expanded somewhat via the creation of new estates, the opening of bannerland, and commoner migration and settlement (Katō 1953a, 595; Sudō 1972a, 451). Officially registered farmland reached fourteen million *mu* by the 1720s, though actual acreage was probably closer to twenty million *mu*. With this land in production, and the population still relatively sparse, Manchuria's agricultural surplus was bound to have grown as more settlers arrived, while the rationale behind the ban on food exports was ever less pertinent. Consequently, in 1749 limited exports of soybeans were permitted and in 1779 all restrictions on soybean as well as grain exports were removed (reintroduced only in times of local famine—see Chapter 9).

This chapter discusses the ecological and structural basis and content of the Manchurian trade under the Qing. The following chapter examines the state's maritime trading policy in Manchuria as well as merchant organizations and their operations in the Manchurian trade. While it is clear that Manchuria partook in an empire-wide division of labor, it is also evident that this division of labor remained largely confined to exchange between peasants of different regions and did not develop into the classic Smithian exchange of cheap town-based manufacturers for agricultural goods (Wu 1983, 99). In the Qing interregional trading system, Manchuria imported woven cotton cloth and exported coarse grains such as millet and sorghum as well as raw soybeans and some soybean beancake. The latter is a residue from pressing oil from the soybean and was used in south China as a fertilizer. Yet, as this chapter will show, Manchuria's ability to export these goods was far less than recently argued by revisionist scholars such as Li Bozhong (1998) and Kenneth Pomeranz (2000) who have argued that beancake fertilizer made mostly from Manchurian soybeans propelled an agricultural revolution in China's Jiangnan region. Thus, in the process of examining the content and growth of Manchuria's trade, I develop estimates of Manchuria's agricultural productiveness and its export capacity, using available yield data and revised population and acreage numbers that adjust for the fact that Qing authorities systematically undercounted both people and land (see Appendix A).

Empire-Wide Long-Distance Trade in the Qing and Manchuria's Place In It

Together with rural manufactured cotton cloth, grain and beans made up more than two-thirds of the value of all Chinese long-distance trade in the early nineteenth century (Wu 1983, 99–100, tables 1 and 2). Wu Chengming (1983, 103) estimated the total volume of grain and beans entering the long-distance trade routes in the mid-Qing at some thirty-six million *shi*, of which six million was procured and moved by the state. More recently, Guo Songyi (1994, 46) estimated that the volume of grain and beans in long-distance trade was between 46.5 and 57.5 million *shi* in roughly the same period (cf. Fang 2000, 399). As for cotton cloth, Wu (1983, 99, table 1, 106) estimates 305 million bolts moved within China's long-distance markets, along with an additional 2.5 million catties of unworked cotton.[2]

The greater part of the long-distance trade in grain and cotton cloth moved between peasant households (Wu 1983) and was driven primarily by peasants in the core regions of the empire such as the north China plain, Yangzi delta, and Lingnan having to make up for their grain deficits through exports of their household manufactures.[3] With the available arable land in the cores largely filled, and having reached the upper limits to the productivity of land in grain cultivation, peasants in the longer-settled cores turned to the grain stores of the more recently settled peripheries.[4] With fewer people per unit of land, the peripheral regions such as Manchuria, Huguang, Guangxi, the Sichuan basin, and Taiwan held grain surpluses that could be exported without threatening local food supplies—with one important qualification. Once population growth in the periphery began to put pressures on land and thereby eat into its grain surplus, the capacity to maintain exports declined.[5] To purchase this grain, peasants in the cores had to produce and exchange inexpensive household manufactures such as cotton cloth. The grain-exporting peripheries were the cores' ghost acres—this was the arable land that made continuation of the cores' patterns of growth and levels of urbanization possible.

The cores' turn to domestic manufacturing was not an indication of the advancement of the division of labor in a Smithian fashion, insofar as it was associated with declining rather than rising daily earnings for labor (Brenner and Isett 2002, 631–632). The recommencement in the first half of the eighteenth century of a rapid rise in grain prices, felt not only in the cores but also in the peripheries—where it was carried through trade networks—signaled a decline in grain output per person and deepening of grain deficits in the cores. Unable to raise grain output fast enough, and finding that stagnating grain yields and returns on labor did not warrant additions of labor to grain cultivation, peasants turned to household manufacturing or proto-industrial production. In turning to domestic manufacturing in this way, however, peasants had to accept returns on their labor that were no better than in agriculture and were often worse. They were compelled to take the lower returns to labor because of the fact that their farming plots had shrunk in size and could no longer guarantee subsistence in grain (Brenner and Isett 2003). For cotton cloth, the most commonly exchanged manufactured item in long-distance trade, the returns on labor were half or less of those of the returns on rice cultivation (Brenner and Isett 2002, 631; 2003; Pomeranz 2002, 548; Huang 2002, 517–518). Undoubtedly, if they could they would have remained in grain production. But because in theory peasants might extend their work longer, proto-industrial activity had the potential to maintain household or even raise total income, all things being equal.

All things were not equal, however. Because of the decline in labor productivity in agriculture and a concomitant fall in discretionary income (i.e., the onset of a typical Malthusian-Ricardian growth pattern), grain prices rose faster than the prices for household manufactures such as cotton cloth. As more and more household income was taken up by grain, less was available for nonessential items. Cloth, silk, and sugar prices all rose at a slower pace than that of grain (Kishimoto 1997, 126–127, 139, 144; Rowe 2001, 157–158). The result was a predictable and dramatic secular fall in relative earnings of as much as sixty percent between 1750 and 1860 for proto-industrialists (Brenner and Isett 2002, 639–640; Pomeranz 2000, 290, 323–326).[6] Reflecting on this phenomena, Pomeranz (2000, 22) rightly notes that China's peasantry had entered a proto-industrial cul-de-sac. But the effects were not equally felt in the empire. Those in the peripheries clearly benefited from this change in the terms of trade so long as they could continue to produce grain surpluses. All things being equal, the relative value of their labor (expressed in grain) rose vis-à-vis the value of proto-industrial labor (in domestic manufactures). The peripheries were better off than the cores since, as Mark Elvin (1999, 142–173) argues, they continued to have unclaimed resources available.

But, it was the economic pattern exhibited in the cores that made possible the grain surpluses in the peripheries. That is to say, it was population growth combined with partible inheritance that led to decreased holding size in the cores and drove peasants to open marginal lands and unsettled regions where nonmarginal land was still available. By extending the area under cultivation in this fashion, greater overall populations were sustainable. This pattern of extensive growth via colonization is a long-recognized hallmark of late imperial economic growth, the value of which was understood by Qing authorities who encouraged colonization, at least up to a point (Ho 1959, 136–168; Perkins 1969, 184–186; Rowe 2001, 218–221; Perdue 1987, 86–89).[7] Thus, the peripheries were key to the viability of the long-term pattern of growth in the late imperial period as both absorbers of excess population and providers of grain (Jiang 1992, 42–48). In essence, it was the dispossessed younger brothers, uncles, and cousins who migrated to the peripheries who in turn fed their families back home. Intensive growth in places like Jiangnan and the north China plain was predicated upon extensive growth on the frontier.

Manchuria's place within Qing trading networks was that of an importer of cotton goods (finished and unfinished piece goods as well as some quantities of unspun cotton) and an exporter of grain (millet, sorghum, and wheat), soybeans, and soybean-based products, the most important of which was beancake fertilizer.[8] As early as the Yongzheng and into the Qianlong eras, authorities memorialized that in return for grain, soybeans, and beancake fertilizer, Manchuria imported cotton cloth and raw cotton, along with smaller amounts of sugar, earthenware, and paper (GDZ-YZ 1977, vol. 6. 404–408; GDZ-QL 1982, vol. 37. 120–121).[9] The importance of cotton cloth in the Manchurian trade is manifest in the fact that the eighteenth-century term "southern goods" (*nanhuo*), which referred to goods moving from Jiangnan to the north, came to be associated closely with cotton cloth (cited in Fan 1992, 277). Shanhaiguan customs reports dated to the second decade of the nineteenth century record that cotton, grain, and soybeans provided the bulk of the region's customs duty. The report notes that, whereas exports of Manchurian tobacco, grain alcohol, sesame, and cotton accounted for a tiny proportion of export duty, the main sources of revenue were exported sorghum (*gaoliang*) and soybeans and imported southern goods—the most important of which we know was cotton cloth: "Merchant mariners bring southern goods to the [northeastern] ports to sell. This [trade] depends on the shipment of sorghum and soybeans to the south. Merchants plan to have goods to ship back and forth and so there is circulation [*liutong*]" (HZ 1824.7.27).

Explaining Manchuria's Dependency upon Cotton Imports

Manchuria imported cotton because beyond the coastal counties of the Liaodong peninsula the short growing season prohibits cotton cultivation (Chao 1977, 14). Still, the ecological barrier to its cultivation was not immediately recognized by the state. Writing on the rural conditions in Manchuria in the early years of the emperor Qianlong's reign, He Qizhong (1992), whose essay is included in the canonical collection *Anthology of Statecraft Writing*, was puzzled by the fact that peasant households did not manufacture cotton cloth. Looking for ways to improve the living standards of common folk, he hoped to encourage greater self-sufficiency by preaching the benefits of the Confucian adage "men cultivate and women weave." Writing in 1745, He Qizhong remarked:

> Reviving the spinning and weaving of cloth [among the common folk] is a way to relieve the people. When considering the livelihood of the common folk, food and clothing are immediate priorities and attending to such fundamentals requires a plan. Though farming and weaving are both essentials, how is it that in all districts of Fengtian the land is plentiful and suited to cotton, yet the price of cotton cloth is double that below the wall [north China]? Tracing causes to their roots, it is most probably the case that a great number of [the northeast's] bannermen and commoners cultivate cotton but they do not comprehend the benefits of weaving it themselves. They sell the raw cotton to merchants who then export it to other provinces. Thus unable to derive the benefits from growing cotton themselves, they have the expense of buying cloth every year. Order the Fengtian military governor and prefect . . . to have weaving frames made and disseminated. (He Qizhong as cited in He Changling 1992, 861–862)

He Qizhong's essay is of interest for two reasons. First, it expresses officialdom's concern that peasants who did not participate in the canonical gender division of labor between spinning and weaving (women's work) and cultivating (men's work) suffered unduly, both economically and morally. On the one hand, in this idealized form the household was able to produce the grain and cloth it consumed, while meeting its tax obligations to the state. When "men plowed and women wove," the social and fiscal foundations of state power were secured. On the other hand, as Susan Mann has argued, women and older girls who wove were inculcating appropriate feminine virtues in an association between womanly labor and moral edification that went back to ancient times (1997, 143–144; cf. Ebrey 1993, 132). He Qizhong's recommendation echoed both concerns.

Second, and more importantly for this study, He Qizhong was convinced that it was ignorance in the domestic art of cotton spinning and weaving that prevented peasants in the northeast from making their own cloth. They grew cotton, he insisted, but were too foolish to know how to spin and weave it themselves. Consequently, merchants profited from the ignorance of the common folk, another commonly held ideological position.

For all his knowledge of the banner system, and despite his research into the "banner livelihood problem," He Qizhong was apparently uninformed about conditions in the northeast. In the first instance, it would be odd indeed if the "commonfolk" did not know how to spin or weave since many had migrated from north China, where cotton growing and cotton work were long-standing occupations. In the second instance, there is no evidence to suggest that peasants in Fengtian grew cotton in substantial enough amounts to clothe themselves, even if they had been able to spin and weave it themselves.

That this was so is fairly apparent from the local gazetteers. Despite the genre's tendency to include accounts of women's work in spinning and weaving as evidence of local conformance with universal notions of feminine goodness, there are no surviving descriptions of cotton cultivation or spinning and weaving in Manchuria's Qing era gazetteers.[10] As Mann (1997) and Francesca Bray (1997) have shown, there is no reason to doubt that had women in rural Manchuria engaged in cotton spinning and weaving this fact would have been celebrated by local authorities as evidence of Manchuria's conformity to the universal ideal.[11]

The reason women did not weave was simply that, with the exception of southernmost Jinzhou and the south edge of the Liaodong peninsula, the climate of the northeast was unsuited to cotton, which is a thermophilic plant. While the cotton plant requires a cumulative annual temperature (the sum of the mean daily temperatures for consecutive days in which the temperature is ten degrees Celsius or more) of at least three thousand degrees Celsius, Manchuria only has a cumulative annual temperature of less than a thousand degrees Celsius (Xu 1991, 14; Yang 1991, 112). The northerly spread of cotton cultivation in late imperial China thus stopped in southernmost Manchuria (Chao 1977, 14; MMK 1928b, 42–44). This was observed by the reverend Alexander Williamson who traveled in the northeast in the 1860s and found that whereas cotton grew in the southernmost districts of Jinzhou, Haicheng, Gaizhou, and Liaoyang, further inland and to the north the climate was unsuited to its cultivation (Williamson 1870, vol. 2, 41).[12] The British consular to Niuzhuang in 1880 noted that cotton was cultivation in the vicinity of that town, but only enough for local consumption (GB.CR 1971, vol. 13, 484). In other words, it was because men in Manchuria generally did not cultivate cotton, as the Confucian canon encouraged, women could not work it up. Moreover, as colonization spread further north beyond the warmer climes of the Bohai coast, where some cotton could be grown, the proportion of land in cotton fell off dramatically. Manchuria, with its particularly harsh climate and short growing season, was one of the few parts of the empire where Han Chinese lived in significant numbers and were ecologically dependent upon cotton imports.

Though cotton was not grown in the northeast, there was tremendous demand for it. As others have shown, cotton had become the fabric of choice in rural China by the sixteenth century, and the inability of peasants in the northeast to grow it issued in an early dependency upon imports (Chao 1977, 63; Huang 1990, 44–45). In Ming times, peasant settlers in the southern reaches of the northeast were already importing cloth from Shandong and as far away as Jiangnan (Jing and Luo 1978, 50–51; Fan 1998, 218; Zhang 1988, 154; Huang 1985, 112). With the resurgence of coastal trade in the eighteenth century, following reversals associated first with the Ming-Qing transition and then with the Qing coastal blockade that was not lifted until 1685, trade links were reestablished and cotton imports came once again from Shandong and Jiangnan. In the eighteenth and nineteenth centuries, as more and more settlement occurred beyond the southern districts where cotton cultivation was possible, Manchuria's dependency upon cotton imports only grew.

The exceptions to the general rule were the imperial cotton estates (*mianzhuang*), all of which were located on the warmer southern edge of Fengtian, that produced raw cotton for state consumption. On closer examination, however, it turns out that the imperial cotton estates were not so much evidence of cotton cultivation in the northeast as exceptions that demonstrate its general absence. Altogether, there were forty-six imperial cotton estates in the mid-eighteenth century and another five attached to the Shengjing Board of Revenue; they supplied the imperial workshops with raw cotton for the production of state cloth (Yi 1993, 232–233; Diao 1993, 80–81). It is unlikely, however, that even these estates produced much raw cotton, and of course the cloth that was woven was for imperial consumption, not for sale locally. The total cotton rent garnered on a Shengjing Board of Revenue cotton estate was a mere seven hundred catties (SJTZ 1965, 1229). Even assuming a very low yield of thirty-five catties per *mu*, each estate would have needed to plant just twenty *mu* in cotton to meet the rent quota. All of the cotton estates of the Shengjing Imperial Household Department combined paid an annual rent of twelve thousand catties of raw cotton, requiring the planting of a mere 350 *mu* in cotton (QHS 1991, 914 [1197]).[13] The various cotton estates were clearly not producing significant amounts of raw cotton for regional consumption, and by the end of the nineteenth century rents in cotton were commutable to cash anyway.

In a study of interregional trade, William Rowe posits that the Qing empire was made up of four distinct ecological macroregions, each characterized by its own macroagricultural regime. Trade in goods such as sugar, rice, and tea suited to one but not the other flowed between these regions (Rowe 1985, 271–

273). While it should be pointed out that this ecological division of labor cannot in general explain why cotton and grain, suited to vast areas of the empire, constituted the most important items of trade empire-wide, it does explain Manchuria's peculiar dependency upon cotton imports. That dependency lasted through the end of the dynasty when cotton cloth and yarn constituted about three-quarters of the value of all of Manchuria's imports (MSCZ 1906, vol. 2, 505).

Explaining Manchuria's Importation of Woven Cloth

Qing sources not only point to the fact that Manchuria's households did little cotton spinning and weaving, they also suggest that cotton cloth made up the greater part of cotton goods imported by Manchuria (Fan 1992, 227). The Japanese source that shows cloth goods constituted most of all imports at the end of the Qing also shows that cloth imports exceeded those of yarn and unspun cotton combined (MSCZ 1906, vol. 2, 505).[14] The ecological obstacles to cotton cultivation notwithstanding, why did Manchurian peasants not import raw or spun cotton in quantities sufficient to support a native manufacturing industry?

To explain this, the historian Zhang Zhongmin (1988, 154) has picked up on He Qizhong's canard to explain Fengtian's demand for cotton cloth woven in and exported from the Yangzi delta. According to Zhang, there was both an insufficient number of carpenters in the northeast who could construct the necessary looms and a shortage of knowledgeable spinners and weavers. This, he argues, made for higher production costs in Fengtian relative to Taicang, Songjiang, and Shanghai. Consequently, Fengtian peasants favored imported over their own native cloth. This argument simply ignores the fact that spinning and weaving skills were widely disseminated among the Zhili and Shandong peasants who migrated to the northeast. This was especially so among migrants from Baoding, Shuntian, Tianjin, the north Lu plain, Dengzhou, and Laizhou who made up Manchuria's earliest and most persistent settlers. Not surprisingly, those few who could get a hold of cotton yarn were able to weave it and did so with skills that apparently matched weavers in and around Shanghai (GB.CR 1971, vol. 13, 484). Zhang's argument also ignores the fact that crude spinning and weaving tools used by peasants were inexpensive and small, making them easily transportable (Chao 1977, 33–34).

The reason for the low levels of cotton work among Manchurian households was that there was simply not enough locally grown cotton or unprocessed or spun cotton circulating in China's long-distance markets to supply the households of the northeast with the raw materials otherwise needed. To the extent that spinning and weaving skills were absent in Manchuria it was because immigrant peasants could not easily pass them on. The explanation for the lack of household manufacturing in the northeast has therefore much to do with conditions in the cores and the market for raw and spun cotton there. In short, peasant behavior in the empire's cotton-growing/manufacturing regions, along with rural property regimes that prevented merchants from interjecting themselves between cotton growers and manufacturers (often of the same household), meant that most cotton entered the long-distance trade routes already worked up into cloth (Huang 1990, 84).

Because peasant households could earn more total money by spinning and weaving up the cotton they grew and then trading it than they could from selling the raw or spun cotton to merchants or other peasants, those who cultivated cotton preferred to weave as much of it as possible into cloth on their own. In this way they made the higher total earnings that accrued to weavers over cotton growers and spinners (Huang 1990, 84–85; Pomeranz 2000, 102, 320–322). The upshot was that most cotton entered the market only after it had been processed into cloth (Huang 2002). Empire-wide, about 2.5 million catties of unspun cotton entered the long-distance trade networks, while less than one percent of spun yarn was ever marketed (Wu 1983, 99, 106; Xu 1990, 264, 320, table B5; 1992, 53; Zhang 1988, 157, 159–160). Moreover, much of the raw or spun cotton that was marketed was swiftly bought up locally by the very poorest peasants—many of whom were entirely or close to being landless. These partially and wholly landless peasants were eager to get the raw materials they needed to eke out a living (Bray 1997, 212–225; Fan 1998, 26–30, 160–161). Or, it was exported over a shorter distance to neighboring areas such as Fujian and Guangdong where peasants were also eager to add to their incomes through domestic manufacturing because they too were reduced to living on small plots (Fan 1998, 73; Zhang 1988, 161). At the end of the day, there was little surplus raw or spun cotton available for export.

On the "demand side," it is my sense that because peasants in Manchuria were able to secure their full subsistence through agriculture due to their larger holdings, they were not compelled to take up household manufacturing of any sort. The local gazetteers from the Qing are telling in this regard: they make no reference to peasant by-employment and Chinese scholars of the region have been unable to unearth any evidence either (Zhang 1990, 168–172; Yi 1993, 345–348). As late as the end of the Qing dynasty, peasant by-employment in Fengtian was rare and consisted of some silk work on the Liaodong peninsula, some weaving and spinning of hemp throughout the region, winter employment in small-scale for a very few, and rural oil mills (Xu 1989, 1564, 1578–1582). This pattern continued so that in the 1930s "women's work"—known locally as *kang*-work (*kang huo*), because it was done sitting on the heated earthen beds or *kang*—consisted of mending shoes and sewing clothes, but not spinning or weaving (Zhang Guizhi and Liu Hongxi, 1994). They were better off buying the woven cloth produced by low-wage labor of women and children working in Jiangnan, than buying up raw or spun cotton and weaving it themselves. Thus, for instance, when north China raw cotton was available for export in the eighteenth century, it did not travel the short distance to Fengtian but took a much longer journey to Jiangnan, where it was used by Songjiang peasants eager to supplement home-grown cotton in spinning and weaving.[15]

Rural property regimes also had an effect on the content of the cotton trade. Local merchants in the cotton belts of Jiangnan and Shandong who purchased household manufactured cloth did not have leverage (economic or political) over the domestic manufacturing realm. They were consequently unable to separate raw cotton cultivation from domestic work or to break up the different stages of processing leading up to and including weaving—steps that were necessary if more unspun and spun cotton were to be moved into the markets. While there certainly were merchant putters-out who bought raw cotton and sold it to peasant spinners and weavers, especially among the poor peasants of the Jiangnan paddy zone who did not grow cotton (the poor and widows seem to have been a major source of putting-out production [Bray 1997, 223; Shih 1992, 128]), most of the cultivation and manufacturing of cotton remained under the control of individual peasant households (Elvin 1973, 276–277; Huang 1990, 2002). Given merchants' inability to induce peasants to part with their raw or semiprocessed cotton, they had to make do by buying up the undyed and uncalendered cloth—processing for which peasants did not have the wherewithal—and thereby making their profits entirely from distribution. It was symptomatic of the structure of rural manufacturing and marketing that merchants did not gain a significant foothold in any stage of domestic cotton work until factory-spun yarn entered the picture in the late nineteenth century. Factory-spun yarn was so inexpensive that peasant households quit yarn spinning altogether, selling their raw cotton to mill brokers and buying the spun yarn back to weave domestically (Huang 1990, 119–120).

To sum up, cotton goods—in particular, cotton cloth—were the northeast's principal import during the Qing. The local population had therefore to buy nearly all of the cloth it consumed. That state of affairs held through to the twentieth century, when Japanese surveys show that whereas raw cotton accounted for a mere two percent of the total value of goods marketed by peasants, cotton goods were the single most important purchase as a percentage of the household budget expended on noncapital outlays (NHB 1937, 7–8, 27–28; HBK 1937, 53, 64; NJ Series 1934–36).[16]

Estimates of Cotton Imports

As the population of the northeast grew over the eighteenth and nineteenth centuries, more and more cotton cloth had to be imported to clothe the local population. In turn, exports of grain and soybeans also had to grow to pay for these imports. The necessary conditions were thus established for what would become one of the empire's most lucrative trading routes by 1800 (Fan 1998, 58, 217–220, 238). However, no data of the volume or value of Manchuria's cotton imports exist until the late nineteenth century. The annual customs reports sent from Shanhaiguan customs office to the emperor give total excise receipts only. More generally, the customs reports sent to Beijing are of no use for measuring changes in the value or volume of trade over time. It is clear that once the tax quota was fixed, tax revenue remained within a very narrow range. The actual excise collected between 1778 and 1843 ranged from 1,199,000 *taels* in 1843 and 1,863,000 in 1797, whereas between 1798 and 1841 the duty collected ranged narrowly from 1,523,000 to 1,598,000 *taels*, with the exception of 1812 when it was 1,438,000 taels.[17]

However, given that by far the greater part of the cotton consumed locally in the northeast was imported, it is possible to generate crude but reasonable estimates of the volume of cotton cloth and raw cotton imported by estimating how much was consumed. The foremost authority on the subject, Xu Xinwu (1990, 229, 324, table B5), estimates that before the Opium War 1.3 bolts were consumed per person per year for nonweaving households and 2 bolts by the 1930s. Using this range, and assuming that all cloth was imported, then a simple calculation suggests that cloth imports were between 1.4 and 2.2 million bolts in 1750, 2.6 and 4 million in 1800, 6.9 and 10.6 million in 1850, and 18 and 28 million in 1900 (see Table 8.1). The need for cotton padding added to ginned cotton imports. Chao Kang (1977, 231) estimates that, for the early twentieth century, 1.3 pounds of ginned cotton, or 1.18 catties, were consumed per person for various forms of padding.[18] This suggests imports of about 1.3 million catties, 2.36 million catties, 6.2 million catties, and 16.5 million catties for 1750, 1800, 1850, and 1900 respectively.

Manchuria's dependency upon cotton imports posed no problem to the peasants of the northeast. With land plentiful and people scarce, the northeast region was able to generate surpluses of grain and soybeans to be traded for cloth and other items, despite the low productivity of its agriculture. The cost of the cloth was easily covered by exports, or so it appears from the few cotton prices we have. In 1815, the Qing state undertook to move banner households from China Proper and around southern Manchuria to a newly created colony in present-day Jilin, at Shuangchengbao. According to official records of the colony, each colonist was outfitted with four bolts of white cloth at a cost of six

TABLE 8.1

Crude Estimates of the Demand for Cotton Cloth

(bolts)

Year	1.3 bolts per person	1.5 bolts per person	2 bolts per person
1725	1,209,000	1,395,000	1,860,000
1750	1,430,000	1,650,000	2,200,000
1775	2,015,000	2,325,000	3,100,000
1800	2,600,000	3,000,000	4,000,000
1825	4,225,000	4,875,000	6,500,000
1850	6,890,000	7,950,000	10,600,000
1875	11,310,000	13,050,000	17,400,000
1900	18,200,000	21,000,000	28,000,000
1910	23,400,000	27,000,000	36,000,000

EXPLANATORY NOTE: total consumption based on estimated population size shown in Appendix A. Estimates for per capita cloth consumption are Xu Xinwu's (Wu 1990, 324), who argues that in the mid-nineteenth century nonweaving households consumed 1.3 bolts per person annually, whereas weaving households consumed 1.5 bolts per person. By 1936, consumption of cloth in weaving household reached two bolts per person (229). This table includes all three per capita consumption estimates to give a range of possibilities.

taels: thus, one bolt of white cloth cost the state 1.5 *taels* (Li 1990, 16). Assuming these were standard market bolt sizes, four would have been enough to make a single set of clothes and an outfit could be expected to last three or four years (Xu 1990, 324). Circa 1815, Manchuria's population was roughly 2.6 million. Assuming the northeast imported all the cloth it consumed and each peasant annually required 1.3 bolts, it would have imported a minimum of five million *taels* worth of cotton cloth in a year. According to the same official source, one *shi* of grain cost 2.5 *taels*; at these prices, the northeast had to export just over two million *shi* of grain to purchase the cotton cloth it imported, this at a time when Manchuria could probably export as much as 4.5 million *shi* in grain and beans combined (see Tables 8.2 and 8.3). To these clothing needs would have to be added the cloth required for a heavily padded winter jacket as well as the raw cotton used to stuff clothes and the yarn used to sew and mend them. Those might raise the cost of cotton imports by fifty percent, but certainly no more. It seems therefore that Manchuria was easily able to sustain the levels of grain and soybean exports necessary to meet regional cotton needs.

Estimates of Grain and Soybean Exports

By the 1820s, most of Manchuria's grain and soybean exports were going to Jiangnan, though some went directly or were transshipped at Jiangnan to Fujian and Guangdong (GCJY 1993, 1197). There are two commonly cited observations by Jiangnan officials of the amount of the combined exports of grain and soybeans shipped from northern China to Jiangnan in the first decades of the nineteenth century. Xie Zhanren estimated that no less than ten million *shi* of grain, soybean, dates, and pears were exported from Fengtian (Guandong) and north China (Shandong and Zhili) combined to Jiangnan annually (as cited in He 1992, 1155). Bao Shichen, recording conditions in 1804, claimed by contrast that "ever since the ban on coastal trade was lifted in 1685, annually more than ten million *shi* of wheat and soybeans are exported from Guandong [Fengtian] to Shanghai."[19] It is to be noted that whereas Xie's estimate was of imports from north and northeast China in a number of goods, Bao was only estimating shipments of wheat and beans and only those from Manchuria. These are both considerable amounts, but the question remains whether they are valid; for both Xie and Bao were engaged in a bureaucratic debate over the best means to transport grain between north and south China and both were active advocates of maritime transportation (see below).

Most estimates of the absolute levels and content of the Manchurian trade come from scholars working in regions of the Qing empire that either imported goods from or exported them to the northeast. Among contemporary scholars, Fan Jinmin's study of Jiangnan trade posits that Manchuria exported to Jiangnan about four to five million *shi* of soybeans, but hazards no estimate of grain exports (Fan 1998, 153). Also focusing on Jiangnan, Wang Yeh-chien has concluded that in the late eighteenth century Manchuria annually exported to that region ten million *shi* of soybeans and grain combined (Wang 1989, 430). He has further estimated that Jiangnan received from Manchuria and north China combined annual imports of fifteen million *shi* of soybeans and grain (Wang 1992, 38).[20] In his study of Jiangnan, Li Bozhong estimates that Manchuria alone annually exported ten million *shi* of soybeans prior to 1850, and no more than five million *shi* of grain (Li 1998, 210 n 37). Between 1800 and 1850, Jiangnan was the principal though not sole destination for Manchuria's exports, so in each case these figures must come close to approximating the sum total or the greater part of Manchuria's exports at the time.

What are we to make of these contemporary estimates, ranging from four to ten million *shi* of beans in the early nineteenth century? Li Bozhong's (1998) estimate of ten million *shi* of soybeans in addition to a smaller amount of grain is certainly the greatest. Li's estimates of Manchuria's exports are part of his more specific claim of real growth in Jiangnan agriculture in the eighteenth century. Li claims peasants in Jiangnan raised yields while not raising labor inputs by applying labor-saving and yield-raising beancake fertilizer made primarily from imported Manchurian soybeans. Li argues that this so-called fertilizer revolution occasioned a significant rise in labor productivity. By addressing the way that Li backs up his estimate of Manchuria's soybean exports, and by correcting his errors, we can show what might reasonably be concluded about levels of both soybean and grain exports.

Though Li cites the estimates of the Qing officials Bao Shichen and Xie Zhanren to support his claims, because his interpretations of their numbers are open to question (see below), he supports his claim by working back from estimates of Manchurian soybean output in the early twentieth century that he derives using yield and acreage data provided by Dwight Perkins (Li 1998, 210 n 37; Perkins 1969, 258, table C.13; 280, table D.15). Li concludes on the basis of these numbers that Manchuria produced about 28.9 million *shi* of soybeans in the years 1914–1918. To take into account the fact that Heilongjiang was little settled in the Qing, and therefore not capable of contributing much in the way of exports, Li adjusts this figure downward to 20.7 million *shi* for Jilin and Liaoning provinces alone. On the basis of that figure, he then suggests that in the first half of the nineteenth century Manchuria was fully capable of exporting ten million *shi* of soybeans, or half as much as his 1914–1918 figure.

In making this estimate, however, Li does not investigate soybean yields in the Qing, nor does he seriously consider how much land was under cultivation in the nineteenth century. Nor does he account for the proportion of soybeans that were consumed within Manchuria and therefore not available for export. The result is an estimate of soybean exports for the first half of the nineteenth century that is far greater than was reasonably possible.

To begin, we can compare Li's claim that in 1914–1918 Jilin and Liaoning together produced 20.7 million *shi* of soybeans with the findings of the investigating arm of the Southern Manchurian Railway, which, at that time, was capturing the entire soybean trade for Japanese economic interests. That study shows that total Manchurian output (including production from all three provinces) was eighteen million *shi* and that the surplus available for trade was fourteen million *shi*. By working from the assumption that all 20.7 million was available for export, Li has overstated his base figure by nearly fifty percent. It also means that Li's estimate of the total volume of Manchurian soybean exports in the early nineteenth century is nearly three-quarters the amount Japanese researchers found was in fact available for export from the entire northeast in the late 1910s (Kameoka 1921, 110). Yet, it is widely recognized that more settlement occurred in the fifty years after 1875 than the two centuries prior.

Turning to his method, we find that Li has greatly overstated Manchuria's export capacity for both the early twentieth century and the Qing because he begins with an uncritical acceptance of Dwight Perkins's (1969) soybean yield figure for the 1930s (1.1 *shi* per *mu*) and then assumes without comment an equivalent yield was possible a century earlier. Perkins's yield figure is not only too high for the Qing, it is too high for the early twentieth century. Japanese studies of Manchurian soybean production in the first two decades of the twentieth century show conclusively that the average yield was 0.5 *shi* per *mu* (Settai and Ito, 1920, 14–16, table 2). This was also the conclusion of the 1909 examination of Fengtian agricultural conditions conducted by Western-trained Chinese agronomists (FNDS 1909, 3.3. 49–60). Li's reliance on Perkins's data alone means he has overstated production in the twentieth century by one hundred percent. All else being equal, this also means that Li has overstated his estimate of soybean production and exports for the first half of the nineteenth century by the same degree.

Just as problematic is the fact that Li makes no provision for Manchuria's temporal and spatial pattern of colonization and settlement. Presumably, this means that he assumes that the area under cultivation in the early nineteenth century was half that of the early twentieth century. Using a yield of 0.5 *shi* per *mu*, we can say that to produce Li's estimated ten million *shi* of soybeans in the early nineteenth century, there had to have been twenty million *mu* of land planted in soybeans. If true, this was eighty percent of all land registered for taxation circa 1820, and fifteen percent more land than was officially registered in 1780. To be sure, land registered for taxation in the Qing fell well short of actual cultivated acreage, but Li does not make this argument, nor does he try to derive plausible acreage figures to support his estimates.

Yet, even reasonable adjustments to the numbers do not support Li's numbers. Using the acreage figures provided in Appendix A as the denominator, and assuming a generous yield of 0.5 *shi* per *mu*, we find that Li's estimated soybean exports would have required about forty-five percent of all cultivated land circa 1825, just over half of all farmed land in 1800, and nearly all farmed land in 1750, when Jiangnan's "fertilizer revolution" was supposedly already in full force and when all available land in Jiangnan was already under cultivation (Li 1998, 19–20, 26–27). Even if the estimates of production levels developed in this study understate actual output by a reasonable margin of error, these percentages are so high that Li's figures cannot be salvaged. There simply would not be sufficient land remaining for Manchuria's peasants to both pay for the cost of agricultural production and ensure their own subsistence (taking into consideration the need for peasants to bank against poor grain harvests) after devoting so much land to soybeans.[21]

Furthermore, it is clear that, *pace* Li, Manchuria did not export all or close to all of its soybean output in either the twentieth century or the Qing. Again, Japanese investigators studying Manchuria in the early 1920s found that before soybeans got to market, peasants had already consumed one-quarter as food (either unprocessed or processed into cooking oil or tofu—a soybean product) and for seed (the latter accounted for only four percent) (Settai and Ito 1920, 19–23, table; MMZ 1922–23, vol. 3, 170–171).[22] A household survey from the 1930s shows that about fifteen percent of soybeans harvested were consumed directly by those who produced them as food and seed, though it says nothing of what percentage was exported (NJ-Series 1934–1936). Finally, one study suggests that twenty-eight percent of soybean production was consumed in Manchuria, and seventy-two percent was exported (Tsao 1930, 942–943). It is not possible to say for sure what proportion of the soybean harvest was consumed in Manchuria in the Qing, but it is clear that soybeans were an important part of the peasant diet at the time. The soybean was important enough that in the eighteenth century the state limited the volume of soybeans exportable in order to protect local food supplies: "there are many districts [in Fengtian] where the bannermen and commoners depend upon the soybean for food" (SC Guangxu 4.19; Katō 1953a, 600–601). Any estimate of exports must, therefore, take regional consumption into account and, given developments in transportation, soy oil manufacturing, market networks, and world demand after 1900, it seems more than likely that the percentage of soybeans marketed by peasants in the twentieth century exceeded that of the Qing. I assume that the amount consumed locally in the Qing was at least equivalent to the amount consumed in the 1920s, or about twenty-five percent.

There are two further problems with Li's assumptions. Li not only fails to consider the cost of production—the proportion of the harvest that had to be retained to resume production the following year—but also assumes peasants in the nineteenth and twentieth centuries planted the same proportion of their land in soybeans. First, Japanese surveys from the 1930s show that production costs took at least thirty percent of soybean output and without sources from the Qing I assume the same applied then.[23] Second, there is every reason to believe that peasants planted less of their land in soybeans in the nineteenth century than in the early twentieth century, when it reached twenty percent (MMZ 1922–23, vol. 3, 256, 269). In all likelihood, in the Qing about fifteen percent of cultivated land was planted in soybeans.[24]

All this adds up to the fact that Li's estimate is far too high. It therefore fails to support the plausibility of his interpretation of the Qing official Xie Zhanren's writings on ocean-going trade in the nineteenth century, to which we now turn. Though Li Bozhong references Qing official Bao Shichen, a rough contemporary of Xie, his argument rests squarely on his use of Xie's essay "A synopsis on maritime transportation" (in He 1992, 1154–1159). Li's interpretation of Xie Zhanren deserves some attention, as does Xie's essay. As Li acknowledges, Xie states in his essay that "ten million *shi*" of beans, grain, pears, and dates were exported from the north to Jiangnan annually (cited in He 1992, 1155). In order to make his case for twenty million *shi*, ten million of which came from Manchuria, Li claims that Xie was expressing the volume of trade in the Guandong *shi*. The Guandong *shi* was a unit of measurement used exclusively in the northeast and typically was two and a half times greater than the standard *shi*, though it might be only twice as large depending upon the port of exit (SC Guangxu, 6.13–15). Once converted to the standard *shi*, the total combined export from the north and northeast becomes twenty-five million standard *shi* (Li 1998, 209 n 35).[25]

Li's contention that Xie was expressing the trade in Guandong *shi* is, however, suspect. As Li acknowledges Xie Zhanren states clearly enough that "northern grain, soybeans, pears and dates are transported to Jiangsu and Zhejiang in the amount of no less than ten million *shi*" (cited in He 1992, 1155).[26] Nowhere does Xie tell us that he used the larger Guandong *shi*, even though he knew the difference between the two measures as a specialist in maritime transport. He provides a conversion rate only later in the essay, under a different subheading when discussing the wages paid to sailors and troubadours (cited in He 1992, 1158).[27] The question thus arises, if Xie were estimating the volume of trade using the larger Guandong unit why did he fail to make that clear? This would have been essential because the essay was written for an audience that included nonspecialists, as well as the sovereign, none of whom would have had reason to presume that Xie was using anything but the standard *shi*. Moreover, as Xie evidently understood, while the Guandong *shi* was used in the northeast it was not employed to measure the volume of goods exported from north China ports that were also included in this estimate. Consequently, there was no reason for Xie to use Guandong *shi*. *Pace* Li Bozhong, there is every reason to believe that Xie, knowing the difference between the two measurements and wishing to avoid confusion, reported in the standard *shi*. In short, Xie was clearly reporting that all imports from the north, including those from Manchuria, amounted to ten million standard *shi*.

What then, do we make of Bao Shichen's roughly contemporary claim that Jiangnan imported annually ten million *shi* of soybeans and wheat from Manchuria alone? As Xue Yong (forthcoming) reminds us, Bao was a fervent advocate of coastal shipping and engaged in a heated bureaucratic debate over the comparative efficiencies of moving grain by sea and by the inland Grand Canal. And, as Xue shows, both sides in the debate produced figures that supported their claims.[28] Bao's reports on the freight capacity of Jiangnan's ocean-going vessels exceeds that of his opponents by one hundred–fold, a clear sign that numbers were being falsified to prove political positions.[29] And, we know that Bao himself was not immune from exaggeration: his assertion that Manchuria exported ten million *shi* of grain and beans every year "*since 1685*" was not only unsubstantiated but quite fantastic. Given the exaggerated nature of that claim, on what basis can we accept Bao's assertion that ten million *shi* was moved annually in his day? I believe we cannot and that Xie Zhanren's estimate of ten million *shi* of goods from Manchurian *and* north China combined is far more plausible.

Fortunately, this conclusion is independently supported by a general survey of the northeast conducted by the Imperial Household Department and included in *Policies on the Imperial Enterprise.* As part of mid-nineteenth-century efforts to tax commerce throughout the empire, the Imperial Household Department ordered Manchuria's Shengjing military governor and Fengtian prefect to study local trade for the purpose of implementing the new *lijin* (likin) tax. The *lijin* was introduced initially as a temporary means to raise funds for the military suppression of the Taiping Rebellion (1851–1864) and was levied on all goods that moved through internal trade networks. Items taxed included those destined for the coastal ports as well as those moving overland or on river barge to other inland markets. The tax captured all trade in grain and beans. According to the joint report, circa 1855 (thirty years after Xie's commentary on coastal trade and fifty years after Bao's) the total amount of grain and beans *together* moved by merchants through the northeast (including that headed for ports as well as local markets) amounted to "no less than several million *shi*." That estimate demonstrates that soybean exports in the first half of the nineteenth century certainly fell short of ten million *shi* and were probably in the range suggested below (GCJY 1993, 1188).

Estimating Soybean Output and Amounts Available for Export

Some questions still remain: how much soybean and grain was exported and how did exports change in volume and content over time? Following the method outlined in the critique of Li Bozhong's numbers, estimates of soybean production and soybean exports, as well as grain production and exports, can be deduced for the eighteenth and nineteenth centuries. Using revised acreage figures provided in Appendix A and assuming fifteen percent of the land was planted in soybeans before 1900 and twenty percent thereafter, and deducting production costs (thirty percent), we can determine that the annual soybean surplus was under 1.5 million *shi* in the late eighteenth century, rose to three million in the first half of the eighteenth century, topped four million in 1875, and reached seven million by 1900. Assuming that seventy-five percent of soybeans harvested were exported, then the average annual exports of soybeans would have been about 1 to 1.5 million *shi* in the late eighteenth century, would have risen to about 2.5 million *shi* in the first half of the nineteenth century, reached three million by 1875, and surpassed five million by 1900.

With this approach, we find that estimates for the late eighteenth century are supported by contemporaneous soybean customs receipts that came from a special investigation of the Shanhaiguan customs offices. The Shanhaiguan customs office collected excise on all duty-paying goods leaving and entering the northeast by sea and overland caravan. Customs receipts for the years 1776–1777, 1777–1778, and 1778–1779, collated in the reign of the Guangxu emperor in the *Pamphlet on the Administration of the Shanhaiguan Customs Office*, were used by Katō Shigeshi (1953a) in his early study of Manchurian trade (SC Guangxu, 4.19–20). Palace memorials located in the First Historical Archives collection provide additional figures for 1774–1775 and 1775–1776 and confirm the *Shanhaiguan Customs Office* reports numbers for 1776–1777 (HZ 1778.10.22).[30] Together, these receipts show that total soybean and beancake exports averaged 1.1 million (standard) *shi* per annum between 1774 and 1779, a figure that turns out to be nearly identical to the revised estimated exports of 1.122 million *shi* (see Table 8.2).

Li Bozhong and Pierre-Etienne Will have suggested without explanation that the reports collected in the *Shanhaiguan Customs Office* report undercounted by a sizable margin actual soybean exports, even though their original source for this, Katō, makes no such inference (Will 1990, 218; Li 1998, 113; Katō 1953a, 600–606). There are, however, reasons to believe that these reports did not undercount revenue by a significant margin. Palace memorials discussing the investigation show that the reports that produced these figures were the result of an extraordinary investigation into the Shanhaiguan customs office ordered by the emperor, overseen by the Board of Revenue, and conducted over five years. They were not standard reports which give only total customs duty tallies without specifying the nature of the goods taxed. The reports were instead detailed investigations into the Shanhaiguan customs offices and their operations. The purpose of the inquiry was to measure the levels of trade, make sure there was no collusion between local officials and merchants to cheat the privy purse of revenue, and gauge whether an increase in the soybean excise tax would harm trade. The investigation pulled in all appropriate civil and banner officials in the northeast and, according to palace memorials, included close official inspections of all merchant ships leaving the northeast ports over the duration of the investigation. The authorities' examinations of vessels were then checked against customs duties collected and all discrepancies were investigated (HZ 1775.2.25; 1779.10.22). Because of the unusual nature of these reports, there is in fact good reason to believe the figures come fairly close to actual export levels.

The customs data collected after 1862 by the Imperial Maritime Customs (IMC) office at Niuzhuang are of still better quality and with some adjustments support these estimated figures. The IMC office collected duties on all soybean products exiting Niuzhuang by foreign ship. From mid-century to the turn of the twentieth century, the great majority of soybeans and soybean products leaving Manchuria were exported through Niuzhuang (U.S. CR Dispatch 236, March 11, 1904). But it was not until the last two decades of the nineteenth century that foreign steamships came to dominate the shipment of processed and unprocessed soybeans (Chao 1983, 10; Sun 1969; Lie 1981, 119–120). By 1901, however, about eighty percent of the processed and unprocessed soybeans left Manchuria on foreign steamboats through Niuzhuang (Lie 1981, 120). The IMC figures, therefore, for the last decade of the nineteenth century come close to representing the entire volume of soybean exports. Adjusting them to account for the portion carried on native junks, we obtain a figure of six million *shi* circa 1890 compared to my revised estimate of 5.2 million.[31]

Aside from the fact that estimates of exports based on revised acreage figures align very closely with customs receipts figures bracketing the period between 1780 and 1900, and concur with the sense of the 1855 report on the *likin* commercial tax, there are other reasons to believe that these estimates are reasonable. First, my estimates for the end of the Qing are also supported by Japanese investigations of soybean cultivation conducted by the investigating arm of the South Manchurian Railway company circa 1910. According to that study, total output was between ten and twelve million *shi*, compared to my estimate of eleven million *shi* for the same year (after adding back the cost of production to give a total output figure) (cf. Table 8.2; KT 1912, 29). Second, Manchuria's principal region of soybean cultivation—and indeed agricultural production more generally—in the Qing was the Liao river basin (which included the Da, Qing, Chai, Fan, Taizi, Jun, and Xinkai tributaries of the Liao). The total soybean production of the basin in the 1850s would have come close to the total production of the region, certainly that part which went for export. In the 1920s, the Liao basin produced an estimated 3.6 million *shi* of soybeans, while my revised estimate of total soybean production in Manchuria in 1850 is 3.4 million (Settai and Ito 1920, 16–18). Given the much lower yields achievable in the Qing era and the fact that large areas of not only Manchuria but even the Liao river basin had poor links to the coast at that time, the comparison suggests my figures may overstate exports for the late Qing.[32]

Second, though there is the possibility that the method used to estimate acreage understates actual farmed area in the eighteenth and nineteenth centuries, it is unlikely that it has underestimated on an order that may bring estimates of grain and soybean exports up to the levels suggested by Li Bozhong and others. Moreover, there is reason to believe that the revised export figures in Table 8.2 have overstated soybean production by using yield data from the 1920s for the eighteenth and nineteenth centuries. Qing grain yields were as much as half those of the twentieth century, and presumably Qing soybean yields were lower too, though how much lower cannot be determined with the sources on hand. Furthermore, as noted in the previous chapter, not all arable

TABLE 8.2

Crude Estimates of the Net Volume of Soybean Output (A) and Exports (B)

(*shi*)

Year	A	B
1725	918,750	689,063
1750	1,155,000	866,250
1775	1,496,250	1,122,188
1800	1,942,500	1,456,875
1825	2,362,500	1,771,875
1850	3,150,000	2,362,500
1875	4,200,000	3,150,000
1900	7,000,000	5,250,000
1910	8,400,000	6,300,000

EXPLANATORY NOTE: Column A assumes fifteen percent of the land is in soybeans before 1900, and twenty percent after 1899 and production costs took thirty percent of soybean output (MMZ 1922–23). Japanese studies from the early twentieth century suggest production costs fell between thirty-five and thirty-nine percent of output (MNK 1942; SNS 1937). Column B assumes seventy-five percent of soybean output was exported from Manchuria. Soybean yields are taken to be 0.5 *shi* per *mu* for the entire period, though yields were certainly lower in the eighteenth and nineteenth centuries. See Appendix B. Acreage taken from Appendix A.

land in the Qing was cultivated every year; in some districts perhaps as much as one-third of the land was rotated in fallow annually. This fact would reduce the estimates of soybean production further still. Finally, Manchuria's transport systems in the Qing were such that regions north of Tieling and Kaiyuan and villages far from the Liao river and its tributaries would have had a much more difficult time moving soybeans to market in the late eighteenth and nineteenth centuries than in the 1920s. There would undoubtedly have been some wastage as a result. As the following chapter shows, soybeans were stored inland when transportation was disrupted by spring rains and at the ports when ships waited for the harbors to thaw and for favorable winds. Yet the numbers presented here assume all peasants produced for the market, peasants consumed in the Qing as much of their own soybeans as they did in the 1920s, no land was fallow, and there was no wastage.

Estimating Grain Output and Amount Available for Export

The revised figures show that soybean exports were considerably less than what many scholars working on regions other than Manchuria have for the most part estimated were exported by the northeast. On the other hand, it is also clear that Manchuria was perhaps capable of exporting more grain than has been generally assumed. What this in turn suggests is that perhaps a greater percentage of Manchurian export trade was made up of grain than previously maintained.

While it has long been recognized, on the basis of Qing observers, that Manchuria exported grain as well as soybeans and beancake, it has generally been assumed by scholars without explanation that beans constituted the greater part of these shipments.[33] The assumption has been based largely on qualitative evidence that is far from definitive. Observations and commentaries usually describe Fengtian exports using the generic term "northern goods" (*beihuo*). By the early nineteenth century, "northern goods" was synonymous with grain and beans, but of course included other items such as jujubes and pears (Fan 1992, 277 n 88). Officials striving for greater precision listed exports as soybeans, other beans, grains, and pears among other items. In these instances as well, however, officials never specified which item made up the greater part of the trade.

On the other hand, there is evidence of a tremendous hunger for imported grain emanating from Manchuria's primary export markets, first in north China and subsequently in Jiangnan (Xu Tan 1998a; Wang 1989). Wang Yeh-chien has estimated Jiangnan's grain production fell short of what was required to feed its population by eighteen to nineteen percent (Wang 1989, 429, table 2; also see Ch'üan and Kraus 1975, 64–65), while Fang Xing (1996, 91–98) shows that about forty percent of the grain consumed by Jiangnan peasants in the High Qing were the imported and less desirable coarse or mixed grains of the sort Manchuria exported.

Manchuria, moreover, was in a position to export considerable amounts of grain. Not taking into account the effects of fallow farming, the grain needs of livestock, grain converted into alcohol, or spoilage, exportable surplus may have fallen just short of three million *shi* in the second half of the eighteenth century and reached perhaps three to four and a half million *shi* in the first half of the nineteenth century. After taking the fallow into account, exportable grain surplus was perhaps just under two million *shi* in the last quarter of the eighteenth century, three and a half million by 1850 and fell to under a million *shi* by 1900. Thereafter exportable surplus appears to have fallen off to 1910.

Turning to total grain and soybean exports, the estimates presented in tables 8.2 and 8.3 suggest that circa 1775 Fengtian total surplus of grain and beans was about four million *shi*, assuming no land in fallow. Circa 1804, when Bao Shichen estimated that total Manchuria imports to Jiangnan were about ten million *shi*, depending on whether one accounts for the fallow, the total surplus was in fact between four and five million *shi*, and for reasons already stated probably less. By 1850, the estimated surplus was between six and seven million. Given the facts that not all of the grain surplus was marketed or exported, there was some spoilage, and not every year was a good harvest, these estimates come

TABLE 8.3

Crude Estimates of Surplus Grain Available for Export

(*shi*)

Year	Grain surplus	Grain surplus after fallow
1725	1,088,850	718,641
1750	2,356,200	1,555,092
1775	2,829,225	1,867,289
1800	3,694,950	2,438,667
1825	3,034,500	2,275,875
1850	4,676,700	3,507,525
1875	3,320,100	3,320,100
1900	2,499,000	2,499,000
1910	856,800	856,800

EXPLANATORY NOTE: Estimates assume that grain yields rose over time from 0.4 *shi* per *mu* in 1725, to 0.5 *shi* in 1750, 1775, 1800, and 1825; to 0.6 in 1850 and 1875, and 0.7 in 1900 and 1910; average per capita consumption is assumed to have been 2.1 *shi* husked grain, though it is reasonable to assume that consumption was higher in early years and then dropped off as the surplus declined. It is assumed that grain was planted on seventy-five percent of arable, commensurate roughly with twentieth-century data (fifteen percent went to soybeans and another ten percent to other pulses, vegetables, oil seeds, hemp, potato, etc.). Production costs are assumed to have taken thirty percent of output, after Japanese surveys from the 1930s and 1940s (MNK 1942; SNS 1937). It is also assumed husking removed twelve percent of grain volume (Liu and Yeh 1965, 29, table 2). This extraction rate is for sorghum, which has the highest extraction rate of those crops grown in significant proportion in Manchuria. Finally, it is also assumed that fifteen percent of grain was marketed locally, where it remained to purchase salt, cooking oil, and other nonimported items. Fallow assumptions follow from Table 7.2. No effort is made to account for grain consumed by livestock given that no data on the numbers of livestock exist for the Qing. If taken into account, this would reduce further the available surplus.

close to matching the Imperial Household Department's 1856 estimate of "no less than several million" *shi* of beans and coarse grains marketed annually.

Revised Figures Compared to Other Estimates

The revised estimates of the total volume of grain and beans available for export presented here are lower than figures provided by Wang Yeh-chien but comparable in some regards to those provided by Fan Jinmin and Zhang Zhongming. Wang Yeh-chien (1989, 430) figures Fengtian exported about ten million *shi* of grain and beans annually to Jiangnan in the early nineteenth century, compared to my upper estimate of just under five million *shi* for roughly the same period. However, Fan Jinmin (1998, 153), in his comprehensive examination of the Jiangnan trade, believes that soybean imports by sea from north China and Fengtian *together* amounted to no more than four to five million *shi* circa 1800.[34] As for combined grain and bean imports from north China and the northeast entering Jiangnan by sea, Fan believes these amounted to about eleven million *shi* circa 1800, compared to my estimate of four to five million *shi* from the northeast alone (Fan 1998, 66). Zhang Zhongmin (1988, 171) concludes that during the Jiaqing emperor's reign about four million *shi* of beans *and* coarse grains together were shipped from the northeast to Shanghai annually, at a time when Shanghai was the principal port for soybeans and grain imported by sea from the north.[35] If just under half of Fan's estimated eleven million *shi* of soybeans and grain came from the northeast only, then my estimates confirm his as well as Zhang Zhongmin's.[36]

An Overview of the Structure of Demand for Manchurian Food Grains and Soybeans

Despite He Qizhong's lament discussed above that bannermen and peasants in Manchuria suffered because they did not know the arts of spinning and weaving, it was no great hardship for Manchuria's peasants to pay for cotton cloth imports with grain and soybeans exports. The peasants of the northeast had land in abundance. By extending the hinterland into Jilin and then Heilongjiang via colonization, new arrivals as well as those born in the region were absorbed without significantly depleting grain surpluses. By raising yields through the gradual adoption of labor-intensifying techniques (the elimination of fallow farming, greater application of manures, more intensive weeding, and even intercropping), peasants in the northeast were able to sustain healthy grain surpluses well into the nineteenth century, even in the face of steady and brisk population growth. While there appears to have been a decline toward the end of the nineteenth century in grain surplus (though perhaps not in soybeans), colonization at the end of the Qing and into the twentieth century appears to have turned this trend around—if such a trend ever existed.

Simultaneously, as the result of independent developments, demand for Fengtian foodstuffs and soybeans in the longer-settled cores of the empire grew. In the early eighteenth century, this demand emanated first from the north China core region (Xu 1998a). By 1750, however, Jiangnan had perhaps superseded north China as the biggest importer of Fengtian grain and beans (Fan 1992, 275–276). The supersession of north China by Jiangnan as the principal market for Manchuria goods was symptomatic of a general pattern of intensifying competition between the cores for the grain surpluses of the peripheral zones. Thus, by the 1840s more and more of Manchuria's soybean exports were going to Zhejiang, Fujian, and Guangdong, where beancake was used on sugarcane fields. With the commencement of the Taiping Rebellion, Fujian and Guangdong replaced Jiangnan as the primary markets and remained so until the twentieth century. In the twentieth century, the south accounted for sixty-five to eighty percent of soybean exports, while Shanghai and Shandong each accounted for a mere ten percent (Lie 1981, 7).

Predictably, the result of the rising competition for grain and soybeans was rising empire-wide prices. Wang Yeh-chien suggests that Jiangnan demand for grain was the chief engine of price inflation as grain prices elsewhere followed the delta's upward (Wang 1992, 52–54). In the cores of the empire, the approach of the limits of economic expansion via population growth and labor intensification had begun to issue in a sharp rise in grain prices and a steady worsening of the terms of trade for producers of some of the cores' key manufactured exports.

Symptomatic of this trend were the relative decline in the price of cotton and cotton cloth and, therefore, the fall in real wages for cotton spinners and weavers. This was a fairly typical manifestation of the Malthusian pressures on prices felt not only in China but in parts of Europe too, and it lead to what Pomeranz (2000, 206–207, 241) has rightly called the proto-industrial cul-de-sac at both ends of Eurasia; as prices for grains rose and took a greater percentage of the family purse, the demand for nonfood goods fell, leading to declining relative prices for cotton goods and the like (Brenner and Isett 2002, 639–640; cf. Zhang 1988, 206, 215; Fan 1998, 162–163).[37]

The fall in real wages of domestic manufacturers of cotton cloth was undoubtedly a windfall for Manchuria's peasantry as long as they could maintain the same level of grain surplus as before. All things being equal, Manchuria's peasants who used their grain to buy cloth were required to expend less and less labor in grain production to obtain the same quantity of cloth over time. To put it another way, the same amount of labor in grain cultivation was, with the passage of time, able to purchase more and more cloth. Still, all things were undoubtedly not equal. The fact that labor productivity in grain cultivation in the northeast was also falling may have negated some (or all) of this effect, though in the absence of cotton cloth price series for Manchuria the relative change in purchasing power of Manchurian grain producers cannot be measured. It does seem, however, that Manchuria was running an export surplus that would mean that peasants were benefiting from the turn in their favor of the terms of trade, and most certainly grain producers in Manchuria witnessed a far slower decline in returns to their labor than cotton manufacturers in Jiangnan. By the 1860s, the value of Manchuria's exports by foreign vessels at the primary port of Yingkou-Niuzhuang, which by one estimate accounted for half of the trade at the time, exceeded its imports by eighty percent (Williamson 1870, vol. 2, 47).

Also symptomatic of the worsening ratio of labor to land in the cores were the rising demand and rising prices for Manchurian soybeans, also felt across the eighteenth century. This demand emanated first from Jiangnan's cotton fields, then its paddy fields, and later from the sugarcane and paddy fields of the southeast provinces of Fujian and Guangdong. Thus, not only were peasants elsewhere paying higher prices for Manchurian grain over time, they were also forced to pay higher and higher prices for the soybeans used to render beancake fertilizer in order to sustain or raise yields on their own fields.[38] The price of beancake in Jiangnan rose from perhaps five hundred cash per catty in 1750 to two thousand cash per catty by 1820 (Li 1998, 85, table 5.3). In 1808 one *shi* of soybeans brought five *taels* in Jiangnan (Deng 1996, 47).[39] Manchurian peasants benefited doubly, therefore, from the cores' rising demand for grain. Just as rising grain prices were symptomatic of rising grain deficits, so rising beancake (and soybean) prices were symptomatic of the same grain shortfalls.

Thus, for instance, in Jiangnan's paddy zone the approaching limits to the land's population-carrying capacity in the eighteenth century pushed peasants to double-crop rice with wheat and other crops to raise total output. That turn to double-cropping, contemporaries noted, put greater stress on the land and threatened to reduce rice yields (Li 1998, 86; Ellis and Wang 1997, 184–188, 190–191; Huang 2002, 508 n 8). To counter these effects, peasants piled on fertilizers (Ellis and Wang 1997, 184–188). Some fertilizer, like manure and canal sludge, required a significant increase in labor inputs, while beancake required less labor but was very expensive.[40]

In Jiangnan's cotton belt the analogous but earlier turn to cotton cultivation required greater use of fertilizers to replenish soils quickly exhausted by year-after-year cropping of nutrient-hungry cotton. At first, Jiangnan received its soybeans and beancake from Anhui and the Shandong peninsula. But the capacity of these regions to sustain let alone increase exports over time was limited by yields and arable area. Thus, from the late eighteenth century on, more and more of Jiangnan's soybeans came from the northeast (Wang 1989, 430; Fan 1998, 67; Fan 1992, 273).

Given beancake's tie to household grain sustenance in the delta, the cost of beancake to peasants followed the price of grain up in the eighteenth century. Consequently, as with Manchuria's grain producers, so Manchuria's soybean growers found they too were able to purchase more and more cloth with the same amount of soybean product.

Kenneth Pomeranz (2000, 242–253) has explained England's ability to undergo an Industrial Revolution in terms of its access to underutilized resources in its colonial possessions. He claims that North America provided the ginned cotton that England's industry needed but which its agricultural sector could not supply without having to abandon grain cultivation to the detriment of its food supply. But in arguing this way, Pomeranz ignores the very similar "palliatives" of China's peripheries to its cores, even while acknowledging, for instance, the importance of beancake fertilizers, produced from imported beans, to the agriculture of the cores (2000, 98–99, 226, 289; 2002, 582–584). The Qing state encouraged peasant colonization of the peripheries in the eighteenth and nineteenth centuries, and in many instances financed it through tax holidays, no less than some states in Europe financed early imperial expansion. It understood that this was a palliative to overpopulation as well as a source of new revenue (Rowe 2001, 56–57). The state assisted peasant settlement in Hunan, Sichuan, Guangxi, Yunnan, and Guizhou and eventually on Taiwan, sometimes removing or eradicating local aboriginal tribes in the process directly or through its inaction to prevent it. All of these regions then became major suppliers of grain and beans to the cores, by virtue of convenient waterways (Guo 1990, 41–45; Jiang 1992, 42–48). And, even though the Qing state forbade peasant colonization of many areas including Manchuria, the fact that peasants did settle there, and the fact that the state permitted the export of grain and soybeans after 1770, went some way to alleviating pressures on Jiangnan land (Wang 1989). Just as Pomeranz asks counterfactually what would have happened to its grain production if England had to produce its own cotton, we might ask analogously what would have happened if Jiangnan had to produce all the grain and soybeans it consumed? Presumably, huge amounts of land would have been removed from cotton cultivation, causing the collapse of cotton work and incurring enormous impoverishment as a significant source of income disappeared (Duchesne 2004, 61–65, 70–71). The problem for China's cores was, as this study of Manchuria shows, that the peripheries themselves had structurally determined limitations on their growth.

The Qing state consequently took a strategic stance vis-à-vis the empire-wide spread of the trading network and the extension of particular trading lanes. Its overriding concern was ensuring grain security for the populations (especially of the cores), an unsurprising fact given the agrarian basis of the empire. As Manchuria's grain and soybean surpluses were first registered and then grew, the Qing state would tap into these to help sustain the populations of longer-settled and more densely populated cores where grain deficits were endemic as early as the 1700s. Poorly fed peasants were, quite simply, more prone to rebellion and rioting and as R. Bin Wong, Pierre-Etienne Will, and others have shown, the famine relief system was a fundamental state concern and its implementation a form of social control (Will 1990; Will, Wong and Lee 1991). To the degree that the maintenance of regional and local grain security played an integral role in the maintenance of social order, the state was directly concerned with how and by whom grain was moved (Will 1990, 56, 178–182, 212). The Qing was not, as Chapter 9 will show, a laissez-faire state when it came to the question of grain and the grain markets—especially in Manchuria. While the state may have lacked the bureaucratic capacity to control trade outright, authorities were well positioned on the highways and at trading entrepôts to affect trade in ways that served—however partially—the state's interest in maintaining price stability.

CHAPTER NINE

State, Merchant, and the Organization of the Manchurian Trade

THAT THE VOLUME and value of goods traded throughout the empire in the high Qing was large in absolute terms is beyond doubt. It is also evident that the bulk of goods freighted along interregional transport routes was moved by private merchants, not the state. By one estimate, in the early and mid-Qing four times as much grain—unsurprisingly the most traded commodity in the empire—moved through the markets than was moved by the government (cited in Rowe 2001, 157). The ability to move large volumes was a singular achievement of the late imperial economy. It should also be stated that going back to the Ming dynasty the social and political standing of the merchant class rose along with the expansion of trade, until its highest echelons entered the social and political realm of the literati. Yet, despite various interpretations of the levels of dynamism evident in trade and among merchants, there is a general consensus among scholars that growth in the absolute levels of interregional trade and an accompanying increase in merchant wealth and social prestige in the Qing were not sufficient to sustain real economic growth over the long run.[1]

There were, I would suggest, two reasons why trade did not initiate economic expansion. First, the productivity of labor in agriculture remained low, a fact manifest in the relative levels of trade in all important food. Guo Songyi (in Fang et al., 2000, 399) estimates that in the early nineteenth century eleven percent of total grain output made it into the market, whereas Wu Chengming (1983) estimates ten percent of rice was marketed. The low relative levels of surplus were of course an indirect manifestation of the low productivity of labor in agriculture, and a fact that circumscribed the deepening and furthering of specialization in rural manufacturing, limited the extent of urbanization, and ultimately precluded the appearance and deepening of the classical division of labor between town and country, or between town-based industry and rural agriculture.[2] In the end, the low *relative* levels of grain exchanged in the Qing could only sustain a limited development of the intra- and interregional division of labor and urbanization (e.g., Beattie 1979, 12, 49). This is captured in the fact that even in the Yangzi delta where peasants were expending ever more time spinning and weaving cloth, these same households continued to devote energy to farming grain.

Second, whereas merchants in the Qing made ample profits—on the basis of the growing regional disparities in grain production and consumption that increasingly marked the era—there is no evidence that those profits made their way into production in ways that facilitated real economic growth (Fan 1998; Zhang 1996). Therein lies a crucial distinction between economies exhibiting Ricardian-Malthusian dynamics and those that grow in a Smithian fashion: until merchant capital (and capital more generally) moves beyond the confines of circulation to enter into the production/manufacturing process, that capital will not issue in sustained economic expansion characterized by ongoing increases in labor productivity (Tilly 1992, 17; Brenner 1977, 56–57). Though Chinese merchants in the late imperial period "invested" in land, they did so as rentiers with the goal of securing a steady income in rent. They did not on the whole do so as farm "managers," which would have entailed some sort of reorganization of agricultural production along more efficient lines. Though merchants forwarded capital and inputs to peasant households engaged in household or proto-industrial manufacturing, they did not step in to restructure the manufacturing process in ways that would lower the cost of production to generate sustained improvements in the productivity of manufacturing.[3] Similarly, merchants did not generally invest their capital in urban enterprises in ways that would expand manufacturing and pull in labor from the countryside.[4] In short, merchants and merchant capital are historically necessary but not sufficient factors for sustained economic development.

As Fang Xing argues, trade and merchant wealth in the Qing era were paradoxically the manifestations of the regional dearth of production in grain not (real) growth (in Xu and Wu 2000, 382). They were the outcome of the inability of agricultural producers in the population-dense cores to match rising grain demand (manifested in rising grain prices) with equivalent or better increases in grain output and rising labor productivity in grain production. Unable to feed themselves, the cores became dependent upon grain imports. Those imports were provided in turn by the peripheries such as Manchuria, which by virtue of their later settlement and lower population densities were able to sustain moderate grain surpluses, up to a point.

This brings us to another point. Given the ultimate limits to the productiveness of Chinese agriculture, and the dependency of the cores on basic food imports, food supply was a major policy concern of the Qing state. William Rowe

(2001, 155) has recently called it "the most important policy area in Qing China" before the advent of the threat from the West. Authorities consequently expended great energy and time monitoring grain supplies, the grain trade, and merchant activities (Will 1990; Will, Wong, and Lee 1991; Li and Dray-Novey 1999). As regional grain deficits mounted in the eighteenth century, the Qing state sought to strengthen the system of grain stores or granaries it had inherited from the Ming, to better redistribute grain to peasants following weak harvests (Will, Wong, and Lee 1991, 37–40). However, toward the end of the eighteenth century, as the level and scope of grain deficits grew beyond the organizational capacities of the state, Qing authorities increasingly turned to merchants to facilitate the circulation of grain from surplus to deficit regions of the empire (Will, Wong, and Lee 1991, 91; Dunstan 1996). In effect, the cost of maintaining regional food supplies was put onto the peasantry who demanded grain most.

Despite the turn to merchants, precisely because grain surpluses remained inadequate and yet crucial to securing social order in the cores, Qing officials and sovereigns, while understanding the utility in allowing merchant-orchestrated "grain circulation" (*migu liutong*), nonetheless could not afford to adopt a laissez-faire or Liberal stance on the grain trade. There was too much at stake for that. Authorities understood that whereas the merchant desire for profit drove the circulation of grain, they also understood that merchant interests were not synonymous with those of the state. Official discussions of grain circulation were couched in a language that therefore prioritized the state's need to move grain in ways that best secured the "people's livelihood" (*minsheng*), not in ways that secured merchant private interests (Rowe 2001, 176–185, 202–204, 214). Official discourse expressed the realization that while social and hence political stability rested on a sufficiently fed peasantry, the volume of grain entering the market was low relative to the consumption needs of the population (Will 1990, 177, 209–210; Mann 1987, 20). Under these conditions, the Qing state reserved for itself the right to intervene in the grain trade in order to secure social stability and to badger and discipline merchants whenever their interests were contrary to its own (and those of the people).

Manchurian Grain Trade Policy in the Eighteenth Century

In the eighteenth century, a central policy concern at court and in the northeast was whether the Fengtian could sustain grain and soybean exports—and at what levels—without compromising regional grain security (Katō 1953a; Sudō 1972; Furichi 2000). Those concerns stemmed from significant and growing demand for Manchurian food grains that emanated first from the north China provinces of Zhili and Shandong, as well as Beijing, and by the end of the eighteenth century from Jiangnan and farther south. The question the imperial court posed to the authorities in Manchuria was whether agricultural production there was vital enough to bear the unrestricted export by merchants of food crops.

Guarding against excessive food grain exports was a common concern for officials governing in China's peripheral regions (Perdue 1987; Will 1990). The movement of grain between regions or districts in response to rapid price spikes, and—by implication—the movement of grain from the jurisdiction of one bureaucrat to that of another, always carried the potential of pitting local and regional officials against one another and/or against the central state as each sought to protect his own grain stores and keep grain prices within his district under control. From the perspective of local officials—a view the sovereign critically described as "narrow" (*suojian shuxiao*)—mandatory grain relief procurements and grain relief exports had the potential to undermine their capacity to maintain social order in their jurisdictions, as grain exports abroad led to rising grain prices at home. From the sovereign's self-styled panoptic perspective, however, control over the movement of grain was an essential tool to achieving political stability. The sovereign was willing to export grain from one region, and tolerate the resulting moderate price rises and accompanying hardships there, if the exports restored order in a neighboring region suffering from more threatening shortages and facing graver social and political disruption.

The resulting tensions between the interests of local authorities and those of the court were structurally determined by the limits of peasant-based agriculture (and the limited means at hand for maintaining social and political order). The movement of grain between (and within) regions was therefore something authorities and the Qing sovereign had to visit and revisit as the relative weight of the population between cores and peripheries underwent change in an overall context of empire-wide population expansion that exceeded food supplies (Rowe 2001, 156–158; Will, Wong, and Lee 1991, 75–92).[5]

North China Grain Shortages and Early Demand for Fengtian Grain

Pierre-Etienne Will has noted the correlation between interregional trading patterns and state-orchestrated famine relief efforts. Citing Wang Yeh-chien's (1973) study of the Qing land tax, Will notes that in the Qing the developed cores exported their populations, capital, and manufactured goods to the developing peripheries, which sent grain in return. Not surprisingly, those same peripheries such as Hunan, Sichuan, Taiwan, and Manchuria also sent grain relief to the cores. That they could do so was because their lower population densities made possible fairly regular grain surpluses (Will 1990, 302–303, 298–299, table 20).

By 1700, grain deficits were a structural feature on the developed north China plain and by the 1720s those deficits were placing demands on Manchuria's slim but growing surpluses. This was a marked reversal of the traditional relationship between the two regions. In the mid- and even late Ming dynasty, Shandong and Zhili (*Bei Zhili*) were for the most part self-sufficient in grain and even produced enough to sustain small exports to southern Manchuria, where Ming military colonies guarded the borders against the Tungusic tribes. However, by the early eighteenth century population expansion and the turn to non-grain crops such as cotton in north China, without corresponding increases in the area under cultivation and matching improvements in grain output, had transformed the Zhili-Shandong region from grain-exporter to grain-importer (Xu 1998b, 311–313, 316–325; Zhang 1993b, 170; Zhao 1995, 44). It seems that by the early 1700s the population on the north China plain had recovered from the downturn caused by wars and famines associated with the Ming-Qing transition. By the mid-eighteenth century, if not earlier, population levels had surpassed the Ming high-water mark (Huang 1985, 322, table B.1; Perkins 1969, 207, table A.4).[6] The demand for imported food was a permanent feature of larger parts of the north China plain by that point in time.

A pattern of labor intensification via cotton cultivation and domestic manufacturing coupled with out-migration on to the ecologically fragile and less productive soils of the Shandong highlands and peninsula merely intensified the region's need for Manchurian food crops.[7] Peasants on Shandong's Lu plain, who witnessed an average decline in per capita arable land, responded by intensifying grain cultivation and introducing winter wheat, which permitted a move from one crop a year to three crops in two years, and by planting more sweet potatoes (Huang 1985, 62–63, 110–111, table; Xu 1998b, 32–42). There were limits to how much more labor could be absorbed in agriculture, however, and so peasants took up the cultivation and processing of cotton, which allowed the expenditure of more labor, to bring in extra income. Had grain production responded better to labor intensification concomitantly with the turn to cotton, then theoretically the conversion of land to cotton cultivation would have not given rise to grain deficits. But grain output did not rise sufficiently, so the spread of cotton cultivation only served to deepen Zhili-Shandong's need for grain imports.[8]

Despite the turn to cotton cultivation and domestic manufacturing to round out incomes on the more productive soils of western and northwestern Shandong, some peasants found themselves with insufficient land and so left to settle on the central Dong mountains and coastal lands of the Shandong peninsula. Those settling in the hillside areas found that the marginal soil of their new surroundings were unsuited to grain production, no matter how hard they strove to farm it.[9] They compensated by cultivating the sweet potato, which was suited to the hills and poorer soils, and devoting the remainder of their land and physical efforts to cash crops like peanuts and soybeans, as well as the raising of mulberry trees for sericulture. The sale of these crops raised the cash needed to buy grain (Xu 1998b, 60–68, 80–81, 324–325; Huang 1985, 116–117).[10]

A similar process unfolded on the coastal lowlands of the Shandong peninsula where peasants confronted the difficulty of surviving on small plots and thin soils. Similarly unable to sustain themselves through grain production, these peasants also planted sweet potatoes on part of their land and grew soybeans and other cash crops on the rest to exchange for imported grains. It seems that they also bought raw cotton (which they could not grow) from peasants on the neighboring Lu plain to spin and weave (Xu 1998b, 81–82, 92; Fan 1998, 74). While most of the cloth woven in this way was consumed directly, small amounts were produced for export to the northeast and the cash earned was used to purchase Fengtian grain (Xu 1998b, 48, 92). Thus, developments internal to Shandong had given rise to significant grain deficits by the 1720s.

Compounding problems on the north China plain was the presence of the capital at Beijing. With its population bloated beyond the carrying capacity of regional grain production by the presence of the state bureaucracy and its officers, and those who attended to their needs, the capital required regular grain shipments from throughout the empire (Skinner 1977b, 238–239; Li and Dray-Novey 1999, 996–997, 1000–1001). Mounting grain deficits on the north China plain in the eighteenth century and the food demands of the capital led to regionwide grain prices that were significantly higher than those in neighboring Fengtian. When famine struck the north China plain, which it did often in the Qing, the gap between prices on the north China plain and Fengtian widened further still.

Shandong merchants seeking the arbitrage profits to be had by purchasing cheap Fengtian grain to sell at high prices in north China were drawn to the granaries in the northeast from their home ports at Tianjin, Dengzhou, Laizhou, and Qingzhou. Without controls Manchurian grain would have flowed steadily across the Bohai to north China. In fact, even with prohibitions that were placed on exports in the eighteenth century, smugglers plied the waters that separated Fengtian from Tianjin and the Shandong peninsula (Katō 1953a, 600–601). The dilemma thus confronting authorities in the eighteenth century was whether to permit exports of Manchurian grain—and risk rising prices and social instability in Fengtian in order to moderate prices in north China—or to prohibit exports altogether, securing grain self-sufficiency and political control in the northeast but burdening north China peasants with higher grain prices.

The Politics of Manchurian Food Exports: Regional and Interregional Food Security in Northern China in the Eighteenth Century

For the first seven decades of the eighteenth century, Manchuria's officials lobbied to maintain the ban on grain and bean exports, maintaining that excessive exports from the northeast would empty Manchurian grain stores, raise local grain prices to unbearable levels, and thereby threaten regional political stability (e.g., FTTZ 2003, 600; GZSL 1964, 1743–1744 [115]; 3025 [206]; QHS 1991, 254 [288]). For most of the eighteenth century, Manchuria's regional authorities maintained that agricultural productivity was too low to allow for unlimited exports. By the end of the seventeenth century, production remained so close to subsistence levels that poor harvests in 1693, 1694, and 1695–96 necessitated extra deliveries of grain to Fengtian from north China (SJTZ 1965, 180–182; SZSL 1964, 2213–2214 [164], 2247 [167]; Sudō 1972a, 441). A bad harvest in 1710 prompted the Kangxi emperor to note: "this year We feel deeply because the Shengjing district experienced such a famine that it was difficult to come by even a few grains" (SJTZ 1965, 135–136 [2]).

To be sure, grounds for continuing the prohibition against food crop exports receded as the population grew, more land was brought under the plow, and total agricultural output rose. Yet these processes were slow, prompting regional officials to remain cautious. When the Kangxi emperor recommended in 1722 that merchants be permitted to trade freely in Manchurian grain because "for many years now the harvest in the region of Shengjing has been abundant, the price of grain very low, and the people have taken to wasting it," regional authorities, who remained unconvinced, argued successfully for the ban's continuation (Yi 1993, 257). As late as 1738, the vice secretary of the Board of Revenue Shuangxi reiterated the need for the ban on coastal exports of grain, citing the "Regulation on grain in the coastal counties and departments of Fengtian" (*Fengtian yanhai zhou-xian mishi li*). He justified continuing the policy by citing his concern that exports would raise grain prices in Fengtian (GZSL 1964, 1221–1222 [75], 1238 [76]). Consequently, it was not until 1749 that the state permitted *limited* exports of soybeans and not until 1772 that the prohibition against grain and controls on bean exports were lifted.[11] That did not signal the end to official concerns, however. Regional authorities continued to monitor local harvests and grain price movements and acted quickly to halt all exports when local grain self-sufficiency appeared threatened (Furichi 2000, 71, 80–81 n 10).

Thus, the first indication of improvements in the levels of food grain production was the decision in 1749 to permit exports of soybeans from Manchuria. That decision came nine years after the governor general of Jiangnan had petitioned successfully for an end to the empire-wide ban on seafaring trade in soybeans and coarse grains that had dated to 1685, though was evidently not fully enforced. According to the governor general's memorial on the topic, the empire-wide ban kept soybean prices high in Jiangnan and so harmed peasants who depended upon soybeans for food. The governor general pointed out that the original purpose of the ban on sea-going trade in grain had been to stop its export outside the empire. However, he argued, because demand for soybeans and coarse grains came from within the empire, the ban only harmed native peasants. It was subsequently lifted by imperial order (GZSL 1964, 1733 [114]).

Nine years later, the ban on the export of Manchurian soybeans was lifted on the grounds that it also harmed peasant welfare. However, northeast authorities, concerned that agricultural production in the region remained inconsistent, insisted on restrictions. First, export quotas were to be enforced which restricted large vessels to carrying two hundred *shi* of soybeans and small vessels to one hundred *shi* (SC Guangxu, 4.13, 15; HZ 1775.2.25; Katō 1953a, 600–601). Second, regional authorities were permitted to reinstate the ban whenever poor harvests were reported in Fengtian. These same officials often referred to the 1749 edict as a temporary lifting of the ban, in an obvious strategy to maintain a tight control on soybean exports (HZ 1775.2.25). The reason given for these restrictions was that peasants in the northeast still depended upon soybeans for food (Katō 1953a, 600–601). While millet was the staple of the peasant diet, the importance of the soybean to peasant diet was noted by regional authorities.[12] In a memorial dated to 1765, superintendent Jinlan, of the Shanhaiguan customs office, which monitored and taxed trade out of the northeast, petitioned the throne to remove all limits on the amount of soybeans each vessel could carry out of port. Echoing the governor general of Jiangnan, Jinlan argued that the export quotas imposed in 1749 were harmful to peasant livelihood both in and outside the northeast. Jinlan was instructed by his superiors to investigate the matter further. Upon re-examining the circumstances, and the feasibility of unrestricted soybean exports, he reversed his initial position and concluded that the limits should remain in place. Jinlan's report concluded:

> in the investigation of the matter of soybeans, it is [found to be] the case that in many districts [of Fengtian] the banner and commoner populations depend upon it for their sustenance. It is therefore necessary to continue following the previous regulations and

limit [exports] in accordance with the quota. There is no need to raise the matter further. Local officials therefore are ordered to examine cargo and provide "bean licenses" to all junks that pass through the ports. After leaving port, records are to be compiled and copies are to be sent to the importing provinces so that those at both ends are informed. Jointly dispatch a banner and civil official every month to examine matters to ensure that such bad customs as bribery and extortion are not occurring. (cited in Katō 1953a, 600–601)[13]

Evidently, while agricultural conditions had improved sufficiently to justify some exports of soybeans by mid-century, regional authorities remained unconvinced of the ability of the northeast to sustain unrestricted exports of food crops while maintaining stable food prices. Thus, Pierre-Etienne Will is incorrect when he argues that the 1749 quota was intended not to limit exports but to facilitate tax collection (Will 1990, 218 n 117). Presumably, he believes that the task of collecting excise revenue was made easier by standardizing shiploads. But it is clear from Jinlan's memorial of 1765 that officials understood the quota to function as a restriction on the amount of soybeans leaving the northeast and intended it to protect local food supplies (cf. Katō 1953a, 600–601).[14] There were good reasons for officials to continue their cautious approach in the eighteenth century. In 1762, the Shengjing military governor complained that though Fengtian had been able to produce food grain surpluses, population growth was occurring at a fast enough pace that regional supplies would be insufficient if the harvest failed (cited in Will 1990, 195). As late as 1807, at a time when grain exports were permitted and surpluses were higher still, the Fengtian Military Governor Fujun memorialized that a bad harvest had reduced output by forty percent in Fengtian. That was sufficient to wipe out the entire surplus and, as Furichi Daisuke shows, the military governor responded by ordering merchants in Manchuria to release their grain stores locally and temporarily stop all exports (Furichi 2000, 71, 80–81 n 10; FTTZ 2003, 757).[15]

The dilemma confronting Manchuria's authorities in the eighteenth century was quite simple: Manchuria did not have a deep hinterland from which to draw grain when poor harvests depleted grain stores or set off famine in longer-settled areas of southern Fengtian. Moreover, absent an alternative to agricultural incomes, peasants in Manchuria could not pay the price that would have been necessary to divert to the northeast that grain heading from the empire's other grain-exporting peripheries to grain-hungry Zhili-Shandong, Jiangnan, and Lingnan. Absent its own hinterland, and with the north China plain and capital soaking up most of the otherwise accessible surplus grain, Manchuria had nowhere to go for grain in times of need. Its authorities were therefore wary of allowing too much grain to leave. This continued to be the case even after the restriction on food crop exports was lifted in 1772. In the late eighteenth and nineteenth centuries Manchuria's authorities continued to stop exports whenever local grain supplies were threatened (Sudō 1972a, 448, 453–454).

The ban on food crop exports did not, however, cover state procurements (*cai mai*) of grain, which were shipped on merchant vessels. Those shipments were first discussed in 1715 in response to a particularly bad harvest in neighboring Zhili province, but the proposal was rejected. Though the Fengtian military governor at the time memorialized that grain could be shipped from coastal Fengtian to Zhili, the Kangxi emperor refused, not willing to risk grain shortages in the northeast. The first sanctioned shipment of state-procured grain left port in the late summer of 1723, when one hundred thousand *shi* of grain was transported to Tianjin to replenish grain stores there. Two years later, in the middle of the 1724–25 Zhili famine, one hundred thousand *shi* left the northeast for Tianjin after Manchurian officials investigated the local harvest and found it sufficient (QHS 1991, 254 [288]; FTTZ 2003, 627–628). In the late fall of 1730, heavy rainfall damaged the harvest in the Shandong districts of Qing, Lai, and Deng just as peasants began the work of harvesting their crops. In response, two hundred thousand *shi* of Fengtian grain from the granaries of its coastal ports was delivered to Shandong by merchant junks. By the following year the famine had still not abated and another two hundred thousand *shi* was shipped (Sudō 1972a, 442). In 1743–44, famine again struck north China, this time in Zhili. A little less than one hundred thousand *shi* was delivered as relief from Jinzhou in late 1743 and another seventy-one thousand the following spring from Fengtian (Will 1990, 158).[16]

Clearly, a pattern had emerged by mid-century. When confronting famine in north China, authorities there sent appeals for Fengtian grain relief. On receiving the memorials, the sovereign instructed northeast authorities to gauge local grain supplies and estimate how much could be shipped without seriously raising Fengtian grain prices. The prohibition against Fengtian exports was temporarily lifted and merchants were then enlisted to move state-procured and privately purchased grain to where it was needed for famine relief. For most of the eighteenth century, Fengtian functioned not as an entrepôt for trade so much as a "granary" for provisioning relief grain to famine-struck north China and filling depleted granaries in the environs of the capital (Furichi 2000, 55–56, 61–62, 64–65; Li and Dray-Novey 1999, 996–997, 1000–1001).[17]

Lifting the ban to facilitate state procurements did not signal a move toward freer or liberal trade policy, however. In each instance the ban was lifted provisionally while exports were closely monitored so as not to threaten the stability of Fengtian grain prices (e.g., GZD-QL 1982, vol. 16, 914). Merchants received licenses from the state to move a specified quantity of grain. On arriving in north China they were required by officials there to show the license before unloading their stock. The grain was then placed in state granaries and the state orchestrated its distribution among the famine-stricken areas. On those occasions, merchants were clearly deployed by the state to assist it in its policy goals (GZSL 1964, 1744 [115]; 3025 [206]; 4159–4160 [87]; also see Furichi 2000, 57–59; Will 1990, 157–158, 222–224).

A clear understanding of eighteenth-century administrative and strategic thinking is provided in the policy discussions that surrounded a series of disasters and famines that struck north China in mid-century. At the center of these policy debates was the feasibility of opening Fengtian to grain exports as a measure of relief to stricken areas.

In late 1747, in the aftermath of two years of poor harvests, floods in the "eastern provinces" (Zhili, Shandong, and Shuntian prefecture) prompted the Qianlong emperor to order Fengtian and Shandong officials to look into the possibility of recruiting merchants to obtain grain from the northeast as part of famine relief efforts. According to accounts in the veritable records:

> [in the past] the Grand Secretary Zhao Qinglu memorialized to request the temporary rescinding of the prohibition against exporting Fengtian grain, to allow merchants to make shipments and so assist in Shandong's relief. That contravened existing regulations so that after the Grand Secretary et al. discussed the matter it was decided to uphold the regulation [banning exports]. To date, the sealing of the ports has been strict. It is intended to stop treacherous merchants from smuggling and facilitate the controlling of evil brigands. But last year there was a flood in Shandong. Today, grain is needed to relieve all aspects of the famine. If Fengtian is opened to ocean trade, but inspections are rigorous enough to stop smuggling, then those areas struck by disaster will benefit. A missive was therefore sent to Alidai, the governor of Shandong, and to Daledanga, the Shengjing military governor, to check whether this was possible and to see how much Fengtian grain could be exported and to examine how the [export] licenses might be apportioned, how to carry out inspections of grain exports to Shandong, and how to prevent merchants from smuggling. The price of grain in Fengtian is not to be allowed to rise rapidly. If these concerns can all be met, then immediately proceed [with allowing licensed exports] and report to the emperor. Because the eastern provinces are suffering disasters, this is to be allowed but it is to be a one-time policy. It is not to be treated as precedent in the future. (GZSL 1964, 4159–4160 [287])

Following an investigation of local grain supply, Fengtian authorities concluded that because allowing exports would raise Fengtian grain prices too swiftly and threaten social stability, the ban on exports of Fengtian grain would remain in place. The request for state procurements was denied.

The following spring, however, Shandong's Dengzhou, Laizhou, and Qingzhou suffered another crop failure (Katō 1953a, 597). Because the suffering localities were less accessible by the overland routes that stretched from western Shandong and Zhili, Shandong Governor Gao Wen asked that shipments of grain be sent directly by sea from Fengtian to the northern coast of the Shandong peninsula. This time the Shengjing Military Governor reported that Fengtian prices were low and stores of more than two hundred thousand *shi* were available. Shipments were permitted and continued into 1749 (GZSL 1964, 5135 [339]; also see Katō 1953a, 597; Will 1990, 224 n 135). Over two years, a total of 360 thousand *shi* was shipped by merchants enlisted by Fengtian authorities to move grain (Sudō 1972a, 447).

In 1750–51, famine struck again. This time more than seventy districts were affected in Tianjin, Zhili, and again in eastern Shandong (GDZ-QL 1982, vol. 1, 662–664). Again, the governor of Shandong requested that the ban on Fengtian grain exports be lifted temporarily (GDZ-QL 1982, vol. 1, 665). Citing the precedent of 1747, he argued that "great benefits will derive from enlisting merchants to come to buy grain, ship it eastward, and sell it in places near the coast at the two prefectures of Dengzhou and Laizhou." The governor noted that "the movement in and out of ports all along the coast will be monitored and inspected" and that "after the following year's spring wheat harvest the situation will be re-assessed and [on the basis of this assessment] an end [to shipments] can be requested. If the amount of grain in Fengtian does not change much, then more can be exported depending on the military governor." There was evidently sufficient grain, the Fengtian Prefect having just reported an excellent harvest (GDZ-QL 1982, vol. 1, 642), and merchants were permitted to purchase and ship a total of two hundred thousand *shi* to Shandong (Sudō 1972a, 447).

It is clear from these instances of famine relief efforts in north China that relevant officials at the highest levels of the Qing bureaucracy in the mid-eighteenth century were acutely aware of the sensitivity of Fengtian grain supplies and prices to any exports. But, they were also aware by the end of the century that grain output was no longer keeping up with local demand (RZSL 1964, 1544 [111]). Given those conditions, Fengtian authorities, including the Shengjing Military Governor and the Fengtian prefect, were eager to maintain modest levels of grain stores and reluctant to release grain for export unless good harvests were reported (Katō 1953a, 596–597; Sudō 1972a, 446; Will 1990, 224 n 135). When grain shipments were permitted, the approving authority emphasized in his instructions that the ban on exports was being lifted provisionally.

By 1760, however, the emphasis on "provisional" was dropped in official communications, a fact that Will believes signaled the de facto end of the export prohibition, even though the formal abrogation did not come until 1772 (Will 1990, 224). That suggests, to be sure, the rising confidence of regional authorities in the productive capacities of the region. Even so, as noted, regional officials continued to be cautious. They monitored exports and harvests closely and quickly closed ports to exports whenever poor harvests in Fengtian were reported. Floods in Liaoyang, Haicheng, and Gaiping in 1802 destroyed homes and forty percent of crops, compelling the Shengjing Military Governor Fujun to reinstate the ban on exports (FTTZ 2003, 750–751). In 1803, a plague of locusts that destroyed crops in "all districts in Fengtian and Jinzhou" sent grain prices to very high levels, again prompting officials to seek remedies. In his exhaustive examination of Manchurian export trade up to the 1840s, Sudō Yoshiyuki noted full or partial prohibitions on exports due to poor harvests and/or price spikes in 1788, 1806, 1807, 1808, 1816, 1822, and 1836 (Sudō 1972a, 448, 453–454). Though Manchuria could produce sizable grain surpluses (see chapter 8), that surplus was thin on a per capita basis such that the state continued to work to secure food supplies in the northeast to the best of its means, even as it opened a greater space for merchants in grain circulation.

The State and Interregional Trade at the End of the Eighteenth Century

Pierre-Etienne Will, in his study of the Qing bureaucracy and its famine relief efforts, has written that bureaucrats reacted with ambiguity at best when eyeing the commercial terrain of the eighteenth century (Will 1990, 211–212, 208–225). Whereas trade in theory moved grain from where it was plentiful (cheap) to where it was needed (dear), whether commercial redistribution worked in practice to ensure food security for the empire was an empirical question open to official judgment. Undoubtedly the state oversaw an expansion of the role for merchants in the circulation of food. But it was also clear to bureaucrats (and merchants) that their interests were not one and the same. Just as merchant profit seeking under certain conditions moved grain to where it was needed, it could also undermine food security as merchants colluded to hoard supplies and profiteer. Thus, while the Qianlong emperor could state of merchants in the abstract that "to harm the merchants is to harm the people" (*bing shang yin er bing min*) (Will 1990, 213), individually they were just as often found to be treacherous and traitorous (*jian shang*) (Will 1990, 216–217; Rowe 2001, 199). At any point in time the prevailing official view depended to a large extent upon the relative alignment of merchant behavior with bureaucratic interests.

As the late eighteenth century unfolded, the need to free merchants to circulate grain was overdetermined by regional developments in population, agricultural productiveness, and related food supplies. It is widely recognized that whereas population tripled over the course of the Qing, cultivated acreage only doubled and gains in land yields, though significant, were ultimately insufficient in the cores to secure the food supplies of the those populations (Zhao

1995; Fang et al. 2000). The upshot was the advent of regional grain shortages, rising grain and land prices relative to other commodities and labor, and increasing importance of trade to the food security of the politically most sensitive parts of the empire (north China, Jiangnan, and Lingnan) (Chao 1986, 216–217; Jiang 1992, 85–131; Wang 1989, 426, 429, 455; Zhang 1988, 163). The later-settled peripheral zones such as Huguang, Sichuan, Guangxi, Taiwan, and Manchuria could be depended upon for grain imports up to a point, given their much lower ratios of labor to land and, consequently, their more "substantial" food surpluses (Jiang 1992, 42–48). The contrast between the Jiangnan core and Manchurian periphery was captured in the writings of Charles Gutzlaff. Gutzlaff traveled to both regions in the 1830s and noted that grain was plentiful in the northeast, but even the most bountiful harvest in Jiangnan was sure to be completely consumed by the large local population (Gutzlaff and Ellis 1834, 307–308).

Given the unfolding economic landscape of the eighteenth century, it is easy to see how a structural dependency upon commercial exchange—and merchants—in both times of feast and famine, took shape. Thus, for the Qing bureaucracy, guaranteeing the movement of grain from areas of surplus to areas of chronic shortage was a political imperative made necessary by threats of social disturbances (Will 1990, 61, 180, 209, 215).[18] Famine relief was in essence a means of social control. Yet, the Qing state was constrained in its ability to orchestrate so many movements of grain over such great distances between so many parts of the empire, notwithstanding the tremendous optimism and can-do-ism of the eighteenth-century bureaucrat. The state had little choice but to turn to merchants to circulate grain in bad as well as good years (Will 1990, 179, 181, 211–215, 278–279; Rowe 2001, 162, 176–183). As Susan Mann puts it in her study of merchants and the Qing state: "State policies protecting and fostering trader's activities . . . aimed not at improving the status of merchants, but at preserving the agrarian social order" (1987, 20). Such developments were evident in Manchuria, where a combination of increased absolute productiveness of the regional economy—driven by labor intensification and land extension—coupled with the recognition of the mounting importance of Manchurian soybeans and grains for other parts of the empire, pushed regional authorities in the late eighteenth century to rely increasingly upon merchants to buy and export food crops privately while reducing (though not eliminating) government procurements (Furichi 2000, 61–63).

Yet, despite the state's greater reliance upon merchants to circulate grain, this did not signal the precipitation of a Chinese "Liberalism," as Helen Dunstan (1996) has suggested in her study of Qing statecraft thought.[19] Classical liberalism is committed to the notion that the self-interest of the individual is congruent with that of the broader society; it relegates the role of the state to that of legal guarantor of the social relations that therefore enables the pursuit of self-interest. Thus, the Liberal social order comes into being through the seemingly anarchic actions of individuals who in pursuing their private economic interest nonetheless produce a self-regulating civil society (see McNally 1988, 152–208). No such ideological claims or vision can be attributed to officials of the Qing state; the Qing sovereign and his bureaucratic staff had a very different world vision. Their function, as they saw it, was *to create* a social and political order in which human behavior would come to mirror principles of moral conduct that were idealized but *not yet realized.* But because the prevailing social conditions obstructed the realization of those goals, bureaucrats could not suppose that individual interests would create a self-regulating social and moral order.

Undoubtedly, a certain pragmatism might prevail over moral certainties, and William Rowe (2001) has made the case for Chen Hongmou's support of merchant solutions to problems of supply and demand disequilibria as a pragmatic position. It remained the case, nonetheless, that even Chen Hongmou could not imagine a self-regulating society; thus Rowe argues that Chen came to his position because he saw it as the best means for securing the necessary preconditions for a moral order (213–214). In the view of the Qing and its officials, therefore, self-interest in the marketplace was not sufficient to remove "treacherous merchants" who profiteered on the backs of the people. By contrast, it is a core tenet of Liberalism that the market will indeed regulate such people out of business. Moreover, Liberalism makes this claim while putting the question of ethics and morality to one side. In Liberal thought, the state's core moral stance, if it can be said to have one, is in essence "disinterest"; a very different position from that held by the Qing state. To draw again from William Rowe (2001), the pro-market stance of some mid-eighteenth-century officials was "less one of *letting* the market accomplish its task than of *making* it do so" (162, italics in original). If a European corollary is desired, then Qing advocacy for merchants and market solutions to the problems of grain supply and demand should be seen as mirroring the concerns of the eighteenth-century French physiocrats.[20] Their concern too was first and foremost the *creation* of a moral order upon which laissez-faire trade policies could then bring about the public interest. The problem for France, as the physiocrats saw it, was that that moral order had not yet been achieved (McNally 1988, 85–151).

This sort of ambiguity in the attitudes of Qing authorities toward merchants is evident in a report filed on merchant activity in Fengtian in 1794, more than two decades after the legalization of the grain trade and removal of all restrictions on soybean exports. In the spring of that year, all signs pointed to a poor harvest in Zhili and Shandong (HZ 1794.6.7). There had been little to no rain after the planting of the fields and the indications were that seeds were not germinating. Anticipating a poor harvest in north China, in the first three months of spring in 1794, from the beginning of the third to the end of the fifth lunar month, merchants from Hejian, Tianjin, and Wuding had come to Fengtian to buy up grain in the hope of making windfall profits in Zhili and Shandong. Fengtian's harvest the year before had been exceptionally good and merchant stores there were quite full. Fengtian authorities consequently reported a significant increase in grain exports in the late spring and early summer of 1794: whereas in a year of normal harvests, Fengtian might export 50 to 60 thousand *shi* a month in the spring, it was observed that in 1794 as much as 220 thousand *shi* had left port in a two-month period between the third and fifth months. Rather than selling the harvest at a nice profit in the summer months, however, merchants closed ranks and hoarded it over the summer in an effort to drive prices up higher still. The actions of authorities to encourage more shipments only made the situation worse. In an effort to encourage exports from Fengtian to north China, the court provisionally reduced the taxes levied on vessels leaving Fengtian ports. Rather than alleviate the upward pressure on north China grain prices, authorities believed their actions only encouraged merchants to purchase and hoard more grain in efforts to raise their profits further still. Finally, in mid-summer the state acted against the merchants. It ordered that "in the matter of shipping beans, wheat, millet and grain, exports [from Manchuria] are to be allowed in accordance with the market price; but it is strictly forbidden to hoard even a little, have others hoard for you, or to put up obstacles blocking the release [of grain]" (HZ 1794.6.7).

Whether state reprisals had the desire effect is unclear. But here in short was expressed the source of bureaucratic ambiguity toward trade and merchants. Whereas authorities wanted and in fact needed grain to move in accordance with prices, *so long as a region could sustain grain exports without endangering its own grain security*, they also recognized that the very merchants who orchestrated the circulation of grain were prone to do so in ways that purposely deepened food shortages and drove up prices and profits (Zhang 1990, 202). It is clear that the same trading organizations that helped merchants to move grain and other goods and to regulate trade were also used to hoard and manipulate markets. In good times this was less problematic, but in times of poor harvests the behavior of merchant "cabals" threatened the political order. For example, in 1743, at the height of the 1743–44 famine that struck north China, the Board of Revenue received reports from the Shengjing Military Governor Ertu of "treacherous merchants monopolizing grain" (*jianshang tun liangshi*) in Fengtian and then smuggling it out of the northeast (GZSL 1968, 3025 [206]). Ertu commanded officials to investigate and break up these cabals.

Such problems were not limited to the eighteenth century. In 1822, for instance, the Shengjing Military Governor Song Lin reported that "treacherous merchants" in Fengtian responding to a harvest failure in north China by hoarding grain with the design to drive prices up further. The governor had to step in to prohibit all further exports in order to bring prices under control in Fengtian (XZSL 1964, 546 [29]). Thus, despite greater reliance upon merchants, Qing authorities in the northeast and elsewhere were compelled for ideological as well as institutional reasons to continue to monitor and influence the grain trade in ways that promoted its paramount stake in the creation of a moral order, on the one hand, and establishment of social stability and political power on the other.

Merchants, Merchant Organizations, and the Manchurian Trade

The political cost to the state of yielding a greater role in grain circulation to merchants was to permit merchants to organize themselves into guilds and other associations for the purpose of controlling trade and, to the best of their abilities, minimizing their risks and securing their profits. Merchants were in fact the only Qing social group allowed to organize associations for the promotion of their economic and social interests, a legal privilege not even granted to the literati who staffed the bureaucracy (Negishi 1953; Mann 1987, 23–24; Zhang 1996, 136–148). The costs to the merchants for these privileges were twofold. On the one hand, merchants were required to pay the customs duty. Merchant guilds and associations were required to cooperate in the collection of commercial taxes from their own members. On the other hand, merchants were expected to stabilize the market while ensuring the circulation of grain to secure the "people's livelihood." The alliance between the large merchant houses and the state was of course not an easy one. But this does not gainsay the fact that it served both parties well enough, especially given the alternatives. The state did not wish to devote the resources needed to move the volumes of grain necessary to secure political control of the empire, while merchants did not wish to compete with the state or have the state overly restrict the movement of goods on whose trade merchant profits depended.

Guilds and merchant associations were thus key to both merchant and state interests. For merchants, these associations helped to secure profits. There was always the tendency to overexport, given the possibility for individual merchants to profit by moving more goods. However, if too many goods were moved, or other merchants and shippers waiting in the wings entered into the trade, prices would fall and merchants' profits could succumb to intensified competition and price cutting. Merchants thus sought to control their numbers by limiting entry into trade, which they did by forming organizations that kept nonaffiliated merchants out of the market. The Qing state was willing to accept those arrangements so long as they yielded stable markets, on the one hand, and merchants profits did not create undue hardship, on the other.

With state backing, therefore, large merchant houses organized themselves into associations for managing trade that, in the Qing, took several forms. Some merchants organized around native places (*shangbang*) and others around lines of trade (*hang*) (Jernigan 1905, 206–211; Zhang 1996, 136–148). Still others, such as the merchant shippers associated with shipping guilds (*chuan bang* and *chuanhang*) and state-chartered market brokers (*yahang*), organized around their functions in the market (Zhang 1996, 59–88). In each case, merchant associations established institutionalized meeting halls (*huiguan*) in the principal cities where they traded. The large merchant houses invariably held simultaneous affiliations with two or more merchant organizations, holding membership within a native *shangbang* as well as a commodity guild, for instance, in an effort to maximize their social and political influence at critical nodes in the trading nexus.

Merchant native-place alliances (*shangbang*) and occupational guilds (*hang*) were corporate and self-governing bodies granted discretionary powers by the state. They adjudicated disputes among members—though they often had recourse to the state's courts—ensured stable market prices, established rules of trade, and limited competition. They were also delegated powers by the state to assess and remit commercial taxes, powers that merchants and their associations in turn used to strengthen their control of the marketplace (Mann 1987, 23–24; Zhang 1990, 70–88, 137–148). Finally, merchant associations helped curry favor with local authorities in return for political protections. They provided authorities with lucrative trade investment opportunities in return for their political cooperation in the policing of the marketplace and protection of their market position (Fan 1998, 220, 264–265).

Big Merchants and the Manchurian Trade

In the eighteenth and most of the nineteenth centuries, China's coastwise trade in Manchurian goods was dominated by big merchant houses from Shandong. Merchants from Shandong and Manchuria's Guandong region constructed a joint hall in Shanghai as early as 1660, establishing one of the earliest permanent merchant presences in Songjiang. Of the Shandong merchants, those from the peninsula's coastal prefectures of Dengzhou and Laizhou, and of Qingzhou, were the most prolific and successful. They controlled the coastal trade in grains, beans, and cotton cloth between north China and Fengtian and between Fengtian and the Jiangnan ports of Liuhegang and Shanghai. On the basis of that trade, by the second half of the eighteenth century, they were among the wealthiest and most powerful merchants in the empire, with an institutional presence not only in their export markets in the north and northeast but also their principal import markets in Jiangnan (Zhang 1993b, 180; Zhang 1996, 187–191; Fan 1998, 218–219).

By the 1750s, grain, beans, and cotton cloth constituted the bulk of goods traded in the empire. The Shandong merchants who controlled the Manchurian export trade in these items were known collectively as the Dongqi (or Jiaodong) merchants. Their rise to prominence was supposedly due to a combination of fortuitous geography and the poor ecology of their native place. Their propitious location on the Shandong peninsula provided easy access to the port city of Tianjin, which not only served the capital at Beijing but also sat at one end of the Grand Canal. The Dongqi merchants also had immediate access to the Bohai (Zhili Gulf), which is formed by the Liaodong and Shandong peninsulas, and from there to the eastern seaboard, which stretches to Jiangnan and Lingnan to the south. It was the poor ecology of the Shandong peninsula that apparently provided the Dongqi merchants with the early trading opportunities that would later serve them so well. Taking advantage of the fact that peasants on the Shandong peninsula were compelled by poor and thin soils to trade soybeans and other suitable cash crops for grain, the Dongqi merchants established an early foothold in the coastal trade of these items (Fan 1992, 274–275; Zhang 1993b, 170, 174–175). Explaining the Dongqi merchants rise to prominence, the Shandong Governor Chen Shiguan in the Yongzheng era wrote:

> the soils along the [Shandong] coast are hard and infertile, so that six or seven out of ten districts plant beans. Every year, non-native merchants from Tianjin, Jiangsu, and other regions come from the east carrying goods and many purchase the beans which they carry back along the coastal sea lanes to sell to tofu shops and oil mills. The beancakes which are made [from pressing oil] are used widely to fertilize the fields. Those who are not engaged in these activities purchase millet and wheat[21] for distilling and making noodles . . . because the mountain roads [between the Shandong peninsula and the Lu plain] are uneven, making transportation by carts difficult, goods to sell cannot be moved between neighboring districts. All trade therefore requires going to sea and circulating. (GZD-YZ 1977, vol. 6, 409)[22]

From their perch on the Shandong peninsula, the Dongqi merchants first dominated the circular trade within the Bohai, moving goods between Niuzhuang, Tianjin, and Qingzhou. The number of ships plying between Fengtian and Tianjin were reported to have reached "hundreds per year" by 1740 (TFZ 1968, 30. 2505). Thereafter, the Dongqi merchants expanded the scope of their trading to the south, taking advantage of the Qing exemption of Shandong soybeans from the ban on coastal trade in food crops (Will 1990, 218). As early as the 1720s, merchants from ports on the Shandong peninsula carried beans, raw cotton, jujubes, and other so-called northern goods (*beihuo*) from Shandong to the south. By mid-century, coarse grains such as millet and sorghum as well as beans were most prominent. On the return leg they brought so-called southern goods (*nanhuo*). By mid-century those included small quantities of paper, earthen, sugar, tea, and other such items. But by far the biggest item brought back to the north was coarse peasant-produced Jiangnan cotton cloth (GZD-YZ 1977, vol. 6, 404–408; Zhu 1990, 80). Thus, several decades before the Qing state lifted the twin bans on exports of Manchurian soybeans and grain, the Dongqi merchants had an established presence between the Yangzi and the Liao rivers, trading in the very commodities—grain, beans, and cotton cloth—that would come to constitute the bulk of the Manchurian trade by the end of the century (Zhang 1993b, 182; Fan 1998, 153, 161, 219; Zhang 1996, 189–190; Zhang 1988, 251, 260).

In the Shunzhi era the Dongqi merchants built an association hall in Suzhou. When the hall was reconstructed in 1777 there were 290 merchants affiliated with the Dongqi group operating in the city, which was at that time the center of Jiangnan's grain and cotton cloth trade (Zhang 1993b, 182; Fan 1998, 218). To deepen their organizational reach, the Dongqi merchant group had formed alliances with sections of the Jiangsu merchants, opening jointly managed guild halls from which to monitor and control the importation and wholesale of grain and soybeans in the Yangzi delta. At the end of the eighteenth century, after the port at Liuhegang silted up and the center of Jiangnan trade moved away from Suzhou to Shanghai, the Dongqi merchants became prominent members of Shanghai's soybean guild (*douhang*), which controlled the wholesale distribution of imported and locally produced soybeans (Fan 1998, 218–219, 235; Zhang 1988, 251, 260; Zhang 1993b, 185). To secure state favor, the Dongqi merchants established close relations with Jiangnan authorities by taking on certain semi-official functions. The Dongqi merchant group provided local officials with militia to assist in the maintenance of local order and provided an armed escort to state shipments of government species (Fan 1998, 220, 264–265). While developing their presence in Jiangnan, the Dongqi merchants were no less busy deepening their links with Manchuria. Initially, they did so by bringing southern goods such as earthernwares, paper, cotton cloth, and velveteen to Fengtian and by assisting the state in its efforts to move famine-relief grain from Fengtian to north China (JZZ 1976, 651). Before trade was legalized, many undoubtedly also partook in the endemic smuggling of soybeans and grain out of the northeast, a practice that earned official displeasure, but nonetheless gave the merchants an institutional presence in Fengtian (HZ 1749.12.4). By the time Manchurian grain exports were permitted in 1772, the Dongqi merchants thus had a presence both in the northeast and Jiangnan, which would facilitate their consolidation of control over the Manchurian trade thereafter.

Whereas the Dongqi merchants had begun trading within the Bohai and between Shandong and Jiangnan, with the passage of time the trade between Fengtian and Jiangnan came to prominence. In redirecting their activities, it appears the Dongqi merchants were reacting to rising demand for grain in Jiangnan. Mounting population pressure had issued in rapidly rising grain prices in the densely populated Yangzi delta. The concomitant turn by Jiangnan peasants to cotton manufacturing, made necessary by declining holding size and their subsequent need to round out their subsistence by working in cotton textiles, only added to Jiangnan's grain hunger by taking land out of grain cultivation. Even as demand for grain grew in Zhili and Shandong, it grew faster still in Jiangnan. Indeed, Jiangnan had an insatiable appetite for imported grain by mid-century such that historian Wang Yeh-chien (1989, 1992) argues the region was setting the pace for the empire-wide rise in grain prices by pulling in grain from an expanding catchment area. From the middle of the eighteenth to the middle of the nineteenth centuries, grain prices in Fengtian followed those in Jiangnan upward, as the two regions became more interdependent.[23]

The supersession of the Shandong-Jiangnan trade by the Fengtian-Jiangnan trade was realized by the third decade of the nineteenth century, when Gutzlaff noted in his description of his 1832 voyage up the Yangzi river to Shanghai that the merchants he passed along the way were headed "principally to the habours of Leaou-tung [Liaodong], or Mantchou tartary [Manchuria], from whence they import oil-cakes and peas [*sic*] . . . whilst they export silk and other manufactures of Keang-nan [Jiangnan]" (Gutzlaff and Ellis 1834, 281; cf. Gutzlaff 1838, 172–173). Given the facts of increasing agricultural settlement and the concomitant expansion of grain and soybean production in the northeast, the limitations of north China's agricultural productiveness at the end of the eighteenth century, and the demand for Fengtian grain and soybeans in Jiangnan, it is evident why Shandong merchants increasingly devoted their energy to trading directly between Fengtian and the Yangzi delta.

That shift in trade networks was also propelled by the northeast's growing appetite for cotton cloth, particularly for Jiangnan cotton. In the sixteenth and early seventeenth centuries, Shandong was the principal supplier to Fengtian of cotton cloth. However, by the late eighteenth century, if not earlier, all of Shandong exports of cloth combined could at best have met no more than one-third of Manchuria's needs, and we know that some of Shandong's export cloth was unavailable to the northeast. According to one estimate, in the Qianlong and Jiaqing periods, Shandong exported annually between 300,000 and 500,000 bolts to the north, northwest, and Manchuria combined, at a time when Manchuria's annual demand was perhaps two million or more bolts (Xu 1998a, 327–329). This points to a sizeable unmet market for cotton cloth in Manchuria. Not surprisingly, therefore, by the mid-eighteenth century Jiangnan cloth exports were meeting much of the northeast's demand.

If circa 1800 half of Shandong's total exports of a half-million bolts went to the northeast, this would have meant a shortfall of perhaps two million bolts annually, a shortfall that Jiangnan could fill. Assuming the growth of Shandong cloth exports did not keep pace with growing demand for cloth in Manchuria—a highly probable scenario—and a low annual per capita rate of cloth consumption in the northeast of 1.3 bolts, then Fengtian was importing from Jiangnan more than 2 million bolts by 1800 and more than 6 million bolts by 1850. At this conservative rate of consumption, Fengtian was importing about six percent of the total Jiangnan output just prior to the Opium War (cf. Li 1998; Xu 1992; Fan 1998; Huang 1990). Most of Fengtian's cloth imports, however, were provided by Songjiang prefecture, which in the late eighteenth century exported in excess of six million bolts (perhaps as many as ten million) (Zhang 1988, 154).[24] Fengtian's demand for Songjiang and Taicang cotton cloth was noted by officials in the 1770s (GZD-QL 1982, vol. 37, 120–121; also vol. 38, 724–726). By the early nineteenth century, the northeast had emerged as one of the most important markets for Songjiang cloth, capable of effecting the price of Songjiang cloth and peasant livelihood there. When a bad harvest struck Fengtian in 1823, for instance, trade between the northeast and Jiangnan came to a standstill and prices for Jiangnan cloth and yarn both fell dramatically, harming Songjiang households (Zhang 1988, 154; Fan 1998, 74–75). By the 1830s, Songjiang annually produced about twenty-seven million bolts, perhaps ten million of which went to the north (Li 1998, 109; Xu and Wu 1985, 277–279; Fan 1998, 74).[25] If the bulk of Manchuria's cloth came from Songjiang prefecture, then the Manchurian market on the eve of the Taiping Rebellion consumed perhaps sixty percent or more of the prefecture's cloth exports. Manchuria's demand for Jiangnan cotton cloth clearly enhanced the Fengtian-Jiangnan trade, providing Dongqi and other merchants with a profitable commodity to carry on their return to the northeast.

Shandong's supersession by Jiangnan as Manchuria's principal market was symptomatic of a general pattern of intensifying competition between the cores for the grain surpluses of the peripheral zones. Predictably, rising interregional competition for grain issued in rising empire-wide grain prices, that commenced in the early eighteenth century and coincided with a rise in population from perhaps 150 to 270 million between 1700 and the 1770s (Rowe 2001, 156). Yet, despite the shift in markets, Shandong's Dongqi merchants managed to retain their dominant position in Manchurian trade, a position they appear to have held until the second half of the nineteenth century. They achieved this by virtue of the early establishment of institutional arrangements that secured for them access to both Manchurian export crops as well as Jiangnan grain and bean markets. They enhanced their market position further by establishing alliances with Jiangnan merchants and government officials.

Manchuria's Hinterland Trade and Hinterland Merchants

In her study of Qing merchants in north China, Susan Mann (1987) shows how in the eighteenth century state efforts to reform local markets by strengthening the liturgical role of merchants ended with the state ceding to them significant powers over the marketplace. The liturgies became "hegemonic structures," Mann argues, using the taxation powers granted to them by the state to dominate markets, promote the interests of partners and family members, and exclude competitors. While Mann suggests these structures may have in the process brought some stability to markets, they did so, she insists, by eliminating competitors and by protecting commercial interests (52–93). Those powers were enhanced by the presence at nodal points in the market of merchant associations and guilds that worked to fix prices and control markets. While the state may have insisted in law that "market prices" (*shijia*) prevail, as the historian Jing Junjian notes, brokers were very successful in fixing prices (Jing 1994, 61; cf. Mazumdar 1998, 312; Golas 1977, 571).

Evidence on merchant activities in Manchuria is unfortunately scant and the sorts of sources Mann (1987) used in her study of north China markets are not available for the northeast until quite late. Nonetheless, the sources that are available for the Qing and early twentieth century point to merchants in the northeast having established political control over local markets through a combination of their roles as liturgical tax farmers and their establishment of closed associations and guilds. That this was so is not surprising when we note that the majority of Manchuria's hinterland merchants were from Zhili and Shandong, where Mann shows such strategies were well honed by the early Qing (DSD 1987, 39, 191, 210; Zhang 1993b, 180–181). Just as peasants brought their ways of regulating property and so forth to the Manchurian countryside, so merchants from north China brought their ways of doing business.

Until the arrival of the railway to Manchuria at the end of the nineteenth century, access to hinterland products and markets was provided by the Liao river and its tributaries. In the early Jiaqing period, the Qing official Bao Shichen noted that "merchants from throughout the empire" had opened up shop in Fengtian's Guandong region, where the mouth of the Liao river provided access to hinterland markets (1968, 1. 44). The importance of the Liao river was recognized by Qing authorities in 1707 when they established Fengtian's first imperial customs office at the port of Niuzhuang, which at that time sat at the river's mouth. Though the Qing customs office remained at Niuzhuang, as silting changed the morphology of the river mouth so the location of the main port moved south. It was relocated from Niuzhuang to Tianzhuangtai in the early nineteenth century and from there to Yingkou by mid-century.[26] From those ports, shallow-draft river barges were able to travel five hundred miles up river, a journey which took fifteen days upstream and six downstream. The entire Liao river basin including the Hun and Taizi rivers was navigable for some eight hundred miles (Adachi 1925, 241). The Liao river system thus linked Fengtian's major entrepôt at Niuzhuang-Yingkou with inland riverside towns such as Tieling, Kaiyuan, Xinmintun, Tianzhuangtai, and Shenyang (Shengjing), that in turn served as emporiums for gathering up grain and beans from the surrounding countryside (Zhang 1990, 167–172). By the 1840s, Shenyang was the center of the inland grain trade, the site where merchants gathered to buy, store, and transship grain and soybeans: "of the grain that comes from beyond the borders [Jilin, Heilongjiang, and eastern Mongolia], most is stored in Shenyang. Xinmintun is of second importance and Liaoyang is third. It passes through these places on the way to ports, from where it is then shipped to relieve the people's food needs in Zhili and Shandong" (GCJY 1993, 1197).

The work of moving goods from the hinterland to Niuzhuang-Yingkou began in the late summer, in the ninth lunar month, and ended in the late winter, in the second lunar month (HZ 1824.7.27; also KT 1912, 73). Reverend Williamson, who traveled in Manchuria in 1864, 1866, and 1877, noted: "it is during the winter that the great bulk of the pulse-crop is brought down to the seaports, and there stored for shipment when the rivers open" (Williamson 1870, vol. 2, 26). Following the harvest of soybeans and grains, a mad rush commenced as hinterland merchants began to move goods to port before dropping winter temperatures froze the Liao river. Once ice made the river passage impossible, merchants and teamsters switched to slower caravans of large carts pulled by horses and mules that traversed the frozen roads and even the frozen rivers. As much as possible of the work of moving goods to the coast had to be completed before the spring thaw. This turned the dirt roads into mud that was too deep for heavily laden carts to pass and caused the rivers to flow too dangerously for the shallow-draft barges to pass. All inland transportation was suspended until the late spring or early summer (HZ 1824.7.27; CGCJY 1993, 1197–1198).[27] Once the river rapids had subsided and the roads were again passable, stores of grain and soybeans that had been warehoused over the winter in hinterland towns for want of enough carts and barges were released and moved to the coast (HZ 1824.7.27; Adachi 1925, 242).

The working calendar of the big merchants was fixed by the change in seasons too. By the time the new harvest of grain and soybeans began to arrive in Niuzhuang in early winter, the harbor itself was frozen and the port closed to ships. Grain and soybeans reaching Niuzhuang at that time had to be stored until the following spring when the harbor ice broke and ocean-going junks could enter the port and be loaded. In the third lunar month, the work of the big merchants and merchant-shippers began as they moved grain, soybeans, and other items from Fengtian to Shandong and Jiangnan. Shipping was halted however in the sixth month when the winds turned and not recommenced until the eight lunar month when they turned again. Shipping ended once again in the tenth month when the ports froze (HZ 1824.7.27; cf. GB.CR 1971, vol. 3, 488).

To obtain the commodities they moved, the Dongqi and other merchant shippers operated in alliance with hinterland merchants known as *liangzhan* ("grain mercantile") who operated out of the inland emporium towns such as Xinmintun, Liaoyang, Tieling, Kaiyuan, Tianzhuangzi, and Shengyang and who orchestrated the movement of goods to the coastal entrepôt. Many *liangzhan* were themselves from the same districts as the Dongqi merchants, a fact that most probably made cooperation easy (DSD 1987, 210). Working below the *liangzhan* were petty brokers and itinerant merchants who bought grain and soybeans directly from the villages and delivered them to the market towns. Thus, a functional hierarchy of merchants stretched over the Manchurian countryside, with some merchants going down to the villages to buy items, others gathering and storing grain in the towns, and still others transporting these goods to the coast (NHB 1937, 45–46, 73).

Just as the merchant associations and guilds were key to the success of the big merchant houses at the apex of that hierarchy, so too the *liangzhan* organized themselves into political communities to advance their position in the hinterland markets, to reduce and eliminate competition, to stabilize prices, and to squeeze out profits from those below. In the early days of the Qing, the most prominent of the merchant groups in Manchuria was the renowned Shanxi *shangbang*, which had an established presence in Shenyang as early as the Qianlong era. By the 1820s, the Shanxi merchants were said to control the inland soybean and grain trade, moving all but one-quarter of the soybeans headed ultimately for Yingkou-Niuzhuang, through their granaries in Shengjing (Lie 1981, 151; Zhang 1993b, 23, 27). Shandong merchants also had an early presence in Manchuria's hinterland trade dating to at least 1707, when the

Kangxi emperor on tour of the region noted that "there are Shandong persons everywhere, either engaging in trade or tilling the land" (SZSL 1964, [115]). As late as the twentieth century, when solid data are first available, the Shanxi, Shandong, and Zhili *shangbang* accounted for two-thirds of all hinterland grain dealers, the remainder belonged primarily to the more recently founded Jilin *shangbang* (Lie 1981, 148, 150–151; cf. Zhang 1993b, 180–181).

At nodal points in the inland trading system, merchants from various native *shangbang* also came together to form commodity guilds. Like the *shangbang*, the guilds functioned to control merchant behavior, regulate the markets, and reduce competition among merchants. But unlike the *shangbang*, they did so by controlling trade in specific items and services. Accordingly, each guild had strict regulations on who could trade in the items the guild oversaw and how. Those rules as well as other market regulations and controls were enforced by the guild corporate body, which was funded and staffed by guild members who also supported the construction and maintenance of halls and other buildings where guild business was handled. Hinterland trade in grain and soybeans was within the purview of the grain guild (*lianghang*), which was formed by *liangzhan* at nodal points in the market system (FTTZ 2003, 2642–2643, 2651; Xu 1989, 1584). The *liangzhan* combined the powers of their *shangbang* and guild associations to police the market, establish market rules, and limit competition among members (FTTZ 2003, 2642). They even controlled their own militia to assist in the enforcement of rules and order (FTTZ 2003, 816), and merchants were not averse to using brute force to assert command in the marketplace. It was reported in 1849, for instance, that the inland merchants and shippers operating in the northeast's largest inland grain entrepôt of Tianzhuangtai and Mogouying—just upriver from Niuzhuang—employed violence to monopolize marketplaces. They employed local brigands to enforce their monopolies and to conduct private vendettas, while they sought political protection by consorting with employees of the local *yamen* (FTTZ 2003, 823). It should be noted that these merchant tactics were not the product of Manchuria's frontier environment, where the state's presence was perhaps weaker, though that may certainly have facilitated such behavior. In north and south China merchants, landlords, and lineage groups consorted with those with gentry connections and official market brokers (the *yahang*) to command markets (Mann 1987, 44–48, 72–93, 181–182; Mazumdar 1998, 315–322, 359–362, 392).

The guilds and merchant associations prevented unaffiliated merchants from entering their line of trade or market thresholds and, according to the Republican-era *Fengtian Complete Gazetteer*, sought to "correct bad business practices and raise profits . . . by binding members from competing against one another unreasonably" (FTTZ 2003, 2651). Toward those ends, merchants in a guild or association shared information on market conditions and informed each other of changing circumstances. Their success in maintaining organizational cohesion and protecting their markets had much to do with their location in the commercial hierarchy. In contrast to the petty merchants and peasants who delivered goods to the market and who were scattered across the countryside by virtue of their market niche, *liangzhan* operations were concentrated at nodal points in the transportation network where self-policing was logistically simpler. Under those conditions it was easier for *liangzhan* to form associations and guilds and to control the marketplace (Lie 1981, 155–156; MT 1921, 118–119; FTTZ 2003, 2642–2643, 2651). Moreover, because merchant corporate bodies actively limited entry into the trade, and because the capital requirements for setting up shop as a *liangzhan* were great, the *liangzhan* were simply far fewer in number than petty merchants and therefore easier to self-organize and self-police. At the end of the Qing, there were six hundred *liangzhan* operating in the northeast at a time when the total population was fourteen million and seven to eight million *shi* of beans alone were moving through the trading system (FTTZ 2003, 2651). In essence, their small numbers and location in the market network occasioned a natural monopsony which was then strengthened by associations and commodity guilds.

The *liangzhan* merchants had one further, very important, advantage over petty merchants and the like that came within their liturgical functions. As noted, it was the Qing practice to deputize merchants to collect and remit commercial taxes and in return those merchants were granted monopoly rights to mediate commercial transactions and collect a broker's fee. These liturgical merchants, known as *yahang*, used their state-granted powers to collect commercial taxes and mediate transactions to favor those associated with particular merchant associations and, thereby, colluded in fixing prices. They of course were willing to do this because they themselves belonged to the same corporate bodies and used their alliances with particular merchants for self-enrichment (Zhang 1996, 80–83; Mann 1987, 44–48; Jing 1994, 61).

In the northeast, *yahang* were at work in major market towns such as Tieling, Liaoyang, and Shengjing as early as the mid-eighteenth century and continued to operate until the end of the dynasty, collecting commercial taxes on tobacco, livestock, grain, and other commodities (SJTZ 1965, 1239; TLZ 1985, 774; LYZ 1985, 741). In the grain trades, local authorities designated *liangzhan* to act as *yahang*. The *liangzhan* were a natural choice because of their institutional presence at critical points in the hinterland trading system and their established membership in commercial associations and guilds (MT 1921, 118). The latter of course provided them with the institutional framework for garnering the commercial tax and for policing their state-granted broker monopolies, and the former gave them the experience they needed to mediate sales and collect the tax.[28] The *liangzhan* merchants who performed tax-collection functions combined that state-delegated authority with the private powers of their associations and guilds to maintain market stability. But in stabilizing the market, they also limited competitive bidding for goods, kept competitors out, and ensured that trade was monopolized by associated merchants.

While horizontal alignments between *liangzhan*, constituted through merchant political communities, worked to advance the reproduction of merchant capital and the control of the larger inland merchants over the intraregional exchange of grain and soybeans, vertical arrangements between *liangzhan* and petty merchants served to maintain the flow of capital into the countryside and the removal of grain and soybean surpluses to the ports. Those merchants were known by various titles (*jingji*, *jiechede*, *zaojingji*, and *shuijingji*), depending upon their mode of operation, and though they dealt in small quantities of grain and soybeans, they were numerous and as a body constituted an important player in trade. According to Japanese investigations, forty-five percent of all grain marketed in southern Manchuria in the 1930s passed through their hands (NHB 1937, 45–46). Yet, despite their obvious importance to the trade, petty merchants remained highly dependent upon the *liangzhan*. In the latter half of the nineteenth century, nearly all soybeans (ninety-five percent) that reached Manchuria's major regional entrepôt of Niuzhuang-Yingkou passed through the hands of the *liangzhan* (Lie 1981, 149; MSRS 1931, 11, 73–76). The *liangzhan* were able to forge ties with and enforce discipline on petty merchants to ensure the bulk of goods passed through them. They achieved this through debt (advance payments) and by contractual obligations.

Many petty merchants it seems were short of capital and so compelled to turn to the better-funded *liangzhan* for loans. The *liangzhan* willingly forwarded capital in return for securing their stocks in advance (NHB 1937, 45–46, 73). But, if the *liangzhan* could not discipline petty merchants through debt, they tried to contract them as agents to buy on their behalf. The merchant associations in turn enforced these contracts, even to the extent of punishing those *liangzhan* who tried to lure petty merchants into breaking contractual agreements with other *liangzhan* (Lie 1981, 156).

With restrictions on competition between *liangzhan* enforced by the merchant associations, one of the few avenues open to *liangzhan* to gain at each other's expense was to capture or soak up more of the agricultural surplus by disciplining the petty merchants with whom they traded. By vertically binding petty merchants through debt and contracts, the more successful *liangzhan* were able to aggregate greater reserves of grain and beans, profiting by handling greater amounts.

Hinterland Merchants and Peasant Access to Markets

Undoubtedly, individual merchants made substantial fortunes in the Manchurian trade, and certainly substantial volumes of capital were accumulated in the hands of merchants as peasant colonization proceeded and the region's total surplus rose. The question remains, however, whether merchant capital made its way into the production process as investments in new tools and methods that sustained ongoing improvements in production, or whether earnings were simply reinvested in ways that, while profitable to merchants, did not systematically advance productivity gains. Studies of other parts of the empire have shown that Qing merchants did not on the whole invest in ways that might have sustained improvements in agricultural or proto-industrial production. In his excellent study of the Fujian tea trade, Robert Gardella finds that merchant capital was not a source for investment in technological improvement and organizational restructuring—tools remained simple and crude and production remained primarily based on small-scale peasant producers with an output in the 1940s of an average of a mere two hundred catties. He describes the expansion of the tea trade as "extensive growth without structural change," to describe the growth of volume in the tea trade, the accumulation by merchants of tremendous wealth through exchange, and the response on the part of producers to demand, but the absence of any innovation in production methods (Gardella 1994, 45, 46, 53–54, 74–81, 171–174). In her study of sugar production in south China, Sucheta Mazumdar (1998, 324–329) comes to a very similar conclusion, showing that merchants in the sugar trade preferred to use their control over markets to make their profits rather than investing in improving production and lowering their costs.

What Gardella, Mazumdar, and others demonstrate is that individually merchants found that peasants could not be expected—nor could they be required—to innovate in ways that would systematically lower the cost of agricultural and proto-industrial products and secure for some merchants a price advantage over their competitors. This again, I believe, was the upshot of the prevailing property system which shielded peasants from the competitive pressure that would have resulted from their full dependency upon the market. Because merchants could not depend upon peasants to innovate in ways that would lower costs and raise labor productivity in an ongoing fashion, these same merchants were unwilling to invest in either proto-industrial or farming activities. When they did forward peasants money, they did so at high rates of interest that allowed peasants to achieve simple reproduction but generally nothing more (Jing 1994, 78–80; Liu 2000, 187, 201–202; Mazumdar 1998, 311–312, 331–333).

Given their institutional power in the market, however, there were structural incentives and means for *liangzhan* to maximize their own profits by suppressing peasant earnings. The *liangzhan* were of course pressured to reduce peasant earnings because the big merchants to whom they sold dominated the grain and soybean trade and were similarly organized to control trade and limit competition among buyers at the few entrepôts serving the northeast. By virtue of their position in the trading hierarchy, big merchants had alliances and knowledge of prices in Tianjin, Shanghai and beyond unavailable to the *liangzhan* and used these advantages and other organizational strengths to squeeze out profits from the *liangzhan*. To eke out profits, the *liangzhan* in turn brought grain and soybeans from the peasantry using similar strategies (Lie 1981, 88). Not only did hinterland merchant associations and guilds proscribe competition between buyers by establishing monopsonies at the points of collection, but their knowledge of market conditions at the ports and larger major market towns—and, conversely, the peasants' lack thereof—also permitted *liangzhan* to squeeze peasants.

Qing officials were aware of the ways by which merchants in the northeast colluded to raise their profits. They tried unsuccessfully to stamp out one such practice known as *maikong maikong* (speculative exchanges) because of its deleterious effects on grain prices and supplies. In 1822, as the Manchurian grain trade was coming into its own, Shengjing Military Governor Ihao sought to ban the practice because, he maintained, it drove up local grain prices daily until "the people found it harder and harder to eat" (cited in Zhang 1990, 198, 203). Evidently the ban had no effect, because in 1835 local officials indicted the practice again, giving the following account of how it worked:

> In Fengtian, Jinzhou, and other districts there are treacherous merchants who have established business with such names as Supreme Harmony, Heavenly Peace, and Lasting Prosperity et cetera. They bring partners together to *maikong maikong*. They make price conjectures and induce one another to arrange purchases and grain delivery dates without circulating any items. The arranged purchases are then bought and sold among the other business establishments. Using this method, they make their profits. In this manner, prices are purposely increased such that the price of grain rises daily and commoners find it hard to get enough food. Merchants in the grain-producing areas, hearing of these practices, don't come to the market and in the neighboring provinces the market prices rises because of this. This kind of malevolent practice is greatly related to the empoverishment [of the people]" (XZSL 1964, 4951 [276]).

The account tells how a few of the large regional merchants—large enough that their businesses' names were known to the authorities—organized to corner the grain market. They did this by making speculative purchases from smaller hinterland merchants on the future grain harvest. The hinterland merchants in turn used the cash they raised to make "preemptory purchases" or "advance" from peasants (see below). Once the speculators had successfully cornered grain supplies, and thereby driven up the grain price, they began to sell their purchases to other merchants. Such methods were not particular to the northeast: they were common to merchants in other parts of the empire and stemmed from the same imbalances in power between big and small merchants on the one hand and between merchants and peasants on the other (Mazumdar 1998, 329–332; Mann 1987, 44–48, 72–93, 181–182).

Merchants could also benefit from the "natural monopsony" stemming from the difficulty of moving grain and soybeans out of the region. As Qing officials noted, most of the hinterland grain and soybeans that made its way into the market was bought up by the rural merchants by the Chinese new year (HZ 1824.7.27). But because merchants could not move their inventories fast enough, prices tended to fall very rapidly as peasant surpluses moved into the market and supplies swelled. The postharvest price of grain could be as much as one-fifth the summer high price and yet only the most well-heeled peasants could afford to wait until the spring to sell their grain (NHB 1937, 35). The hinterland merchants therefore quickly purchased the bulk of their grain when prices were tumbling. By the time the larger hinterland merchants were selling their grain at the entrepôt in the spring, however, grain prices had risen considerably as regional supplies fell, allowing them to capture the difference. Given their organizational power and the natural monopsonies that formed in the countryside, merchants at all levels received the lion's share of trade revenue. Of the revenue from the mid-nineteenth-century soybean trade, about one-third covered expenses of bringing the soybeans to market (transport and customs duty), more than half was divided between hinterland and entrepôt merchants as their income (profit), and a mere one-tenth went to the peasant producers (Lie 1981, 154–155).

The other means by which merchants extracted profits from peasants was through loans. These were forwarded to peasants as either simple loans that required the repayment of the original sum plus interest or more commonly in the form of advance purchases of agricultural items. Loans were also the one vehicle available to merchants to require peasants to produce for the market, since the loans had to be repaid. The advance or preemptory purchase was the most effective tool for securing peasant output.[29] Known variously as *pi maimai*, *mai qingtian*, or *maiqing maiqing*, merchants used preemptory purchases to secure access to and guarantee control over part of the agricultural output well in advance of the harvest (MT 1921, 12; 1926, 32; MMZ 1922–23, 5.77–78; MSRS 1931, 36–39). The loan was usually advanced in the spring and repayment in kind was expected at the time of harvest (Wang 1987, 42; HBK 1937, 30–38; Kameoka 1921, 126). The practice is illustrated in a legal case cited by Zhang Yaomin (1990). According to the court records, Yu Kunbao was a *liangzhan* merchant operating from Shenyang in the 1830s, which by this time was the center of the inland grain and soybean trade (cf. GCJY 1993, 1197). Every spring and summer he sent several agents into the countryside to buy grain and beans from peasants, well before harvest. In 1838, however, he was unable to call in the harvest when more than twenty-five households owed him a total of nearly five hundred *taels*. The matter ended up in court, though Zhang does not provide details of the final judgment (in Zhang 1990, 204–205). The hinterland merchants, in turn, traded on preemptory purchases ahead of the harvest. Petty merchants sold the contracts in advance to *liangzhan* and *liangzhan* sold them to the big merchant houses in Shenyang and Niuzhuang (Xu 1989, 1096). Preemptive purchases were thus closely tied with the aforementioned practice of *maikong maikong*, a fact noted in a 1907 memorial to ban the speculative exchange. Fengtian Governor Xu Shichang memorialized that it was an outgrowth of the long-standing practice of preemptory purchases. Xu wrote: "investigations show that beans and grain have long been the most cultivated crops in Fengtian. In the past, non-native merchants groups monopolized commodities (*tunhuo*) by the method of setting the price beforehand but completing the exchange afterwards. The practice of *maikong maikong* developed from this" (Xu 1989, 1096).

Twentieth-century accounts of the preemptive purchase show that petty merchants, often using money secured from *liangzhan* and merchant shippers, made their purchases early in the year before the desired crops had fully matured, often when crops were just pushing through the topsoil. Before advancing the payment, the merchant inspected the fields where the crops lay and gauged the land's productivity. If the crop in question had sprouted, the merchant also gauged its quality. On the basis of this assessment, the merchant offered a price for the crop that was always well below the current and estimated future market value. If the peasant agreed, he took the cash and a contract was signed acknowledging receipt of payment and stating the terms by which the crop was to be delivered (HBK 1937, 30–35).

Merchants were clearly taking a risk when they entered into these arrangements. Crop failure, such as that which affected the aforementioned merchant Yu Kunbao, or peasants' refusal to heed the agreement could result in significant losses. Risks were compounded by the fact that merchants were given to contracting with many individual households simultaneously, many of whom would fail to repay following a bad harvest. In addition, the money could have been earning interest if not advanced, so merchants needed to cover that lost opportunity as well. To ensure profitability and cover the cost of risk, merchants predictably paid a very low price for the grain and soybeans. Accounts of the price paid vary; sources from the 1930s show the price paid was as high as seventy to eighty percent of the autumn market value to as low as twenty to forty percent and fifty to sixty percent, with studies of the early twentieth century citing lower percentages still (NHB 1937, 73; HBK 1937, 32; Kameoka 1921, 126; MT 1926, 32; Lie 1981, 161). The difference between the cash advanced and the final value of the crop was in effect interest, making the "advanced payment" akin to a loan rather than a contracted purchase. At forty percent of harvest value, a merchant made a 150 percent profit on every successful transaction. At eighty percent, he still made a twenty-five percent profit. In normal years, benefits accrued therefore disproportionately to the merchants making these loans. In fact, with the merchant paying such a small proportion of the autumn crop value, a weak but not devastating harvest could bring them big rewards since the difference between the purchase and sale price (raised by the weak harvest) was that much greater.

The interest charged on ordinary loans was comparable. It is widely accepted by historians that even though the state fixed interest at no more than three percent per month, merchants and pawnshop owners regularly secured higher rates than that (Jing 1994, 78–80; Liu 2000, 187, 201–202). Two separate sources suggest that in the mid-eighteenth century interest on loans to merchants in Fengtian was thirty percent per annum. Peasants who had far less in the way of security certainly paid higher (Zhang 1996, 102; Zhang 1990, 197). In twentieth-century Manchuria, interest paid by peasants was compounded three to four percent per month (MS 2000, 452; Zhang 1996, 102–105). These levels are comparable to those of the empire as a whole. In perhaps the most thorough study of the cost of capital in late imperial China to date, Liu Qiugen suggests annual interest usually exceeded thirty percent, with monthly rates of three to five percent most common (Liu 2000, 178–181, 184–188).[30]

For peasants who took these loans, the cash received was critical to their survival, though it seems reasonable to conclude from the level of interest rates that only desperate peasants took loans. Loans provided cash that was often needed to begin production, hire wage laborers, buy seed, pay land taxes (which were due in the spring), cover unpaid rent, replace tools and other means of production, and cover basic subsistence needs (HBK 1937, 34–35). The conditions under which such loans were made, and the "interest" charged, could not possibly have allowed for anything more than the maintenance of production at previous levels, however. Merchant loans that went to peasants in Manchuria and other parts of China were not a means for advancing and improving productivity in the economy. They were at best a means to ensure simple reproduction. Indeed, much of the debt that peasants in Manchuria and elsewhere took on was not for production but for the most basic consumption needs (Table 9.1; Lie 1981, 162–163).

In the twentieth century, debt was most commonly taken on in the spring

TABLE 9.1

Debt and Reasons for Debt in Qing Homicide Cases

Year	Prefect/County	Reasons	Amount	Interest
1792	Fengtian	pay house rent	24,700 cash	
1794	Fengtian, Changtu	purchase grain	1,500 cash	
1796	Jilin, Boduna	clothing and food	6,500 cash	
1796	Fengtian	without means	6,000 cash	
1798	Fengtian, Xingjing	loan	40,000 cash	
1820	Fengtian, Jinzhou	purchase alcohol	15,000 cash	
1820	Fengtian, Jinzhou	loan	18,000 cash	
1820	Shengjing	purchase grain	13,000 cash	
1821	Fengtian, Kaiyuan	a pawn	3,500 cash	
1821	Fengtian, Kaiyuan	drama/brothel	400 cash	
1869	Fengtian, Guangning	grain	10,000 cash	
1870	Fengtian, Xinmin	purchase land	15,000 cash	
1872	Fengtian, Xinmin	purchase a horse	12,0000 cash	
1873	Fengtian, Tieling	not stated	19,000 cash	10,000 cash
1876	Fengtian, Jinzhou	loan	4,000 cash	
1876	Fengtian, Jinzhou	purchase meat	2,900 cash	
1877	Fengtian, Changtu	loan	8,000 cash	
1878	Fengtian, Changtu	pay rent	300 strings	
1878	Fengtian, Fuzhou	purchase sundries	25,000 cash	
1878	Fengtian, Xinmin	purchase a donkey	25,000 cash	
1879	Fengtian, Xingjing	make ends meet	3,000 cash	
1879	Fengtian, Xingjing	loan	2,000 cash	
1879	Fengtian, Xinmin	medical expense	7,500 cash	

SOURCES: XT (*xingke tiben*) in the First National Archives, Beijing.

and summer months when household grain reserves were at their lowest and peasants used the cash to purchase food. Debts were also incurred at random moments during the year to cover the expense of a funeral or a wedding. A 1930s survey of 569 households in southern Manchuria shows how borrowed money was spent. All in all, of the debt for which expenses were specified, thirty percent of the money borrowed went to subsistence and ceremonial items, a similar amount went to pay off previous debts, and about sixteen percent to purchase farm tools and equipment and other production expenses (NKFS 1937, 55–56, 95, 119). Another thirty percent went to support businesses in towns. But, as the survey points out, a few well-off households (about ten percent of all households) had taken on more than eighty percent of such debt. Thus, for the average peasant subsistence and ceremonial purchases accounted for most debt. The same appears to have been the case in the Qing. The most commonly stated reason for borrowing or owing money cited in Qing debt-related homicide cases was to purchase food, clothes, or sundries, or simply to "make ends meet." Unspecified debts for very small amounts were presumably also used to cover these sorts of expenses (see Table 9.1).

While grain merchants could rely on peasants' need for cash in the spring to make preemptive purchases and, in this way, pull a part of the peasants' labor into the market in order to secure the goods they needed to turn a profit in trade, unless peasants were willing/required to sell the greater part of their labor in advance—in other words, to commit the greater part of their holdings and productive efforts to one crop dedicated to the market—the extent to which merchants could enforce a regime of market dependency through debt remained limited. Even if they could, given the interest rates it is not clear that anything would have come of it. Therein lay the structural constraints of the credit system. Whereas peasant indebtedness was the one vehicle through which merchants could enforce some degree of market dependency upon peasants in the late imperial economy, debt was most commonly taken on for subsistence and similar non-productive investment. Furthermore, the rates of interest levied were high enough to preclude ongoing productivity gains when such investment was used for tools, buying land, and the like.[31] Because the high cost of capital precluded most peasants from accumulating at the end of the day, loans by merchants to peasants did not so much advance the productive process as merely permit it to continue in the same vein. In essence this was a typically "peasant route" to market reliance. It was propelled initially by poverty often associated with declining holding size, and the need to accept terms of exchange that systematically undermined any attempt/necessity to accumulate and improve.[32]

Trade, Merchants, and Agriculture in the Qing

A number of Western scholars have pointed to the absolute and relative amounts of grain in Qing China's long-distance trade to support their claims of the highly developed character of the late imperial Chinese economy (Wong 1997, Pomeranz, 2000, Rowe 2001). It is, however, the burden of their position that the proportion of total grain exchanged was undeniably low in the Qing, at between ten and fifteen percent of total grain production (Wu 1983; Guo 1994, 46; Fang et al. 2000, 399). Thus, even though William Rowe (2001) contends that eighteenth-century China "was one of the most highly commercialized [agrarian economies] in the world," he acknowledges that the amount of rice traded empire-wide was a mere ten percent of all rice produced (157).[33]

The relevant figure for gauging and comparing China's historical level of commercialization is of course the relative and not the absolute amount of trade—it is the relative number that speaks to the productivity of labor in farming and most importantly the ability of the economy to sustain people working outside of agriculture. By any accounting, the relative level of commercialization in the Qing economy was low. The proportion of grain traded did not grow across the Qing and the variety of goods traded in inter-regional trade remained more or less unchanged, suggesting a limited and constrained regional division of labor. As Fang Xing (2000) notes, the trade was built primarily on insufficient grain production in the cores and thus driven by "penury not plenty" (in Xu and Wu 2000, 382). Far from being one of the most commercialized economies of the early modern period, Qing China was certainly no more commercialized than the economically laggard regions of continental Europe. By comparison, in England, with only thirty-five percent of its population in agriculture circa 1800, and only ten percent of the population still claimants to the land and therefore with direct access to their output (Allen 1992, 2000), somewhere in the order of ninety percent of *all* agricultural output (grain, meat, and dairy) must have been marketed.[34]

Much of the grain moving through China's long-distance market of course came not from China's densely populated cores but from its peripheral regions. Like China's other peripheries, Manchuria was able to export grain and other food crops such as soybeans by virtue of its later settlement. The northeast and other frontiers benefited from a favorable ratio of land to labor that enabled peasants to produce surpluses in grain sufficient to sustain exports (Jiang 1992, 42–48). Though the surplus per capita was usually quite slim, the fact there were many producers made for large overall surpluses. Consequently, some peripheries such as Huguang found their export capacity increasingly strained by rising population (Jiang 1992, 66). But in the northeast, the vast unsettled areas of Jilin and Heilongjiang helped sustain Manchuria's exports over the entirety of the Qing. A combination of gradual labor intensification in the longer settled south of Manchuria and the extension of arable land in the north sustained both the rising settled population and the grain surplus, while favorable river systems permitted the movement of those goods to the coast. The great demand for Manchurian grain and beans emanating first from north China, then Jiangnan, and finally Lingnan, and the arbitrage profits that that demand occasioned, established the necessary conditions for sustaining merchant activity and the Manchurian trade.

In the context of rising grain prices and mounting regional deficits in the eighteenth and nineteenth centuries, the decision by Qing officials to remove limits on grain and bean exports did not signal a turn to free trade liberalism, as suggested by Helen Dunstan (1996), but rather a pragmatic approach to feeding the empire's densely populated cores. The Qing state did not possess the institutional capacity to orchestrate the movement of so much grain over such great distances. While it is shown by Will, Wong, and Lee (1991) that the Qing state did not withdraw from its accepted role in the intra- and interregional redistribution of grain until the nineteenth century, it is evident that by the first half of the eighteenth century structural grain deficits in Shandong-Zhili, Jiangnan, Fujian, and Guangdong were greatly straining bureaucratic efforts to distribute grain under normal conditions. Institutionally and fiscally unable to move the volumes of grain that were demanded, Qing officials commenced their reliance upon merchants to move grain as early as the mid-eighteenth century. In that sense, I would argue that the "integration" of markets along the eastern seaboard was the upshot of the structural constraints on agricultural productiveness in the economic cores. Robert Marks (1998, 257–258), in his study of Guangdong, has suggested that the parallel movement of grain prices across regions signaled the arrival by the second half of the eighteenth century of an advanced and modern market system to south China. However, as Sucheta Mazumdar (1998) has pointed out, there remains the question of how market integration affected production. The fact of price correlation across neighboring regions says little about how production was organized in either place, or whether producers in response to prices altered their production habits—or, more importantly, their methods—in ways that drove sustained improvements in the productivity of labor in agriculture (Mazumdar 1998, 393; cf. Gardella 1994, 171–172). Indeed, everything suggests that peasants in the cores were unable to raise output sufficiently in response to rising grain prices so that deficits continued to mount (Jiang 1992). The fact that prices correlated between regions simply demonstrates that merchants were able to seek out arbitrage profits.

Chapter 7 showed how Manchurian peasants "responded" to rising relative grain prices in the eighteenth and nineteenth centuries not by improving labor productivity through the reorganization of farming units or the better application of tools but by intensifying labor inputs and extending arable land. Subsequently, productivity of labor and perhaps output of grain per person in the population declined. There is no indication that peasants in the northeast responded to Manchuria's integration with far-off markets by reorganizing production or applying labor-saving tools that would raise the proportion of the product they could market and thereby raise their incomes. There is also no such indication for Jiangnan or Lingnan. Yet this is precisely how English farmers reacted first to falling prices from 1660 to 1750 and to rising grain prices thereafter (Thirsk 1984, 183–216; Allen 2000, 20, table 8). Despite rising population after 1750—when in conjunction with the Industrial Revolution England's population commenced an unprecedented period of rapid growth after a long period of very slow growth—English farmers became ever more efficient, producing ever more grain with ever less labor, and did so well before modern chemical inputs or machines became available. Grain imports were not significant until the 1820s, by which time the Industrial Revolution was well on its way and England could finance its grain imports by means of its increasingly competitive industrial exports (Thirsk 1978, 1984; passim; Overton 1996, 88–128; Brenner and Isett 2002, 644, n 41).

In conclusion, Manchurian peasants were integrated into the market under conditions that facilitated merchant extraction of the agricultural surplus but did not advance their capacity to improve labor productivity. First, the cost of capital remained high and while the method of preemptory purchase gave peasants needed startup capital at the beginning of the season, the cost was too great to allow anything but simple economic reproduction. Second, merchants organized into guilds and associations at the higher levels of the trading system and were able to use their knowledge of markets and prices to accrue to themselves the greater part of the earnings from trade, leaving peasants with a tiny fraction. Third, merchants were unwilling to invest the large sums of capital needed to improve agricultural production because they had no means to ensure a return on their capital. Because peasants held full possession in land as owners and secure tenants they could not be disciplined into producing optimally for the market—that is, they could not be required to use the machines and tools in an optimal fashion. Merchants were thus inclined to take advantage of peasants' minimal standards of living to lend money at high interest rates rather than make investments in improving agriculture. Finally, peasants benefited the least from trade given natural and man-made monopsonies. Thus, despite the integration of regional markets across long distances, peasants found themselves unable to respond to the rising market for their goods by saving, reinvesting, and reorganizing production in ways that raised the productivity of their labor.

Conclusion

Critiques and Alternative

THIS STUDY BEGAN by examining the Qing dynasty's restructuring of the Manchurian countryside in service of its imperial needs. It emphasized that the Qing state formed an agricultural regime that on the one hand facilitated the vertical expropriation of surplus from land-bound peasants by the Conquest Elite. In the first decades of Qing rule, the state appropriated farmland in southern Manchuria, combined these lands into large manors, and bound the land's former cultivators to the new manors as serfs. The manors provided important rent income to the Qing aristocracy and the imperial family, and helped cover some of the cost of regional administration. On the other hand, the new regime helped defray some of the cost of supporting the growing banner population and provisioned regional garrison towns by putting demobilized troops to farm work. Large areas of land were thus set aside to create agricultural colonies for the settlement of demustered and rusticated bannermen. A small number of nominally free commoner peasants were allowed to remain in the northeast, but further migration from China Proper was initially restricted and then banned outright in order to prevent the sinicization of the region. Furthermore, to preserve the new agrarian regime the state segregated commoners, bannermen, and serfs and prohibited the formation of horizontal social and economic relationships (intermarriage, the exchange of land, and the exchange of labor) between them.

This study went on to show that the imperial court and the regional bureaucracy were ultimately unable to maintain this agrarian regime, leaving a peasant-dominated economy with low overall levels of state/elite extraction. There were several reasons for this. For one thing, the Qing state did not have the institutional presence on the ground that was necessary to police rural communities and enforce prohibitions intended to preserve the land system. For another, the aristocracy and emperor delegated oversight of their estates to hereditary bailiffs over whom they had little social control, despite the existence of what was—in principle—a significant degree of juridical authority. Finally, the serfs and rusticated bannermen themselves actively welcomed settlers from China Proper and partook in the subterranean exchange of land and labor. Under propitious conditions, rural communities succeeded in desegregating themselves. Through subterfuge and deceit they changed the social and economic character of their communities while successfully keeping the state at arm's length. This was possible because peasants turned to long-established customary practices to regulate and mediate their own affairs, practices they maintained and defended through homegrown village institutions. The result of these achievements was that peasants in Manchuria replicated essential elements of the north China pattern of property relations.

In the course of the eighteenth century, Manchurian villages came to be dominated by smallholding peasants who held customary possession of the land. Landlordism in Manchuria took a very different form than in Jiangnan and Lingnan, where gentry landlords who lived in the urban areas and often held bureaucratic office in some other part of the empire were commonplace. In Manchuria tenants rented land *primarily*, though not exclusively, from a class of petty rentier landholders who, for the most part, remained in the countryside. All in all, this was a pattern not too dissimilar in its outline to north China, where peasants for the most part also held direct and nonmarket access to the land they worked.

Finally, this study examined the long-term consequences for the economy of this set of social property relations, which took shape in the foregoing political contestation between peasant and the state. By virtue of their strong claims to the land, peasants were able and inclined on the one hand to avoid risks and eschew market specialization, and on the other hand to pursue social goals (particularly in family formation) that, while perfectly rational, were nonetheless incommensurate with the requirements of sustained economic development. Not dependent upon the market and thus shielded from the competitive constraint that market dependency would have implied, peasants did not have to innovate or match the productive abilities of others in order to maintain household integrity. As a result, peasants were not obliged to adopt or make improvements in agriculture to raise their labor productivity.

By virtue of their larger farms, early settlers were under no pressure to be productive in terms of yields or labor output. They found that they could support themselves and their families by labor-extensive and low-yielding farming methods. They did this *not* because they had insufficient labor or draft animals (in fact they may have had more of the latter). We know that in the twentieth century peasants with holdings of thirty *mu* achieved far higher yields, yet their households were no larger than those of the eighteenth century. Early settlers worked the land extensively because on the one hand these methods were less strenuous and therefore preferable and on the other they wished to lay claim to as much land as possible with the understanding that they would pass land on to their sons. Thus blessed with large holdings in the eighteenth century, early settlers abandoned the labor-intensive, high-yielding farm methods of north China for labor-extensive, low-yielding systems.

But these methods could not be sustained permanently given that household formation practices privileged the division of property among sons and therefore led predictably to a decline in the average holding over time. Consequently, peasants found that in order to maintain the same standard of living as before they had to raise output. But because their patrimony was shrinking over time, they could only do so in ways that made for greater and greater labor inputs for fewer and fewer returns to their work. Rising population density, the subdivision of farms, and the regular division of liquid assets and tools obliged peasants to raise the intensity of their work to sustain the same standard of living as before.

Having mapped out the long-term pattern of social and economic change in Manchuria, it is now time to turn to the more speculative task of examining how the approach taken here challenges the dominant interpretations of economic change in the Chinese historiography. The field of Chinese economic history is dominated by two schools of thought. One branch of scholarship works in the neo-classical or Smithian tradition to argue that economic development accompanies the expansion and deepening of the trade-based division of labor. The other branch operates within the neo-Malthusian (or Ricardian-Malthusian) tradition to argue that patterns of change in the rural economy reflect shifts in the relative prices of land and labor that accompany periods of population expansion and contraction. While both paradigms offer powerful analytical tools for understanding certain patterns of economic change over long periods of time, I would argue that neither school of thought provides a full account of why these patterns should occur in the first place.

Smithian and Malthusian Growth

The continued importance of Adam Smith, and the Smithian or neo-classical economic model of development he inspired, to the study of economic dynamics is well founded. It could be said that Smith was the first to uncover the mechanisms responsible for sustained economic growth and to suggest why economic actors find it in their rational self-interest to behave in ways that correspond to the requirements of sustained economic growth (Brenner 1986,

1997). For Smithians, and the neo-classical model Smith inspired, economic growth (rising output per unit of labor input) is occasioned by a generalized pattern of economic behavior that results in ongoing and constant cost cutting throughout the economy. This approach maintains that the economy grows because, à la Smith, economic actors find it in their best interest to specialize in what they do best: to improve the production process (by reorganizing, breaking up, and simplifying tasks) and to search out and adopt the latest labor-saving technology (Smith 1976, 11–14, 96, 292, 297–298).[1]

The Smithian model explicitly maintains that these mechanisms are normalized throughout society by "choice," in the first instance. But the model also implicitly maintains that they are sustained by "necessity," in the second instance. First, individuals *choose* to specialize in order to capture the gains from trade occasioned by the productive capacities of others (Smith 1976, 15).[2] Thus, Smith and the Smithians understand that specialization results from the natural tendency of humans to "truck, barter, and exchange." Second, once individuals choose to specialize they are required to accumulate and innovate in a systematic and ongoing fashion in order to continue specializing, or face the sanction of failure. That is to say, because they are economic specializers individuals can be expected to behave in ways that underwrite sustained economic development of the whole.[3] Thus, for Adam Smith economic growth did not commence with the introduction of this or that innovation (whether the steam engine or double-entry bookkeeping), shifts to new sources of energy, the extraction of surplus from colonies or peripheral regions, or the appearance of new organizational forms such as the factory, bank, or merchant corporation (Brenner 1997, 9–12). What Smith uncovered was that economic development occurs when through specialization his mechanisms are normalized so that people are required to innovate in ways that systematically cut costs and ipso facto raise the productivity of labor. But, what Smith and the Smithians do not explain was how this pattern of behavior becomes normalized in the first place.

The problem with Smith and the paradigm he has inspired is the unwarranted assumption that what is required of individuals for sustained economic growth *to begin* is precisely what they will elect to do *in the first place* because it is in their interest to do so. Correspondingly, the model assumes that so long as the market exchange of goods grows because of rising demand, specialization, accumulation, and innovation *naturally* follow. The claim that individual economic behavior can be expected to correspond in this fashion precisely with the requirements of economic growth assumes, however, an economy of specializers already subject to the competition. Yet, the social conditions that are needed to subject economic producers to competition cannot be *historically* assumed. There are after all a host of reasons why producers might not elect to specialize and subject themselves and their household's integrity to competition.

Put another way, it is only when Smith's assumptions about the social character of production hold true that the mechanisms that drive economic growth can be expected to operate. Conversely, Smith and the Smithian account fail to account for why some economies fail to grow in real terms *despite* the appearance of the division of labor. It was the inability of the Smithian model to explain prolonged historical periods of economic stagnation (and even decline) that moved an entire generation of scholars beginning in the 1950s to look to Smith's first major critic, Thomas Malthus.

Responding to what he considered was Smith's ill-placed faith in the division of labor, Malthus proposed his "iron law," that holds that whereas population always grows geometrically, labor productivity grows arithmetically. The predictable outcome of these divergent tendencies is that population tends to outstrip resources until the point when this imbalance is corrected by a fall in population. Rising mortality rates brought on by starvation, disease, and war reduce population until the equilibrium between resources and people is again restored. The outcomes of Malthus's "iron law" are long temporal waves alternating between economic expansion and contraction as population grows, reaches the economy's demographic carrying capacity, and is corrected. These waves are what neo-Malthusians call Phases A and B respectively.

One only need look as far as Thomas Malthus's critique of Smith to comprehend first the full implications of Smith's mechanisms for growth and second Smith's failure to account for the social conditions that might elicit those mechanisms. For Malthus, Smith's mistake was to assume that his mechanisms would begin to operate with the appearance of the division of labor, thereby issuing in a pattern of sustained economic growth characterized by ever-higher levels of output that rise at rates faster than increases in the total population. Thus, whereas Smith assumed the division of labor would initiate economic growth Malthus countered that, *despite* the division of labor, population grows faster than improvements in output. Indeed, Malthus found no reason whatsoever to assume that the division of labor would initiate *any* improvements in labor productivity: he claimed *pace* Smith that there was a tendency for wealth to diminish, for the economy to stagnate, and for population to outstrip the capacity of the land to feed it until its growth was checked and reversed. As Malthus saw it, the problem with Smith's model is that it assumes growth is for all intents and purposes natural to the way people operate in the market (Malthus 1985, 183–191; also see McNally 1993, 76–77, 84). Malthus argued against Smith that the long-term economic trend is toward declining output per capita and falling standards of living (Malthus 1985, 71).

If economic stagnation was not immanent in the mechanisms uncovered by Smith, this cannot be said of Malthus's "iron law," in which the very mechanisms that propelled economic expansion were precisely those that led inexorably to stagnation and collapse. To be sure, Malthus acknowledged that there were means by which societies through the actions of individuals might delay the onset of demographic contraction by controlling family size and by raising the population carrying capacity of the land. As population grows through so-called Phase A, and households are obliged to survive on smaller and smaller plots, Malthus suggested that people will take steps to limit the number of children born, as well as those who survive much beyond the time of birth. They might reduce family size by having fewer children and by infanticide (what Malthus called "exposure") (1985, 76, 89).

Malthus also recognized that cultivators could improve tillage to support more people on the same amount of land. But because the impetus to "improve" agriculture commences, for Malthus, at the point in time when labor is already abundant and cheap (when the relative cost of labor to land is low), cultivators will naturally favor cheaper labor-intensive farming methods that raise the productivity of land (grain yields) even as these same methods drive down labor productivity (1985, 77).[4] Ultimately, Malthus claimed, neither controlling family size nor increasing the amount of labor in farming were sufficient to prevent the onset of economic stagnation, a subsistence crisis, and the population reversal that was bound to follow. What Malthus understood, therefore, was that Smith's mechanisms for growth were *not* natural to the market economy.

Both the Smithian and Malthusian paradigms are at their core market-driven models; but each assumes different generalized patterns of social and economic behavior, giving rise to different outcomes. Smith assumed that because people are naturally inclined to specialize in what they do best they would systematically reallocate their labor in ways that gave them higher returns and that would pari passu raise labor productivity. Malthus assumed that because the rate of population growth naturally supersedes that of gains in productivity there is an inexorable tendency toward the systematic intensification of labor for diminishing returns. But if the Smithian paradigm can neither account for the many observable historical cases of economic stasis, nor the conditions under which its mechanisms come to prevail, so the Malthusian paradigm can neither account for the equally observable historical cases when the demographic obstacle to growth is transcended, nor the conditions under which these obstacles can be expected to prevail. For all their genius, both men described patterns of growth that they failed to explain. They failed to provide *historical* accounts of the origin of the patterns they were trying to explain because each began with certain *ahistorical* or transhistorical assumptions concerning human behavior. These assumptions are reproduced in the works of contemporary neo-Smithian and neo-Malthusian histories.

The Smithian Paradigm in Chinese History

Given eighteenth-century China's abundant trade in grain and peasant-manufactured goods, the complex of long-distance trade routes through which these items flowed, and the dense networks of urban centers that characterized some of China's microregions, it is easy to see why the Smithian paradigm has had such a strong appeal among economic historians of China. The Smithian account turns, as noted, on the appearance and intensification of the division of labor that accompanies the expansion of trade, and historians have long observed these developments at work in China's most densely populated and urbanized core regions. It is hardly surprising, therefore, that works of a Smithian bent would attribute economic dynamism and growth to those commercial developments.

Arguing that China's late imperial economy showed positive signs of economic growth, R. Bin Wong (1997), Li Bozhong (1998), Kenneth Pomeranz (2000), among others, have thus maintained that Chinese producers, like their European counterparts, took advantage of the development of market opportunities to reallocate their labor in a Smithian fashion. In other words, they reallocated their labor from one specialization to another specialization that yielded a higher rate of return, *ipso facto* raising the productivity of their labor (Wong 1997, 13; Pomeranz 2000, 98–99, 226, 212–213, 215; Li Bozhong 1998, 99–115).[5] Thus, these scholars also posit that—far from pressing down on the economy—demographic growth in China, accompanied by the rise and growth of market exchange, enabled economic growth. It did so because the growing population made for ever-larger and increasingly dense markets that were spread over ever more diverse agro-ecologies and that provided opportunities for producers to specialize in the production of those things they did best. By taking advantage of the gains to be had by trade in this fashion, peasants in the eighteenth century witnessed growth in their "wages" (returns to days worked) and a rise in total household incomes that issued in improving standards of living and rising demand for more goods. In short, it is claimed that China experienced a pattern of Smithian growth.

However, these same scholars also acknowledge that China in the late imperial era experienced no qualitative breakthrough to sustained economic growth driven by constant rises in labor productivity and characterized by a rising proportion of people living in urban areas and working outside of agriculture (i.e., in manufacturing). Thus, they must explain why a period of expansive market-driven growth in the eighteenth century came to an end in the nineteenth century. To do so, they argue that expansion was ultimately brought to a close by Malthusian resource constraints and changing state priorities. Thus, though the recent reworking of the Smithian paradigm is clearly positioned as both a departure from and a critique of an earlier generation of scholars who work in the neo-Malthusian paradigm, it concurs with those scholars that economic expansion in China ran up against constraints to self-sustaining growth (Wong 1997, 17, 32; Pomeranz 2000, 12, 22, 206–207, 241).

Where the revisionist argument differs, however, is in its insistence that, despite this economic dead end or stasis, peasants continued to enjoy standards of living well above mere subsistence levels. This was due to the high productivity of their labor in agriculture and their ability to extend the number of hours they worked in sideline manufacturing (particularly, though not exclusively, cotton spinning and weaving). The end of imperial China's Smithian growth was *not* therefore due to declining peasant household income per se because, at least in the most commercialized regions of the empire, it is claimed this did not fall (or did not fall any more than incomes in Europe in the same period). Rather, the late imperial economy was unable to make a breakthrough to sustained growth because of unique "resource constraints" that prevented what would have otherwise been an unimpeded shift to industrial production in the European/English fashion.

It is important to note that what is being argued is that had China the same access to inorganic coal resources and agricultural imports as Europe/England, its economy would have *naturally* followed the European/English pattern. Stated differently, it is held that the European/English pattern of economic development is what occurs when such resource constraints do not intervene (Pomeranz 2000, 207). Despite the seemingly conjunctural claims of "fortune" and luck, the underlying paradigm to which Pomeranz is appealing is a version (albeit, highly original) of the resource constraint model of neo-classical economics: that is, in the presence of market exchange, economic growth is natural and continues apace until it comes up against a resource constraint—the absence of some input. Until the point in time when another source or a substitute is found, the economy rests at a stationary state. Thus, the absence of a qualitative breakthrough in China is explained as the result of a lack of accessible coal or the failure to make use of inorganic fuels and technologies (Pomeranz 2000, 207; cf. Wong 1997, 52) or a lack of colonial possessions from which to extract, directly and indirectly, the resources necessary to move the economy to higher levels of productivity (Pomeranz 2000, 19–20, 23, 264; cf. Wong 1997, 130–131).

Yet, for all their claims to the contrary, R. Bin Wong and Kenneth Pomeranz, among others, note that labor intensification for declining returns was not simply a regular feature of China's economy in the nineteenth century but had been throughout the late imperial period, even in its most advanced regions. Thus, while Wong (1997) begins, rightly enough, by defining Smithian growth as "productivity gains attending the division of labor and specialization," and suggests moreover that these mechanisms operated in late imperial China as much as in early modern Europe, he nevertheless accepts that trade may not have elicited productivity gains in China (16–19, 228). Thus, Wong is not convinced that there was sustained rising per capita income attending labor intensification and suggests that: "Growth [in China] may have been extensive [the substitution of labor for capital, i.e., through labor intensification] much of the time, leading to an increase in total production, rather than intensive [the substitution of capital for labor], with an increase in per capita productivity" (Wong 1997, 19). By this Wong can only mean that productivity of labor did not grow over the long run and nor did real wages, which presumably fell as is typical of labor intensive growth (cf. Wong 1997, 29, 30, 32, 50).[6]

Wong is, I believe, correct to say that growth in late imperial China was driven by labor intensification, or the substitution of labor for capital. Attempts to show otherwise have, I would argue, failed. The most sustained attempt to demonstrate real growth to date is offered by Li Bozhong (1998). Yet, when his calculations are corrected for serious omissions,[7] the evidence marshaled by Li to make the case for rising labor productivity in agriculture in Jiangnan shows in fact that labor productivity stagnated at best and most probably fell (Brenner and Isett, 2003, 235–236).[8] Wong and Pomeranz also believe this was true for Chinese peasant manufacturing, which they compare in logic and outcomes to the "involutionary" processes associated with proto-industrial production in Europe, and which Pomeranz rightly terms an economic cul-de-sac (Wong 1997, 41–42; Pomeranz 2000, 206–207, 241). In accord with much of Wong's analysis, Pomeranz holds that China *as a whole* may have experienced a long, sustained decline in *real* wages and labor productivity. Citing Chao Kang's admittedly thin wage data, which suggest a slow but steady fall in real wages after the twelfth century, Pomeranz also concludes that "the amount of labor needed to buy a given quantity of rice increased steadily between about 1100 (when cultivated land land-to-population ratios were at their most favorable) and at least 1800" (Pomeranz 2000, 95; cf. Chao 1986, 216–217). As for agriculture in the Jiangnan region, which is the focus of Pomeranz's comparison to Europe's most advanced economic cores, in *The Great Divergence* he marshals no evidence to argue for rising labor productivity in agriculture.[9] Moreover, Pomeranz's data also point to the involutionary nature of sideline manufacturing in cotton and silk, where daily earnings were lower than for agriculture and falling relatively over time. In cotton spinning and weaving, daily earnings were already half that in agriculture in 1750 and fell further in relative terms over the next century. The implication of this for wages in manufacturing is quite clear. As more and more peasant labor shifted into manufacturing between 1750 and the 1840s (and it does seem that peasants in Jiangnan at least were increasing the hours they worked spinning yarn and weaving cloth), real wages from cloth manufacturing were steadily falling instead of rising (Pomeranz 2000, 319; 2002, 548; cf. Brenner and Isett 2002, 631–632, 640).

It should be evident, therefore, that—the Smithians' claims to the contrary—their own work points to an absence of Smithian growth that, to reemphasize, is conventionally understood as the reallocation of labor and capital from one specialization to another that would yield the highest rate of return and labor productivity. In fact, the pattern of growth they describe could not be more neo-Malthusian: for example, the long-term tendency for demographic expansion to come up against the limited capacity of the agricultural economy to improve productive forces, making for declining productivity of labor in grain production, and the tendency for the demand for basic necessities and land to come up against supplies (Wong and Lavely 1998). Commercial rents rose, food prices increased, and the terms of trade increasingly favored agricultural as opposed to manufactured goods. Wong and Pomeranz acknowledge as much and therefore make much of the evidence that European economic development in the early modern period was as "involutionary" (i.e., as labor intensifying for lower daily returns) as China's in order to make their claims of equivalence between Europe and China stick (Wong 1997, 30, 41–42; Pomeranz 2000, 91–106).[10]

Breaking Free of Malthusian Constraints in the Early Modern World: England, Smithian Growth, and Agrarian Capitalism

It is a fact long observed among historians of Europe that large swaths of that region experienced no real growth in the early modern period, despite the intensification of market and dense urban networks (particularly in northwest Europe) and the rising total volume and variety of goods in trade. It was because of this that several generations of scholars, beginning in the 1950s, faced with the "paradox" of dense markets without economic growth, in response turned away from the Smithian model that had up to that point dominated the historiography and turned instead to the demographic or neo-Malthusian interpretation. By the 1960s, that model had achieved a sort of orthodoxy in the field.[11]

However, it has also been long observed that within Europe the economies of England (and the northern Netherlands [the Low Countries]) departed company with those of the continent in the seventeenth century and that thereafter the gap between English development in particular and that of the rest of the continent grew steadily until the late nineteenth and early twentieth centuries (Brenner 1985b [1982]; de Vries 1976, 63, 75).[12] To be sure, many explanations have been put forward for England's exceptionalism. But, what is clear is that *pace* Wong and Pomeranz, England's economy in the early modern era (1600 to 1800) never approached stagnation, let alone crisis, nor did it come even remotely close to approaching a Malthusian proto-industrial cul-de-sac à la China (Pomeranz 2000, 126, 206–207, 216, 223–224, 241; Wong 1997, 29).[13]

Yet, drawing upon the work of England historian E. A. Wrigley (1988), it is claimed that growth in agricultural productiveness was constrained *everywhere* in the early modern or preindustrial world by the resource limits imposed by what Wrigley calls the "organic economy." In this view, it is claimed that because the land provided not only all of the food for the population, but also all of the basic raw materials (by way of plants and animals), growth runs up against the limits of the land's productivity. Growth hits a ceiling because the "organic economy" cannot furnish agriculture with the sorts of tools and other inputs, especially modern fertilizers, that are needed after a certain point to sustain increases in both the productivity of land and of farm labor (Wong 1997, 50, 279–280). But, Wrigley never argues, as both Wong and Pomeranz suggest he does, that England was careening toward either ecological or demographic crisis, or that it was coming up against resource constraints and therefore approaching a "stationary state" before 1750 and the advent of the Industrial Revolution.[14] Indeed, what Wrigley does argue is that well prior to the transition to an "inorganic economy," characterized by the greater reliance upon "inorganic" inputs such as coal and steam, England had passed through a prolonged period of what Wrigley calls the "advanced organic economy" (Wrigley 1988, 34–57, especially 54–56; cf. Brenner and Isett 2002, 645–646).

Wrigley (1988) makes crystal clear that "Smithian Growth" was already instantiated in "the nature and extent of the changes taking place [in England] in the two centuries preceding the conventional date of the industrial revolution; the kind of growth that was in the mind of Adam Smith when he wrote the *Wealth of Nations*" (34). Wrigley describes this growth path thus:

> The single most remarkable feature of the economic history of England between the later sixteenth and the early nineteenth centuries was the rise in output per head in agriculture. Population more than doubled: the number of men engaged in farm work rose only slightly, and, given that the country remained broadly self-sufficient in food, it follows that out per head must have roughly doubled to levels well above those found elsewhere in Europe. (35)

It is Wrigley's argument that this growth path—like every growth path in Smith's view—was in the last analysis circumscribed by the limited supply of natural resources and would ultimately have returned England to the "stationary state, "but that, as it happened, the advent of coal-steam technology opened up vast new vistas of development that allowed England and the world to defy the resource constraint for centuries." Nevertheless, Wrigley is at pains to emphasize that "the average man engaged in agricultural in 1800 was producing far more than his predecessor in 1600 rather than substantially less as might have been expected based on the principle of declining marginal returns, "and that "increased output per head was of great strategic importance in relation to the course of real incomes and, more generally, to structural change in the economy" (35).

Wrigley's findings are indeed supported by four decades of historical research that shows England experienced sustained growth in labor productivity across the early modern period, and that this growth formed the basis of even more vigorous expansion in the eighteenth and nineteenth centuries once the Industrial Revolution commenced. Furthermore, this research has demonstrated the uniqueness of England's developmental trajectory within Europe.[15] From 1500 to 1750, before the onset of the classic period of the Industrial Revolution, England's economy experienced real growth, leaving behind all of continental Europe, except the northern Netherlands. In the hundred years after 1750, the productivity gap between England and continental Europe grew greater still, leaving behind even the Low Countries.[16] It was in large part these advances that made possible much more than the Industrial Revolution. It made for rising urbanization, rising real wages, and significant coal consumption well before its onset. It was an expression of the vitality of England's eighteenth century economy that Britain's coal industry grew up alongside farming and industry in the sixteenth and seventeenth centuries, rather than rescuing Britain from an involutionary path in the nineteenth century, as Wong and Pomeranz argue. By the end of the seventeenth century coal was more widely used in England than anywhere else in Europe (Hatcher 1993, 54–55, 409–458, 547–556).

It cannot be stressed enough that the entirety of these developments occurred in what was still substantially an "organic economy." Studies in English agrarian history show that improvements were achieved through the spread and adoption of inexpensive or already known best farming methods—methods that were in many instances known in the fifteenth century or were borrowed from continental Europe, but were applied during this period in new ways that initiated and then sustained ongoing improvements in the productivity of labor. England's first "Agricultural Revolution" (1600–1850) was based among other things on the adoption of new crops such as turnips, trefoil, lucerne, clover, and sanfoin; the adaptation of new field systems and crop rotations such as the Norfolk four-course and convertible husbandry, both of which greatly improved soil fertility and increased income from beef and dairy; the ever greater use of the horse to keep labor inputs under control, even as more careful tillage systems were adopted; and the rising efficiencies that came with growing farm size, which by 1800 averaged 150 acres.[17] These and other innovations were the backbone of pre-1850 developments in English agriculture; for the most part the costs were low and the methods were entirely "organic" (Thirsk 1984, 188–189, 193; Allen 1992; Campbell and Overton 1993, 41; Overton 1996, 105–121, 193–195; Kerridge 1967, 181–221, 267–310; Jones 1967, 6–21; Brenner 1985b [1982]). Indeed, it was not until the second half of the nineteenth century, a century into the classical period of the Industrial Revolution, that steam power could be used efficiently in farming[18] and that modern "inorganic" phosphate fertilizers were available to farmers (Overton 1996, 127, 193).[19]

Despite the fact that improvement was entirely "organic," and despite the fact that England's population grew at an astonishing rate after 1750, the proportion of England's population that remained in farming steadily fell. This was possible because of the continued rise in labor productivity in farming. Here, recent work by Nicholas Crafts, Robert Allen, E. A. Wrigley, Mark Overton, and Gregory Clark (1993, 1999, 2004) has strengthened, modified, and fleshed out the findings of an earlier generation of scholars. Nicholas Crafts (1985) concludes of trends in English agriculture up to 1850 that "the economy [of England] generally had the ability to cope domestically with increased demand for food and release labour from agriculture without experiencing food-price rises, while achieving respectable, but not high, rate of growth of per capita income" (121). What made this possible, Robert Allen shows, was a twenty-four percent increase in the productivity of English labor in agriculture between 1700 and 1800 (when his study ends) (2000, 20, table 8); and, as E. A. Wrigley (1985) shows, a further increase in agricultural labor productivity of forty percent between 1800 and 1850. Taking a long view, Mark Overton suggests labor productivity in English agriculture rose twenty-six percent between 1750 and 1800 and a further twenty-one percent between 1800 and 1850 (Overton 1996, 86, table 3.11; 1996a).[20]

Rising labor productivity in agriculture meant fewer and fewer laborers were needed to feed England's population, making possible the early commencement and dramatic growth of the proportion of people employed in other trades. Already by 1600, thirty percent of England's population worked outside agriculture (surpassing China's urbanization rates circa 1840 by four hundred percent). By 1700, the number had risen to forty-five percent, and by 1800 it had reached sixty-four percent (Wrigley 1985, table 7.4). This was achieved, moreover, with *minimal* food imports. In the early eighteenth century, England was still an exporter of grain, even though forty-five percent of the population was no longer farming. As late as 1837–1846, by which time England's total population was close to three times what it had been in 1700 and the proportion of the population outside agriculture had surpassed two-thirds (Wrigley and Schofield 1981, 208–209, table 7.8), a mere twelve percent of wheat consumed in England was imported.[21]

Despite the rapid rise in labor implied by these trends toward the increase of population and nonagricultural employment, as well as the enormous upward pressure on grain prices that resulted from the runs of bad harvest, the outbreaks of war, and Europe-wide population growth, especially between the 1780s and 1815, nominal wages still managed to keep up with the cost of living between 1780 and 1815. Real wages then increased by about thirty percent between 1815 and the mid-1850s (Feinstein 1998, 642–643). Because of the response of English agriculture to the growing demand for food, discretionary income grew along with real wages which in turn encouraged greater and greater investments in manufacturing, commerce, and transportation in particular (Crafts 1985, 122, table 6.3).[22] Predictably, the manufacturing sector of the economy grew as a percentage of gross domestic product while agriculture shrank correspondingly.[23]

This stands in contrast to China, including its more prosperous regions such as Jiangnan, as well as much of continental Europe. Not only were real wages apparently declining in China as a whole (Pomeranz 2000, 95), but the steady decline in terms of trade of cotton cloth and the resulting decline in real daily wages of cloth manufacturers would strongly suggest that, as a proportion of gross domestic product, manufacturing in the proto-industrial core of Jiangnan was either stagnant or falling.[24] In Jiangnan, peasants' exchange of cotton cloth for grain imported from the peripheries took place on increasingly *disadvantageous* terms, since it took increasingly more peasant labor in cotton manufacturing to purchase any given amount of grain—even as all prices began to fall in the nineteenth century. By 1850, cotton-weaving households had to weave sixty percent more cloth than in 1750 just to make the same incomes as before (Brenner and Isett 2001, 639–640). By contrast, England's turn to food imports after 1810 (which it received from continental Europe, not its colonies) was an indication of the strength of its position vis-à-vis other European economies, not its weakness; England was able to finance ever more grain imports by increasing its highly competitive industrial exports (Brenner and Isett 2002, 644; Crafts 1985, 126).

What the historical example of England shows is that *properly understood* Smithian mechanisms were capable of sustaining economic growth well before the onset of the Industrial Revolution; this of course is precisely what E. A. Wrigley (1988) himself argued in his work that serves as a conceptual framework for both Pomeranz and Wong. Wong (1997) seems to acknowledge as much when he points to differences between what can only be understood to be a pattern of Smithian growth that he recognizes occurred in parts of early modern Europe and an involutionary pattern that he ascribes to China; he writes that "European food supply conditions were transformed *in the eighteenth century by productivity growth* and in the nineteenth century especially after 1850, by market integration made possible by the development of railroads and shipping. China experienced *no remotely similar set of changes before the 1980s*" (228, emphasis added).

To argue, as Wong does (1997, 50, 58), that there was nothing inevitable about England's transition from a successful and growing agrarian economy to an industrial economy does not of course gainsay the widely held proposition that an industrial revolution would not have occurred without an advancing agricultural sector. Industrialization after all did not occur ex nihilo. Up to 1750 and the onset of the classical period of the Industrial Revolution, English manufacturing developed in a Smithian fashion alongside and in conjunction with ongoing improvements in productivity of labor in agriculture. From the fifteenth through the early seventeenth centuries, the most dynamic section of English industry—the production of undyed and undressed cloth—had grown as heavily export-oriented, in response to the demand for luxury textiles of the continental European elite. However, during the seventeenth and eighteenth centuries, as output per person in agriculture made for cheaper food, there emerged a wide range of consumer-goods industries to meet a growing domestic market for manufactures.[25] The expansion of manufacturing in England accompanied, and was furthered, by the increasingly intense specialization of arable farmers in grain and their sloughing off of manufacturing. On the flip side of the same coin, manufacturing in England was typically undertaken *not* by peasant producers to make ends meet, but by market-dependent commercial pastoral or dairy farmers as a by-employment, or by capitalist manufacturers taking advantage of relatively loose labor markets in nonarable agricultural regions. Unlike their peasant counterparts in Europe (and China)—and their own medieval predecessors—English manufacturers tended from the start to be separated from direct access to their means of subsistence and, as a consequence, dependent upon the market and subject to the competitive constraint (Brenner 1985a [1976], 53–54; 1985b [1982], 299, 301).

As a result, English manufacturing expanded and changed in response to the growth and shifting character of market demand and comparative costs, rather than in response to the need of peasant agriculturalists to make up for their grain deficits and secure subsistence by selling textiles on the market, no matter how low—and declining—the rate of return (Brenner and Isett 2002, 635). It would seem evident that the pattern of economic expansion experienced in the period from 1600 to 1800 was indeed Smithian in nature. It was characterized by ever more producer and regional specialization as well as by the ongoing deepening of the classical division of labor—first between industry and agriculture and then between town and country. This issued in constant improvements in labor productivity as economic actors maximized their gains from trade through specialization and searched out and adopted efficiency-raising technologies.[26] The long period of economic expansion that began in the seventeenth century meant that by 1750, England had not only diverged from Europe but also China and its advanced core in Jiangnan (Brenner and Isett 2002; Broadberry and Gupta 2005; Allen, Bassino, Ma et al. 2006).

The Smithian character of England's economic expansion in the century and a half *before* the onset of the Industrial Revolution stands in marked contrast to the character of economic evolution in its own medieval era and the coeval experience of much of continental Europe (Allen 2000, 2001; Maddison 2001). It is not without cause, therefore, that the neo-Malthusian paradigm, which at one time dominated the historiography of medieval and even early modern Europe, was understood in large part as a palliative to the notion that *commercialization* leads to Smithian economic expansion. That is, the demographic interpretation served as a direct critique of the Smithian explanation of the *onset* of sustained economic growth, with its emphasis on the appearance of trade and the division of labor. Historians such as M. M. Postan (1966) and Emmanuel LeRoy Ladurie (1976, 1987) noted that though peasants often benefited from proximity to urban markets, the effects of these were not sufficient to counteract declining standards of living that accompanied population expansion and the subdivision of property (e.g., LeRoy Ladurie 1987, 53–60, 101–108, 125–136). Writing of highly urbanized Flanders, in the vicinity of Ghent, LeRoy Ladurie notes interestingly that: "As a result . . . the diminution in the average area leased for rent corresponded . . . to a sort of optimization of the farmer's labour, on the basis of intensive cultivation in the Flemish, or even Chinese, manner" (59, also 163; cf. Thoen 2001, 111–112). The demographic interpretation posited by the neo-Malthusians, by explaining the cyclical pattern of economic expansion and contraction that followed upon Malthus's Phases A and B, challenged the unilinear notion that trade resulted in economic growth by pointing out how peasant-led commercialization invariably led to economic stagnation or collapse.

The Neo-Malthusian Approach in Chinese History

A very similar challenge to Smithian arguments has been posed implicitly and explicitly by neo-Malthusian or demographic interpretations of China's late imperial economy (Ho 1959; Elvin 1973; Chao 1986; Perkins 1969). There too, these interpreters note, dense urban networks (particularly in the Jiangnan region), urban concentrations of skilled artisans, sophisticated merchant corporations, long-distance trade, peasant-based manufacturing, and commercialized agriculture were insufficient to counteract the effects of population growth, with the result that labor productivity fell steadily in farming and manufacturing. Indeed, it could be said that the defining "paradox" of the field was for some time the notion that commercialization was not accompanied by Smithian economic growth.

Thus, if China's dense regional urban networks and abundant trade serve as points of departure for the neo-Smithian account, its large population serves the analogous function for the demographic interpretation. According to Dwight Perkins's (1969) figures, at the end of the fourteenth century China's population was already in the range of sixty-five to eighty million. There were at most an average of seven *mu* (just over one acre) for every person in the population. By 1750 the population had reached 200 to 250 million, and cultivated land per capita had fallen to less than six *mu*. By the third quarter of the nineteenth century, the population had reached 410 million, while per capita cultivated area had fallen to three *mu*, or less than half an acre per person (Perkins 1968, 216, table A.7; 240, table B.17). These are unequivocally dramatic developments. It is for good reason, therefore, that much of the scholarship of China's late imperial economy begins with population growth and sees it as more determinative than other factors in establishing China's developmental path.

The classic neo-Malthusian statement—the view that population growth led to economic stagnation as households responded to the falling relative cost of labor to land by working harder for lower returns—is the basis for Elvin's (1973) "high equilibrium trap" thesis. That thesis posits an economy of extraordinarily high total productivity along with a population so large that the average person is sustained only at the margins of subsistence; in addition, an equilibrium is constantly reasserted as absolute levels of output increase to meet the demands of the growing population (314). An important contribution of this literature has been to demonstrate, à la Boserup (1965), the remarkable technological creativity of peasants in adopting new means for raising the carrying capacity of the land, particularly in responding to the growing demand for food.

The neo-Malthusian or demographic interpretation has posited that, by virtue of the fact that population tended to grow as fast as or faster than output, the economy could only grow by way of labor intensification or the extension of the area under cultivation. As China's population rose and peasants had less and less land from which to secure their subsistence, they worked harder to raise total output, especially in grain. They collected, mixed, and spread more fertilizers. They added to the hours spent bringing water to their fields. They weeded more frequently, planted a second and even third crop, and expanded the cultivation of new crops such as potatoes and maize. But because the price of their labor was falling relative to land and rents, there was a structural disincentive to the adoption by peasants of labor-saving methods as they sought to raise yields. Predictably, their efforts resulted in ever smaller returns to labor in agriculture (Elvin 1973, 314; Chao 1986, 216–220).

Simultaneously, the neo-Malthusian interpretation argues that those peasants with access to markets sought to make up for declining total incomes by taking up household manufacturing. They did this initially by using seasonally underemployed household labor. As their plots continued to shrink, however, labor that had formerly been employed in farming, but was now redundant, was also shifted into domestic manufacturing. However, the inability of agricultural producers to keep the production of basic grain up with the demand led to a pattern of rising food and land prices and declining terms of trade of manufactured versus agricultural goods. The predictable result was that wages from domestic manufacturing, which were already lower than those in agriculture, continued to fall. In the end, the turn to proto-industrial outlets was an expression of the same involutionary logic that propelled labor intensification in agriculture (Chao 1977, 36).

Clearly, these responses to Malthusian pressures could only guarantee subsistence up to a point. Peasants might try to control fertility and kill off unsupportable children, but these practices would not stop population growth. The continuing rise of population that drove labor intensification in the cores would, with the approach of the limits of this pattern of economic expansion, also propel migration to unsettled or less densely settled lands on the internal and external frontiers of the empire (Chao 1977, 201–208; Ho 1959, 136–195; Perkins 1969, 23–26, 52). Historically, migrants who found they could take up grain cultivation, and who had more land than was necessary to support themselves, often took to labor-extensive farming methods on the frontiers. Even for these peasants, however, the gradual rise in population density and the recommencement of the fall in the relative cost of labor meant that the frontiers would eventually follow the pattern of growth already experienced in the longer-settled cores. In contrast, migrants who found themselves unable to grow grains, because they were on hillside land, for example, often took up commercial activities in lumber or commercial crops like tea. However, they too did so under conditions that often did not permit sustained accumulation and growth and in ways that often led to ecological damage and debilitating effects on neighboring communities (Osborne 1998).

It would seem evident that, by proceeding historically from a point in time when the Chinese population was already very large, and given that labor was already cheap relative to land, the demographic interpretation—for all its descriptive power—does not specify the conditions under which its defining Malthusian-Ricardian mechanisms could be expected to prevail (nor, under what conditions those mechanisms might be transcended). Thus, in his long-term view of more than 1,500 years of Chinese economic growth, Chao Kang (1986, 224–225) concludes that high population pressure on the land—more than any other factor—determined the entirety of China's Malthusian-Ricardian pattern of expansion. It did so first because it rendered labor ever more cheap so that substituting labor for capital (especially tools and draft animals) was the ever more rational course of bchavior, even as that course made for declining returns to labor in farming. The pressures of high population encouraged the self-exploitation of household labor because household labor (especially that of children, women, and the elderly) had next to zero opportunity costs; it always made sense for households to put this labor to work even if its earnings were less than the cost of securing its full subsistence (223).[27] Finally mounting population pressure elicited merchant investments in land (where it provided opportunities for rent squeezing and therefore anti-economic though profitable behavior) and discouraged investments in manufacturing, where, had merchants invested, the growing employment opportunities would have pulled labor out of the peasant household and reversed the Malthusian course (Chao 1977, 38–40).

While Chao sees these conditions as particularly Chinese (1977, 39; 1986, 221), the fact is that similar patterns of economic behavior were to be found on continental Europe in the early modern period, as the revisionists have been at pains to point out. There was nothing historically peculiar about the Chinese practice of combining farming and manufacturing (proto-industry) within the peasant household; it was a widely observable phenomenon throughout early modern Europe, one explored in the large literature on proto-industrialization, for instance (e.g., Kriedte et al., 1981, 23–33, 101–107). Furthermore, the fact that Chinese merchants preferred to invest their capital in trade (buying, transporting, and selling goods) and in land over manufacturing, was again not unique to China in the early modern world (Wood 2002, 74–80; Brenner 2001).

In effect, the neo-Malthusian argument faces two problems. By demurring on the question of family formation and population growth, the model can only explain patterns of development in a post hoc fashion; that is, once a certain population density is achieved, a certain outcome is implied because at that point the relative cost of labor and land has determined what the most rational course of behavior is. While, as should be clear, I believe the pattern of economic expansion in late imperial China was Malthusian or "involutionary," as it is commonly understood, I also believe that the neo-Malthusian paradigm with its emphasis on the relative cost of land and labor is itself unable to account adequately for the origin of this pattern and its long-term trends, or why some economies, notably early modern England, broke out.[28]

Chayanov and Philip Huang's Theory of Involution

While the neo-Malthusians capture the long-term dynamic of China's late imperial economy—successive phases of population increase without a labor-productivity response leading to rising land and food prices and falling labor and manufacturing prices—and also account for the mechanisms that drove the long-term pattern of economic change, they provide only a partial explanation of that dynamic. First, the neo-Malthusians do not explain the conditions that made possible women's early age of marriage and high fertility rates (i.e., they do not explain the demographic pattern). Second, they take the supersession of productivity gains by population increases as a given and do so paradoxically because they accept many of the core assumptions of the Smithian model regarding human economic behavior. With both rises in population and the failure of productivity gains as givens, then it is only rational that economic actors should begin to substitute labor for capital, maximizing their incomes at the cost of productivity gains by substituting those factors that are cheapest.

In two major works on the peasant economy, Philip Huang (1985, 1990) has sought to resolve the central problem of the neo-Malthusian account by arguing that the absence of labor productivity response was itself specific to the workings of the peasant household (Huang 1990, 5–6, 10). Some of Huang's critics have incorrectly labeled him a neo-Malthusian (e.g., Lee and Wang 1999, 19). To be sure, Huang *describes* China's long-term pattern of economic growth as "involutionary," which as a description is essentially equivalent to the account of diminishing marginal returns to labor offered by the neo-Malthusian models of Elvin, Perkins, and Chao. But, whereas those population-based accounts understand the long-term economic trends in late imperial China *strictly* in terms of the demographic dynamic and its effects on factor costs, Huang's account does not lend primacy to the demographic dynamic per se. Rather, Huang's account turns on what he perceives to have been the peasants' shunning of profit-maximizing behavior. Thus he argues, "*even without population pressure*, the peasant family might work for returns lower than the equivalent of market wages for the simple reason that the incentive for working on one's own farm is different from that of working for another as hired labor" (Huang 1990, 10, my emphasis). They did so, Huang argues, because family labor (and presumably its costs) once given was fixed so that households had every incentive to continue using (exploiting) this labor despite the tendency toward diminishing returns to work (1990, 11).

Thus, to those who would argue that Smithian dynamics naturally attend trade-based divisions of labor, Huang counters that peasants operate by a different economic logic or rationality. That logic, rooted in the fact that the peasant household is simultaneously a unit of production and consumption, is antithetical to the requirements of sustained economic development (i.e., systematically precludes the unfolding of Smith's key mechanisms). Deploying the early twentieth-century Russian economist A. V. Chayanov's understanding of peasant economic behavior, Huang argues that because household labor does not receive an immediately calculable wage its *market* cost cannot be taken into account in production decisions (Chayanov 1986, 86–87, 220–223, 226). This fact has a series of ramifications for the economy that Chayanov explored. First, peasants for whom the marginal utility of added output is great give up their leisure time to work harder in the fields (weeding more, adding a second crop, intercropping) and might even add sidelines during the off season. Second, because of the fixed cost of peasant household labor there is a built-in bias in the peasant household toward labor over capital intensification. Third, increases in household income therefore come at the expense of declining marginal productivity of labor.

Huang's argument turns therefore not on the population dynamic, as some of his critics would have it, but on the economic subjectivity of the peasant and the ways that is structured by the institutional arrangements of the household farm. However, as Huang also acknowledges, because peasants tend to marry early and therefore cannot avoid having high relative levels of fertility, the absence of a productivity response leads inexorably to a cheapening of labor relative to land that only intensifies the Chayanovian tendency to use household labor inefficiently. It is at this point that the peasant's Chayanovian logic reinforces and then merges with the neo-Malthusian. But, whereas the Chayanovian model assumes a self-sufficient household, and whereas neo-Malthusian examinations of China's economy have downplayed peasant production for the market, Huang rightly points out that population pressure may compel peasants to seek market outlets for their labor (Huang 1990, 86–88). Where family plots were too small to sustain the household directly or through agriculture, peasants increased the amount of production they devote to the market, especially in household manufacturing, *if that allowed them to meet their consumption needs*. It is just that for peasants at the margins the surpluses thus generated remained small, and diminished economies of scale did not allow for (sustained) improvements in labor productivity.

The problem with Huang's argument, I would suggest, is not to be found therefore in his claim that Smithian mechanisms do not attend the appearance of a trade-based division of labor. Nor is it that population pressure and its effects on relative price movements propel a pattern of labor substitution and labor intensification. Rather, it is located in his account of the origins of the mechanisms that drive the peasant economy. I believe Huang is mistaken when he claims that peasant behavior is distinct from capitalist profit-maximizing behavior *insofar as* it is the fixed cost of household labor (or the fact that the peasant household is both a unit of production and consumption) of the former that precludes labor-saving innovation of the latter.[29] When Chayanov talked of the payoff between work (drudgery) and leisure, at some level this must have been registered as a payoff between the cost of not working and the earnings from work. Costs are therefore recognized, even if they cannot be accurately measured or predicted. It is just that in the economies described by Huang and Chayanov there were no alternatives to farm work that might reap higher wages. There were no higher-wage factory jobs to which peasants might move, for instance. But, Huang's (1990, 86) explanation of the absence of factory jobs turns back on the cheapness of rural wages which are said to be so low that they prevent urban-based manufacturers from entering into production for the rural market.

But if the cheapness of family wages is given by the condition of household production to begin with, and if urban based manufacturing is precluded by cheap rural wages, the question pertains: how did the first economies which were similarly rooted in family units of production industrialize? To resolve the conundrum one must step outside the analytical confines of the peasant family. The problem with the Chayanovian approach is that it deduces from the particular conditions of the peasant household a general theory of the economy, even though it is clear that the general structure of the economy impinges to a great extent on household behavior. Rather than deduce the logic of the extant economy from its units of production one must begin with a general theory of the economy and situate the peasant household therein (Friedman 1980, 166–167).

Of all the interpretations of China's late imperial economy, Philip Huang's (1985, 1990) comes closest to explaining its long-term tendencies. In what is an explicitly speculative gesture, Huang points to the early appearance of a pattern of family formation that kept China on an involutionary pattern of growth. As early as the seventh century B.C., Huang notes, the Chinese monarchy ordered the early marriage of men and women, and in the first century B.C. it ordered the equal division of land among all sons. Those mandates, which subsequently became customary practices, established the basis of a socioeconomic system characterized by early marriage, relatively high fertility, and the subdivision of property (Huang 1990, 325–326). That pattern, coupled with the fixed cost of peasant household labor, overdetermined what Huang refers to as involutionary growth. However, both the origin of this family pattern and how it was reproducable, as well as the structural conditions that trapped labor on the peasant farm, need to be explained if Huang's account is to be complete.

Peasant Possession, Household Formation, and Involutionary Growth in Qing Manchuria

Hill Gates (1996) and Arthur Wolf (2005) give a fuller account of Huang's thinly sketched demographic hypothesis. They argue that the Chinese pattern of universal and early marriage was enforced by parents with the backing of state power. Parents desired children (especially males) for their labor and old-age care, among other reasons They used their authority over their children not only to select marriage partners but also to enforce early marriage as the surest means to maintaining the continuity of the patriline. The imperial state backed this family system because it both secured social order, as parents disciplined their children and dictated their lives, and underwrote continued tax growth via the multiplication of people and farming units. Furthermore, the state's legal recognition and enforcement of the claims of all sons to their father's land, in more or less equal portions, ensured the fragmentation of farms and so assisted in its goal of preventing the rise of landed magnates who could challenge state authority (Gates 1996, 29–41; Wolf 2005, 221–226). A unity of interests between parents and state ensured the reproduction of the family system over the long term.

While I agree that the state supported the system of family formation and property division in law and practice, the fact is that in Manchuria we see similar modes of behavior occurring in regular opposition to the state. State power it would seem was not necessary at all times and in all places to enforce the family system. It is my contention that what secured this family system was first and foremost a set of social property relations that simultaneously configured a particular mode of economic behavior which was itself the principal barrier to economic growth. That property system was in turn defended by peasant communities. A different set of social property relations would have configured a different economic logic that would have in turn entailed a different system of family formation.

The argument that I have made regarding late imperial China posits that (1) early and universal marriage and partible inheritance and (2) an aversion to specialization and accompanying profit maximizing behavior were made possible in the first instance by strong peasant claims to the land (Brenner 1997;

Brenner and Isett 2002, 2003). Those claims were in turn secured politically, in the ongoing struggle over surplus between the state, social elites (gentry/literati, landlords, merchants, and combinations thereof), and peasants, sometimes without state support.

Because its ownership of land was key to continued integrity of the peasant household, this struggle in effect was part and parcel of everyday peasant life. Uncovering that history is, to be sure, a process full of pitfalls. Nonetheless, legal records, in combination with routine administrative reports and twentieth-century ethnographic sources, all point to the fact that peasant communities in Manchuria managed on their own to institutionalize customary practices in land that underwrote their social and economic reproduction. Every effort by the state to restore its vision of the countryside, whether through the removal of settlers or recovery of Qing lands, failed as the state encountered peasant opposition and resistance. We can see a sort of peasant politics at work, even if it is difficult to discern its precise mechanisms and the nature of the beliefs that secured it. What is clear is that through individual acts of defiance and struggle over land rights peasants managed to establish customary claims to land, oftentimes in contradiction to the stated letter of the law.

By virtue of their strong rights to the land, peasants in Manchuria, as in the rest of China where similar conditions prevailed, were able to pursue a variety of goals that were ultimately incommensurate with the requirements of Smithian growth. Indeed, it was in pursuit of these goals that migrants extended to Manchuria a land system that replicated that of north China in its basic form. Having thus secured possession in land, it is clear that peasants in Manchuria were not obliged (nor did they elect) to specialize: they preferred to secure most of their consumption directly, diversifying whenever they could, and selling only their surpluses. In essence, they willingly sacrificed the gains to be had from *full* specialization in favor of security. In order to provide for their own social insurance in old age or sickness, peasants in Manchuria were obliged to have large families, insofar as their conditions permitted. Moreover, they preferred sons and grandsons over daughters and granddaughters, because sons were responsible for caring for parents, maintaining the patriline, and ensuring the continuation of the performance of ancestral rites.[30] The desire to have sons and grandsons in turn obliged patriarchs to break up the family holding through partible inheritance to enable sons to set up households of their own. Over time, this practice made for ever smaller holdings, and presumably the regular breakup of capital (both liquid and in the form of tools) acquired over the previous generation(s). The combination of large families (at least initially),[31] declining holdings, and the constant breakup of capital that subdivision implied made it very difficult for households to use labor efficiently. It is quite evident, therefore, that despite the initial abundance of land and scarcity of labor in Manchuria there was a gradual and steady decline in per capita acreage and in the size of holdings. Whatever efficiency advantages there were to keeping the patrimony together was regularly undercut by impulses in the other direction as the peasant pattern of subdivision common to China Proper was replicated in the northeast (cf. Wakefield 1998).

But, it is not farm size per se that explains the absence of development in Manchuria. The absence of development was in the first instance due to the peasants' ability to avoid specialization, made possible by their direct and strong hold over their land. I argue that, by virtue of peasants' choice to avoid specialization, to secure subsistence first, and to market only their surpluses, they were not obliged to improve their techniques in ways that raised the productivity of their labor.[32] In essence, because they were not sufficiently dependent upon the market for labor, land, tools, and their main source of food sustenance (grain), they were not subject to price/cost-cutting pressures that drive Smithian growth. Moreover, because of the tendency toward declining holdings and declining or stagnant capital stock, peasants found that in order to raise output and sustain the same standard of living, they were obliged to work harder for lower returns to their labor. Growth in Manchuria thus came in the first instance through labor intensification, affirming the "involutionary" narrative.

That said, the gradual process of labor intensification followed upon the initial extensification of labor. When peasants first settled in Manchuria, rather than choosing to maximize their incomes by adopting labor-saving tools and draft animals that would have allowed them to farm large areas and secure large surpluses, they chose instead to operate large farms and work very little for very low yields and reduced surpluses. This goes against all Smithian assumptions. Indeed, the Smithian interpretation would expect, given the large trade in Manchurian soybeans and grain, well established by the 1770s, that cultivators would have tried to adopt farming methods not too unlike those followed by seventeenth-century English yeoman. That is, they would have elected to operate large farms using the wage labor of landless migrants and applied labor-saving tools and methods as the surest means to improving their gains from trade. Such a system of agriculture did not, however, take hold, in large part because landless peasants themselves could acquire land of their own and so were unwilling to work for others. Rather than ceding their own holdings, for the reasons outlined above, it is clear that Manchuria's early settlers preferred to work their own large farms with as little effort as possible for yields that were at times one-fifth those achieved by their relatives in north China.

Only after more migration and the natural increase of the settled population did peasants begin to raise yields. But they did so in ways that required ever greater exertions of effort that produced ever smaller returns to labor. For example, the shift from fallow farming (in which a portion of the land was rested each year in order to restore soil fertility) to permanent farming (in which the land was only rested during the winter months) was not an indication of "improvement" in the Smithian sense of innovation in pursuit of higher levels of labor efficiency. Rather, it followed the typical Malthusian pattern that was exhibited in parts of Europe in the late medieval and early modern eras as farming there underwent very similar developments. It was only as peasant farms shrank in size that they began to make the shift to higher yielding methods. To be sure, those were improvements of a very important kind. They ensured that in Manchuria as in parts of Europe the carrying capacity of the land would improve and thus made possible the ever greater population and the maintenance of ever larger absolute volumes of trade and urban populations.

However, the gradual shift to permanent cultivation obliged Manchuria's peasants to work harder. First, they found that in order to crop land without resting it they had to apply fertilizer. They gathered everything available to them, from their own waste to rotting vegetable matter and animal waste. They stored it and mixed it before carting it to their fields where they applied it by hand. Next, they found that in order to maximize the amount of nutrients released by the fertilizers that went to the crop, they had to weed more intensively. They began with one weeding a year and eventually weeded three times a year. For the same reasons, in extreme cases they also took to weeding out those plants that showed early signs of illness, weakness, or deformity so as to lessen the waste of soil nutrients. Because they did all this with the same rudimentary tools, the predictable outcome was that labor inputs in Manchuria rose disproportionately faster than yields. Surpluses therefore rose in absolute levels, but not relative to total production. The urban population may have also grown in absolute numbers (we do not have reasonable numbers for the northeast), but it is clear that as a percentage of the entire population it most probably remained little changed; as a result, by 1900 perhaps eight percent of the population lived in towns of more than five thousand people, a smaller proportion than lived in towns of more than ten thousand in early nineteenth-century Europe.

Eventually, peasants found that no matter how hard they worked they could not secure their basic subsistence and had to find other avenues for survival. Typically, when peasants in late imperial China were confronted with these pressures, they took to household manufacturing to produce items they could sell to urban markets or to other peasants, either through merchants or directly. As is well documented, by the Qing the most important of these sidelines was the spinning and weaving of cheap cotton cloth. Here, however, Manchurian peasants were at a disadvantage. Cotton did not grow in Manchuria except in the southernmost reaches of Liaodong and Jinzhou prefectures and, for structural reasons explained earlier, very little raw cotton or cotton yarn was released to China's long-distance trade. Manchuria's peasants were, therefore, unable to turn to domestic cotton work to supplement their incomes.

It is unlikely that in the eighteenth century, and most probably for the first half of the nineteenth century as well, this caused Manchuria's peasants hardship. As this study noted, the fact that the terms of trade between manufactured and agricultural goods were increasingly in favor of the latter meant that peasants in Manchuria had to expend less and less of their time in farming to import their cotton cloth. But it did mean they had to forgo a sideline that would have added to their income. This meant that those whose holdings had shrunk close to what was minimally required to guarantee full subsistence did not have available to them an important avenue for sustaining incomes.

Peasants in Manchuria facing high population pressure had to migrate. This highlights that the second principal means by which the region's economy grew, aside from labor intensification in agriculture, was by way of extending total arable area. However, because the same property relations tended to obtain within Manchuria's own frontiers as in its longer-settled areas, the same pattern of holding subdivision and labor intensification was reintroduced with every new round of migration and settlement.

As the revisionists have pointed out, there was nothing particularly "Chinese" about this Malthusian-Ricardian or involutionary pattern of growth. They are certainly correct in pointing to similar patterns in much of early modern Europe. As noted, the "Malthusian" interpretation as represented in the historiography of Europe in works by Slicher van Bath (1964), LeRoy Ladurie (1976, 1987), and Postan (1966) had indeed become a sort of orthodoxy by the 1960s (Brenner 1985a [1976], 1985b [1982]). The demographic interpretation remained alive and well into the 1980s with the commencement of a new wave of research on "proto-industrialization." Whereas that work began as a way of locating a transition in the organization of production that lay temporally and schematically between agriculture and industry (Mendels 1981), much of the research that followed ended by reaffirming (as it elaborated upon) the basic Malthusian interpretation. It did so because the peasants' turn to domestic manufacturing came to be understood not as an expression of the Smithian division of labor but of the need to compensate for the steady decline in the productivity of labor in agriculture that was a common feature of the early modern economy. As the work on proto-industrialization showed, peasants were obliged by the shrinking of their agricultural income to take up domestic manufacturing even as this implied lower returns to their labor (Pollard 1981, 72; Kriedte et al., 1981, 100, 111; Van de Wee 1988, 347; Brenner 2001, 307–308).[33]

It should be evident that ascribing to those economies the label Smithian, as the revisionists do, is to overlook what I believe were Smith's key contributions. As Robert Brenner (1986) notes, Smith's genius was to locate the essence of modern economic growth in *the generalized adoption, across the economy, of certain specific forms of individual economic behavior and the adoption of a certain approach to economic life on the part of individuals as standard*. Modern economic growth thus takes place where, and because, the economy is constituted by individuals who, *as the norm*, systematically maximize their price-cost ratio by means of cost-cutting through ever deeper specialization, the systematic reinvestment of surpluses, and the obsessive adoption of the latest techniques. For Smith, then, the *differentia specifica* of modern economic growth or economic development is not this or that once-and-for-all improvement in the accessibility of factors of production, the scope of the division of labor, or the availability of productive forces.

To assume, however, that these mechanisms apply transhistorically to all market economies is to assume a unitary human type—*homo economicus*—who, if gains can be made from trade, will exploit these opportunities in ways that bring about constant economic growth. On the other hand, if, as the revisionists claim, institutions matter, why is it that they seem not to matter in this regard? That is to say, why is it that only a single economic logic is assumable, despite the multitude of institutional arrangements that weigh upon individuals as they navigate their use of the market? Simply stated, the revisionists believe that humans will always choose to exploit resources in the most efficient manner possible and, in so doing, that they will sooner or later establish institutional arrangements that facilitate this. I would suggest that "institutions" matter precisely because they may lead to individually rational sorts of behavior that are nonetheless systematically un-Smithian and therefore establish fundamental barriers to Smithian growth from the outset. Ironically, the upshot of this line of argument is that despite their tremendous attentiveness to "institutional" difference between China and the West, the Smithians have reaffirmed in the realm of theory much of the very Eurocentrism they seek to displace in the field of historicism.[34] In explaining the long-term economic dynamics of most of the world's people over the last five hundred years or so, they have adopted the Smithian model and in so doing they have collapsed the totality of this vast human experience into a univocal and trans-historical economic model.

REFERENCE MATTER

Population and Cultivated Area in Qing Manchuria

The necessary condition for the sinicization of Manchuria was, as scholars all recognize, Han migration and settlement. Nonetheless, gauging not only the temporal and spatial dimension of migration and settlement, but even measuring changes in absolute population numbers and area of cultivated land, are very difficult tasks.

For the Qing era, the historical scholarship has accepted without comment the officially registered numbers of people and tax-paying farmland, a habit which goes back to the seminal research of Japanese scholar Sudō Yoshiyuki (Sudō, 1944, 139, 148, 173–174, 198–201, 208).[1] The unquestioning acceptance of these numbers is surprising, especially given that historians such as Sudō and Zhao Zhongfu all note the Qing state's poor record of achievement in policing and keeping track of changes in landholding patterns and in uncovering illegal settlement and squatters (Sudō 1944, 197–209, 225–235; Zhao 1998, 200–208, 686–687). These failings, after all, were what made possible the devolution of Qing lands into the hands of commoners. Even Qing administrators recognized their own failure to register the population fully. The 1736 edition of the Shengjing gazetteer, a basic source of information on early eighteenth-century Manchuria, states that an estimated one-quarter to one-third of all land in Manchuria went unregistered in the Yongzheng era (cited in Sudō 1944, 200).

Peasants throughout the Qing empire sought to keep their land and themselves off the tax rolls and household registries in order to avoid payment of both the land and poll taxes. But, in Manchuria, where commoners were forbidden to settle and acquire Qing land, there were extraordinary reasons for not declaring property ownership and for keeping people off the official population registries. The thinly stretched rural agents who operated between the *yamen* and village and were charged with maintaining tax rolls and household registries found it very difficult to ferret out illegal settlers. Regional official Yehande explained the institutional problems in registering populations and farmed land when he wrote: the "*cuiling*, *xiangyue*, and *paitou* in the localities of Fengtian can not be everywhere at once" and despite the implementation of the *baojia* system "commoners from the outside have continued to settle here for many years. Among them, there are those who have been registered in the county records and rolls, and there are those who have not" (cited in Yamamoto 1941, 30, 32 n.1). Moreover, as has been documented here, because many of these agents were themselves implicated in facilitating illegal settlements and land sales, they had good reason to keep illegal settlers and illegally cultivated lands off the books.

Given that the state did not deploy enough local agents to police and register the commoner population, and given that this population had far greater incentive to remain off these registers than most, there is good reason to believe official figures significantly undercount both the actual population and the area of land under cultivation in the Qing.

Revising Population Data

To correct for underreporting of population, I assume that while official registries do not track the actual levels, some of these figures capture rates of change over time. These rates are then used to estimate Manchuria's nineteenth- and eighteenth-century population by working backward from secure twentieth-century population data which were collected by modern states. This is to be sure not an unproblematic method. However, absent sound Manchurian prefectural and county level gazetteer population data for the Qing, this method must suffice for now (see Table A.1).

Estimating the 1900 Population Baseline

I begin by devising, from 1910s to 1930s data, a plausible population figure for 1900. In so doing, I have discounted Thomas Gottschang's (1982) estimated population of 24 million for that year a figure. His numbers for the period 1891 to 1942 are all considerably greater than those suggested by modern censuses conducted in the same period. No less an authority on Manchuria than Zhao Zhongfu (1998, 688–689) cites seven different censuses for the years 1912, 1915, 1919, 1921, 1923, 1927, and 1930, each of which gives figures that are considerably lower than Gottschang's estimates for the same dates. Furthermore, the amount of cultivated area recorded by separate surveys for the period 1900–1930 could not have supported populations of the magnitude estimated by Gottschang. For these reasons I have rejected his figures and gone with the more conservative census numbers.

The first "modern" census of the northeast was conducted in 1908 by reforming governor general of the northeast Xu Shicheng. In 1907, the imperial court appointed Xu to take up the newly created civil governor-generalship of the "Three Eastern Provinces" and he set about fulfilling his mission to bring the region's administrative structures in line with the rest of the empire and to modernize its legal, policing, education, and commercial structures as part of broader late Qing reforms that were mirrored in other parts of the country (Enatsu 1991, 50–55). One of Xu's first commands was to order a thorough counting of the population and farmland. Xu was operating under orders of the Ministry of Interior (*Neizheng bu*) which in 1906 had called for all provinces to provide an accounting of their populations. The so-called *Neizheng bu* census was the first modern census conducted in Manchuria, though the findings are not without problems. The results of the survey suggested a population of nearly fifteen million (see Table A.2).[2]

The 1908 survey was undoubtedly the most thorough to date, but when contrasted with later population figures collected by the Japanese colonial state it seems that the 1908 census undercounted by several million. To derive a reasonable population figure for 1900, it is therefore best to work back not from the 1908 headcount but from the better numbers gathered by the Japanese colonial state and later statistical analyses.

TABLE A.1

Qing Registered Population and Tax-Registered Land

(persons and *mu*)

Year	Registered population	Tax-registered land
1724	422,000	7,317,000
1726		14,013,488
1741		
1788[a]	974,667	
1812	1,243,984	22,874,541
1820	2,491,438	23,174,869
1862	3,165,000	
1887		30,075,426
1893		32,000,000
1897	5,736,000 (6,136,000)[b]	
1898	6,943,000	

SOURCES: *Population*: 1788, 1812, 1820, 1862, and 1897 from Liang (1980, tables 82, 85, 86, 88); 1898 from Chao (1983, table 1, 6); *Registered land*: 1753, 1812, 1820, 1887 from Liang (1980, table 64); 1893 from Perkins (1969, table B.14, 236). Perkins's tax-registered land for 1893 is taken from Qing official figures but includes his own upward adjustment to account for underreporting. His "1913" acreage figure is for 1914; I have used Perkins's cultivated acreage figure for 1930 as opposed to Chao Kang's (1983 tables 2, 9) smaller figure of 188,640,000); 1908 from Sun (1969).

EXPLANATORY NOTE: Figures are numbers of persons and area of farmland registered (captured) in Qing official registries for tax purposes and suffer from significant underreporting. Figures for the post-1912 period are from various sources, including state census figures and survey results cited in secondary literature.

[a] Actual years covered are 1786–1791.

[b] For Fengtian and Jilin only. If, however, we assume Heilongjiang's registered population rose as fast as that of Jilin in the intervening years (1.12% per annum from 1812 to 1897), then Heilongjiang's registered population would have risen from 167,616 in 1820 to 400,000 in 1897, giving a total recalculated "registered" population of 6,136,000.

TABLE A.2

Twentieth-Century Registered Population and Farmland

(persons and *mu*)

Year	Registered population	Registered Farmland
1908	17,055,000	120,000,000
1910	17,942,000	
1912	18,415,714	
1915	20,112,100	123,000,000
1924	25,700,000	164,000,000–183,000000
1930	31,030,000	206,000,000

SOURCES: *Population*: 1898, 1908, 1910, 1930 from Chao (1983, tables 1, 6) and Wynne (1958, 17, Table III.A); 1912 from Liang (1980, tables 82, 85, 86, 88; cf. MMZ 1922–23, 209–211); 1915 from MMZ (1922–23, 226); *Farmland*: 1908 from Sun (1969); 1915 (actual number for 1913) and 1930 from Perkins (1969, table B.14, 236), the higher 1924 figure is from Adachi (1925, 141).

In his study of Manchuria's twentieth-century economy, Sun Kungtu (1969), using figures gathered by others, including the researchers of Japan's Southern Manchurian Railway Company, holds that Manchuria's population circa 1900 was about nine million (1969, 21, Table 3). There are reasons, however, to believe that Sun's estimated population for 1900 is too low in light of later numbers. Researchers for Japan's Southern Manchurian Railway Company and other colonial entities as well as statisticians working with the 1908 Ministry of Interior census concluded separately that the northeast's population was around eighteen million in 1910 and by 1924 had reached just under twenty-six million (Wynne 1958, 17, Table III.A). In light of the Japanese numbers for 1910 and 1924, Sun's estimated nine million people in 1900 implies that the population of the northeast grew faster between 1900 and 1910 than between 1910 and 1924, at a rate of 7.18 percent per annum compared to 2.66 percent per annum respectively.

There is no reason to believe that the population grew faster in the decade after 1910 than it did in the decade before, however. First, railway and steamer links between China Proper and Manchuria developed more after 1910 than before. Second, given the near full cessation and reversal of migration first in 1900, following the Boxer Rebellion and Russia's occupation of southern Manchuria, and then in the two years 1904 and 1905, during the Russo-Japanese War fought in the northeast, there is good reason to believe that overall the population grew more slowly between 1900 and 1910 than the politically and socially more stable period from 1910 to 1920. Both considerations imply a higher population for 1900 than Sun provides.

To estimate the population figure for 1900, I assume the population grew at the same rate between 1900 and 1910 as it did between 1910 and 1930, or 2.76 percent per annum. I then work back from our 1930 figure. We thereby arrive at an estimated 1900 population just under fourteen million. This is the same figure cited from Soviet Union estimates by the U.S. Bureau of the Census for 1900 (Wynne 1958, 17). With the figure of fourteen million as the 1900 population base, we can work back to the eighteenth century.

Estimating Population Between 1750 to 1900

The extent of underreporting of population in the Qing is immediately evident in the headcount for the year 1897, even after adjustments to this figure are made to include the population of Heilongjiang. The official Qing records of 1897 suggest a population of only 5.7 million (or about 6.1 million after adjusting for Heilongjiang). If this number were in fact correct, it suggests an extraordinary rate of population growth of 8.65 percent per annum in the last decade and a half of Qing rule. To be sure, intervening developments in railway construction—the completion of first rail links between north China and Manchuria in 1902 and the Harbin-Dalian line in 1903[3]—the turmoil caused in north China by the Boxer uprising, and the end of the ban on commoners' purchase of Manchu land in 1907, each may have caused a sudden spurt in migration to the northeast. But, it is just as likely that the Boxer Rebellion, which spread to southern Manchuria from north China, Russia's subsequent occupation of the northeast, and the ensuing Russo-Japanese War of 1904–1905 significantly depressed migration, as they did Manchuria's export trade.

To compensate for undercounting in the Qing, I have chosen to use the rates of growth of the registered population as a proxy for growth rates of the actual population and use these rates to calculate back from the 1900 baseline figure. One problem with this method is determining which officially recorded population numbers to use in calculating the rate of growth. For example, officially registered population in the middle of the nineteenth century was 2.9 million and grew by 1.36 percent per annum between 1850 and 1897, when it reached 5.7 million, but between 1870 and 1897 officially registered population grew 2.08 percent, and so on.

In his study of Qing population records and land tax registries, Liang Fangzhong (1980) provides registered population figures for Fengtian and Jilin for the years 1812 and 1897 which I use to measure the rate of growth in population in the nineteenth century. Because Liang's 1897 figure does not include Heilongjiang, it is necessary first to make adjustments which I do by assuming Heilongjiang's population grew at the same rate as Jilin's. Using Liang's numbers and adjusting to include Heilongjiang, officially registered population grew from 1.244 million in 1812 to 6.136 million in 1897, or at an annual rate of 1.9 percent per annum. Turning now to the second half of the eighteenth century, using Liang's numbers again, registered population grew from 974,667 in 1788 (1786–1791) to 1,243,984 in 1812, suggesting a rate of growth of 1.02 percent per annum.

I use these two growth rates to estimate population numbers from 1900 back first to 1800 then to 1725 to achieve the results shown in Table A.3.

Estimating Farmed Acreage

The Qing land tax registries capture only those lands the state managed to record for tax purposes and therefore grossly underestimate actual cultivated acreage. To develop reasonable estimates of actual acreage I have applied methods and logic similar to that used to develop estimates of the Qing population.

Estimating the 1900 Farmland Baseline

The 1900 base figure assumes that the area of cultivated land grew between 1900 and 1930 at a rate similar to the period between 1908 and 1930, or about 2.5 percent per annum. This method gives an area of farmland of just under ninety-eight million *mu* in 1900, which I round up to one hundred million *mu*.

TABLE A.3

Revised Population, Farmland Area, and Farm Size for Manchuria, 1725–1910

Year	Population (1,000 persons)	Farmed land (1,000 *mu*)	Arable per capita	Average family farm size
1725	930	17,500	19	113
1750	1,100	22,000	20	120
1775	1,550	28,500	18	110
1800	2,000	37,000	19	111
1825	3,250	45,000	14	83
1850	5,300	60,000	11	68
1875	8,700	80,000	9	55
1900	14,000	100,000	7	43
1910	18,000	120,000	7	40

EXPLANATORY NOTE: Figures for years after 1900 are population and acreage provided by government and other sources. All other figures are revised estimates based upon the methodology described above. All numbers are rounded off. The "1910" acreage figure is Sun's (1969) 1908 figure rounded up. Average farm size assumes a household of six persons, the average family size among the Daoyi bannermen as calculated by Lee and Campbell (1997) and slightly smaller than the figure 6.63 provided by the 1912 census (Liang 1980, table 86, 268–271).

Estimated Farmland for the Qing

The Qing land registries suggest a very slow rate of increase in area cultivated in the nineteenth century, a mere 0.32 percent per annum from 1812 to 1887, from about twenty-three million to thirty million *mu*, and just less than 0.5 percent per annum between 1726 and 1887. Since registered population grew in excess of one percent per annum, and often significantly higher, the slow rate of increase in registered land if applied to estimating actual acreage would have resulted in a precipitous and unlikely decline in per capita acreage over the nineteenth century. My inclination is to assume that farmland area grew a little slower than population over the very long term. This would give a slightly slower rate of growth than population, a phenomenon observable on other Chinese frontiers. Between 1725 and 1900 revised population grew at 1.57 percent per annum and so I assume a one percent growth rate in acreage over the same period.

APPENDIX B

Crop Yields in the Qing and Republican Eras

Table B.1 overleaf shows crop yield figures in standard *shi* per *mu* collected from various records; Table B.2 shows crop yields collated from the *Agricultural survey of all Fengtian province* (FNDS 1909), which gives yields for twenty-one counties in present-day Liaoning province; and Table B.3 provides yields from a Japanese survey of agricultural conditions conducted in the 1920s. For comparison, recent estimates of yields by Guo Songyi suggest yields in eighteenth- and nineteenth-century Manchuria averaged 0.5–0.6 and 0.7–0.8 *shi* respectively (see Table B.4), though rent data suggest yields were on average under 0.5 *shi* (in Fang et al. 2000, 342, table 1.55, 344).

TABLE B.1

Crop Yields in Manchuria, 1642–1909

(*shi* per *mu*)

Period	Crop	Yields	Location	Source
1642	Millet	0.54	Shenyang	Perkins (1969, 332
1707	Millet	0.25–0.5	Ningguta	Yang Bin (1993, 46)
1820s	Grain	0.4–0.5 (in a good year)	Jilin	Saying'e (1939, 191)
1908	Millet	0.3–0.7	Jilin	Kong (1990, 317)
	Sorghum	0.4–0.8		
	Wheat	0.2–0.4		
	Soybeans	0.25–0.7		
1909	Millet	0.29–1.1	Fengtian	Xu (1989, 1528)
	Sorghum	0.56–1.5		
	Wheat	0.6–1.0		
	Maize	0.46–1.6		
	Soybeans	1.2		
1909	Millet	0.5	Fengtian	See Table B.2
	Sorghum	0.6		
	Wheat	0.3		
	Soybeans	0.5		
Average	Millet	0.52		
	Sorghum	0.73		
Pre-1900 average	Millet	0.43		
	All grain	0.43		
1908–1909 average	Millet	0.66		
	Sorghum	0.89		
	Soybeans	0.50		
	Wheat	0.62		
	Maize	1.01		

TABLE B.2

Crop Yields in Liaoning Province circa 1909

(*shi* per *mu*)

County	Millet	Sorghum	Wheat	Soybean	Maize
Chengde	0.45	0.65	0.30	0.55	—
Xingren	0.70	0.71	0.60	0.70	—
Liaoyang	0.57	0.70	0.30	0.61	1.00
Haicheng	0.65	0.62	0.55	0.50	—
Gaiping	0.45	0.45	—	0.45	0.55
Liaozhong	0.40	0.31	0.20	0.40	0.30
Tieling	0.52	0.63	0.31	0.50	0.75
Kaiyuan	0.55	0.80	0.35	0.65	—
Xinmin	0.45	0.50	0.20	0.45	—
Zhen'an	0.35	0.42	0.19	0.40	—
Changtu	0.56	0.60	0.20	0.65	—
Huaide	0.70	1.00	0.50	1.00	0.60
Kangping	0.25	0.40	0.40	0.40	—
Liaoyuan	0.60	0.70	0.35	0.55	—
Xi'an	0.70	0.70	0.30	0.50	0.60
Xifeng	0.55	0.80	0.35	0.60	0.80
Guangning	0.50	0.50	0.40	0.40	—
Panshan	0.65	0.60	0.25	0.30	—
Yaonan	0.65	0.50	—	0.40	0.60
Xingjing	0.45	0.63	0.23	0.60	—
Faku	0.60	0.70	0.30	0.60	0.50
Average	0.52	0.615	0.33	0.53	0.63

SOURCE: FNDS 1909, 3.3. 49–60.

TABLE B.3

Crop Yields in Manchuria, circa 1920s

(unhusked *shi* per *mu*)

Year	Crop	Yield	Location	Source
1925	Soybeans	0.56	Fengtian	Adachi (1925, 151)
1920	Soybeans	0.56	Fengtian	Settai and Ito (1920, 14–16, table 2)
		0.50	Jilin	
		0.52	Heilongjiang	
1923	Sorghum	0.67	South Manchuria	MMZ (1922–23, 254–276)
	Soybeans	0.56		
	Millet	0.63		
	Wheat	0.31		
	Maize	0.58		
	Sorghum	0.57	Central Manchuria	
	Soybeans	0.47		
	Millet	0.57		
	Wheat	0.34		
	Maize	0.59		
	Sorghum	0.58	North Manchuria	
	Soybeans	0.49		
	Millet	0.58		
	Wheat	0.38		
	Maize	0.60		

TABLE B.4

Crop Yields in Southern and Central Manchuria circa 1925 by Field Quality and Place

(*shi* per *mu*)

Place / field quality	Soybeans	Sorghum	Millet	Wheat
Jinzhou				
poor	0.26	0.27	0.2	
middling		0.5	0.5	
good		0.7	0.7	
Wafangdian				
good	0.7	0.8	1.1	
Qiongyue				
sandy	0.4	0.4	0.4	
heavy	0.7	0.7	0.7	
Gaiping				
poor	0.6	0.8	0.8	
good	0.8	1.0	1.0	
Dashiqiao				
poor	0.4	0.4	0.4	
good	0.6	0.8	0.8	
Yingkou				
good	0.5	0.6	0.6	0.6
Liaoyang				
good	0.8	0.7	0.7	0.6
Fengtian				
middling	0.6	0.6	0.8	0.4
Kaiyuan				
good	0.8	1.2	1.2	0.6
Tieling				
good	0.5	0.8	0.8	
Siping				
good	0.9	1.0	1.0	0.8
Gongzhuling				
good	0.9	0.96	0.96	1.0
Changchun				
good	0.8	0.9	0.96	1.0

SOURCE: MT (1925, 11–12).

Notes

Introduction

1. Though the nature of the outcomes of this process of integration of Manchuria into the world economy are disputed, the fact that Manchuria's economy was significantly restructured by foreign trade and investment and then Japanese colonialism is not in dispute. For accounts of these changes, see Ramon Myers (1976, 1982), Louise Young (1998).

2. For the general approach adopted here, see Brenner (1985a [1976], 1985b [1982], 1986, 1997, 2001). For this approach, with respect to the study of agrarian social-property relations and long-term economic development in the Yangzi delta, see Brenner and Isett (2002, 2003) and in south China (principally Guangdong), see Mazumdar (1998, 7, 58, 192–294).

3. Robert Brenner's thesis took off from the insights offered by Maurice Dobb (1947) in his classic *Studies in the Development of Capitalism*. Following Marx, Dobb rejected arguments that explained the advent of sustained economic development (capitalism) in terms of preexisting or transhistorical economic laws. Instead, he posited that economic development must be understood to be the result of a very particular set of social arrangements that determine how economic actors obtain access to the land, labor, and tools that they require to reproduce themselves. Moreover, it was Dobb's original insight that the appearance of that set of social arrangements particular to capitalism (or more accurately the demise of social arrangements featured in feudalism that were contrary to requirements of development) cannot be understood as the outcome of the economic processes or mechanisms that drive sustained economic development when it occurs (41–42). In this fashion he broke the link, prominent among both Marxian and Smithian models, between the appearance of trade or commercial activity and the commencement of sustained economic growth. Where Brenner departs from Dobb is in explaining not the demise of precapitalist (in the European case feudal) social relations but in the appearance of capitalist ones. Whereas Dobb understood the hollowing out of European feudalism to be the result of political struggles between the main classes of lords, merchants, and peasants, he explains the onset of capitalism in Europe as a process of evo-

lution made possible by the disappearance of feudal fetters on the economy and driven by commercial pressures.

4. For the original text and full argument, see Brenner and Isett (2002, 2003).

5. Five major monographs on the subject of Manchu ethnicity and ethnicity more generally in the Qing have appeared in recent years. My understanding of these matters is derived from those works: they include James Millward's (1998) study of Qing colonization of the northwest, Evelyn Rawski's (1998) examination of the institutions and practices of the Qing ruling house, a succession of studies on the constructed nature of Manchu ethnicity and Qing ideology by Pamela Crossley (1999), Edward Rhoads's (2000) study of the institutions of the Qing banner system, and Mark Elliott's (2001) study of the banner system and the instantiation of Manchu ethnicity in the Qing.

6. The fact of the Qing's Manchu origin brought new imperial goals to the late imperial political system that informed in new ways the long-standing tension between emperor and bureaucracy. Michael Chang (2001) has documented, for instance, the tensions between emperor and bureaucracy over "imperial touring." He shows that whereas the bureaucracy quoted classical Chinese sources to argue against the tours as wasteful extravagance, the Kangxi and Qianlong emperors, both of whom went on extended tours of the empire, insisted on touring as specifically Manchu style of rule. Similarly, James Millward (1998) has shown how the Qianlong emperor brushed aside bureaucratic concerns over the costs of the campaigns waged to incorporate Xinjiang within the Qing empire. According to Millward, whereas civil officials not only complained of the expense but also questioned the policy, the Qianlong emperor brushed aside such concerns. For Qianlong, the extension of Qing power into central Asia was only natural given the Manchu's steppe origins.

7. William Rowe's (2001) account of the political life and philosophy of Chen Hongmou gives emphasis to both ideological and pragmatic commitment of eighteenth-century officialdom to maintaining and improving the "people's welfare" (*minsheng*). If Chen was ideologically committed to improving the people's welfare, he also understood the practical benefits of a well-fed peasantry for the maintenance of social stability (or, in Confucian lexicon "social harmony"). Even so, Chen's pragmatism in this regard was guided by what Rowe sees as his fundamental and unyielding commitment to Confucian ideology and tenets (204).

8. Though the Qing state encouraged the colonization of frontier regions, it did so *in principle*. Under certain conditions, it forcefully prohibited colonization. In deciding when and where to allow colonization, the state weighed strategic interests as well as financial costs. Because the frontier areas were often places where colonists competed with aborigines for resources, they were also politically unstable places. Aborigines rebelled, settlers and aborigines fought pitched battles, and the state had to respond to restore order. Frontiers were also places where bandits hid and where controlling social institutions such as the patriarchal family were attenuated. To maintain control under these conditions required a strong state presence, which made frontiers expensive places to administer. When deciding whether to promote or prohibit colonization, the Qing state weighed the cost (in revenue as well as less tangible strategic costs) of extending its presence on to the frontier regions against the potential revenue to be gained from reclaimed land. When costs were too great, the state simply prohibited colonization and

local authorities refused to recognize settlers' property claims (Shepherd 1993, 181, 208, 214).

9. This revisioning of the Qing state contrasts starkly with an earlier historiography that portrayed the late imperial state as stifling entrepreneurship and economic growth. For example, Albert Feuerwerker's (1958) study of the Mandarin-industrialist Sheng Xuanhuai or Etienne Balazs's (1964) study of the Chinese bureaucracy and economy.

10. Other notable exceptions to the "limited reach of the state" thesis were political crimes and rebellions of ideological or military significance. In his account of an eighteenth-century crime of sedition, Philip Kuhn (1990) has documented how the emperor could harness the full powers of the bureaucracy to tremendous effect. In the case documented by Kuhn, bands supposedly roamed the countryside treasonously removing the queues that male subjects wore as a sign of their loyalty and obeisance to the Qing. Concerned that these acts were expressions of anti-Qing resistance, the Qianlong emperor single-mindedly devoted the full energies of the bureaucracy to root out the principals involved. Though this was an impressive demonstration of the emperor's authority and reach, it was an extraordinary instance much like famine relief efforts. As Kuhn documents, the Qianlong emperor was successful in his efforts to whip the bureaucracy into action in the case of the "soulstealers" because he devoted all his energy to the task.

11. On the autocratic power of the late imperial sovereign over the bureaucracy, see two studies by Benjamin Elman (1992, 1993). In both pieces, Elman shows how emperors used the examination system as a tool for eliciting ideological conformity among officials.

12. Vivienne Shue (1988, 84–85) provides a useful synopsis of this view. G. William Skinner (1977c, 341) discusses the tension between the late imperial monarch's dependency upon gentry and merchants as "informal agents of bureaucratic government" and the threat these agents posed to the sovereign's control, and how the sovereign sought to secure his authority. Min Tu-ki's (1989) discussion of the critique of bureaucratic government developed by the Ming scholar and official Gu Yanwu shows how late imperial bureaucrats were themselves aware of the state's relatively weaker control over local affairs in comparison to the pre-Song state.

13. William G. Skinner (1977a) took the limits of imperial reach to be the result of coordination problems within the bureaucracy. He argued that as the number of administrative units grew so did the physical distance between central and local administrators, making it increasingly difficult for the state's center to control its lower levels. He also argued that as the number of officials increased the ability of the monarch to control his bureaucracy diminished. Finally, the state's ability to extract resources to pay for its own expansion was constrained by the state's limited reach. Over the long run, therefore, the bureaucracy did not grow to keep up with the expansion of the empire's size and the rising density of its population. In Skinner's well-known proof of the phenomenon, late Han dynasty rulers had 1,180 county level units to administer a population of sixty million, whereas late Qing rulers controlled a population of 425 million (seven times more people) with a mere fifteen percent increase in county level units, which reached 1,360 (19–20).

14. That this was the case is not all that surprising; a number of historical works have pointed out how peasants hid certain aspects of their customary affairs from the

state. In the sale of wives, for instance, even though such arrangements were illegal, peasants used contracts and go-betweens to arrange sales (Sommer 2005.); and of course disciples and practitioners of various sectarian religions that the state deemed heterodox, and against which local authorities waged suppression campaigns, hid their day-to-day ritual activities from official eyes (Naquin 1985, 257–260).

15. For an important contrary opinion, see Sucheta Mazumdar's (1998) study of south China.

16. Helen Dunstan (1996) has gone further than previous scholars to locate market-based solutions to the problem of grain distribution in the writings of the Statecraft thinkers of the Qing dynasty. Those solutions amounted to, in her view, a Chinese variant of Liberalism. But, as William Rowe counters, first there was no place in the economic discourse of the day for "schools of thought" and any attempt to find them, he rightly argues, "is an *a posteriori* creation" (2001, 506 n 149). Second, the moral discourse and policy solutions were more akin to those of the French physiocrats than Liberalism (Rowe 2001, 213–214).

17. The Chinese variant of the representation of the sovereign as the provider of food to his subjects is evident in several ritual practices that revolved around preparing the land, planting, and harvesting (Zito 1997, 130–132; Rawski 1998, 211–212).

18. I will return to examine the relationship between trade and economic growth in the conclusion to this study. For an extended criticism of the view that merchants/trade and the division of labor propel economic development, see Ellen Meiksins Wood (2002, 11–21, 73–94). Even those scholars in the field of Chinese history who have adopted a neo-classical viewpoint show either explicitly or implicitly that the appearance and deepening of the division of labor was insufficient for determining economic growth (Rawski 1972, 96–99; Wong 1997, 17, 32; Pomeranz 2000, 12, 22, 206–207, 241).

19. There are numerous studies in English on Japanese efforts to transform the Manchurian economy in the twentieth century. Louise Young (1998, 183–240) provides an excellent overview and analysis of the nature, goals, and reasons for Japan's efforts to transform the economy. Also see Kutsuji Nakagane's (1989) analysis of the Manchukuo state and industrial development and Yoshihisa Matsusaka's (2000) study of the economic and colonial functions of the South Manchurian Railway. Matsusaka briefly discusses the range of South Manchurian Railway's Research Bureau activities (15–16).

20. See Ramon Myers (1976) for both a description of these surveys—what they include and how they were conducted—and an excellent outline of rural conditions (see especially pp. 592–596).

Chapter 1

1. These phrases appear again and again in gazetteers, the dynastic history, official writings, and imperial edicts. The phrase *faxiang zhi di* appears in Wang Yipeng's 1659 essay included in the *Anthology of Statecraft Writings* (He 1992, 862, [35]). Wang wrote, "Our dynasty has established its capital at Yanjing [Beijing]; though its place of origin is in Liaoyang [*ce Liaoyang faxiang zhi di*]." The Chinese phrase *Manzhou genben zhi di* appears, for example, twice in a 1740 imperial edict. The Qianlong emperor noted that "Shengjing is the *locus genesis* of the Manchu" and that the "Fengtian region is the Manchu's place of origins" (GZSL 1964, 1743 [115]).

2. On the relationship, real and imagined, between Manchu cultural habits and Qing power see Robert Lee (1970, 20–23, 41–77) and Mark Elliott (2000, 617–619). See the work of Pamela Crossley (1987, 776–778; 1989, 85, 91–93) on the topics of Manchu genealogies, the construction of ethnic and racial differences, and the construction of imperial ideology in the later half of the eighteenth century.

3. Summing up the consensus in the 1970s, Joseph Fletcher wrote: "Four principal motives have been adduced to explain Ch'ing (Qing) effort to preserve the banner and tribal character of Kirin (Jilin) and Heilungkiang (Heilongjiang). One was to hold open a place to retreat for the dynasty, should the need arise for Manchus to abandon China; another was to maintain a military reservoir of banner troops untouched by Han Chinese cultural influence so as to bolster Manchu dominance among the immense population of China; a third was to guard the government's monopoly on the production of ginseng, furs, pearls, and gold; and a fourth was to preserve Manchu culture and the Manchu dynasty's ancestral traditions" (1978a, 39). Fletcher's own opinion on the matter was, as he acknowledged, shaped by Robert Lee's (1970) earlier study of the northeast. But, because the geographic focus of Robert Lee's study was Jilin and Heilongjiang, where peasant colonization was far less extensive before the late nineteenth century, Lee has little to say on the economic importance of the land system in Fengtian (Liaoning) to the monetary and fiscal needs of the Conquest Elite and state. Elliott has revised Lee's original position to include protection of the bannerlands in southern Manchuria as one of the Qing goals (Elliott 2000, 618), though the focus of Elliott's study on ethnic identity leads him (appropriately) to emphasize cultural over other motivations in his account of Qing administration of that region (also see Elliott 2001, 67–68).

4. Green Standard forces were reduced from 900,000 to 600,000 following the end of the Rebellion of the Three Feudatories (1673–1681). Banner forces at that time numbered between 200,000 and 350,000 (Kessler 1976, 108).

5. To prevent acculturation of the Conquest Elite, in the late seventeenth and eighteenth centuries the Qing ruling house maintained that elite Manchus devote their energies to honing their military abilities and maintaining their Manchu language while it encouraged them to shun the literary pursuits favored by Han officials (Crossley 1990, 24–26). The court was evidently quite successful in that regard, and few Manchus acquired the highest of the civil service degrees—the *jinshi* (Chu and Saywell 1984, 51–52).

6. Crossley (1990) shows that alongside martial skills (such as archery and horsemanship), which were the primary concerns of the Kangxi emperor, the Qianlong emperor gave equal weight to the mastery by Manchus of the Manchu language, thereby shifting the "standards of identity from military servitude to cultural life" (24).

7. For more on the Qianlong emperor's understanding/vision of the Manchu homeland and the closing of Manchuria to Han migration, see Elliott (2000, 618–619).

8. Pamela Crossley (1987) argues that the Qianlong emperor's frustration over the growing signs of bannerman acculturation to Han ways may have stemmed less from fear of military emasculation as from a new political agenda: the desire to "force a comprehensive cultural structure upon the Qing polity, with the emperor as its integrating center" (779). Crossley's argument does not require that we discard the older paradigm. Mark Elliot (2001, 257–263), for instance, cites memorials from the Kangxi and Qianlong eras that point to Qing fears that Manchu acculturation to Han customs also meant a loss of military abilities. If we understand political hegemony to operate simultaneously

at the Gramscian levels of both "consent" and "force," rulership is secured insofar as rulers elicit compliance through both ideological work *and* physical violence (Gramsci 1971). Any degrading of Manchu martial skills (whether real or assumed) represented to the monarch a net diminution of the dynasty's ability to secure hegemony by force—by waging war, suppressing rebellion, and policing the population—even as new *ideological* means for achieving consent were in the offing.

9. The original insight is William G. Skinner's (1978, 308). He argues that there was an inverse relationship in regional space between "revenue" and "defense" such that in the cores of the empire such as Jiangnan the military concerns of the field administration were minimal, whereas revenue concerns were paramount. On the frontiers, however, field administrators were principally concerned with defense against unincorporated peoples.

10. That old rationales no longer applied does not gainsay the fact that rationalizations for Han exclusion had real purchase at an earlier moment, when the challenges and issues confronting the Qing were very different. One must hold out the possibility that had the dynasty permitted Han settlement of Manchuria beginning in the seventeenth century, the worst fears of the dynasty may have come to fruition. Nonetheless, what Fletcher found puzzling was not that the Qing pursued the policy of Han exclusion in the seventeenth and eighteenth centuries, but that it did not abandon it in the nineteenth century. Recent scholarship on Qing rule suggests, however, that Fletcher was incorrect to view the continuation of Han exclusion into the nineteenth century as an unnecessary anachronism. The works of Crossley (1990, 1987, 1999) and Elliot (2000) suggest the ideological and institutional imperative for Han exclusion remained well into the nineteenth century. The institutions of dyarchic rule were constitutive elements of the Qing constitution that could not be easily abandoned and, so long as imperial discourse conceived of the empire as a multiethnic realm, in which people were defined by genealogical, linguistic, and geographical differences, that was held together by a transcendent sovereign, a need for clear boundaries between Han and Manchu and between commoner and banner would have had purchase with the Qing ruling house.

11. On the destruction of farmland caused by the Ming-Qing transition and the attending peasant uprisings, see Guo Songyi (1991, 228–239). Available sources suggest a significant proportion of land under cultivation in 1600 was abandoned by 1644 in the north China provinces of Shandong, Zhili, and Shanxi. Reports cited by Guo suggest as much as sixty to seventy percent of farmland was abandoned in Zhili, more than half in Shandong, and fifteen percent in Shanxi. On the desperate conditions of state revenues and the impending fiscal crisis of the Qing state in the 1650s, see Xu (1990, 91–92). Xu states that there was a shortfall of about one million silver *taels*, with revenues of 14,859,000 and expenditures of 15,734,000 taels. In the years between 1644 and 1660, there were total deficits of more than twenty-seven million *taels*. Most of this was apparently due to tax arrears in Jiangnan (Wakeman 1985, 1061–1062, n.152).

12. Decrees encouraging migration and resettlement were promulgated in 1649, 1651, 1652, 1656, 1657, and 1660. On the first three occasions, officials were commanded to "seek out and recruit the landless and regardless of their native place have them open waste land [*shi min kaiken huangdi*] and grant them permanent proprietorship" (cited in Li 1987, 19–20).

13. Similar policies were pursued in Sichuan, also beginning in 1653 (Ho 1959, 139).

In Manchuria, the specific rank bestowed depended upon the number of colonists recruited and whether the person already held civil or military rank (SJTZ 1965, 1160). Historical studies mention three individuals who were so rewarded and subsequently memorialized in their home county gazetteers (Xu 1990, 92; Yi 1993, 197).

14. To be sure, the palisade was by most accounts fairly permeable. Many peasants simply bypassed designated border crossing points by working their way over the ditches and through the willow stockades. Nonetheless, the palisades served the vital function of demarcating the geographical boundary separating legal and criminal settlement, thus marking the jurisdictional borders between the southern part of Manchuria, administered by the Fengtian military governor and an area in which commoners lived legally, and northern and central Manchuria, administered by the Ningguta military governor, where commoners could not settle (Zhang 1999, 81).

15. Note that the *Shengjing Complete Gazetteer* incorrectly totals the amount of Qing land in Fengtian and Jinzhou as 1,367,804 *shang* (SJTZ 1965, 1233–1234 [24]). The correct figure, based on the total of garrison town bannerland, is 2,367,804 *shang*. Zhao Lingzhi (2001) and Yi Baozhong (1993) maintain, contra Sudō Yoshiyuki (1944, 1972b), the highly plausible position that land recorded under the emperor Yongzheng as "bannerland" (*qidi*), and listed in the 1736 edition of the *Shengjing Complete Gazetteer*, includes not only formal bannerland—small land grants to rusticated bannermen—but also manor land (*zhuangdi* or *zhuangtian*) of the imperial estates, Qing nobility, and Shengjing bureaucracy (Zhao 2001, 208). Sudō assumed that land recorded as *qidi* in the *Shengjing Complete Gazetteer* was land formally set aside for rusticated bannermen and therefore did not include manorial lands. Zhao Lingzhi and Yi Baozhong reckon that the figures of 2.65 and 14 million *mu* include both forms of land. There is very good reason to concur with them. It was commonplace for administrators to lump "manor" and "banner" land together in their memorials. The formal expression "banner land conditionally purchased by commoners" (*min dian qidi*) referred to both land farmed by rusticated bannermen and to manorial land that had been bought by commoners. It was therefore possible that the compiler of the 1736 *Shengjing Complete Gazetteer* similarly conflated these forms of land. Whatever the case, it is evident that the total area dedicated to use by the Manchus grew considerably under the Kangxi emperor.

16. There are numerous studies which outline in part or whole the "negotiations" that marked the early days of Qing rule and the processes by which Qing imperial authority was established in China Proper. See for example Hillary Beattie (1979, 13–17, 44–47), Li Wenzhi (1993, 22–37, 81–145), and Sucheta Mazumdar (1998, 201–217). This is the subject of much of Frederic Wakeman's (1985) two-volume study (414–508, 1074–1127).

17. Much of what is known of early Ming society is taken from official accounts and state decrees and must be interpreted with some skepticism. Nonetheless, it still stands that late Ming agrarian social relations were marked by juridical and customary restrictions on the liberties of the greater body of producers, whether laborers, tenants, or owner-operators.

18. The notable exceptions include the serf laborers of Anhui province and the Pearl river delta described and discussed by Sucheta Mazumdar (2001, 93–94) as well as a variety of remnant *nupu* attached mostly to gentry and noble households (Jing 1993).

19. There are many studies showing these developments for different parts of the

empire. General surveys include the works of Yang Guozhen (1988, 91–122), Philip Huang (2001, 102–107), Zhou Yuankang and Xie Zhaohua (1986, 288–337), Li Wenzhi (1993, 81–145), Fang Xing (1992, 66–69), and Shi Zhihong (1994, 45–81). On the southeast, see Sucheta Mazumdar (1998, 193–230); on the Yangzi Delta, see Kathy Walker (1999, 69, 78, 80–82) and James Shih (1992, 131–155); and on south China more broadly, see Evelyn Rawski (1972, 19–24).

20. In 1644 Regent Dorgon decreed an end to "plunder" of land and institutionalized a formal system for its allotment (Kessler 1976, 15). Though the new land allotment method aimed to reduce friction between Manchu and Han Chinese, it also effectively gave to the emperor a monopoly over the distribution of largesse. This was useful in his efforts to rein in his nobles.

Chapter 2

1. Circa 1910, officially registered bannerland amounted to 18.5 million *mu*, while total arable area was closer to 120 million *mu* (Xu 1989, 1099). The general demographic makeup was correspondingly transformed. There were perhaps eighteen million inhabitants by 1910, of whom no more than two million and probably fewer were rusticated bannermen and serfs. In 1940, the Japanese registered 2.68 million "indigenous Manchus" in a population of 43.2 million, or about six percent of the total population (Chikusa 1964, vol. 1, 1).

2. Note that Diao Shuren (1993, 116–117) has mistakenly transcribed the acreage figure from the 1726 *cadastre* results. His figure of 1,367,804 *shang* should read 2,367,804 (cf. Zhao 2001, 207–208).

3. Given the sources at hand, estimates of population are very rough. This figure is derived from Edward Rhoads who states that for every garrisoned bannerman circa 1850 there were twenty dependents (Rhoads 2000, 34).

4. Similar colonial efforts were made in other parts of the Qing empire. Fang Yingkai and James Millward have provided accounts of efforts by the Qing to form soldier and peasant colonies in the far northwest that look in form very much like the banner colonies in the northeast (Fang 1989, passim; Millward 1998, 50–52).

5. Initially, there were eleven garrisons in Fengtian and one in Jilin. By 1700, this number had grown to fifteen and six respectively with an additional garrison in Heilongjiang. By the late Jiaqing era, the number of garrisons in the northeast had grown to forty-three and the number of garrisoned soldiers to approximately fifty thousand (Diao 1993, 46, 118–119; Lee 1970, 33; Sudō, 1944, 182; Zhao 2001, 199–203, 214, 219). The situation remained roughly unchanged until the end of the dynasty.

6. Initially, bannerland and manorial land could not be sold outside the banner: "the land of the official manors and soldiers are not to be exchanged outside the banner; the soldiers are to cultivate the land themselves and can not sell it all" (*guanyuan bingding dimu, bu xu yueqi jiaoyi; bingding benshen gengdi, bu xu quan mai*) (Wang 1990, 75). After 1758, however, the transfer of property between members of the banner population was sanctioned, though the sale of banner or manor land to commoners remained illegal (Wang 1990, 75). In 1729, a ban on conditional sale of bannerland to commoners was specified in the regulations (QHS 1991, 1019 [159]). In 1808, the conditional sale of bannerland to commoners was criminalized under the Qing Code, the new sub-statute

making formal law what was already the case under the regulations of 1680, 1689, and 1729. The 1808 sub-statute 95.11 reads: "As for banner land and banner houses, none of these may be conditionally purchased by commoners." (DC 1970).

7. See Edward Rhoads (2000) for a brief yet detailed account of the disposition of banner population throughout the empire, both garrisoned and rusticated (27–42; also see Lee 1970, 36–39).

8. The phrase to "make a living" appears often in Qing court records together with the terms "cultivate" (*gengzhong*) or "hire out" (*gu*). That the state spoke of rusticated bannermen as "cultivating land for a living," while rusticated bannermen spoke of themselves in these same terms, demonstrates both the state's expectation and rusticated bannermen's recognition that they worked the land for their sustenance and were, therefore, of a different social type to the garrisoned bannermen. Also see essays on banner welfare in the *Anthology of Statecraft Writings* (He 1992, 874, 879).

9. Edward Rhoads (2000, 36–37) provides an account of this regulation when applied to garrisoned bannermen.

10. As in many matters, when administering corporal punishment the Qing made distinctions between those attached to a banner and those who were commoners. Whereas commoners sentenced to beatings received strokes from either a light or heavy bamboo stick, depending on the severity of the crime, persons attached to a banner received lashes of the whip (Bodde and Morris 1967, 77, 80–81). The whip was the preferred method of punishment of the pre-Conquest Manchus and was continued after the founding of the Qing dynasty, when it was applied to all those affiliated with the banner system, including bannermen, their bondservants, and serfs (97, 217). Bannermen, their bondservants, and serfs were also singled out for different treatment in the application of penal servitude and military exile, which was commuted in these instances to the wearing of the *cangue* (96).

11. According to the Military Board's regulations in the Jiaqing edition of the *Collected Statutes*, banner populations living in the countryside who illegally left their villages were to be punished in the same manner as banner populations living in Beijing who committed the same crime (Sudō 1972b, 401).

12. According to Elliott (2001), maintaining dependents and provisioning horses took the greater part of the total monies allotted to supporting the banner armies.

13. The fourteen Statecraft school essays on "Banner livelihood" are collated in section ten of the Board of Revenue Policies in the *Anthology of Statecraft Writings* (He 1992). Topics covered range from proposals on improving living conditions of rusticated bannermen to expanding the policy of rustication and creation of new colonies.

14. See Chen's essay "Plans on the livelihood of the Manchu soldiers and people" (*Manzhou bing min shengji shu*) in the *Anthology of Statecraft Writings* (He 1992).

15. In his early career under the Qianlong emperor, Liang Shizheng was one of the emperor's most trusted officials, developing expertise in banner and Manchu matters even though he himself was Han.

16. In addition to Ste. Croix on serfdom (1981, 158–159, 250–255) see Anderson (1974, 147–148) and Bloch (1966, 86–90).

17. In Pamela Crossley's (2002) account of the Qing Conquest Elite at the end of the eighteenth century, its core or "central population" included the imperial lineage, titled Manchu and Mongol families, eminent lineages of the Chinese-martial banners, com-

manders of the Eight Banners and the banner garrisons and some high-ranking Chinese civil officials. The common families of the Eight Banners, by contrast, were "marginal" groups and rusticated bannermen certainly ranked lowest among the Eight Banner common families. Many were of the Han-Martial banners, a caste that was increasingly marginalized itself within the banner system. Across the eighteenth and nineteenth centuries, the Han-Martial bannermen were increasingly removed from the rolls and thrown into the general Chinese civilian population (356). Nevertheless, however distant socially and politically from the general banner populations, or from those in the Manchu and Mongol banners, rusticated bannermen remained in the system.

18. As Pamela Crossley (1990) notes, bannermen were understood, and even understood themselves, to be their emperor's "slaves," bound in military service. But, she also notes that the "master-slave" relationship in this case never took on the "external forms of servitude," except in extreme circumstances (15). This was obviously quite different from serfdom, in which the "master-serf" distinction was key to both its social function and reproduction.

19. The fate of the *tokso* manors before 1644 is unclear. Roth-Li (1979) argues that on coming to power Nurgaci's son Hung Taiji sought to reclaim these manors from the various *beile* lords, to both reduce friction between Chinese civilians and Manchus and to weaken *beile* power by attacking their fiscal base (24–25). She (1975) also claims the *tokso* were abolished in 1625 (89). More recent work by Chinese scholars shows, however, that the number of *tokso* or manors increased in the mid 1630s, and were distributed among the Manchu *beile* lords (Yi et al. 1992, 29–31).

20. The area of land occupied by the official estates remained more or less at this level. By the 1880s, there was 265,124 *mu* of government manor land (Liang 1980, 385 n 6; also see Wu et al. 1992, 74). The area occupied by the imperial manors declined, however, to 700,000 *mu* by the end of the eighteenth century, thereafter staying at this level. The decline in imperial manorial lands was due to the largesse of the Qianlong emperor, who rewarded members of the aristocracy with manors taken from his own holdings (Diao 1993, 63; Wu et al. 1990, 50).

21. *Zhuangding* caught fleeing or having absconded from a manor were thus subject to punishment upon recapture—one hundred lashes of the whip for the first offense, one hundred lashes and forty days of the *cangue* for the second, and death for the third (Yang and Zhou 1986, 227; Diao 1993, 107). Article One of the 1956 Convention of the United Nations defines serfdom as "the condition of status of a tenant who is by law, custom or agreement bound to live and labour on land belonging to another person and render some determinate services to such other persons, whether for reward or not, and is not free to change his status" (UN 1956). I use this definition as a model for determining the appropriate rendition of *zhuangding* into English.

22. Note that the land tax burden estimated by Wang Yeh-chien is for the last decades of the dynasty. The actual burden in the eighteenth century as a percentage of output was, he argues, higher by two-thirds (cf. Wang 1973, 113). Nevertheless, this fact would have not closed by very much the large gap in burden between the land tax and manor rents.

23. Two separate statutes defined the crime and fixed the degree of punishment for selling manor land. One refers to serfs of the imperial house and the other to serfs of the aristocratic houses. The former serfs who sold manor land were punishable under

Statute 93 of the Qing Code: "Whoever steals another's fields or houses and sells them, or takes another's unusable fields or houses and exchanges them, or falsely declares another person's fields and houses to be his own, or who falsely writes a cash sale price into a contract of conditional sale (*dianmai*), or who occupies wrongfully another's fields or houses will be punished in instances when the amount of land is one *mu* or less, or the number of rooms is one or less, with fifty strokes of the light bamboo. For each additional five *mu* or three rooms, one degree [of punishment] is to be added, the punishment not exceeding 80 strokes of the heavy bamboo and penal servitude of two years. *If the fields and houses belong to an official, then it is to be two degrees higher*" (emphasis added). According to jurist Xue Yunsheng's commentary on the Qing Code, Statute 93 was adapted from the Ming Code with clarifications added.

24. Thus, a person of *jian* status who committed a crime against a person of *liang* status received harsher treatment than a *liang* person who committed the same crime against a *jian* person. For a discussion of the *jian-liang* binary and the legal implications, see Jing (1993).

25. Crossley (1999, 90–128) demonstrates the increasingly precarious and unstable nature of the classification *nikan* from the conquest of Liaodong in 1620 to the reign of Qianlong.

26. Thus, Millward (1998, 153) finds that *minren* was used in Xinjiang to refer to both Han and Tungans.

27. The imperial requirement that regional administrators separate Manchuria's communities was repeated on many occasions. In the first month of 1715, for instance, the Kangxi emperor reiterated the need to separate the banner and commoner communities: "[i]n Fengtian, bannermen and commoners mingle indiscriminately [*zachu*] so that the number of trouble-makers and instances of theft and murder are many. It is necessary to demarcate the boundaries, following the lay out of the military garrisons. Only when bannermen and commoners dwell separately will no problems arise [*qi min fenju fang ke wu shi*]" and so Kangxi commanded that "the Fengtian military governor and prefect are to have bannermen and commoners both inside and outside the towns dwell separately" (SZSL 1964, 3494 [262]; also see SZSL 1964, 3542 [266]; GZSL 1964, 1743 [115]).

28. The intent of the 1680 and 1689 decrees contrasted sharply with the state's active promotion of colonization, with few strictures, in such areas as the middle and upper Yangzi regions, the southwest (Yunnan and Guizhou), and western Guangxi. For examples of open colonization, see studies by Guo Songyi (1994), Perdue (1987), and Vermeer (1998). But, it does echo, though for a very different rationale, the state's concern for unregulated settlement on Taiwan, where the primary concern was open hostility between aboriginal people and Han settlers (Shepherd 1993).

29. Restrictions on where peasants could live and farm were not altogether absent in China Proper, to be sure. In the middle and lower Yangzi regions, for instance, local and regional officials put upland areas off bounds to peasants for fear of the damage they caused to ecological stability (Leong 1997, 157). On Taiwan, where Han settlement led to conflict with the aboriginal populations, local and regional officials sought to control where Han resided (Shepherd 1993, 142–146, 148–154; Meskill 1979, 33, 42–43).

30. In 1908, there were 1.8 million Han bannermen in the northeast, most working land as rusticated bannermen—three-quarters of the Han bannermen in Fengtian were

rusticated bannermen and presumably the proportion of rusticated bannermen was similar in Jilin and Heilongjiang (Enatsu 1991, 13). The banner population of Daoyi, which forms the basis of several of James Lee and Cameron Campbell's studies (1992, 1997), was ethnically Han.

Chapter 3

1. There were of course important exceptions to the general rule. On the frontiers where strategic military concerns were a state priority, a small military administration was often established in advance of peasant migration and settlement (Skinner 1978, 45–50). See, for instance, John Shepherd's (1993, 137–154, 182–208, 396–397) study of the colonization of Taiwan and Peter Perdue's (1987, 59–92) study of settlement in Hunan, as well as Ann Osborne's (1994, 11–30) work on the Anhui-Zhejiang border region.

2. In 1653, a military governor was appointed to Ningguta to oversee the north. This governor's seat was relocated to Jilin in 1676. The territory overseen by the Ningguta military governor proved too vast for effective administration and, in 1683, a third military governor was assigned to the garrison town of Aigun, on the Amur. Logistically difficult to supply and too exposed to Russia forces in the area, the Aigun military governor's seat was relocated first to Mergen and then Qiqihar in 1699 (Lee 1970, 59–60, 65; Zhao 1998, 192–193).

3. The boards were those of Rites, War, Revenue, Punishment, and Works. Unlike Beijing, there was no Board of Personnel in Shengjing. The Qing court, located in Beijing, did not entrust Manchuria's regional government with the task of selecting and assigning officials to administer its own offices and territories. That power was jealously guarded by the sovereign, who insisted that all assignments to Manchuria's regional government be made in Beijing under his supervision. See Robert Lee (1970, 61–62) on official appointments, on how they were made, and on changes to how they were made.

4. Within the banner hierarchy, the garrison commandant was subordinate to the assistant commandant (*xieling*), who in turn was subordinate to the deputy lieutenant general (*fudu tong*), who reported to the lieutenant general (*du tong*). The military governor (*jiangjun*) always held the rank of lieutenant general (Lee 1970, 25–28, 59–60, 63–65).

5. On the structures of rural control in the banner zones, see Sudō Yoshiyuki (1944, 178–194), Yamamoto Yoshimitsu (1941, 12–18), and Robert Lee (1970, 59–77).

6. One Guandong *shi* was equal to 2.5 standard *shi*; one *shang* was equal to six *mu* in Fengtian. In the eighteenth century, one *shang* (six *mu*) yielded at best three *shi* of beans, while yields as low as 1.5 *shi* per *shang* were commonplace. Initially, the bannerland tax was collected in kind, though later commuted to cash. A peasant would not put all his land in beans because such pulse crops were regarded as a supplement to the grain staple (*zhu shi*). Most land was planted in millet or sorghum, which were together the mainstay of the peasant diet in Manchuria. Circa 1700, a peasant planting his land in millet could hope to harvest about 0.8 standard *shi* of millet per *mu* at very best, though a yield of 0.5 *shi* or under was far more common. One *shi* was valued at about four cash circa 1700, according to Sudō Yoshiyuki (1944, 151). (Sudō states that one Guandong *sheng* of millet was worth about 0.1 cash circa 1700, so that a standard *sheng* of millet was worth about 0.04 cash, making a standard *shi* worth about four cash.) One Guandong

sheng of black beans had a market value of about 0.06 cash circa 1700. With six *mu* to the *shang*, the black bean tax on bannerland was the equivalent of 0.01 cash per *mu* after conversion (Sudō 1944, 151). Thus, a bannerman putting his land in millet, paying his taxes in cash rather than kind, and achieving a yield of 0.5 *shi* of millet per *mu* might expect to pay a mere half of one percent of his total harvest in tax circa 1700. Even assuming an acceptable lowest millet yield of 0.2 *shi* per *mu*, the burden of the tax on bannerland would only just exceed one percent, at 1.25 percent.

7. The 1724–1725 *qingcha* was the full survey of population and land overseen by provincial officials to uncover unreported land (*yindi*, lit. "hidden land") that was cultivated but not registered for tax payment.

8. The structures of rural control in the banner village are far from clear from the sources at hand. Japanese scholar Yamamoto Yoshimitsu (1941), who provided the only comprehensive account of local Qing administration in the northeast, drew heavily on descriptions of the administration of bannerland and villages in Zhili province found in the Tong county gazetteer, suggesting that there was in all likelihood a significant degree of similarity between banner village oversight in the northeast and north China. According to Yamamoto, the banner villages in Tong county were formed into thirty-two *pai* with each *pai* under the supervision of a *lingcui*. Each banner village was headed by a *shoubao*, or *tunmu*, who was charged with assisting the *lingcui* and *zuoling* in both tax collection and policing. How closely Manchuria's banner villages approximated those of Tong county in their organization is hard to say. But, evidence in legal court records from Manchuria corroborates much of Yamamoto's account. Numerous legal cases from the Qianlong period, for instance, mention *lingcui* and *shoubao* in their capacity as local constabulary. For example, in a 1762 case of attempted rape in a banner village in the vicinity of the Fenghuang garrison, the *shoubao* reported the crime and a *lingcui* was commanded to hold the suspect in custody until the trial convened (XT 1762.2.5).

9. In this study, I use the archaic English meaning of "bailiff," which refers to an estate steward or overseer.

10. The Accounts Department (*kuaiji si*) of the Shengjing Imperial Household Department directly administered the imperial estates of Fengtian prefecture, which included estates in the environs of the towns of Xingjing, Liaoyang, Tieling, Jinzhou, and Gaizhou. The Accounts Department was originally known as the Directorate of Palace Eunuchs (*neiguan jian*). Its name was then changed to the Palace Provisions Commission (*xuanjiao yuan*) in 1760, and the Accounts Department in 1777. The smaller Jinzhou Imperial Household Department, which was subordinate to the Shengjing Imperial Household Department, oversaw the imperial estates of Jinzhou, Yizhou, Ningyuan, and Guangning. This sole duty of this institution was minding the estates in the Jinzhou region, while the Shengjing Imperial Household Department was also responsible for the general affairs of the imperial household. Under Qing regulations, nine prompters (*cuiling*) from the Shengjing Imperial Household Department and three from Jinzhou were charged with overseeing the collection and remittance of rent from the bailiff of all imperial estates (Diao 1993, 62, 66–68; Yi 1993, 118).

11. Enatsu's (1989) significant account of the founding of the manor in Junjiatun is based on a unique Japanese ethnographic survey conducted in the twentieth century, which combined historical sources with interviews.

12. The Qing legal system provided for different degrees of punishment for crimes that crossed status and familial boundaries (Bodde and Morris 1967, 30, 33, 183; Ch'ü 1961). Thus, for example, it is widely cited that bondservants who struck their masters received a higher degree of punishment than a commoner who struck another commoner. In this case, the crime of striking another was considered a greater crime when committed by a status inferior against a status superior.

13. Substatute 93.5 of the Qing Code prohibited the selling by a bailiff of his master's property.

14. Bailiffs, for instance, were not always prohibited from taking the civil service exam, a privilege universally denied to serfs because of their *jian* status. In regulating the right of bailiffs to sit for the exam, the Qing Code distinguished between those bailiffs who were appointed to the post for "meritorious behavior" (*chengling* bailiffs, such as the Jun household studied by Enatsu Yoshiki) and those who received their office after "submitting to vassalage" (*touchong*). Substatute 76.21 of the Qing Code states that while *chengling* bailiffs could sit for the civil service exam, *touchong* bailiffs could not (Statute 76.21; also see QD 1989, 511). The critical difference, from the perspective of the state, was the issue of how the bailiff entered the banner system. The Chinese term *touchong* refers to an action by which a person "submitted" voluntarily to vassalage under a bannerman's household. Most often, the person who voluntarily submitted was seeking the protection and patronage of the household head. By Manchu tradition, this act rendered the person a slave. It was the *touchong* bailiff's standing as a slave, therefore, that made him ineligible to sit for the exam (on *touchong* see Kessler 1976, 28).

15. In total, a serf circa 1700 with a standard sixty *mu* allotment paid in rent, tribute, and head tax the equivalent of twenty-four standard *shi* of grain, at a time when grain yields averaged about 0.5 *shi* per *mu* and a standard holding was sixty *mu*. Even if yields were as high as 0.7 *shi*, a yield which was only achievable under the best of conditions, the rate of expropriation was still the equivalent of half the entire grain output of one serf household (Yang and Zhou 1986, 306–307).

16. There is some discrepancy in the secondary works on the amount of rent in grain collected. Yi Baozhong et al. (1992, 134) suggest that each manor of 720 *mu* paid in rent 120 granary *shi*. Since one granary *shi* was 0.28 standard *shi*, the take in rent would have been a mere forty-six *shi* if Yi et al. are correct. (For granary (*cang shi*) to standard *shi* conversion rate, see QDTD [1988, 415]; Zhao [2001, 291–292].) But, Diao Shuren (1993, 74, 85) gives the rent as 432 granary *shi*, or 120 standard *shi*. In support of Diao, some sources in fact specify that rent on the grain manors of the crown and regional government circa 1700 was 120 standard *shi* (QDTD 1988, 386–388). Diao's figure of 120 standard *shi* appears to be the correct one.

In the early eighteenth century, the manors were reorganized into four grades according to the rank of the bailiff and rents reset. After 1730, on government grain manors, first-ranked bailiffs were required to remit 382 granary *shi*. A second-ranked manor remitted 370 *shi*, a third-ranked 352 *shi*, and fourth-ranked 192 *shi* (QHS 1991, 372–373 [289]). After 1715, on crown manors rents were set at 320 granary *shi* for first-ranked bailiffs, 290 for second-ranked, and 260 for third- and fourth-ranked (Wu et al. 1990, 65). In addition to rents, serfs on the crown and government manors of Shengjing continued to pay customary annual tribute in a variety of items, including geese, ducks, eggs, hay, lamp oil, and labor services (Zhao 2001, 288; Diao 1993, 68).

17. The next round of administrative expansion took place under Yongzheng. In 1727, three offices of civil administration were established at Yongji, Qinning, and Changning in central Manchuria. Qinning county was soon subsumed by Yongji department, while Changning department was disbanded;, its Han commoner population subsequently came under the authority of the military vice commander-in-chief in Ningguta. By the end of the eighteenth century, while the civil bureaucracy in much of present-day Liaoning was more or less in place, suggesting a stabilization in settlement there, the civil bureaucracy of central and northern Manchuria remained attenuated. Not until after the mid-nineteenth century were there any additions to the civil administration of Jilin and Heilongjiang provinces. During the nineteenth and twentieth centuries, the most rapid expansion of the civil bureaucracy in the northeast was centered in these two provinces. Increases in migration and settlement led to the establishment of no fewer than forty new civil administrative offices in present-day Jilin between 1877 and 1910 (Niu 1990, 79–119).

18. See Hilary Beattie's (1979) study of local power in Anhui's Tongcheng county during the Ming and Qing; see Hsiao Kung-chuan's (1960) study of rural control and the methods used by the state to ensure local gentry did not take control of the *lijia* and *baojia* system, while nonetheless remaining subject to them (for example, pages 45–49, 67–69, 85). Also see Esherick and Rankin's (1990, 5–7) discussion of state and elites.

19. See for instance Georges Duby's (1976, 33–42, 54–58) study of serfdom in medieval Europe, particularly chapter two.

Chapter 4

1. For instance, see Yang Guozhen (1988, 20), Li Wenzhi (1993, 16–18, 113), H. Franz Schurmann (1956, 507–509, 515–516), Peter Perdue (1987, 150), and Sucheta Mazumdar (1998, 217–230).

2. For the development of layered rights to property outside the northeast, also see Zhou and Xie (1986, 44–59), Huang (2001, 71–118), Liang Zhiping (1996, 107–110) and Chen Keng (1987).

3. Statute 93 stipulated the appropriate level of punishment for those who stole land. The statute began: "Whoever illegally sells fields or buildings belonging to another; or disposes of fields and buildings not belonging to him; or falsely claims the real estate of another as his own; or makes out a contract of conditional sale or sale with a false price; or occupies the fields and buildings of another—in each case, the offender shall receive fifty blows of the light bamboo if the amount of property in question, if land, does not exceed one *mu*, or, if a building, does not exceed a single bay" (cited with changes from Jing 1994, 43). To say that the principal aim of statute 95 was the collection of land tax and not the prescription of land rights is not to say that when magistrates adjudicated cases they did not recognize the payment of the land tax as supporting land claims (see Osborne 2004, 140–142, 154).

4. It was not until the end of the Qing and the Republican era that an attempt to codify land rights came about. See Philip Huang's (2001, 89–98, 107–114) discussion of the ways in which Republican jurists of the early twentieth century sought to forge a new property law that took into account existing customary practices while creating a consistent body of code.

5. Philip Huang (1996), in making his case for the existence of a realm of "civil law" in late imperial China, argues that even though certain principles such as property rights were not guaranteed in law, they were secured in the practice of justice. Thus, local magistrates, he argues, in their adjudication of property and other disputes, acknowledged and supported a positive principle in practice which had the effect of defining and protecting land and other such claims. But, the absence of a positive principle in law meant that there could never be a legal guarantee of any positive principle in practice. Huang's argument therefore begs the questions: how is it possible to speak of a "principle" at work in Qing law when it existed in practice only, and how was it that a "principle" that existed in practice—a practice that was always local—was replicated both *in situ* and spread over vast and socially differentiated jurisdictions of the empire? When local practice and the law were aligned as they were for instance in the arena of household property division and some property claims, then what appears as a legal principle in practice may rather be the product of a simple convergence of local interest and state interest. More problematic are instances detailed in Chapter 5 of land practices that were sanctioned by the community but rejected by the state. In such cases it is much harder to see any principle at work.

6. Despite different interpretations of the Qing property systems, and the relative functions of the state and village in mediating it, there is general agreement that claims to property were secured in the first instance within the village. See Chen and Myers (1976), Huang (1996), Buoye (2000), Perdue (1987), Allee (1994a).

7. See Myron Cohen's insightful description of Chinese land contracts and other such agreements as "documents of understanding," which he suggests are more social than legal "insofar as they are basic instrumentalities in the regulation of social, economic, and religious affairs in daily life." Cohen points out that it is their materiality which lends such documents their formal legal uses (Cohen 2004, 88).

8. Liang Zhiping (1996, 53–55) has similarly argued on the basis of Republican investigations of Chinese customary practice that timing was critically important when changes in the status of land were negotiated. These surveys show that conditionally sold land could not be redeemed, nor leaseholds changed, when work was still being done in the fields. Changes in the status of farmland had to occur after the harvest and before spring land preparation began.

9. Valerie Hansen (1995, 65) shows that the reliance by semiliterate scribes upon boilerplate contracts dates at least to the tenth century.

10. Though the evidence presented by Xu Tan (2000) demonstrates no definitive trend, she concludes otherwise. Xu argues that the right of first purchase remained but was weakened over the Qing dynasty. This is based in part upon the problematic claim that in the pre-Qing era land could not be sold outside the lineage group. There are few data that speak directly to this assertion. Moreover, the national data she presents for the Qing show sales to relatives falling within a fairly constant range over time: accounting for 38.5 percent of land sales in the Kangxi period, twenty-one percent in the Yongzheng era, thirty-four percent in the Qianlong era, and 35.3 percent in the Jiaqing era (in Fang et al. 2000, 1609–1610, table 4.38). The lowest percentage of land sales to relatives was in Hubei and Zhili, with about sixteen percent. The highest rates were in Guangdong, Fujian, and Shanxi with between forty-five to 47.5 percent of sales going to relatives.

11. John Henry Gray wrote in 1878 of the practice in China more generally: "The

person to whom the property belongs must make an offer of it to his father, or to the next of kin, in the event of his father being deceased or declining to purchase. Should all members of his family—the list ending with cousins—be indisposed, or unable to buy the estate, it is then offered for sale to others" (2002, vol. 2, 108–109). While George Jamieson (1921) noted in his examination of Chinese property that by the twentieth century the "right of first purchase" was rarely honored, he also observed that "On the occasion of a sale a score or more of cousins and relatives may turn up all claiming to be interested in the land, and the consent of all of them may be required to give a valid title" (101, 103).

12. In the survey of several individual villages, Japanese investigators found that in Dadaosanhezitun in Heilongjiang, peasants related that there had been cases of nonvillagers whose attempt to buy land was preempted by fellow villagers or kinsmen, even when the village outsider had offered twice the money of the fellow villager or kinsman (MTK 1939, 128); the same surveyors found that in the village of Dayingzi in Jilin the "right of first purchase" was particularly robust (MTK 1939, 107).

13. Wong's claims vis-à-vis some areas of western Europe are clearly disputable. Indeed, it appears that, like late imperial China, the attachment of the French peasantry to their land remained a major barrier to urban and industrial development well into the nineteenth century. Consequently, French industrialization came later and was slower getting off the ground once it began (see LeRoy Ladurie 1976, 76–83, 95–97; 1987, 337–338; Grantham 1978; O'Brien and Keyder 1978, 138, 172–173; Kindleberger 1964, 217, 225–238). Yet, it is clear that in early modern England the dispossession of peasantry (their eradication as a class)—their separation from the land—constituted a significant break in that country's social formation, one that marked off subsequent English developments from both continental Europe and China (Brenner 1985b [1982]; Brenner and Isett 2002, 2003; Chambers 1972, 38–39, table 2; Lindert 1980, 702–704, table 3, 705; O'Brien and Keyder 1978, 132).

14. On the prevalence of the conditional sale see Jamieson (1921, 99–100), Schurmann (1956, 515–516), Yang (1988, 42), Zhou and Xie (1986, 44), Perdue (1987, 138–139), Huang (2001, 71–98).

15. The terms *dian*-maker (for the conditional seller) and *dian*-holder (for the purchaser of the *dian*) are taken from the usage of Chinese jurists who wrote in English in the twentieth century (see McAleavy 1958, 403 n 1).

16. The few historical anecdotes of peasants making a living solely by manufacturing are of landless widows engaged in spinning and weaving (Shih 1992, 125–130). As Susan Mann (1997) shows, these individuals were singled out for praise by members of the literati for their iconic attempts to raise their children while mirroring Confucian ideals of feminine virtue of which "women's handiwork was a normative value" (148, 162, 166). The fact that they were iconic figures deployed as discursive strategies in efforts to demonstrate the orthodox virtues of localities raises suspicion of how representative such examples were (148–149).

17. Thomas Buoye (2000) challenges the notion that the conditional sale was used by peasants desperate to stave off landlessness (94–95). He argues instead that because economic opportunities outside agriculture were sufficiently numerous peasants could use the conditional sale to raise capital for such things as business ventures. Yet he finds only seven examples of *dian*-makers going off to start up a business among his fifty-six

"redemption and sales" homicide cases (94, table 4.). He seeks to explain away the low number of findings by arguing that those who conditionally sold their land for startup capital were less likely to be involved in homicides because they departed their villages after the sale (97–100, 102–104). But this would only explain the low number of such examples if it were *also* the case that these same individuals were unlikely to return home to redeem the land or to collect the *zhaotie*. This is hard to imagine, since the *zhaotie* could be as much as eighty percent the value of the land. Indeed, if the *zhaotie* were unimportant, and the seller was in fact moving into business, why not sell the land outright, collect the full value of the land, and be gone? One would in fact expect the *dian*-maker to return (or send a representative) either to buy back the land or to collect the *zhaotie*, particularly if they had any business acumen (Buoye 2004, 110). In the end, Buoye's perspective is necessarily limited by his dependency on homicide cases. Those who have mined the local archive collections of civil disputes which constitute the bulk of court matters handled by local magistrates, and therefore represent the full spectrum of property disputes, have found that the *dian*-maker was typically a poor peasant hanging onto his land and livelihood through the best possible means (Huang 1996, 36–39; Macauley 1998, 230).

18. Myron Cohen (2004) rightly argues that peasants who sold their land were often in "bad shape" and under "ordinary circumstances" those families selling their land were considered to be "going down socially;" conversely, those who purchased land were considered "ascendant" (cf. Huang 2001, 81 for a similar view.) Cohen argues that the circumstances in which land was sold does not testify to a sentimental attachment to land on the peasant's part, but the "importance of land as a dependable source of income in the rather insecure world of late imperial China" (48). Cohen erroneously, I believe, attributes a "sentimentalist" vision of peasant attachment to land to Philip Huang (2001), when Huang's actual position is that peasant attachment to land was largely dictated by their need to secure subsistence through farming and that normative barriers to sales were for the most part operational at the level of the state (Huang 2001, 81; Huang 1990, 106–108).

19. Young males were typically kept under patriarchal and clan authority as sources of both cheap labor and muscle to protect household and lineage wealth (Mazumdar 1998, 221–223; Lambley 1990; Hsiao 1960, 366–367; Meskill 1979, 54, 210).

20. Huang also notes that he found not a single instance of the application of the 1730 statute among his civil dispute cases for Baxian, Dan-Xin, and Baodi counties (Huang 2001, 92). McAleavy (1958) wrote: "To the last days of the Chinese Empire it was observed that the institution carried on as before [the 1730 and 1753 edicts], and the *dian*-holder's right of redemption enduring without limit of time. . . . Nor did Republican legislation have any stronger influence on custom" (411; cf. TS 1910, 678–679).

21. Ling Chou, a mid-eighteenth-century Qing judicial commissioner in Jiangxi, observed husbands requesting the *zhaojia* on sold wives (Ling 2002, 135). The fact that wife-selling was illegal under the Qing Code meant that the practice of selling wives and demanding *zhaojia* payments on wives sold took on the sort of surreptitious and subterranean character found in the illegal sale to commoners of banner and manorial lands in Manchuria.

22. Li Wenzhi (1993, 512) provides no evidence for his assertion that the 1730 regula-

tion had any impact on either the *zhaotie* or the *zhaojia*. Indeed, in his description of the *zhaojia*, Li presents court records from across the eighteenth century showing that in fact the *zhaojia* continued to be practiced in Hunan (1741), Yunnan (1764), and Zhejiang (1781).

23. For twentieth-century examples of the multiple *zhaojia* see the Republican government's survey of local customs (MS 2000). For instance, see pages 498–499 (Shanxi), 555–556, 560 (Anhui), 626 (Fujian), 645, 672 (Hubei), 699–700 (Hunan). For the geographic range of the practice in the Qing, in addition to Yang (1988), see Macauley (1998, 228–245), Perdue (1987, 138–139), Kishimoto (1997, 266–267), Liang (1996, 107–110), and Huang (2001, 90–91).

24. In principle, the *zhaojia* was also applicable against land sold outright, but I have seen no examples of this in Manchuria because the outright sale was so rare.

25. Japanese surveys of Manchuria show that the *zhaojia* was customarily recognized. For instance, a 1937 survey of property rights conducted as part of a general survey of more than six hundred households found that the *zhaojia* was practiced in all localities (TKK 1937, 248–249). Similarly, a 1939 survey of property relations in six villages showed that in the four villages where there was evidence of the conditional sale the *dian*-maker had the right to request and receive the *zhaojia* (MTK 1939, 31, 68, 103, 158). In the reports on the other two villages no mention was made of whether the *zhaojia* was practiced.

26. McAleavy (1958, 407) states that the *dian*-holder did not have to ask the *dian*-maker for his consent to sub-*dian*.

27. See Chapter 5, note 11 for an explanation of "strings" of cash.

28. The case went to trial after Li Hongyou took the contract but failed to pay the full *zhaojia* amount. Dong killed Li during an argument over the outstanding sum.

29. Thus, as LeRoy Ladurie demonstrates, commercial expansion in sixteenth- and seventeenth-century France was accompanied not with the weakening of peasant and communal rights to land but followed upon the reassertion of more powerful peasant and communal rights (Ladurie 1987, 53–60, 76–82, 117–135; 1976, 98–110, 114–119; see also Brenner 1985b [1982], 284–291, 302–305).

30. The Royal Asiatic Society report on China's land system was compiled by Jamieson (1888) on the basis of reports submitted to him by missionaries working in various parts of China. Jamieson asked these men to answer a short list of questions regarding how land was held and exchanged in their environs. The study is often overlooked by historians of legal and customary law in China, yet it is an illuminating account of property in the Qing.

31. The best-known examples of the Qing assault on gentry power were the infamous tax arrears trials of the early 1660s in which the state prosecuted powerful Jiangnan gentry households that had failed to pay the land tax in its efforts to smash their power, weaken their grip on local society, and even transfer their properties to peasants (Kessler 1976, 34–39).

32. Though the wording of the prohibition spoke only of "bannerland," it also applied to manorial lands. We know this from the court records. This fact looks back to the Qing practice of affiliating all serfs and manor land to the banner of the aristocratic lord who possessed them.

Chapter 5

1. Also see Huang (1985, 322–323, 327) and Xu (1998a, 30–31, tables 2-1 and 2-2).

2. With rising population density, peasants on the north China plain may also have tried to limit the number of children born and to delay the division of household property. Though there is evidence of these practices in China's northeast, there is little evidence for north China (Wakefield 1998, 49, table 4, 162–165).

3. Pierre-Etienne Will cites a 1703 edict to the effect that smallholding peasants in Shandong barely had enough to eat in good years. When famine struck they could only choose between "fleeing" and "dying on the spot" (Will 1990, 66).

4. Famines were reported in 1679–1680, 1701, 1716, 1724–1725, 1737, 1743–1744, 1747, 1748–1749, 1750–1751, 1762, 1801, 1806–1807, 1809, 1823, 1836–1837, 1847, 1855–1856, 1859, and 1877 (Edmonds 1985, 75; Katō 1953a, 597–601; Lu 1987, 27–31; Sudō 1972a, 440–453; Zhu 1990, 80–81).

5. During the massive famine of 1876–79, for instance, 900,000 migrants arrived in Fengtian each year from villages between Shanxi and Shandong provinces, though many of these famine victims returned home after the famine receded (Gottschang and Lary 2000, 47).

6. For north China, I use data compiled by Huang (1985, 323–326, see appendix B, table B.1 and appendix C, table C.1).

7. See Appendix A in this book for an explanation of how these numbers were derived.

8. Presumably, the "forcing of payments" refers to the practice of demanding payments in addition to the original purchase price known as *zhaojia* (see below and Chapter 4).

9. For commentary on related matters, see the following of Fujun's memorials located in the palace archive collection (HZ 1804.6.22, 1804.6.28, 1805.2.20, 1805.7.28).

10. This was not the first time a Nuomizhuang bailiff had been dismissed for failing to fulfill his duties. When the estate was first created by the Kangxi emperor, the title of bailiff was granted to a family surnamed Xing. In 1691, however, the Ma family assumed the office, and the Xing family was demoted to the status of serfs on the estate. The precise cause for this transfer of the office is not stated in the court records (LPA 1815, 25944).

11. A "string of cash" (*diao*) was a commonly used unit of payment. One string nominally bound together one thousand copper coins, each of which had a hole in the center through which the string could pass and thereby bind the coins in a bundle. One thousand copper coins was approximately equal to one silver ounce or *tael* circa 1800, though the rate of exchange between copper and silver varied by place and time depending on usage and amounts in circulation.

12. In 1792 Zhou Bi died and his son Zhou Shixun became bailiff. Though not stated, Zhou Shixun had apparently died in the intervening years between Ma Jin's initial suit, brought in 1799, and Mrs. Zhou's plaint of 1815. Zhou Shixun's son Zhou Lin had subsequently taken on the post of bailiff of Nuomizhuang.

13. According to Mrs. Zhou's plaint, in 1814 serfs were called on to pay more than five hundred strings of cash per household for the wedding of bailiff Ma Jin. According to the plaint, the bailiff supposedly threatened to confiscate the land of any serf who failed to make the payment. One serf, Wang Er, refused to pay. When Bailiff Ma Jin

moved to take his land, a suit was brought and Ma Jin was told by the local magistrate to desist. According to Mrs. Zhou, despite the order, Ma Jin persisted and in the tenth month of 1815 again demanded an extra four hundred strings of cash from every serf (LPA 1815, 24127). It was then that Mrs. Zhou brought suit.

14. At that time, Guo Ruisheng denied having ever paid to the Mas a deposit for the land or having loaned money using land as collateral: "it was absolutely not the case that [I] sold the land conditionally, nor did [I] use [mortgage] the land to borrow money" (*bing wu dianmai yazu zhidi jieqian*) (LPA 1815, 26008).

15. For a description of the practice of sentencing on the greater crime, see Bodde and Morris (1967).

16. For instance, overseeing the imperial manors in Fengtian there were nine prompters (*cuiling*) and two prompter-captains (*cuizhang*) assigned to the Office of Accounts of the Shengjing Imperial Household Department, and three prompters assigned to the Jinzhou Imperial Household Department (Diao 1993, 66–68).

17. The practice of keeping two accounts of illegal land sales in Manchuria appears similar in some interesting ways to the practice common among peasants in China Proper of circulating both "white" and "red" deeds, a practice that evolved as a means of evading the land tax. Peasants who did not wish to pay the transfer fee to the state would exchange land using titles known as "white deeds" (*baiqi*), so named because the paper did not bear the official stamp that was applied in red ink when the transfer fee was paid. Peasants who paid the transfer fee held what were called "red deeds," so named because they bore the state's imprint in red ink. The state was under no obligation to recognize "white" deeds as evidence of property claims (Osborne 2004, 151–152), though it often did. When the use of white deeds was uncovered, the state certainly required that their holders exchange them for red deeds, bearing an official stamp, thereby registering the land for taxation. The state might even demand back-payment of taxes and slap on a fine (Jing 1994, 67; also, see Perdue 1987, 137). The Manchurian practice of hiding the sale of Qing lands to commoners was different in both intent and appearance. First, the "white" deed did not conceal an illegal sale of land, it simply evaded the transfer fee. Second, the language of the "white" deed did not hide the fact that the land was sold by misrepresenting the transaction as something other than a sale. What is similar about the two practices is what stood behind them, however—the belief that communities could under most conditions be expected to handle and resolve disputes so that recourse to the state was unlikely.

18. Bannermen in Manchuria were permitted to rent some land to commoners for a period of three years. The three-year limitation was imposed in 1769 (Diao 1993, 140; Yi 1993, 216). The goal of the three-year limitation was to make the permanent transfer of bannerland to commoners more difficult. First, the three-year limit ensured that commoners could not acquire permanent tenancy through purchases, as was common practice in Qing China Proper (Yang 1988, 94). Second, limiting tenancy to three years made it more difficult for peasants to disguise land sales as leaseholds. Commoners who had worked manor land or bannerland in Manchuria for more than three years had broken the law and this required official investigation. The intent of the new regulation was in part to make it easier for magistrates to spot conditional sales which were being misrepresented as leaseholds—any Han commoner who had worked the same fields for more than three years was now suspected of having in fact purchased the land—and in

part to make it impossible for tenants to obtain permanent rights to the land through the payment of large deposits.

19. In this instance, the seller of the land, serf Su Yi's father, heard the Shengjing Imperial Household Department was conducting a general survey; fearing he would be caught, he reported the illegal sale to local officials.

20. By the eighteenth century, it was common for landlords to require a deposit of some sort from their tenants, though this was more likely to be the case when a tenant bought the right of permanent tenancy (on use of rental deposits to secure leaseholds see Yang [1988, 96–97]). As we saw in the case of Mrs. Ma discussed earlier, for the savvier magistrates stationed in the northeast, the fact that an unusually large deposit had been paid was often a signal that either the land was illegally sold or the leasehold arrangement was permanent.

21. The land deed (i.e., the land sale contract) was in late imperial China the universal means for demonstrating possession of land. It was required to demonstrate ownership when selling land or dividing it among sons, to prove ownership to a village mediator, and to establish ownership in the courts. On Qing land contracts, see Hamashita (1986).

22. Chang Chung-li (1955) only provided numbers for Fengtian. Given that pre-Taiping the vast majority of Manchuria's population lived in Fengtian, and that this remained the case until 1900, Chang's estimate of total Fengtian gentry can be taken as a rough estimate of the total Manchurian gentry. Adding degree-holders from the banner household category would have little impact on the relative number. The total number of degree-holders from the entire eight banners regardless of their residency was 3,219 and 4,325 pre- and post-Taiping (164, table 32). Chang estimates that Fengtian's total gentry population including family members was 10,455 and 24,160 before and after the Taiping (164, table 32), at a time when the northeast's population was three and eight million respectively (Appendix A). Whereas empire-wide the gentry and their families were 1.3 and 1.9 percent of the population for these two periods, they were less than one-tenth of one percent of the population of the northeast, even after taking into account only that proportion living in Fengtian.

23. Liu was clearly losing money in this arrangement, the total rent amounting to 240 *diao* over six years compared to a debt of 280. The records provide no clues as to why Liu would settle for this arrangement. We know that Liu was a farmer himself, since the case records tell us he employed farmhands to assist him in working his own holding. But, perhaps together his holding and the sixty *mu* from Zhang was more than he could manage without having to hire more hands, a project he was unwilling to undertake.

24. Pierre Bourdieu (1977) developed the notion of "social capital" to describe a form of prestige or social standing that he argues moved independently of the circuits of capital and yet can be equally important in the reproduction of class and status to the extent that it is fungible.

25. Some villages in China had "village regulations" (*xiang gui*) which were usually written up by local gentry and then approved by the magistrate. But they did not constitute a body of law per se, but rather an informal set of rules and standards of behavior (Hsiao 1960, 292–293).

26. On the role of mediators in the Chinese village more generally, see Yang (1988, 26–27, 59–71), Liang (1996, 120–126), Duara (1988, 94, 181–191), and Huang (1996, 51–74).

27. Scholars Yi Baozhong (1993) and Diao Shuren (1993) speak only of the policy of buying back bannerland. But, it is clear that the Qianlong policy of redeeming land extended to manor land as well. This is evident in the court records that commonly refer to manor land that the state had redeemed after it was found to have been *min dian qidi* (see the case of Su Chenggui above). A memorial filed in 1773 on the amount of land redeemed, and its cost to the state, includes reports of both bannerland and manor land (HZ 1773. 8.30).

28. Yi Baozhong provides a lower figure of 720,000 *mu* of illegally sold land uncovered by the regional government in 1770, and 970,000 *mu* in the mid-Qianlong period (Yi 1993, 216). There is no feasible means to reconcile the disparities between his source and the original memorial. I am inclined to follow the official memorial.

29. Under the Qing tax code, land that was opened from wasteland and converted to arable land was termed *shengke di*. Literally, this meant "raising to the rank," or the land had been defined as taxable (Jamieson 1921, 104).

30. The burden proved too great for some commoners, however, and in 1799 the penalty tax rate was lowered in some cases, though not all, to three *fen*, in line with the highest tax rate on red-registry commoner and surfeit bannerland (Yi 1993, 251).

31. Standard references have no biographical information on Suonuomucejun, but do list him as Shengjing Military Governor for the years 1780–1782 and member of the Manchu Bordered Yellow Banner. Some sources give his name as Suonuomuceleng, but others give his name as Suonuomucejun, which is the name also attached to his memorials.

32. I was unable to locate the original memorial outlining the policy in the First Historical Archives in Beijing.

33. Thus, in a memorial dated the twentieth day of the second month, 1805, Duo Qing wrote, "[p]reviously, there were frequent imperial commands ordering that bannermen and commoners come forth to report [their land]. However, those that reported were few. As a result, another set of regulations were authorized and it was broadcasted clearly what was beneficial and what was harmful. Now, all those who have yet to come forth and register will naturally do so and there will be no deceit" (HZ 1805, 2.20).

34. There are other examples of state reluctance to remove illegal settlers and squatters from land that had been planted (LPA 1801, 24052; Isett 2004, 163).

35. Something along these lines became official policy in the Jiaqing era. In an effort to provide illegal commoner settlers the wherewithal to return home, under Jiaqing the state allowed commoners caught illegally possessing surfeit land (bannerland that was not part of a banner household's original land grant) to continue cultivating rent- and tax-free for three years. After this, they were required to return the surfeit land to the state and return home. Any red-registry land (a banner household's original land grant) had to be relinquished immediately.

36. Since he was a serf of the imperial household's Plain Yellow Banner, his case was jointly handled by the Shengjing Imperial Household Department, which managed the affairs of the imperial household, and the Shengjing Board of Revenue's Farmland Department, which investigated and adjudicated land disputes involving those attached to bannerland (LPA 1786, 8499, 8508, 8512).

37. Thus, for instance, Partha Chatterjee (1983) suggests that "in all political formations in which there exists an institutionalized sphere of class domination based ulti-

mately on the direct superiority of physical force, it is in constant battle against subordinate forces seeking to assert (perhaps reassert) an alternative mode of power and authority based on the *notion* of the community" (emphasis added, 375). By the "notion of the community," Chatterjee means a prior state or condition, whether real or simply an idea of a more desirable state of existence, in which peasants confronted production on their own, not yet facing off with an expropriating power. It is a condition, he argues, peasants seek to reassert in one form or another after the arrival of interlopers. Chatterjee suggests peasants' desire for a return to this prior state of existence is most vociferously articulated in the language of millenarianism, but is also present in day-to-day customary practices. Chatterjee is aware that peasants may back authoritarian figures in their quest for a return (figurative or real) to this prior mode of social organization.

38. John Shepherd (1993) finds a similar pattern in eighteenth-century Taiwan. To protect aborigine livelihood and to reduce interethnic tensions between settlers and aborigines, the Qing state tried to limit Han settlement by demarcating boundaries that defined the limits of legal settlement. Illegal settlement nevertheless proceeded apace and local officials had to adjust constantly to the changing situation on the ground by redrawing the boundaries (186). This redrawing of the boundaries did not signal an end to the state's desire to control settlement, but rather was an expedient administrative adjustment.

39. Briefly stated, the above discussed case of Su Yi came to light when serf Su Yi's uncle brought a false lawsuit against Chen Jun and his brother accusing them of being his scofflaw tenants and demanding they return the land. The uncle, Su Chenggui, had been convinced to bring the false suit by Bailiff Gu after the Chens had rebuffed Gu's request for a loan. The Bailiff persuaded Chenggui that if he brought the lawsuit, the Chens would return the land to him rather than risk getting caught for having illegally purchased manor land. At first the plot succeeded, and the Chens gave the land to Chenggui. But the *yamen* decided to investigate matters further and thereupon the full account of how the Chens came into possession of the manor land was brought to light. For more on this case, see Isett (2004, 155–158).

Chapter 6

1. The assertion that there was a rise in large-scale farmers hiring wage labor in the Qing is based upon an increase in the number of wage workers who appear in homicide records (Li 1957; Jing and Luo 1978). There may have been less of a dramatic increase in the employment of wage labor between the Ming and Qing than is argued, however. Chao Kang (1986) has pointed out that the rise in the number of cases reflected a procedural change in the way cases were handled by the Board of Punishment. Chao states that Yongzheng legal reforms required that the Board review all cases involving wage laborers during the Autumn Assizes, whereas this had not been the case previously (146). The shift has to do with the Yongzheng reinterpretation of the 1588 *gugongren* statute, which is discussed below.

2. See Jing and Luo (1978). For recent statements on the demise of servile agricultural labor see Xu Tan (in Fang et al. 2000, 1853–1907), Li Wenzhi (1993, 30), and Thomas Buoye (2000, 62–66).

3. Ordinary banner soldiers and bailiffs could legally own slaves, though it is impossible to gauge with any accuracy how many did. Mark Elliott (2001, 228, 462 n 97),

citing the work of others, has suggested that in the pre-Conquest and earliest days of the Qing, banner soldiers had acquired perhaps millions of Han slaves. There is little evidence, however, that after receiving their land grants in Zhili and Manchuria either rusticated bannermen or bailiffs employed slave labor on a significant scale. Wang Zhonghan (1990, 76–77) believes—and I find no reason to fault him—that the great majority of rusticated banner households in the Qing worked their land with household labor. Only a small minority, he believes, owned slaves. Wang also suggests that at the time of the founding of the Qing dynasty banner households that held slaves were in the minority.

4. In his study of legal status in the Qing, Jing Junjian is at pains to show that even as the Qing legal system increasingly narrowed the range of those wage laborers who might be defined as *gugongren*, it continued to recognize the sociolegal status of household bondservants such as bailiffs, slaves, and the large number of estate serfs attached to the households of the Qing aristocracy and the imperial family (Jing, 1993).

5. I wish to thank Matthew Sommer for making the record of the Chen case available to me (Sommer 2000, 96).

6. The arguments of Liu and Xu echo in fundamental ways Paul Sweezy's (1976) classic account of the demise of serfdom/feudalism and the transition to capitalism in England.

7. In China, the eleventh and twelfth centuries too witnessed an expansion of the market and the concomitant spread of bonded tenants (*dianpu*). Not only were bonded tenants more common to the Song dynasty (960–1279) than the preceding Tang (618–907), but their treatment at the hands of their masters appears to have deteriorated over time and with more intensive commercial development (Elvin 1973, 71–80).

8. Also see Thomas Buoye (2000, 62–66). Buoye gives equal weight to commercial developments and class conflict, as do Li Wenzhi (1993, 30) and Xu Tan (in Fang et al. 2000), though they seem to see commerce and trade as the triggers for social and class conflicts. The arguments of Li and Xu are part of a long-standing debate in Marxist historiography over the relative roles in determining historical change of class relations and forces of production. The argument here differs to the extent that I argue the market in labor was a necessary but wholly insufficient condition for determining the direction of change in production relations.

9. The Qing had inherited the Ming tax system but soon began to reform it by eliminating the head or poll tax by merging it into the land tax. With the reforms, landowners provided just over seventy percent of tax revenue to the state down to the end of the eighteenth century (Wang 1973, 80). The merging of the head or poll tax and into the land tax (*tanding rudi*) created the so-called land-head (*diding*) tax. The reform was implemented with significant regional variation so that it was not until the end of the eighteenth century that most of China was covered. In some parts of China the two taxes had already been merged under the Ming Single-Whip reforms (*yitiao bianfa*).

10. Four recently published books have been central to this revision: see Evelyn Rawski (1998), Pamela Crossley (1999), Edward Rhoads (2000), Mark Elliott (2001).

11. These include the records of homicide cases from the First National Archives' *xingke tiben* collection; cases from the Liaoning Provincial Archives' Shengjing Imperial Household Department, as well as the *Ming-Qing dang'an* collection compiled by Zhang Weiren.

12. The distinction between death by strangulation after the assizes and death by de-

capitation after the assizes was based on the severity of the crime. Death by strangulation denoted a capital offense of less severity than death by decapitation. There were five degrees of punishment under the death penalty: starting with the lowest degree, they were strangulation after the assizes, decapitation after the assizes, immediate strangulation, immediate decapitation, and death by slicing (Bodde and Morris 1967, 104, 133–134). Bodde and Morris note that death by strangulation was less severe for socioreligious reasons: "[a]ccording to the tenets of Chinese filial piety, one's body is not one's own property, but a bequest from his parents. To mutilate one's body, therefore, or allow it to be mutilated, is to be unfilial" (92).

13. It would seem that developments in rural Manchuria were quite different from those outlined in Mark Elliott's (2001) account of social developments in the banner populations garrisoned in China Proper. In the garrison cities, Elliott finds that separation and status distinctions that secured for bannermen a unique ethnic identity were maintained (219–225, 230–232).

14. Whereas the emphasis on the transformative and progressive implications of the emergence of the large-scale farming employing wage labor is well placed, comparatively speaking Chinese developments did not look anything like England's. There, the supersession of small farms and the emergence of large ones made a critical contribution to the growth of labor productivity, especially in basic food production (Brenner 1985b [1982], 299–317; Brenner and Isett 2002, 626–627). First, larger farms eliminated the disguised unemployment that had held back England's medieval agriculture. Second, the increase in the size of farms, which continued to grow throughout the eighteenth and nineteenth centuries, reaching unprecedented levels for the early modern era, allowed for the greater use of wage labor and, by this means, could better adjust labor requirements to productive need, seasonal or otherwise (Allen 1992, 218–227; Overton 1996, 127–128).

15. Most recently, Xu Tan revives and develops the thesis of capitalist sprouts in her discussion of the managerial landlord in the edited three-volume study of China's Qing economy. However, whereas for Jing and Luo the emphasis was on the emergence of large-scale, commercial farmers, Xu places more emphasis on the development of wage labor as the critical signal of the emergence of capitalist property relations (Xu Tan in Fang et al. 2000, 1864–1907, especially 1885). Also see Liu Kexiang (1994, 1995), who makes the case for the emergence of managerial farming—by which he means large-scale commercial farming employing wage labor—in the late Qing and early Republican periods. Liu (1994, 1–3, 5–7) argues that managerial farming developed not during the early and mid-Qing but after the Sino-Japanese War and did so in response to developments in urban-based industrialization.

16. Whereas in the Jing and Luo (1956, 1978) account of north China the typical managerial farm was upwards of a thousand *mu*, in his introduction to the English translation of Jing and Luo, Endymion Wilkinson (in Jing and Luo 1978, 17) has shown most of the land (eighty percent) held by the biggest landowners in large estates was in fact rented out by their owners to tenants. Moreover, Philip Huang (1985, 97, 172–174, 177) has shown the typical large holding managed by its owner using wage labor was between one hundred and two hundred *mu*, since anything larger was too unwieldy to supervise effectively. Huang points out that of Jing and Luo's big landlords, those with two hundred *mu* or less on average farmed close to ninety percent of their land compared to

the twenty-one percent of their entire sample. Chao Kang (1983, 143) suggests the "cut off size" was five hundred *mu*: he points out that eighty percent of Jing and Luo's big landowners supervised farming on less than five hundred *mu* (eighty-three acres). Lastly, recent historical work suggests that the percentage of wage labor fully separated from the land in north China was very low, somewhere between eight and just under thirteen percent (Fang et al. 2000, 1863).

17. Yi Baozhong (1993) dates the emergence of large-holding yeoman farmers to the late Qing and Liu Kexiang (1995) to the last decades of the Qing and early twentieth century.

18. Lee and Campbell (1997, 110, table 6.1) find that on average the *largest* of the complex households ("multiple family households") in Daoyi for the period 1792–1873 had seven to thirteen people (actual numbers were 7.2 to 12.5). The average size of all households was 5.9 persons.

19. Robert Lee (1970, 74–76) has shown that the principal administrative goal of the sovereign was to prevent the emergence of a local power elite that might challenge ruling-house claims of hegemony. His argument focuses on how the sovereign divided administrative powers of Manchurian authorities and ensured their financial dependency upon Beijing as ways to preclude such developments. However, the same concerns are clearly evident in how the land system was constructed and policed.

20. The survey covered seventeen north Manchuria villages, a total of 681 households and 4,961 persons. Of the 1,550 who worked in agriculture 258 worked as "year laborers" and were therefore fully dependent upon wages, or five percent of the entire and sixteen percent of the working agricultural population (TKK 1937, 17–18, table 7).

21. Joseph Esherick estimates that in the 1930s fully dispossessed peasants were no more than 10 percent of China's *entire* rural population, and perhaps as low as 8 percent. Esherick's figure is very close to Xu Tan's estimate of 8 to 12.5 percent for the north China plain in the Qing (Esherick 1981, 402; Fang et al. 2000, 1863). Sucheta Mazumdar (1998, 237) finds that in the 1930s and 1940s, 8 percent of the population in the Pearl River delta, less than 5 percent in the Yangzi delta, and 12.5 percent on the north China plain were fully dependent upon wage labor.

22. The proportion of fully market-dependent peasants in Manchuria in the 1930s was indeed comparable to (and perhaps even lower than) that of north China in the Qing, where land was by comparison far more scarce. Xu Tan, for instance, suggests that on the north China plain landless laborers accounted for perhaps eight to 12.5 percent of the entire population, and presumably a higher proportion still of those who labored in the fields (Fang et al. 2000, 1863). She also argues that for China in general day and month laborers outnumbered year laborers in the high Qing (1857).

23. At this level of labor intensity, the same source provides that yields were only between 0.4 and 0.5 *shi* of millet per *mu in a good year* (Saying'e 1960, 191; also see the *Shuangchengbao tuntian jilue* (*Plans for the military colony of Shuangchengbao*) (Li 1990, 165]). Presumably in an average year the yield was less than 0.4 *shi* per *mu*.

24. Yu Bangcai resembles the Xias of Nanyangbao, a small village outside Changchun. According to interviews conducted in 1994, in the 1930s the Xias were large-holding tenants, renting five hundred *mu* (just over eighty acres) of land in the neighboring village of Liujiatun. The Xia household hired two laborers, surnamed Chen and An, who worked for them for a total of five years each. Both laborers came to the Xia family ask-

ing for employment and both were fellow villagers from Nanyangbao. Each year, their contracts began in the spring and ended in the winter (from the twentieth day of the first month to the twentieth day of the last month) (Xia Deyi interview 1994; Xia Dianyou, interview 1994).

25. Data provided by Adachi Kinnosuke show that the average Fengtian (south Manchuria) farm was forty *mu* in 1917, based on Japanese surveys of the time (Adachi 1925, 142, 144). The average holding a decade earlier, at the time of the 1909 Fengtian survey, was probably not much greater.

26. According to the case record Zhang beat his laborer to death when the two men got into an argument. Zhang and laborer Cai were planting beans on the hillside. Zhang guided the plough as Cai walked behind planting. Zhang complained that Cai was not planting straight. Cai got angry and threw the seed basket at Zhang. Zhang struck back and beat Cai with a stick and, three days later, Cai died.

27. Shi hired laborer Wang at the beginning of the sixth month. On the third day, Shi's donkey went astray. He told Wang to look for it but Wang refused, saying the animal would find its own way home. When it did not return the next day, Shi beat Wang, who then died from his wounds.

28. Some of these households lived as far away as north China and every spring sent young males by foot to the northeast where they worked as month, day, and year laborers before returning home with their wages (Amagai 1969, 734–739). Amagai Kenzaburō erroneously suggests that 100,000 migrant laborers made their way from Shandong to Fengtian every spring in early eighteenth century. This number is, however, a misreading of the Kangxi emperor's recollections of a recent journey through south Manchuria. Kangxi did speak of seeing perhaps 100,000 Shandong-ese in Fengtian but he is clearly referring to recent settlers as well as migratory labor.

29. The typical holding by the 1930s was sixty-six *mu* and the typical household had the equivalent of three adult laborers working the land (Myers 1976, 599).

30. The only other place in western Europe where one witnesses rising labor productivity in agriculture in the early modern period is the Netherlands (Allen 2000; de Vries and van der Woude 1997).

31. See note 21.

32. In mid-sixteenth-century France, for example, in the aftermath of the Black Death, a tiny minority of peasants (what LeRoy Ladurie calls "*kulaks*") held holdings as large as fifty to seventy-five acres (300–450 *mu*); but the vast majority held less than forty acres (120 *mu*) and most of these held less than five (30 *mu*) (LeRoy Ladurie 1987, 184).

33. In an analogous way, proto-industrial production developed alongside farming in large parts of the early modern world as a means of rounding out household incomes at a time when land-labor ratios were particularly low. In those instances, peasants were pushed by Malthusian pressures into taking up low-wage household manufacturing even if they would have preferred to stay in food production. They did so, however, because proto-industrial or handicraft production provided them with extra income that ironically tightened their grip on the land, thereby delaying their full separation from the means of subsistence (Kriedte et al. 1981, 39, 41, 100).

Chapter 7

1. Through close analysis of land contracts and ethnographic surveys, Shimizu Kinjirō (1945) demonstrates the north China origin of Manchuria's property system. My analysis of legal cases suggests the same, when compared with various sources on property systems in north China (e.g., Johnston 1986; MS 2000).

2. This Smithian interpretation of China's late imperial economy includes a number of conceptually related works, each of which takes the market to be both the source of the economy's dynamism and the propellant of economic growth. Those studies include works by Evelyn Rawski (1972), Loren Brandt (1989), R. Bin Wong (1997), Li Bozhong (1998), and Kenneth Pomeranz (2000).

3. A number of scholars have applied the neo-Malthusian paradigm to the late imperial period, including Dwight Perkins (1969), Mark Elvin (1973), and Chao Kang (1986). See the Conclusion for further discussion.

4. There were clearly cases when peasants could not secure their full array of food needs directly. Often, this was because their farms had become too small or because they had taken up farming on marginal lands unsuited to food production. In these cases, peasants were rendered dependent upon the market, and may even have been full specializers—i.e., producing a single item such as cotton cloth, sugar, tea, or lumber. But because they came to this end in the climate of a general pattern of declining labor productivity in food production, and therefore rising food prices, there was often no avenue for accumulation and improvement in ways that would have raised their incomes over the short or medium term. In late imperial China, the typical example was the rural cotton spinner-weaver and the silk spinner. As labor productivity in agriculture fell over the late imperial period, the price of grain relative to cotton cloth and spun silk yarn rose. As a consequence, rural manufacturers had no choice but to take a smaller daily wage. They would of course have preferred to stay in grain production, but this was often not possible because of their small plots (Huang 1985, 1990; Brenner and Isett 2001, 2003).

5. A lack of detailed information on cropping patterns in the Qing requires that we rely heavily on twentieth-century data, though some Qing observations are illuminating.

6. A variety of rotations were practiced in the late nineteenth- and early twentieth-century Manchuria. Aside from those described by Yang Tonggui, Alexander Hosie, in the account of his tenure as British Consular General of Niuzhuang for the years 1894–1897 and 1899–1900, describes a three-course rotation of millet, beans, and either wheat, barley, or rice, which he explained was common to "large farms" (Hosie 1980, 180). This rotation is not very different from one in use in the early twentieth century; as described by observers, peasants rotated either millet, wheat, beans, and sorghum or sorghum, beans, and millet (Adachi 1925, 153; Wilm 1927, 1046–1048). Famed Japanese agricultural historian Amano Motonosuke, who worked as a researcher in the northeast before World War Two, noted a number of multi-course rotations that he surveyed in Manchuria. In Jilin province, for instance, he noted four different commonly employed rotations ranging from four-course to six-course rotations that included millet, sorghum, wheat, soybeans, barley, and tobacco. In Fengtian province, he mentions only two three-course rotations that combined millet, sorghum, wheat, soybeans, buckwheat, and wet rice in one form or another. Large farms throughout Manchuria, Amano noted,

often used a simple three-course rotation of sorghum, soybeans, and wheat (Amano 1932, 7).

7. For a discussion of the hardy and resistant qualities of millet and sorghum, see Charles Piper (1924, 300–301, 315–316). Millet and especially sorghum yield more calories than other basic food crops, while the stalks, roots, and chaff were used to meet basic household needs. Sorghum stalks were used as fuel and building materials, sorghum roots as fuel, and stalks and chaff from millet and sorghum to feed animals (Parker 1920, 54). Thus, while sorghum and millet provided greater security against inclement weather and the like, both crops dramatically reduced peasant reliance upon the market as well.

8. Conceptually and analytically, we can conceive of the larger holdings in Manchuria as "composite farms," after Richard Bushmann's (1998, 364–369) analysis of the farming economy of colonial north America. The composite farm was one in which the household expended as much labor as needed to secure directly as full a round of household subsistence needs as possible and only then ventured into commercial production. Thus, the composite farm secured household needs and provided for the descent of property to the next generation before risking any commercial undertakings that might otherwise undermine the household's social goals (365). In the highly commercial world of colonial north American, Bushmann argues, the composite farm flourished, propelling increases in production for subsistence alongside that for the market (368, 369). The composite farm was able to operate in this fashion only because it was relatively large. Bushmann recognizes some farms may be too small to produce items for the market and still have sufficient land left for subsistence production (364). Also see Russell Menard and John McCusker's (1985) survey of the north American colonial economy, particularly pages 297–301.

9. On household division of property among sons both in Qing law and custom see Shiga (1978, 113, 117, 135–136), Gates (1996, 91–93), Wakefield (1998, 155–184), Jing (1994, 54–59), Huang (1996, 25–28, 60–61).

10. It seems that in most peasant marriages very little capital was transferred to a daughter as she left for her husband's house . Marriage was for most peasants contracted with the purchase of the girl. Her parents might wish to save face by providing a dowry; but among peasants, dowries were usually lower in value than the cash received for the daughter (Gates 1996, 128–147; also see Sommer 2000, 176, 184–191 and 63 n 29). Among peasants, daughters-in-law were for all intents and purposes purchased.

11. James Lee and Cameron Campbell (1997, 119–120), for instance, in their examination of household formation and household division among the rusticated bannermen of Daoyi in Manchuria, have neither land records nor household-division records with which to analyze property redistribution.

12. Lee and Campbell (1997, 120) have evidence of one incidence of the "brother's share" in a 1956 household division contract. In that case, the elder son received twice as much land as his younger brother.

13. To the extent that Chinese and Manchurian peasants divided their land more or less equally among sons, they were well within the norm of other peasant societies, where partible inheritance had similar implications for capital accumulation and limits of peasant economic expansion. The classic expression of this is perhaps Emanuel LeRoy Ladurie's work on the French peasantry. In post-medieval France, LeRoy Ladurie shows, farms swiftly succumbed to what he termed morselization, fragmentation, and subdivision following a brief period of holding aggrandizement and engrossment that followed

in the wake of the demographic collapse associated with the Black Death (1976, 84–97; 1987, 161–162).

14. David Wakefield (1998, 208–209) argues that property division among sons, with its emphasis on egalitarian if not equal division of land, was a significant hindrance to the emergence of efficient and market-oriented farms, ensuring that even large, farming landowners saw their wealth dissipate over time.

15. Lee and Campbell (1997) write: "During the nineteenth century, the Malthusian trend of rising resource pressure . . . reduced the frequency of household division, and changed the conditions under which it could occur" (120).

16. The obverse was not necessarily true. While the wealthy were more likely to live in large and complex households, such households were not beyond the reach of the poor (Wolf 2005, 224).

17. Thirty-six *mu* is the generally cited figure for land granted in Fengtian. In Jilin and Heilongjiang, sixty *mu* was apportioned.

18. In the 1820s and 1830s a colony of rusticated bannermen from north China was resettled to Shuangchengbao as part of the efforts to relief poverty in the banner system. In all likely the grand patriarch of the Caiwobaotun (literally, the Cai fortified village) migrated to join those bannermen.

19. Unfortunately, the Japanese ethnographers do not provide given names for each member of the family, and instead assign a letter for each branch of the family and a number for the birth order.

20. It is standard practice among demographers, especially when making comparisons, to adjust the TMFR to take into account the average age of female marriage and other influencing factors (see Conclusion).

21. The TFR is a different measurement than the TMFR. Whereas the TMFR is not weighted for the proportion of women in the population who actually were married, the TFR is. The TFR is therefore lower than the TMFR.

22. Since Lee and Campbell provide only the TMFR for Daoyi we can only surmise as to the TFR. In the turbulent period 1929–1931, a nationwide TMFR of 6.2 was accompanied by a TFR of 5.5 with a population sample size of 50,000; in 1955 a TMFR of 6.2 had a corresponding TFR of 6.0 with a sample size of 300,000 (Lee and Wang 1999, 85, table 6.1).

23. That the population of Daoyi was rusticated bannermen perhaps made for the much earlier exposure to Malthusian pressures: the facts that the community was formed in the earliest days of the Qing by state command and individuals were prohibited from emigrating by banner regulations certainly made for a longer period of population expansion and fewer exits for excess population.

24. In his study of Jiangnan grain supply in the Qing, Wang Ye-chien suggests that forty percent of the household budget went toward essential nonfood costs (1989, 455 n 18).

25. Though Boserup posed her study as a counter to Malthus's, as we shall see, it in fact echoes in striking ways Malthus's own conclusions about how agriculturalists had managed to increase the population-carrying capacity of their lands before his day. Malthus himself pointed to labor intensification and changes in farming methods as the chief means by which some civilizations managed over time to support more people on the same amount of land (Malthus 1985, 77, 86–87).

26. Varying degrees of labor-intensive farming were still observable in the 1920s. In

a survey of the region, Paul Wilm (1927) describes three forms. The most labor-intensive were permanent farming using rotations and annual planting of the same crop. He also observed swidden and fallow farming in eastern Manchuria and Mongolia (1047).

27. In theory, peasants who moved from north China to Manchuria may have experienced a one-off improvement in the productivity of their labor as they took up more labor extensive farming methods, though that remains open to question given the reduced yields that accompanied this shift.

28. The short-fallow system as described by Adachi Kinnosuke (1925) closely resembled the medieval three-field system of northwest Europe. Under that three-field system, a peasant's holding was divided into three fields and every year two fields were planted while the third rested in fallow. Each year the fields were rotated so that within a three-year period each field was under crops for two full years and in fallow for one full year. More intensive and higher-yielding variants of the three-field system divided holdings into as many as twelve parts, thereby increasing total output by reducing the area in fallow at any one time (Campbell 1983). These more intensive variants, however, required greater attention to the maintenance of soil fertility and generally followed the introduction of green manure, the greater application of animal manure, better tillage, and more thorough weeding.

29. If half the land were planted year round and yields were 0.5 *shi*, then after deducting production costs (thirty percent), husking (ten to twelve percent), and essential nonfood expenditures (thirty percent), a family of four would have about 2.1 *shi* each, close to minimum subsistence. Production costs are taken from Table 7.3; extraction rates from Liu and Yeh (1965, 29, table 2). According to Wang Yeh-chien (1989, 437, 455 n 18), the cost of purchasing nonfood essentials took about forty percent of the total grain output.

30. Francesca Bray (1984) notes that given the choice peasants will increase output by extending the area they tend rather than apply more work. But, as land becomes scarce compared to labor, returns on land become much more important than returns on labor, forcing peasants to work harder for disproportionately smaller rises in output (132–133).

31. This is corroborated by the 1919 survey of Manchurian economic conditions conducted by China's Central Bank. Describing agriculture in the Qing, the investigation notes that little manure or other fertilizer was spread, leaving crops to grow "naturally" (DSD 1987, 98).

32. The outer limits of reported area of land worked by a single adult laborer using labor-intensive methods (including triennial spreading of manure, two to three rounds of weeding, and careful tillage) suggest one adult male peasant in the 1930s with a draft animal could farm as much as fifty to seventy *mu* and still attain average yields of the time. Data taken from the largest farms surveyed in twenty-two villages covered as part of a Manchuria-wide investigation of the farming economy suggest that a single adult male with a team of draft animals was capable of working as much as eighty *mu* in some instances, and sixty-plus *mu* is not uncommon (NJ-Series 1934–1936). For instance, in the village of Erdaohezitun, household number 14 had one adult laborer for every eighty *mu* of land. Household number 50 had one laborer for every sixty *mu*. In the village of Huangjiawobaotun, household 15 had one laborer for every fifty *mu*. Though atypical, total yields on the more labor-extensive holdings were comparable to those with more intensive applications of labor (Isett 1998, 338–339, table 8.5).

33. Typically, the *shang* was greater in size in Jilin and Heilongjiang, where it was equal to ten *mu*, than in Fengtian, where it was the equivalent of six *mu*.

34. In this case, Saying'e is probably citing Fujun's report of the establishment of a banner colony in Shuangchengbao in 1810s. According to Fujun, one male with one ox could work one hundred *mu*, but with a second draft ox and a hired year laborer he could work two hundred *mu* (Wang 1990, 21).

35. Historians of rural Europe have long noted the contradictory effects of population growth on the demand and supply of manure. As population grew leading up to and following the Black Death, grain production replaced animal raising (because grain production supported more people per unit of land than animal raising), thereby reducing the supply of manure just as peasants needed more manure to raise or maintain yields (de Vries 1976, 36).

36. Other humus-destroying crops include wheat, maize, and buckwheat, all planted in Manchuria.

37. Peasants who applied more overall fertilizer tended to apply a greater proportion in compost than manure, while those who applied less fertilizer tended to spread a higher proportion of manure than compost.

38. Panshi and Ningcheng counties, which in the 1930s were still fairly remote and not heavily populated by southern Manchurian standards, were both surveyed fairly thoroughly by the Japanese. Table 7.3 shows the results with data added from the NKK 1939 study.

39. It took about two people one ten hour day to spread the typical application of fertilizer on one *shang* (or ten *mu*) in twentieth-century Panshi county (NJ-Panshi 1936b, 242, 260–262). Surveys of Xinmin, Liaoyang, Liaozhong, and Yushu counties, each of which was settled early and were typical of the most intensive forms of cultivation in the twentieth century, show that on average 0.45 of a day was spent gathering, mixing, and preparing manure for every *mu* farmed (NKK 1939).

40. One person with a hoe could weed and thin 1.5–2 *mu* in a day. Only adults could accomplish two *mu*, but many children were also deployed in this labor because it was light work. In the second and third rounds of weeding one adult could complete two or three *mu* in a day. One man with two horses or mules can harrow fifteen *mu* in a day, or seven *mu* with two donkeys. One man could rebuild the ridges and furrows on 3.5–4 *mu* in a day after horse harrowing (NJ-Ningcheng 1936, 205–206). In the 1920s, beans were typically weeded twice, millet three times, and sorghum as many as four times (Wilm 1927, 1048).

41. Bruce Campbell's study of Norfolk, England, shows that by 1292 the average peasant holding was a mere five acres, at a time when ten acres could be worked by one adult male. The open fields went from a three-field system in which one-third of the land was fallow per year to nine- and even twelve-field systems in which one-ninth or one-twelfth of the cultivated area was fallow each year. At the same time, however, the number of livestock fell. First, horses, which are capable of working faster and for longer hours, were replaced by less efficient but cheaper-to-maintain oxen. Later, oxen too were abandoned, and as much as two-thirds of the livestock from the pre-Black Death high were eliminated. This had an obviously deleterious effect on labor productivity as more and more heavy work was performed by human labor and less by animals. Peasants also took to weeding intensively. Whereas weeding was unheard of in the eleventh and twelfth centuries, by 1300 between sixty and eighty percent of the demesne land was

weeded (Campbell 1980, 1983). Higher investments of labor could not be avoided, yet yields in the late medieval Norfolk never broke thirteen bushels per acre, compared to yields of twenty-five bushels achieved in the 1790s with less labor.

42. As LeRoy Ladurie has shown, following a brief period during which peasants had the luxury of large farms, and could therefore farm extensively with heavy emphasis on livestock, population growth drove peasants to take up ever more intensive use of land. This entailed abandonment of fallow farming, shedding of large livestock, more intensive tilling and weeding, and farming of ever more marginal land. For all their "dynamism," these changes nonetheless issued in falling labor productivity (LeRoy Ladurie 1987, 119, 122–123, 125–136).

43. Skinner suggests that nationwide 5.3 percent of the population lived in towns of two thousand or more in the 1840s (1977b, 229); Cao Shuji (2001) posits higher estimates of 7.4 percent in 1776 and 7.1 percent in 1893, again for towns over two thousand (828–829, table). For European figures, see Wrigley (1985, table 7.5), according to whom circa 1750 ten percent of Europe's population lived in towns of ten thousand or more, and eight percent did so circa 1600 (note the urbanization rate of eight percent for Manchuria in 1900 is for towns of five thousand or greater and China for as small as two thousand). In England, the urban population was already 17.5 percent in 1750, though the percentage of the population outside agriculture, supported in manufacturing, was already about fifty percent. In other parts of Europe, rates of urbanization circa 1800–1850 all appear to be higher than Manchuria's in 1910. The urban populations of Spain and Poland were eighteen percent of the population in 1800, Austria thirteen percent, France nineteen percent, and Italy 22 percent in 1850–1870 (Allen 2000, 7, table 1).

44. Chemical fertilizers were not widely used until well after 1850, in part because of the technical problems associated with their manufacture (Russell 1913, 59). Similarly, it was not until the second half of the nineteenth century that steam power was applied to farming (Overton 1996, 127, 193).

45. The more recent cliometric literature on the development of English agriculture provides overwhelming evidence for the dramatic growth of labor productivity in England in 1500–1850 (Allen 2000; Wrigley 1985, 1988; Crafts 1985; Overton 1996; Clark 1999) as well as for the uniqueness of this trend within Europe outside the northern Netherlands. In so doing, it confirms, elaborates, refines, and corrects the insights of the previous, pioneering generation of historians of English agricultural progress (among them Thirsk, 1978, 1984; Kerridge, 1967; Jones 1967, 1968).

46. Agrarian historian Eric Kerridge (1967) provides seven major innovations which raised yields while raising labor productivity (14, 181–325).

47. The eminent historian of English agriculture Joan Thirsk (1987) concludes her study of the period 1500 to 1750, "many of the technical advances that used to be associated with the agricultural revolution in the century between 1750 and 1850 were under way 200 years before" (57).

48. As historians of English agriculture have demonstrated, some of the most important improvements in farming were adopted from continental Europe, particularly Holland (Thirsk 1990, 9, 18, 21, 27–28).

Chapter 8

1. In the early years of the Qing dynasty an empire-wide ban on coastal trade, which lasted from 1655 to 1685, was imposed in part as a countermeasure against rebel Ming holdouts on the island of Taiwan. With the pacification of Taiwan in 1683, the ban was lifted, though not entirely. The court continued to ban the transportation by sea of coarse grains and soybeans until 1740 (GZSL 1964, 1733 [114]).

2. According to Wu Chengming, the remaining trade was primarily made up of salt (15.3 percent of the value of all commodities), tea (7.75 percent), woven silk (4.17 percent), and silk yarn (2.92 percent) (Wu 1983, 100, table 2). There were, to be sure, other goods entering the long-distance trading networks—such as sugar, dates, and fruit—but they accounted for too small a percentage to be included in Wu's macroestimates.

3. On Qing food deficits in the Yangzi delta, see Wang (1989, 428–430). On deficits on the north China plain, see Xu (1998b, 310–325); on deficits in Lingnan (southeast China), see Marks (1998, 252–254) and Mazumdar (1998, 261–263). On China's regional grain deficits more generally, see Guo (1990), Jiang (1992, 23–32), Wang (1989, 426–428; 1992, 67–68), Ch'üan and Kraus (1975, 64–65), and Rowe (2001, 157–158).

4. On the limits to increases in grain output see Zhao Gang (Chao Kang) (1995) for what I believe is the most thorough and systematic examination of grain yields to date. Other studies of grain yields rely on problematic casual observations found in gazetteers and recorded by state officials. These observations often do not distinguish between husked and unhusked yields. In rice-growing regions this is particularly problematic because the difference is in the order of thirty percent. By contrast, Zhao Gang deduces changes in yields using data on the amount of rent paid and provides, therefore, the most systematic and internally consistent numbers. That said, Guo Songyi's more recent analysis of grain yields, which does draw on Qing observations, concurs with Zhao that yields grew only modestly in the Qing cores and that by 1800 they had reached a ceiling there (in Fang et al. 2000, 250, 292, 321, 322).

5. This is, for example, what occurred in the Huguang region of the middle Yangzi toward the end of the eighteenth century. Early settlement in Huguang began in the Ming and by the seventeenth century the region was renowned for its ability to export rice. By the second half of the eighteenth century, however, the good land had all been occupied and peasant subdivision of holdings had begun to cut into surpluses. On the Huguang plain, population pressure was pushing peasants onto Lake Dongting, from which they reclaimed land with elaborate but ecologically unstable dyke systems (Zhang 2006, 38–39). Huguang rice yields, moreover, had topped out by 1800, or earlier. Consequently, a region that had been a major rice-exporting region, supplying grain chiefly to the Yangzi delta and Beijing, found it increasingly difficult to sustain prior levels of grain exports (Jiang 1992, 49–66; Tan 1987, 36–37; Zhang Guoxiong 1993, 44–45; Zhang Jianmin 1987, 60).

6. Such relative movements in prices are typical of the Malthusian pattern of growth and it is this that makes for the proto-industrial cul-de-sac. In the Dutch case, see de Vries and Woude (1997, 25–26).

7. The population booms of the fifteenth and sixteenth centuries and the eighteenth and nineteenth centuries accelerated the pace of colonization and settlement so that from the late Ming on the population living in the long-settled cores fell relative to that in the peripheries (Guo 1990, 31, 33, tables).

8. See the works of Katō Shigeshi (1953a), Sudō Yoshiyuki (1972a), Wu Chengming (1983), and Fan I-Chun (1992) for discussions of this trade.

9. Also see the following memorials: GDZ-YZ 1977, vol. 6, 407; GDZ-QL 1982, vol. 38, 730–731. In addition, see Qi Yanhuai's essay on ocean-going shipping in the *Anthology of Statecraft Writing* (in He 1992, 1160). Qi Yanhuai gives beans and wheat as Manchuria's principal exports, and mentions by name cotton cloth and tea as southern goods that are imported to Fengtian.

10. In his encyclopedic study of Manchurian agriculture from the earliest recorded times to the end of Japanese colonial rule in 1945, which draws on all the available gazetteer evidence, Yi Baozhong (1993, 269–271, 275–276, 351–353) makes no mention of cotton spinning and weaving in the northeast. Similarly, in a study of Manchurian towns and manufacturing, Zhang Yaomin (1990, 178) can only cite a handful of examples of cotton cloth manufacturing among common folk. We might also expect to find mention of cotton and cotton manufacturing in the massive study of the northeast compiled by late Qing reforming governor Xu Shichang in the early 1900s. The work *Governing Proposals for the Northeast*, which covers all three newly created provinces of Fengtian, (Liaoning), Jilin, and Heilongjiang, was undertaken in concert with ongoing political and economic reform of the northeast—one of the late Qing's model reform programs that included efforts to develop local agriculture and industry. Despite its comprehensiveness, the study makes no mention of cotton cultivation or cotton manufacturers (or the need to encourage either), even though it describes the need to expand the cultivation of hemp production for its fiber (Xu 1989). Furthermore, while the 1909 study of farming conditions of every district in Fengtian province does mention cotton cultivation, it shows that few cultivated it and those who did gathered thin harvests. Of the ten locations where cotton cultivation was observed in Fengtian, yields were under thirty-five catties per *mu* in six locations, and only two locations managed yields of eighty catties, the approximate yield of eighteenth-century peasants in Shandong and eastern Songjiang (FNDS 1909, 4.20). As for domestic manufactures, the 1909 study makes no mention of domestic cotton spinning or weaving, though it does list such handicrafts as weaving hemp cloth, processing vegetable and soybean oil, rendering tofu, distilling grain alcohol, and milling wheat flour (FNDS 1909, 5.13–16).

11. Compilers were certainly eager to demonstrate that women in Manchuria conformed to Confucian ideals in other arenas. For instance, a 1736 edition of the *Complete Gazetteer* lists celebrated chaste widows among both the civil and banner-administrated populations.

12. The Pommeranian missionary Charles Gutzlaff, sailing along the Liaodong peninsula in 1833, noted that cotton grew well south of Gaizhou, which lies on the southern edge of the Liaodong peninsula. There he found migrants from Shandong—where peasants had a long acquaintance with cotton cultivation and domestic cotton manufacture—had settled in large numbers (Gutzlaff and Ellis 1834, 418).

13. By the end of the Qing, according to the 1878 *Reference to the Laws and Institutions of Shengjing*, every spring about nine thousand artisans under the Shengjing Imperial Household Departments' three imperial banners were employed to weave 9,500 catties of cotton produced on the cotton estates. No more than 270 *mu* of total cotton estate land was required to produce this amount of raw cotton, even assuming a very low yield of thirty-five catties per *mu* (SD 1995, 599–600 [3]).

14. *The Investigation of Northeast China's Economy* (*Dongsansgeng jingji diaocha lu*),

conducted in the early Republican era, also notes that the value of cotton imports exceeded all others (DSD 1987, 44).

15. By the late eighteenth century, north China cotton was no longer going to Jiangnan, but was being spun and woven locally. The cotton cloth thus produced was consumed by the households that manufactured it and any surplus was sold locally or to the interior (Xu 1998a).

16. According to surveys of agricultural conditions in twenty-two counties, cotton cloth accounted for sixty percent of clothing purchases, and raw cotton less than ten percent. The remaining thirty percent was "other"—which included shoes, hats, etc. (Isett 1998, 405, table 9.3).

17. Total Shanhaiguan customs receipts for the years 1728, 1778, 1797, and 1798 are provided in the *Secret Palace Memorials* cited by Fan I-Chun (1992, Appendix B.5, 335–336). Figures for 1811–1812, 1828–1832, 1834–1837, 1841, and 1843 are located in the Palace Memorials found in the First National Archives.

18. Chao Kang's figures break down as follows: five pounds of cotton per person per eight years for quilts, three pounds for mattress, and three pounds for winter garments (Chao 1977, 364 n 17).

19. Also see Qi Yuanhuai's essay in the *Anthology of Statecraft Writing* in which he repeats Bao's claim verbatim (in He 1992, 1160).

20. Wang Yeh-chien (1989, 430) states that Jiangnan imported a total of ten million *shi* of beancakes, of which several million came from Henan and Shandong, and the rest from Manchuria.

21. These estimates of total output assume twentieth-century yields to have held for the entirety of the eighteenth and nineteenth centuries as well, when all evidence points to yields in the earlier periods that were lower than those of the twentieth century. Also, these numbers assume that all cultivated land was planted in crops, when sources suggest Manchurian peasants practiced fallow farming that left some land out of production each year. These assumptions alone have elevated the results by perhaps as much as twenty percent.

22. Another estimate puts the amount consumed directly by peasants before marketing slightly higher, at twenty-eight percent (Tsao 1930, 942–943).

23. To be sure, peasants might choose to "pay" for some of the cost of production out of other crops or wages earned laboring for others. Even so, it would be pushing the envelope to assume, as does Li, that none of the cost of soybean production came out of soybeans themselves. Accounting for the possibility of a poor harvest, peasants had to devote sufficient land to grain cultivation just to ensure basic household subsistence and could not therefore afford to take too much of the cost out of those crops. For these very reasons, studies of twentieth-century Chinese agriculture conclude that peasants who secured their subsistence directly had to produce twice their minimum food requirements in order to attain food security (Ellis et al. 2001, 102–103).

24. In the 1920s, when twenty percent of the land was planted in soybeans, peasants were feeling the effects of a newly constructed transportation infrastructure and new processing plants especially targeting soybeans that were financed by Japanese capital (Matsusaka 2001, 127–136). With the commencement of World War I, moreover, international demand for soybeans skyrocketed as Europe's armies consumed in huge volumes the glycerine and fatty acids extracted from soybeans needed in the production of explosives, medicines, and soaps (Tsao 1930, 944; Lie 1980, 76–83). The period 1914–1918

was indeed an unusual time when rapidly rising soybean prices ushered in a period of modest prosperity for Manchuria's peasants who were planting more land in soybeans than at any other time. Even so, the proportion of land in soybeans did not rise above one-fifth.

25. Kenneth Pomeranz believes Li Bozhong to be correct and cites the work Wu Chengming and Xu Dixin to support this position (Pomeranz 2002, 584, n 57). He also cites Bao Shichen's tally of ships, their cargo load, and number of voyages to make estimates of goods moved from north to south (Xu and Wu 2000, 362; Pomeranz 2002, 587 n 57). Bao states that 3,500 junks traveled up and down the coast between Shanghai and Niuzhuang-Yingkou three to four times each year carrying between 1,500 and 3,000 *shi* each. Pomeranz then asserts that if these boats were full, then twenty million *shi* of grain could have been shipped from the north to Jiangnan circa 1840. The assumption that all ships were full all the time is however quite extreme. As Xue Yong points out, Qing officials Shi Yanshi and Wei Yuan, both proponents of sea-going transportation, suggest that vessels never loaded to their full capacity because of the risks inherent in carrying too heavy a cargo. Wei went so far as to say that on average vessels carried a little over 1,500 *shi* (cited in He 1992, 1145). There is also reason to believe that not all ships could make the three to four voyages to Fengtian and back each year, and that some northern voyages only went as far as Shandong and Tianjin. The ports of Liaodong were closed to trade five to six months of the year when the ports froze in the winter and when winds were contrary in the early summer (HZ 1824.7.27). This left only six to seven months for operations between Fengtian and Jiangnan.

26. As with many of Qing estimates of the northeast's exports, Xie Zhanren provides no clue as to how he in fact deduces his figure.

27. When discussing shipping volumes, it was common practice for specialists to provide conversion rates when appropriate. Thus, the specialist in shipping and long-distance trade Shi Yanshi did not assume his audience would know the difference between the Guandong *shi* and standard *shi*. He provides an explanation and conversion rate (in He 1992, 1161).

28. Xue Yong (forthcoming) does an admirable job disproving Li Bozhong's (2000) more recent attempt to make the same case by using Bao Shichen's numbers instead of Xie's. In this case, Li argues that the larger Guandong *shi* was so commonly used in Jiangnan—because of the influence of Manchuria's exports there—that officials felt no need to specify this was their unit of measurement. When they spoke of *shi* in reference to goods from the north Li believes that they assumed the reader understood this meant the larger Guandong *shi*. *Pace* Li, Xue shows that not only was Bao Shichen in fact very cognizant of which units he was using, and always made this clear in his writings, it was also his practice to use the official or *guan shi* which was equivalent to the standard *shi*. Xue cites Bao to this effect: "Every traveling merchant who establishes a trading house in the Northeast has a shop in Shanghai. The Shanghai broker would write down the freight charges [for the shipping of his goods] in the shop. Measured by *guanhu* [official *hu*], each *shi* would be charged 300–400 *wen*" (Xue forthcoming). Here Xue shows that it was Bao's practice to use the official *shi*, which was equivalent to Jiangnan's standard *shi*.

29. Xue Yong (forthcoming) provides further confirmation of the greater plausibility of Xie Zhanren's claims in a discussion of the technical and logistical problems of sea

transportation in the High Qing. I wish to thank Xue for providing his article in manuscript form.

30. These figures come from two separate Qing sources that overlap for the years 1776–1777. The first source is a 1778 palace memorial that covers the years from 1774 to 1777 (HZ 1778.10.22). The reported customs revenue from beancake and beans for those years are as follows: 1774–75, 18,825 *taels*; 1775–76, 23,052 *taels*; 1776–77, 26,881 *taels* (HZ 1778.10.22). The second source, which was used by Katō Shigeshi (1953a) and from which Adachi Keiji (1978) and others have deduced customs duty collected, is the *Pamphlet on the Administration of the Shanhaiguan Customs Office*. This was a review conducted in the Guangxu period of the history of the Shanhaiguan customs office and provides data on soybean excise tax collected in the northeast for the years 1776–1779. The reported customs revenue from beancake and beans for 1776–77 was 26,881 *taels*; 1777–78, 27,029 *taels*; and 1778–1779, 28,133 *taels* (SC Guangxu, 4.20). The *Shanhaiguan Customs Office* and the palace memorials report the excise tax rate on soybeans was 0.022 *taels* per standard *shi*. I have followed Katō (1953a) and Adachi (1978) and converted all exports to unprocessed soybeans. The tax rate itself is clearly levied on standard *shi* so that all estimates of exports derived from the levels of duty are in standard *shi* as well.

31. Adjusting Sun Kungtu's (1969) data (taken from all IMC reports for the northeast's major ports) to give a five-year moving average centered on the year in question, total soybean exports (soybeans, beancake, and soybean oil) by 1890 exports were 4.5 million *shi*, 5.5 million in 1895, and 6.4 million in 1900. Given the nature of the available data, the fifteen percent discrepancy between the crude estimates presented in Table 8.2 and the IMC data are not sufficient to be of concern. The difference may result from an underestimation of the amount of soybeans carried by foreign vessels, from an underestimation of total farmland, or an underestimation of the percentage of land planted in soybeans at the very end of the nineteenth century. If the estimated figures for all years before 1900 were raised by fifteen percent to bring them in line with IMC 1900 data, the result would not be a significant enough increase in the estimates provided here to bring them anywhere near in line with the much higher numbers suggested by Wang Yeh-chien (1989), Wang Yejian and Huang Guoshu (1998), and Li Bozhong (1998).

32. On the relationship between Japanese railway construction in the twentieth century and the soybean trade in Manchuria see Yoshihisa Matsusaka (2001, 127–136). Matsusaka demonstrates that the Southern Manchurian Railway company was directly engaged in developing and profiting from the soybean trade, constructing railroads, and other in-land infrastructure with the goal of moving the center of trade from the Chinese-controlled port of Niuzhuang to the Japanese-controlled port of Dalian. In these efforts, the company exceeded all expectations.

33. See for example Wang Yeh-chien's (1989, 430) work on Jiangnan's grain supply and Li Bozhong (1998, 113–114) on the amount and content of imports. Also see Ch'üan and Kraus (1975, 66) who articulate the commonly held position that the bulk of Jiangnan imports from Manchuria came in the form of soybeans and very little of it in grain.

34. Fan Jinmin (1998, 271–272) derives this number from customs receipts collected at the Liuhegang customs office through which all northern goods shipped by sea had to pass. Customs receipts for that port therefore record all legal imports of northern goods by sea to Jiangnan.

35. Shanghai was by this time the destination of Manchurian exports to Jiangnan,

Suzhou having lost its entrepôt status in the sea-going trade in grain and beans due to the silting up of its harbor at Liuhegang (Fan 1998, 273).

36. Any further discrepancy between the revised estimated figures and those of Qing observers such as Bao and Xie may in part be explained by the fact they overlooked the exports of indigo (GCJY 1993, 1189). Though not much is known about the volume of this export, it was perhaps quite considerable. On his travels through Manchurian in 1867, the reverend Alexander Williamson noted that "[i]ndigo is produced in immense quantities to the north of Mouk-den (Mukden or Shenyang). We met strings of carts of seven and eight mules each, day after day, in our journeys, conveying this commodity to the south for sale and exportation." According to Williamson, each cart was capable of carrying two thousand catties of indigo and they passed twenty to forty a day and, according to their local informants, this level of movement was kept up for six weeks as the crop was sent to Niuzhuang and from there it was exported (Williamson 1870, 42, 153). There is no evidence of a Qing dyeing and calendering industry in the northeast, yet large quantities of this crop were clearly grown and carted to the Niuzhuang entrepôt for export. Certainly, there was demand for indigo used in the dyeing industries of Jiangnan (located first in Suzhou and later Shanghai). If Manchuria was importing finished cottons from Jiangnan and was producing only a little locally, then most of the indigo was indeed for export. A bulky commodity, if exported in large enough quantities, it could easily have taken up a fairly significant space on sea-going junks.

37. On a similar price phenomenon in Holland, see de Vries and Woude (1997, 25–26). On England's avoidance of the proto-industrial cul-de-sac, see Clark and Van Der Werf (1998) and Brenner and Isett (2002). In China's Jiangnan region, Fan Jinmin (1998, 162–163) dates the worsening terms of trade to the 1820s. While cotton prices entered into a deep and extended slump in the early 1820s, this relative downturn in cloth prices had in fact come at the end of a prolonged period of steady decline in relative prices of cloth dating to the mid-eighteenth century. After 1820, terms of trade simply worsened for cotton weavers at a faster pace than before. Fan Jinmin suggests that where they could, peasants even gave up cotton cultivation, returning to grain (Fan 1998, 162–163).

38. The dregs remaining after oil is extruded from the soybean is seven percent nitrogen by weight and makes a good inorganic fertilizer, with one kilo of beancake raising unhusked grain output by a kilo (Brenner and Isett 2003).

39. I thank Xue Yong for bringing this source to my attention.

40. On the turn to intensive use of fertilizer see Huang (2002), Brenner and Isett (2002, 622; 2003, 235–236), Li (1984, 27–29, 33), Zhao (1995, 48–49), and Ellis and Wang (1997, 184–188, 190–191). On labor use for manure and canal mud, see Ellis and Wang (1997) and Cao (1996). There is no evidence that beancake actually raised labor productivity. On this, see Brenner and Isett's (2003) critique of Li Bozhong's attempt to demonstrate this.

Chapter 9

1. Despite very important differences in their interpretations of the possibilities and levels of economic growth in Qing China, studies of the eighteenth and nineteenth centuries by Evelyn Rawski (1972), Philip Huang (1985, 1990), Fang Xing (1986), Chao Kang

(1986), Peter Perdue (1987), Li Wenzhi (1993), Mark Roberts (1998), R. Bin Wong (1997), Sucheta Mazumdar (1998), Lynda Bell (1999), Kenneth Pomeranz (2000), among others, have variously demonstrated that commercial expansion was not a sufficient condition for sustained economic growth, understood as rising labor productivity.

2. In two widely cited studies, historians E. A. Wrigley (1985) and Robert Allen (2000) use changes over time in rates of urbanization and nonagricultural employment as indirect measurements of changes in the productivity of labor in English and European agriculture. Quite simply stated, in a closed system with small or no imports of grain, for a larger and larger proportion of a given population to be supported outside agriculture there must be an increase in the productivity of labor of those that remain in agriculture.

3. See David Landes's (1986) classic statement of how merchants/proto-industrialists can combine production, break up tasks, and improve tools to match competitiveness and secure higher profits and in the process advance labor productivity.

4. See, for example, the most thorough study to date of Jiangnan trade, merchants, and urban development, by Fan Xinmin (1998). Fan shows unambiguously that merchants in Jiangnan, China's most urbanized region, remained outside of production, using their capital to circulate but not produce goods. Studies of rural manufacturing have also concluded that merchant operations also remained outside of production for the most part. See, for example, Robert Gardella's (1994) analysis of tea cultivation and preparation in northern Fujian; Sucheta Mazumdar's (1998) analysis of sugar manufacture in China's southeast; Daniels (1983) and Isett (1995) on sugar manufacture on Taiwan; and Nishijima (1984) on merchant putting out in Jiangnan cotton.

5. For the discussion of these tensions within the bureaucracy, and particularly on the conflicts between the sovereign's global vision and the local bureaucratic narrow view, see Will (1990, 215). On the rising disequilibria between the demand for grain and its production, leading to rising grain prices across the eighteenth and nineteenth centuries, also see Jiang (1992, 185–203).

6. By the eighteenth century, the ratio of land to people was very low in Shandong, at 2.19 *mu* per capita in the central mountain belt; just under 3.5 on the peninsula; 3 on the northern Lu plain; and between 4 and 4.5 on the western Lu plain (Xu 1998b, 77, table 2.16). By 1820, Shandong's population had reached just under twenty-nine million and cultivated area was 96 million *mu*, giving a land-labor ratio of 3.33 *mu* per person (Xu 1998b, 31, table 2.2). In Zhili, the situation was not much better. Cultivated area increased little in the early eighteenth century and none at all thereafter, while population continued to grow with only modest if any improvement in yields (Huang 1985, 323, table B.1, 327, table C.1; Perkins 1969, 207, table A.4, 234, table B.12). Li Hua in his study of the rise of the Shandong *shangbang*, while acknowledging important regional variation, nonetheless concludes that high population density and ecological sensitivity led to a contradiction between grain demand and grain supply. Citing the Kangxi-era gazetteer for Qingzhou, Li argues that a family of the average eight persons worked thirty *mu*. The typical yield was 1.28 *shi* per *mu*, giving about 4.8 *shi* per person per year, which he points out was enough to support a household in good times. But in times of poor harvest, Li maintains, this output was clearly not enough (in Zhang Haipeng 1993 , 170–171).

7. On the ecology of the north China plain, see Huang (1985, 57–6), Xu (1998b, 10–12), Lu (1987, 27–31), as well as Jean Oi and Pierre-Etienne-Pierre Will (1992, 322–326).

8. The turn to cotton on the Shandong Lu plain was, I suggest, analogous to the earlier shift to cotton cultivation and domestic cotton work in Jiangnan's cotton belt. Neither instance constituted a Smithian reallocation of labor to lines that yielded the best price/cost ratio, but rather signaled a declining capacity of peasant labor to acquire not only nonessentials but essentials as well (Huang 1985, 111–114, 191–195).

9. Thus, Dengzhou prefecture, which is seventy percent mountains and hills, was already short of grain by the early eighteenth century. Peasants in Fenglai county, it was said, could not meet their own grain needs even in good years, while the gazetteer of Huang county recorded: "in good years there is not enough grain to provide sustenance for the year" (Xu 1998b, 198; 1998a, 36).

10. According to Philip Huang, who cites the State Statistics Bureau of China, one *mu* of land planted in sweet potatoes yielded 263 catties versus 114 for wheat, 170 for sorghum, and 60 for millet (Huang 1985, 117 n; Perkins 1969, 276–279). However, sweet potatoes required two to three times the labor (Huang 1985, 116). In terms of market value, the cultivation of the sweet potato certainly represented a decline in returns on labor; though in terms of caloric yield the switch to sweet potatoes meant peasants could survive with relatively smaller amounts of land devoted to food production.

11. See Furichi Daisuke's (2000, 53–60) discussion of the shifts in export policy in the eighteenth and early nineteenth centuries.

12. In seventeenth-century Ningguta, millet, *beizi*, Russian wheat, and wheat were the main sources of caloric intake (Li Debin 1987, 55). In the 1890s, the British Consular General of Newchwang (Niuzhuang) Alexander Hosie observed that millet was "the staple food of the population and the principal grain feed of the numerous animals," while traveler H. E. M. James noted in 1888 that the staple food was "millet boiled with various condiments" (Hosie 1905, 174; James 1968, 137–138).

13. Also see the discussion in the *Pamphlet on the Administration of the Shanhaiguan Customs Office* for references to the fact that peasants in Manchuria depended upon the soybean for food (SC Guangxu, 4.15).

14. Though the language is less transparent than that of Jin Lan's memorial, a later discussion of the decision to end all restrictions on exports suggests that indeed the quota on soybean exports was intended to limit exports, not to facilitate the collection of the excise tax as Will suggests. It is stated: "in the first month of 1772 the Military Governor Heng[lu] petitioned to allow merchants to export soybeans without limits" (SC Guangxu, 4.19). The use of the term "limits" suggests that the intent of the 1749 policy was in fact to restrict how much soybean was leaving.

15. It was roughly at this time that the Qing specialist on grain transportation and trade, Xie Jieshu, ridiculed the notion proposed by some that the state could procure as much as three million *shi* in the northeast, stating at best it could hope to buy several hundred thousand in and around Beijing and Manchuria combined (in He 1992 [47]).

16. Between 1722 and 1772, the export of state-procurements from Fengtian were permitted in 1722, 1724, 1725, 1729, 1730, 1744, 1747, 1748, and 1750 (Sudō 1972a, 439–459).

17. Lillian Li (1992) suggests that in the eighteenth century one million *shi* of grain was shipped annually to Beijing from Fengtian.

18. Will writes: "To be sure, this [the imbalance between grain supply and demand] is a phenomena that must be considered fundamental to the Chinese economy of the period, and the examples taken from crisis situations simply mark its extremes. Gener-

ally speaking, supply was *never* able to meet demand or, more precisely, the stimulation of demand on supply *always* threatened to stretch supply beyond its capacity" (1990, 209).

19. In her study of the canonical Statecraft school of thought, Helen Dunstan (1996) has come closest to suggesting the Qing state adopted a Liberal stance on trade. See Rowe (2001, 506 n 149).

20. On the parallels between the eighteenth-century Qing official Chen Hongmou and the French physiocrats, see Rowe (2001, 213–214). These ideological commitments (in both France and China) reflected the structural limits of agricultural productiveness in both countries; as long as empire-wide grain surpluses were slim (only about ten to fifteen percent of Chinese food grain, including that paid as rent, ever made it into the market; the rest was consumed directly by the peasants who produced it [Guo 1994]) the Qing state was just one or two poor harvests away from social unrest. On agricultural productiveness, grain surpluses, and problems of grain supply in eighteenth- and nineteenth-century France, see Steven Kaplan (1982, 62–70) and Judith Miller (1999, 1–24).

21. The original source actually states "rice (*mi*) and wheat (*mai*)," though in this instance *mi* clearly refers to millet not rice, the latter not cultivated in eastern Shandong.

22. Similar sentiments were expressed in 1750 by the Shandong governor when explaining why sea traders were needed to bring grain to eastern Shandong to relieve a famine (GZD-QL 1982, volume 3, 665).

23. While the late eighteenth-century pull of the Jiangnan market on Manchurian grain and soybean exports has long been noted, its effects on grain prices in Fengtian has more recently been confirmed and elaborated using more complete price information. Katō Shigeshi (1953a) and Sudō Yoshiyuki (1972a) were the first historians to map both the growth in volume of trade and shifts in markets for Manchurian goods. Sudō even argued, on the basis of a few price observations, that Fengtian grain exports to Zhili and Shandong moderated price swings there (448). Building on the findings of Katō and Sudō, Adachi Keiji (1978, 45–51) mapped the shift in market demand for Manchurian soybeans from Jiangnan to the southeast beginning in the late eighteenth century and then realized by the middle of the nineteenth century. Using qualitative sources, Fan I-Chun (1992, 273–274) has mapped the early shift in demand for Manchurian grain and beans from north China to Jiangnan in the middle of the eighteenth century. Subsequent to these works, price studies by Wang Yeh-Chien (1992) and James Lee et al. (1990) show how Fengtian prices followed secular price trends led by the Yangzi delta, though how closely they matched is not yet clear.

24. Zhang Zhongmin's (1988, 154) estimates of cotton cloth exports to Manchuria and north China are approximate. His figure of three million bolts exported from Chongming is from the "early Qing" and the similar figure of three million bolts from Shanghai is for the early nineteenth century. From this and other unstated sources he concludes exports were about ten million to Shandong and Manchuria.

25. According to Fan (1998, 74), Songjiang prefecture supplied cotton cloth to both Manchuria and Fujian; Changshou supplied Zhejiang, Fujian, as well as Huaiyang and Shandong.

26. When Great Britain signed the Treaty of Tianjin in 1858 its negotiators mistakenly assumed the Fengtian entrepôt was still at Niuzhuang where the Qing customs office was. They therefore demanded access to trade through Niuzhuang, where the for-

eign-run Imperial Maritime Customs office was also established, even though the port was many miles to the south at Yingkou (IMC 1904, 1–2).

27. Late nineteenth- and early twentieth-century observations by Westerners confirm the poor conditions of Manchuria roads from the spring to the summer. See for example Reverend Alexander Williamson's description dating from the 1860s; he wrote that "one day's rain will often make the roads utterly impassable for carts; and the wight caught in such misfortune has a sad time of it—his cart floundering out of one black pool into another, now in the roads, then in the fields, plunging and splashing at the rate of a mile an hour—men, beasts, and carts covered in mud." By contrast, in the winter, when the land was frozen, "[c]arts go in a straight line wherever they please" (Williamson 1870, vol. 2, 24, 26). Later in the same recollections, Williamson describes an overland journey in April on a stretch of the road from Yingkou to Shengjing—the same road on which much of the hinterland grain passed on its way to export: "the roads were frightful, not from stones but from mud, which was up to the axle; at one time the tracing mule was floundering in a pool, and at another the tram mule was up to the neck and nearly drown; requiring not only that we should dismount, but that the men should strip and dig. . . . The carters took all these annoyances quite coolly; they were accustomed to such disasters and had the most ingenious expedients for getting us out of our difficulties" (Williamson 1870, 133, and see 135). Also see the account of travel in Manchuria written by Dugald Christie, a medical missionary posted to Shenyang (Mukden) in 1883. According to Christie, "Towards the end of November the port of Newchwang (Niuzhuang), the one gate to Manchuria, 'closed' and remained ice-bound for at least four months." He continues, "[i]tinerating tours were and are often taken in winter, when the roads are frozen hard and the cart can rattle over them or along the ridges of the bare brown fields." In the spring, "the cart bumps and toils in the mud and deep ruts." In the summer "come the heavy rains, the streams are swollen and hard to ford, the roads become rivers or quagmires" (Christie 1914, 66).

28. It was common Qing practice to deputize *yahang* from among guild merchants. When the center of the soybean trade in Jiangnan relocated to Shanghai, it was merchants of Shanghai's Bean Guild (*douhang*) who acted as *yahang* and collected commercial taxes on the soybean trade (Zhang 1994, 88).

29. Very similar practices were found in other parts of China. In the sugarcane-growing districts of Guangdong and Taiwan, sugar merchants and sugar mill managers made advance purchases of sugar cane, while in the tea-growing region of Minbei peasant households producing tiny quantities of tea "mortgaged" it to petty merchants before it was harvested (Mazumdar 1998, 324; Gardella 1994, 46; Zhang 1996, 104). In these cases peasants also took cash payment several months before the crop was harvested, but had to accept earnings that were considerably lower than if they had sold the harvest themselves.

30. Rates of interest charged in twentieth-century Manchuria were not too different from rates charged in contemporaneous north China and Jiangnan (Huang 1985, 176–177; 1990, 108–109). Though the Qing state prohibited interest rates above three percent per month and total interest that exceeded the loan, officials were unable to enforce the statute because, the Qianlong emperor explained, there were too many offenders for the courts to handle (Jing 1994, 81; Huang 1994, 150). Interest rates in Qing Jiangnan ranged from twenty to twenty-four percent per annum and were as high as ten percent

per month (Pan 1995, 97, 108). William Rowe (2001, 285) cites the Qing official Chen Hongmou, whose hallmark career was devoted to bettering the conditions of peasants, to the effect that private loans for grain taken in the spring and repaid in the fall were for thirty to forty percent. Qing observer Wei Jirui noted interest rates of ten, twenty, and thirty percent. He also observed that peasants borrowing twenty or thirty *taels* were required to pay two to three hundred *taels* at the end of a year (cited in Zhang 1996, 102–103).

31. A very similar logic is evident in parts of Jiangnan. According to Pan Ming-te (1995) peasants in Jiangnan with holdings too small to produce a surplus in grain and short of cash took loans to purchase startup seed and fertilizer, as well as raw cotton and yarn which they could work up. At the end of the year, though they had attained their goal of meeting subsistence, many peasants were nonetheless without sufficient capital to restart production the following year. They thus returned again to money lenders and merchants for a new purse of start-up capital, and so on and so forth (73–129). Pan (1995, 111) argues that peasants' ability to borrow money was key to their survival but was often the basis of peasant prosperity. The burden of his thesis, however, is that some of his household models (Pan constructs schematic households and assumes key parameters such as production and capital costs) show peasants achieving not much more than "simple reproduction" (i.e., some of the models show households achieving subsistence but unable to accumulate capital) (97).

32. One-time or one-off improvements are of course common to all peasant societies. But what distinguishes these "advancements" from those that are truly revolutionary is the fact that the latter are ongoing, systematic, and constant, leading to ongoing and constant improvements in labor productivity; whereas the former are sporadic and often not followed by further changes at all.

33. Taking a very different view of the meaning of the expansion of trade following the seventeenth century, Hillary Beattie (1979, 49) concludes that there was no significant fundamental change in the economy and that much of both the increase in absolute levels of trade and variety of items traded can be explained by population expansion. Most significantly, she notes that manufacturing was not becoming more "sophisticated."

34. I thank Robert Allen for providing this figure. The estimate of the proportion of output marketed could be adjusted in a number of obvious ways; nonetheless, this must be the order of magnitude (personal communication from Robert Allen to Robert Brenner, February 17, 2004).

Conclusion

1. Thus, Smith was quick to point out that the rising wages that follow from productivity improvements are more than compensated by rising labor productivity: "There are many commodities . . . which, in consequence of these improvements [in technologies], come to be produced by so much less labor than before, that the increase of its price is more than compensated by the diminution of its quantity" (1976, 96).

2. In Smith's words, "It is the great multiplication of the productions of all the different arts, in consequence of the division of labor, which occasions, in a well-governed society, that universal opulence which extends itself to the lowest ranks of the people.

Every workman has a great quantity of his own work to dispose of beyond what he himself has occasion for; and every other workman being exactly in the same situation, *he is enabled to exchange a great quantity of his own goods for a great quantity, or, what comes to the same thing, for the price of a great quantity of theirs*" (1976, 15, emphasis added).

3. It is clear that Smith himself did not hold that his mechanisms (deepening specialization, furthering division of labor, and improvement) were sufficient to sustain growth over the very long run, arguing instead that economic expansion was ultimately constrained by what he called the "extent of the market" and the tendency toward a "stationary state" (Smith 1976, 83). Yet, Smith never laid out an adequate theory of what he called the "stationary state" or its appearance; rather Smith simply deduced it from his observations of economies of his day that had ceased to expand by his count (106). Whatever one makes of Smith's "stationary state," there is nothing contained in his account of the "mechanisms" of growth that insists upon it per se: that is to say, economic decline or stagnation are not immanent in his account of the mechanisms behind growth. After all, the very same competition that for Smith propelled prices to their "natural" resting point, also drove the deepening of specialization, the breaking up of tasks, the application of machinery and other innovations, all in the quest to cheapen the costs of production, that would in theory sustain growth (11–14).

4. Many scholars have strangely attributed to Malthus a static vision of agricultural productiveness. Esther Boserup (1965) is perhaps the classic misstatement of Malthus. She famously criticized Malthus for not allowing for the possibility of "improvements," arguing that mounting population pressure drives cultivators to raise total output by expending greater effort in farming. These efforts raise yields, which in turn allow the population to rise to a new level, and so on. While she posits this position as a refutation of Malthus, it is quite clear that Malthus himself recognized this very same pattern and that, like Boserup, Malthus argued that such efforts lead to diminishing returns to labor. Boserup even concedes that the failure to raise agricultural output sufficiently will lead to population reversal à la Malthus; though she rightly points out that a population may fall well below Malthus's equilibrium point and fail to recover (62).

5. The application of the Smithian paradigm to the study of Chinese economic history is, of course, not new. Earlier exemplary studies include works by Evelyn Rawski (1972, especially 139–163), Loren Brandt (1989), and Thomas Rawski (1989).

6. Also see Evelyn Rawski (1972, 140–142).

7. In short, Li Bozhong (1998, 139–140) fails to take into account the cost of fertilizer that was required to provide the increase in yields and labor productivity he claims occurred between the seventeenth and nineteenth centuries. The central tenet of Li's argument is that the turn to new oilcake fertilizers (principally soybean beancake) in eighteenth-century Jiangnan agriculture gave peasants a boost in yields without increasing labor inputs disproportionately (112–114). But, in his mathematical proof Li does not account for the full cost of fertilizer for the nineteenth century—in so doing he either assumes in his mathematics that beancake is replacing other fertilizers or inadvertently fails to take into account the additional production cost that the spreading of beancake logically entailed. But, it is widely known, as Li (1984) himself acknowledges, that beancake did not replace other fertilizers—rather it was an additional fertilizer spread after other manures. The cost of the beancake must therefore be added to the cost of the other fertilizers already and still in use in order to achieve the full cost of fertilizer needed to

get the boost in yields he argues occurs in the eighteenth century. Once we deduct the cost of the beancake Li believes was required to give the increase in rice yields from the total output, labor productivity in the early nineteenth century is in fact slightly lower than in 1600. But, there are still other problems with Li's proof. Li assumes that soybean beancake fertilizer was as effective in raising yields as chemical fertilizers, a claim he basis on the rough equivalency of their nitrogen content by volume. Using Perkins's (1969) estimates of yield response to chemical fertilizers, Li comes to an estimated yield response on a *mu* of rice paddy of 0.50 *shi* of grain for every addition of forty catties of beancake applied (Li 1998, 114). Actual experiments with beancake performed in the 1990s, however, suggest the grain yield response to beancake fertilizer was in fact half this amount, or about 0.25 *shi* in husked rice (Brenner and Isett 2003, 236; He 1998, 165). If we take that into account, we find that there is a still greater decline in labor productivity. (In fact the gains in rice yields from the beancake hardly outweigh the cost of the beancake itself, suggesting that the actual value of beancake to peasants came from the fact that it helped maintain soils that were under greater pressure as peasants in the paddy zones turned to double-cropping and those in the cotton belt turned to mono-cropping cotton. The strain on soil structure in the paddy zone that came with double-cropping was recognized by Qing observers and has been verified by contemporary soil analyses [Li 1998, 96; also see Ellis and Wang 1997].) On the economic logic of beancake fertilizer use in Jiangnan agriculture, see Brenner and Isett (2003, 236), Ellis and Wang (1997, 185, 190–191), Huang (2002, 508 n 8). Finally, citing a well-known 1820s account of farming in Jiangnan's Songjiang region, Li believes that the addition of the second winter wheat crop increased labor inputs by a mere three days per *mu* while adding another one *shi* of grain. But, twentieth-century data on labor inputs (which Li uses in making his estimate of days in rice cultivation) suggest that winter wheat required seven to eleven days of labor annually per *mu*. Other scholars of Jiangnan agriculture in the Qing, though well aware of Li's 1820s source, prefer to use twentieth-century data or Qing sources on wheat cultivation in other parts of the empire which they evidently feel are more accurate (Zhang 1988, 62; Huang 2002; Cao 1996, 94, table 4.4). Once Li's figures are corrected for these mistakes, the returns to labor are lower circa 1800 than in 1600.

8. A decline in output per worker in agriculture was predictable given the requirements of sustaining high levels of output on small plots. As peasants in Jiangnan turned to double-cropping rice and wheat, they were required to pile on vast amounts of fertilizer. The revisionists have stressed beancake, because of the ease with which it was applied, but have apparently neglected to fully account for its cost (see above) and have overstated its effects (Brenner and Isett 2003, 235–236). They have also neglected the clearly documented addition of large amounts of animal manures, human excrement, compost, and canal mud that were gathered, mixed, hauled to the fields, and spread two to three times a year. This work required large amounts of labor (Ellis and Wang 1997, 184–186, 190–191). Similarly, a secular decline in real earnings in cotton domestic manufacturing was predictable given the stagnation or decline in daily returns in agriculture. Because productivity in agriculture did not rise, grain prices rose (or rose relative to other peasant manufactures); as a result, disposable income available for nonfood goods shrank.

9. The only statement on the question in Pomeranz's *The Great Divergence* is relegated to a single paragraph and an accompanying footnote. The footnote by all appear-

ances suggests he accepts that labor productivity fell. Pomeranz writes, "[t]he difference between the cost of beancake and purchased manure [which ordinarily would have been mixed from farm waste, rather than bought] was probably one month's total wage for a laborer. . . . Depending on how scattered one's plots, [the substitution of beancake for manures] might have saved a substantial portion of a month's labor" (2000, 98 n 140).

10. James Lee and Wang Feng (1999) also champion the Smithian account of early modern China, finding no reason to dispute the claims that labor productivity in late imperial China fell. Yet, in their critique of Huang's "involutionary" account of China's development (more on which below), they suggest that in "some parts of China, output per workday, though not per year, may indeed have decreased" (175 n 52). They then concede to Huang by suggesting that even if this were also the case in Jiangnan, the decline in hourly income from rice was offset by income gained from work in proto-industry, so that "annual output and annual income also increased." While Lee and Wang are correct that annual output rose, they may be wrong to suggest that peasants raised total incomes by working harder. Much of that extra work went into proto-industrial activities and it is clear that in the most important sector—household cotton cloth manufacturing—wages were falling rapidly enough that peasants would have had to double the time they spent making cloth between 1750 and 1840 just to keep incomes steady (Brenner and Isett 2002; 639–640; Pomeranz 2000, 290, 323–326).

11. For example, see Slicher Van Bath (1964) on Europe generally, LeRoy Ladurie (1976, originally published in 1966) on southern France, and Habakkuk (1958) and M. M. Postan (1966) on England and Britain.

12. For recent demonstrations of this, see Allen (2000) and Maddison (2001).

13. It is important to note that Pomeranz makes this claim vis-à-vis English agriculture on the basis of two studies, neither of which supports his conclusions in substance or in sentiment (see Duchesne 2004, 61–62). One of those is a study of grain yields for England by Gregory Clark (1991) and the other, by Mauro Ambrosoli (1997), is a general survey of agricultural conditions in western Europe from the fourteenth to the nineteenth centuries. Citing these works, Pomeranz claims that yields in English agriculture had stagnated between 1750 and 1850 (2000, 216), that a major technological breakthrough was required to alleviate the situation (126), and that overworking the land had caused soil degradation (223), all propelling England toward agrarian stagnation from which it was rescued by the onset of the industrial revolution and new inputs (206–207, 241). Neither Clark nor Ambrosoli suggest this was the case, however. In the critical period from 1750 to 1850, when England's population doubled, Clark estimates that English grain yields rose 3.5 bushels per acre, when they had risen 5.5 bushels in the period from 1600 to 1700 (Clark 1991, 455). Thus, Clark's data suggest only that the pace at which yields were rising had slowed; they had not stagnated. As for Ambrosoli's study, as Duchesne notes, he never disputes the seventeenth-century agricultural revolution thesis made famous by Eric Kerridge, E. L. Jones, and Joan Thirsk among others. In fact, Ambrosoli (1997, 394) is in perfect agreement with the now commonly held view of two agricultural revolutions in England: the first leading up to 1850 and the second subsequent to 1850.

14. The only evidence Wong cites for stagnant wages in England is David Levine's study of family formation in the period before and during the Industrial Revolution. Levine's otherwise excellent work is not a study of wages (Wong 1997, 29). Levine's position on wages is contradicted by a mass of work that has focused on both labor produc-

tivity growth and real wage growth over the same period. Between 1600 and 1750 real wages in England increased thirty-five to forty percent (Coleman 1977, 102, table 9; Wrigley 1985, 700–701, table 4; cf. Clark 2004, passim).

15. Among the most prominent works are those of Joan Thirsk (1978, 1984), Eric Kerridge (1967), E. L. Jones (1967, 1968), Robert Allen (2000), Nicholas Crafts (1985), Mark Overton (1996), and Gregory Clark (1999).

16. In 1750 labor in English agriculture was twice as productive as labor in French agriculture, three times as productive as labor in German agriculture, twenty-five percent higher than in Belgian agriculture, and fractionally better than in the Netherlands (Allen 2000, 20, table 8). By 1851 the nearest country to England in terms of labor productivity in agriculture was the Netherlands, where labor was only half as productive (Clark 1999, 211, table 4.2).

17. More significantly, across the seventeenth and eighteenth centuries most farms were well above the average in size. In the Midlands, by the early sixteenth century, when the average farm was sixty acres, seventy percent of farms were larger than average and half of all farms were greater than one hundred acres (Allen 1992).

18. Until 1850 water power was the most important source of nonanimal energy employed even in manufacturing. Steam (and thus coal) power superseded water only after 1850 (Landes 1993, 144). Steam power did not enter into agriculture until later still.

19. Not until 1842 was a means found for extracting phosphates from mineral matter and it was not until 1879 that a process was discovered for removing phosphates from iron during its conversion to steel; even so, farmers had to wait to 1885 before the benefits of phosphates extracted from iron were made available to them (Russell 1913, 58–59).

20. Mark Overton (1996) sums up his findings (and those of the literature more generally) thus: "there are grounds for claiming the period 1700–50 as *more* revolutionary than the following half-century. But both periods were outpaced by developments in the first half of the nineteenth century" (37, emphasis added).

21. Deane and Cole estimate that circa 1750 six percent of English gross domestic grain production was exported (1962, 65, table 17). E. L. Jones (1981, 68) estimates that fifty years later, circa 1800, ninety percent of England's population was fed on food produced within Great Britain. As late as 1815, by which time Pomeranz (2000, 216) suggests English agriculture was already floundering between overpopulation and an impending ecological backslide, a mere 6.4 percent of the value of England's agricultural income in grain, meat, and butter was imported. Even then, seventy percent of England's "imports" came not from the Americas or continental Europe but from Ireland, where advanced English agriculture had already taken root in some parts following Cromwell's conquest (Thomas 1985, 743, table 2; Wood 2002, 152–156).

22. R. Bin Wong (1997) to the contrary, there was nothing "involutionary" about England's long-term turn to manufacturing. On this point, Gregory Clark and Ysbrand Van Der Werf (1998) have shown that England's turn to manufacturing did not entail declining returns to labor or falling wages. While workers often did labor longer hours in factory employment, the productivity of their labor only rose as did their wages, albeit more slowly than productivity gains. Clark and Van Der Werf are confirming, therefore, earlier statements to this effect (cf. Pollard 1981; Crafts 1985; Deane and Cole 1962).

23. According to Crafts (1985, 122), the greatest decline in the rate of investment in agriculture occurred in the four decades from 1791 to 1830, between which time agriculture's share of fixed capital investment fell from 32.6 percent to 12.8 percent. The diver-

sion of investment away from agriculture to industry, commerce, and transportation did not, however, prevent agriculture from continuing to improve through the period 1800 to 1850, even as it fell as a proportion of GDP.

24. If household incomes were unchanged, it was only because the economy was becoming highly "involuted" (i.e., peasants were spending vast time spinning and weaving to make up for the decrease in their manufacturing wages).

25. See, for example, Thirsk (1978), Jones (1967, 1968), John (1965), Eversley (1967).

26. It cannot be overemphasized that Jiangnan peasants (as well as peasants in continental Europe) who turned to household manufacturing were not maximizing their gains from trade in the Smithian fashion because of the *disadvantageous* terms of trade for their products.

27. Thus, Chao Kang writes: "in the Chinese family labor was a truly fixed productive factor even in the long run. This helps explain why the Chinese domestic production system had a tendency to harbor surplus labor. Instead of discharging redundant labor, the family kept it in production even when the marginal earning fell below subsistence cost" (1977, 39; cf. 1986, 223).

28. In her study of the economy of south China, Sucheta Mazumdar concludes with a very similar criticism of the "involutionary" thesis (1998, 404–405).

29. Frank Ellis's (1988) critique of the Chayanovian model farm is correct to point out that it pertains in its fullest expression in the absence of a capitalist labor market. The model focuses on the decisions as to cropping output and labor input in a household that cannot hire labor out, or at least has minimal and only seasonal opportunities to do so. Consequently, production decisions depend upon farm size and the age structure of the household (the number and work capacity of laborers and the household's consumption needs). It presumes therefore no urban or town-based manufacturing employment possibilities (35, 116–117, 137).

30. There has been much debate on the subject of fertility rates in late imperial China (see the exchange between Cameron Campbell, Wang Feng, and James Lee (1999, 2002) and Arthur Wolf (2001). One point of contention is the numerical value of historical fertility rates; another is whether Chinese families were controlling fertility deliberately or whether environmental and other factors reduced fertility. It does appear that the Total Marital Fertility Rate (which accounts for only married women) was higher in Europe than in China, though perhaps not as high as Lee and Wang suggest (see below). What is clear is that the total fertility rate (TFR—the relevant number for gauging the effects of fertility on population growth because it takes into account both married and unmarried women of child-bearing age) in late imperial China was higher than in Europe (Lee and Wang 1999, 84). The reason for these differences between TFR and TMFR is largely because European women married at much older ages than Chinese women and far more European women never married than Chinese women, behavior which will make the TFR significantly lower than the TMFR. The average age at which Chinese women married was close to eighteen, whereas in some European populations it was twenty-five or older. Whereas in China female marriage was universal (i.e., close to one hundred percent of Chinese women married and were therefore, in the language of demographers, "exposed" to the "risk" of pregnancy at a very early age), in Europe large numbers of women and men never married at all. Consequently, early modern European populations, and England in particular, had lower TFR than contemporaneous

China. Thus, any advantages Chinese households had in lower TMFR washed out in the aggregate.

In England, the female celibacy rate was twenty-five percent across the seventeenth century and eleven percent during the first half of the eighteenth century while the average age of women at marriage was twenty-six between 1600 and 1750. This made for a significant difference between the TMFR and TFR, which were 7.4 and 4.38 respectively for the century and a half before the Industrial Revolution (Coleman and Salt 1992, 15–19, tables 1.2 and 1.3). On the flip side of the same coin, the difference in China between TMFR and TFR is historically far less. Thus, when in 1955 the TMFR was 6.2 the TFR was 6.0 (Lee and Wang 1999, 85, table 6.1). This all suggests that prior to the onset of the Industrial Revolution England's population was growing far more slowly than that of China.

As for the manner in which Lee and Wang construct the TMFR it should be noted that because of such differences in marriage patterns, to use the TMFR in a meaningful, comparative way it is common demographic practice to standardize the data to distinguish nuptiality effects from fertility effects, but Lee and Wang do not do this. Instead, they use a crude TMFR, which is far less desirable (see Shyrock and Siegel 1975, 485–487, 513). The crude TMFR unduly biases figures in favor of China, making it an unacceptable unit of comparison. Because of the way the figure is calculated (it is a synthetic number derived from summing the number of births per woman in the population for different age cohorts [often from ages twenty to forty-nine] and not a measurement of the number of children actually born to the average married woman), it significantly dilutes the effect of the much later age at which European women married. While Chinese women on average married at about eighteen or less in the late imperial period, in early modern England the average female age of marriage was about twenty-six between 1600 and 1750 (Coleman and Salt 1992, 15–19, tables 1.2 and 1.3). Of course, the later average age at which English and European women in general married meant a shortened period of time in which they were "at risk." To show how the crude TMFR biases in China's favor, Ricardo Duchesne (2003, 538–539), citing Livi-Bacci (2000), points out that given an average age of marriage of eighteen, English women in the period from 1600–1700 would have delivered 7.3 children (which is close to the figure attributed by Lee and Wang [1999] to English women); but at twenty-five years of age—the actual age at which the average woman in England married before the onset of the Industrial Revolution—the figure falls to 5.3. The same bias effect can be seen in other continental European populations; once the TMFR is calculated at the average age of marriage, the rate drops considerably. By including cohorts of European women in their lower twenties, who were in fact hardly ever married, while neglecting the large number of Chinese women who were married before twenty, Lee and Wang have made Chinese TMFR look that much lower by comparison.

31. As the amount of land per person diminished it would obviously become more difficult to follow the norms of subdivision and in turn have many children. Population growth could thus be expected to slow down.

32. My argument here differs from that posited by James Reardon-Anderson's (2005) study of Manchuria, though his conclusion—that there was no secular rise in labor productivity in the Qing period—concurs with my findings stated here and in my earlier dissertation (1998). Reardon-Anderson argues first that Manchuria's farms were

large enough that what he holds to be the standard account for nongrowth, with its focus on the smallness of Chinese farms, can not hold (2005, 9). Two points need to be made before addressing his argument. First, he cites Philip Huang (1985, 1990) and Sucheta Mazumdar (1998) as both arguing that the small size of Chinese farms was a barrier to growth, though in fact neither of them make any such claim. Huang's argument is first and foremost about economic rationality and how that determines choices and ultimately the trajectory of growth or non-growth. Similarly, Mazumdar's argument is also concerned with uncovering peasant economic behavior. In contrast to Huang, however, she shows how economic behavior in the Qing was configured by extant social property relations in ways that prevented economic growth, as I also argue here. Second, Reardon-Anderson can not make the argument that Manchuria was different structurally from the rest of China because farms there were uniquely large. The largest farms in the twentieth century most often did not exceed sixty acres, a size small by eighteenth century English standards. More importantly, most farms were less than ten acres by this time. Nor were farms significantly bigger in the Qing, when average farms were perhaps twenty acres at their height in size. Small farm size was of course a barrier to growth, though I agree that that alone can not explain outcomes (see Brenner 1985b [1982], 315–317).

Reardon-Anderson explains the absence of growth in terms of the persistence of certain peasant patterns of social and economic behavior, initially borne by the settlers from their north China homes to their new homes (9). But, as is so often the case with culturalist accounts of this sort, the answer simply begs the question of why the persistence of that behavior. Is it simply a cultural preference? More importantly, that explanation simply displaces the question further back in time and to a different place. One must ask: why did growth not occur in north China?

33. In his far-ranging study of European industrialization between 1760 and 1970, Sidney Pollard (1981) captures the proto-industrial dynamic: "Both landlord and putter-out did well out of the early proto-industrial family, but the family itself moved into a position of low-wage employment that would turn into a poverty trap when its allocation of land declined with rising population induced by the process itself" (72).

34. See Joseph Bryant's (forthcoming) discussion of polycentricism and his critique of the logic of the "radical contingency" position that is entailed in much of the revisionist historiography.

Appendix A

1. There is an across the board acceptance of Qing population and arable figures. The examples of the unquestioning use of these numbers are in fact too numerous to cite in full. A few examples taken from the more important works will suffice (Diao 1993, 46–47, 116–119; Enatsu 1980, 67–68, citing Sudō's work; Lu 1987, 20; Wang 1991, 328–329, 331, 338; Xu 1990, 102; Yi 1993, 211, 218–219, 311; Zhang 1998, 59).

2. Sun Kungtu (1969) accepts this number as does Wang I-Shou (1971). For a discussion of official population statistics, see Wynne (1958).

3. The Harbin-Dalian line, built by the Southern Manchuria Railway company, was completed in 1903 but did not begin running until 1907 (Chao 1983, 5).

References and Sources

Archival materials are cited in the following fashion. Materials from the First National Archives collection of memorials, the *xingke tiben*, *xingbu tiben*, and *hubu zouzhe*, are cited as XT, XB, and HZ respectively. The *xingke tiben* and *hubu zouzhe* are cited by Western calendar year, lunar month, and day. The *xingbu tiben* are cited either by the original archived case number or Western calendar year, lunar month, and day (depending upon the state and form of my sources). Materials from the Liaoning Provincial Archives' Shengjing Imperial Household Department collection are cited as LPA and those from the Jilin City Archives as JCA. For these materials, the citation is followed by the Western calendar year and the original archived case number. MQ refers to the *Zhongyang Yanjiuyuan Lishi Yuyan Yanjiusuo xian cun Qing dai Neige Daku yuan cang Ming-Qing dang'an* (Ming-Qing documents from the Qing Dynasty Grand Secretariate Archive in the Possession of the History and Language Research Institute, Academia Sinica). Taibei: Academia Sinica. Each case is identified by the original serial number. References to the statutes and substatutes of the Qing Code are cited according to the format provided in Huang Tsing-cha's edition of Xue Yun-sheng's *Duli cunyi* (DC 1970).

Field Interviews

Xia Deyi and Xia Dianyou. (1994). Elderly men interviewed in Liujiatun, Jilin. March 9, 1994.

Zhang Guizhi and Liu Hongxi. (1994). Elderly women interviewed in Liujiatun, Jilin. March 12, 1994.

Works Cited

Adachi, Kinnosuke. (1925). *Manchuria: A Survey.* New York, Robert M. McBride & Company.

Adachi Keiji. (1978). "Daizu kasi ryūtsū to Shindai no shōgyōteki nōgyō" (The circulation of soyabean cake and commercial agriculture during the Qing). *Tōyōshi kenkyū* 37.3: 35–63.

Allee, Mark A. (1994a). *Law and Society in Late Imperial China: Northern Taiwan in the Nineteenth Century*. Stanford, Stanford University Press.

Allee, Mark A. (1994b) "Code, Culture, and Custom: Foundations of Civil Case Verdicts in a Nineteenth-Century County Court." In Kathryn Bernhardt and Philip Huang, ed., *Civil Law in Qing and Republican China*. Stanford University Press. 122–141.

Allen, Robert. C. (1992). *Enclosure and the Yeoman: The Agricultural Development of the South Midlands, 1450–1850*. Oxford, Clarendon Press.

Allen, Robert C. (1999). "Tracking the Agricultural Revolution in England." *Economic History Review* 52: 209–233.

Allen, Robert C. (2000). "Economic Structure and Agricultural Productivity in Europe, 1300–1800." *European Review of Economic History* 3: 1–25.

Allen, Robert C. (2001). "The Great Divergence of European Wages and Prices from the Middle Ages to the First World War." *Explorations in Economic History* 38: 411–447.

Allen, Robert, C, Jean-Pascal Bassino, Debin Ma, Christine Moll-Murata, and Jan Luiten van Zanden. (2006). "Wages Prices and Living Standards in China, Japan, and Europe, 1738–1925." Presented at Economic History Workshop Programme, Warwick University.

Amagai Kenzaburō. (1969). *Chūgoku tochi monjo no kenkyū* (Studies in Chinese land documents). Tōkyō, Keisō shobō.

Amano Motonosuke. (1932). *Manshū keizai no hattatsu* (The development of the Manchurian economy). No place of publication.

Amano Motonosuke. (1985). *Chūgoku nōgyō shi kenkyū* (Research on the history of Chinese agriculture). Tōkyō, Ochanomizu shobō.

Ambrosoli, Mauro. (1997). *The Wild and the Sown: Botany and Agriculture in Western Europe, 1350–1850*. Cambridge, Cambridge University Press.

Anderson, Perry. (1978). *Passages from Antiquity to Feudalism*. London, Verso.

Anderson. Perry. (1974). *Lineages of the Absolutist State*. London, Verso.

Balazs, Etienne. (1964). *Chinese Civilization and Bureaucracy*. New Haven, Yale University Press.

Bao Shichen. (1968). *An Wu Sizhong (Four Treatises on the Governance of Wu)*. Taibei, Wenhai chubanshe.

Barfield, Thomas J. (1989). *The Perilous Frontier: Nomadic Empires and China, 221 BC to AD 1757*. Oxford, Blackwell Publishers.

Beattie, Hilary. (1979). *Land and Lineage in China: A Study of T'ung-Ch'eng County, Anhwei, in the Ming and Ch'ing Dynasties*. Cambridge, Cambridge University Press.

Bell, Lynda S. (1999). *One Industry, Two Chinas: Silk Filatures and Peasant-family Production in Wuxi County, 1865–1937*. Stanford, Stanford University Press.

Berend, T. Ivan. (2003) *History Derailed: Central and Eastern Europe in the Long Nineteenth Century*. Berkeley, University of California.

Bernhardt, Kathryn. (1992). *Rents, Taxes, and Peasant Resistance: The Lower Yangzi Region, 1840–1950*. Stanford, Stanford University Press.

Bernhardt, Kathryn. (1999). *Women and Property in China, 960–1949*. Stanford, Stanford University Press.

Bernhardt, Kathryn, and Philip C. C. Huang. (1994). *Civil Law in Qing and Republican China*. Stanford, Stanford University Press.

Broadberry, S. N. and B. Gupta (forthcoming). "The Early Modern Great Divergence:

Wages, Prices, and Economic Development in Europe and Asia, 1500–1800. *Economic History Review.*

Bloch, Marc. (1966). *French Rural Society: An Essay on Its Basic Characteristics.* Berkeley, University of California Press.

Bodde, Derk, and Clarence Morris. (1967). *Law in Imperial China: Exemplified by 190 Ch'ing Dynasty Cases Translated from the Hsing-an hui-lan.* Philadelphia, University of Pennsylvania Press.

Boserup, Esther. (1965). *The Conditions of Agricultural Growth: The Economics of Agrarian Change under Population Pressure.* Chicago, Aldine Publishing Company.

Bourdieu, Pierre. (1977). *Outline of a Theory of Practice.* Stanford, Calif., Stanford University Press.

Bourgon, Jérôme. (2004). "Rights, Freedoms, and Customs in the Making of Chinese Civil Law, 1900–1936." In William C. Kirby, ed., *Realms of Freedom in Modern China.* Stanford, Calif., Stanford University Press.

BQ. (1985). *Ba qi tongzhi* (Complete gazetteer of the eight banners). Changchun, Dongbei shifan daxue chubanshe. Reprint.

Brandt, Loren. (1989). *Commercialization and Agricultural Development in East-Central China, 1870–1937.* Cambridge, Cambridge University Press.

Bray, Francesca. (1984). *Science and Civilisation in China: Agriculture.* Cambridge, Cambridge University Press.

Bray, Francesca. (1997). *Technology and Gender: Fabrics of Power in Late Imperial China.* Berkeley, University of California Press.

Brenner, Robert. (1977). "The Origins of Capitalist Development: A Critique of Neo-Smithian Marxism." *New Left Review,* I/104, (July–August 1977): 25–92.

Brenner, Robert. (1985a [1976]). "Agrarian Class Structure and Economic Development in Pre-Industrial Europe." In T. H. Ashton and C. H. E. Philpin, eds., *The Brenner Debate: Agrarian Class Structure and Economic Development in Pre-Industrial Europe.* Cambridge, Cambridge University Press.

Brenner, Robert. (1985b [1982]). "The Agrarian Roots of European Capitalism." In T. H. Ashton and C. H. E. Philpin, eds., *The Brenner Debate: Agrarian Class Structure and Economic Development in Pre-Industrial Europe.* Cambridge, Cambridge University Press.

Brenner, Robert. (1986). "The Social Basis of Economic Development." In John Roemer, ed., *Analytical Marxism.* Cambridge, Cambridge University Press.

Brenner, Robert. (1993). *Merchants and Revolution: Commercial Change, Political Conflict, and London's Overseas Trade, 1550–1653.* Princeton, Princeton University Press.

Brenner, Robert. (1997). "Property Relations and the Growth of Agricultural Productivity in Late Medieval and Early Modern Europe." *Economic Development and Agricultural Productivity.* Amit Bhaduri and Rune Skarstein. Cheltenham, UK, Edward Elgar.

Brenner, Robert. (2001). "The Low Countries in the Transition to Capitalism." In Peter Hoppenbrouwers and Jan Luiten van Zande, eds., *Peasants into Farmers? The Transformation of Rural Economy and Society in the Low Countries (Middle Ages-Nineteenth Century) in Light of the Brenner Debate.* Turnhout, Belgium: Brepols.

Brenner, Robert, and Christopher Isett. (2002). "England's Divergence from China's Yangzi Delta: Property Relations, Microeconomics, and Patterns of Development." *Journal of Asian Studies* 61.2: 609–662.

Brenner, Robert, and Christopher Isett. (2003). "Yinggelan yu Zhongguo changjiang sanjiao zhou de fencha: caichan guanxi, weiguan jingjixue, yu fazhan xingshi" (England's Divergence from China's Yangzi Delta: Property Relations, Microeconomics, and Patterns of Economic Development). *Zhongguo xiangcun yanjiu* 2: 217–282.

Brockman, Rosser H. (1980). "Commercial Contract Law in Late Nineteenth-Century Taiwan." In Jerome Cohen, R. Randle Edwards, and Fu-mei Chang Chen, eds., *Essays on China's Legal Tradition*. Princeton, Princeton University Press. 76–136.

Brook, Timothy. (1998). *The Confusions of Pleasure: Commerce and Culture in Ming China*. Berkeley, University of California Press.

Bryant, Joseph. (forthcoming). "The West and the Rest Revisited: Debating Capitalist Origins, European Colonialism, and the Advent of Modernity." *Canadian Journal of Sociology*.

Buck, John Lossing. (1937). *Land Utilization in China: Statistics*. Shanghai, University of Nanking.

Buoye, Thomas. (2000). *Manslaughter, Markets and Moral Economy*. Cambridge, Cambridge University Press.

Buoye, Thomas. (2004). "Litigation, Legitimacy, and Lethal Violence." In Madeleine Zelin, Jonathan Ocko, and Robert Gardella, eds., *Contract and Property in Early Modern China*. Stanford, Stanford University Press. 94–119.

Bushman, Richard Lyman. (1998). "Markets and Composite Farms in Early America." *The William and Mary Quarterly*. 55.3: 351–374.

Campbell, B. M. S. (1980). "Population Change and the Genesis of Commonfields on a Norfolk Manor." *Economic History Review* 2.33: 174–192.

Campbell, B. M. S. (1981). "The Regional Uniqueness of English Field Systems? Some Evidence from Eastern Norfolk." *Agricultural History Review* 29.1: 16–28.

Campbell, B. M. S. (1983). "Agricultural Progress in Medieval England: Some Evidence from Eastern Norfolk." *Economic History Review* 2.36: 26–46.

Campbell, B. M. S. (1991) "Land, Labour, Livestock and Productivity Trends in English Seigniorial Agriculture, 1208–1450."' In B. M. S. Campbell and M. Overton, eds., *Land, Labour and Livestock: Historical Studies in European Agricultural Productivity*. Manchester, Manchester University Press. 144–182.

Campbell, B. M. S. (1995). "Progressiveness and Backwardness in Thirteenth- and Early Fourteenth-Century English Agriculture: The Verdict of Recent Research." In Jean Marie Duvosquel and E. Thoen, eds., *Peasants and Townsmen in Medieval Europe. Studia in Honorem Adriaan Verhulst*. Gent, Snoeck-Ducaju & Zoon. 558–559.

Campbell, B. M. S., and Mark Overton. (1993). "A New Perspective on Medieval and Early Modern Agriculture: Six Centuries of Norfolk Farming c.1250–c.1850," *Past & Present*, 141: 38–105.

Campbell, Cameron, Wang Feng, and James Lee. (2002). "Pretransitional Fertility in China." *Population and Development Review* 28.4: 735–750.

Canny, Nicholas. (1998). "The Origins of Empire: An Introduction." In Nicholas Canny, ed., *The Oxford History of the British Empire*, vol. 1: *The Origins of Empire: British Overseas Enterprise to the Close of the Seventeenth Century*. Oxford, Oxford University Press.

Cao Shuji. (2001). *Zhongguo renkou shi: Qing shiqi* (China's population history: the Qing period). Shanghai, Fudan daxue chuban she: Xinhua shudian, Shanghai faxing suo.
Cao Yonghe. (1991). *Taiwan zaoqi lishi yanjiu* (Historical research on early Taiwan). Taibei, Lianjing chubanshe.
Cao Xinsui. (1996). *Jiu Zhongguo Sunan nongye jingji yanjiu.* (Research on the agricultural economy of southern Jiangsu in traditional China). Beijing, Zhongyang biandu chubanshe.
Chambers, Jonathan. (1972). *Population, Economy, and Society in Pre-industrial England.* London, Oxford University Press.
Chang, Chung-li. (1955). *The Chinese Gentry.* Seattle, University of Washington Press.
Chang, Michael. (2001). "A Court on Horseback." Ph.D. thesis. San Diego, University of California.
Chang, Te-chang. (1972). "The Economic Role of the Imperial Household (Nei-wu-fu) in the Ch'ing Dynasty." *Journal of Asian Studies* 31.2: 243–273.
Chao, Kang. (1977). *The Development of Cotton Textile Production in China.* Cambridge, Mass., Harvard University Press.
Chao, Kang. (1983). *The Economic Development of Manchuria: The Rise of a Frontier Economy.* Ann Arbor, Center for Chinese Studies, University of Michigan.
Chao, Kang. (1986). *Man and Land in Chinese Economic History: An Economic Analysis.* Stanford, Stanford University Press.
Chatterjee, Partha. (1983). "More on Modes of Power." In R. Guha, ed., *Subaltern Studies II.* Delhi, Oxford University Press. 311–349.
Chayanov, A. V. (1986). *The Theory of Peasant Economy.* Madison, University of Wisconsin Press.
Chen Keng. (1987). "Zhongguo budong chan jiaoyi de zhaojia wenti" (The question of "zhaojia" in the exchange of real estate property in China). *Fujian luntan* 5: 29–35.
Ch'en, Fumei and Ramon H. Myers. (1976) *Customarty Law and the Economic Growth of China during the Ch'ing Period."* Ch'ing-shih Wenti. 3.5: 1–32.
Chikusa Tatsuo. (1964–1967). *Manshū kazoku seido no kanshū (The Customs of the Manchurian Family System).* 3 vols. Tōkyō, Yiritsusha.
Chikusa Tatsuo. (1978). "Succession to Ancestral Sacrifices and Adoption of Heirs to the Sacrifices: As seen from an Inquiry into Customary Institutions in Manchuria." In David C. Buxbaum, ed., *Chinese Family Law and Social Change in Historical and Comparative Perspective.* Seattle, University of Washington Press: 151–175.
Chu, Raymond W., and William G. Saywell. (1984). *Career Patterns in the Ch'ing Dynasty: The Office of Governor-General.* Ann Arbor, Center for Chinese Studies University of Michigan.
Chü, Tung-tsu. (1961). *Law and Society in Traditional China. Paris, Mouton.*
Chü, Tung-tsu. (1962). *Local Government in China under the Ch'ing.* Cambridge, Mass., Harvard University Press.
Ch'üan Han-sheng, and Richard A. Kraus. (1975). *Mid-Ch'ing Rice Markets and Trade: An Essay in Price History.* Cambridge, Mass., East Asian Research Center Harvard University: Harvard University Press.
Clark, Gregory. (1991). "Yields per Acre in English Agriculture, 1250–1860: Evidence from Labour Inputs," *Economic History Review* 44: 445–60.

Clark, Gregory. (1993). "Labour Productivity in English Agriculture, 1300–1860." In B. M. Campbell ed., *Land, Labour, and Livestock: Historical Studies in European Agricultural Productivity*. Manchester, Manchester University Press.

Clark, Gregory. (1999). "Too Much Revolution: Agriculture in the Industrial Revolution, 1700–1860." In Joel Mokyr, ed., *The British Industrial Revolution. An Economic Perspective*. Boulder, Colo., Westview Press.

Clark, Gregory. (2004). "The Long March of History: Farm Laborers' Wages in England 1208–1850." University of California–Davis, Working Paper.

Clark, Gregory, and Ysbrand Van Der Werf. (1998). "Work in Progress? The Industrial Revolution." *Journal of Economic History* 58.3: 830–843.

Coleman, D. C. (1977). *The English Economy, 1450–1750*. Oxford, Oxford University Press.

Coleman, David, and John Salt. (1992). *The British Population: Patterns, Trends, and Processes*. Oxford, Oxford University Press.

Cohen, Myron. (2004). "Writs of Passage in Late Imperial China: The Documentation of Practical Understandings in Minong, Taiwan." In Madeleine Zelin, Jonathan Ocko, and Robert Gardella, eds., *Contract and Property in Early Modern China*. Stanford, Stanford University Press: 17–36.

Crafts, N. F. R. (1985). *British Economic Growth During the Industrial Revolution*. Oxford, Clarendon Press.

Crossley, Pamela K. (1987). "*Manzhou yuanliu kao* and the Formalization of the Manchu Heritage." *Journal of Asian Studies* 46.4: 761–790.

Crossley, Pamela K. (1989). "The Qianlong Retrospective on the Chinese-martial (*hanjun*) Banners." *Late Imperial China* 10.1: 63–107.

Crossley, Pamela K. (1990). *Orphan Warriors: Three Manchu Generations and the End of the Qing World*. Princeton, Princeton University Press.

Crossley, Pamela. K. (1994). "Manchu Education," in Benjamin Elman and Alexander Woodside, eds., "*Education and Society in Late Impeiral China, 1600–1900*. Berkeley, University of California Press.

Crossley, Pamela. K. (1999). *A Translucent Mirror: History and Identity in Qing Imperial Ideology*. Berkeley, University of California Press.

Crossley, Pamela. K. (2002). "The Conquest Elite of the Ch'ing Empire." In Willard J. Peterson, ed., *The Cambridge History of China*, vol.9: *The Ch'ing Empire to 1800*. Cambridge, Cambridge University Press.

Daniels, Christian. (1983). "The Handicraft Scale Sugar Industry and Merchant Capital in South Taiwan, 1870–1895." *Tōyō Gakuho* 64.3–4: 65–102.

Deane, Phyllis, and W. A. Cole. (1962). *British Economic Growth, 1688–1959*. Cambridge, Cambridge University Press.

DC. (1970). *Du li cun yi* (Lingering doubts after reading the substatutes). Taibei, Chinese Materials and Research Aids Service Center.

Deng Yibing. (1996). "Qingdai qianqi yanhai yunshuye de xingshuai" (The rise and decline of commercial shipping in the early Qing). *Zhongguo shehui jingji shi yanjiu* 3: 40–52.

Diao Shuren. (1991). "Ming he Qing qianqi dongbei de jingying yu kenzhi" (The management and opening of the Northeast during the Ming and Qing). In Li Shutian., ed., *Zhongguo dongbei tongshi* (A complete history of northeast China). Jilin, Jilin wenshi chubanshe.

Diao Shuren. (1993). *Dongbei qidi yanjiu* (Research into the bannerlands of the northeast). Jilin, Jilin wenshi chubanshe.

Ding Yizhuang. (1991a). "Qingdai bianjiang tunken jiqi chengxiao" (Qing frontier colonies and their outcomes): "Dongbei guanwai diqu de kaifa he tunken" (The opening and colonization of the northeast region). Wang Yuquan, Liu Zhongri, Guo Songyi, and Lin Yongkuang, eds., *Zhongguo tunken shi* (The history of colonies and land-opening in China). Beijing, Nongye chubanshe. Vol. 2, 326–342.

Ding Yizhuang. (1991b). *Manzu de funü shenghuo yu hunyin zhidu yanjiu* (Research on the lives and marriage system of Manchu women). Beijing, Beijing daxue chubanshe.

Dobb, Maurice. (1947). *Studies in the Development of Capitalism*. New York, International Publishers.

DSD. (1987). *Dongsansheng jingji diaochao (Survey of the Northeastern economy)*. Shen Yunlong, ed., *Jindai Zhongguo shiliao congkan*. Taibei, Wenhai chubanshe.

Duara, Prasenjit. (1988). *Culture, Power, and the State: Rural North China, 1900–1942*. Stanford, Stanford University Press.

Duby, Georges. (1976). *Rural Economy and Country Life in the Medieval West*. Columbia S.C., University of South Carolina Press.

Duchesne, Ricardo. (2003). "Malthus and the Demographic Systems of modern Europe and Imperial China." *Review of Radical Political Economies* 35.4: 534–542.

Duchesne, Ricardo. (2004). "On the Rise of the West: Researching Kenneth Pomeranz's 'Great Divergence.'" *Review of Radical Political Economies* 36.1: 52–81.

Dunstan, Helen. (1996). *Conflicting Counsels to Confuse the Age: A Documentary Study of Political Economy in Qing China, 1644–1840*. Ann Arbor, Center for Chinese Studies, University of Michigan.

Ebrey, Patricia. B. (1993). *The Inner Quarters: Marriage and the Lives of Chinese Women in the Sung Period*. Berkeley, University of California Press.

Edmonds, Richard L. (1985). "Northern Frontiers of Qing China and Tokugawa Japan: A Comparative Study of Frontier Policy." Chicago, University of Chicago, Department of Geography, Research paper.

Elliott, Mark. C. (2000). "The Limits of Tartary: Manchuria in Imperial and National Geographies." *Journal of Asian Studies* 59.3: 603–646.

Elliott, Mark C. (2001). *The Manchu Way: The Eight Banners and Ethnic Identity in Late Imperial China*. Stanford, Stanford University Press.

Ellis, E. C., and Wang S. M. (1997). "Sustainable Traditional Agriculture in the Lake Tai Region of China." *Agriculture, Ecosystems, and Environment* 61: 177–193.

Ellis, E. C., R. G. Li, L. Z. Yang, and X. Cheng. (2000). "Nitrogen and the Sustainable Village." In S. R. Gliessman, ed., *Agroecosystem Sustainability: Developing Practical Strategies*. CRC Press, Boca Raton, FL. 95–104.

Ellis, Frank. (1988). *Peasant Economics: Farm Households and Agrarian Development*. Cambridge, Cambridge University Press.

Elman, Benjamin. (1992). "Political, Social, and Cultural Reproduction via the Civil Service Examinations in Late Imperial China." *Journal of Asian Studies* 50.1: 7–28.

Elman, Benjamin. (1993). "Where is King Cheng?: Civil Examinations and Confucian Ideology During the Early Ming, 1368–1415." *T'oung Pao* 79: 23–68.

Elvin, Mark. (1973). *The Pattern of the Chinese Past*. Stanford, Stanford University Press.

Elvin, Mark. (2004). *The Retreat of the Elephants: An Environmental History of China*. New Haven, Yale University Press.

Elvin, Mark and Liu Ts'ui-jung, eds. (1998). *The Sediments of Time*. Cambridge, University of Cambridge Press.

Enastu, Yoshiki. (1991). "The Rise of the Fengtian Local Elite at the End of the Qing Dynasty." Ph.D. thesis, Department of History. Ann Arbor, University of Michigan.

Enatsu Yoshiki. (1980). "Shinchō no jidai, tōsanshō ni okeru hakki ki shōen no shōtō ni tsuite no ikkōsatsu" (A preliminary investigation of the bailiffs to the manors of the Eight Banners in the northeast during the Qing era). *Shakai keizai shigaku* 46.1: 59–76.

Enatsu Yoshiki. (1989). "Kyū Kinshū kanshō no shōtō to eitenko" (Permanent tenants and village bailiffs of the manor in old Jinzhou). *Shakai keizai shigaku* 54.6: 753–894.

Esherick, Joseph. (1981). "Number Games: A Note on Land Distribution in Prerevolutionary China." *Modern China* 7.4: 387–411.

Esherick, Joseph, and Mary B. Rankin. (1990). *Chinese Local Elites and Patterns of Dominance*. Berkeley, University of California Press.

Eversley, D. E. C. (1967). "The Home Market and Economic Growth in England, 1750–1780." In E. L. Jones and G. E. Mingay, eds., *Land, Labour, and Population in the Industrial Revolution*. New York, Barnes and Noble.

Fan, I.-Chun. (1992). "Long-distance Trade and Market Integration in Ming-Ch'ing Period, 1400–1850." Ph.D. thesis, Stanford, Stanford University.

Fan Jinmin. (1998). *Ming Qing Jiangnan shangye de fazhan* (The development of Jiangnan commerce in the Ming and Qing). Nanjing, Nanjing daxue chubanshe.

Fang Gongqian. (1993). *Jue yu ji lüe* (Records from a distant land). Jilin, Jilin wenshi chubanshe.

Fang Shiji. (1985). *Longsha jilüe* (Records from the Heilongjiang). Harbin, Heilongjiang renmin chubanshe.

Fang, Xing. (1983). "Lun qingdai qianqi dizhu zhi jingji de fazhan" (On the development of the landlord economy in the early Qing). *Zhongguo yanjiu* 2: 88–99.

Fang Xing. (1986). "Lun Qingdai nongmin shangpin shengchan de fazhan" (Concerning the development of peasant commodity production in the Qing). *Zhongguo jingji shi yanjiu* 1: 53–56.

Fang Xing. (1992). "Qingdai qianqi fengjian dizu lü" (On the rate of feudal rent in the early Qing). Zhongguo jingji shi yanjiu 2: 61–69.

Fang Xing. (1996). "Qingdai Jiangnan nongmin de xiaofei" (Rural consumption in Qing Jiangnan). *Zhongguo jingji shi yanjiu* 3: 91–98.

Fang Xing, Jing Junjian, and Wei Jinyu. (2000). *Zhongguo jingji tongshi: Qingdai jingji juan* (The economic history of China: the Qing economy). 3 vols. Beijing, Jingji ribao.

Fang Yingkai. (1989). *Xinjiang tun ken shi* (The history of the opening of Xinjiang). Wulumuqi, Xinjiang qingshao nian chubanshe.

Faure, David. (1989). *The Rural Economy of Pre-Liberation China: Trade Expansion and Peasant Livelihood in Jiangsu and Guangdong, 1870–1937*. Hong Kong, Oxford University Press.

Feinstein, Charles H. (1998). "Pessimism Perpetuated: Real Wages and the Standard of Living in Britain during and after the Industrial Revolution." *Journal of Economic History* 58.3: 625–658.

Feng Shaoting. (1994). "Supplemental Payment in Urban Property Contracts in Mid to Late Qing Shanghai." In Madeleine Zelin, Jonathan Ocko, and Robert Gardella, eds., *Contract and Property in Early Modern China*. Stanford, Stanford University Press. 209–229.

Feuerwerker, Albert. (1958). *China's Early Industrialization: Sheng Hsuan-huai (1844–1916) and Mandarin Enterprise*. Cambridge, Mass., Harvard University Press.

FCZS. (1914). *Fengtian quan sheng caizheng shuoming shu (A description of Fengtian finance policy)*, ed. Jingji xuehui. Beijing, Caizheng bu (Ministry of Finance).

FNDS. (1909). *Fengtian quan sheng nongye diaocha* (Agricultural survey of all Fengtian province). Ma Weiyuan. Fengtian, Fengtian nongye shiyan chang.

FO. (1920). Foreign Office: *Manchuria*. London, H.M. Stationary Office.

FTTZ. (2003). *Fengtian tongzhi* (The complete gazetteer of Fengtian). Shenyang, Liaohai chubanshe. Reprint.

Fletcher, John. (1978a). "Ch'ing Inner Asia, c. 1800." In Denis Twitchett and John K. Fairbank, eds., *The Cambridge History of China*, vol. 10, part 1: *The Ch'ing Dynasty, 1800–1911*. Cambridge, Cambridge University Press. 35–106.

Fletcher, John. (1978a). "Sino-Russion Relations, 1800–1862." In Denis Twitchett and John K. Fairbank, eds., *The Cambridge History of China*, vol. 10, part 1: *The Ch'ing Dynasty, 1800–1911*. Cambridge, Cambridge University Press. 318–350.

Friedmann, Harriet. (1980). "Household Production and the National Economy: Concepts for the Analysis of Agrarian Formations." *Journal of Peasant Studies* 7: 158–183.

Fu Yiling. (1961). *Ming-Qing nongcun shehui jingji* (The economy of rural society in the Ming and Qing). Beijing, Renmin chubanshe.

Furichi, Daisuke. (2000). "Chūgoku tōhoku no chiiki keisei to shinchō gyosei: 18–19 seiki Seikyō ni okeru saibai sōmō seisaku to kanryōsei" (Regional formation and the Qing government in China's Northeast: State procurements, granary policy and the bureaucratic system in eighteenth and nineteenth century Shengjing). Ph.D. thesis, Humanities and Social Sciences, Tōkyō, Tōkyō daigaku, daigakuin jinbun shakaikei kenkyūka.

Gardella, Robert. (1994). *Harvesting the Mountains: Fujian and the China Tea Trade, 1757–1937*. Berkeley, University of California Press.

Gates, Hill. (1996). *China's Motor: A Thousand Years of Petty Capitalism*. Ithaca, Cornell University Press.

GB.CR. (1971). *Commercial Reports*. Irish University Press, Area Studies, British Parliamentary Papers. Shannon, Irish University Press.

GCJY. (1993). *Guochao jianye chuji jilue* (Records of the Dynastic founding enterprise). Beijing, Beijing daxue chubanshe.

GDZ-YZ. *Gongzhong dang* (Secret palace memorials). *Yongzheng chao zou zhe* (Draft memorials of the Yongzheng emperor); Taibei, Guo li gu gong bo wu yuan. Published series 1977–1999.

GDZ-QL. *Gongzhong dang* (Secret palace memorials). *Qianlong chao zou zhe* (Draft memorials of the Qianlong emperor). Taibei, Guo li gu gong bo wu yuan. Published series 1982–.

Golas, Peter. (1977). "Early Ch'ing Guilds." In G. W. Skinner, ed., *The City in Late Imperial China*. Stanford, Stanford University Press. 555–580.

Gottschang, Thomas, and Diana Lary. (2000). *Swallows and Settlers: The Great Migration from North China to Manchuria*. Ann Arbor, University of Michigan Press.

Gottschang, Thomas R. (1982). "Migration from North China to Manchuria: An Economic History, 1891–1942." Ph.D. thesis, Department of History, Ann Arbor, University of Michigan.

Gramsci, Antonio. (1971). *Selections from the Prison Notebooks.* New York, International Publishers.

Grantham, George. (1978). "The Diffusion of the New Husbandry in Northern France, 1815–1840." *Journal of Economic History* 38.2: 311–337.

Grantham, George. (1980). "The Persistemce of Open-Field Farming in Nineteenth-Century France." *Journal of Economic History* 60.3: 515–531.

Gray, John Henry. (2002). *China: A History of the Laws, Manners, and Customs of the People.* 2 vols. New York, Dover Publications. Reprint.

Guo Songyi. (1982). "Qingdai guonei de haiyun maoyi" (Coastal trade in the Qing). *Qing shi luncong* 4: 92–110.

Guo Songyi. (1990). "Qingdai renkou liudong yu bianjiang kaifa" (The movment of populations and the opening of frontiers in the Qing period). In Ma Ruheng and Ma Dazheng, eds., *Qingdai bianjiang kaifa yanjiu* (Research on the opening of the frontiers in the Qing period). Beijing, Zhongguo shehui kexue chubanshe. 10–51.

Guo Songyi. (1991). "Qing chu shehui jingji yu Qing zhengfu de tunken zhengce" (Government land reclamation policies and the social economy of the early Qing). In Wang Yuquan, ed., *Zhongguo tunken shi* (The history of colonization in China). Beijing, Nongye chubanshe.

Guo Songyi. (1994). "Qingdai liangshi shichang he shangpin liang shuliang de guce" (An estimation of the size of the grain market and commodified grain in the Qing). *Zhongguo lishi yanjiu* 4: 40–49.

Gutzlaff, Karl F. A., and W. Ellis. (1834). *Journal of three voyages along the coast of China, in 1831, 1832, & 1833, with notices of Siam, Corea, and the Loo-Choo Islands.* London, [s.n.].

Gutzlaff, Karl F. A. (1838). *China opened: or, A display of the topography, history, customs, manners, arts, manufactures, commerce, literature, religion, jurisprudence, etc., of the Chinese empire.* 2 vols. London, Smith, Elder and co.

GZSL. (1964). *Da Qing Gaozong huangdi shilu* (The veritable records of the great Qing Gaozong [Qianlong] emperor). Taibei, Taiwan huawen shuju. Reprint.

Habakkuk, H. J. (1958). "The Economic History of Modern Britain." *Journal of Economic History*, 18.4: 486–501.

Hamashita, Takeshi. (1986). *Toyo bunka kenkyūjo shozō: Chūgoku tochi monjo mokuroku, kaisetsu.* Tōkyō: Tōkyō daigaku tōyō bunka kenkyūjo fūzoku tōyōgaku Bunken Sentā.

Hansen, Valerie. (1995). *Negotiating Daily Life in Traditional China: How Ordinary People used Contracts, 600–1400.* New Haven, Yale University Press.

Harrell, Stevan, ed. (1995). *Chinese Historical Microdemography.* Berkeley, University of California Press.

He Changling. (1992). *Huangchao jingshi wenbian* (Anthology of statecraft writings). Published as *Qing jingshi wenbian.* Beijing, Zhonghua shuju. Reprint.

He Ping'an. (1999). *Zhonguo youji feiliao* (China's organic fertilizers). Beijing, Nongye chubanshe.

Heijdra, Martin. (1998). "The Socio-economic Development of Rural China during the Ming." In Denis Twitchett and Frederick W. Mote, eds., *Cambridge History of*

China, vol. 8, part 2: *The Ming Dynasty, 1368–1644*. Cambridge, Cambridge University Press. 417–578.

HBK. (1937). *Hanbai narabini kōnyū jijō hen* (On the circumstances of sales and purchases). Shinkyō (Changchun), Kokumuin jitsugyōbu rinji sangyō chōsakyoku.

Ho, Ping-t'i. (1959). *Studies on the Population of China, 1368–1953*. Cambridge, Mass., Harvard University Press.

Hoang, Peter. (1888). "A Practical Treatise on Legal Ownership." *Journal of the China Branch of the Royal Asiatic Society of Great Britain and Ireland* 23: 118–174.

Hobsbawm, Eric J. (1999). *Industry and Empire: The Birth of the Industrial Revolution*. New York, The New Free Press.

Hong Huanchun. (1988). *Ming Qing Suzhou nongcun jingji ziliao* (Sources on the agrarian economy of Ming-Qing Suzhou). Suzhou, Suzhou guji chubanshe.

Hosie, Alexander. (1910). *Manchuria: Its People, Resources and Recent History*. Boston and Tokyo, J. B. Millet Company.

Hostetler, Laura. (2001). *Qing Colonial Enterprise: Ethnography and Cartography in Early Modern China*. Chicago, University of Chicago Press.

Hsiao, Kung-chuan. (1960). *Rural China: Imperial Control in the Nineteenth Century*. Seattle, University of Washington Press.

Hsu, Cho-yun. (1980). *Han Agriculture: The Formation of Early Chinese Agrarian Economy, 206 B.C.–A.D. 220*. Seattle, University of Washington Press.

Huang, Philip C. C. (1985). *The Peasant Economy and Social Change in North China*. Stanford, Stanford University Press.

Huang, Philip C. C. (1990). *The Peasant Family and Rural Development in the Yangzi Delta, 1350–1988*. Stanford, Stanford University Press.

Huang, Philip C. C. (1994). "Codified Law and Magisterial Adjudication in the Qing." In K. Bernhardt and P. C. C. Huang, eds., *Civil Law in Qing and Republican China* Stanford, Stanford University Press. 142–186.

Huang, Philip C. C. (1996). *Civil Justice in China: Representation and Practice in the Qing*. Stanford, Stanford University Press.

Huang, Philip C. C. (2001). *Code, Custom, and Legal Practice in China*. Stanford, Stanford University Press.

Huang, Philip C. C. (2002). "Development or Involution in Eighteenth-Century Britain and China? A Review of Kenneth Pomeranz's *The Great Divergence: China, Europe, and the Making of the Modern World Economy*." *Journal of Asian Studies* 61.2: 501–583.

HZG. (1965). *Heilongjiang zhi gao* (Draft gazetteer of Heilongjiang). Taibei, Wenhai chubanshe. Reprint.

IMC. (1904). *Imperial Maritime Customs: Decennial Reports, 1892–1901*. Shanghai, Statistical Department of the Inspectorate General of Customs.

Isett, Christopher. (1995). "Sugar Manufacture and the Agrarian Economy of Nineteenth-Century Taiwan." *Modern China* 21.2: 233–259.

Isett, Christopher. (1998). "State, Peasant and Agrarian Change on the Manchurian Frontier, 1644–1940." Ph.D. thesis, Department of History, Los Angeles, University of California.

Isett, Christopher. (2004). "Village Regulation of Property and the Social Basis for the Transformation of Qing Manchuria." *Late Imperial China* 24.1: 124–186.

James, H. E. M. (1968). *The Long White Mountain or a Journey in Manchuria: With some Accounts of the History, People, Administration and Religion of that Country.* New York, Greenwood Press. Reprint.

Jamieson, George. (1888). "Tenure of Land in China and the Condition of the Rural Population." *Journal of the China Branch of the Royal Asiatic Society* 23: 59–118.

Jamieson, George. (1921). *Chinese Family and Commercial Law.* Shanghai, Kelly and Walsh Ltd.

Jernigan, T. R. (1905). *China in Law and Commerce.* London, Macmillan & Co.

Jiang Jianping. (1992). *Qingdai qianqi migu maoyi yanjiu* (Research on the grain trade in the early Qing). Beijing, Beijing daxue chubanshe.

Jiang Tao. (1993). *Zhongguo jindai renkou shi* (A history of China's population). Hangzhou, Zhejiang renmin chubanshe.

JTZ. (1986). *Jilin tongzhi* (Complete gazetteer of Jilin). Jilin, Jilin wenshi chubanshe. Reprint.

Jing Junjian. (1983a). "Ming-Qing liangdai nongye gugong falü shang renshen lishi guanxi de jiefang" (The hired agricultural laborer's legal liberation from personal dependency during the Ming and Qing dynasties). In Li Wenzhi, Wei Jinyu, and Jing Junjian, eds., *Ming-Qing shidai de nongye zibenzhuyi mengya wenti* (Questions on agricultural capitalist sprouts in the Ming-Qing period). Beijing, Zhongguo shehui kexue chubanshe.

Jing Junjian. (1983b). "Ming-Qing liangdai 'gugong ren' de falü diwei wenti" (The legal status of the "gugongren" in the Ming and Qing dynasties). In Li Wenzhi, Wei Jinyu, and Jing Junjian, eds., *Ming-Qing shidai de nongye zibenzhuyi mengya wenti* (Questions on agricultural capitalist sprouts in the Ming-Qing period). Beijing, Zhongguo shehui kexue chubanshe.

Jing Junjian. (1993). *Qingdai shehui de jianmin dengji* (The status of 'mean people' in Qing society). Hangzhou, Zhejiang renmin chubanshe.

Jing Junjian. (1994). "Legislation Related to the Civil Economy in the Qing Dynasty." In Kathryn Bernhardt and Philip C. C. Huang, eds., *Civil Law in Qing and Republican China.* Stanford, Stanford University Press. 42–84.

Jing Su and Luo Lun. (1959). *Qing dai Shandong jing ying di zhu de she hui xing zhi* (The social system of managerial landlordism in the Qing Shandong). Jinan, Shandong renmin chubanshe.

Jing Su and Luo Lun. (1978). *Landlord and Labor in Late Imperial China: Case Studies from Shandong.* Cambridge, Mass., Harvard University Press.

John. A. H. (1965). "Agricultural Productivity and Economic Growth in England, 1700–1760." *Journal of Economic History* 25.1: 19–34.

Johnston, Reginald F. (1986). *Lion and Dragon in Northern China.* Hong Kong, Oxford University Press. Reprint.

Jones, E. L. (1967). "Editor's Introduction." In E. L. Jones, ed., *Agriculture and Economic Growth in England, 1650–1815.* London, Methuen.

Jones, E. L. (1968). "The Agrarian Origins of Industry." *Past & Present* 40(July): 58–71.

Jones, E. L. (1981). "Agriculture, 1700–80." In Roderick Floud and Donald McCloskey, eds.,vol. 1: *1700–1860.* Cambridge, Cambridge University Press. 66–86.

JZFZ. (1985). *Jinzhou fu zhi* (Jinzhou prefectural gazetteer). *Liaohai congshu* (Compendium of books from the Liao sea) Shenyang, Liao-Shen shushe. Reprint.

JZZ. (1976). *Jiaozhou zhi* (Jiaozhou Prefectural Gazetteer). Taibei, Taiwan chengwen chubanshe. Reprint.

Kameoka Seiji. (1921). *Manshu daizu no kenkyu* (Research on the Manchurian soybean). Dairen, Minami Manshu tetsudō kabushiki kaisha.

Kaplan, Steven L. (1982). *The Famine Plot Persuasion in Eighteenth-Century France.* Philadelphia, American Philosophical Society.

Katō Shigeshi. (1953a). "Kōki-Kenryū jidai ni okeru Manshū to Shina hondo tono tsū shō ni tsuite" (Trade between Manchuria (northeast China) and China (Proper) in the Kangxi and Qianlong eras). In Katō Shigeshi, ed., *Shina keizaishi kōshō* (Studies in Chinese economic history). Tōkyō, Tōyō bunko. 2: 595–616.

Katō Shigeshi. (1953b). "Manshū ni okeru daizu, mamemochi seisan no yurai ni oite" (The origins of soyabean and beancake production in Manchuria). In Katō Shigeshi, ed., *Shina keizaishi kōshō* (Studies in Chinese economic history). Tōkyō, Tōyō bunko. 2: 688–699.

Kerridge, Eric. (1967). *The Agricultural Revolution.* London, George Allen & Unwin.

Kessler, Laurence D. (1976). *K'ang-Hsi and the Consolidation of Ch'ing Rule, 1661–1684.* Chicago, University of Chicago Press.

Kishimoto Mio. (1997). "Min-Shin jittai ni okeru 'zhaojia huishu' mondai" (The problem of "zhaojia" and "huishu" in the Ming and Qing). *Chūgoku: Shakai to Bunka* 12: 263–293.

Kishimoto Mio. (1998). "Tsuma o uttewa ikenai ka? Min-Shin jidai no baisai/tensai kankō" (Is it prohibited to sell a wife? The custom of selling/pawning wives in the Ming-Qing era). *Chūgoku shigaku* 8: 177–210.

Kindleberger, Charles. (1964). *Economic Growth in France and Britain: 1851–1950.* Cambridge, Mass., Harvard University Press.

KKK. (1937). *Koyō kankei narabi ni kankō hen: 1934 nendo nōson jittai chōsa hōkokusho* (On employment relations and practices: report on the 1934 investigation of actual village conditions). Shinkyō (Changchun), Jitsugyōbu rinji sangyō chōsa kyoku.

Kochanowicz, Jacek. (1989). "The Polish Economy and the Evolution of Dependency." In Daniel Chirot, ed., *The Origins of backwardness in Eastern Europe: Economics and Politics from the Middle Ages until the Early Twentieth Century.* Berkeley, University of California Press.

Kong Jingwei, ed. (1990). *Qingdai dongbei diqu jingji shi* (The economic history of the northeast region during the Qing). Harbin, Heilongjiang renmin chubanshe.

Kong Jingwei. (1963). "Qing chu zhi jiwu zhanqian dongbei guotian qidi de jingying he mindian yiji mindi de fazhan" (The management of state and banner land and the development of commoner lands and commoner tenancy from the early Qing to the Sino-Japanese war). *Lishi yanjiu* 4: 67–90.

Kriedte, Peter, Hans Medick, and Jürgen Schlumbohm. (1981). *Industrialisation before Industrialisation: Rural Industry and the Genesis of Capitalism.* Cambridge, Cambridge University Press.

KT. (1912). *Manshū daizu ni kansuru chōsa* (Investigation of the Manchurian soybean). Dairen, Kantō tōhokufu minseibu shouka..

Kuhn, Philip A. (1990). *Soulstealers: The Chinese Sorcery Scare of 1768.* Cambridge, Mass., Harvard University Press.

Kula, Witold. (1976). *An Economic Theory of Feudalism.* London, New Left Books.

KYZ. (1985). *Kaiyuan xianzhi (Kaiyuan county gazetteer). Liaohai congshu* (Compendium of books from the Liao sea). Shenyang, Liao-Shen shushe. Reprint.

Kwon, Grace. (2002). *State Formation, Property Relations, and the Development of the Tokugawa Economy (1600–1868).* New York, Routledge.

Lachmann, Richard. (1987). *From Manor to Market.* Madison, University of Wisconsin Press.

Lambley, Harry. (1990). "Lineage Feudling in Southern Fujian and Eastern Guangdong." In Jonathan Lipman and Stevan Harrell, eds., *Violence in China: Essays in Culture and Counterculture.* Albany, State University of New York Press.

Landes, David. (1969). *The Unbound Prometheus: Technological Change and Industrial Development in Western Europe from 1750 to the Present.* Cambridge, Cambridge University Press.

Landes, David. (1986). "What do Bosses Really Do?" *Journal of Economic History* 46.3: 585–623.

Landes, David. (1993). "The Fable of the Dead Horse." In Joel Mokyr, ed., *The British Industrial Revolution.* Boulder, Colo., Westview Press.

LeRoy Ladurie, Emmanuel. (1976). *The Peasants of Languedoc.* Chicago, University of Illinois Press.

LeRoy Ladurie, Emmanuel. (1987). *The French Peasantry, 1450–1660.* Berkeley, University of California Press.

Lee, James, and Cameron Campbell, et al. (1995). A Century of Mortality in Rural Liaoning, 1774–1873. In Stevan Harrel, ed., *Chinese Historical Microdemography.* Berkeley, University of California Press. 163–182.

Lee, James and Cameron Campbell, et al. (1992). "Infanticide and Family Planning in Late Imperial China: The Price and Population History of Rural Liaoning, 1774–1873." In Thomas G. Rawski and Lillian M. Li, eds., *Chinese History in Economic Perspective.* Berkeley, University of California Press. 145–176.

Lee, James, and Cameron Campbell. (1997). *Fate and Fortune in Rural China: Social Stratification and Population Behavior in Liaoning, 1774–1873.* Cambridge, Cambridge University Press.

Lee, James, and Wang Feng. (1999). *One Quarter of Humanity: Malthusian Mythology and Chinese Reality, 1700–2000.* Cambridge, Mass., Harvard University Press.

Lee, Robert H. G. (1970). *The Manchurian Frontier in Ch'ing History.* Cambridge, Mass., Harvard University Press.

Lenin, V. I. (1956). *The Development of Capitalism in Russia.* Moscow, Foreign Language Press.

Leong, Sow-theng. (1997). *Migration and Ethnicity in Chinese History: Hakkas, Pengmin, and Their Neighbors.* Stanford, Stanford University Press.

Levine, David. (1977). *Family Formation in an Age of Nascent Capitalism.* New York, Academic Press.

Li Bozhong. (1984). "Ming Qing shiqi jiangnan shuidao shengchan jiyue chengdu de tigao" (Intensification of Jiangnan wet-rice cultivation in the Ming-Qing period). *Zhongguo nongshi* 1: 24–37.

Li Bozhong. (1998). *Agricultural Development in Jiangnan, 1620–1850.* New York, St. Martin's Press.

Li Bozhong. (2000). *Jiangnang de zaoqi gongye* (Jiangnang's early industry). Beijing, shehui kexue wenxian chubanshe.

Li Debin. (1987). *Heilongjiang yimin gaiyao* (An outline of migration to Manchuria). Harbin, Heilongjiang renmin chubanshe.

Li, Lillian. (1982). "Introduction: Food, Famine, and the Chinese State." *Journal of Asian Studies* 41.4: 687–707.
Li, Lillian M. (1992). "Grain Prices in Zhili Province, 1736–1911: A Preliminary Study." In Thomas G. Rawski and Lillian M. Li, eds., *Chinese History in Economic Perspective*. Berkeley, University of California Press. 69–99.
Li, Lillian, and Alison Dray-Novey. (1999). "Guarding Beijing's Food Security in the Qing Dynasty: State, Market, and Police." *Journal of Asian Studies* 58.4: 992–1032.
Li, Lillian. M. (2000). "Integration and Disintegration in North China's Grain Markets, 1738–1911." *Journal of Economic History* 60.3: 665–699.
Li Qiao. (1985). "Baqi shengji wenti shulue" (Discussion the problem of the eight banner's welfare). *Lishi dang'an* 1: 91–97.
Li Shutian. (1990). *Shuangchengbao tuntian jilue* (Plans for the colonization of Shuangchengbao). Jilin, Jilin wenshi chubanshe. Reprint.
Li Tingyu. (1978). *Fengtian bianwu jiyao* (A summary of frontier affairs of Fengtian). Taibei, Wenhai chubanshe.
Li Wenzhi. (1957). *Zhongguo jindai nongyeshi ziliao*, vol. 1: *1840–1911* (Source materials on the agricultural history of modern China, 1840–1911). Beijing: Sanlian chubanshe.
Li Wenzhi. (1963). "Qingdai qianqi de tudi zhanyou guanxi" (Land relations in the early Qing dynasty). *Lishi yanjiu* 5: 75–109.
Li Wenzhi. (1993). *Ming-Qing shidai fengjian tudi guanxi de songjie* (The loosening of feudal property relations in the Ming-Qing period). Beijing, Zhongguo shehui kexue chubanshe.
Liang, Ernest P. (1982). "China, Railways and Agricultural Development, 1875–1935." Chicago, Research Paper, University of Chicago, Department of Geography.
Liang Fangzhong. (1980). *Zhongguo lidai hukou, tiandi, tianfu tongji* (Statistical data on household registries, agricultural land, and land tax in Chinese history). Shanghai, Shanghai renmin chubanshe.
Liang Zhiping. (1996). *Qingdai xiguan fa: shehui yu guojia* (Qing customary law: society and state). Beijing, Zhengfa daxue chubanshe.
Liang Shizheng. (1992). "Baqi tun zhong shu" (Account of village and farming of the Eight Banners). In He Changling, ed., *Huangchao jingshi wenbian* (Anthology of statecraft writings). Published as *Qing jingshi wenbian*. Beijing, Zhonghua shuju. Reprint.
Lie Huier. (1981). *Dongbei de douhuo maoyi, 1907–1931* (The northeast's trade in soyabean goods, 1907–1931). Taibei, Guoli Taiwan shifan daxue lishi yanjiu suo.
Lindert, Peter H. (1980). "English Occupations, 1670–1811." *Journal of Economic History* 40.4: 685–712.
Ling Chou. (2002). "Xijiang shinie jishi" (Recorded matters concerning the administration of Nie district in Xijiang). *Xuxiu siku quanshu*. Shanghai, Shanghai guji chubanshe 882: 1–166. Reprint.
Liu Kexiang. (1994). "Zhongguo jindai de dizhu gugong jingying he jingying dizhu" (Landlord and labor management and managerial landlords in modern China). *Zhongguo jingjishi yanjiu* (supplement): 1–50.
Liu Kexiang. (1995). "Qingmo he beiyang zhengfu shiqi dongbei diqu de tudi kaiken he nongye fazhan" (Land-opening and agricultural development in the northeast during the periods of the decline of the Qing and the warlord government). *Zhongguo jingjishi yanjiu* 4: 83–105.

Liu Qiugen. (2000). *Ming Qing gaoli dai ziben (Usury capital in the Ming and Qing)*. Beijing, Shehui kexue wenxian chubanshe.

Liu, Ta-Chung, and Kung-Chia Yeh. (1965). *The Economy of the Chinese Mainland: National Income and Economic Development, 1933–1959*. Princeton, Princeton University Press.

Livi Bacci, Massimo. (1992). *A Concise History of World Population*. Cambridge, Blackwell.

Livi Bacci, Massimo. (2000). *The Population of Europe: A History*. Oxford and Malden, Blackwell.

Lu Yu. (1987). *Qingdai he minguo Shandong yimin dongbei shilue* (Historical account of the migration of Shandongese to Manchuria in the Qing and Republican eras). Shanghai, Shanghai shehui kexue xueyuan chubanshe.

LYZ. (1985). *Liaoyang zhouzhi (Liaoyang department gazetteer). Liaohai congshu* (Compendium of books from the Liao sea). Shenyang, Liao-Shen shushe. Reprint.

Ma Ruheng and Ma Dazheng. (1990). *Qingdai bianjiang kaifa yanjiu* (Research into the development of frontiers during the Qing). Beijing, Zhongguo shehui kexue chubanshe.

Macauley, Melissa. (1998). *Social Power and Legal Culture: Litigation Masters in Late Imperial China*. Stanford, Stanford University Press.

Maddison, Angus. (1998). *Chinese Economic Performance in the Long Run*. Paris, OECD (Organization for Economic Cooperation and Development).

Maddison, Angus. (2001). *The World Economy. A Millennial Perspective*. Paris, OECD (Organization for Economic Cooperation and Development).

Malthus, Thomas. (1985). *An Essay on the Principle of Population*. London, Penguin Books.

Mann, Susan. (1987). *Local Merchants and the Chinese Bureaucracy, 1750–1950*. Stanford, Stanford University Press.

Mann, Susan. (1997). *Precious Records: Women in China's Long Eighteenth Century*. Stanford, Stanford University Press.

Marks, Robert. (1998). *Tigers, Rice, Silk, and Silt: Environment and Economy in Late Imperial South China*. Cambridge, Cambridge University Press.

Marx, Karl. (1976). *Capital*, vol. 1. New York, Penguin Press.

Matsusaka,Yoshihisa Tak. (2001). *The Making of Japanese Manchuria, 1904–1932*. Cambridge, Mass., Harvard University Press.

Mazumdar, Sucheta. (1998). *Sugar and Society in China: Peasants, Technology, and the World Market*. Cambridge, Mass., Harvard University Press.

Mazumdar, Sucheta. (2001). "Rights in People, Rights in Land: Concepts of Customary Property in Late Imperial China." *Extreme- Orient, Extreme-Occident* 23: 89–107.

MC. (1906). *Manshū chishi* (The Topography of Manchuria). Tōkyō, Maruzen kabushiki kaisha.

McCusker, John and Russell Menard. (1985). *The Economy of British America, 1607–1789*. Chapel Hill, University of North Carolina Press.

McAleavy, Henry. (1958). "Dien in China and Vietnam." *Journal of Asian Studies* 17.3: 403–415.

McNally, David. (1988). *Political Economy and the Rise of Capitalism: A Reinterpretation*. Berkeley, University of California Press.

McNally, David. (1993). *Against the Market: Political Economy, Market Socialism and the Marxist Critique*. London, Verso.

Meijer, Marinus J. (1980). "Slavery at the end of the Ch'ing Dynasty." In Jerome Cohen, R. Randle Edwards, and Fu-mei Chang Chen, eds., *Essays on China's Legal Tradition*. Princeton, Princeton University Press. 327–358.

Menzies, Nicholas K. (1994). *Forest and Land Management in Imperial China*. New York, St. Martin's Press.

Meskill, Johanna M. (1979). *A Chinese Pioneer Family: The Lins of Wu-feng, Taiwan, 1729–1895*. Princeton, N.J., Princeton University Press.

Millward, James A. (1998). *Beyond the Pass: Economy, Ethnicity, and Empire in Qing Central Asia, 1759–1864*. Stanford, Stanford University Press.

Miller, Edward, and John Hatcher. (1978). *Medieval England*. London, Longman.

Miller, Judith A. (1999). *Mastering the Market: The State and the Grain Trade in Northern France, 1700–1860*. Cambridge, Cambridge University Press.

Min Tu-ki. (1989). *National Polity and Local Power: The Transformation of Late Imperial China*. Cambridge, Mass., Harvard University Press.

MKK. (1938). *Manshū ni okeru kosaku kankei: 1934–36 nōson jittai chōsa hōkokusho* (Tenant relations in Manchuria: report on the investigation of actual village conditions). Shinkyō (Changchun), Manshū tosho kabushiki kaisha.

MMZ. (1922–23). *Man-Mō zensho* (Complete study of Manchuria and Mongolia). Daren (Dalian), Man-Mo Bunka Kyōkai.

MNK. (1942). *Shuyō nōsanbutsu seisanhi ni kansuru chōsa hōkokusho* (Report on the investigation of the production costs of major crops). Shinkyō (Changchun), Manshu nōsan kōsha.

MNS. (1937). *Manshū nōson shakai jittai chōsa hōkokusho* (Report on the investigation of Manchuria's rural society). Manshū teikoku daidō gakuin.

Moulin, Annie. (1991). *Peasantry and Society in France since 1789*. Cambridge, Cambridge University Press.

MS. (2000). *Minshi xiguan diaocha baogao lu* (Abstracts of report on the investigation of civil matters and practices). Beijing, Zhongguo zhengfa daxue chubanshe. Reprint.

MSCZ. (1906). *Manshu chishi* (Gazetteer of Manchuria). Tōkyō, Maruzen kabushiki kaisha.

MSRS. (1931). *Manshū ni okeru ryōsen* (Manchuria's grain merchants). Dairen (Dalian), Minami Manshū tetsudō kabushiki kaisha.

MT. (1914). *Manshū kyūkan chōsa hōkokusho* (Report on the survey of Manchurian customs). 9 vols. Dairen (Dalian), Minami Manshu tetsudō kabushiki kaisha.

MT. (1924). *Manshū ni okeru yubōgyō* (Oil mills of Manchuria). Dairen (Dalian), Minami Manshu tetsudō kabushiki kaisha.

MT. (1925). *Manshū zairai nōgyo* (Manchuria's traditional agriculture). Dairen (Dalian), Minami Manshu tetsudō kabushiki kaisha.

MT. (1926). *Soya beans in Manchuria*. Dairen, South Manchuria Railway Company.

MT. (1928a). *Manshū no kōryō* (Manchuria's sorghum). Dairen (Dalian), Minami Manshu tetsudō kabushiki kaisha.

MT. (1928b). *Manshū no menka* (Manchuria's cotton). Dairen (Dalian), Minami Manshu tetsudō kabushiki kaisha.

MT. (1942). *Hokuman nōgyo kikō dōtai chōsa hōkoku: daichi hen: Hinkō shō, Koran ken, Mōka son, Mōka ku* (Report of the survey of the structure of north Manchurian Agriculture, part one, Mengjia district, Mengjia village, Hulan county, Binjiang province). Minami Manshu tetsudo kabushiki kaisha. Tōkyō, Hakubunkan.

MTBB. (1939). *Manshū tochi kyūkan to tochi baibai keiyaku gairon* (Outline on research of Manchurian customs and land sale contracts), ed. Sugimoto Kichigorō. Manshū takushoku kōsha tochika. No place of publication.

MTDG. (1935). *Manshū nōson no jittai: chūbu Manshū no ichi nōson ni tsuite* (Actual Village conditions in Manchuria: regarding one village in central Manchuria). Shinkyō (Changchun), Manshū teikoku daidō gakuin.

MTK. (1939). *Manshū tochi kankei chōsa hōkokushūroku* (Report on the investigation of Manchuria's land relations). Shinkyō (Changchun), Chiseki seirikyoku.

MTKK. (1939). *Manshū tochi kankei to tochi baibai keiyaku* (Manchurian land relations and land sale contracts). Unknown.

Myers, Ramon H. (1970). *The Chinese Peasant Economy: Agricultural Development in Hopei and Shantung, 1890–1949.* Cambridge, Mass., Harvard University Press.

Myers, Ramon. (1976). "Socioeconomic Change in Villages of Manchuria During the Ch'ing and Republican Periods: Some Preliminary Findings." *Modern Asian Studies* 10.4: 591–620.

Myers, Ramon H. (1982). *The Japanese Economic Development of Manchuria, 1932–1945.* New York, Garland Publishing, Inc.

Naquin, Susan. (1985) "*The Transmission of White Lotus Sectarianism in Late Imperial China.*" In David Johnson, ed., *Popular Culture in Late Imperial China.* Berkeley, University of California Press.

Nakagane, Katsuji. (1989). "Manchukuo and Economic Development." In Peter Duus, Ramon H. Myers, and Mark R. Peattie, eds., *The Japanese Informal Empire in China, 1895–1937.* Princeton, Princeton University Press. 133–157.

Negishi Tadashi. (1953). *Chūgoku no girudo* (The guilds of China). Tōkyō, Nihon Hyoronsha.

NHB. (1937). *Nōsanbutsu hanbai jijō hen: Kōtoku ninendo Nan-Man nōson jittai chōsa hōkokusho* (On the conditions of the agricultural commodities markets: report on the 1935 investigation of actual village conditions in southern Manchuria). Shinkyō (Changchun), Jitsugyōbu rinji sangyō chōsa kyoku.

NKK. (1939). *Nōka keiei keizai chōsa* (Survey of farming household management and economy). 3 vols. Shinkyō (Changchun), Manshūkoku sangyōbu.

Niida Noboru. (1943). *Shina mibunhō shi* (A History of China's status law). Tōkyō, Sayūhō Kankōkai.

Niida Noboru. (1962). *Chūgoku hōseishi kenkyū: dorei nōdo hō, kazoku sonraku hō* (A study of Chinese legal history: law of slave and serf, and law of family and village). Tōkyō, Tōkyō daigaku shuppankai.

Niu Pinghan. (1990). *Qingdai zhengqu yangai zongbiao* (A complete guide to the changes in Qing administrative districts). Beijing, Zhongguo ditu chuban she.

NYZ. (1985). *Ningyuan zhou zhi* (Gazetteer of Ningyuan department). *Liaohai congshu* (Compendium of books from the Liao sea). Shenyang, Liao-Shen shushe. Reprint.

Nishijima, Sadao. (1984). "The Formation of Early Chinese Cotton Industry." In Linda Grove and Christian Daniels, eds., *State and Society in China: Japanese Perspectives on Ming-Qing Social and Economic History.* Tokyo, Tokyo University Press.

NJ-Ningcheng county. (1936). *Nōson jittai chōsa hōkokusho: kobetsu chōsa no bu, Neijō gen* (Report on the investigation of actual village conditions: household investigations, Ningcheng county). Rinji sangyō chōsa kyoku.

NJ-Panshi county. (1936). *Nōson jittai chōsa ippan chōsa hōkokusho: kobetsu chōsa no bu, Banjaku gen* (Report on the investigation of actual village conditions: household investigations, Panshi county). Rinji sangyō chōsa kyoku.

NJ-Taonan county. (1936). *Nōson jittai chōsa ippan chōsa hōkokusho: Chōnan gen* (Report on the investigation of actual village conditions: household investigations, Taonan county). Rinji sangyō chōsa kyoku.

NJ-Series. (1934–1936). *Nōson jittai chōsa hōkokusho: kobetsu chōsa no bu* (Report on the investigation of actual village conditions: household survey section). 21 vols. Shinkyō (Changchun), Rinji sangyō chōsa kyoku.

NJC. (1937). *Nōson jittai chōsa sōgō kobetsu chōsa kōmoku* (Investigation topics for total household survey in surveys of actual village conditions). Shinkyō (Changchun), Manshū tosho kabushiki kaisha.

NK. (1937a). *Nōgyo keiei hen–1934 nendo nōson jittai chōsa hōkokusho* (On farm management: report on the 1934 investigation of actual village conditions). Shinkyō (Changchun), Jitsugyōbu rinji sangyō chōsakyoku.

NK. (1937b). *Nōgyo keiei hen* (On farm management). Shinkyō (Changchun), Jitsugyō bu rinji sangyō chōsakyoku.

NKFS. (1937). *Nōka no fusai narabini taishaku kankei hen* (Rural household debt and loan relations). Shinkyō (Changchun), Jitsugyōbu rinji sangyo chōsakyoku.

NSS. (1937). *Nōson shakai seikatsu hen–1934 nendo nōson jittai chōsa hōkokusho* (On village social life: report on the 1934 investigation of actual village conditions). Shinkyō (Changchun), Jitsugyōbu rinji sangyō chōsakyoku.

O'Brien, Patrick, and Caglar Keyder. (1978). *Economic Growth in Britain and France, 1780–1914: Two Paths to the Twentieth Century*. Boston, George Allen and Unwin.

Oi, Jean, and Etienne-Pierre Will. (1992). "North China: Shandong during the Qianlong Period." In Etienne-Pierre Will, R. Bin Wong, and James Lee, eds., *Nourishing the People: The State Civilian Granary System in China, 1650–1850*. Ann Arbor, University of Michigan Center for Chinese Studies Publications. 321–388.

Ocko, Jonathan. (2004). "The Missing Metaphor: Applying Western Legal Scholarship to the Study of Contract and Property in Early Modern China." In Madeleine Zelin, Jonathan Ocko, and Robert Gardella, eds., *Contract and Property in Early Modern China*. Stanford, Stanford University Press. 178–208.

Osborne, Anne. (1998). "Highlands and Lowlands: Economic and Ecological Interactions in the Lower Yangzi region under the Qing." In Mark Elvin and Liu Ts'ui-jung, eds., *The Sediments of Time*. Cambridge, Cambridge University Press. 203–234.

Osborne, Anne. (1994) "The Local Politics of Land Reclamaition in the Lower Yangzi Highlands." *Late Imperial China*. 15.1 (June): 1–46.

Osborne, Anne. (2004). "Property, Taxes, and the Protection of Rights." In Madeleine Zelin, Jonathan Ocko, and Robert Gardella, eds., *Contract and Property in Early Modern China*. Stanford, Stanford University Press. 120–158.

Overton, Mark. (1996). *Agricultural Revolution in England: The Transformation of the Agrarian Economy, 1500–1850*. Cambridge, Cambridge University Press.

Oxnam, Robert B. (1970). *Ruling from Horseback: Manchu Politics in the Oboi Regency, 1661–1669*. Chicago, University of Chicago Press.

Oyama, Masaki. (1984). "Large Landownership in the Jiangnan Delta Region During the Late Ming-Early Qing Period." In Linda Grove and Christian Daniels, eds., *State and Society in China: Japanese Perspectives on Ming-Qing Social and Economic History*. Tokyo, Tokyo University Press. 101–163.

Paladin, Ann. (1991). *The Chinese Spirit Road: The Classical Tradition of Stone Tomb Statuary*. New Haven, Yale University Press.

Pan, Ming-te. (1995). "Rural Credit Market and the Peasant Economy (1600–1949)." Ph.D. thesis, Department of History, University of California, Irvine.

Parker, Edward C. (1920). *Field Management and Crop Rotation*. St. Paul, Minn., Webb Publishing.

Patterson, Orlando. (1970). "Slavery and Slave Revolts: A Socio-historical Study of the First Maroon War, 1655–1740." *Social and Economic Studies* 19: 289–325.

Patterson, Orlando. (1982). *Slavery and Social Death: A Comparative Study*. Cambridge, Mass., Harvard University Press.

Perdue, Peter C. (1987). *Exhausting the Earth: State and Peasant in Hunan, 1500–1850*. Cambridge, Mass., Harvard University Press.

Perkins, Dwight H. (1969). *Agricultural Development in China, 1368–1968*. Chicago, Aldine.

Piper, Charles. (1924). *Forage Plants and Their Culture*. New York, Macmillan.

Pollard, Sidney. (1981). *Peaceful Conquest: Industrialization of Europe, 1760–1970*. Oxford, Oxford University Press.

Pomeranz, Kenneth. (2000). *The Great Divergence: Europe, China, and the Making of the Modern World Economy*. Princeton, Princeton University Press.

Pomeranz, Kenneth. (2002). "Beyond the East-West Binary: Resituating Development Paths in the Eighteenth-century World." *Journal of Asian Studies* 61.2: 539–590.

Postan, M. M. (1966). *The Cambridge Economic History of Europe*, vol. 1: *The Agrarian Life of the Middle Ages*. Cambridge, Cambridge University Press.

Price, Roger. (1975). *The Economic Mondernisation of France*. New York, John Wiley & Sons.

Price, Roger. (1996). "Railways and the Development of Agricultural Markets in France: Opportunity and Crisis, c. 1840–c. 1914." In Peter Mathias and John Davis, eds., *The Nature of Industrialization: Agriculture and Industrialization From the Eighteenth Century to the Present Day*. Oxford, Blackwell Publishing.

QD. (1989). *Qingdai de qidi* (Qing bannerlands*)*. Beijing, Zhonghua shuju.

QDTD. (1988). *Qingdai tudi zhanyou guanxi yu diannong kangzu douzheng* (Property relations and tenant anti-rent struggles during the Qing). Beijing, Zhonghua shuju.

QHS. (1991). *Qing huidian shili* (Collected statutes of the Qing). Beijing, Zhonghua shuju. Reprint.

QHZ. (1983). *(Qin ding) Da Qing huidian zeli* (Collected precedents of the great Qing). *Qinding siku quanshu*. Taibei, Taiwan shangwu yinshu guan. Reprint.

Ravenstein, Ernest George. (1861). *The Russians on the Amur; its discovery, conquest, and colonization, with a description of the country, its inhabitants, productions, and commercial capabilities*. London, Trubner.

Rawski, Evelyn S. (1972). *Agricultural Change and the Peasant Economy of South China*. Cambridge, Mass., Harvard University Press.

Rawski, Evelyn S. (1998). *The Last Emperors: A Social History of Qing Imperial Institutions*. Berkeley, University of California Press.

Rawski, Thomas. (1989). *Economic Growth in Pre-War China*. Berkeley, University of California Press.
Reardon-Anderson, James. (2000). "Land Use and Society in Manchuria and Inner Mongolia during the Qing Dynasty." *Environmental History* 5.4: 503–530.
Reardon-Anderson, James. (2005). *Reluctant Pioneers: China's Expansion Northward, 1644–1937*. Stanford, Stanford University Press.
Reed, Bradly. (2000). *Teeth and Talons: County Clerks and Runners in the Qing Dynasty*. Stanford, Stanford University Press.
Rhoads, Edward J. M. (2000). *Manchus and Han: Ethnic Relations and Political Power in Late Qing and Early Republican China, 1861–1928*. Seattle, University of Washington Press.
Roth, Gertrude. (1979). "The Manchu-Chinese Relationship, 1618–1636." In Jonathan Spence and John E. Wills, eds., *From Ming to Qing: Conquest, Region and Continuity in Seventeenth-Century China*. New Haven, Yale University Press. 3–38.
Roth-Li, Gertraude. (1975). "The Rise of the Early Manchu State: A Portrait Drawn from Manchu Sources to 1636." Ph.D. thesis, Department of History, Cambridge, Mass., Harvard University.
Rowe, William. (2001). *Saving the World: Chen Hongmou and Elite Consciousness in Eighteenth-Century China*. Stanford, Stanford University Press.
Rösener, Werner. (1994). *The Peasantry of Europe*. Oxford, Blackwell.
Rozman, Gilbert. (1982). *Population and Marketing Settlements in Ch'ing China*. Cambridge, Cambridge University Press.
Russell, Edward J. (1913). *The Fertility of the Soil*. Cambridge, Cambridge University Press.
RX. 1976). *Rongcheng xianzhi* (Rongcheng county gazetteer). Taibei, Wenhai chubanshe. Reprint.
RZSL. 1964. *Da Qing Renzong huangdi shilu* (The veritable records of the great Qing Renzong [Jiaqing] emperor). Taibei, Taiwan huawen shuju. Reprint.
Sakatani, Yoshiro. (1980). *Manchuria: A Survey of Its Economic Development*. New York, Garland.
Satō, Yoshitane. (1924). *Daizu no kakō* (Soybean processing). Dairen, Minami Manshū tetsudō kōgyōbu nōmuka.
Saying'e. (1939). *Jilin waiji* (Miscellaneous records from Jilin). Shanghai, Shangwu yingshu chuban. Reprint.
SC. (Guangxu). *Shanhaiguan chaoguan juezheng bianlan* (Pamphlet on the administration of the Shanhaiguan customs office). No place of publication.
Schurmann, H. Franz. (1956). "Traditional Property Concepts in China." *Far Eastern Quarterly* 15.4: 507–516.
Scott, James. 1990. *Domination and the Arts of Resistance: Hidden Transcripts*. New Haven, Yale University Press.
Settai Hatsuro and Ito Bunjurō (1920). *Manshū daizu* (The Manchurian soybean). Dairen-shi, Man-Mō bunka kyōkai.
SD. (1995). *Shengjing dianzhi beikao* (Reference to the laws and institutions of Shengjing). Shanghai, Shanghai guji chubanshe. Reprint.
Shepherd, John R. (1988). "Rethinking Tenancy: Explaining Spatial and Temporal Variation in Late Imperial and Republican China." *Comparative Studies in Society and History* 30.3: 403–431.

Shepherd, John R. (1993). *Statecraft and Political Economy on the Taiwan Frontier, 1600–1800*. Stanford, Stanford University Press.

Shi Zhihong. (1994). *Qing dai qianqi de xiaonong jingji* (The economy of the small peasant in the early Qing). Beijing, Zhongguo shehui kexue chubanshe.

Shiga Shūzō. (1967). *Chūgoku kazokuhō no genri* (The principles of the Chinese family law). Tōkyō, Sōbunsha.

Shiga Shuzo. (1978). "Family Property and Law of Inheritance in Traditional China." In David C. Buxbaum, *Chinese Family Law and Social Change in Historical and Comparative Perspective*. Seattle, University of Washington Press. 109–150.

Shih, James C. (1992). *Chinese Rural Society in Transition: A Case Study of the Lake Tai Area, 1368–1800*. Berkeley, Institute of East Asian Studies, University of California.

Shimizu Kinjirō (1945). *Kei no kenkyū: Man-Shi tōchi kankō kihan ni tsuite* (A study of contracts: regarding the standard land norms of Manchurian and China). Kyōto, Daigadō.

Shue, Vivienne. (1988). *The Reach of the State: Sketches of the Chinese Body Politic*. Stanford, Stanford University Press.

SJTZ. (1965). *Qinding Shengjing tongzhi* (Official Compilation of the complete gazetteer of Shengjing). Taibei, Wenhai chubanshe. Reprint.

Skinner, G. William. (1964–65). "Marketing and Social Structure in Rural China." *Journal of Asian Studies* 24.1: 3–44, 2: 195–228, 3: 363–399.

Skinner, G. William. (1977a). "Introduction: Urban Development in Imperial China." In G. William Skinner, ed., *The City in Late Imperial China*. Stanford, Stanford University Press. 3–31.

Skinner, G. William. (1977b). "Regional Urbanization in Nineteenth-Century China." In G. William Skinner, ed., *The City in Late Imperial China*. Stanford, Stanford University Press. 211–273.

Skinner, G. William. (1977c). "Cities and the Hierarchy of Local Systems." In G. William Skinner, ed., *The City in Late Imperial China*. Stanford, Stanford University Press. 275–351.

Skinner, G. William. (1978). "Cities and the Hierarchy of Local Systems." In Arthur Wolf, ed., *Studies in Chinese Society*. Stanford, Stanford University Press.

Slicher Van Bath, B. H. (1964). *The Agrarian History of Western Europe, AD 500–1850*. New York, St. Martin's Press.

Smith, Adam. (1976). *An Inquiry into the Nature and Causes of the Wealth of Nations*. Chicago, University of Chicago Press.

Smith, Richard M. (1984). *Land, Kinship, and Life-cycle*. Cambridge, Cambridge University Press.

SNS. (1937). *Shuyō nōsanbutsu seisanhi* (Major Crop Production Costs). Shinkyō (Changchun), Jitsugyōbu rinji sangyō chōsa kyoku.

Sommer, Matthew. (2000). *Sex, Law, and Society in Late Imperial China*. Stanford, Stanford University Press.

Sommer, Matthew. (2005). "Making Sex Work: Polyandry as a Survival Strategy in Qing Dynasty China." In Bryna Goodman and Wendy Larson, eds., *Gender in Motion: Divisions of Labor and Cultural Change in Late Imperial and Modern China*. Oxford, Rowman & Littlefield. 29–54.

Sommer, Matthew. (forthcoming). *Wife Selling in Qing Dynasty China: Survival Strategies and Judicial Interventions*. Stanford, Stanford University Press.

Song Zexing and Liu Changxin. (1987). *Zhongguo renkou: Liaoning fence* (The population of China: Liaoning volume). In Liu Rui, ed., *Zhongguo renkou* (The population of China). Beijing, Zhongguo caizheng jingji chubanshe.

Spence, Jonathan, and John Wills, eds. (1979). *From Ming to Qing: Conquest, Region, and Continuity in Seventeenth Century China*. New Haven, Yale University Press.

Spence, Jonathan D. (2001). *Treason by the Book*. New York, Viking.

SSL. (1964). *Da Qing Shezu huangdi shilu* (The veritable records of the great Qing Shezu [Shunzhi] emperor). Taibei, Taiwan huawen shuju. Reprint.

Ste. Croix, G. E. M. de. (1981). *The Class Struggle in the Ancient Greek World: From the Archaic Age to the Arab Conquests*. Ithaca, Cornell University Press.

Sudō Yoshiyuki. (1944). *Shindai Manshū tōchi seisaku no kenkyū* (Research into state policy toward Manchu land during the Qing). Tōkyō, Kawade shōbō.

Sudō Yoshiyuki. (1972a). "Shindai no Manshū ni okeru ryōmai no sōun ni tsuite" (Manchuria's Tribute Grain Shipments in the Qing). *Shindai higashi Ajia shi kenkyū* (Historical research of east Asia during the Qing). Tōkyō, Nippon gakujutsu shinkōka. 439–459.

Sudō Yoshiyuki. (1972b). "Shindai zenki ni okeru hakki no sonrakusei" (Village order under the eight banners in the Qing period). *Shindai higashi ajia shi kenkyū* (Historical research of east Asia during the Qing). Tōkyō, Nippon gakujutsu shinkōka. 349–412.

Sun, Kungtu C. (1969). *The Economic Development of Manchuria in the First Half of the Twentieth Century*. Cambridge, Mass., Harvard University Press.

Suzuki Shobe. (1938). *Manshū no nōgyō kikō* (The structure of Manchuria's agriculture). Tōkyō, Hakuyōsha.

Sweezy, Paul. (1976). "A Critique." In Rodney Hilton, ed., *The Transition from Feudalism to Capitalism*. London, Verso.

SZSL. (1964). *Da Qing Shengzu huangdi shilu* (The veritable records of the great Qing Shenggzu [Kangxi] emperor). Taibei, Taiwan huawen shuju. Reprint.

Tan Tianxing. (1987). "Qing qianqi Lianghu diqu liangshi chanliang wenti tantao" (On the problem of foodgrain production in the 'Lianghu' region in the early Qing). *Zhongguo nongshi* 3: 29–37.

Tanaka, Masatoshi. (1984). "Popular Uprisings, Rent Resistance and Bondservant Rebellions in the Late Ming." In Linda Grove and Christian Daniels, eds., *State and Society in China: Japanese Perspectives on Ming-Qing Social and Economic History*. Tokyo, Tokyo University Press. 165–214.

Thirsk, Joan. (1978). *Economic Policy and Projects: The Development of a Consumer Society in Early Modern England*. Oxford, Clarendon Press.

Thirsk, Joan. (1984). *The Rural Economy of England*. London, Hambledon Press.

Thirsk, Joan. (1987). *England's Agricultural Regions and Agrarian History, 1500–1750*. Houndsmills, Basingstoke, Macmillan Education.

Thirsk, Joan. (1990). *Chapters from the Agrarian History of England and Wales, 1500–1750*. Cambridge, Cambridge University Press.

Thoen, Erik. (2001). "A 'Commercial-Survival Economy' in Evolution: The Flemish Countryside and the Transition to Capitalism (Middle Ages–19th century)." In Peter Hoppenbrouwers and Jan Luiten van Zande, eds., *Peasants into Farmers? The Transformation of Rural Economy and Society in the Low Countries (Middle Ages-Nineteenth Century) in Light of the Brenner Debate*. Turnhout, Belgium, Brepols.

Thomas, Brinley. (1985). "Escaping from Constraints." *Journal of Interdisciplinary History* 15.4: 772–753.

TFZ. (1968). *Tianjin fuzhi* (Tianjin Prefctural Gazetteer). Taibei, Taiwan xuesheng shuju. Reprint.

Tilly, Charles. (1992). *Coercion, Capital, and European States, AD 990–1990.* Cambridge, Mass., Blackwell.

Titow, J. Z. (1969). *English Rural Society, 1200–1300.* London, George Allen and Unwin.

TKK. (1937). *Tochi kankei narabi ni kankō hen: 1934 nen Minami Manshū nōson chōsa hōkokusho* (On property relations and practices: report on the 1934 investigation of actual village conditions in southern Manchuria). Shinkyō (Changchun), Manshū tosho kabushiki kaisha.

TLZ. (1985). *Tieling xianzhi* (Tieling gazetteer). *Liaohai congshu* (Compendium of books from the Liao Sea). Shenyang, Liao-Shen shushe. Reprint.

Torbert, Preston. M. (1977). *The Ch'ing Imperial Household Department: A Study of Its Organization and Principal Functions, 1662–1796.* Cambridge, Mass., Council on East Asian Studies, Harvard University.

TS. (1910). *Taiwan shihō, dai ikkan jō* (Private law in Taiwan, volume 1). Kobe, Rinji Taiwan kyūkan chūsakai.

Tsao, Lian-en. (1930). "The Marketing of Soya Beans and Bean Oil." *Chinese Economic Journal* 7.3: 941–971.

UN. (1956). "Supplementary Convention on the Abolition of Slavery, the Slave Trade, and Institutions and Practices Similar to Slavery." Adopted by a Conference of Plenipotentiaries convened by Economic and Social Council resolution 608(XXI) of 30 April 1956 and done at Geneva on 7 September 1956. Available on line at http://www.ohchr.org/english/law/slavetrade.htm#wp1047545.

U.S.CR. *United States Consular Reports, United States. Department of State Consular Dispatches: Newchwang, 1875–1906.* Record Group 59.2.2 (Consular Correspondences), National Archives Microfilm Publication No. 115, 7 Reels.

Verbiest, Ferdinand. (1686) *A Journey of the Emperor of China into East-Tartary in the year 1682.* London, Freeman Collins.

Vermeer, Eduard. (1998). "Population and Ecology along the Frontier in Qing China." In Mark Elvin and Liu Ts'ui-jung, eds., *Sediments of Time: Environment and Society in Chinese History.* Cambridge, Cambridge University Press. 235–279.

Vries, Jan de. (1976). *The Economy of Europe in the Age of Crisis, 1600–1750.* Cambridge, Cambridge University Press.

Vries, Jan de. (1984). *European Urbanization, 1500–1800.* Cambridge, Cambridge University Press.

Vries, Jan de, and A. van der Woude. (1997) *The First Modern Economy. Success, Failure, and Perseverance of the Dutch Economy, 1500–1815.* Cambridge, Cambridge University Press.

Wakefield, David. (1998). *Fenjia: Household Division and Inheritance in Qing and Republican China.* Honolulu, University of Hawai'i Press.

Wakeman, Frederic. (1985). *The Great Enterprise: The Manchu Reconstruction of Imperial Order in Seventeenth-Century China.* Berkeley, University of California Press.

Walker, Kathy Le Mons. (1999). *Chinese Modernity and the Peasant Path: Semicolonialism in the Northern Yangzi Delta.* Stanford, Stanford University Press.

Wang Gesheng. (1987). "Qingdai dongbei dadou shangpin hua guochen yu ziben zhuyi jingji de chansheng, fazhan" (The unfolding in the northeast of soybean commodification in the Qing and the origins and development of capitalism). In Kong Jingwei, ed., *Dongbei dichu zibenzhuyi fazhan shi yanjiu* (Studies on the historical development of capitalism in the northeast region). Harbin, Heilongjiang chubanshe.

Wang, I-Shou. (1971). "Chinese Migration and Population Change in Manchuria, 1900–1945." Ph.D. thesis, Department of Geography. Minneapolis, University of Minnesota.

Wang Yuquan. (1991). *Zhongguo tunken shi* (The history of colonies and land-opening in China). Beijing, Nongye chubanshe.

Wang, Yeh-chien. (1973). *Land and Taxation in Imperial China, 1750–1911*. Cambridge, Mass., Harvard University Press.

Wang, Yeh-chien. (1989). "Food supply and grain prices in the Yangzi delta in the eighteenth century." The Second Conference on Modern Chinese History. 3 vols. Taibei, Academia Sinica. 2: 423–462.

Wang, Yeh-chien. (1992). "Secular Trend of Rice Prices in the Yangzi Delta, 1638–1935." In Thomas Rawski and Lillian Li, eds., *Chinese History in Economic Perspective*. Berkeley, University of California. 35–68.

Wang Yejian (Wang Yeh-chien) and Huang Guoshu. (1989). "Shiba shiqi zhong Zhongguo liangshi gongxu de kaochao" (An investigation of grain supply and demand in mid-eighteenth century China). *Jindai Zhongguo nongcun jingji shi lunwenji* (Collection of works in modern Chinese agrarian economic history). Taibei, Academia Sinica.

Wang Zhonghan. (1990). "Qingdai qidi xingzhi chutan" (Preliminary investigations of the nature of bannerland in the Qing). In Wang Zhonghan, ed., *Qingshi xinkao* (A new history of the Qing). Shenyang, Liaoning daxue chubanshe. 71–86.

Weale, Putnam B. L. (1904). *Manchu and Muscovite*. London, Macmillan.

Wee, Herman van der. 1988. "Industrial Dynamics and the Process of Urbanisation and De-Urbanisation in the Low Countries in the Late Middle Ages to the Eighteenth Century: A Synthesis." In Herman van der Wee, ed, *The Rise and Decline of Urban Industries in Italy and the Low Countries (Late Middle Ages–Early Modern Times)*. Leuven, Leuven University Press. 307–381.

Wei Ming. (1932). *Dongbei de maoyi* (The northeast trade). Shanghai, Zhonghua shuju.

Wiens, Mi Chu. (1980). "Lord and Peasant in China: The Sixteenth to the Eighteenth Centuries." *Modern China* 6: 3–39.

Will, Pierre-Etienne. (1990). *Bureaucracy and Famine in Eighteenth-century China*. Stanford, Stanford University Press.

Will, Pierre-Etienne, R. Bin Wong, and James Lee. (1991). *Nourish the People: The State Civilian Granary System in China, 1650–1850*. Ann Arbor, University of Michigan Center for Chinese Studies Publications.

Williamson, Alexander. (1870). *Journeys in North China, Manchuria, and Eastern Mongolia with Some Account of Corea*. London, Smith Elder.

Wilkinson, Endymion. (1978). "Introduction." In Jing Su and Luo Lu, eds., *Landlord and Labor in Late Imperial China: Case Studies from Shandong*. Cambridge, Mass., Harvard University Press. 1–38.

Wilm, Paul. (1927). "Agriculture in Manchuria and Mongolia." *Chinese Economic Journal* 1.12: 1044–1058.

Wolf, Arthur P. (1985). "Fertility in Pre-Revolutionary Rural China." In Susan B. Hanley and Arthur Wolf eds., *Family and Population in East Asian History*. Stanford, Stanford University Press.

Wolf, Arthur P. (2001). "Is There Evidence of Birth Control in Late Imperial China?" *Population and Development Review* 27.1: 133–154.

Wolf, Arthur P. (1970). "Chinese Kinship and Mourning Dress." In Maurice Freedman ed., *Family and Kinship in Chinese Society*. Stanford, Stanford University Press.

Wolf, Arthur P. (2005). "Europe and China: Two Kinds of Patriarchy." In Theo Engelen and Arthur Wolf, eds., *Marriage and the Family in Eurasia: Perspectives on the Hajnal Hypothesis*. Amsterdam, Aksant Academic Publishers. 215–238.

Wolf, Arthur P. and Huang Chieh-shan. (1980). *Marriage and Adoption in China, 1845–1945*. Stanford, Stanford University Press.

Wong, R. Bin. (1997). *China Transformed: Historical Change and the Limits of European Experience*. Ithaca, Cornell University Press.

Wong, R. Bin, and Peter Perdue. (1983). "Famine's Foes in Ch'ing China." *Harvard Journal of Asiatic Studies*, 43.1: 291–332.

Wong, R. Bin and William Lavely. (1998). "Revising the Malthusian Narrative: The Comparative Study of Population Dynamics in Late Imperial China." *Journal of Asian Studies* 57.3: 714–748.

Wood, Ellen Meiksins. (2002). *The Origin of Capitalism: A Longer View*. London, Verso.

Wood, Ellen Meiksins. (2003). *Empire of Capital*. London, Verso.

Wood, James. (1994). *Dynamics of Human Reproduction: Biology, Biometry, Demography*. New York, Aldine de Grute.

Wrigley, E. A. (1985). "Urban Growth and Agricultural Change: England and the Continent in the Early Modern Period." *Journal of Interdisciplinary History* 15: 683–728.

Wrigley, E. A. (1988). *Continuity, Chance, and Change: The Character of the Industrial Revolution in England*. Cambridge, Cambridge University Press.

Wrigley, E. A., and R. S. Schofield. (1981). *The Population History of England, 1541–1871: A Reconstitution*. Cambridge, Cambridge University Press.

Wu Chengming. (1983). "Lun Qingdai qianqi woguo guonei shichang" (On the domestic Chinese marketplace in the early Qing). *Lishi yanjiu* 1.96–106.

Wu Yanyu. (1992). *Qingdai Manzhou tudi zhidu yanjiu* (Research on the Manchurian land system during the Qing period). Jilin, Jilin wenshi chubanshe.

Wu Yanyu et al. (1990). *Dongbei tudi guanxi yanjiu* (Research on property relations in northeast China). Jilin, Jilin wenshi chubanshe.

Wu Zhenchen. (1985). *Ningguta ji lüe* (Records from Ningguta). Harbin, Heilongjiang renmin chubanshe. Reprint.

Wynne, Waller. (1958). "The Population of Manchuria." *International population statistics reports*. Washington D.C., U.S. Department of Commerce, Bureau of the Census.

Xiao Guoliang. (1981). "Shachuan maoyi de fazhan yu Shanghai shangye de fanrong" (The development of junk trade and flourishing of Shanghai commerce). *Shehui kexue* 4: 118–122.

Xu Guohua. (1991). "Natural Environment." In Xu Guohua and L. J. Peel eds., *The Agriculture of China*. Oxford, Oxford University Press.

Xu Dixin and Wu Chengming. (1985). *Zhongguo zibenzhuyi de mengya* (On the sprouts of Chinese capitalism). Beijing, Renmin chubanshe.

Xu Xinwu and Wu Chengming. (1990). *Jiu minzhu zhuyi geming shiqi de Zhongguo zibenzhuyi* (Chinese capitalism in the era of the old democratic revolution) Beijing, Renmin chubanshe.

Xu Dixin and Wu Chengming. (2000). Chinese Capitalism, 1522–1840. New York, St. Martin's Press.

Xu Shichang. (1989). *Dongsansheng zhenglüe* (Governing proposals for the Northeast). Jilin, Jilin wenshi chubanshe. Reprint.

Xu Shuming. (1990). "Qingdai Dongbei diqu tudi kaiken shulue" (The opening of land in the northeast region during the Qing). In Ma Ruheng and Ma Dazheng, eds., *Qingdai bianjiang kaifa yanjiu* (Research into the development of frontiers during the Qing). Beijing, Zhongguo shehui kexue chubanshe.

Xu Tan. (1995). "Ming-Qing shiqi Shandong de liangshi liutong" (The circulation of Shandong grain in the Ming and Qing periods). *Lishi dang'an* 1: 81–88.

Xu Tan. (1998a). *Ming Qing shiqi Shandong shangpin jingji de fazhan* (The development of the commercial economy in Ming-Qing Shandong). Beijing, Zhongguo shehui kexue chubanshe.

Xu Tan. (1998b). "Qingdai qian-zhong qi de yanhai maoyi yu Shandong bandao jingji de fazhan" (Coastal trade and the development of the economy of the Shandong peninsula in the early and middle Qing periods). *Zhongguo shehui jingji shi yanjiu* 2: 33–45.

Xu Xinwu. (1992). *Jiangnan tubu shi* (A history of Jiangnan native cloth). Shanghai, Shanghai shehui kexue yuan chubanshe.

Xu Xinwu. 1990. "Zhongguo ziran jingji de fenjie" (The breakup of the natural economy of China) in Xu Dixin and Wu Chengming eds. *Jiu minzhuzhuyi geming shiqi de Zhongguo zibenzhuyi* (Chinese capitalism in the period of the old democratic revolution). Beijing, Renmin chubanshe. 258–332.

Xue, Yong. (forthcoming). "A "Fertilizer Revolution"? —A Critical Response to Pomeranz's Theory of "Geographic Luck." *Modern China.*

XZSL. (1964). *Da Qing Xuanzong* [Daoguang] *huangdi shilu* (The veritable records of the great Qing Xuanzong [Daoguang] emperor). Taibei, Taiwan huawen shuju. Reprint.

Yamamoto Yoshimitsu. (1941). "Kyū Manshū ni okeru gōson tōchi no keitai"(The form of village control in traditional Manchuria). *Mantetsu chōsa geppo* 11: 1–56.

Yan, Yunxiang. (1996). *The Flow of Gifts: Reciprocity and Social Networks in a Chinese Village.* Stanford, Stanford University Press.

Yang Bin. (1993). *Liubian jilüe* (Records from the Willow Palisades). Jilin, Jilin wenshi chubanshe. Reprint.

Yang Shenghua. (1991). "The Ten Agricultural Regions of China." In Xu Guohua and L. J. Peel, eds., *The Agriculture of China.* Oxford, Oxford University Press.

Yang Tonggui. (1967). *Shen gu* (Shenyang tales). Taibei, Wenhai chubanshe. Reprint.

Yang Guozhen. (1988). *Ming-Qing tudi qiyue wenshu yanjiu* (Research on Ming and Qing land contracts and documents). Beijing, Renmin chubanshe.

Yang Xuechen and Zhou Yuankang. (1986). *Qingdai baqi wang gong guizu xingshuai shi* (The history of the formation and decline of the Qing eight-banner aristocracy). Shenyang, Liaoning renmin chubanshe.

Yang Xuechen. (1963). "Qingdai qidi de xingzhi ji qi bianhua" (The nature of bannerland and its change in the Qing dynasty). *Lishi yanjiu* 3: 175–195.

Yelling, J. A. (1977). *Common field and enclosure in England, 1450–1850.* Hamdon, Conn., Archon Books.

Yi Baozhong et al. (1992). *Qingdai Manzhou tudi zhidu yanjiu* (Research on the Manchurian land system in the Qing dynasty). Jilin, Jilin wenshi chubanshe.

Yi Baozhong. (1993). *Zhongguo dongbei nongye shi* (A history of agriculture in northeast China). Jilin, Jilin wenshi chubanshe.

Young, Louise. (1998). *Japan's Total Empire: Manchuria and the Culture of Wartime Imperialism.* Berkeley, University of California Press.

Zelin, Madeleine. (1986). "The Rights of Tenants in Mid-Qing Sichuan: A Study of Land-Related Lawsuits in the Baxian Archives." *Journal of Asian Studies* 45.3: 499–526.

Zelin, Madeleine. (1984). *The Magistrate's Tael: Rationalizing Fiscal Reform in Eighteenth-century Ch'ing China.* Berkeley, University of California Press.

Zhang Guoxiong. (1993). "Ming Qing shiqi Lianghu waiyun liangshi zhi guocheng, jiegou, diwei kaocha" (An examination of the position, structure, and procedures of Lianghu grain exports in the Ming and Qing). *Zhongguo nongshi* 12.3: 40–46.

Zhang Haipeng. (1993). *Zhongguo shi da shangbang* (China's ten great merchant associations). Hefei, Huangshan shushe chubanshe.

Zhang Jianmin. (1987). "'Huguang shou, tianxia zu' shulun" (A discussion of [the proverb] "Huguang's harvest meets the empire's needs"). *Zhongguo nongshi* 4: 54–61.

Zhang, Jiayan. (2006). "Environment, Market, and Peasant Choice: The Ecological Relationship in the Jianghan Plain in the Qing and the Republic." *Modern China* 32.1: 31–63.

Zhang Jie. (1999). "Liutiao bian yinpiao yu Qingchao dongbei feng jin xin lun" (A new account of the Willow Palisade and the Qing's closure of the northeast). *Zhongguo bianjiang shi yanjiu* 1: 78–85.

Zhang Jinfan. (1988). *Qing ruguan qian guojia falü zhidu shi* (A history of the Qing state's legal system prior to 1644). Shenyang, Liaoning renmin chubanshe.

Zhang Jinfan. (1998) *Qingdai minfa zonglun* (General account of civil law in the Qing). Beijing, Zhongguo zhengfa daxue chubanshe.

Zhang Limin. (1998). "'Chuang Guandong' yimin chao jianxi" (A general account of "forcing the Guandong pass" and the high-tide of migration). *Zhonguo shihui jingji shi yanjiu* 2: 57–64.

Zhang Mingxiong. (1986). "Ming-Qing shiqi Taiwan nongye yanjiu zhi tantao" (An investigation of Taiwan's agriculture during the Ming and Qing periods). *Taiwan wenxian* 37: 1–19.

Zhang Yaomin. (1990). "Chengzhen xingqi yiji shougongye, jinrongye, he shangye" (The revival of market towns and handicrafts, finance and trade). In Kong Jingwei, ed., *Qingdai dongbei diqu jingji shi* (The economic history of the northeastern region during the Qing). Harbin, Heilongjiang renmin chubanshe. 167–210.

Zhang Zhongmin. (1988). *Shanghai: cong kaifa zouxiang kaifang, 1368–1842* (Shanghai: from settlement to opening, 1368–1842). Kunming, Yunnan chubanshe.

Zhang Zhongmin. (1996). *Qian jindai Zhongguo shehui de shangren ziben yu shehui zai shengchan* (Merchant capital and social reproduction in early modern China). Shanghai, Shanghai shehui kexue yuan chubanshe.

Zhao Gang (Chao Kang). (1995). *Qingdai liangshi muchan liang yanjiu* (Research on the productivity in grain of land in the Qing period). Beijing, Zhongguo nongye chubanshe.

Zhao Lingzhi. (2001). *Qing qianqi baqi tudi zhidu yanjiu* (Research on the land system of the eight banners in the early Qing). Beijing, Minzu chubanshe.

Zhao Zhongfu. (1998). "Jindai Dongsansheng yimin wenti zhi yanjiu" (Research on the question of migration in Modern Northeast China). In Zhao Zhongfu, *Jinshi Dongsansheng yanjiu lunwen ji* (Collection of research articles on Modern Northeast China). Taibei, Chengwen chubanshe.

Zhou Yuying. (1999). "Cong wenqi kan Ming-Qing Fujian tudi dianmai (Examining the conditional sale of land in Ming-Qing Fujian through contracts). *Zhongguo shi yanjiu* 2: 131–139.

Zhou Yuankang and Xie Zhaohua. (1986). *Qingdai zudian zhi yanjiu* (Research into the Qing system of tenancy). Shenyang, Liaoning renmin chubanshe.

Zhu Chengru. (1990). "Qingdai Liaoning haiyun ye de fazhan ji qi yingxiang" (The development and effects of Liaoning sea-going trade in the Qing). *Liaoning shifan daxue bao* 2: 79–83.

Zito, Angela. (1997). *Of Body & Brush: Grand Sacrifice as Text/Performance in Eighteenth-Century China.* Chicago, University of Chicago Press.

ZWZ. (1908). *Zhangwu xian [xiangtu] zhi* (Gazetteer of Zhangwu County), *Fangzhi zonghe ziliao* (Collected gazetteer resources), vol. 12 *(Liaoning*, number 2*)*. Nanjing nongye daxue, Zhonguo nongye yichan yanjiu shi.

Glossary

baiqi 白契
bangqing 幫情
banlazi 半拉子
baojia 保甲
baoyi 包衣
baozhang 保長
baqi shengji 八旗生計
baqi xia tun zhongdi renhu 八旗下屯種地人戶
beihuo 北貨
Beijing 北京
beile 貝勒
beizi 稗子
bing 兵
bing liwan jianran hanren xiqi 並力挽漸染漢人習氣
bing mo xieli wenqi yi wu baoren 並末寫立文契亦無保人
bing shang yin er bing min 病商因而病民
bing wu dianmai yazu zhidi jieqian 並無典賣押租指地借錢
Bodune 伯都訥
Bohai 渤海
buju nian xian 不拘年限
buxu neidi liumin zai xing touyue chukou 不許內地流民再行偷越出口
cai mai 採買
cang shi 倉石
canling 参領
cha zhengjing zhi shi kao quan zai zhongjian ren, yimian chengshou 差爭淨之事考全在中間（見）人一面承受
Changchun 長春
changgeng 長耕
changgong 長工
Changning 長寧
Changshou 常熟
Changtu 昌圖
changzu 長租
chendi 陳地
Chengde 承德
chenggong 成工
chengling 承領
chengshou wei 城守尉
chongcha 重杈
Chongming 崇明
chuanbang 船幫
chuangguan 闖關
chuanhang 船行
chuanmen'er 串門兒
ci xi liang jia qingyuan, bing bu fanhui zhengjing 此係兩家情願，並不反悔爭淨
da banlazi 大半拉子
Daqing he 大清河
Dashiqiao 大石橋
dasi yin pu 打死伊僕
datian 大田
Dengzhou 登州
dian 典
dian 佃
dian huo qian nian 典活千年
dian zhu 典主
dianmai 典賣

dianpu 佃僕
diao 吊
dibao 地保
diding 地丁
Dongqi 東齊
Dongsansheng 東三省
dou 斗
douhang 豆行
du tong 都統
duan 段
duangong 短工
Faku 法庫
fan jiazhong suoyou xi wei guanwu 凡家中所有係爲官物
faxiang zhi di 發祥之地
Feihu 飛戶
Fenghuang 鳳凰
fengjian 封建
Fengtian 奉天
Fengtian si 奉天司
Fengtian yanhai zhouxian mishi li 奉天沿海州縣米食例
fenjia 分家
fu buguo san dai 富不過三代
fu dutong 副都統
Fujian 福建
Fushun 撫順
Fuzhou 復州
Gaiping 蓋平
Gaizhou 蓋州
gaoliang 高梁
gaoxing shangliang wanxi 高興商量玩戲
genben zhi di 根本之地
gengzhong 耕種
gong chen zhi jia 功臣之家
gongfu shi 工夫市
Gongzhuling 公主嶺
gu 雇
guan nei 關內
guan shi 官石
guan wai 關外
guan zhuang 官莊
Guandong 關東
Guandong sheng 關東升
Guangdong 廣東
Guangning 廣寧
Guangxi 廣西
Guangzhou 廣州
guanhu 官斛
guanyuan bingding dimu, buxu yueqi jiaoyi: bingding benshen gengdi, buxu quanmai 官員兵丁地畝，不許越旗交易；兵丁本身耕地，不許全賣
gugong 雇工
gugongren 僱工人
Haicheng 海城
hang 行
Heilongjiang 黑龍江
hongce di 紅冊地
Huaide 懷德
Huaiyang 淮揚
huang zhuang 皇莊
huangdi 皇地
huangdi 荒地
huangfen 黃糞
Huguang 湖廣
huhun tiantu xishi 戶婚田土細事
huiguan 會館
huimin 回民
huishu 回贖
huji neiren 戶籍內人
Hulan 呼蘭
Hun he 渾河
huomai 活賣
huozu 活租
ippan kichi (Japanese) 一般旗地
jiafu di 加賦地
jian 賤
jian shang tun liangshi 奸商囤糧食
jiangjun 將軍
Jiangnan 江南
jianran 漸染
Jiaodong 膠東
Jiaozhou 膠州
jiazhong pinhan 家中貧寒
jiechede 接車的
Jilin 吉林
jingji 經記
jingying dizhu 經營地主
jinshen dizhu 縉紳地主
jinshi 進士
Jinzhou 錦州
Jinzhou 金州
juemai 絕賣

jun-xian 郡縣
Kaiyuan 開遠
kanchi (Japanese) 官地
kanghuo 炕活
Kangping 康平
kichi (Japanese) 旗地
kongkou wuping lizi wei zheng 恐口無憑立字爲證
kuaiji si 會計司
Laizhou 萊州
liang 良
liang zhuang 糧莊
lianghang 糧行
liangzhan 糧棧
Liao he 遼河
Liaodong liumin kaiken li 遼東流民開墾例
Liaodong zhaomin shouguan li 遼東招民收官例
Liaoyang 遼陽
Liaoyang faxiang zhi di 遼陽發祥之地
Liaozhong 遼中
lijia 里甲
lingcui 領催
Liuhegang 六河港
liumin ri jian jiazeng, zhi shi manzhou jiu su 流民日見加增，致失滿洲舊俗
liutong 流通
lizhang 里長
long xing zhi di 龍興之地
mai 麥
mai qingtian 賣青田
maikong maikong 買空賣空
maiqing maiqing 買青賣青
Manzhou bing min shengji shu 滿洲兵民生計述
manzhou genben 滿洲根本
mei qian shiyong 沒錢使用
mi 米
mian zhuang 棉莊
migu liutong 米穀流通
min 民
min kaiken huangdi 民開墾荒地
min yudi 民余地
mindi 民地
mindian qidi 民典旗地
ming dian an mai 明典暗賣
minjie 民界
minren 民人
minren bu ying jie dian qidi 民人不應借典旗地
minsheng 民生
mintun 民屯
Mogouying 沒溝營
mu 畝
nanhuo 南貨
neiguan jian 內管監
neizheng bu 內政部
niangong 年工
Ningcheng 寧城
Ningguta 寧古塔
Ningyuan 寧遠
niulu 牛彔
Niuzhuang 牛莊
nongtian si 農田司
nu 奴
nubi 奴婢
nubi ou jiazhang 奴婢毆家長
nupi ou liangren zhi si 奴婢毆良人致死
nupu 奴僕
paitou 牌頭
paizhang 牌長
panfei 盤費
Panshi 磐石
pi maimai 批買賣
pu 僕
qi chan 旗產
qi min fenju fang ke wu shi 旗民分居方可無事
qi min za chu 旗民雜處
qidi 旗地
qidi maimai zhangcheng 旗地買賣章程
qihu xia tun gengzhong 旗戶下屯耕種
qijie 旗界
qing 頃
qing miao zai di 青苗在地
qingcha 清查
qingyuan mai 情願賣
Qingzhou 清州
Qinning 秦寧
Qiqihar 齊齊哈爾
qiren 旗人
qiren zhongdi du ri 旗人種地渡日

qitun 旗屯
renshi bing mei chou 認識並沒仇
ri qu yu xia 日趨於下
rigong 日工
Rongcheng 榮城
Shaanxi 陝西
Shandong 山東
shang 垧 or 晌
shangbang 商幫
Shanghai 上海
Shanhaiguan 山海關
Shanxi 山西
she 社
Shengjing 盛京
shengke di 升科地
shenli 申里
Shenyang 瀋陽
shi 石
shigeng 世耕
shijia 市价
shijia zhang 十家長
shilang 侍郎
shipu 世僕
shoubao 守保
shoudi 熟地
shoudian 收典
Shuangchengbao 雙城堡
shuijingji 水經記
shumin dizhu 庶民地主
sichan 私產
Sichuan 四川
simai 死賣
Siping 四平
sizi chujing 私自出境
sizu 死租
Songhuajiang 松花江
Songjiang 松江
sui 歲
suo hao wu chou 所好無仇
suojian shuxiao 所見殊小
Suzhou 蘇州
Taicang 太倉
Taiwan 臺灣
Taizi he 太子河
tanding rudi 攤丁入地
Taonan 洮南
Tianjin 天津
Tianzhuangtai 田莊台
Tianzhuangzi 田莊子
Tieling 鐵嶺
ting qi zi bian 聽其自便
tong zuo tong chi 同坐同吃
tongtun 同屯
tou qiren wei dong 投旗人爲東
touchong 投充
tun qihu 屯旗戶
Wafangdian 瓦房店
wang zhuang 王莊
wen 文
wu zhu-pu mingfen 無主僕名分
Xi'an 西安
xia tun qiren 下屯旗人
xia tun zhongdi 下屯種地
xia tun zhongdi 下屯種地
xiang gui 鄉規
xiangbao 鄉保
xiangyue 鄉約
xianmai quan 先買權
xiaode shi qiren zhongdi du ri 小的是旗人種地渡日
xiaoji xiao 驍騎校
xiansan 閑散
xieling 協領
Xifeng 西豐
xindi 新地
Xingjing 興京
Xinjiang 新疆
Xinmin 新民
Xinmintun 新民屯
Xiongyue 熊岳
xiuxian fa 休閒法
Xiuyan 岫岩
xuanjiao yuan 玄教院
yahang 牙行
yanglao di 養老地
yangmin 養民
Yangzi 楊子
yezhu 業主
yi fan lun 依凡論
yi fu 一夫
yi gugongren lun 依僱工人論
yin zhengyong bu zu 因徵用不足
yindi 陰地
yingcha 迎杈

Yingkou 營口
yitian liangzhu 一田兩主
yitiao bianfa 一條鞭法
Yizhou 義州
yong shi 傭市
yongdian 永典
yongdian 永佃
yonggeng 永耕
Yongji 永吉
yongyuan gengzhong 永遠耕種
yongyuan gengzuo 永遠耕做
yuan bu yu handi xianglian
原不與漢地相連
yudi 餘地
yuegong 月工
za chu 雜處
zai wai maigong duri 在外賣工渡日
zaojingji 早經記
zeng liang wei ye 增糧爲業
zhaojia 找價
zhaotie 找貼
Zhejiang 浙江
Zhen'an 鎮安
zheng fengsu 整風俗
zhengcha 正杈
zhengshen qiren 正身旗人
Zhili 直隸
zhongdi wei zhu 種地爲主
zhongjian ren 中間人
zhongren 中人
zhu 主
zhu pu zhi fen 主僕之分
zhuandian gei 轉典給
zhuang 莊
zhuangdi 莊地
zhuangding 莊丁
zhuangtian 莊田
zhuangtou 莊頭
zhuren 主人
zhushi 主食
ziji 自己
zongli 總里
zu 租
zuoling 佐領
zuyi 族遺

Index

In this index an "f" after a number indicates a separate reference on the next page, and an "ff" indicates separate references on the next two pages. A continuous discussion over two or more pages is indicated by a span of page numbers, e.g., "57–59."